Publication of the Ernest Oppenheimer Institute
of Portuguese Studies of the University of the Witwatersrand
Johannesburg

PORTUGAL

AND THE

SCRAMBLE FOR

AFRICA

1875 - 1891

ERIC AXELSON

One-time research officer
Ernest Oppenheimer Institute of Portuguese Studies
University of the Witwatersrand, Johannesburg

WITWATERSRAND UNIVERSITY PRESS
JOHANNESBURG
1967

Witwatersrand University Press
1967

Printed in the Republic of South Africa
By L. S. Gray & Co. (Pty) Ltd, Johannesburg

Set and Printed in 10 on 12pt Times Roman

PREFACE

The pages that follow were made possible by the generosity of the Board of the Ernest Oppenheimer Institute of Portuguese Studies at the University of the Witwatersrand, Johannesburg, and the Trustees of the Calouste Gulbenkian Foundation, to whom I express my most grateful thanks.

A full year, 1960, was spent in Portugal and England, and subsequently a visit was paid to the province of Moçambique. I thank the authorities and staffs of those archives and libraries where I worked, especially of the Arquivo Histórico Ultramarino, the archives of the Portuguese Foreign Office, and the Arquivo Histórico de Moçambique; of the library of the Sociedade de Geografia de Lisboa; and of the Public Record Office, British Museum, and the Institute of Commonwealth Studies of the University of London. In all of these institutions I received unfailing courtesy and the most efficient assistance. That too was the experience of Miss Anne Stupart, who kindly searched for me in the Rhodesian Archives.

This monograph is a factual expression of research; it does not pretend to be a history. Its modest purpose is to gather together some of the information available about the partition of south-central Africa in so far as Portugal was concerned; to supply some details additional to those already published; and to indicate some of the sources to facilitate further research. I am conscious of the excellent work published regarding certain areas of this field, notably by Dr A. J. Hanna and Professor Roland Oliver, and more recently (since this work was started and partly written) by Dr R. T. Anstey and Mr P. Warhurst. But there is still need for much more research before anything approaching a comprehensive history of the partition of Africa can be attempted, even from the European point of view. Among the most urgent needs is more research in the archives of the Portuguese Foreign Office which, beyond the publications of Dr Jose de Almada, remain almost completely unexplored by historians.

Professor J. S. Marais has very kindly read some of the chapters and made valuable comments; needless to say he is in no way responsible for the short-comings of the present book.

I am indebted to Mrs E. M. Cotty for typing the manuscript and to Mrs M. A. Hutchings, Publications Officer, not only for her painstaking correction of the proofs but also for seeing the book through the press; to Mr P. Alton for drawing the final map; and to my wife for tracing the map of Tungue and for designing the dust-cover.

University of Cape Town
Rondebosch
December 1965

ACKNOWLEDGEMENTS

Transcripts, and two photographic reproductions, of Crown-copyright records in the Public Record Office appear by permission of the Controller of H.M. Stationery Office, to whom is made grateful acknowledgement. The reference numbers of the volumes containing quoted records are FO 403/17, 108, 110, 111, 127, 143, 144, 146, 147, 148, 157, 163; FO 541/23; and CO 806/238, 240, 267, 268, 287, 302.

Acknowledgement is also made to Mrs P. Lewsen and the Council of the Van Riebeeck Society for permission to quote from *Selections from the Correspondence of J. X. Merriman 1870–1890*, I, 1960. (Publication No. 41.);

Dr Jose de Almada and the Imprensa Nacional, Lisbon, for the reproduction of map No. LXXIII in *Tratados aplicáveis ao Ultramar, Mapas apensos ao volume V*. Lisbon, 1943;

The Imprensa Nacional, Lisbon, for reproduction of illustrations from Augusto de Castilho, *Relatorio da viagem da canonheira Rio Lima de Lisboa a Moçambique . . . 1884–1885*. Lisbon, 1889; and *Relatorio da Guerra da Zambezia em 1888*. Lisbon, 1889;

Edward Stanford, London, for maps reproduced from K. Johnston, *Africa*. London, 1880.

CONTENTS

PLATES

ABBREVIATIONS

A	Acting
Adm.	Admiralty
Af.	Africa
AHM	Arquivo Histórico de Moçambique (Lourenço Marques)
AHU	Arquivo Histórico Ultramarino (Lisbon)
ALC	African Lakes Company
Bol.	*Boletim*
BSAC	British South Africa Company
C	Command
CO	Colonial Office
Comm.	Commercial
CP	Confidential Print
CPT	Consulado de Portugal no Transvaal
Dir.	Director
do.	ditto
Ext.	Externo
extr.	extract
FO	Foreign Office
GG	Governador geral, Governor-general
Gov.	Governador, Governor
JAH	*Journal of African History*
LB	Livro Branco
LPL	Legação de Portugal em Londres
Min.	Ministro
Moç.	Moçambique
NA	Natal Archives
n.d.	no date
Nec.	Necessidades (Ministry of Foreign Affairs, Lisbon)
Neg.	*Negocios*
Off.	Official
PRO	Public Record Office
Rep.	Repartição
RGS	Royal Geographical Society
RSEA	*Records of South-Eastern Africa*
SAR	South African Republic
SGL	Sociedade de Geografia de Lisboa
Sec.	Secretário
SNA	Secretary of Native Affairs
S of S	Secretary of State
SPZ	Sobernia de Portugal na Zambézia
ST	Slave-trade
tel.	telegram
USA	United States of America
V	Vice

PORTUGAL IN SOUTH-EAST AFRICA 1875-1878

The year 1875 was one of great promise for the Portuguese territories in Africa. Andrade Corvo, scholar, writer, scientist and statesman, added to his portfolio of Foreign Affairs that of Marine and Ultramarine Affairs, so there was every prospect that his enlightened policies would be applied to the Portuguese possessions in Africa.[1] These possessions were vast. They stretched on the east coast from Delagoa Bay, the Portuguese ownership of which was confirmed that year by the MacMahon award, to Cape Delgado. On the west, they extended from Cape Frio to Ambriz, and the Portuguese strenuously asserted claims to territory farther north, about the mouth of the Congo. Every good Portuguese also assumed a broad belt across Africa linking the provinces of Angola and Moçambique to be Portuguese by priority of exploration, or at least reserved for Portuguese exploitation. There was no other European power in Africa south of the equator other than Great Britain, whose colonies of the Cape of Good Hope and Natal were flanked to the north by the Boer republics of the Orange Free State and the South African Republic. Hostility in that quarter seemed inconceivable. But by 1891 Portugal had been humiliated by her ancient ally; she had been deprived of her swathe across Africa; she had been confined to rigidly demarcated territory and forced to surrender areas claimed as Portuguese to Britain and the British South Africa Company, to France and the Congo Free State.

The sheer extent of Portuguese territory in Africa, the small white population, the nature of that population, and the comparative lack of administrative and material development made Portugal extremely vulnerable during the period of the scramble for Africa.[2]

On the east coast of Africa the capital was still Moçambique, an island which the Portuguese had occupied since 1507; they had taken it to serve as a marine station and its harbour in 1875 remained the busiest on the coast.[3] Beneath the walls of the great four-bastioned sixteenth-century fortress of São Sebastião sprawled a number of impressive and glaringly white stone buildings, among them the one-time Jesuit convent which was now the residence of the

1 J. de Andrade Corvo, *Estudos sobre as provincias ultramarinas* (Lisbon, 1883–87), 4 vols. · J. de Almada, *A politica colonial de João de Andrade Corvo* (Lisbon, 1944.)
2 The expression "scramble" for Africa became popular after *The Times* had used it in a leading article in 1884 (19/9/84, weekly edition.)
3 In 1874, 70 sailing ships and 25 steamers called, a total tonnage of 27,644. Forty French vessels totalled 5,610 tons, 34 English 18,256, 8 Portuguese 1,995 (*Boletim Official*, Moçambique, 7/8/75, p. 199).

Governor-general of the province.[4] Around the bay on the mainland stretched farms and country residences of Portuguese; but their influence did not extend more than a few miles along the coast or inland, and beyond lay Makua chiefs and cross-breed sheikhs who lived in complete independence.[5]

Ibo island, one of the Querimbas, was the seat of an administrative district to the north. The Portuguese considered the northern boundary of the province to be Cape Delgado, a boundary acknowledged by Great Britain in a treaty with Portugal in 1817.[6] A treaty negotiated by Portugal with an envoy of the Imam of Oman and Zanzibar in 1828 declared that Portuguese territory included Tungue, the bay to the south of Cape Delgado, while Arab possessions terminated at Mugau north of that Cape; but this treaty was never ratified.[7] An Arab settlement on the shores of Tungue Bay acknowledged Portuguese sovereignty until 1853,[8] when the local sheikh revolted, and paid allegiance to the Sultan of Zanzibar, who set up an administrative post there. The Governor-general of Moçambique sailed to Zanzibar in 1861 to negotiate a treaty, but the Sultan refused to admit the Portuguese claims to Cape Delgado, declaring the Minangani (which flows into Tungue Bay) to be the boundary.[9] The Portuguese conferred the grand cross of the Order of the Tower and the Sword on Bargash in 1875,[10] but this produced no softening in the Sultan's attitude. Arab influence penetrated southwards to Quissanga, on the mainland opposite Ibo and the district's thirty-seven soldiers could do but little to protect pro-Portuguese traders.[11] The question became aggravated when the Sultan strengthened his custom post at Tungue, and leased land on its shores for a British factory. The British Government declined to take sides in the dispute[12] much to the relief of Morier, the British minister in Lisbon, who had feared interference on the Sultan's behalf which would have prejudiced the efforts he was making towards persuading the Portuguese to adopt a more liberal commercial policy in Moçambique.[13] The Governor-general of Moçambique, however, saw the unscrupulous hand of England in the Sultan's manoeuvres. He considered that the repeated journeys of Elton, the British consul at Moçambique, along the coast and into the interior could not be unofficial, and that the consul must have entered into relation with the chiefs; he was sure that the Sultan must by some secret treaty have ceded his rights to Great Britain; and he had heard a rumour that the British Government was planning

---

4 See A. Lobato, *A Ilha de Moçambique* (Lourenço Marques, 1945).

5 Corvo, 2, p. 224.

6 Additional Convention, 28/7/1817 to Treaty 22/1/1817, Livro Branco, *Negociações com o Zanzibar* (1888), p. 5.

7 J. Gray, *History of Zanzibar from the Middle Ages to 1856* (London, 1962), pp. 174–8; Convention, 28/3/28, *Negociações com o Zanzibar*, pp. 6–8.

8 No salary, however, appears to have been paid the sheikhs of Tungue after 1847 at the latest; J. de B. Carrilho, 20/9/84, memo, *Negociações com o Zanzibar*, pp. 26–7.

9 J. Tavares de Almeida to Minister, 8/2/62, ibid., pp. 13–16.

10 J. Kirk to Derby, 10/3/75, 42, Foreign Office Confidential Print, 2915, pp. 127–8; Governor-general to Minister, 31/3/75, 80, AHU, Moç., Pasta 29.

11 GG to Min., 17/2/76, 50, AHU, Moç., Pasta 30.

12 Derby to Morier, 21/2/77, 17 ST, CP 3686, p. 182.

13 Morier to Derby, 20/4/77, 29, ibid., p. 237; 31/5/77, 50, ibid., pp. 267–8.

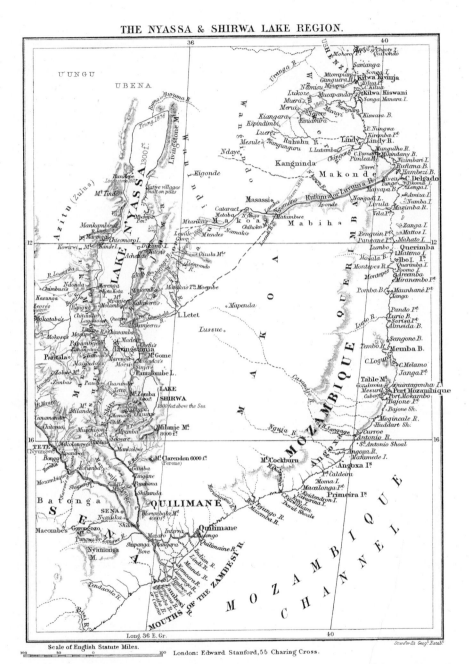

1   The Nyasa area (map by Edward Stanford, in Stanford's Compendium of Geography and
    Travel: K. Johnston, *Africa*. London, 1880)

to plant 2,000 married colonists on the shores of Lake Nyasa, with Tungue as a base.[14]

A new Governor-general, Maria da Cunha, proceeding from Portugal by way of the Red Sea, called at Zanzibar, where he informed the Sultan that he had instructions to negotiate a new commercial treaty, which would also define the limits of Portuguese territory at Cape Delgado. Bargash professed willingness to come to an agreement. But when Cunha reminded him of this in a letter from Moçambique, hoping he would commit himself in writing, he diplomatically replied that it was better known in Moçambique than in Zanzibar exactly which lands belonged to Portugal.[15] When word of these overtures reached London, the Foreign Office instructed Morier to sound the Portuguese Government as to its intentions. Morier replied that since Britain had recognized Cape Delgado as the boundary in 1817, for him to advert to the subject now would arouse the suspicion if not the hostility of Portugal.[16]

To counteract the growing influence southwards of the Arabs the Portuguese authorities decided to establish a government post at Mocimboa.[17] Shortly afterwards the chief of Medo, who lived inland from Quissanga, on a caravan route to Lake Nyasa, submitted to Portuguese vassalage. He had twice gone to the aid of Quissanga, in 1874 and 1876, when that town had been attacked by Maviti tribesmen. But in 1878 there was another such raid, which devastated Quissanga, with the death of some fifty men and the abduction of many women and children. The Governor of Ibo placed a small force in Quissanga, but it was no more than a token of Portuguese sovereignty.[18]

South of Moçambique the next centre of Portuguese administration was Angoche; the Governor resided in a rude thatched hut, and his authority did not extend beyond his garden.[19]

Quelimane, a town of some consequence on the estuary of that name, with a detachment of eighty-five troops, was the main port of entry to the Zambezi. But its importance must not be exaggerated. In 1874 its custom-house yielded only 3,653 milreis (of which 2,722 came from foreign vessels).[20]

Up the Zambezi, Sena, which had received a charter of municipal government in the sixteenth century, was in a state of almost complete decay. The residents totalled only four. Trade was virtually non-existent. It was the seat of a military command (represented by one soldier). Two bastions of the fort of S. Marçal had been recently rebuilt, but the curtain wall had collapsed, and only a line of stakes marked the perimeter. Within were four stone huts. Two of these served as barracks, a third as a magazine, despite the thatched roofs; in the fourth, under tiles, were stored the ornaments from the churches, which

14 GG to Min., 12/6/77, 137, and 24/8/77, 199, AHU, Moç., Pasta 30.
15 GG to Min., 2/11/77, 264, AHU, Moç., Pasta 30, and 17/4/78, 87, ibid., Pasta 31.
16 Morier to Salisbury, 31/5/78, 15, CP 3928, p. 124.
17 Perry de Camara to GG, 29/11/77, 120, from Ibo; GG to Min., 19/1/78, 14, AHU, Moç., Pasta 31.
18 Termo de Vassalagem, 23/6/78, *Termos de Vassallagem*, pp. 21–2; GG to Min., 24/12/78, 2/299, 31/12/78, 302, AHU, Moç., 1 Repartição, Pasta 1, 15/8/78, 182, AHU, Moç., Pasta 31.
19 Corvo, 2, pp. 144, 381.
20 *Bol. Off.*, 6/3/75, pp. 58–9. A milreis was worth approx. 1s. 6d.

were no longer in existence. The only recent government expenditure had been on the erection of a flag pole. Because of Sena's ruinous condition, and the unhealthiness of its situation, there were periodic suggestions that the place should be abandoned and the seat of administration transferred across the river to the Manganja hills.[21]

Tete, the capital of Zambezia, contained a number of stone houses, most of them thatched. Its fort on the bank of the river was dilapidated; that on the hill at the back of the town had been completed only in 1874. The town was the headquarters of the battalion of Caçadores 2, which had a strength of 296 at the beginning of 1875 (less 37 detained in the cells), of whom 118 were stationed in Tete. None of the officers was white; and most of the soldiers were *degredados*—men who had been banished or convicted of crime.[22]

Portuguese influence extended up the Zambezi as far as Zumbo, where authority had been re-established in 1863; this authority was exercised by a non-white *capitão-mor*, who began to repair the long abandoned fort and barracks, which housed twenty-one troops.[23]

The most remarkable feature of the Zambezi area was the institution of *prazos* of the Crown. In the seventeenth century conquered land had been occupied by the Portuguese responsible, or under grant from the Portuguese authorities for services rendered on payment of a nominal rent. In the eighteenth century the Government to encourage white immigrants had limited these estates to areas three leagues[24] by one and less if the soil were mineraliferous, and had granted them to Portuguese-born women on condition that they married Portuguese men; *prazos* could pass for three generations, each time to the eldest daughter on like conditions. These conditions were soon forgotten and the holders were only nominally white. A decree of 1832 abolished the *prazos*;[25] but the holders refused to acknowledge such abolition. A decree of 1838 declared that vast areas of the Zambezi were almost depopulated, and uncultivated, owing mainly to the vicious system of *prazos* and it forbad any new concession.[26] A report of the Conselho Ultramarino in 1854 announced that an area larger than Portugal had been divided among a handful of families. Many of the holders were absentees, so authority was exercised by agents. These governed as absolute despots, to the point of reducing women and children to slavery and selling them. Enslavement, and flights to escape enslavement, had depopulated the country. Those who remained had to pay annual tribute to their feudal lord, who was seldom white; they could not so much as dispose of their produce without his permission, and they had to buy inferior cotton goods at his own price. One *prazo*, Gorongosa, was a hundred leagues long; another, Boror, ninety. Yet rental from the 200 registered *prazos* brought in a total of only 3,200 milreis a year.[27] As a consequence of

21 Report of Obras Publicas, *Bol. Off.*, 16/1/75, p. 10; Corvo, 2, pp. 229–30; GG to Min., 11/7/78, 2/159, AHU, Moç., 1 Rep. Pasta 2.
22 Relatório of Acting Governor, *Bol. Off.*, 31/1/75, p. 17.
23 Corvo, 2, p. 252. *Bol. Off.*, 6/3/75, pp. 55–6, notes the resignation of the *Sargento-mor*.
24 A league was approximately 3½ miles.
25 Decree of 13/8/32, Ribeiro Sousa, *Regimen dos prazos da Coroa* (Lourenço Marques, 1907), pp. 10–12.
26 Decree of 6/11/38, ibid., pp. 13–14.
27 Consulta, 1/9/54, ibid., pp. 174–9.

this report, a law declared the *prazos* to be abolished; the natives on them were to be freed from all personal obligations and services, and to be subject only to the general laws; they were to receive the right to fifty hectares each, and to pay only 1$600 milreis per hut per year.[28] But again the holders refused to abandon their *prazos*, and in 1875 conditions on the Zambezi were the same as those which had given the Conselho Ultramarino such concern twenty years before. The Governor-general complained not only of the negligible financial return from them but of the absolutism of these feudal potentates who could sentence to death with impunity; he urged that no more *prazos* be granted, and that on the expiration of the existing leases the land be divided among the *colonos*.[29] The position had in fact deteriorated, because some of the *prazo* holders were at war not only with each other but with the Portuguese Government.

The most notorious of these rebels was the lord of Massangano, António Vicente da Cruz, nicknamed Bonga (the wild cat), who had massacred a force sent to take him prisoner, among the victims being the Governor of Tete himself. A punitive expedition failed to take Bonga's stockade but a third expedition, well equipped with artillery, got as far as beseiging it. The defenders sallied out and butchered half the attacking troops. A fourth expedition, largely composed of volunteers from Portugal, met with no success; the rebels attacked it while it was returning, and turned the withdrawal into a rout. These Bonga wars destroyed Portuguese prestige. Great was the joy when in January 1875, an emissary from Bonga arrived in Tete to propose peace. The Portuguese Government granted him a pardon, and peace was officially signed in August of that year.[30] And there was great relief when another powerful and often hostile *prazo*-holder, of Macanga, submitted at the end of 1875.[31]

One of the most notorious *prazo*-holders was Manuel António de Sousa, a native of Portuguese India, who had come to south-east Africa in about 1853. At the age of eighteen, he had married the daughter of an uncle who had been a resident of Sena, and with her dowry he financed caravans into the interior. He established himself on the slopes of Mount Gorongosa; his lair which, impregnably defended by rocks and precipices and cannon once saw 50 men repel 3,000, was known from his Goan origin as Gouveia. When it suited him he made his levies available to the Government which, in 1863, made him *Capitão-mor* of Manica and Quiteve; he co-operated against Bonga, because he wished to destroy that rival potentate. But he thought nothing of murder; and he was beyond the reach of the law, for the Government did not

28 Decree of 22/12/54, ibid., pp. 16–19.
29 Corvo, 2, pp. 228 and 235, quoting the Relatório of General José Guedes de Carvalho e Meneses.
30 Corvo, 2, pp. 235–42; F. G. de Almeida de Eça, *História das Guerras no Zambeze Chicoa e Massangano (1807–1888)* (Lisbon, 2, 1954), *passim.*; GG to Min., 2/3/75, 30/3/75, 100, AHU, Moc., Pasta 29.
31 Termo de Submissão . . ., *Bol. Off.*, 24/1/76, pp. 15–16.

have the force to restrain him, and feared to provoke him to revolt.[32]

But now there arrived on the Zambezi men whose activities seemed to the authorities to present almost as serious a threat to Portuguese influence as the Bongas and the António de Sousas. These were Protestant missionaries. In 1858 David Livingstone had been sent to the Zambezi as British consul for the east coast of Africa south of Zanzibar territory and the independent districts in the interior; and at the same time he had been given command of an expedition to explore eastern and central Africa. He found what any Portuguese on the Zambezi could have told him, that the Quebrabasa rapids were an insuperable barrier to navigation. While waiting for a more powerful steam-launch, he ascended the Shire River and reached Nyasa. He visited the Makololo on the Zambezi above the Victoria Falls, and on his return to the mouth of that river met Bishop MacKenzie and six missionaries sent out by the Universities' Mission to plant a station in the area of Nyasa. Livingstone, after trying to reach Nyasa by way of the Rovuma, guided MacKenzie's party to the Shire highlands, which were much disturbed by warfare, for the Yao were encroaching on the Manganja. Livingstone explored the western side of Nyasa. On his return to the mouth of the Zambezi he was joined by James Stewart, a strong Free Churchman, who had read arts, theology and medicine in Edinburgh and had found a personal message in *Missionary Travels and Researches in South Africa*. Livingstone had proposed the establishment of stations on the Zambezi beyond Portuguese territory; there was scope for various sects, including "that most energetic body the Free Church of Scotland"; the country was so extensive that there was no fear of clashing: "only let the healthy locality be searched for, and fixed upon". The Free Church turned down Stewart's plea so he organized an influential committee which sent him out to reconnoitre the area, meet Livingstone, and choose the most suitable site for a mission—and prepare a report for the Cotton Supply Association of Manchester. He ascended the Shire and visited the highlands. But the more he saw of Livingstone the more disillusioned did he become, until he consigned *Missionary Travels* to the turbid waters of the Zambezi. He reported to his committee that conditions in the area were unpropitious for missionary work. That was the experience of the Universities' Mission which after the death of the bishop and three missionaries withdrew to Zanzibar. Livingstone returned to Africa on his final journey. At his funeral in Westminster Abbey, Stewart vowed that he would revive the idea of a mission to south-central Africa, and that he would call it Livingstonia. The Foreign Missions Committee of the Free Church of Scotland now accepted his proposal, and the Established Church of Scotland which had already been considering a mission in central Africa decided to avail itself of the opportunity to establish a station in the

32 GG to Min., 21/7/75, 179, 27/7/75, 203, AHU, Moç., Pasta 29; Lima Moura to Sec., Sociedade de Geografia de Lisboa, 9/2/85, from Vila Gouveia, *Boletim* of the SGL 1885, pp. 496–500; Moraes Pinto to do., 23/12/85, ibid., 1886, pp. 9–13; Castilho, GG, 17/3/87, instruções, AHU, Moç., 1 Rep. Pasta 2; J. de Azevedo Coutinho, *Manuel António de Sousa* (Lisbon, 1936), pp. 11–14.

same general area.   Lieutenant E. Young, a bombardier who had been a member of the Livingstone Zambezi expedition, obtained leave of absence from the Navy and was charged with the duty of placing a steamer on Lake Nyasa and choosing a site for a mission station which Stewart would later lead.[33]

Young left England in May 1875, accompanied by Rev. Dr Robert Laws, six artisans and a seaman; and a further artisan who was to choose a site for the Church of Scotland mission.   The party sailed with the blessing of the British Government, which declared the motives to be the promotion of commerce and civilization which would lead to a suppression of the slave traffic in the Nyasa district.   The Portuguese Government instructed its Governor-general in Moçambique to render the party any assistance it might need in its passage through Portuguese territory.   Warned by Elton that customs duties might cripple the finances of the mission, the British Government, whilst admitting that it had no right to claim an exemption from customs, suggested that a remission of duties would be a proof of the friendliness of Portugal towards the mission. This was eventually conceded.[34]

The far-sighted Corvo appreciated the complications that might result from this settlement of foreigners at the southern end of Nyasa, and in July his Government ordered the Governor-general to establish a garrison at some convenient point on the Shire, which would guarantee possession of the river as far as its source in Nyasa.   The Governor-general replied that this was impossible: the mouth of the Shire was under Portuguese dominion, but the tribes up the river were not, and he did not have the force to subdue them.[35] The actions of the missionaries on their arrival in the province did nothing to set the Governor-general's mind at rest.   Their schooner chartered in Cape Town entered the Zambezi by the Inhamissengo (Congone) mouth, which was not a recognized port of entry, and where there was no custom-house.   The party assembled the steam-launch *Ilala*.   Making no effort to report their arrival to the authorities in Quelimane, they ascended the Zambezi.   Nor did they report to the military Commandant at Sena, but promptly ascended the Shire, where they made contact with those Makololo who had been abandoned in that area by Livingstone, and who, granted land on the lower Shire by the Portuguese, had intermarried with the local inhabitants, multiplied, and become local potentates.[36]

These actions seemed ominous to the Governor-general. He had received

33 J. Stewart, *Livingstonia, its origin* (Edinburgh, 1894); J. P. R. Wallis (ed.), *Zambesi Journal of James Stewart 1862–3* (London, 1952); D & C. Livingstone, . . . *The Zambezi and its Tributaries* (London, 1865); R. Coupland, *Kirk on the Zambesi* (London, 1928); J. P. R. Wallis (ed.), *The Zambezi expedition of David Livingstone, 1858–1863* (London, 1956), 2 vols.
34 R. Bourke to Elton, 28/5/75, 1 ST, CP 2915, p. 326; F. de S. Lencastre, Sec. Geral, Moç., to Governors Quelimane, etc., 11/5/75, ibid., p. 355; Derby to Lytton, 28/5/75, 1, pp. 290–1; Corvo, portaria, 28/6/75, ibid., p. 295; Elton to Derby, 20/7/75, 12 ST, ibid., pp. 354–5; Corvo to Lytton 8/9/75, ibid., p. 295; Derby to Lytton, 15/9/75, 9, ibid., p. 294; Lytton to Corvo, 30/9/75, ibid., p. 296; Corvo to Lytton, 10/12/75, ibid., p. 305; E. D. Young, 19/2/75, *Proceedings RGS*, 1876, p. 451–4 with a map of Nyasa and remarks by H. Waller.
35 GG to Min., 16/9/75, 251, AHU, Moç., Pasta 29.
36 E. D. Young, *Nyassa*; 2 ed. (London, 1877), pp. 16–39.

no instruction to remit the customs duties, so it appeared that the missionaries were attempting to defraud the revenue; and since they were professing to establish not only a religious but an industrial mission, he feared that Portuguese commerce would suffer. More serious were the possible political consequences. The missionaries' first engineer had been H. Faulkner, an Englishman who incited the Makololo to seize the *prazo* of Goma until killed by men of a rival chief. The Governor-general therefore feared that these foreigners would continue their intrigues, incite the Makololo to attack Portuguese subjects, and subvert other tribes to rebellion. He feared they might themselves become the victims of disorders they provoked, and so cause an international incident.[37] Nor was the Governor-general reassured to hear that Bishop Steere, of the Universities' Mission, had gone to Lindi, whence he was planning to push a chain of stations to Nyasa; and that Elton was to open a direct route to the lake from the Moçambique coast.[38]

After great efforts the *Ilala* was floated on Nyasa. Young found a harbour sheltered from the prevailing winds near the tip of the Maclear promontory where on 18 October 1875 Livingstonia came into existence.[39] The pioneer party of the Established Church laid out the site of their mission station at Blantyre, and in 1878 the first missionary arrived.[40]

South of the Zambezi, the next Portuguese authority was at Sofala, the scene of the first Portuguese occupation on the coast in 1505, and from where the first penetration to the interior had taken place. The fort still stood, though it urgently needed repair, the nominal home of a detachment of troops, but it was no longer the capital of the district of Sofala. In fact, by this time, in the whole of the Sofala area, complained the Governor-general, there was not a single Portuguese resident, there was not a mulatto; there was not a single literate native. The seat of government had been removed, from fear of attack by Umzila's Landeens, to the island of Chiloane, and the authority of the Governor did not extend to the mainland. Chiloane was the headquarters of a battalion of Caçadores 3, with a strength of 129, which had a further detachment on the island of Bazaruto. The district had no external trade, but a custom-house had been newly erected in Chiloane.[41]

The next Portuguese centre to the south was Inhambane, described in 1871 as being a "considerable place" with a number of Portuguese inhabitants—but no Portuguese women. Thanks to Laforte, the most powerful of the local residents, Umzila's men had been repulsed, and the Portuguese controlled a strip some 70 miles long by 15 across.[42]

37 GG to Min., 27/9/75, 303, and 23/12/75, 230, AHU, Moç., Pasta 29; and 24/1/76, 28, ibid., Pasta 31.
38 Elston to Derby, 15/9/75, 27, CP 2915, pp. 396–7.
39 E. D. Young, pp. 59–60, 76.
40 See, e.g. A. Hetherwick, *The Romance of Blantyre* (London, [1931]).
41 GG to Min., 202, AHU, Moç., Pasta 30, *Bol. Off.* 16/1/75, p. 10; Corvo, 2, p. 254, report of Obras Publicas, ibid., p. 256; relatório of A-Gov. Sofala, 30/9/75, *Bol. Off.* 31/1/76, p. 20.
42 St V. Erskine, 'Journey to Umzila's, South-East Africa, in 1871–1872', *Journal RGS, 1875,* pp. 52–3; Corvo, 2, p. 257.

Inland from Inhambane lay the kingdom of Gaza. The original Gazaland had been at the southern end of the Lebombo range. Forced to flee from the Zulus in about 1819 Chief Shoshongane and other survivors of his Nguni clan headed northwards into Tongaland. Shoshongane, or Manikusa as the Portuguese called him, sacked Lourenço Marques, pillaged Inhambane, Sofala and Sena, and became paramount over the country between Delagoa Bay and the Zambezi. When he died in 1856 there was dispute between two of his sons, Umzila, the eldest, and successor by Tonga law, and Mawewe (or Mueva), the eldest son by the great wife, and the successor by Nguni law. Umzila, who had been banished to the Transvaal, appeared at Lourenço Marques in 1861, and requested the assistance of the Portuguese against their common enemy, Mawewe, which assistance he received after professing himself a vassal of the Portuguese Crown. The Governor assembled a force and overwhelmed the army of Mawewe in a pitched battle at Moambe, near to the Komati River, in August 1862.[43] The unsuccessful claimant tried to persuade the Natal Government to intervene on his behalf. The Lieutenant-governor replied curtly that he had no authority to communicate with the Governor-general on political matters.[44]

In 1870 it was Umzila who sent a deputation to Natal, asking that colony to accept him as "ally, friend and tributary". He proposed trade between the two territories, with the exportation from Gazaland of ivory and labour. He suggested that an officer be sent to discuss these matters, who should travel by sea to the mouth of the Limpopo, whither he would send a present of ivory. He further proposed that a certain chief, subject of the Government of Natal, who was a relative of his, be established between Gazaland and the Swazis, his enemies, who had supported Mawewe, in what would become a buffer territory, and which would facilitate communication between Gazaland and Natal. Shepstone, the Secretary of Native Affairs, asked the messengers whether Gazaland was not subject to Portugal, but this they denied. Shepstone pointed out that the Portuguese might object to the entry of a ship into the mouth of the Limpopo, and the diversion of the ivory trade, but the deputation declared simply, "Umzila is the King; the Portuguese are women." Umzila was most impressed that the Natal Government had been able to restrain the Zulus from attacking the Swazis; he was confident that it could similarly prevent the Swazis from attacking the Shangaans: "Umzila says, that I am a girl wishing to become a bride, and be married like the Zulu and the Amaswazi brides have been, to a strong and vigorous husband, who is able by his word only to protect me."[45] The Lieutenant-governor replied readily accepting Umzila's offer of friendship, but "Civilized White Nations are always careful not to interfere with the rights of each other. The Portuguese Government across the sea is in friendly alliance with the English Government across the sea, which

43 O'Neill to Rosebery, 4/7/86, 18 Af., C 6459, pp. 256–7; A. T. Bryant, *Olden Times in Zululand and Natal* (London, 1929), pp. 446–57.
44 A statement by the messengers of Langa, 21/10/62, a draft reply, 20/11/63, Natal Archives, SNA 1/6/2, Nos. 121–2.
45 T. Shepstone, SNA, statements, 16/8/70, C 6495, p. 198.

owns Natal, and whatever may be the feelings of Umzila and his people towards the representatives of the Portuguese Government with whom he has to do, the Lieutenant-governor of Natal must be careful not to disregard the rights which that Government has itself laid down as its rights." There were difficulties too in sending a ship to the mouth of the Limpopo, lest this infringe Portuguese regulations. It seemed advisable to have more information on the situation, and to obtain this the Governor sent St Vincent Erskine, who had already carried out an exploration of the lower courses of the Limpopo.[46]

There was fear in Pietermaritzburg that Erskine's mission would cost more than the promised ivory, so Erskine offered to pay the expenses of the trip in return for the ivory.[47] He arrived in Lourenço Marques in July 1871. The Governor declared that Umzila was a Portuguese subject, who was not competent to receive a foreign mission; he refused Erskine permission to land at the mouth of the Limpopo, and insisted that Erskine go to Moçambique to discuss the matter with the Governor-general. The Governor's attitude was partly influenced by fear lest Lourenço Marques lose the fifteen shillings a passport paid by labourers in transit; and he also feared British aggrandizement. On Elephant Island in Delagoa Bay were four British subjects who maintained that they were on British soil, and Erskine urged the Natal Government to occupy the southern end of Delagoa Bay, to which Britain had already laid claim. Erskine continued to Inhambane, where he found a more obliging governor who allowed him to traverse Portuguese territory though disclaiming responsibility for his safety were he to pass beyond.[48] He marched southwards to meet his interpreter and porters with trade goods who were proceeding from Lourenço Marques, and he made a new survey of the lower Limpopo, reporting that it was difficult of entry, but had 60 miles of navigable water.

Since Umzila now proved unco-operative he was unable to travel up the Limpopo. He returned to Inhambane where he exceeded his instructions by planning the actual transportation of labourers to Natal.[49] He then set out directly for Umzila's kraal, which was near the source of the Buzi River, on the southern slopes of the Chimanimani mountains. For weeks Umzila refused to receive him; rude messages from Umzila were answered by ruder replies from Erskine. When eventually he met the Paramount Chief, Umzila declared that he was dissatisfied with his present; he had wanted a shipload of guns, and nothing else. He refused to allow his subjects to depart as labourers to Natal; and he declared that the buffer territory was in the possession of another tribe. So far from presenting a shipload of ivory, Umzila gave only forty-two tusks. Erskine returned to Natal by way of Lydenburg, his mission a complete failure.[50]

46 T. Shepstone, statement, 18/8/70, C 6495, pp. 199–200.
47 Erskine to Shepstone, 12/5/71, NA, SNA 1/1/21.
48 Erskine to Shepstone, 3/7/71, from Lourenço Marques, C 6495, pp. 200–3, and 22/7/71, from Inhambane, ibid., pp. 204–7.
49 Erskine to SNA, 19/11/71, from Inhambane, and minute by SNA, Natal Archives, SNA 1/1/23, in No. 17.
50 Erskine to SNA, 23/2/72, from Inyambane's kraal, NA, SNA, 1/1/23, in No. 17; and 30/11/72, C 6495, pp. 307–16; for his narrative see Erskine, 'Journey to Umzila's . . . pp. 45–128.

Having assessed the potentialities of Gazaland, however, Erskine returned in 1875 on his own account. He gave Umzila one hundred tower muskets and powder and obtained a concession to hunt elephants. A dispute arose and only by a display of force was Erskine able to send his ivory to Inhambane. He demanded that Umzila be destroyed, and though he reckoned the chief commanded 2,000 muskets he considered that the forces of Inhambane and Lourenço Marques were ample for the purpose; he tried to enlist the aid also of the Natal Government against Umzila.[51] He failed to secure the sympathy of the British authorities since other Englishmen were able to travel freely in Gazaland while the Portuguese had no desire to goad Umzila into active hostility.[52] As it was, they soon had their hands full, subduing tribal fighting in the neighbourhood of Závora;[53] and before long there were greater dangers. António de Sousa compelled Umtasa, chief of the Manica area, to proceed against Landeens who were raiding *prazos* in the neighbourhood of Sena. Umzila assembled tribesmen to oppose Sousa's force. One subordinate chief in the neighbourhood of Inhambane failed to send his quota of warriors. Umzila abandoned his kraal and ominously descended towards the lower Limpopo; his main motive was to overawe those Tongas who were falling under Portuguese influence.[54]

Umzila in 1878 made another approach to the Natal Government. He asked for certain goods to be sent him by sea, and for them to be accompanied by a discreet person who would listen to what Umzila had to say. The administration collected the goods asked for, but the Lieutenant-governor replied curtly that he could not send them by sea since there was no steamer going to Umzila's country; the messengers must convey them.[55]

Though no port yet served Gazaland, the mouth of the Limpopo River seemed admirably suited for that purpose. Portuguese authorities were in fact receiving reports that English contraband runners were already using it. Augusto de Castilho, the energetic Governor of Lourenço Marques, urged the need for a proper hydrographic survey of the river mouth and the establishment of a custom post.[56]

Lourenço Marques was situated on Delagoa Bay, the finest harbour between Cape Town and Moçambique. From the days when the survivors of the Trichardt Trek had stumbled into Lourenço Marques, South African Boers had regarded Delagoa Bay as the natural port of the Transvaal. Pretorius, the President of the South African Republic, in 1868 declared the annexation of a strip of land a mile wide on each side of the Maputo River as far as the shores

51 Erskine to Gov. Inhambane, 28/8/75, CP 2915, pp. 403–4; Erskine to Elton, 31/8/75, ibid., pp. 401–2.
52 Elton, Erskine, 30/9/75, CP 2915, pp. 405–6; GG to Min., 2/10/75, 264, AHU, Moç., Pasta 29.
53 GG to Min., 17/3/76, 77, CP 2915, Pasta 30.
54 GG to Min., 29/10/76, 261, CP 2915, do. 26/5/78, 124, ibid.
55 J. W. Shepstone, A-SNA, 2/1/78, statement, NA SNA 1/6/1 No. 34, C 6495, p. 216, and reply to H. Bulwer, 4/2/78, ibid., pp. 216–7. The goods were 15 wool blankets, 11 shawls, 8 lbs of copper beads, 21 lbs of blue beads, 4 knives and forks, 5 butchers' knives.
56 A Castilho, Gov. Lourenço Marques, to Sec. Geral, 13/8/75, *Bol. Off.* 9/10/75, p. 240.

of Delagoa Bay.[57] Portugal protested, and Pretorius withdrew. The Portuguese consul in Cape Town visited Pretoria in 1869, and negotiated a treaty of peace and commerce. Portugal conceded complete freedom of commerce to Transvaal subjects in all goods except slaves, arms and ammunition. In return, the South African Republic acknowledged Portuguese sovereignty over the country bordering Delagoa Bay, down to latitude 26° 30′ south. The treaty defined the boundary.[58] It was also agreed to open a road, and the eventual construction of a railway was discussed. A Portuguese delegate reconnoitred a route for this railway line across Swazi territory. The Transvaal Government appointed a commissioner, Moodie, to survey an easier route by way of the Komati valley. Realization of these plans would transform Lourenço Marques.[59]

Lourenço Marques had been described by Erskine as a "mass of grass huts, reed fences, decayed forts, rusty cannon, small proportion of Europeans, and large half-castes, Banyans, Mussulmans, Brahmins, Tongas, slaves and freed men, sand dunes, narrow streets, flat-roofed houses, and coco-nut trees and stench." It was enclosed by a recently constructed wall about six feet high, protected by bastions at intervals. Abolition of the slave-trade, and the death or the retreat of the elephants, had ruined commerce; the Portuguese kept largely behind their walls, and had no knowledge of the high and healthy ground beyond. Erskine had no doubt about the course of events: "The future of Delagoa Bay under Portuguese rule can be but decay and death; but under a Teutonic race, a more glorious future may await it. That it will fall under one or other of those races by force or diplomacy there can be but little doubt."[60]

The population of Lourenço Marques a few years later was 458, of whom 295 were men. Of these 93 were European Portuguese, 83 Asiatic Portuguese, 66 African Portuguese, and 28 European foreigners. All of the European Portuguese were soldiers or officers or officials; of the other Portuguese nearly all were *degredados*. Those who were not civil servants traded; there was not a single farmer or other producer of primary products.[61]

Most Britons shared Erskine's view as to the fate of Delagoa Bay. Englishmen had raised the Union Jack on Inhaca Island in 1861, and Britain

57 C 1361, p. 33.
58 Treaty, signed 29/7/69, by A. du Prat, Pretorius, etc., ratified 21/8/70. The boundary ran along the 26° 30′ south parallel of latitude to the Lebombo mountains. It followed the crest of the Lebombo range to the poort cut by the Komati River. From there it ran north-north-east to the Pokiones Kop, north of the Olifants River, thence north-north-west to the nearest point of the Umbovo River, to a Chicundo hill and thence to the junction of the Pafuri and the Limpopo.
59 J. J. Machado, 'Caminho de Ferro de Lourenço Marques á fronteira do Transvaal', *Bol. SGL*, 1880, pp. 71–3; S. W. A. Forssman, *Guide for Agriculturists and Capitalists, Speculators* . . . (Pretoria, 1874), which includes a list of customs duties in force at Delagoa Bay.
60 Erskine, 'Journey to Umzila's', pp. 48–9; Erskine to Shepstone, 3/7/71, from Lourenço Marques, C 6495, p. 201. The new defensive line had been started in 1867, and finished in 1869. A residence had been bought for the governor in 1873; a custom-house was built in 1874 (*Bol. Off.* 9/1/75, p. 3). A fire swept through much of Lourenço Marques in 1875; among the 52 subscribers to alleviate the distress was Herbert Rhodes (*Bol. Off.* 2/10/75, p. 234.)
61 Corvo, 2, p. 261.

claimed the territory south of Delagoa Bay. She strongly protested against the Treaty of 1869. Natal merchants thoroughly appreciated the danger to their trade with the Transvaal were Delagoa Bay to be developed and communications improved between the Bay and the interior. The Natal Government was also concerned, because a considerable portion of the Colony's revenues came from dues levied on goods in transit to the Transvaal. Portugal and Great Britain agreed in 1872 to submit the question of title to the area in question, between Delagoa Bay and latitude 26° 30′ S, and between the sea and the Lebombo hills, to arbitration by Thiers, the President of the French Republic.[62]

The discovery of gold in the neighbourhood of Lydenburg and Pilgrim's Rest added greatly to the importance of Delagoa Bay.[63] A party of Australian miners, for instance, landed at the Bay,[64] and Forssman, the Portuguese consul in the Transvaal, urged the encouragement of communication and trade between there and the gold-fields. He appointed an Austrian, Nellmapius, as Portuguese vice-consul on the fields, and the promotion of commerce, Forssman pointed out, could of course best be done by the construction of a railway.[65] Increase in commerce would benefit not simply the traders: from the flourishing centre of Lourenço Marques Portuguese influence would expand southwards and westwards; and expanding customs revenues would bolster the province's desperately weak finances, and render possible general development in the province. Castilho encouraged these schemes.[66] The prospects of collaboration with the South African Republic seemed bright. In April 1875 the Transvaal Government appointed an engineer to make a preliminary survey for a railway. It also gave a concession to Nellmapius to start road transport between the border and the gold-fields and it sent a delegation, including Nellmapius, to Moçambique to discuss methods of improving communications and commercial relations. The Governor-general extended the road concession to Portuguese territory, and the Lourenço Marques and South African Republic Transport Service came into being. The goods so transported which passed the frontier post established at Castilhopolis were mainly food and drink— especially drink for the thirsty miners—and arms and gunpowder.[67]

In June 1875 the British Foreign Office received secret information that the arbitration award would be against Britain; and that Burgers, President of the Transvaal, was about to set out on a secret mission to Portugal to buy Delagoa Bay, and obtain guarantees from Germany, the United States and

62 Protocol, Lisbon, 25/9/1872, *RSEA* IX, pp. 59–62.
63 For a description of a journey between Delagoa Bay and Lydenburg in 1873 see E. Cohen, 'Erläutende Bemerkungen zu der Routenkarta Reise van Lydenburg . . .', (*Zweiter Jahresbericht der geographische Gesellschaft in Hamburg 1874–75*, Hamburg, 1875), pp. 173–286, and map facing p. 236.
64 GG to Min., 26/9/74, 174, AHU, Moç., Pasta 29.
65 Forssman to Min., 19/10/74, 10, Nec., Consulados de Portugal no Transvaal, 1, 1874–1890; and 18/1/75, 1 ibid.
66 GG to Min., 29/3/75, 79 and 29/3/75, 119, and 20/5/75, 126, AHU, Moç., Pasta 31.
67 GG to Min., 2/6/75, 161, and 28/6/75, 175, 176, and 22/7/75, 192, 27/7/75, 206, AHU, Moç., Pasta 29; GG to Min., 22/7/75, 2/924 AHU, Moç., 2 Rep. Caixa 1; Forssman to Min., 21/6/75, 6, Nec., CPT 1; Nellmapius to Forssman, 13/8/75, Civil 33, Nec., CPT 1; *Bol. Off.* 6/11/75, p. 257.

Russia to safeguard this acquisition.[68] The Secretary of State for Foreign Affairs promptly instructed Lord Lytton, the British minister in Lisbon, to propose that Portugal and Britain enter into a mutual agreement by which, whichever way the award might go, the successful power would give the defeated claimant the opportunity to acquire the territory by purchase or for some other consideration. The Portuguese Government agreed.[69] MacMahon, who had succeeded Thiers, officially issued his verdict on 24 July 1875.[70] Britain announced that she would loyally abide by the award, but the opinion was expressed that if Britain had known how important Delagoa Bay was to become she would never have agreed to arbitration.[71]

With increase in the popularity and status of Lourenço Marques came suggestions that a British vice-consul[72] and an English minister of religion[73] be stationed there. Elton urged the British Government to try and purchase the Bay, or obtain its cession. The main reason he advanced was the reckless sale of guns and gunpowder, lead and spirits. Between the beginning of January and October 1875 no less than 15,000 guns were sold to tribes bordering on Natal and the Transvaal; most had passed into the hands of the Zulus. Of the traders only two were Portuguese; the others were English or Germans or Netherlanders. Portugal was not developing the place; despite 3 per cent tax for public works added to the customs duties, nothing had been done beyond the construction of a causeway across the marsh leading to the town, a wall for the useless fort, a small custom-house, and an inexpensive lighthouse: there was no wharf, nor was there any building on the healthy heights overlooking the bay. No Portuguese lived outside the city walls, two miles beyond which Portuguese influence was non-existent. "No control whatever is exercised over the neighbouring chiefs, and the oaths of allegiance sworn by some few of them lately, represent, each of them, one act in a series of drunken dances and farces which it would be a disgrace to permit in a civilized town." If Britain could acquire Delagoa Bay, Elton urged, there would be development; and Zululand would be encircled; the tractable Tongas lay between the Bay and the turbulent Landeens of Gazaland; and if Britain extended her borders northwards to the Limpopo there would be a useful source of labour for the British colonies, which would be of great value in the attainment of confederation.[74]

Carnarvon, the Secretary of State for the Colonies, had revised plans to

68 C. J. Uys, *In the era of Shepstone* (Lovedale, 1933), p. 146, 153.
69 Lytton to Corvo 14/6/75, Theal, *Records of South Eastern Africa.* IX, pp. 262–3. Corvo to Lytton, 17/6/75, *RSEA* IX, pp. 264–5.
70 Sentence, *RSEA* IX, pp. 266–8.
71 Saldanha to Min., 20/6/75, 17 A, Nec., Legação de Portugal em Londres, Caixa 42, who side-lined an extract to this effect from *News of the World.*
72 Elton to Derby, 26/6/75 CP 2915, p. 350.
73 GG to Min., 8/7/75, 177, AHU, Moç., Pasta 29. In accordance with the laws of the country no Protestant place of worship might have the external appearance of a church. The Governor-general commented on the difference between the foreigners, anxious to educate and civilize, and the Portuguese in Moçambique, whose padres were illiterate and immoral.
74 Elton to Derby, 30/7/75, Consular 47, CP 2915, pp. 406–7; 2/10/75, 10, pp. 409–10; 25/10/75, 11, pp. 415–7; –/10/75, 12, pp. 419–20; J. P. Ablett to Elton 21/10/75, pp. 418–9.

federate the South African colonies and states. If the Transvaal were to acquire Delagoa Bay, she would become so independent that she could refuse to be coerced into federation. The alternatives were for Great Britain to acquire Delagoa Bay, and force the Transvaal into joining the confederation by raising still further the import and export duties—or else Britain could assume direct control of the Transvaal.[75]

Burgers proceeded to Europe. In Amsterdam he obtained promise of a loan for the railway. In Lisbon he failed to gain the cession of Delagoa Bay, but he came to an agreement over the construction of a railway, and negotiated a new treaty which confirmed the freedom of trade between the Transvaal and Portuguese territory, and limited import duties on goods in transit to 3 per cent, which could be raised to a maximum of 6 per cent if necessary to cover the interest and amortization on the costs of construction of the railway line.[76] Natal merchants saw ruin staring them in the face, and they stepped up their anti-Portuguese propaganda. They had an ally in Pine, the Lieutenant-governor, who had seen some hope as long as communication was restricted to wagon transport, which was prejudiced by a belt of tsetse fly; but if a railway were built the great superiority of the port of Delagoa Bay over Durban would enable it almost to monopolize the trade to the Transvaal.[77]

The Government of Moçambique had been chronically short of money, and it seemed impossible that Portugal would ever be able to find the amount necessary for the construction of the Portuguese section of the railway line. But the brisk trade in arms and ammunition was beginning to make Moçambique solvent; an under-secretary in the Foreign Office then had an idea: Carnarvon's conference to discuss federation was shortly to meet in London and if the conference could be persuaded to object to this traffic "we shall be justified in putting very strong pressure upon the Portuguese Government to prohibit the importation of arms through Delagoa Bay. This would impoverish them and might lead to some arrangement for our getting possession of the place." The suggestion appealed to the permanent under-secretary, who added, "A strong effort should again be made to ascertain for what money consideration Portugal would give up Delagoa Bay. We could offer a great deal of Natal money for a purchase of such vital importance to her."[78]

Carnarvon's London conference had no result because the Cape Prime Minister boycotted it; the Transvaal was not represented; and the President of the Orange Free State walked out whenever the question of federation was brought forward. The conference was no sooner over than an alternative line of action suggested itself to the Colonial Office which saw the possibilities of a more positive course of action.[79]

75 Uys, pp. 116–7.
76 J. van der Poel, *Railways and customs policies in South Africa, 1885–1910* (London, 1933), p. 5; for the Treaty of 11/12/75, J. de Almada, *Tratados* (Lisbon, 1947), V, p. 342.
77 Uys, pp. 116–7.
78 Uys, p. 156, who quotes minutes by Malcolm and Herbert, dd 21 and 22/2/76.
79 Uys, p. 173; A. Aylward, *The Transvaal To-day* (Edinburgh, 1878), pp. 45–6; C. W. De Kiewiet, *The imperial factor in South Africa* (C.U.P., 1937), p. 100.

Sekukuni, chief of the Bapedi tribe, which occupied an area between the Steelpoort and Olifant's River, considering himself to be independent, declined to pay taxation. One of his followers forbad the cutting of timber for mine props on his land. This was declared to be an act of rebellion, and when a German missionary falsely reported that his station had been burned down, the Republican Government, desiring to push the Lourenço Marques railway line across his land, declared war on Sekukuni. Burgers, to the consternation of his burghers, led the Republican forces in person. His three columns met with initial successes, but an attack on Sekukuni's stronghold failed disastrously. There was a great loss of white prestige, and there was no knowing what the consequences might be.[80] Forssman considered that there was a possibility of the Swazis and Zulus being drawn into a general war; he urged that white immigrants be sent to Lourenço Marques, which should also be supplied with troops and artillery.[81] It was exactly this danger of a general war which afforded the Colonial Office the pretext that it had been looking for, and Carnarvon gave Shepstone, the Natal representative at the London conference, discretionary authority to annex the Transvaal.[82]

Forssman considered such annexation to be inevitable because of Natal's jealousy of the growing prosperity of Lourenço Marques, and appreciation of the development that would come to the Transvaal's back country after the building of the railway line.[83] This was also the opinion of the Governor-general of Moçambique, who warned his minister that there were no limits to the ambitions of England; the English had taken advantage of the war to bring about stoppage of work on the railway; and they would not be content until they had brought the Transvaal, and Lourenço Marques, under their dominion. He considered that the English had been largely responsible for instigating the Sekukuni war, and he reported that Herbert Rhodes had tried to smuggle a piece of artillery ashore near Lourenço Marques for that chief.[84] At the beginning of January 1877, Shepstone crossed the Transvaal border. In February the Transvaal concluded a peace with Sekukuni. It was not until 12 April that Shepstone proclaimed the annexation of the Transvaal. He had desired to annex all land up to the Zambezi and as far west as 25° longitude, but a legal adviser dissuaded him from this.[85]

In a letter to Herbert, the Permanent Under-secretary of Colonial Affairs, Shepstone exclaimed, "You have now got the Transvaal and a magnificent acquisition it is; the Orange Free State must soon follow, but I hope that Delagoa Bay will follow first because it is the natural sea port of this country, and must be had if possible."[86]

80 Barkly to Carnarvon, 14/7/76, C 1748, pp. 63–4; 25/8/76, pp. 100–1; 31/8/76, p. 113.
81 Forssman to Min., 2/8/76, 6, Nec., CPT 1.
82 Carnarvon to Shepstone, 23/9/76, C 1748, pp. 103–4.
83 Forssman to Min., 10/10/76, 3, Nec., CPT 1. The growing prosperity of Lourenço Marques was well illustrated by district receipts, 1875–6; Angoche, 85 milreis; Sofala, 98; Bazaruto, 255; Sena, 861; Tete, 7, 786; C. Delgado, 8,428; Lourenço Marques, 24, 263 (*Bol. Off.*) 25/9/76, p. 262.
84 GG to Min., 29/10/76, AHU, Moç., Pasta 30; and Castilho, Lourenço Marques, to A-President Joubert, 29/9/75, Uys, pp. 194–5.
85 Uys, pp. 212, 242, 247, 391, 431.
86 Uys, p. 157.

At first Shepstone, appreciating its importance to the economy of the Transvaal, was in favour of building the railway line. He issued a proclamation that his administration guaranteed all bona fide contracts made by the previous Government. But Natal pressures were too great and three months later he was condemning the building of the Lourenço Marques railway line.[87] His action aroused great indignation in Portugal.[88] Castilho saw in it further warning of England's unscrupulous behaviour towards small nations. But material already bought with £75,000 of the Portuguese subsidy would take the railway beyond the Lebombo mountains, and for a further £150,000 a total length of eighty miles of line could be built. Moodie, now the managing director of the Lebombo Railway Company, assured him that an immediate start would be made and ten miles would be constructed that winter.[89] It was essential, however, that adequate police and troops be sent, for with the construction would come an influx of foreigners, and any disorders would be a pretext for foreign intervention. The Lebombo Railway Company had its seat in Pretoria, with a nominal capital of £110,000. Only about £600 was subscribed by the general public; the remainder of the capital was £82,000, subscribed by the SAR Government, the proceeds of the Amsterdam loan. The new administration now declared that the railway project would be ruinous to the country; it suspended all current expenditure on the scheme, apart from what was necessary to safeguard the material already at Delagoa Bay, and referred the matter to London.[90] The Colonial Office, on Shepstone's advice, declared the railway scheme to be "reckless and hopeless": it was wildly extravagant and entirely beyond the Transvaal's resources. The Transvaal was bankrupt, and the administration refused further payments to Moodie.[91] Morier expressed the British Government's lack of sympathy with the scheme and asked the Portuguese Government to rescind the agreement made with Burgers. Though the Portuguese Government had come to power on a retrenchment of public works programme, it had quickly seen the advantages of the railway; it had voted the funds asked for by Castilho, and it refused to be stampeded by the British minister.[92] Ninety per cent of the population of the Transvaal wanted the railway; but, Forssman reaffirmed, Shepstone and his fellow officials, being

87 Uys, p. 157. The chief promoter of the Natal railway was his son-in-law, whilst its solicitor was his son.
88 Morier to Derby, 19/5/77, tel., CP 3686, p. 250.
89 Castilho to GG, 18/5/77, Civil 2, AHU, Moç., Pasta 30; R. T. Hall to G. Pigot Moodie, 13/4/77, Pretoria, CP 4302, pp. 87–8.
90 N. Swart, A-Government Secretary, Pretoria, to General Managing Director, Lebombo Railway Company, 23/5/77, CP 4302, p. 89. It put forward an adverse report by an army engineer, Brooke, who had had no experience of railway construction or of the country (Hall to Moodie, 8/6/77, CP 4302, p. 89–91). Another army engineer, C. Warren, travelled down the Nellmapius road to Lourenço Marques; he decided the railway would cost more than had been estimated, up to £3,000,000 to take it to the highveld, but it would materially help in the development of South Africa (C. Warren to Frere, 29/6/77, PRO, African No. 135; and The Gold Regions in the Transvaal to Delagoa Bay, Nec., CTT 1.)
91 Malcolm to Pauncefote, 25/5/77, CP 3686, p. 270; Gould to Derby, 7/8/77, 54 ST, CP 3686, p. 286; Herbert to Pauncefote, 13/8/77, ibid., p. 313.
92 Morier to Derby, 1/7/77, 45 ST, CP 3686, p. 277; 4/7/77, 47 ST, p. 280; GG to Min., 13/7/77, 169, AHU, Moç., Pasta 30; Derby to Morier, 14/9/77, 63 ST, CP 3686, p. 312; Morier to Derby, 22/11/77, 64 ST, CP 3686, p. 320.

civil servants from Natal, would do nothing to prejudice the interests of Natal.[93] This railway dispute was to undermine relations between Portugal and Britain for many years.

Many Britons also viewed the Portuguese policy in Moçambique with hostility on humanitarian grounds, for the colony was commonly regarded as a dumping ground for convicts, and an area where slavery still survived. The exact position could not be determined, the Governor-general admitted in his annual report for 1875. Apart from the impossibility of estimating the native population, no statistics had been kept of the coming of Europeans during recent years. This had been regarded as unnecessary, because all new arrivals of consequence were known by name: most were officers and officials, plus a rare trader. The bulk of the new arrivals were *degredados*. Between 1832 and 1875, 2,836 *degredados* were known to have reached Moçambique; and in 1875 there were 358 *degredados* on Moçambique Island alone. Though emigration from Portugal had averaged 8,584 a year between 1866 and 1871, and somewhat more than that in the years thereafter, virtually none had come to Portuguese Africa.[94]

Nor was it known how many slaves or near slaves there were in Moçambique. When in 1854 a decree had freed state-owned slaves and defined the rights and obligation of *libertos*, there were 40,086 registered slaves in Moçambique. A decree of 1856 had abolished slavery in northern Angola, Cape Verde and Macau; one of 1858 declared that all remaining slaves in the Portuguese possessions would be liberated in twenty years. In 1869 a decree fixed 27 April 1877 as the date of final liberation of *libertos*. Thanks to Corvo's enlightenment a law of April 1875 declared that slavery would be extinguished the following year. But it was not proclaimed in Zambezia, and a clandestine slave-trade even continued, so that the Governor-general of Moçambique in his report for 1875 estimated that some 2,000 to 4,000 slaves a year were being exported from Moçambique.[95] This question of slavery, and lack of welfare and education in Moçambique (there were only 332 at school in the entire province in 1874) made it easy for Portugal's enemies to appeal to moral and humanitarian arguments when they wished to deprive her of territory.

Another factor was soon to cloud relation between Britain and Portugal— the activity of an individual. Cecil Rhodes was laying the foundations of his future fortune. In 1877 he made a remarkable will declaring that his estate was to be used for "the establishment, promotion and development of the Secret Society, the true aim and object whereof shall be the extension of British rule throughout the world, the perfecting of a system of emigration from the United Kingdom and of colonization by British subjects of all lands wherein the means of livelihood are attainable by energy, labour and enterprise, and especially the occupation by British settlers of the entire Continent of Africa . . ."

93 Nellmapius to Gov., Lourenço Marques, 7/10/77, 3, AHU, Moç., Pasta 31; GG to Min., 20/11/77, 266, ibid.; Forssman to Min., 8A, 5/12/77, 15/7/78, and 16/7/78, Nec., CPT 1.
94 Corvo, 1, pp. 331–2; *Bol. Off.* 3/7/76, p. 165–6, Relação dos degradados: 7 from Portugal, 69 from Goa, in 1875.
95 Corvo, 1, pp. 336, 344–6, 428; Supplementary law, 29/4/75, *Bol. Off.* 29/1/76.

The will was fantastic and unrealizable; his fortune was not yet made; but this was a declaration of policy to see the map of Africa coloured red.[96] Once he found the fortune and the power collision would be inevitable with any person, group or state that stood in his way.

Portugal's immediate difficulties, however, arose, not from foreign intervention but from the pusillanimity of some of the members of her own parliament.

96 J. G. Lockhart and C. M. Woodhouse, *Rhodes* (London, 1963), pp. 69–70.

2

THE LOURENÇO MARQUES TREATY OF 1879

Livingstone and philanthropists of his time had laid emphasis on the importance not only of Christianity but of commerce in the civilizing of Africa. The Zambezi, in particular, was described in glowing and exaggerated terms as a highway into the interior.[1] As a result, when missionary reinforcements went to Nyasaland in 1876, a would-be trader, Cotterill, accompanied the party with the intention of making the route by way of the lower Zambezi and the Shire a commercial reality. At the request of the British Government, which insisted that the Nyasa area lay outside Portuguese dominion, the Portuguese Government granted Cotterill many facilities, and remitted the customs duties on his goods.[2] Cotterill on arriving at Livingstonia did not confine his activities to trade. He reported to the Secretary of State for Foreign Affairs that there were now twenty-three British subjects in the country of whom seventeen were white, and he declared "we are all of the most decided opinion that no permanent good can be effected until the region of Lake Nyasa is placed under British jurisdiction. We have a right to the country by discovery, and by first occupation."[3]

But before the crisis over sovereignty came to a head there was a clash over access to the Nyasa area. This clash became inevitable when in August 1875 the Portuguese Government granted a monopoly of steam navigation on the Zambezi and the Shire for thirty years to two traders.[4] Corvo, informing Morier of this, added that his Government asserted Portuguese sovereignty over those two rivers, and all territories in eastern Africa within the limits declared by the treaty of July 1817. Morier pointed out that this could be construed to mean a claim to the whole territory between the Indian Ocean coast and Angola. With the authority of the Secretary of State, he intimated to Corvo that Her Majesty's Government had no desire to enter into a discussion regarding the precise limits of Portuguese territory in east Africa; they did not question the full sovereignty of Portugal over the *coastal* territory between Cape Delgado and Lourenço Marques; "but with regard to the vast interior of the African continent, respecting which no treaties exist, they do

1 e.g. D. Livingstone, *Missionary Travels and Researches in South Africa* (London, 1857), pp. 673–5.
2 A. J. Hanna, *Beginnings of Nyasaland and North-Eastern Rhodesia 1859–95* (Oxford, 1956), pp. 107–10.
3 H. B. Cotterill to Derby, 30/10/76, CP 3686, pp. 174–5; Min. to GG, 12/6/76, 228, *Bol. Off.* 21/8/76, p. 220, did not arrive in time, and so much correspondence ensued to obtain a refund of the duties paid (Cotterill to Derby, 3/2/77, CP 3686, p. 268).
4 Min. to GG, 5/6/76, 220, 5/6/76, *Bol. Off.* 21/8/76, p. 219.

not admit that the idea of sovereignty can be dissociated from that of a bona fide occupation and *de facto* jurisdiction of a continuous and non-intermittent kind."[5] Cotterill was assured that the British Government had no reason to believe that the Portuguese Government had any intention of asserting any claim of sovereignty over Lake Nyasa, adding that it would not look with indifference on any attempt on the part of the Portuguese Government to take possession of that lake, or interfere with free access to it, or free navigation on it, by British subjects.[6] Morier, informed that this was the point of view of the British Government, battled against the monopoly;[7] then, to his embarrassment, he learned that the concession had been acquired by an Englishman, who had the effrontery to ask the British Secretary of State whether the Portuguese Government would have the power to protect the monopoly against interference by other nations.[8] Derby assured him that the British Government did not recognize any Portuguese right to exclusive navigation of the Zambezi and Shire, and asserted the right of access to Nyasa by British subjects by way of the Shire.[9]

Morier was authorized to come to an agreement with Corvo as to the system of dues to be imposed on goods in transit to and from the interior, and Corvo appointed a special commission.[10] Morier urged that the high tariff then obtaining be drastically reduced, and that the complex, vexatious and dilatory methods of clearing goods through customs be reformed. He urged that the duties be reduced to the level in the Sultanate of Zanzibar, namely, 5 per cent, including port and local dues, otherwise trade into the interior might be tempted to use this alternative route, and Portugal lose both revenue and development.[11] Corvo fell from office before the commission presented its report but the new Government fully appreciated Morier's arguments and accepted the commission's recommendations that port dues be abolished, duties be reduced from the existing 26–30 per cent to a maximum of 10 per cent *ad valorem;* transit dues of 3 per cent be introduced and the coastal trade be opened to all flags, with a 50 per cent preference to Portuguese commerce.[12] The decree of 30 July 1877 based on this report declared that these measures would prevent foreign trade from deserting Portuguese coasts; and it was partly to avoid political complications that the new tariff was being adopted. The decree added that the internal frontier passed through the confluence of the Ruo and the Shire Rivers.[13] Some in Natal shuddered at this liberal policy, but in the end the

5 Hanna, *Beginnings*, pp. 110–2.
6 Pauncefote to Cotterill, 7/2/77, CP 3686, p. 175.
7 Derby to Morier 7/2/77, 13 ST, CP 3686, p. 174; Min. to Sampayo, 30/1/77, ibid., pp. 204–5; Derby to Morier, 12/3/77, 18 ST, ibid., p. 203.
8 H. Vignoles to Tenterden, 27/2/77, CP 3686, p. 209.
9 Derby to Vignoles, 10/3/77, CP 3686, p. 209; Vignoles to Pauncefote, 15/3/77, ibid., p. 218; Pauncefote to Vignoles, 12/3/77, p. 218.
10 Corvo to Morier, 9/2/77, CP 3686, p. 206.
11 Morier to Corvo, 28/2/77, CP 3686, pp. 206–7.
12 Morier to Derby, 12/3/77, 16 ST, CP 3686, p. 210, 23/3/77, 22 ST, ibid., pp. 225–6, 29/3/77, 23 ST, ibid., p. 228, 17/4/77, 27 ST, CP 3686, pp. 233–4; *Commercio do Porto*, 26/4/77, ibid., p. 243; Morier to Derby, 11/5/77, 39 ST, ibid., pp. 251–2; Gould to Derby, 18/8/77, 58 ST, ibid., pp. 293–4.
13 J. de Almada, *Corvo* (Lisbon, 1944), pp. 27–8.

official point of view was that though Natal had no transit duties, but charged 6 per cent on most goods for the interior, the route from Durban was so well established that the new tariff would not acutely affect Natal trade.[14]

The monopoly of steam navigation on the Zambezi and the Shire remained irksome. The English company sent an agent to Lisbon, but Morier did all in his power to foil him, pointing out to the authorities that the original concession had lapsed, and with the tariff reformed it would be a grave anomaly to bar free trade from the Zambezi and its tributaries. The Minister for Foreign Affairs agreed that approval had not been given for transfer of the concession. The concessionaire undertook to admit any ship the British Government might require on the Zambezi—provided it did not trade—but Morier would not consider such a paltry concession. It was not until August 1878 that the monopoly finally lapsed and "every vestige of un-freedom" disappeared from the Zambezi.[15]

One physical obstacle remained, and that was the absence of a through channel from the Cuacua to the Zambezi except during floods, necessitating at other times of the year portage for several miles to Mazaro. Machado, the energetic Director of Public Works in Moçambique, contemplated digging a canal. Such a canal, he urged, would have immense economic, political, and strategic advantages.[16] Another handicap to traffic was the number of Landeens who still infested the Mazaro area, and periodically raided the *prazos*. Machado urged the building of some two-storey block houses to confine them.[17]

The Portuguese authorities were gravely perturbed by a journey to Nyasa carried out by Elton, which seemed to advertise official British interest in the area. Elton reported to the British Secretary of State that Portugal exercised no jurisdiction whatsoever beyond, or even as far as, the northern extremity of the Morrumbala marsh. The Portuguese had no legitimate communication with the Makololo and occasionally, he alleged, Portuguese colonists on the Zambezi would dispatch parties to raid outlying Manganja villages and the Makololo, but the agents who led them were disowned when they were unsuccessful.[18] Elton ascended to Blantyre by a newly built road. He met leading chiefs and urged them not to indulge in slave-trading. Dr Stewart conducted him in the *Ilala* to the northern end of the lake, whence he set out to explore to the coast, since the London Missionary Society was interested in this route, and a commercial-philanthropic organization under Sir William Mackinnon

14 Bulwer to Carnarvon, 13/11/77, CP 3928, p. 98.
15 Morier to Derby, 20/4/77, 28 ST, CP 3686, pp. 234–5; and 21/4/77, 30 ST, ibid., pp. 238–9; Pauncefote to Vignoles, 25/4/77, p. 273; Morier to Derby, 25/4/77, 32 ST, p. 240; and 26/4/77, 33 ST, pp. 241–2; Derby to Morier, 26/4/77, 37 ST, p. 231; Gould to Derby, 12/8/77, 56 ST, p. 257; Vignoles to Derby, 16/10/77, pp. 316–7; Morier to Derby, 20/11/77, 63 ST, p. 318; Pauncefote to Vignoles, 6/12/77, p. 321; Morier to Salisbury, 9/7/78, 19 ST, and 21/9/78, CP 3928, p. 150.
16 J. Machado to Dir. Geral, 14/8/77, 33, AHU, Moç., Pasta 30.
17 GG to Min., 11/7/78, 158, AHU, Moç., Pasta 31.
18 Elton, Livingstonia, to Derby, 12/9/77, 40, CP 3928, pp. 188–9.

2 Fortress S. Caetano of Sofala (from A de Castilho, *Relatorio da viagem da canonheira Rio Lima de Lisboa a Moçambique . . . 1884–1885*. Lisbon, 1889)

Fortaleza de S. Caetano de Sofalla—Faces Norte e West (desenho original de Aug. de Castilho

had actually started to build a road from Dar-es-salaam to the northern end of Nyasa. But Elton did not live to reach the coast.[19]

The Portuguese were also intensely resentful of the violent criticism of them and their actions, or inaction, by Young, who, now back in civilization, publicly urged that the Portuguese should never be allowed to assume control over Nyasa. Morier felt constrained to write to him that while fully appreciating the object of the Nyasa settlers, "I find fault with the spirit of hatred, malice and uncharitableness against Portugal and the Portuguese with which you, as the mouthpiece of the commercial-missionary settlement of Lake Nyasa, have thought fit to inspire all your utterances since you returned to civilized life."[20]

While Young's pronouncements were producing turmoil in Portugal the committee responsible for Livingstonia was considering increasing its steamer service and asked the British Government to obtain certain assurances as to navigation and trade.[21] Morier pointed out that the application of the Moçambique tariff to transit traffic postulated two custom-houses: a port of entry and a port of exit. There were then no custom-houses in the interior of Africa, and to raise the matter would be to raise the vexed question of an internal frontier to the Portuguese dominions. The Moçambique tariff had purposely left the matter obscure, declaring that the tariff generally was not to be applied above the confluence of the Shire and the Zambezi (which, literally applied, would exclude Tete and Zumbo). In the circumstances it would be safer to try and induce the Portuguese Government to establish a custom-house at that confluence, to clear goods in transit which had entered through the existing custom-house at Quelimane.[22]

Morier wrote to Salisbury that the negotiation required very careful and delicate handling, but diplomacy was prejudiced by the reckless attitude of some of the more prominent promoters of the scheme.

> The Nyasa settlers are, I believe, highly meritorious persons, possessing in an eminent degree the qualities likely to ensure success in their peculiar undertaking, namely religious zeal, in combination with that keen insight into matters of business by which North Britons are distinguished. They deal in Gospel truths and calicoes, and obtain in exchange, baptisable infants, Sunday scholars, wax, ivory, and other native products, doing, in addition, really valuable service by keeping a sharp outlook upon the slave-trade in the interior.

They had settled in a no-man's-land, for while Great Britain had refused to admit that the Portuguese could claim that territory, Great Britain had never claimed it herself. There was acrimonious controversy as to who had been the first white man to sight Nyasa. Morier considered it certain that the lake was as known to the Portuguese in the sixteenth century as it was unknown to them in the nineteenth. Morier therefore avoided this stumbling block by

19 Elton to Derby, 13/10/77, CP 3928, p. 190; Hanna, *Beginnings*, pp. 55–6; Anstey, p. 70.
20 Morier to Young, 31/12/77, CP 3928, p. 121.
21 Salisbury to Morier, 18/4/78, 8 ST, CP 3928, pp. 106–7.
22 Morier to Salisbury, 28/4/78, 10 ST, CP 3928, pp. 112–3; Morier to Corvo, 3/5/78, ibid., pp. 114–5.

declaring that Britain refused to recognize Portuguese sovereignty because of the lack of bona fide occupation and *de facto* continuous exercise of jurisdiction. Morier feared collision, not on the lake itself, but in connection with the waterway to the lake, over which Portugal had asserted rights, which had been unequivocally disputed by the British Government. But the settlers had to pass through Portuguese territory. It would have seemed natural for them to cultivate good relations but some of their more active members seemed to have inherited the animosity of Dr Livingstone against the Portuguese, and vilified everything connected with Portuguese dominion in Africa. The Portuguese Government had granted special facilities for Young's expedition, and for Cotterill to trade. The settlement afforded an opportunity of raising the whole question of opening up the interior of Africa by way of the Zambezi. Corvo had proved most co-operative over the steamship monopoly, the tariff, free trade, free cabotage, and low transit dues. But everything was being prejudiced by "the pyrotechnic displays of bombardier missionaries". Young was still making violently abusive speeches against the Portuguese, declaring that the settlers in Nyasaland would never submit to Portuguese authority and the sooner the Portuguese in south-east Africa were substituted by Englishmen the better. This had provoked violent debates in the Cortes, and aroused the bitterest feelings, and removed Corvo from the Colonial Office, where he had been replaced by Thomaz Ribeiro, a poet of some merit, who was chiefly known politically for the violence of his attacks on the British. Morier considered that the foolish chauvinism of irresponsible agents should be repudiated by their employers, or the question might rapidly assume an international character. Already the Nyasa settlers were making common cause with the native tribes against the Portuguese, and furnishing them with arms and ammunition, instigating them to oppose Portuguese penetration into the interior. Morier had no doubt that "these gallant missionaries, with their bibles and their swords, and, above all, their Makololo allies well stockaded on the lower Shire, would prove a match for any Portuguese armies that should be so foolish as to attack them." But there was a better way of achieving the desired end. Commercial development would give the settlement a new importance; "With this importance it will grow, and with this growth will necessarily come British jurisdiction, and, with British jurisdiction and the unfurling of the British flag, British territorial rights and sovereignty."[23]

This assertion of British sovereignty was brought a step nearer by the formation of the Livingstonia Central African Company (Limited). This Company, started by the efforts of J. and F. Moir, who were appointed joint managers, became responsible for the trading side of the mission's endeavours. It bought a paddle steamer, the *Lady Nyasa*, which was to run a two-monthly service between Mazaro and the foot of the Shire rapids, and might also pay periodic visits to Tete.[24]

23 Morier to Salisbury, 14/5/78, 12 ST, CP 3928, p. 116; and 15/5/78, 13 ST, pp. 119–20.
24 Salisbury to Morier, 31/7/78, 24, CP 3928, p. 132; F. Moir, *After Livingstone* (London, [1923], pp. 7–9; and microfilm of journals by Moir in possession of Gubbins Library, University of the Witwatersrand, Johannesburg.

Morier now formally proposed that a custom-house be established at the confluence of the Zambezi and the Shire. He regretted the death of Elton; no successor had been appointed; and he "could foresee nothing but confusion if the bellicose missionaries of the lake and the mulish officials of the Portuguese colony are left to settle these questions between themselves . . ."[25]

A graver question arose over the sale of arms to the Zulus. Cetewayo was going far towards reviving Chaka's military organization but equipping his impis with more modern weapons. An average of 20,000 percussion guns, 500 breech-loading rifles, and 10,000 barrels of gunpowder, were sold each year in Lourenço Marques, where the trade brought great profit, for a musket cost eight shillings, customs duties were 2s. 3d., and it sold for 24s. Two-thirds of the guns, it was estimated, reached the Zulus.[26] The South African Republic had laid claim to territory in the north-west of Zululand, but its war with Sekukuni diverted its attention. Shepstone had supported Cetewayo against the Transvaal claims and brought pressure to bear on the Zulu chief to prevent him from attacking the Republic (while using the threat as an argument for annexation). Great was his indignation when Shepstone, having taken over the Transvaal, declared himself in favour of the Transvaal land claims. Shepstone told London that war with Zululand was inevitable, and the sooner it came the better. Carnarvon, in view of complications elsewhere, wished that it be postponed, and Cetewayo was persuaded, in January 1878, to agree to arbitration of his border dispute.[27]

Confident of the outcome of the arbitration, and that war was inevitable, Frere sent an agent to Lourenço Marques to remind the Governor of the old alliance between Portugal and England and to request the Portuguese authorities to forbid the sale of arms to the Zulus.[28] Frere also asked as a matter of urgency for diplomatic overtures to be made in Lisbon. Morier reminded Salisbury that in 1876 he had approached the Portuguese Government about the advisability of controlling the sale to natives of arms and ammunition imported through Lourenço Marques; Corvo had declared that he was very anxious for the two governments to come to an agreement, but the Colonial Office had declared the moment to be inopportune. It was, therefore, impossible to address a remonstrance to the Portuguese Government. But Corvo was still Minister of Foreign Affairs, and he was still co-operative; though Morier's request reached him on Good Friday, he sought out Ribeiro, the Colonial Minister, at midnight so that the necessary orders might leave a few hours later on a mail ship for southern Africa.[29] These orders were obeyed and no more arms or ammunition were sold to natives at Lourenço Marques. Cetewayo sent an embassy to Lourenço Marques to protest, declaring that the Zulus and the Portuguese had been friends long before the English had intruded, and inquiring

25 Morier to Salisbury, 21/9/78, 35 ST, CP 3928, p. 150.
26 O'Neill to Salisbury, 5/8/79, PRO, FO 179/215; Thompson, V/Consul, Lourenço Marques, to O'Neill, 22/9/79, ibid.
27 R. Coupland, *Zulu Battle Piece: Isandhlwana* (Oxford, 1948), pp. 21–32 and C 1748, 1961, 1883, 2079, 2220.
28 Castilho to GG, 17/3/78, 178, AHU, Moç., Pasta 31.
29 Morier to Salisbury, 19/4/78, 4 ST, CP 3928, p. 109 and 20/4/78, 9 ST, p. 110.

whether the once great King of Portugal was now taking orders from the Queen of England.[30] Arms and munitions were largely diverted to Inhambane, whence quantities made their way to Gazaland and tribes bordering on the eastern Transvaal; one merchant alone was reputed to have sold ninety cases each containing twenty guns in one day.[31]

In these anxious days inhabitants of Natal and the Transvaal maintained that it would be a safeguard if Great Britain could acquire control of Delagoa Bay; their wishful thinking gave rise to reports that negotiations between the Portuguese and British Governments had resulted in an arrangement by which Delagoa Bay was to be exchanged for a British port in India, plus the payment of £190,000. The English inhabitants of Lourenço Marques, when these rumours reached them, became so overbearing that the Governor had to request an official denial of the reports.[32]

The British Government meanwhile was impressing on the Portuguese the community of their interests, warning them of general agitation among the tribes in south-east Africa directed against the whites, and declaring that only Great Britain had adequate means to prevent a general insurrection. Morier, requesting that the ban on the sale of arms (some of which were said to be paid for by the Russian Government) be extended to Inhambane, reminded Corvo of the Portuguese proverb, "When you see your neighbour's beard on fire, you soak your own."[33] Castilho, at least, was fully aware of the danger. He warned Lisbon of a terrible war which could not help but have far-reaching consequences on the Portuguese colony.[34] His reports helped to make his Government receptive to proposals from Britain.

Owing to this fear of the Zulus, and of concerted black action, and with an eye on the welfare of the Transvaal, the Colonial Office in August 1878 declared to the Foreign Office that it was advisable to come to a clear understanding with Portugal over Delagoa Bay. The best solution, of course, would be the cession of Delagoa Bay, but since that was out of the question, negotiations were essential. There was much to be said for declaring Delagoa Port a free port, but to avoid objections from Natal it might be preferable to come to an agreement by which customs duties would not exceed those paid at British ports.[35] Salisbury concurred, and it was arranged that Shepstone, who was due to visit England, should call at Lisbon and confer with Morier,[36] who was instructed to sound the Portuguese Government on the conclusion of a treaty of commerce and navigation which would be to the mutual benefit of the British and Portuguese possessions in South Africa. Morier at about this time telegraphed London that Corvo was largely sympathetic and that he

30 Castilho to GG, 5/8/78, 52, AHU, Moç., Pasta 31.
31 Morier to Salisbury, 11/7/78, 20 ST, CP 3928, p. 129; Nellmapius to Sec. to Government, Pretoria, 1/8/78, p. 155; Morier to Salisbury, 7/9/78, 30 ST, p. 143.
32 Castilho to GG, 5/9/78, 69, AHU, Moç., Pasta 31; GG to Min., 25/9/78, 230, ibid.
33 Morier to Corvo, 13/9/28, CP 3928, pp. 145–6; Morier to Salisbury, 16/9/78, 33 ST, p. 146 and 34 ST, pp. 146–8.
34 Castilho to GG, 9/9/78, 74, AHU, Moç., Pasta 31; GG to Min., 25/9/78, 229, ibid.
35 R. H. Meade to Sir J. Pauncefote, 17/8/78, CP 4302, pp. 1–2.
36 Pauncefote to Meade, 24/9/78, CP 4302, p. 2; Salisbury to Morier, 24/9/78, ST 28, ibid., p. 2.

believed that if there were a widespread native uprising in south-east Africa, the Portuguese Government would be prepared to grant free passage of troops through Lourenço Marques, in a manner similar to that provided for in a treaty concerning Goa, which had been recently negotiated; but Anglo-Portuguese relations would be still more improved if Lourenço Marques were the terminus of a British railway.[37] So anxious were the Portuguese Government and Portuguese public opinion to see this railway materialize that Morier appreciated that with this as a bargaining factor many concessions could be obtained.[38] The Secretary of State for War considered it most advisable that permission be immediately obtained for the passage of British troops through Delagoa Bay should it be decided to embark on operations against the Zulus.[39] Salisbury accordingly told Morier that since Portugal had applied for a renewal of negotiations about Goa, "if possible, at the same time commence and conduct, *pari passu*, negotiations for Lourenço Marques railway."[40] Corvo agreed to the principle of negotiation for the Lourenço Marques railway, but until Morier knew exactly what the Colonial Office wished to obtain, he could not fix the definite bases.[41] Salisbury instructed Morier to apply for permission for British troops to pass through Portuguese territory for operations against the Zulus.[42] The High Commissioner forbade Shepstone to leave South Africa in those unsettled days.[43] Morier was left to initiate the negotiations alone. The Portuguese Government promptly announced its willingness to permit the passage of British troops; but it naturally expected Britain to co-operate with the Portuguese forces in repelling any attacks to which Portuguese territory might be exposed. Morier drew a distinction between defensive operations and landing troops to march across Portuguese territory for offensive operations against Zululand. He sounded a warning however that it would be well for the military authorities carefully to weigh the advantages of landing troops at Lourenço Marques against the possible disadvantages of extending the area of hostilities and increasing the white property to be defended.[44]

Morier's conversations with Corvo were most friendly.[45] The King of Portugal, in his speech from the Throne at the beginning of 1879, announced that negotiations were in progress for a treaty which would draw closer relations between Lourenço Marques and the Transvaal.[46] The Colonial Office however had decided that it was sufficient for the time being to express to the Portuguese Government the readiness of Great Britain to go to their aid in the defence of Delagoa Bay should there be any unfortunate consequences from making Delagoa Bay a base for operations against the Zulus, and a grant of reciprocal

37 Morier to Salisbury, 3/10/78, tel., CP 4302, pp. 2–3; and 3/10/78, ST 41, p. 3.
38 Morier to Salisbury, 23/10/78, ST 45, CP 4302, p. 6.
39 R. Thompson to Branston, 22/10/78, CP 4302, p. 5.
40 Salisbury to Morier, 25/10/78, CP 4302, p. 5.
41 Morier to Salisbury, 29/10/78, tel., CP 4302, p. 5.
42 Salisbury to Morier, 5/11/78, CP 4302, p. 6; Morier to Corvo, 15/11/78, p. 8.
43 Shepstone to S of S for Colonies, 11/11/78, FO 179/215.
44 Corvo to Morier, 24/11/78, CP 4302, p. 8–9; Morier to Salisbury, 25/11/78, 76 Confid., ibid., pp. 7–8; and 25/11/78, 77 most confid., pp. 9–10.
45 Morier to Salisbury, 4/12/78, ST 49, ibid., pp. 11–5.
46 2/1/79, FO 179/216.

rights.[47] Shortly afterwards the Colonial Office decided that the time was not opportune for negotiations with Portugal.[48] Meanwhile events in Natal were moving rapidly to a climax. The British commission, appointed in January 1878 to arbitrate on the disputed frontier, found in favour of the Zulus. But its report was kept secret for months, and revealed only on 13 December, when it was accompanied by an ultimatum from Frere to the Zulus to comply with certain demands which they could not accept. On 11 January 1879 British troops crossed the Tugela.[49]

The absence of any Colonial Office opinion seemed ominous to Morier,[50] but he proceeded to draft out a "treaty between Great Britain and Portugal for the development of commerce in South Africa and the more effectual suppression of the slave-trade on the East coast and in the Interior of the African Continent." It provided for the granting of reciprocal freedom of commerce and navigation; the pivotal article, 4, conceded to Great Britain the use of Delagoa Bay for both commercial and military purposes, with the right, on conditions to be agreed on, "to embark and disembark troops, stores and munitions of war at Delagoa Bay and the free passage of such to her Majesty's dominions across the dominions of His Most Faithful Majesty." The next articles bound the two governments jointly to build the projected railway, the details to be left to a joint commission to meet in Delagoa Bay; as Corvo had already conceded complete immunity from dues and charges to goods in transit, interest and amortization were to be guaranteed by customs duties. An article requiring interchange of information about slave-trading operations and joint action in certain circumstances Morier intended "as a gentle irritant to act as a corrective to the normal torpor of Portuguese officialdom." Another clause provided for the two countries to adopt identical rules regarding the importation of arms and munitions and their sale to the natives.[51]

It is worth following the fortunes of this treaty, because had it been accepted and ratified, in its amended form, the relations between Portugal and Great Britain would have been drastically changed, and the critical events of subsequent years might have been avoided.

The Colonial Office did not like the linking of the railway question, which it described as being possibly impracticable or uneconomic, and certainly a source of political embarrassment, to the right to land troops at Delagoa Bay. It accordingly requested the Secretary of War to reconsider whether the advantage of using Delagoa Bay was so great from a military point of view as to justify the risk.[52] Morier pointed out that his instructions had been to "commence and conduct negotiations for the Lourenço Marques railway";

47 Herbert to Pauncefote, 12/12/78, CP 4302, pp. 15–6.
48 Herbert to Pauncefote, 16/1/79, CP 4302, pp. 18–20.
49 Coupland, *Zulu Battle Piece*, pp. 40–1, 57–9; GG to Min., 4/1/79, 2/3, AHU, Moç., Rep. Pasta 1.
50 Morier to Salisbury, 18/1/79, ST 4, CP 4302, pp. 21–3.
51 Morier, draft of Treaty, c. 27/1/79, CP 4302, pp. 26–30; Morier to Salisbury, 27/1/79, ST 6, ibid., pp. 24–5.
52 Herbert to Pauncefote, 28/1/79, CP 4302, p. 31, and Herbert to Thompson, 28/1/79, pp. 31–2; Salisbury to Morier, 30/1/79, ST 7, ibid., p. 21.

he had naturally assumed that this had been definitively decided upon by the British Government, and he had made it the basis of his negotiation. If the question of the railway was to be left open, his negotiations would bear the stamp of bad faith.[53] Salisbury telegraphed to him that he had misunderstood his instructions; there was nothing even provisionally committing the Government to pay for the railway; only Parliament could advance funds for such a purpose and that only after a careful survey.[54]

Morier, of course, had never assumed that the British Government would take full responsibility for the financing of the railway, only that it would co-operate with the Portuguese authorities. The railway clause could easily be made dependent on the results of survey and parliamentary exigencies; he re-drafted the article accordingly.[55] There was now freedom of action as far as the building of the railway was concerned since the Moodie contract had lapsed.[56]

The disaster of Isandhlawana, in February 1879, when 800 English soldiers were killed, caused consternation in Portugal. The predominating public opinion was that England should have left well alone: she had thrust her heel into a hornet's nest; without adequate strength she had annoyed the Transvaal, and seized Zulu kraals; there was fear lest Delagoa Bay be overwhelmed in a common disaster. The attitude of the Government was sympathetic however, and Corvo was convinced that events emphasized the necessity for inter-colonial co-operation; he regretted that earlier negotiations had not been followed up, for the mere landing of British troops at Lourenço Marques would have sufficed to prevent the concentration of the Zulu force on the Natal frontier.[57] But the War Office now decided that there would be no advantage in landing troops at Delagoa Bay to take the Zulus in the rear.[58] Morier still considered the times particularly propitious to negotiate a general agreement with Portugal.[59] The Colonial Office however remained unconvinced; it considered the first necessity was to bring the Zulu war to a successful conclusion.[60] Corvo had wanted to present to the Cortes the Goa and Lourenço Marques treaties simultaneously; but he could not further delay the former, so the urgency to complete the negotiations for the Lourenço Marques one fell away.[61] Salisbury decided, "Events in South Africa have made conclusion of treaty with Lourenço Marques railway impossible for the present."[62] Morier, intimating this decision to Corvo, did not dare give a reason, lest it seem that Great Britain was incapable of re-establishing order and security, and there might be loss of confidence in

53 Morier to Salisbury, 5/2/79, tel., CP 4302, pp. 32–3; and 5/2/79, ST 11, pp. 36–41.
54 Salisbury to Morier, 6/2/79, ST 13, CP 4302, p. 33.
55 Morier to Salisbury, 7/2/79, tel., CP 4302, pp. 33–4; and 7/2/79, ST 15, ibid., pp. 42–3; and 7/2/79, 16 ST, ibid., pp. 43–6; and 7/2/79, ST 17., ibid., pp. 46–8; the new article, pp. 48–9.
56 Morier to Salisbury, 10/2/79, 18 ST, CP 4302, p. 18.
57 Morier to Salisbury, 15/2/79, ST 19, CP 4302, pp. 50–2.
58 F. Russell, memo., 24/2/79, CP 4302, p. 67; Thompson to Herbert, 11/3/79, p. 67.
59 Morier to Salisbury, 8/3/79, 22 ST, CP 4302, pp. 55–6.
60 Meade to Pauncefote, 11/3/79, CP 4302, pp. 53–4.
61 Morier to Salisbury, 11/3/79, 23 ST, CP 4302, p. 54.
62 Salisbury to Morier, 12/3/79, 21 ST, CP 4302, p. 55; and 17/3/79, 24 ST. ibid., p. 57 F.

Britain's omnipotence. Morier could not help but express his keen regret that the negotiation should be interrupted. The railway article, as re-drafted, merely pledged the two governments to undertake at some future date the joint construction of a railway after careful examination by a joint commission; there would be other advantages obtained for Great Britain; and the harbour would be available for debarkation of British troops, and they would be granted transit, should it ever be deemed necessary if not to Zululand, then to any threatened district in the Transvaal, by the very shortest line. The mere fact that this right was in existence would help to prevent native organization.[63] Morier proceeded to London on leave where he did much lobbying for his projected treaty. He pointed out that the real grievance of the Boers was the persistent manner in which Britain had resisted all their efforts to gain access to the sea. Refusal to proceed with the railway planned by Burgers was one of the real and most effective causes of the opposition to British rule in the Transvaal.[64] So strong was this disaffection that Boers had entered into secret communication with the Zulus to make common cause in resisting British invasions of their countries.[65] The railway, even Frere now accepted, was a practical possibility.[66] Morier's efforts met with considerable success; the Foreign Office authorized him to resume negotiations of general principles, though practical steps towards securing the railway could be postponed until after the restoration of tranquillity.[67]

The Portuguese Foreign Office made certain emendations to the draft treaty, which did not alter the substance, but which were to establish the appearance of completely formal reciprocity. Morier remarked that in view of "the vanitous susceptibility of the Portuguese Cortes this is a matter of considerable importance."[68] The Colonial Office now withdrew its objection to resumption of negotiations, though it declared that as far as the railway was concerned no action even of a preliminary kind was possible until the Zulu war was over and the territories and dominions of South Africa re-constituted.[69] Morier was authorized to sign the treaty as amended but ratification would be postponed until political and economic relations between Great Britain and the South African colonies were more definitely adjusted, and the assent of the local authorities had been received to such portions of the treaty as might require it.[70]

Morier returned to Lisbon on the night of 27 May 1879.[71] At noon the next day he saw Corvo, who observed that he had returned not an hour too

63 Morier to Salisbury, 14/3/79, 32 ST, CP 4302, pp. 60–1.
64 Morier, memo., 4/4/79, CP 4302, pp. 62–5.
65 GG to Min., 5/5/79, 126, AHU, Moç., Pasta 32; and 10/5/79, 4, 1 Rep. Pasta 1.
66 Frere to Beach, 20/3/79, CP 4302, pp. 78–9 enclosing R. T. Hall to W. Littleton, 10/3/79, ibid., pp. 79–80, estimating that 106 miles, to the Transvaal border, 3′ 6″ gauge, would cost £53,740.
67 Morier to Saurin, 10/4/79, FO 179/215; Pauncefote to Saurin, 12/4/79, CP 4302, p. 66; Saurin to Corvo, 14/4/79, FO 179/217.
68 Morier, memo., London, 15/5/79, CP 4302, pp. 68–70.
69 Herbert to Lister, 21/5/79, CP 4302, p. 76.
70 Lister to Herbert, 22/5/79, CP 4302, p. 77; Herbert to Lister, 23/5/79, ibid., p. 77; Salisbury to Morier, 23/5/79, ibid., pp. 77–8.
71 Morier to Salisbury, 27/5/79, 32, FO 179/216.

soon: a ministerial crisis was pending, and the storm would burst at any moment; he asked if the treaty might be signed the next day. Morier tried to persuade him that he was morally bound to remain in office till parliament had sanctioned it.[72] By an exchange of notes it was agreed that ratification would be postponed.[73] On 30 May 1879 the treaty was signed,[74] and the Government resigned.[75]

Morier expressed forcibly to the King of Portugal that it was most unfair that the Fontes ministry, which had inaugurated an entirely new system in colonial relations between Great Britain and Portugal, should resign at the very moment when this new system was to pass from theory into practice. Had the ministry remained in power a fortnight longer both the Lourenço Marques and the Goa treaties would be safe. The only hope for these treaties now lay with the King, who was the sole connecting link between the past and the present. The King observed that Corvo had spoken in the same sense, and he undertook to urge on Braamcamp, the new Prime Minister, the importance of at once proceeding with the treaties.[76] But Braamcamp, "an old man with deficient vitality," though cordial to Morier, declared that the majority still lay with the Fontes party, the Regeneradores. Fontes professed his co-operation, but though the Goa treaty was passed, the new Government refused to present the Lourenço Marques treaty and adjourned the Cortes until the new year.[77] Salisbury fully appreciated Morier's political difficulties, and expressed to him the high sense of the British Government for his energy, tact and judgment displayed in the negotiation of the treaty.[78]

Morier asked Braamcamp if he would apply the treaty clauses without waiting for the legislative approval of the treaty as a whole. This the Prime Minister agreed to do and he issued orders for Portuguese naval forces to come to an agreement with the British naval forces for joint action in suppressing the slave-trade; but he invoked the terms of an old treaty, of 1842, not that of 1879.[79]

Braamcamp decided to go to the country, and as the time for the elections approached a violent campaign opened in the press against the new treaty. This Morier condemned as a transparent manoeuvre. Morier thought that this uncompromising attitude was distasteful to the "aged, amiable and anaemic mediocrity who at present acts the part of Prime Minister in this country," but he was impotent to restrain his irresponsible partners. Dantas, the Portuguese

72 Morier to Salisbury, 28/5/79, tel., CP 4302, p. 91; and 28/5/79, ST 48, ibid., pp. 94–5.
73 Morier to Corvo, 29/5/79, CP 4302, p. 100; and Corvo to Morier, 29/1/79, ibid., p. 101.
74 Tratado . . ., *Neg. Ext.* . . . 1880, pp. 381–94.
75 Morier to Salisbury, 30/5/79, tel., CP 4302, p. 92.
76 Morier to Salisbury, 1/6/79, CP 4302, pp. 102–3.
77 Morier to Salisbury, 7/6/79, Commercial Confid. 24, FO 179/216, and 8/6/79, tel., ibid.; and 8/6/79, Comm. 27, ibid.; and 11/6/79, Comm. 29, CP 4302; and 12/7/79, ibid., pp. 104–5.
78 Salisbury to Morier, 28/7/79, CP 4302, pp. 105–6.
79 Braamcamp to Morier, 26/8/79, FO 179/217; Morier to Salisbury, 29/8/79, FO 179/216; Braamcamp to Morier, FO 179/217; Morier to Salisbury, 29/9/79, 67 ST, FO 179/216.

minister in London, agreed that the outcry against the treaty was absurd, and raised only for party purposes.[80]

The Portuguese Government chose this time to re-assert its claims to territory on the west coast of Africa.[81] Morier suggested that the British Government declare that it would entertain no formal discussion on the Congo question until the Lourenço Marques treaty had been ratified, and the Government had shown its readiness to continue with the policy of friendly inter-colonial intercourse of its predecessors.[82] He had great hopes in this lever, and, optimistic that the treaty would be shortly passed, he asked whether the colonial authorities in South Africa had sanctioned those articles which required their endorsement.[83] Though the Zulu war was now over, and Cetewayo a prisoner, the Secretary of State for the Colonies had considered the continuance of native disorders justified him in not bringing the treaty to the notice of the colonial governments;[84] and until their replies were received, the British Government could take no steps towards ratification.[85] This delay was regretted by Morier, for he was confident that if the two treaties could be presented simultaneously to the Cortes there was every prospect that the Lourenço Marques one would also be accepted; and he feared that Natal, covetous of keeping duties she levied on goods in transit to the Transvaal, and jealous of Delagoa Bay, would impose difficulties.[86] All the while the language of the Portuguese press became more unbridled.[87] Salisbury decided that it was unnecessary to wait for colonial approval—and in fact the South African authorities raised no formal protest against the treaty[88]—and when the Secretary for the Colonies concurred, the Portuguese Government was informed that ratification could take place immediately.[89] Knowing that there were strong anti-treaty elements in the cabinet, Morier feared he might not be able to summon the Portuguese Government to ratify without making some reply to the demand for Congo negotiations; but he confined himself to expressing the wish that the Government would consider itself strong enough to ratify the work of its predecessor. This piqued the minister to the desired end.[90] Though Salisbury declined to authorize the opening of negotiations on the Congo question,[91] the treaty was

80 Morier to Salisbury, 6/10/79, 60 ST, CP 4302, pp. 108–9; and 17/10/79, 70 ST, ibid., pp. 111–2; Salisbury to Morier, 22/10/79, FO 179/214; Salisbury to Morier, 10/11/79, Comm. 94, ibid., pp. 115–6.
81 See p. 51.
82 Morier to Salisbury, 14/11/79, 74 ST, CP 4302, p. 117; Salisbury to Morier, 15/11/79, tel., ibid., p. 114 and CP 4786, p. 6; Morier to Salisbury, 19/11/79, ibid., pp. 7–9.
83 Morier to Salisbury, 13/12/79, 81 ST, CP 4302, pp. 117–8, CP 4786, p. 12.
84 Herbert to Pauncefote, 12/1/80, CP 4302, pp. 130–1 and CP 4786, pp. 12–3.
85 Salisbury to Morier, 15/1/80, tel., CP 4302, p. 131.
86 Morier to Salisbury, 12/2/80, 9, CP 4302, pp. 132–4.
87 Morier to Salisbury, 12/3/80, 13, CP 4786, p. 14.
88 T. Upington, opinion, Cape Town, 19/3/80, CP 4302, pp. 152–3; W. Lanyon Pretorius to Wolseley, 20/3/80, ibid., p. 156; Bulwer to Wolseley, 27/3/80, FO 179/218; Wolseley to CO, 29/3/80, ibid., p. 149.
89 Pauncefote to Herbert, 19/3/80, CP 4302, pp. 141–2; Pauncefote to Morier, 25/3/80, 24, CP 4786, p. 18 and tel., ibid., p. 142.
90 Morier to Braamcamp, 26/3/80, CP 4302, p. 144, and CP 4781, p. 19; Morier to Salisbury, 26/3/80, CP 4302, pp. 143–4; Morier to Salisbury, 30/3/80, pp. 147–8.
91 Salisbury to Morier, 21/4/80, 34, CP 4302, p. 151.

submitted to the Cortes, on 20 April 1880.[92] Once Braamcamp had taken the plunge, he was anxious for the treaty to be brought before the house as soon as possible, to stop political controversies and press declamation.[93] As opposition mounted, Morier made it clear that the responsibility would not be his if the treaty failed to pass the Cortes; particularly did he regret the opportunity that would be lost of redressing the very great injustice to the Boers, of deliberately cutting them off from the sea, of diverting the money they had contributed to the railway to other causes, of making the railway material they had bought rust on the shores of Delagoa Bay.[94] The newspaper campaign against the treaty became more and more intensified, but Morier trusted to Braamcamp's loyalty, for he had a reputation for "a character in inverse ratio to his intellectual capacity." But Braamcamp could not fight the rising tide, and he decided to adjourn the Cortes. Morier took the strongest exception to this, declaring that he could not allow such a slight to be put on the English Crown. Braamcamp expressed astonishment at Morier's haste in trying to get the treaty passed, and declared it would come to debate the following year.[95] Morier did some lobbying and obtained promises of support of the treaty from the followers of the Duke of Avila, who occupied a middle place between the contending parties. The Cortes was to close within twenty-four hours, so Morier sent Braamcamp a private letter enclosing the draft of an ultimatum, protesting that the Portuguese Government would, in a most flagrant manner, have broken her word solemnly plighted to Great Britain; and Portugal would have slighted the British Crown, in as much as the ratification, signed by the august hand of Her Majesty, and bearing the Great Seal of Great Britain, had been left lying in the British Legation. This was a situation he, as representative of the Queen, could not accept, and he demanded that the session be prolonged so that the treaty might be submitted to it, and that the Government use all the means at its disposal to get it passed. He requested an answer that day, or he would have to request the British Government for instructions as to how he should act in this grave and unforeseen situation. Braamcamp surrendered, and prolonged the session.[96] But after an emergency caucus meeting of his party he declared that there was no guarantee that the treaty would be accepted. He asked whether Morier insisted on a vote in such circumstances, or whether the debate might be adjourned until the next session of the Cortes, in January 1881. Morier insisted that the engagement be fulfilled to the letter.[97]

92 Morier to Salisbury, 21/4/80, CP 4302, p. 151; Braamcamp, Project of Law 170 A, 21/4/80, FO 179/220; Braamcamp to Morier, 21/4/80, FO 179/222.
93 Morier to Salisbury, 22/4/80, 33, CP 4302, pp. 153–4; see e.g. *Journal des Colonias*, 1/5/80, pp. 160–2, which asserted that the Treaty showed complete contempt for Portugal as an independent nation, and that it was a flagrant injustice to her commercial interests.
94 Morier to Granville, 6/5/80, 38, CP 4302, pp. 157–60.
95 Morier to Granville, 20/5/80, CP 4302, p. 163; Morier to Braamcamp, 27/5/80, pp. 167–70; Morier to Granville, 27/5/80, pp. 165–7; Morier to Braamcamp, 28/5/80, pp. 170–1; Morier to Granville, 28/5/80, p. 170; Morier to Braamcamp, 29/5/80, pp. 172–3; Morier to Granville, 29/5/80, pp. 171–2; Braamcamp to Granville, 30/5/80, pp. 173–4; Morier to Granville, 30/5/80, 54, p. 174.
96 Morier to Braamcamp, draft, 1/6/80, CP 4302, p. 176; Morier to Granville, 1/6/80, 57, pp. 175–6.
97 Morier to Granville, 2/6/80, 58, CP 4302, pp. 176–8; and 3/6/80, 61, p. 178; and tel., 3/6/80, p. 164; Braamcamp to Morier, 3/6/80, pp. 190–1.

The treaty was presented at a secret session of the Cortes, at which Braamcamp spoke courageously in defence of the treaty. But he asked the Portuguese minister in London whether the British Government indeed attached so much importance to having the treaty ratified at that session. Granville, the Secretary of State for Foreign Affairs, declared that it could not be left in suspense for another six months. Braamcamp appealed to Morier, in a painful scene, declaring that the Avila party was withdrawing its support, and the treaty and the Government would both be lost. The distraught Braamcamp announced his intention of resigning, but Morier insisted that a vote be taken first. The King refused to accept Braamcamp's resignation. The next day, 5 January 1880, the Cortes accepted a private member's motion that the legislative committee of the house examine the constitutional legality of the treaty, which was thereby shelved until the session of 1881, and virtually rejected. Morier exclaimed in disgust, "The Portuguese are not so much men, as weak-brained hysterical women, and when they fancy they have had the best of it in any transaction or encounter, they become wholly unmanageable." But Morier still had a game to play. He wrote to Granville, "The Portuguese Government must be intimidated by Her Majesty's Government"; on second thoughts he toned this down to "The Portuguese Government should be disquieted by what they hear from London." He promptly followed this up by visiting London and giving verbal explanations.[98] Pauncefote, however, critically re-examined the treaty, which, he realized, conferred substantial advantages on Great Britain, while all that Portugal received were the hypothetical gains to be derived from the joint control of the harbour and railway of Delagoa Bay. The advantages were all on the British side, as the Portuguese press and Parliamentary opposition had not failed to emphasize.[99] Now that the treaty seemed unobtainable, and the prospects for federation were receding, the Colonial Office became the more anxious for the treaty to be obtained, and Kimberley, the Secretary of State for the Colonies, demanded that every effort be made to obtain ratification of the railway article in some shape or form.[100]

Now however came a turning point. Sabugosa, the Minister of Marine and Ultramar, resigned, and Januário took the office on condition that the Lourenço Marques treaty was signed, which he did from his personal friendship with Corvo and the King, and the conviction that this would lead to important improvements for the province of Moçambique.[101] When therefore the Portuguese minister in London announced that his Government was prepared to come to an agreement which, without altering the treaty materially, would remove the principal objections to it, there was a sympathetic reception of his proposals. Particularly did the Portuguese Government object to the treaty being in perpetuity, and the clauses about the unconditional entry and passage

98 Morier to Granville, 4/6/80, 62, ibid., pp. 179–80; Granville to Morier, 4/6/80, tel., p. 164; Morier to Granville, 5/6/80, 63, pp. 180–2; and 6/6/80, 66, pp. 184–6, and 8/6/80, tel. 69, FO 179/220; and 11/6/80, tel. 71, ibid., and 17/6/80, tel., ibid.
99 Pauncefote, memo., 26/6/80, CP 4302, pp. 202–3.
100 Herbert to Pauncefote, 1/7/80, CP 4302, p. 203.
101 Vansittart to Granville, 5/7/80, 88, FO 179/220; and 9/7/80, 89, CP 4302, p. 205; Morier to Granville, 17/8/80, 106, CP 4395, pp. 4–5.

of British troops, the right of British naval forces to police territorial waters, and British interference in the organization of colonial tariffs. It suggested a term of twelve years; and with concession on the other points, it was convinced that the Chambers would accept the treaty.[102] Kimberley was inclined to agree, provided that the arrangements for the railway were of a permanent nature to ensure security for the capital invested, and that goods in transit should pass free of duty. Granville instructed Morier to re-open negotiations in Lisbon, accepting that the treaty proper was terminable after twelve years.[103] These negotiations opened in August. At the second conference Morier insisted that the railway, being a permanent undertaking, should not be subject to transitory conditions. Braamcamp agreed to extend the term beyond twelve years, and subsequent negotiation centred on what this length should be, Braamcamp suggesting the period, whatever that might be, to pay off the cost of the railway, Morier demanding perpetuity. The Foreign Office suggested 99 years, but eventually, to ensure the passage of the treaty, after repeated consultations with the Colonial Office, it accepted Braamcamp's suggestion, but a ministerial crisis, and the necessity for referring every stage of the negotiation to the Colonial Office, and Morier's insistence, until overruled, on perpetuity, delayed the negotiations. In return for giving up the principle of perpetuity, the Portuguese Government undertook to make the treaty a cabinet matter, to ensure its passing the Cortes, and on 31 December 1880 the ministers signed an additional article and protocol embodying these negotiations.[104]

But in the middle of December 1880 the Boers of the Transvaal had declared their independence. A British column was attacked near Bronkhorstspruit, and the British garrisons in the main towns became virtually invested. Burghers gathered to close the road from Natal at Laing's Nek.[105] In Portugal there was widespread sympathy for the Transvaal, especially in the ranks of the Radical party then in power. Portugal had never been formally informed of the British annexation of the Transvaal, and was still in treaty alliance with the South African Republic. Were the treaty passed, Great Britain would be able to demand the right to send troops through Delagoa Bay to fight the Boers. There was renewed opposition to the treaty, which intensified after a British column had been repulsed at Laing's Nek. The Government, faced with growing political discontent, had no desire to precipitate a crisis and though the diplomatic committee of the House of Deputies reported in favour of the treaty, the Government did nothing to implement its promise to introduce the necessary bill.[106]

Opposition to the treaty mounted. The Democratic or Republican Party, which had been in alliance with the Government, turned against it and

---

102 Granville to Morier, 5/7/80, CP 4302, pp. 204–5.
103 Herbert to FO, 19/7/80, CP 4302, pp. 209–10; Granville to Morier, 4/8/80, 72 and 73, ibid., p. 214.
104 Braamcamp and Morier, 'Minutes of a Conversation', 17/8/80, CP 4395, pp. 6–10; and 17/9/80, ibid., pp. 15–19; Morier to Granville, 18/9/80, 115, ibid., pp. 13–15. The negotiations are detailed in CP 4395, pp. 19–86; Additional Article, CP 4506, pp. 8–9; Final Protocol, pp. 9–12; Morier to Granville, 31/12/80, 166, pp. 12–14.
105 C 2783, 1881.
106 CP 4506, pp. 18–39.

concentrated attack on the terms of the treaty. Its chairman declared that the King was in Morier's power; this British Bismarck must be driven from the country, and the King called to account. Even a number of Regenerador leaders, former colleagues of Corvo, opposed the treaty. Morier appealed to the King to use his influence, while the British Government made a formal request that the treaty be introduced into the Cortes. It was eventually introduced into the House of Deputies on 24 February. A member of Avila's middle party moved an amendment that discussion be postponed until the war in the Transvaal was at an end. On 25 February the debate was adjourned over carnival time. On 26 February the African commission of the now influential Society of Geography of Lisbon welcomed the growing opinion in England favourable to the restoration of independence and autonomy to the Transvaal; it urged the Portuguese Government to maintain the most scrupulous neutrality, and postpone any resolution on the treaty.[107] And on 27 February came the British disaster at Majuba. When the deputies re-assembled they did so under the guns of a British fleet which had steamed up the Tagus. The organ of the Republican party declared that there was a secret compact between the King of Portugal and his English relatives to sell his Portuguese possessions piecemeal to Great Britain, and demanded that the debate be adjourned until the fleet had left the Tagus. There were public demonstrations and disorders, in the course of which a number of people were injured. There were cries of "Down with the Ministry"; and "Down with the King, long live the Republic." Troops, both cavalry and infantry, were called out, and a guard placed over the British Legation. Morier however was convinced that this was not a popular movement, but an opposition to the Government artificially instigated by Fontes. The Regeneradores demanded in the Cortes that the debate be postponed until the war in the Transvaal was over, and unsuccessful in this, left the House. On 8 March the deputies passed the treaty by 74 votes to 19.[108]

There were renewed demonstrations against the treaty, and against the Government, especially on Sunday, 13 March. There were more Republican shouts. Stones were thrown at the police; mounted gendarmes made several charges, and one man was killed and several wounded. The next day there were scenes of great confusion in the House of Deputies, when extracts from the *Morning Post* and *The Times* were read out, reporting the vote in favour of the treaty, and falsely declaring that Lourenço Marques had now been ceded to Great Britain. The Government was naturally reluctant to send the bill to the House of Peers, where there was a hostile Regenerador majority. Morier tried to persuade the Prime Minister that there was no point in postponing the issue, for whatever the course of events, Great Britain would reserve to herself control of the foreign affairs of the Transvaal. He warned the Portuguese Government that the Triumvirate then governing the Transvaal had their eyes on Delagoa Bay, and that they were asserting the right of the Transvaal to expand to the Zambezi; that the only chance of Portugal to remain

107 *Parecer, Bol. SGL*, 1881, pp. 328–31.
108 CP 4506, pp. 37–74.

undisturbed in south-east Africa was under the protection of Great Britain. At the same time he tried to persuade the British Government to make a public announcement that as soon as the Lourenço Marques treaty had been ratified Britain would initiate *pourparlers* for the negotiation of the Congo treaty so desired by Portugal. The anti-Government agitation continued. Morier urged the Prime Minister to send the bill to the House of Peers before he quitted office, but on 23 March the Government resigned.[109]

Sampaio became the new Prime Minister. He had been a member of the Fontes ministry, and Fontes remained the power behind the scenes. Fontes however was anxious to woo public opinion and so would not become head of a government which might be obliged to enact an unpopular piece of legislation. Sampaio accepted no responsibility for the treaty, though he had been a member of the cabinet which had authorized it. He brought Dantas back from London and appointed him as Acting Minister of Foreign Affairs with the specific task of persuading Morier to postpone the treaty. Morier demanded that the treaty go to the House of Peers; and he suggested to the Secretary of State for Foreign Affairs that hints should be dropped that if the vote were adverse, Britain would no longer be represented by a minister in Lisbon, and that she might even denounce the seventeenth-century treaty of alliance with Portugal. By now the anti-treaty agitation was turning pronouncedly anti-English. Spain was no longer the traditional enemy; in fact there were the stirrings of a pan-Iberian Republican feeling. Dantas maintained that if the debate were not postponed there would be movements which would have to be suppressed by force. Morier still considered that the agitation was artificial, and insisted that the treaty go forward. Dantas resigned and returned to London, where he met with success. Kimberley agreed that since the Transvaal commission was about to return independence to the Transvaal there was no point in proceeding with the treaty. Granville concurred, on the understanding that the treaty was postponed, and not abandoned. The Portuguese Government, in great relief, dissolved the Cortes.[110] It was soon to turn its attention to Africa again, this time to the west coast.

109 Ibid., pp. 89–181.
110 PRO, FO 63/1100, 1101, 1102, 1103, 1129.

3

THE CONGO 1875–1884

Luanda, the capital of Angola, in 1875 still enjoyed the reputation of being the most beautiful city on the west coast of Africa. It had an excellent, if undeveloped, harbour, substantial buildings, and many of the amenities of civilization. But its old prosperity, based on the slave-trade, had passed; now it existed on the export of wax, ivory, oil, coffee and copra. Dues had to be paid on most exports; and there were heavy import duties on articles of foreign manufacture, especially of non-Portuguese origin, while goods imported in non-Portuguese bottoms paid extra duties, of up to 30 per cent. Many Portuguese were economically compelled to emigrate from Portugal each year; but few went willingly to the Portuguese possessions in Africa. Most of those who came were *degredados*, and the majority of Luanda's white population of about 1,000 were criminals, past or present. Officials were grievously underpaid, and many extorted what they could from black and white alike; travellers of the time commented bitterly not only on the irksomeness of the local regulations, but on the venality of the officials.

A steamer and barge service, started by an American, linked Luanda with the mouth of the Cuanza, which river was navigable to Dondo. There was an administrative post at Pungo Andongo. The limits of Portuguese authority were at Malange and Duque de Bragança, but traders frequented Cassange, on longitude 18° east.

South of Luanda there were small stations on the coast, at Amboim, Novo Redondo, Egito and Catumbela. There was no settlement at the grand port of Lobito, but on the shores of the open roadstead at Benguela was Angola's second to most important town, well laid out, with some substantial buildings, and what passed as a fort even though its guns were honeycombed with rust. The area produced sugar, cotton and dried fish, while wax and ivory were also exported. Inland, on the plateau, were posts at Caconda and Galangue, while the limit of Portuguese authority was at Bié, but three or four enterprising traders, or their mulatto or negro agents, penetrated far into the interior in search of slaves and ivory. Cameron in 1875 travelled in the company of such a caravan from the Zambezi to Bié. Holub, on the upper Zambezi at much the same time, recorded,

> I accepted a Portuguese trader as guide, and had also the opportunity of observing that the countries between Angola, Mossamedes and Benguela, also among the great lakes as far down as the Victoria Falls of the

Zambezi, are well known to the Portuguese traders, both the white and the Mambari, i.e. the mixed race, that they know every tribe and chief, all the rivers and mountains, and the good or bad character of those with whom you have to deal; in short, I found this "terra incognita" well known to them.

Moçâmedes, which had a fort and a number of stone houses, was the centre of a fishing industry, and the port for settlers established on the Cela plateau. Otherwise the town had but little to recommend it, for the cold current which brought it piscatorial wealth robbed it of moisture, so that it was situated on an extension of the Namib Desert.

The southern boundary of Angola was usually accepted as being the parallel of 18° south, in desert which extended to the settlements at the mouth of the Swakop River and at Walvis Bay.

The most northerly district of Angola was Ambriz, which, however, could be approached only by sea since intervening tribesmen refused to allow any Portuguese to travel overland between Libongo (famed for its bitumen) and Ambriz. Liverpool concerns had established trading stations here in the middle of the century. In 1855 the Portuguese authorities had annexed the place and promptly applied their high duties. The trading houses moved across the Loge River to Kinsembo. The Governor-general was persuaded to reduce duties at Ambriz to 6 per cent, and as a result much trade returned to the town, which boasted, beyond the custom-house, a fort, the walls of a church, and the only iron pier in Angola. Exports comprised ground-nuts, baobab fibre (for paper making), coffee, sesame, rubber, ivory and palm kernels.

North along the coast were other factories, mainly foreign owned, but with Portuguese employees, at Ambrizete, Lucunga, Mangue Grande and Cabeça da Cabra.

Inland, a fort had been built at Bembe, to cover the extraction of copper which had still been in progress in 1873, but shortly afterwards the mining and the fort were abandoned.

Farther inland, and only some seventy-five miles short of the Congo, was São Salvador. This was no longer the extensive city where the Paramount Chief of the Congo tribe had welcomed the first missionaries to central Africa in 1491, and where a Christian kingdom had flourished early in the sixteenth century. Now the town contained only two hundred huts and the chief, who was not of the direct line, commanded the allegiance of only a few kraals in the immediate vicinity. Portuguese occupation had continued to 1866. Since that date the only Portuguese to visit the place were occasional priests, mulatto as often as not. Lieutenant Grandy passed through in 1873 on his quest for Livingstone but he could not reach farther than Tungwa, sixty miles to the north, because of the opposition of tribesmen who feared that white occupation would follow and they would lose the carrier trade between the interior and the coast.

At the southern entrance to the Congo, Ponta do Padrão commemorated the discovery of the river by Diogo Cão. The original pillar had been shattered in the seventeenth century, and a replica erected in 1856 had been overthrown by the scour of the currents. A foreign factory had opened in the early 1870's near the site of Santo António, but the independent Musurongos had sacked and burnt it. Across the river, six miles away, lay the southern point of Banana, a two-mile-long sand spit, the shelter of which provided the entrance port to the Congo, visited regularly by English steamers, while on the peninsula Netherlands, French and English trading houses maintained depots for their factories up the estuary. Sheer walls of mangroves, cut by labyrinthine creeks, lined the lower course of the river as far as Porto da Lenha, some forty-five miles from Banana, where half a dozen factories stood on piles. Above here the banks became clearer with bushes, trees, and palms, to Boma. The last slave ship had sailed from Boma in 1868, and now there was an even more remunerative trade in palm-oil and kernels and ground-nuts. Competition was forcing the houses to establish factories farther upstream. But above Boma the river became narrower, confined between lofty hills, and the strength of the current complicated communication.[1]

North of the Congo, there were factories on a number of bays, roadsteads and river-mouths, notedly at Cabinda, Chiloango, Ponta Negra, and Sette Cama. At Gaboon, there was a French settlement; but the length of coast from Gaboon to Ambriz belonged to no European power. To most of this coast Portugal asserted claim.

In 1783 a Portuguese expedition had built a fort at Cabinda, a slaving roadstead frequented by French, English and Netherlands vessels. The next year a French naval squadron arrived, and its commander demanded that the commandant restore the previous state of affairs: the slave-trade was common to all the powers of Europe; this trade, he declared, stretched from the equator to Cabo do Padrão at least, if not to Luanda, for Portugal's exclusive rights extended only southwards from Luanda.[2] The Portuguese garrison withdrew and the fort was destroyed. The Portuguese Government protested. Recourse was had to arbitration, and the Convention of Madrid, 30 January 1786, obliged Portugal to recognize the slave-trading interests of all European nations from 5° 12' south latitude to the Congo; but the French plenipoteniary denied that the French naval expedition had had any intention of disturbing or diminishing the rights of sovereignty which Portugal still claimed over the territory. As for the territory south of the Congo, the French Government, without acknowledging Portuguese claims, would not permit French subjects to trade there, provided the governments of other powers similarly restricted their subjects. The Portuguese representative declared the rights of his country

1 J. Monteiro, *Angola and the River Congo* (London, 1875), 2 vols.; V. L. Cameron, *Across Africa* (London, 1877), 2 vols.; W. H. Bentley, *Pioneering on the Congo* (London, 1900), 2 vols; H. H. Johnston, *George Grenfell and the Congo* (London, 1908), 2 vols; R. F. Burton, *Two Trips to Gorilla Land and the Cataracts of the Congo* (London, II, 1876); E. H. Holub, *Journey through Central South Africa from the Diamond Fields to the Upper Zambezi* (London, 1881).
2 Almada, *Tratados*, III, p. 410.

3 Angola (map by Edward Stanford, in Stanford's Compendium of Geography and Travel: K. Johnston, *Africa*. London, 1880)

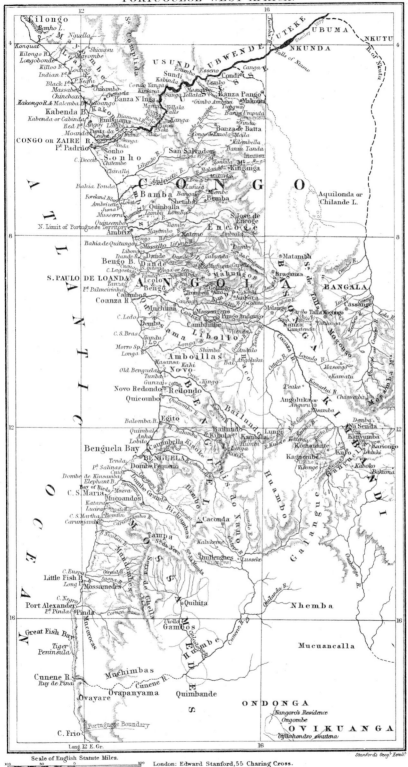

not only to the coast of Angola, but to the interior, from beyond Cassange to the extremity of the district of Benguela.[3]

In the treaty between Great Britain and Portugal in 1810 for the suppression of the slave-trade Portugal recorded that she did not renounce her rights over Cabinda and Malembo.[4] This treaty was replaced by one signed in Vienna on 22 January 1815, in which Portugal undertook to prohibit to her subjects traffic in slaves north of the equator, but permitted that traffic in possessions of the Portuguese Crown south of the equator.[5] An additional convention, signed on 28 July 1817, defined this area on the west coast as situated between 8° and 18° south, and "those territories on the coast of Africa on the south of the equator, over which His Most Faithful Majesty has declared that he has retained his rights, namely—the territory of Malembo and Cabinda upon the eastern [sic] coast of Africa, from 5° 12′ to 8° south latitude."[6]

Portugal's constitutional charter of 1826 included Cabinda and Malembo as dependencies of the Crown.[7] The British Government protested against the occupation of Ambriz in 1855. It eventually acquiesced in the occupation since Ambriz was close to 8° but threatened to use naval force against any Portuguese occupation north of the Loge. When, in July 1856, the Cortes proclaimed the abolition of slavery in Ambriz, Cabinda, and Malembo six months after a government administration should be established there, the British Government again forbad the occupation of those territories.[8]

In 1870, during the Franco-German war, the ship *Hero* belonging to the mercantile marine of the Confederation of North Germany, and under charter to a Netherlands trading association, arrived at Banana. A French warship, *La Diligente*, followed her into harbour, and on 15 September took her prisoner. The German minister in Lisbon protested to the Portuguese authorities: Banana was Portuguese territory, and the *Hero* had been taken in neutral waters; the seizure had been contrary to the law of nations, and he requested Portugal to take the necessary steps.[9] The French authorities released the ship. These actions implied both German and French recognition of Portuguese sovereignty.

At the end of 1875 the Portuguese Government decided to re-assert Portuguese claims to the coastline between 5° 12′ and 8° south. The Portuguese minister in London in January 1876 read to the Secretary of State for Foreign Affairs extracts from a dispatch and memorandum by Corvo which presented the *de facto* and *de jure* Portuguese case, based on the legality and necessity for effectual occupation and dominion of the disputed territories.[10] Derby declared to the Portuguese representative that neither Britain nor Portugal

3 Convention, Hertslet, memo., 20/4/83, CP 4807, p. 45; G. Sousa Dias, *Os Portugueses em Angola* (Lisbon, 1959), pp. 245–52; R. S. Thomson, *La Fondation de l'Etat Indépendent du Congo* (Brussels, 1933), pp. 121–2; Reeves, pp. 10–11; Corvo, I, pp. 199–200.
4 CO, Africa No. 2 (1883), p. 1.
5 Ibid; and Almada, *Tratados*, I, pp. 5–9.
6 Convention, Hertslet, p. 955; eastern was corrected to western in 1819.
7 Africa No. 2 (1883), p. 36.
8 Ibid., pp. 60–4.
9 Brandebourg to Avila, 27/12/70, CP 5019, p. 8.
10 Corvo to Saldanha, 4/12/75, *Negocios Externos* . . . 1876, pp. cli–cliv, and Memorandum, pp. clv–clxiii; Saldanha to Min., 6/1/76, 1A, Nec., Legacão de Portugal em Londres, 42 (1875–7).

obtained any advantage from occupying savage lands, but he promised to examine the Portuguese case, and then make reply;[11] in the meantime the instructions to British cruisers to oppose any attempt by Portugal to extend her sovereignty north of Ambriz would not be altered. In October 1876 Derby repeated his promise to enquire into the matter.[12] That year the Netherlands Government applied to the Portuguese Government for exequaturs for vice-consuls to be appointed at Cabinda and Malembo, but the British Government intervened, declaring that this would be to acknowledge the Portuguese claims to the territory, and the Netherlands withdrew their request.[13] In reply to a Netherlands application for clarification of the position on the Congo and in Cabinda and Malembo Derby declared firmly that Britain had never recognized Portugal's inchoate rights to these territories, which were founded only on prior discovery and had never been perfected by possession; they had lapsed by non-use, and the native tribes in the meantime had repudiated Portuguese sovereignty, and had made treaties with Great Britain. Britain therefore opposed, and would continue to oppose, any attempt on the part of Portugal to occupy the territory in question, or to interfere with the freedom of British trade with the natives.[14]

British official action in the area now intensified and treaty-making with chiefs increased. Ostensibly these treaties were to aid in the suppression of the slave-trade. But the treaties acknowledged the chiefs' sovereign rights, and so were directed against Portuguese claims. The British consul at Luanda, for example, requested that among the presents to be sent to the Queen of Ambrizete should be a velvet robe trimmed with gold lace, and a crown—"but a theatrical tinsel crown will be quite good enough."[15]

Simultaneously, Portuguese naval craft were redoubling their visits to the coast and up the Congo estuary; and their officers were informing the natives that the country belonged to the Portuguese Crown. The Governor-general of Angola in September 1876 issued a proclamation requiring the coasting trade between all Portuguese possessions on the west coast of Africa to be carried in Portuguese bottoms. The British consul considered that the primary purpose of the proclamation was to bring to the attention of European countries the rights of sovereignty claimed by Portugal north of Ambriz. Morier pointed out to Corvo how injurious this measure would be to Portuguese commerce, since there was insufficient Portuguese shipping to handle the trade. Corvo agreed it was most unfortunate to apply this exaggerated principle of national cabotage at the very moment when trade was developing, and the Governor was instructed to withdraw the proclamation.[16]

That some civilized control there had to be was illustrated by several incidents in 1877. In the first, a factory belonging to a Portuguese at Quisanga

11 Quillinan to Corvo, 24/1/76, 1 A, Nec., LPL 42.
12 Braamcamp to Morier, 28/11/79, CP 4786, pp. 10–1.
13 Hertslet, memo., 20/4/83, CP 4807, p. 45.
14 Derby to Bylandt, 27/1/77, CP 4807, p. 171.
15 Hopkins, Ambrizette, to Derby, 11/11/76, CP 3686, p. 162.
16 Sampayo to Min., 8/1/77, 7A, Nec., LPL 42; Derby to Morier, 8/1/77, 1 ST, CP 3686, p. 159; Morier to Derby, 10/1/77, 5 ST, ibid., pp. 166–8; Custodio Duarte, circular to consuls, 10/2/77, Luanda, ibid., pp. 228–9; Irvine & Co. to Salisbury, 3/4/78, CP 3928, p. 157.

was burnt. Suspicion fell on some slaves who were tortured, but they revealed nothing. Many were shot. The remainder were fastened to a long chain, put in a boat and sent to Scott, a mulatto from St Helena who had a station near Boma. Scott had them thrown into the river. Two days later the officers of a British gun-boat enjoyed the hospitality of this British subject. When their ship was leaving her anchor fouled a chain to which forty corpses were found attached.[17]

At Ambrizete, an attempt was made to break into the powder store of an English trading house. The agent seized a suspected negro, and chained him; the prisoner died. The agent feared retaliation from the victim's friends, and when a Portuguese gun-boat called at Ambrizete he asked for protection, to the intense indignation of the British consul in Luanda, who exclaimed that it was such incidents that gave the Portuguese pretext for interference; he forbad British traders to imprison natives, and to appeal to the Portuguese.[18]

In a third incident a United States schooner, the *Joseph Nickerson*, ran aground off Cape Padrão. The local chief's son and two companions volunteered their assistance and the master sent out a kedge anchor, hoping to winch the vessel free. But men from nearby villages swarmed around the vessel and cut the cable. Being unarmed, the crew fled and found refuge in Banana. The next day ten Netherlands traders and 150 of their men, in two steam-launches and nine boats, crossed to the wreck. They killed the only two men found aboard her, and burnt the nearest village. At the request of the master they then fired the schooner.

When word of these events reached Luanda the British consul requested a British naval vessel to proceed to the scene and its commander to hold an enquiry and take such steps as he thought fit. Lieutenant Keppel of the *Avon* sent out bluejackets who fired at the local tribesmen with rifles and rockets and destroyed six villages. The consul eulogized the commander's "just, prompt and praiseworthy action."[19]

But the Governor-general of Angola strongly protested against Keppel's action as a flagrant attack on Portuguese sovereign rights on a coast proclaimed as Portuguese in the country's constitutional charter which had been internationally recognized.[20] In the House of Deputies too there were protests against this bombarding and burning of what were described as Portuguese villages. Corvo, in his reply, declared that the Congo was within the limits of Portuguese territory as recognized by Great Britain, whose Government, however, opposed Portuguese occupation of it; but he hoped that this resistance would yet be overcome.[21] Morier promptly declared that the British Government had never admitted the Portuguese claims and the British plenipotentiary who negotiated the 1817 agreement had carefully distinguished between the

17 W. H. Bentley, *Pioneering on the Congo* (London, 1900), 1, pp. 46–8.
18 Hopkins to Derby 16/4/77, 21, CP 4786, pp. 3–6.
19 Keppel to Hopkins, 4/1/77, CP 4786, p. 1; Keppel to Commodore, Cape of Good Hope and West Coast Station, [4/1/77], p. 1; Hopkins to Derby, 9/1/77, 5, ibid., p. 1.
20 C. A. de Almeida e Albuquerque to Hopkins, [2/77], CP 4786, p. 3; and Hopkins to Derby, 1/3/77, 5, ibid., p. 3.
21 Precis of debates, 28/2/77, CP 3686, pp. 212–3.

territories possessed by the British Crown, and those over which the Portuguese King declared he retained his rights.[22]

Corvo was ousted from power and Avila e Bolama became the new Minister of Foreign Affairs. He assured Morier he would continue Corvo's general policy. Morier warned him not to occupy the territory in dispute.[23] Gouveia, the new Minister of Marine and Ultramar, emphasized the embarrassing position in which the authorities of Angola were placed by the outrages on the Congo, the hostile attitude of the British consul, and the unfriendly attitude of the British Government. He urged that England and Portugal, in the general interests of humanity and civilization, should come to a settlement on this question.[24]

Morier, instructed to draw up a memorandum on the Congo, found to his surprise that the Portuguese claims were stronger than the British Government had assumed them to be; in fact, the British Government had no solid or international bases on which to resist them. In the absence of any concurrent claim by Britain or any other power, more harm than good would be done in preventing the establishment of a responsible European jurisdiction in the region. The present state of affairs was becoming untenable. A definite settlement must be attempted and that could come about only by friendly agreement between the two governments or by recourse to arms or by arbitration. Morier naturally favoured agreement; and he thought a very fair arrangement could be reached. Shortly before quitting office, Corvo had remarked to him that he was desperately anxious for a settlement of the Congo question, partly to round off Portuguese territory in west Africa, but most of all because of the humiliating position in which Portugal was placed of being debarred, by threat of arms, from territory which the constitution declared to be an integral part of the monarchy. Corvo added that all he wished for was the line of the Congo; any extension beyond that would be a fatal encumbrance. Morier suggested that Britain should recognize the Portuguese claims, and Portugal in return should cede from the mouth of the Congo northwards to 5° 12′ south to Britain, who would thereby obtain the right bank and full command of the mouth. Portugal should be compelled to control traffic and commerce according to the regulations laid down for the control of the British section of the coast; in view of the docility which the Portuguese had always shown, such a plan would give Britain virtual control of commerce on the west coast of Africa. Of course, there would have to be manoeuvres to make the proposal come from Portugal, but Morier was sure that he could achieve this if, as seemed likely, Corvo returned to power.[25]

Such was the Morier plan; but it was overthrown by an Englishman who had acquired United States nationality. Stanley, under the patronage of the *New York Herald* and *Daily Telegraph*, had struck inland from Bagamoyo, circumnavigated Victoria Nyanza, discovered Lake Edward, and continued to

22 Morier to Avila e Bolama, 10/3/77, CP 3686, p. 214; Morier to Derby, 13/3/77, 18 ST, ibid., pp. 211–2.
23 Morier to Derby, 15/3/77, 20 ST, CP 3686, pp. 216–7.
24 G. F. Gould to Derby, 4/8/77, 53 ST, CP 3686, pp. 284–6.
25 Morier, London, memo., 17/8/77, CP 3686, pp. 288–91.

Lake Tanganyika. Though he failed to recognize the Lukuga as the head stream of the Congo, he struck the Lualaba, and followed the course of the Congo. Reduced at the end of his journey to great extremities from lack of food, he was refreshed with beer, champagne and plum pudding rushed from Boma, where there were now half a dozen factories, and a white population of eighteen, eleven of them Portuguese. He reached the sea on 12 August 1877.[26] His despatch, published in the *Daily Telegraph* on 17 September, focussed the attention of Europe and the United States of America on the Congo region. The manufacturers of the world, who were suffering from increased competition and a trade recession, became excited by his description of the unclothed savages of central Africa, whom he estimated to number some two hundred million, simply waiting to be supplied with manufactured goods; here was a vast potential market. The scramble for Africa was on.

Stanley, on his arrival in Europe, was met by commissioners of Leopold II of Belgium, who informed him that the King had summoned a conference in Brussels in September 1876, at which representatives of Belgium, Germany, France, England, Austria-Hungary, Italy and Russia had met, and founded an International African Association, with national committees in various countries. At a meeting in July 1877, attended by representatives of Belgium, Germany, France, Austria-Hungary, the Netherlands, Spain and the United States, it had been decided to send an expedition via the east coast of Africa to establish a "hospitable and scientific station" on or near Lake Tanganyika, from which a subsequent expedition would explore towards the Atlantic. The commissioners called for Stanley's co-operation. In November he met financiers and industrialists convened by Leopold, who commissioned him to return to the Congo, collect more information about the river and its basin and report to their Comité d'Études du Haut Congo.

Stanley reached the Congo in August 1879, his published purpose threefold: philanthropic, scientific and commercial. He himself declared he had "the novel mission of sowing along its banks civilized settlements, to peacefully conquer and subdue it, to remould it in harmony with modern ideas into National States, within whose limits the European merchant shall go hand in hand with the dark African trader, and justice and law and order shall prevail . . ."[27] His instructions from Strauch, president of the Comité, required him to obtain concessions of ground for stations and roads, and envisaged the eventual establishment of "a republican confederation of free negroes . . . such confederation to be independent except that the King, to whom this conception and formation was due, reserved the right to appoint the President, who should reside in Europe."[28]

Ascending the river, Stanley selected a site for a station at the limit of navigation, at Vivi, on the north bank. As soon as the station had been established, in January 1880, he started building a road for the transport of a

26 Newton to Derby, 24/8/77, Luanda, CP 3686, pp. 314–5; H. M. Stanley, *Through the Dark Continent* (London, 1878), 2 vols.
27 H. M. Stanley, *The Congo and the founding of its Free State* (London, 1885), 1, pp. 59–60.
28 Ibid., pp. 53–3.

steam-launch to operate on the upper river. His choice of the north side of the river for the station and road implied his recognition of Portuguese rights to the lower left bank. At Isangila the vessel was again launched on the Congo. It steamed to Manyanga, where another road was started, this time on the south side. As he approached Stanley Pool, great was his chagrin to encounter a Senegalese sergeant bearing a tricolour, escorted by two Gaboon sailors, who showed him a copy of a treaty made by Brazza.[29]

Savorgnan de Brazza, a Frenchman of Italian birth born in Rio de Janeiro, had in 1875-8 explored with two companions the upper waters of the Ogooue. Pushing on alone, he had partially descended the Alima and Licona, which proved to be tributaries of the Congo. Commissioned by the French Committee of the African Association and by the French Government, he had returned to Gaboon to trace the course of the Alima to the Congo, and to establish stations, one on the Ogooue, and the other on the Congo. His first, founded in June 1880, came to be called Franceville. He decided to follow the Lefini River to the Congo. There, on 10 September 1880 he made a treaty with King Makoko. He descended the Congo to Stanley Pool where, in October 1880, he hoisted the French flag at what came later to be called Brazzaville. Two days later he took possession of the territory between the Djoue and Impiela Rivers. He tried to explore a new route to the coast, heading westwards to the headwaters of the Niari, but finding the route too hazardous he returned to the Congo, and followed it down-stream. He had met Stanley on the way, who had entertained him, but he had made no reference to the treaty. He returned to Gaboon. His steamer for the Congo and reinforcements had not arrived, so he returned to the interior to relieve the stations so far established, and to build a road for the seventy-five mile portage between the Ogooue and the Alima. He then explored the alternative route to the coast, by way of the Niari.[30]

Stanley, on his arrival at Stanley Pool, appreciated the force of Brazza's treaty: the Djoue River flowed into the Congo fifty yards below the first rapids which marked the exit from the pool; the north bank of the pool was closed to him. He turned to the south bank, where on 1 December 1881 he founded Leopoldville. He continued his explorations inland.[31]

The activities of Brazza prompted Leopold to send a second expedition to west Africa, to prevent the French from opening up the Kouilou-Niari route to Stanley Pool. But its leader, Peschuel-Loeche, lingered in Vivi, where Stanley, returning ill down the Congo, found him. Loeche bore a commission placing him in command should Stanley be disabled, so Stanley promptly handed over to him and proceeded to Europe,[32] where he reported to the committee of the International Association of the Congo, a fictitious body, for there was now no

29 Ibid., pp. 292–5.
30 *Proceedings RGS*, 1882, pp. 226, 509–13; N. Ney, ed.,*Conférences et lettres de P. Savorgnan de Brazza sur ses tres explorationes dans l'ouest africaine, de 1875 à 1876* (Paris, 1887); D. Neuville and Ch. Bréard, *Les voyages de Savorgnan de Brazza: Ogôué et Congo (1875–1882)* (Paris, 1884).
31 Stanley, *Congo*, especially, pp. 231–4; Thomson, *Fondation*, pp. 78–80.
32 Stanley, *Congo*, pp. 447–9; Thomson, *Fondation*, pp. 86–7.

longer any international participation, and the title simply cloaked the identity of Leopold.[33]

Leopold entreated Stanley to return to the Congo forthwith and take the most active measures to forestall the French in as wide an area as possible. He was to consolidate the ground won, and obtain "the concession of their authority from all the chiefs along the route, and such other rights as they may possess, which could be obtained by others to oppress us who pioneered the way." After only six weeks in Europe he left for the Congo. Arriving at Vivi in December 1882, he found that Peschuel-Loeche had defected. He sent Elliott to Isangila, whence he was to open a line of stations along the Niari and the Kouilou, to seal off the French in Gaboon and along the Ogooue from the lower Congo. Then, realizing that that would take time, Stanley sent van der Velde to the mouth of the Kouilou, where he erected a station, and made treaties with neighbouring chiefs, as far as the rapids which proved to block navigation twenty-eight miles up-stream. He succoured the Elliott expedition, which had established three stations. Stanley further instructed Hanssens to establish a line of communication between Manyanga and the Niari, which led to the founding of two further stations, after which he went in support of the Elliott expedition.[34] These moves effectively closed the Kouilou-Niari area against the French—but only for the time being.

Portugal had not been invited to the Brussels Conference of 1876. This slight naturally produced a painful impression on the Portuguese, who prided themselves on having produced the first African explorers, and on the vast tracts of equatorial Africa which still remained to them. The result was to arouse the Government and thinking people to a sense of realities and to direct attention to their long neglected African possessions.[35] The Sociedade de Geografia de Lisboa came into being as a result of "recognition of the urgent necessity and imperious duty imposed on Portugal by her traditions, by her situation as the second colonial power in Europe, and by her economic and political interests beyond the seas, to enter definitively into an expansionist movement . . ."; its particular role was to stimulate public interest to a comprehension of the national interests and duties. The most urgent necessity was to send a scientific expedition to the interior of Africa and open it to commerce, for the sake of Portuguese prestige and European civilization.[36] The Society petitioned the King to take a more active interest in African affairs, and urged a "definitive rectification" of the boundaries of Portuguese territories in Africa.[37] Violent criticism of Portuguese policy, and even presence, in Africa, by Cameron

33 Thomson, *Fondation*, p. 89.
34 Stanley, *Congo*, pp. 462–76; Thomson, *Fondation*, pp. 95–6; Elliott, 'Exploration et organisation de la Prov. du Kwilou-Niali', *Bull. Soc. Geog. Belg.* 1886, pp. 101–22; van der Velde, 'La Rêgion du Bas-Congo et du Kwilou-Niali', *Bull. Soc. Geog. Belg.*, 1886, pp. 347–412.
35 Morier to Derby, 26/2/77, 11 ST, CP 3686, p. 183.
36 Actas, 7/7/76, *Bol. SGL*, 1876, pp. 11–12, 47.
37 SGL to Rei, 16/10/76, *Bol. SGL*, 1887, pp. 19–23.

and Young, further irritated, and stimulated, Portuguese public and parliamentary opinion.[38]

Major Serpa Pinto, who had seen service on the Zambezi in 1869, and Lieutenant H. Capelo reached Luanda in August 1877, where they met their colleague, Lieutenant R. Ivens. Their original instructions, drawn up by a Government-appointed Geographical Commission, provided for them to make a hydrographic survey of the watershed between the Congo and the Zambezi basins, and the country between Angola and Moçambique. Subsequently, they were required to pay more attention to the Cuango and sources of that river, the Cubango and the Cunene. Having difficulty in raising sufficient porters, Pinto went to the mouth of the Congo, where he encountered Stanley on his emergence from the continent, and conducted him and his party to Luanda. In view of the success of Stanley's journey, the Portuguese explorers decided to avoid the Congo area; they determined to go to the mouth of the Cunene, ascend that river, study the sources of the Cuanza and Cubango, determine whether the latter river entered the Zambezi, and travel by way of lakes Bangweolu and Nyasa to Moçambique. Subsequently, still unable to raise sufficient porters, they decided to leave the coast at Benguela, and recruit more porters at Bié. On that journey there were bitter disagreements between Pinto and his companions, and at Bié the party split. Capelo and Ivens travelled north-eastwards to the headwaters of the Cuanza, and explored lengths of that river northwards to approximately the latitude of S. Salvador. Pinto headed south of east, crossed the headwaters of the Cuando and reached the Zambezi at Lialui. Hearing that the missionary Coillard was at Pandamatenka waiting for permission to enter the Rotse country Pinto made for his camp, hoping to be able to borrow goods which would enable him to continue down the left bank of the Zambezi to Zumbo, and thence to Quelimane. Coillard had no goods to spare, and invited him to withdraw with him and his family southwards, across Bechuanaland.[39]

The Pinto-Capelo-Ivens expedition, though it failed to realize its instructions, filled in many geographical details and fixed many points with precise observations; more important, it kept African affairs in the public eye, and reassured national pride that Portugal was really playing a part in the opening and civilizing of the continent.

Some of the increased activity was directed to the south of Angola, consequent on events in south-west Africa. Ichaboe had been annexed by Britain in 1861, and in 1866 eleven further guano islands off the south-west African coast were annexed to the Cape Colony, though the Queen assented only in 1873.[40] In 1876 the Cape Government sent Palgrave, a magistrate, to investigate conditions in south-west Africa. His report declared that the Cape Colony

---

38 Morier to Derby, 13/2/77, 9 ST, CP 3686, pp. 179–80; 27/2/77, 12 ST, pp. 183–5; GG to Min., 28/4/77, 103, AHU, Moç., Pasta 30.
39 L. Cordeiro, 'Expediçao geographica Portugueza á Africa Central', *Bol. SGL*, 1877, pp. 126–38, 1878, pp. 204–8; Actas, 4/7/77 *Bol. SGL*, 1878, pp. 274–5; Serpa Pinto, *How I crossed Africa* (London, 1881), 2 vols; H. Capello and R. Ivens, *From Benguella to the territory of Yacca* (London, 1882), 2 vols.
40 G. M. Theal, *History of South Africa*, IV, p. 229.

desired to expand its frontiers northwards to the Portuguese border for three reasons: the general desire of expansion common to all colonies; to prevent trekking Boers from founding autonomous communities which, if on the coast, might maintain their independence from British rule; and to prevent the Portuguese from spreading southwards. After meeting the chiefs of Damaraland he advocated that the Cape Colony should set aside a tract of country as a native reserve, the northern boundary of which would march for sixty miles along the Cunene River.[41] The British Government did not accept all Palgrave's recommendations, but Carnarvon did approve the annexation of Walvis Bay, "thus the only door of entrance to very large regions in which the Colony is materially interested should be placed in the custody of Great Britain." On 12 March 1878 the Union Jack was hoisted at Walvis Bay, and four hundred square miles immediately adjacent were annexed to Great Britain.[42] When a copy of the Palgrave report reached Lisbon there was the strongest exception to his reference to the Portuguese and fear lest the annexation of Walvis Bay be but a preliminary step to the implementation of his other recommendations. Corvo protested particularly against the drawing of a frontier on the Cunene which lay far north of the boundary of 18° south acknowledged in the conventions of 1815 and 1817. Morier could only deplore the language of the report and assure Corvo that it was absolutely inexplicable how a British official could perpetrate such a suggestion in direct contradiction of well-known treaty arrangements; Morier added that the British Government would never tolerate such an infringement by a local government of British treaty stipulations.[43] He suggested to London that the Imperial Government advise the exuberant young manhood of the young British colony, "Keep the commandments. Remove not your neighbour's landmark. Covet not that which is not yours. But, if you do, don't do it in public."[44]

Reports reached Lisbon of penetration by traders from south-west Africa into the south of Angola and that forty-three Portuguese traders resident at Moçâmedes had asked the British consul in Luanda for British annexation of that district.[45] A Portuguese gun-boat surprised an English cutter making a clandestine call at an unauthorized port in southern Angola.[46] The Governor-general sent a gun-boat to examine all the ports, bays, and anchorages as far

41 Morier to Salisbury, 3/9/78, 29 ST, CP 3928, p. 141.
42 Theal, V, pp. 107–16; at p. 115 Carnarvon to Frere, 23/1/78.
43 Morier to Salisbury, 28/8/78, 28 ST, CP 3928, p. 139.
44 Morier to Salisbury, 3/9/78, 29 ST, CP 3928, p. 141. He added, "There is a story told of a French diocese, celebrated for the austere morality of its clergy and the absence of scandals rife elsewhere. A legend arose to the effect that these results were to be attributed to certain words of a strange and mystic importance which the holy father at the head of the diocesan seminary was wont to whisper into the ear of each departing priest. At last the mystery was explained, and the magic words were discovered to be of the simplest kind. They were these: 'Soyez chaste, mais soutout soyez prudent'."
45 Morier to Salisbury, 13/6/78, 18 ST, CP 3928, p. 126; Salisbury to Morier, 20 ST, ibid., p. 127. The British consul ignored the communication, and the Secretary of State approved his action.
46 Salisbury to Morier, 5/11/78, 40 ST, CP 3928, p. 166.

south as Walvis Bay,[47] while a party from the same gun-boat explored the mouth of the Cunene.[48]

The passage of the Boers northwards through south-west Africa[49] prompted Frere to urge that the boundary between British and Portuguese possessions in south-west Africa be defined, but the Secretary of State for Foreign Affairs declared a favourable opportunity for such a negotiation had not arrived.[50] It was in vain that Frere urged the annexation of a strip of land, five to ten miles across, along the entire coast from the Cape Colony to the Portuguese boundary, and that the latter should be definitively demarcated. The British appreciated that there was no harbour north of Walvis Bay which the Boers could occupy; in any case the Boers were now reported to be in Portuguese territory; and to propose delimitation of the boundary with Angola would be to arouse Portuguese suspicions, and prejudice the prospects of the Delagoa treaty, which was a matter of much more immediate importance to Britain and South Africa than the acquisition of extra colonial territory on the western coast.[51] But such an annexation would have forestalled the German annexation of south-west Africa.

German travellers were active in and beyond Angola at this time. They added considerably to geographical knowledge,[52] and their work was acceptable to the Portuguese. But the travels of some other foreigners, and especially of Protestant missionaries, were regarded as affronts to national pride, especially when they were made from the seat of the old Catholic kingdom of S. Salvador.

In May 1877, four months before the publication of Stanley's historic despatch, and influenced by the work of Cameron and Grandy, a benefactor offered the Baptist Missionary Society money if the Society would start missionary work on the Congo. Two missionaries in the Cameroons, Grenfell and Comber, paid a quick visit to the lower Congo at the beginning of 1878, and returned for a longer reconnaissance in the middle of that year. They were well received by King Pedro V; but attempting to reach Stanley Pool they were turned back at Tungwa, the people of which "had never seen white men who were not traders"[53]—an acknowledgment that Portuguese traders had operated in that area. Comber reported in England, and in 1879 a mission station was established, under his leadership, at S. Salvador. Members of this mission carried out numbers of journeys which, with their missionary activities, helped to concentrate more English attention on the Congo, and to give religious and

47 L. Hunt, Consul, Luanda, to Salisbury, 6/12/78, PRO, FO 179/215.
48 A. de Almeida Lima to Commander, Naval Station, Moçâmedes, 1/1/79, *Bol. SGL*, 1880, pp. 9–17; A. M. da Silva, commander, *Tamega*, to Commander, Naval Station, Moçâmedes, 10/1/79.
49 J. C. Hepburn, Shoshong, to Shepstone, 14/8/78, CP 3928, pp. 178–80; anon., 'Os Boers na costa occidental', *Bol. SGL*, 1880, pp. 117–8; G. P. J. Trümpelman, Die Boer in Suid-Wes Afrika (*Archives Year Book 1948*), pp. 33–9.
50 Beach to Frere, 21/9/79, CP 4302, p. 108.
51 Beach to Frere, 25/12/79, CP 4302, pp. 129–30; Meade to Pauncefote, 27/12/79, ibid., p. 128. For the Boers in Angola see F. Amaral and J. B. F. de Almeida, 'Apontamentos para a historia do estabelecimento da colonia agricola S. Januario nos terrenos de Humpata', *Bol. SGL*, 1881, pp. 304–17, 456–67.
52 See e.g. E. Lux, *Von Loanda nach Kimbuandu* (Vienna, 1880); P. Pogge, *Im Reiche des Muata Jamvo* (Berlin, 1880); H. O. Schütt, *Reisen im süd-westlichen Becken des Congo* (Berlin, 1881).
53 Bentley, 1, p. 81.

humanitarian circles in England a feeling of vested interest already possessed by commercial concerns.[54]

As a counterblast, the Portuguese authorities were soon to organize a Roman Catholic mission to S. Salvador. A Portuguese gun-boat conveyed its members to Noqui; its presents to the King, and a letter to him from the King of Portugal, indicated the official nature of the mission. The British consul in Luanda had no hesitation in declaring that its main purpose was to try and restore Portuguese influence in that country and by degrees to establish a permanent authority over the Congo.[55]

The Portuguese authorities could not understand why Britain should continue to resist their claims. The slave-trade was dead, there were no other claimants to the territory and in the interests of humanity and civilization it was essential that European control should be extended over the area.[56] Further disorders underlined their contention. A new king of Ambrizete was hostile to the traders and the Portuguese and French agents appealed for Portuguese protection, the English for British naval support. The Governor-general warned the British consul that no bluejackets were to be disembarked unless British buildings or lives were being actually attacked or threatened. In these circumstances of insecurity and uncertainty it would be infinitely preferable if Portuguese jurisdiction were extended north of Ambriz.[57]

It was accordingly not surprising that the Portuguese Government should again approach the British about the advisability of coming to an agreement over the Congo.[58] Morier, the diplomat, saw the possibility of exerting pressure to secure the passage of his Lourenço Marques treaty[59] but Braamcamp, the Prime Minister and Minister for Foreign Affairs, anticipated him. In a note, he marshalled the Portuguese arguments, and urged the necessity for coming to a common agreement with other nations so that her frontiers might be positively fixed and recognized.[60] Morier assured him that there was no lack of willingness on the part of the British Government to discuss the question, but he thought it unlikely it would enter into any formal examination of the matter until the Lourenço Marques treaty had been finally settled.[61] Braamcamp resorted to the prevarications over the Lourenço Marques treaty which have been already noted; and Morier declined to reply to this Portuguese note of 28 November 1879 until he heard that there was reasonable expectation of the Lourenço Marques treaty being submitted to the Cortes. Morier regretted that until

54 Cohen to Granville, 10/12/80, 31, FO 149/224; T. J. Comber, 'Brief account of recent journeys in the interior of Africa', *Proceedings RGS*, 1881, pp. 20–6, and 'A boat journey round Stanley Pool', *Proceedings RGS*, 1884, pp. 71–5; Bentley; H. H. Johnston, *George Grenfell and the Congo* (London, 1908), 2 vols; R. M. Slade, *English-speaking missions in the Congo Independent State (1878–1908)* (Brussels, 1959), pp. 35, 42.
55 Cohen to Granville, 25/1/81, 8, PRO, FO 179/223; 'Missão portuguesa do Congo', *Bol. SGL*, 1881, pp. 294–7; A Barroso, Relatório, 15/7/81, *D. António Barroso*, pp. 1–13.
56 W. G. L. Hunt, Consul, Luanda, to Salisbury, 3/10/78, CP 3928, p. 181.
57 Hunt to Salisbury, 10/4/79, and 14/4/79, and 19/7/79, PRO, FO 179/215.
58 Salisbury to Morier, 31/10/79, 66 ST, CP 4786, p. 6, reporting a conversation with Dantas.
59 Morier to Salisbury, 14/11/79, 73 ST, tel., CP 4302, p. 114, CP 4786, p. 6.
60 Braamcamp to Morier, 28/11/79, CP 4786, pp. 10–11.
61 Morier to Salisbury, 6/12/79, 80 ST, CP 4786, pp. 9–10; Salisbury to Morier, 24/12/79, 80 ST, ibid., p. 12.

three years previously Portugal had used her sovereign rights over the vast African seaboard mainly to exclude, to her own detriment and cost, the commerce and industry of other nations; even then only a small portion of her recognized possessions in east and west Africa were being effectively occupied and permanently settled. He questioned the historical rights asserted by Portugal, but agreed that circumstances had changed, and the question was well suited to amicable settlement between the two governments; in view of the popular feelings on both sides, however, the negotiations would have to be carried on with great delicacy and care.[62]

But just when these negotiations were about to begin, there came a change of government in England. Salisbury left the authorization of the negotiations to his successor[63] and this Granville was in no hurry to grant. Another incident, the murder of the master of a Portuguese coaster at Cabinda,[64] kept the subject fresh in the minds of the Portuguese Government; but most of all was it worried by the activities of the International Association.

The day before Braamcamp and Morier signed the additional article and protocol to the Lourenço Marques treaty, the Portuguese minister asked Morier the views of the British Government as to the Congo negotiations. Morier had still received no new instructions[65] but in compliance with authority given him by Salisbury in January 1880, he drew up a draft treaty which he submitted to the new Secretary of State for Foreign Affairs. By this, the Queen would recognize Portuguese sovereignty from 18° south to the mouth of the Congo, and use her good offices to obtain similar recognition from other powers; commercial relations between the two countries in regard to such of that coast as was not yet occupied by Portugal would be the subject of a separate convention; a joint commission would investigate and report on questions connected with the relations of native tribes and the vested interests of settlers on the unoccupied portion of the coast, and the two crowns jointly would determine how to deal with these rights and interests; for twelve years a mixed commission would deal with all matters connected with the slave-trade; the King of Portugal, while maintaining his claim to sovereignty over the coast from the mouth of the Congo to 5° 12′ south, would consent to exercise his sovereign rights in common with the other governments whose subjects possessed recognized commercial establishments within the region on the right bank of the Congo; on matters connected with navigation and policy the Congo would be managed in common by the two crowns; and the term of the treaty would be for twelve years, renewable for further periods of twelve years.[66]

The reaction of Kimberley, the Secretary of State for the Colonies, was

---

62 Morier to Salisbury, 13/3/80, 13, CP 4786, p. 14; Morier to Braamcamp, 26/3/80, confid., CP 4302, pp. 144–6, CP 4786, pp. 20–2.
63 Pauncefote to Morier, 6/4/80, 28 tel., CP 4786, p. 22.
64 Cohen to Granville, 20/9/80, Luanda, CP 4786, pp. 30–1; Granville to Morier, 9/11/80, 39 ST, FO 179/219; Cohen to Salisbury, 10/12/80, 30, FO 179/224. The Portuguese sent a warship to Cabinda, but the accused were eventually acquitted for lack of evidence (Cohen to Salisbury, 18/2/81, 12, FO 179/224).
65 Morier to Granville, 20/1/81, 10, CP 4786, p. 31.
66 Morier, draft Treaty, CP 4506, p. 149, enclosed in Morier to Granville, 20/4/81, 101, ibid., p. 148 and CP 4786, pp. 36–7.

that considering the proceedings of the Portuguese Government in connection with the Lourenço Marques treaty and the hostile feeling in Portugal against England, it was not desirable at that time to take any steps in the matter.[67] Granville passed this opinion on to Morier, but expressed no view of his own.[68] The negotiations hung fire.

A British firm trading on the Congo chartered a ship to take salt from Lisbon to Cabinda. The Portuguese authorities refused to allow her to load, declaring Cabinda to be a Portuguese port, and trade between Portugal and the Portuguese possessions was reserved for Portuguese bottoms. The firm requested the British minister to intervene. Morier pointed out to Granville that the Portuguese constitutional charter declared Cabinda to be Portuguese territory, so legally the decision was correct; but in the meantime everybody suffered: the British firm, the German shipowners, the Portuguese salt merchants, and the people of Cabinda.[69]

Brazza's operations prompted Serpa, the new Minister for Foreign Affairs, in October 1882 to urge that an arrangement be come to between Great Britain and Portugal regarding the territories about the mouth of the Congo. This would strengthen the position of Portugal in any territorial claim that might be put forward by France. He suggested a simple interchange of notes, to obviate the arguments that would be sure to be raised in the Cortes.[70] He followed this up with a despatch to Dantas for communication to the British Government, drawing attention again to the insecurity and near-anarchy prevailing about the Congo mouth, and summarizing the attempts made by Portugal to persuade Britain to come to an agreement. This was now more necessary than ever before in view of Brazza's explorations and French pretensions. France was a friendly power, but there was danger that French public opinion, and the apparent abandonment of those regions by Portugal, might drive the French Government to act contrary to justice and international law.[71] At the same time Portugal made "friendly representations" to the French Government.[72]

The Netherlands Government heard rumours of this overture and enquired whether there was any truth in it. Granville denied that there had been any recent negotiations on the subject, but admitted that the British Government would favour some arrangement with the Portuguese. The British aims were only to secure freedom of trade and navigation to all nations, and the extinction of slavery. It invited the Netherlands Government and the governments of other nations with the same interests to communicate their views.[73] Publication of Brazza's Treaty with Makoko[74] caused the Chamber of Commerce of Manchester to urge the British Government to use its earliest endeavours, in concert

67 Wingfield to Pauncefote, 23/4/81, CP 4506, p. 139.
68 Granville to Morier, 30/4/81, 52, CP 4506, p. 150, CP 4786, p. 38.
69 Morier to Granville, 12/5/81, 125, FO 179/226.
70 Baring to Granville, 19/10/82, 15 ST, FO 179/231.
71 Serpa to Dantas, 8/11/82, communicated 22/11/82, CP 4785, p. 14.
72 Serpa to Chargé d'Affaires, Paris, 20/11/82, CP 4785, pp. 36–7.
73 Granville to Bylandt, 14/11/82, CP 4785, p. 6.
74 Lyons, Paris to Granville, 19/11/82, 81 ST, CP 4785, p. 9.

with other governments of Europe and the USA, to ensure that the territorial and sovereign rights of the natives of the Congo be respected and maintained without any interference by any power in the existing freedom of navigation and commerce.[75] Now other British commercial concerns began to protest against the possibility of Portugal acquiring Congo lands.[76] Dantas assured Granville that Portugal would not impose any commercial monopoly over those areas and that his Government was animated by the most liberal ideas in regard to the navigation of the Congo.[77]

The French House of Deputies ratified the Brazza Treaty with Makoko. The Minister of Foreign Affairs declared that the area ceded to France lay outside the Portuguese possessions which had been clearly defined in the treaty of 1786, and a gun-boat, the *Sagittaire*, was leaving at once for west Africa to secure the first results of Brazza's labours.[78] These proceedings, and an article in *Le Temps* which advocated the French occupation of land north of the Congo, greatly disturbed the Belgians,[79] but still more did it disturb the Portuguese Government which became more desirous than ever of coming to agreement with England.[80] And the British Government shared its apprehensions lest annexation of territory by France should lead to the establishment of a commercial monopoly which would be detrimental to British trade.[81]

Granville accordingly decided that British policy in this matter might be reversed. The slave-trade had ceased in the area in dispute, and there were no other objections that Britain could justly raise. It was now French action that threatened British commerce. Granville was prepared to come to an agreement with Portugal on condition that the trade and navigation of the Congo were guaranteed free to all nations, with exemption from all river dues or tolls and with very low maximum customs duties; that due consideration be given to the privileges enjoyed by British subjects under treaty arrangements with native chiefs; that Portuguese possessions in and around Whydah, on the Dahomey coast, be ceded to Britain; and that arrangements be made for the navigation of the Zambezi, as provided for in the unratified Lourenço Marques treaty.[82]

As the implications of the French acquisition of land at Stanley Pool became appreciated, commercial interests became more and more worried, and Jacob Bright asked in the Commons for a Government assurance that territorial changes on the Congo would leave unimpaired the freedom of commerce between Great Britain and that region.[83] When word leaked out that the Foreign Office was favourably considering Portugal's overtures, British commercial interests moved into action in support of the *status quo;* they brought pressure to bear on

75 Chamber of Commerce, Manchester to Granville, 13/11/82, CP 4785, p. 617.
76 Hatton and Cookson, Liverpool, to Sir Chas. Dilke, 20/11/82, CP 4785, p. 12. The Company's imports and exports into and from this area had totalled £69,523 in 1879; £126,876 in 1880; £133,420 in 1881; and £87,333 for the first half of 1882.
77 Dantas to Serpa, tel., 22/11/82, tel., communicated 22/11/82, CP 4785, p. 19.
78 Legum to Granville, 22/11/82, 83 ST, CP 4785, p. 19.
79 Lumley to Granville, 25/11/82, 4 ST, CP 4785, pp. 22–3.
80 Baring to Granville, 23/11/82, 20 ST, CP 4785, pp. 26–7.
81 Granville to Lyons, 25/11/82, 87 ST, CP 4785, p. 28.
82 Lister to Herbert, 25/11/82, CP 4785, pp. 21–2.
83 28/11/82, CP 4785, p. 27; C. H. Aston to Granville, 27/11/82, ibid., p. 27.

members of parliament urging them not to recognize Portuguese sovereignty over the disputed territory.[84]

But Kimberley now concurred with Granville. He suggested that Britain insist that British subjects be put on a footing of equality with Portuguese subjects in the acquisition of land, the conduct of missionary operations, and the like. As for the transfer of Whydah, he wished this to be extended to cover the acquisition of Portuguese rights or claims wherever they might be between 5° west and 5° east longitude; he further suggested obtaining from Portugal a declaration that she had no claims in South Africa south of 18° south latitude on the west side, and 26° 30′ south on the east side; and he thought that Portugal should be made to understand that where her claims to the coast were admitted, she was not entitled to unlimited territory inland.[85]

Morier, though he was no longer accredited to the court in Lisbon, urged on the British Government the expediency of coming to an agreement with Portugal, at least in regard to the territory south of the Congo, on the lines of his draft treaty. The French activities rendered the opportunity particularly favourable for obtaining concessions from Portugal, in return for which the Portuguese possessions on the west coast could be opened to free commerce and navigation. He suggested the advisability of including France in the arrangements provided Portuguese sovereignty south of the river was recognized.[86]

In the middle of December 1882, Granville conveyed to the Portuguese minister in London the British Government's readiness to enter into negotiations for British recognition of Portuguese sovereignty over the west coast between 8° south and 5° 12′, on the conditions which he and Kimberley had elaborated.[87] The Portuguese Minister of Foreign Affairs received the news with much satisfaction, and expressed his Government's acceptance of the bases of agreement proposed by Granville. He declared that the Portuguese Government had never entertained the idea of monopolizing the navigation of the great African rivers, or of raising difficulties in such navigation by foreigners: the freedom of great commercial highways was now recognized as a principle of international law. He saw difficulties in defining the inland extent of Portuguese jurisdiction; Portugal had no claim to increase her already vast dominions, but she could not accept a situation which would place her in unfair circumstances compared with other nations.[88] On second thoughts, Portugal had doubts about the cession of Whydah, fearing a revolt of public opinion, whilst the militant expression "missionary operations" would have to be replaced by "religious worship."[89]

84 J. Irvine, Liverpool, to Granville, 29/11/82, CP 4785, pp. 32–3; Elder Dempster & Co., to Gibson, 28/11/82, pp. 33–4; Whitby, Westminster, to Granville, 2/12/82, pp. 37–8; Incorporated Chamber of Commerce, Liverpool, to Granville 5/12/82, p. 38; Holt to Granville, 11/12/82, pp. 38–9; Chamber of Commerce and Manufacturers, Glasgow, to Granville, 18/12/82, p. 44.
85 Herbert to Lister, 1/12/82, CP 4785, pp. 35–6.
86 Morier, Madrid to Granville, 7/12/82, CP 4785, pp. 40–2.
87 Granville to Dantas, 15/12/82, CP 4785, p. 43; Granville to Baring, 21/12/82, ibid., p. 45.
88 Serpa to Dantas, 26/12/82, CP 4785, pp. 45–6.
89 Dantas 10/1/83, memo., CP 4785, pp. 48–9.

Derby had no objection to certain alterations suggested by Portugal, but considered that Britain should continue to demand the cession of Whydah; in consideration for this he would withdraw his insistence on the declaration about expansion inland to which Portugal objected.[90] An inspired article in the *Diario de Noticias* stating that the dismantled fort of Whydah was being surrendered in return for British recognition of Portugal's claims started preparing Portuguese public opinion for the surrender.[91] The British Government was worried to learn that a new Moçambique tariff was being introduced, which would greatly increase customs duties,[92] but the Portuguese Government ordered the Governor-general to suspend the new tariff[93] so the list of 1877 could still be accepted as that which would apply to the Congo. A clause about suppressing the slave-trade needed to be re-written to avoid wounding Portuguese susceptibilities,[94] and there was disagreement about the wording of two other articles.[95]

The anti-treaty agitation was now gathering momentum and questions were asked in both the Commons and the Lords about the negotiations.[96] The arrival of a report from the British consul in Luanda which revealed that the number of Portuguese factories in the Congo area was small compared with the number of English, Netherlands, French and German[97] prompted Granville to take a stronger line. Rumours that a number of Portuguese gun-boats were being sent to the coast, possibly to take possession of it by force, may also have disquietened him, though Serpa made haste to declare that no naval expedition

90 Herbert to Lister, 17/1/83, CP 4785, p. 54; E. Hertslet, Memo. on Whydah, 12/1/83, ibid., pp. 49–50.
91 Wyke to Granville, 17/1/83, 2 ST, CP 4785, pp. 54–5.
92 Granville to Dantas, 20/1/83, CP 4785, pp. 55–6.
93 Dantas to Granville, 29/1/83, CP 4785, pp. 56–7; Dantas to Lister, 5/2/83, pp. 58–9.
94 Dantas, memo., 20/2/83, CP 4785, p. 76.
95 Dantas to Granville, 10/3/83, CP 4785, p. 93.
96 e.g. Chamber of Commerce, Manchester, to Granville, 29/1/83, CP 4785, pp. 57–8; James Irwin and Co., Liverpool, to Granville, 14/2/83, pp. 63–4; African Lakes Company, Glasgow, to Sir J. Kirk, 15/2/83, p. 75; deputation from African Association, Liverpool, to FO, 21/2/83, p. 77; C. H. Aston, Birmingham, to Granville, 22/2/83, p. 80; J. E. Hutton, Manchester, to Lister, 3/3/83, p. 82; Chamber of Commerce, Warrington, to Granville, 5/3/83, CP 4807, pp. 1–2; *Manchester Examiner* 6/3/83, CP 4785, pp. 97–8; British & Foreign Anti-Slavery Society to Granville, 9/3/83, p. 95, quoted in Commons, 8/3/83, pp. 87–8 and in Lords, 9/3/83, p. 91; Chamber of Commerce, Manchester, to Granville, 12/3/83, p. 96; Chamber of Commerce, London to Granville, 14/3/83, p. 100.
97 Between the Loge and the Congo were factories at Kinsembo, Mussera, Ambrizette, Muculla, Quinzan, Cacongo and Cabeça da Cobra; of the total of 29 only 2 were Portuguese; 1 German, 1 Belgian, 5 Netherlands, 9 French, 11 English. At Banana were the head establishments of the Dutch Trading Company, the French houses and the Congo and Central African Company recently formed in Liverpool. On the left bank were a French and a Netherlands station at Mussoco; at Noqui, a French and a Portuguese. On the right bank were two English; a French and a Netherlands at Ponta de Lenha; and of the 9 at Boma were a Belgian, a Netherlands, 2 French, 2 English and 3 Portuguese. North of the Congo were factories at Cabinda, Black Pt, Loango, Landana and Mazumba; of the total of 17, there were a French, 2 Netherland, 3 American and 5 English. The whole trade was carried on almost exclusively with English, Netherlands and French capital; one Portuguese concern alone imported and exported. Exports from the Congo alone were valued at close on £20,000 for the previous year; imports were valued at 8% of the exports — which explained the profits each obtained and the interest of the commercial houses. (Cohen to Granville, 3/1/83, received 17/2/83, CP 4785, pp. 66–7). Further information about factories was given in Lt. Cmdr. Hadley, Luanda, to Rear Admiral Salmon, 16/3/83, CP 4865, pp. 7–8.

would be despatched until after the close of the negotiations.[98] But most of all
did Granville prove to be susceptible to Belgian pressure. Strauch, the President
of the International Association, wrote to him that the stations of the Association were purely philanthropic and scientific; the Association did not trade;
but trade in the area the Association was opening up would be threatened by
the negotiations proceeding between England and Portugal. The vice-president
of the Association wrote to Lord Rosebery along the same lines. Leopold
invited Kirk to Brussels, and in the course of four long interviews informed
him that he already had 50 Europeans and 700 Zanzibaris in the Congo; he
was expecting 300 Hausas and was hoping for 400 Chinese; he would oppose
Portuguese occupation by force. Mackinnon, too, pressed on Granville the
views of Leopold, and gave him a memorandum on the conditions which would
probably satisfy the British commercial community, and at the same time meet
the wishes of the King of the Belgians.[99]

Granville now told Serpa that Britain did not admit Portugal's claims to
sovereignty; Britain was asking for concessions not as a favour, but as a
condition. Portuguese trading stations were in a small minority. Commercial
houses of five nations paid no dues or imposts, other than small contributions
to chiefs; their vessels plied without hindrance; there was free access to the
interior; missionaries were allowed perfect freedom irrespective of creed.
Granville warned that there must be no obscurity; he demanded that there be
no differential dues, no transit duties; there must be complete freedom of trade
and navigation, and equality to missionaries of all creeds. It was necessary to
define extension into the interior, otherwise the differences on the coast would
be extended to the interior. The Sociedade de Geografia de Lisboa was suggesting
that Portuguese claims might extend to Stanley Pool, which emphasized that
severe damage might arise from vague pretensions.[100]

British houses trading to the Congo continued to lobby and inflame public
opinion.[101] Reports that a Portuguese post and health office had been started
at Banana were interpreted to mean that Portugal was assuming administrative
control of the area in dispute,[102] and plans for the civil re-occupation of S.

98 Wykes to Granville, 21/2/83, 9 ST, CP 4785, p. 78; FO to Wykes, 5/3/83, tel., p. 83;
   Wykes to Granville, 6/3/83, 2 Af., p. 92; and 8/3/83, 3 Af., pp. 94–5; and 12/3/83, 4 Af.,
   p. 104.
99 Strauch to Granville, 5/2/83, CP 4785., p. 63; Lambert to Rosebery, 9/2/83, pp. 65–6; Kirk,
   memo., 18/2/83, pp. 74–5; Pauncefote, memo., 26/2/83, p. 79, in which he notes that the
   King of the Belgians was the real proprietor of the Association; and W. Mackinnon,
   memo., 14/3/83, and to Granville, 19/3/83, p. 110. Mackinnon followed this up with a
   memo. of 9/4/83, CP 4807, p. 61, in which he suggested an international commission to
   control the free navigation of the Congo with the King of Belgium as its President.
100 Granville to Dantas, 15/3/83, CP 4807, pp. 101–3.
101 Hutton to Granville, 20/3/83, CP 4807, pp. 3–4; Chamber of Commerce, Dewsbury to
   Granville, 22/3/83, pp. 6–7; Chamber of Commerce and Manufacture, Greenock, to
   Granville, 30/3/83, p. 10; Bristol Incorporated Chamber of Commerce and Shipping
   to Granville, [3/83], pp. 22–3; African Steamship Coy to Granville, 2/4/83, p. 11; African
   Steamship Coy to Granville, 2/4/83, p. 11; H. Jepson, Manchester, to Granville, 4/4/83,
   pp. 23–4; Elder Dempster Coy to Granville, 17/4/83, p. 33; Chamber of Commerce,
   Birmingham, to Granville, 19/4/83, p. 42.
102 Wyke to Granville, 14/3/83, 5 Af., CP 4785, p. 105; and 17/4/83, 21 Af., p. 42; Chamber
   of Commerce, Manchester, to Granville, 18/4/83, p. 34; Wyke to Granville, 21/4/83,
   tel., p. 46; Cohen to Granville, 16/5/83, 7 Af., pp. 55–6; Wyke to Granville, 21/4/83,
   tel., p. 44.

Salvador were regarded as threats to the Baptist mission established there.[103] Partisan opinion was forcibly expressed in a debate in the House of Commons which aroused great indignation in Portugal, and prompted a call by Dantas on Granville. But the Secretary of State refused to explain observations by independent members of parliament.[104] Serpa undertook that everything would remain *in statu quo* pending the conclusion of the negotiations.[105] The Portuguese opposition accused the Government of trucking to the wishes of the British; there was a strong demand for a more aggressive policy and simple seizure of the territory in dispute. The British minister feared that if the Government fell, its successor, backed by over-excited public opinion, which recalled the perfect success of the Ambriz coup, might well adopt such a policy.[106]

Despite this warning, the negotiations dragged on at a snail's pace. Dantas pointed out that it was impossible to define mathematically the effective limits of Portuguese jurisdiction, but he urged Portuguese rights over the ancient kingdom of Congo.[107] Derby still approved of the treaty, but now instead of demanding the cession of Whydah, he declared that he would be satisfied with a declaration that if Portugal ever withdrew from Whydah, Portugal would make over her rights to Britain.[108] The Lords of the Admiralty questioned whether Portugal had any rights in Whydah at all; they had no objection to the treaty, but wisely questioned the settling of the boundary on the Congo at Porto da Lenha; the Congo was navigable to Noqui, and there would be difficulty if a considerable portion of the river were left without control.[109] Even the French Government was asked what it thought about the proposed treaty. The French Minister of Foreign Affairs declared that as matters then stood the French Government did not admit the claims of Portugal to any of the disputed territory. The view of the British Foreign Office was that a bad tenant was better than an empty house, and it was better to let Portugal in at once than for Britain to wake one morning and find that France had occupied the disputed territory.[110] There seemed every danger of such a happening.

Brazza returned to the west coast with 130 men. Among his stores were 8,000 rifles, 20,000 sabres, 12 field-guns, and 40 tons of gunpowder. Beyond this, the French Parliament voted him a grant for the purchase of 100,000 muskets, or arms equivalent in value. The military character of his expedition was completely unjustified by the nature of the natives.[111]

103 Cohen to Granville, 11/1/83, 6 ST, CP 4785, p. 60; Baptist Missionary Society to Granville, 21/3/83, pp. 5–6.
104 Granville to Wyke, 6/4/83, 7 Af., CP 4807, p. 24; Wyke to Granville, 11/4/83, 17 Af., p. 29.
105 Wyke to Granville, 21/4/83, 28 Af., CP 4807, pp. 56–7.
106 CP 4807, 23/4/83, 29 Af., ibid., pp. 57–8.
107 Serpa to Dantas, 24/3/83, CP 4785, pp. 114–5; Dantas, memo, 2/4/83, CP 4807, p. 23.
108 Meade to Lister, 15/5/83, CP 4865, p. 24.
109 Tryon, Sec. to Adm., to Lister, 18/5/83, CP 4865, p. 26.
110 Granville to Lyons, 15/5/83, 22 Af., CP 4805, p. 23; Lyons to Granville, 23/5/83, 35 Af., p. 39; Sir F. Richards, memo., c. 31/5/80, p. 45.
111 W. Carson, Liverpool to Granville, 27/2/83, CP 4785, p. 81; Col. G. Villiers, military attaché, Paris, to Lyons, pp. 92–3; Lumley, Brussels, to Granville, 24/3/83, 2 Af., CP 4807, p. 8; Lyons to Granville, 22/5/83, 33 Af., CP 4865, pp. 34–5.

On 15 March the *Sagittaire* anchored off Ponta Negra. Her commander Cordier proposed a cession of land to the local chief, who refused a present and pointed to the Portuguese flag left by a Portuguese warship. The next day Cordier repeated his proposal at a palaver. The headmen declared that they would cede land on the same terms as to the traders established there—all of whom were Portuguese—but they would not agree to any permanent alienation of land.

On 17 March Cordier landed an armed force, and in the name of the French Republic he hoisted the tricolour. The local traders protested; and the commander of a Portuguese gun-boat, who was soon on the scene, protested on his own authority. Cordier declared that the Portuguese flag which had been flying there had possessed no significance beyond decoration, and the French, in their great civilizing and humanitarian work, had taken possession of land that belonged to no one. The Governor-general of Angola invited the British consul in Luanda to join him in a joint protest, but Cohen replied that the annexation did not affect British commercial interests; he would protest only if there were annexation between 5° 12′ and 8° south; and the matter should be left to higher authority.[112]

There was an attempt to murder a British subject at Nyanga; Portuguese and British gun-boats sped to the scene. Two Portuguese implicated surrendered themselves and were taken to Luanda for trial. The judge ordered their release in the absence of evidence; and in any case there were doubts as to whether they could be tried by Portuguese law, not having been arrested on Portuguese soil. Cohen hinted to Granville that the results would have been very different had a black been charged. He declared that there was no protection for life or property under existing conditions and urged that Britain should exercise control over the disputed territory for the sake of commerce and to prevent hostilities between Brazza and Stanley.[113]

The course of justice was different at Quisanga, where a factory was attacked. The commander of a Portuguese gun-boat found that the local chief had done nothing to apprehend the offenders, so he took the chief to Luanda. Cohen protested against this action; the Governor-general assured him that the chief would not be tried, but simply detained for nine or ten months as an example.[114]

Relations between the Governor-general of Angola and Cohen continued to be strained. In January 1883, van der Velde of the International Association had travelled inland from Noqui to Palabala, on the road to S. Salvador, where there was now a Netherlands factory and a station of the Livingstone Inland

112 A. Loemba and others, Ponta Negra, to GG, Angola, 19/3/83, CP 4865, pp. 14–5; Protest by C. A. de Magalhaes e Silva, Ponta Negra, 19/3/83, p. 12; Cordier's reply, 19/3/83, pp. 12–4; Treaty with King of Loango, 12/3/83, pp. 10–11; Cohen to Granville, 25/3/83, 14 ST, p. 1; Cohen to Amaral, 28/3/83, pp. 3–4; Rear Adm. Salmon, at sea, to Sec. to Adm., 30/3/83, p. 9; Cohen to Granville, 16/4/83, 3 & 5 Af., pp. 30–3; Wyke to Granville, 17/5/83, p. 27.
113 Cohen to Granville, 18/6/83, 8 Af., CP 4865, p. 88; and 12/7/83, 17 Af., p. 94; and 17/7/83, p. 105; and 10/8/83, 23 Af., p. 120.
114 Cohen to Granville, 10/8/83, 24 Af., CP 4865, pp. 121–2.

Mission. There he had made a treaty with the chiefs by which they sold not only land to the Association, but sovereignty over their territory; no other trading concern was to be permitted without the assent of the Association; and tribesmen could be called upon for forced labour. When the treaty was later translated to the chiefs, and explained, they were horrified; they declared they had never intended to alienate their land. The Governor-general of Angola called on the British consul to join him in a joint protest, but it was July before Cohen would admit the existence of such a treaty, and then he saw no grounds for protest.[115] It soon emerged that there was not just one such treaty, but that the emissaries of the Association had been active over a wide area. The most controversial was with the King of Boma, who was alleged to have ceded his sovereign right to the Association in return for two muskets and twenty pieces of stuff; he too denounced it when it was translated and explained to him.[116] All were of the same pattern. All, obtained by intimidation or fraud, conferred sovereign rights on the Association (over territory regarded by Portugal as hers); and all reserved to the Association the exclusive right to trade—to the potential prejudice of international commerce.[117]

Cohen had one cure for all these threats and ills. At his instigation, the British traders at Sette Cama forwarded a petition from the local chiefs begging to be taken under British protection; in fact, the chiefs added, they would view with satisfaction the extension of the Queen's authority to the Congo and as far south as Kinsembo. Cohen urged on Granville the advantages of British annexation of Cabinda, from which it was only sixty miles overland to Boma, and also of Landana and Banana. With these points in British possession, he thought that Portugal might be graciously permitted to exercise jurisdiction as far as the south bank of the Congo. The natives would soon recognize the advantages of British rule, and the Portuguese would be compelled to abandon their vexatious rules and regulations, and their export of slaves thinly disguised as contracted labourers.[118] It was not surprising that the Portuguese Government should protest against the activities of Cohen who, it declared, was inciting the natives in the Congo area against the Portuguese.[119] But there were soon petitions on the Sette Cama pattern, from the chiefs of Mayumba. The British Government could not countenance such proposals.[120] The Association later moved into Sette Cama after making the usual restrictive treaties and despite the customary protests of the chiefs.[121]

115 Cohen to Granville, 16/7/83, 18 Af., CP 4865, p. 103; and 10/9/83, 27 Af., CP 4944, p. 11; and 6/11/83, 40 Af., pp. 80–1, enclosing three treaties, pp. 84–6.
116 Stanley and Winton to Capello, 4/6/84, CP 5019, pp. 52–3; Newton, A-Consul, Luanda, to Gray, 14/6/84, 3 Af., CP 5019, p. 12; Petre to Granville, 19/6/84, 69 Af., CP 5000, p. 137.
117 Lister to Mackinnon, 4/1/84, CP 4960, p. 1; Dantas to Granville, 2/7/84, CP 5019, p. 3; Bocage to Dantas, 31/7/84, pp. 40–2; Dantas to Granville, 4/8/84, p. 27.
118 Cohen to Granville, 6/8/83, 21 Af., CP 4865, pp. 118–9.
119 Baring to Granville, 25/7/83, 59 Af., CP 4865, p. 86; Serpa to Dantas, 1/8/83, pp. 87–8; Cohen to Granville, 15/10/83, 38 Af., CP 4944, pp. 38–9.
120 Cohen to Granville, 12/11/83, 45 Af., CP 4865, p. 94; Currie to Cohen, 31/1/84, 5 Af., CP 4960, p. 14.
121 Edward Bros, Liverpool, to Lister, 22/2/84, CP 4960, p. 39; Congo District Association, Liverpool, to Granville, 17/10/84, CP 5019, p. 71.

Amaral, the Governor-general of Angola, seeing the occupation of one place after another by France and the Association, and apprehensive of British intentions, yet debarred by British threats and the instructions of his Government from any occupation in the disputed zone, determined on his own initiative to annex the coast from Landana on the Chiloango River (which was shown on British Admiralty charts to be immediately north of 5° 12′) northwards to the Massabe River. Brito Capelo, commander of the corvette *Rainha de Portugal*, on 29 September 1883 informed a meeting of chiefs at Landana that numbers of them desired the protection of Portuguese sovereignty; he had come with full powers conferred on him by the King of Portugal to conclude a treaty with them, the eleven articles of which were read out and discussed; if they signed, their own laws and customs would remain unaltered, but if they did not sign another power would come and seize the country. According to the commander of a British gun-boat, who was a spectator of these proceedings, it was rum and cloth that carried the day. The majority of Europeans at Landana were Portuguese, and they naturally viewed with enthusiasm the raising of the blue and white flag. The Minister of Foreign Affairs eventually approved Capelo's action.[122]

Landana was accordingly spared the disorder that rent Muculla. There, the local king objected to the behaviour of Kroomen belonging to the Netherlands factory. The agent's answer was to close the factory and build a mud fort mounting four small cannon. One night tribesmen surrounded the fort. The agent ordered fire to be opened, and the natives replied. The exchanges came to an abrupt end when eight or ten tons of gunpowder in the French factory, which was in the line of fire, exploded. The attackers lost some forty men, while two factories were destroyed and two others severely damaged. A Portuguese gun-boat arrived. Capelo summoned a meeting of traders, at which it was decided to call on chiefs of several neutral villages to produce the king and four of his councillors under penalty of the destruction of their villages and manioc fields. The agent of a British factory returned to the place as the ultimatum was expiring and protested strongly against such wanton action. Capelo was persuaded to direct his reprisals against only the king's villages. These, which had been evacuated, were burnt, and fields of maize and manioc were destroyed. Capelo persuaded the neutral chiefs to elect a new king, on whom he imposed conditions favourable to the traders.[123]

Meanwhile, on 1 June 1883, Granville had communicated to Dantas a draft treaty. The British Government acknowledged the authority of the King of Portugal over the coast between 8° and 5° 12′ and on the Congo as far as Porto da Lenha. Otherwise "the inland frontier shall coincide with the boundaries of the present Possessions of the coast tribes"; this frontier was to be

122 G. A. de Brito Capello, 29/9/83, deed of possession, CP 4944, p. 69, treaty, pp. 70–1; Cohen to Granville, 8/10/83, 32 Af., p. 34; Cohen to Granville, 9/10/83, 33 Af., p. 35; Amaral to Cohen, 10/10/83, p. 36; Baring to Granville, 12/11/83, tel., p. 22 and 19/11/83, p. 34; Cmdr Hammick, *Flirt*, St Helena, to Rear Adm. Salmon, 28/11/83, pp. 79–80.
123 Cohen, Mucalla, to Granville, 8/1/84, 6 Af., CP 4960, pp. 32–3; and 10/1/84, 7 Af., p. 36; and 11/1/84, 8 Af., p. 37; Cmdr Moore, *Frolic*, Luanda, to Sec. to Adm., 12/1/84, pp. 40–2; Cohen to Granville, 15/1/84, 9 Af., pp. 37–8.

defined and demarcated as soon as possible. The territory was to be open to all nations; foreigners would enjoy the same benefits as the subjects of Portugal. Trade and navigation along the coastline and on the Congo and other waterways was to be open to the flags of all nations, and not to be subject to any monopoly, exclusive concession or impediment, nor were customs duties or tolls to be imposed except those agreed upon; the parties further were to agree to appoint a commission to draw up regulations for the navigation, policing and supervision of all rivers. There were to be no duties on goods in transit by land or by water. All forms of religious worship were to be tolerated, and protection afforded to all missionaries. The customs tariff was not for ten years to exceed that introduced into Moçambique in 1877. Legislation for the extinction of slavery and the slave-trade was to be effectively applied. The River Zambezi was also to be open to the trade and navigation of all flags and not subject to any monopoly or exclusive concession or other impediment, or any customs duties, tolls, charges, etc.; it was further to be understood that Portuguese jurisdiction did not extend to the River Shire. If at any time it was in the interests of Portugal to withdraw from Whydah, the cession was to be first offered to Britain.[124]

Serpa and his colleagues were not prepared to accept Porto da Lenha as the limit on the Congo, which would have left a sort of Alsace between there and Vivi, nor would they accept the appointment of an international commission. They preferred to abide by the outright cession of Whydah. They were prepared to accept the application of the Moçambique tariff to territories about to be acquired, but owing to vested interests they could not agree to its extension to Angola, and their re-wording of one article would have made possible the imposition of transit duties. They refused to allow Protestant places of worship to look like churches. And they objected to the withdrawal of sovereignty from the Shire.[125] The Foreign Office appreciated that the treaty, even with the proposed amendments, was so exceptionally liberal that it might be rejected by the Cortes. It decided to substitute Boma for Porto da Lenha. It could not agree to the altered commercial proposal, which would be opposed by the British trading concerns. And it could not give up the commission, without which there would be an outcry in Britain though Baring, the minister in Lisbon, considered it safe to yield on this point, which would help in passing it through the Cortes.[126] Granville demanded complete religious freedom, and insisted that there be no loophole for the imposition of transit duties. In regard to the Shire, the British Government desired to do all in its power to meet the views of Portugal, and would not insist on inserting in the treaty any definite frontier line. It was, however, essential to lay down a frontier custom-house in the effective possession of Portugal; the Moçambique tariff stated this to be at the junction of the Shire and the Zambezi, and this would be acceptable to the

124 Granville to Dantas, 1/6/83, CP 4865, pp. 48–50.
125 Wyke to Granville, 14/6/83, 49 Af., CP 4865, p. 58; Baring to Granville, 22/6/83, 51 Af., pp. 60–1; Serpa to Dantas, 26/6/83, pp. 63–6, and pp. 66–72 the English proposals and Portuguese counter-proposals in parallel columns.
126 Memos by H. P. Anderson, T. V. Lister, and Fitzmaurice, 13, 15 and 18/7/83, CP 4865, pp. 74–6; Baring to Lister, 16/8/83, pp. 107–8.

British Government.[127] Derby was now of opinion that the offer of Whydah could be accepted.[128] The Portuguese Government yielded on all the essential points at issue, except three. It demanded that the question of the Shire be divorced from that of the Congo; that Vivi be made the limit on the Congo; and that if there must be a commission, it should be Anglo-Portuguese.[129]

The British Government accepted the principle of a joint commission, but it refused to divorce the question of the Shire from that of the Congo, knowing that only by such a linkage would it be possible to obtain concessions in south-east Africa. Granville insisted that British trading and missionary settlements at and near Lake Nyasa be secured in their independence and freedom of action, and they must know their position regarding the transit of goods; it was essential to fix the limit of Portuguese jurisdiction in this area. If Portugal agreed to claim no territory more than sixty miles above the confluence of the Shire and the Zambezi, Britain would be prepared to accept Noqui as the limit on the Congo.[130] The Portuguese Government, "in the presence of powerful circumstances", accepted these conditions. It regretted the re-writing of certain articles; it preferred a contingent rather than an absolute cession of Whydah; and it urged the advisability of setting a fixed boundary to its jurisdiction up the Shire, suggesting the confluence of the Ruo with that river.[131] The British Government accepted the Whydah amendment, and the Ruo frontier.[132] Some provisions were re-written. There was a last-minute objection by the Association which demanded, and received, assurance that its station at Ikungula, near Noqui, should be outside Portuguese jurisdiction.[133] Finally, on 26 February 1884, the treaty was signed.[134]

127 Granville to Dantas, 21/8/83, CP 4865, pp. 89–90.
128 Meade to Lister, 6/10/83, CP 4944, p. 1.
129 Dantas to Granville, 28/8/83, CP 4865, pp. 107–10; Lister, minute, 31/8/83, pp. 110–1; Dantas to Granville, 11/9/83, p. 113; Granville to Dantas, 17/9/83, p. 115; Dantas to Granville, 24/9/83, p. 125; Anderson, Lister, Fitzmaurice, Pauncefote, minutes, 8, 9 and 11/10/83, CP 4944, pp. 2–5; Dantas to Granville, 17/10/83, pp. 9–10 and minutes, Lister to Granville, 18/10/83, p. 10; Serpa to Dantas, 20/10/83, pp. 13–7; Granville to Baring, 16/11/83, 44 Af., pp. 27–8; Lister, minute, 4/12/83, p. 61; Fitzmaurice, minute, 6/12/83, p. 62.
130 Granville to Dantas, 7/1/84, CP 4960, pp. 2–3, and 3–7 revised English draft of the Treaty, 14 clauses.
131 Bocage to Dantas, 26/1/84, communicated 31/1/84, CP 4960, p. 14 A–B.
132 Granville to Dantas, 1/2/84, CP 4960, p. 14 C.
133 Dantas to Granville, 11/2/84, CP 4960, p. 28; Anderson, memo. 18/2/84, pp. 29–30; Granville to Petre, 23/2/84, 15 Af., p. 38 B–39; Petre to Granville, 25/2/84, tel., p. 39; and 25/2/84, 12 Af., p. 44.
134 E. Hertslet, *Map of Africa by Treaty* (London, 1894), pp. 713–4.

4

THE BERLIN CONFERENCE 1884–1885

There was an immediate uproar against the Anglo-Portuguese Congo Treaty in Britain and Portugal, France and Belgium, and, before long, in Germany.

In England various chambers of commerce protested that Portugal would impose prohibitive customs duties on foreign imports, and British trade would be ruined.[1] The Liverpool merchants trading with Africa expressed their official opposition more nobly, declaring that the natives, rightful owners of the land, had not been consulted: England had thirteen treaties with chiefs which could not be denounced without reference to the other parties; and Portugal was utterly incompetent to govern her colonies as it was, and advance commerce or civilization.[2] The feeling in Sheffield was that Portugal was utterly incapable of carrying out treaty obligations and she imposed exorbitant taxes on traders and settlers.[3] The Baptist Missionary Society and Baptist Union declared that Portugal had insignificant interests on the Congo and urged the British Government, in concert with other powers possessing interests there, to secure unrestricted navigation, and not allow any one power to obtain exclusive control over the area.[4] The British and Foreign Anti-Slavery Society criticized the inefficient and corrupt character of Portuguese administration in Africa; it accused Portugal of indulging in a slave-trade between Luanda and the islands of S. Tomé and Principe and feared that the treaty would lead to an extension of this nefarious trade.[5] There were letters to *The Times*,[6] there were pamphlets,[7] there were questions in Parliament.[8] Though isolated voices were raised in support of the treaty,[9] there were loudly expressed demands that if the *status*

1 J. F. Hutton, President, Chamber of Commerce, Manchester, to Fitzmaurice, 6/3/84, CP 4960, p. 49; Hutton to Granville, 26/3/84, ibid., pp. 99–100. J. W. Browne, Birmingham, to Fitzmaurice, 29/3/84, ibid., p. 110, complained that on guns and revolvers 6/8 duty had to be paid, which represented 100% of the FOB Liverpool cost. British exports to West Africa in 1883 had totalled £2½m., half of it to ports not under European control (Com. of Privy Council for Trade to Lister, 5/11/84, CP 5033 p.40). See Anstey, ch. VI.
2 Liverpool merchants trading with Africa, memo., 4/4/84, CP 5000, pp. 10–12.
3 J. Bailey, Sheffield, 25/4/84, CP 5000, p. 51.
4 A. H. Baynes to Granville, 3/5/84, CP 5000, p. 73, enclosing petition by Baptist Missionary Society, 25/4/84, pp. 73–4, and memo by W. H. Bentley, 21/4/84, ibid., pp. 74–8, according to whom in 1882 there had been not 26 Portuguese factories, as Serpa had alleged, but only 2, compared with 14 Netherlands, 5 English, 3 French; J. P. Chowa, Baptist Union, memorial 28/4/84, ibid., p. 52.
5 British and Foreign Anti-Slavery Society to Granville, 12/4/84, CP 5000, p. 13.
6 e.g. W. F. Forster, 16/4/84.
7 e.g. Jacob Bright.
8 24 and 27/3/84, 8/4/84, CP 4960, p. 93, and 101, CP 5000, p. 13.
9 e.g. Cotton Spinners Association, Manchester to Granville, 25/3/84, CP 4960, p. 98 and Chamber of Commerce, Bradford, to Granville, 1/5/84, CP 5000, p. 59.

quo could not be maintained, then there should be international control of the lower Congo.[10]

To help counter the growing tide of opposition, the British Government obtained from the Portuguese an undertaking that where fixed duties were provided for in the Moçambique tariff, steps would be taken to ensure that a maximum of 10 per cent would be imposed on cotton and other goods to the Congo except for guns and gunpowder, tobacco and alcohol.[11] This concession, the British Government thought, would greatly help in the acceptance of the treaty by Parliament. In return, the British Government undertook to help Portugal obtain acceptance of the treaty by other powers.[12] Petre, the minister in Lisbon, considered that Portugal was now sincere in trying to suppress the slave-trade. He added that though there were fifty-one Portuguese factories in the Congo area, 61 per cent of the total number, they handled only 10 per cent of the total trade.[13] The critics of the treaty became more and more vociferous. They were not stilled by a declaration in the Lords by Granville that the Portuguese had claimed this particular territory for nearly four hundred years and

> there is no reason why their claim should not be perfectly good, although we have hitherto refused to recognize it. Their claims have not been opposed by any other country and the only reason why they are not now in occupation is this, that we, acting in a high-handed manner, but one justified by the circumstances of the time, with a view to our anti-slavery opinions, gave them to understand that we would use force to prevent their occupation of the territory.[14]

The Portuguese appreciated that with growing opposition the sooner the treaty was debated in the Commons the better it would be.[15] But Fitzmaurice, the Under-secretary of State for Foreign Affairs, was convinced that if the treaty were submitted to the Commons it would be rejected. It was inconceivable to jeopardize the Government on such an issue. He bluntly asked the Portuguese minister in London whether his Government would prefer the treaty to be thrown out by Parliament, or withdrawn, in the hope that time might bring a more favourable result. Dantas was persuaded to agree to such postponement. Fitzmaurice was also dismayed by the growing opposition abroad: a merely dual arrangement between the two countries, unrecognized by other powers, would be futile.[16]

In Portugal itself there was growing clamour against the treaty. So heated was the discussion in the Sociedade de Geografia de Lisboa that the Society found it expedient to declare the subject outside its scope.[17] The grant of

10 Hutton to Fitzmaurice, 30/5/84, CP 5000, p. 120.
11 Petre to Granville, 27/3/84, tel., CP 4960, p. 101.
12 Granville to Petre, 31/3/84, 24 Af., CP 4960, p. 111.
13 Petre to Granville, 13/4/84, 27 Af., CP 5000, pp. 17–8.
14 Bocage to Petre, 9/7/84, CP 5019, p. 10.
15 Petre to Granville, 17/4/84, 37 Comm., CP 5000, p. 39.
16 Fitzmaurice, memo., 23/4/84, CP 5000, pp. 34–5; Granville to Petre, 23/4/84, 35 A Af., pp. 35–6.
17 Actas, 12/5/84, *Bol. SGL*, 1884, pp. 43–4.

sovereignty in the territory to be recognized had been made so conditional that the treaty was regarded as humiliating to national pride; the articles about Whydah and S. Tomé were regarded as particularly repugnant; and commercial houses in Lisbon protested strongly against the abolition of differential duties, and the freedom of navigation which would gravely prejudice their profits. But the Government fully appreciated the advantages of the treaty for Portugal, Angola and the Congo, and was prepared to make the treaty a cabinet matter.[18] It therefore received with great disappointment the despatch from Dantas foreshadowing the abandonment of the treaty. The Portuguese Government felt that the treaty must be debated in the British Parliament before being submitted to the Cortes, and the Cortes was due to rise in the middle of May. It felt further that the state of affairs in the Congo could not continue much longer—there had been renewed disorders at Vivi and Noqui[19]—and if Portugal were to be left to her own resources she would be forced to adopt a policy by which her interests would suffer the least damage. She would be compelled to come to an agreement with France and the African Association, by which, Bocage forecast, France would be left in possession of the whole northern bank of the Congo, the Association would be free to annex in the upper Congo, while Portugal occupied to the south bank. Bocage suggested that the British critics of the treaty might relax their opposition to it if they realized the consequences were the treaty rejected.[20]

This threat greatly disturbed the Foreign Office, which had been anxiously watching the southward march of France down the west coast.[21] The British Government assured the Portuguese that it would endeavour to secure ratification that session, but the debate could not be held before the end of May; and it would regard it as a matter requiring grave explanation if the Portuguese Government allowed the Cortes to rise without first obtaining its ratification.[22] The Deputies' Committee for Foreign Affairs had already presented a report recommending approval of the treaty and it had been placed on the order paper.[23] Now Bocage wondered whether, in an effort to meet foreign criticism, it might not be advisable to invite France and the Netherlands to join the Anglo-Portuguese commission.[24] To this, of course, Britain was perfectly agreeable, because her original proposal had been for an international commission.

18 Petre to Granville, 10/3/84, 20 Af., CP 4960, pp. 66–7; and 18/3/84, 22 Af., p. 90; and 25/3/84, tel., pp. 95–6; 46 Comm., 24/4/84, CP 5000, p. 43.
19 At Vivi, the head of the IAA placed the local chief in irons; and rioting between Hausas and Cabindas had resulted in the death of two (Cohen to Granville, 8/11/83, 43 Af., CP 4944, p. 89). At Noqui there had been a dispute about 'customs' to be paid the chiefs. European traders refused to pay the customary tax, or attend a palaver summoned by the chiefs, but proceeded to levy a tax on carriers bringing down rubber and ivory. The traders sallied out with their armed servants against the villages; several factory workers were killed. Kroomen arrived from Netherlands and French factories at Banana and an attack destroyed many villages and killed and wounded many tribesmen. Commanders of Portuguese and French gun-boats imposed conditions which restored the situation. (Cohen to Granville, 14/3/84, 24 Af., CP 5000, p. 30)
20 Petre to Granville, 25/4/84, 33 Af., CP 5000, pp. 53–4.
21 Anderson, memo., 30/4/84, CP 5000, pp. 61–2.
22 Granville to Petre, 3/5/84, 40 Af., tel., CP 5000, p. 62.
23 Petre to Granville, 1/5/84, 36 Af., CP 5000, p. 66, and 8/5/84, 43 Af., p. 101.
24 Petre to Granville, 2/5/84, 37 Af., CP 5000, p. 71.

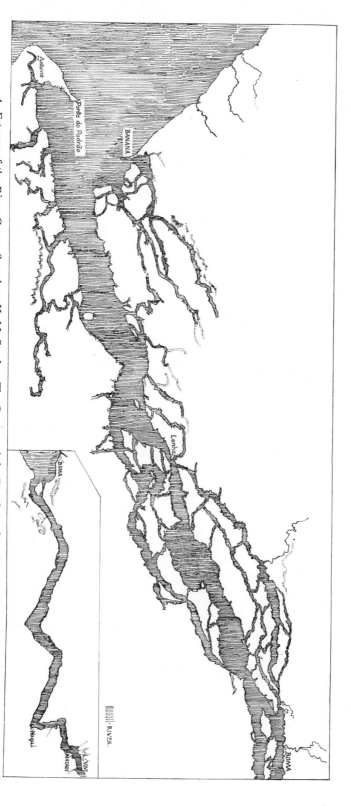

4 Estuary of the River Congo (based on H. M. Stanley, *The Congo and the Founding of its Free State*, 1. London, 1885)

But it was impossible to secure the sanction of these countries before 17 May, when the Cortes was due to rise.[25]

Bocage professed that France was the main opponent. The French Government had made every effort to impress on the Portuguese that her African treaties were innocuous, with such success that at the end of 1882 the Portuguese Government had gone to the length of keeping the French informed of the progress of the negotiations with England. In August 1883, when Portugal had been in the midst of these negotiations, the French minister in Lisbon had proposed to Serpa that the two governments should come to an agreement to delimit their contiguous frontiers in Guinea and the Congo; France would acknowledge Portuguese rights on the Congo, in return for a Portuguese undertaking not to interfere with the settlements of Ponta Negra and Loango.[26] But no agreement materialized. Not long afterwards Charmes, Ferry's confidential adviser on African affairs, sounded the Portuguese representative in Paris as to the possibility of a mutual understanding between the two governments. He declared that the Anglo-Portuguese treaty would hang fire since England was working only for her selfish ends; Portugal and France should divide the lower Congo, France taking everything to the north of the river, Portugal to the south, with the right of unlimited expansion eastwards. But nothing came of these overtures.[27] Once the Anglo-Portuguese treaty had been signed, there was much criticism of it in France.[28] The French Government protested to the Portuguese against negotiating a treaty with Britain alone, to the exclusion of France; France would never recognize the Portuguese claim to the Congo region, and it was necessary for the two governments to come to an understanding. The note complained also of the cession of Whydah, to which, it alleged, France had prior claim.[29] Bocage gave conciliatory and evasive reply, declaring that the joint commission did not preclude French co-operation.[30] The French Government interpreted the Convention of 1786, which conceded France the free right to trade on the Congo, as the right of free trade; it further insisted that no modification or curtailment of the communities secured by this Convention be made without her co-operation and consent.[31]

The greatest change at this time was being effected by Leopold's Association. Whilst there was growing realization in certain circles of the nature of the Association's activities, its waxing prestige and astute diplomacy made it a formidable force. The Foreign Office, after a study of various treaties made by the Association, agreed that it was really a commercial enterprise, and that its talk of humanitarianism and philanthropy was so much claptrap. H. H. Johnston, asked his opinion on his return from a visit to the lower Congo,

---

25 Granville to Petre, 9/5/84, 40 B Af., CP 5000, p. 89; Bocage to Dantas, 9/5/84, tel., p. 101; Granville to Petre, 10/5/84, 11 Af., tel., p. 99; Petre to Granville, 10/5/84, tel., p. 101; and 11/5/84, 45 Af., rec. 16/5, p. 107.
26 Petre to Granville, 17/4/84, 30 Af., CP 5000, p. 38.
27 Granville to Petre, 8/4/84, 30 Af., CP 5000, p. 12; and 29/4/84, 38 Af., pp. 52–3; Petre to Granville, 17/4/84, 30 Af., p. 38.
28 Lyons to Granville, 7/3/84, 25 Af., CP 4960, p. 54.
29 Petre to Granville, 23/3/84, 23 Af., CP 4960, p. 102.
30 Petre to Granville, 25/3/84, 23 Comm., CP 4960, pp. 105–6.
31 Petre to Granville, 11/5/84, 46 Af., CP 5000, pp. 107–8; and 2/6/84, 57 Af., pp. 125–6.

disclosed there could be no doubt that the aim of the Association was a gigantic commercial monopoly; scientific objects were frankly discarded.[32] Stanley, to discredit Portugal and win support for the Association, had revived charges of slave-trading against Portugal.[33] But the Association was much more guilty of the practice. According to Johnston, it bought Kroomen allegedly to free them, but actually to work for it; it treated them as slaves and brutally flogged them for slight offences. Some of these unfortunates ran away from one particular station on the lower Congo. They were caught, and given one hundred blows with a sjambok each, except for the ringleader, who died under six hundred.[34]

But the Association had acquired, by fair means or foul, a number of valuable friends.[35] One such was General Sanford, one-time United States Ambassador in Brussels. Leopold and Strauch enlisted his services and on his return to Washington he used his influence to make propaganda for the Association. He was responsible for the introduction into the Senate, in February 1884, of a resolution declaring to be lawful occupation by the Association of the country drained by the Congo and its tributaries; its flag should be recognized; and an appropriation should be made to send diplomatic or commercial agents to that country. The resolutions were referred to the Committee of Foreign Relations, which recommended that they be indefinitely postponed. Such was Sanford's influence, however, that on 10 April 1884 the Senate acknowledged the flag of the African International Association as the flag of a friendly government.[36] The New York Tribune commented that the United States had acted prematurely and with inconsiderate haste. The Monroe doctrine deprecated meddlesome activity and entangled alliance by the United States in relations with European states; the traditional policy of the American people implied rigorous abstention from the complications of Old World diplomacy. It quoted a remark from The Times that what had been a trust of humanity had become a private speculation; in fact, the State Department had been duped.[37]

Leopold, with consummate skill, now proceeded similarly to dupe the French Government. His representatives rumoured that he had spent a vast fortune in establishing the Association, and he could no longer maintain his subvention, and the Association faced financial ruin. Strauch then wrote to the French Government that the Association had no intention whatever of selling its possessions, but if for unforeseen circumstances it was compelled to realize its assets, it would give France first refusal of those assets—on condition, of

---

32 Anderson, memo., 2/3/84, CP 4960, pp. 46–7, and 13/5/84, with evidence from Ruthven, who accompanied Elliott, p. 102.

33 Baring to Granville, 4/10/83, 71 Af., CP 4944, p. 5, and 28/10/83, 71 Af., p. 17.

34 Lister, minute, 3/3/84, CP 4960, p. 48.

35 Granville, memo., 29/8/84, CP 5033, p. 79.

36 L. S. Sackville West, Washington, to Granville, 30/3/84, CP 5000, p. 22; and tel., 23/4/84, p. 34; and 9/4/84, 4 Af., p. 34; Resolution of Executive Session, Senate, 10/4/84, pp. 63–4; S. E. Crowe, The Berlin West African Conference, 1884–5 (London, 1942), pp. 79–81.

37 New York Tribune, 27/5/84, CP 5000, pp. 131–2. The Portuguese Government drew the attention of the US Government to the international difficulties of recognizing a private company as a friendly power (West to Granville, 30/5/84, 11 Af., p. 127).

course, that the French Government recognized the Association, and undertook in no way to interfere with its authority.[38]

Recognition of the Association as a body possessing sovereign rights in an undefined area of the Congo could only cause confusion and complicate an already extraordinarily difficult situation. In the circumstances Bocage considered that an international conference was almost the only solution: it would be the only effective agency to bring the general concurrence of the powers concerned by the treaty. It only remained to decide which powers should be invited, and whether the invitations should be in Portugal's name alone, or in conjunction with Britain.[39] The British Government, however, did not favour a conference, fearing that the hostility of France would be a stumbling block; it preferred to invite the other powers to sit on an enlarged commission.[40] But the Portuguese Government, without waiting for an expression of the English point of view, on 13 May sent out a circular despatch to its legations in Berlin and Paris, Brussels and the Hague, Madrid, Rome, and Vienna, canvassing the support of the other powers for such a conference.[41]

The British Foreign Office, not knowing of this development, appreciated, "From what has passed since the signature of the treaty, we can see pretty clearly that the opposition in England is mainly founded on distrust of Portugal; in France, on jealousy of England; in Germany and Holland, on dislike to the dual commission and suspicion of the Moçambique Tariff." To meet the English objection, it seemed necessary to extend the powers of the commission; to meet the French objection, and the fear of Germany and the Netherlands, it was necessary to extend the composition of the commission; and to remove suspicion of the tariff it would be as well to introduce a maximum 10 per cent duty. Portugal would agree to the first two of these, but not the third. Agreement could be embodied in a protocol to the treaty. It was premature, however, to consider such a protocol until the opinion of the other powers had been canvassed. Especially was it necessary, Fitzmaurice minuted, that the view of the German Government be known, and whether it desired representation on the commission. Granville agreed on 15 May.[42]

On 1 May, Munster, the German minister to the court of St James, had informed Granville that chambers of commerce in Germany were protesting against the provisions of the treaty, and Bismarck hoped that it would not be proceeded with until its terms had been modified.[43] Granville assured Munster that modifications were being discussed, especially the internationalization of the commission. Munster failed to pass on to Granville a second communication from Bismarck, written on 5 May, enquiring whether the British Government intended coming to a new agreement with Portugal, or seeking an

38 Convention 24/4/84, Hertslet, pp. 207–8; Malet to Granville, tels. 24 and 25/4/84, CP 5000, pp. 37, 46; 27/4/84, 5 Af., p. 46; Crowe, pp. 81–2.
39 Petre to Granville, 11/5/84, 46 Af., CP 5000, pp. 107–8; 28/5/84, p. 122.
40 Granville to Petre, 28/5/84, 52 Af., CP 5000, p. 119.
41 *Africa No. 4* (1885), p. 21, and Crowe, pp. 29, 205–7.
42 Anderson, Fitzmaurice, Lister, Pauncefote, Granville, minutes, 13–15/5/84, CP 5000, pp. 110–1.
43 Granville to Ampthill, 1/5/84, 3 Af., CP 5000, p. 58.

understanding with the powers interested on a new basis. If the latter, Bismarck obviously expected to be approached; and if the former, to be consulted. But the British Government remained in ignorance of Bismarck's attitude.[44] And it was not until 26 May that Granville signed a despatch to the British minister in Berlin in accordance with the resolution of 15 May. He requested the minister to sound the views of the German Government, and enquire whether, if the composition and powers of the commission were widened, and a maximum duty of 10 per cent imposed (except on guns and gunpowder, tobacco and brandy) the German Government would be prepared to support the treaty.[45] But such measures did not interest German traders, whose interests were mainly spiritous,[46] or Bismarck, who was favourably considering the Portuguese suggestion.

Bismarck, moreover, was becoming increasingly exasperated at not receiving an answer to his enquiry of 5 May, a seeming slight which only added to his hostility to England. At the beginning of 1883 Bismarck had asked the British Government whether it would protect a German settlement at Angra Pequena, and he had indicated that if Britain refused, he would reserve his right to take the bay under German protection. He had repeated his enquiry at the end of 1883, but had still received no answer from the British Government. Moreover, Bismarck was being carried along by a growing colonial movement, propaganda for which was being actively fomented by the newly formed German Colonial Society. At the end of April he authorized the German consul at Cape Town to proclaim that German establishments north of the Orange River were under the official protection of the German Government. There were serious differences between the German and British Governments over Fiji, and Egypt. Now, by the Anglo-Portuguese treaty, Britain seemed to be arrogating to herself the distribution of land in Africa. Another despatch written by Bismarck early in May generally surveying the colonial differences between the two governments, was also not communicated by Munster. When the German Colonial Society protested against the treaty, he replied that its complaints were fully justified. A German hint that the cession of Heligoland would help resolve the differences between the two governments evoked no response from Granville. Bismarck approved the organization of the German New Guinea Company and sent Nachtigal to west Africa with instructions to annex the Cameroons; the latter could be at the expense of British interests, but Nachtigal was instructed to respect the rights of France, with which Government Bismarck now came to an understanding. Bismarck saw advantage in such a conference as that which Bocage suggested. The French Government approved the idea, provided the discussions were limited to trade and navigation, and the internationalization of the commission; being still optimistic of being able to come to agreement with Portugal, it stipulated that territorial questions be excluded. The German and British Governments became further estranged when Bismarck heard, early

44 Crowe, pp. 28–9.
45 Granville to Ampthill, 26/5/84, 5 Af., CP 5000, pp. 118–9, CP 5023, pp. 1–2.
46 Crowe, p. 103.

in June, that the Cape Government had recommended the assumption of formal British control over the entire coastline of south-west Africa, from the Orange River to Walvis Bay, including Angra Pequena. Vital German interests, Bismarck decided, could not be sacrificed to English goodwill.[47]

On 7 June 1884 Bismarck wrote a despatch to Munster who actually communicated it to Granville, on the 14th. This declared that the Anglo-Portuguese treaty had no chance of being universally recognized even with the modifications proposed by the British Government. Even the Portuguese Government had appreciated this, and had put before certain powers the suggestion of a conference. If such a conference took place, Germany would be prepared to be represented. Germany was not, however, prepared to acknowledge the possession of previous rights as a basis of negotiation. To Germany, Portugal had no stronger claim to the lower Congo than any other power whose traders frequented it. Trade in those areas had been free to all alike, without restriction: Germany shared the fear of the merchants of all nations that the action of Portuguese officials would be prejudicial to trade, and Germany would not agree to the handing over of the administration of the territory to such officials. The limiting of customs duties to a maximum of 10 per cent would not compensate for such an extension of the Portuguese colonial system. Even if the general opinion of Portuguese officials was exaggerated there was no reason why the existing freedom and equality of trade should be changed in favour of Portugal, to the detriment of other nations.

> In the interests of the German crown, therefore, I cannot consent that a coast which is of such importance and has hitherto been free land should be subjected to the Portuguese colonial system. We are, however, ready and willing to co-operate in obtaining a mutual agreement by all the powers interested in the question, so as to introduce in proper form into this African territory by the regulation of its commerce the principles of equality and community of interests which for long have been so successfully pursued in the Far East.[48]

Granville decided that it was more essential to try and come to an understanding with Germany over the Egyptian question than to claim south-west Africa and to maintain the Anglo-Portuguese treaty. When he informed Dantas that there was no point in proceeding further with the treaty the Portuguese minister reluctantly agreed. In this decision Granville was also influenced by the revelation that Portugal had been pursuing the question of an international conference behind Britain's back.[49] It now became known that Bismarck had entered into negotiations to recognize the International Association.[50] Britain

47 Crowe, pp. 37–57; Fitzmaurice, pp. 347–52; C 4190; Ampthill to Granville, 2/5/84, 111, CP 5000, p. 68; and 16/5/84, a Af., p. 111; Petre to Granville, 25/5/84, 52 Af., p. 121.
48 Bismarck to Min., 7/6/84, CP 5000, p. 128 and CP 5023, pp. 2–3; communicated to FO on 14/6/84.
49 Granville to Petre, 20/6/84, 65 Af., CP 5000, pp. 134–5; Petre to Granville, 29/6/84, 75 Af., CP 5019, p. 7.
50 Malet to Granville, 21/6/84, 9 Af., CP 5000, p. 136; Ampthill to Granville, 25/6/84, 174, p. 142.

made an attempt to maintain that portion of the treaty relating to the river commission by giving it powers comparable to the Danube Commission. But the Portuguese Government objected, holding that this would be equivalent to an abdication of her claims of sovereignty. The Portuguese Prime Minister admitted that it was useless to ratify the treaty so long as Germany maintained her attitude, but he was still optimistic that some analogous arrangement might be come to. He sent telegrams to Berlin, Paris, London and the Hague declaring that Portugal maintained her claims to sovereignty and that she would give every guarantee for free navigation and unprejudiced commerce.[51]

Bocage correctly attributed the miscarriage of the treaty to Bismarck's hostility, which was directed more against Britain than against Portugal. He interpreted a German enquiry made in May as to Portugal's intentions as an invitation to throw over her engagements with Britain and cast in her lot with Germany. Petre thought that if left to her own devices Portugal would naturally seek to make the best terms she could, considering her own interests and security, and she was most likely to come to an arrangement with France.[52] The Portuguese Government clung tenaciously to the bases of the treaty, and foreseeing some of the difficulties that might confront Portugal at a conference made one last attempt to achieve its ends by negotiation. It sent Serpa, the previous Minister of Foreign Affairs, on a secret mission to Paris and Berlin. It authorized him to make every concession if only Portuguese sovereignty were recognized.[53] In Paris Serpa found resentment that France had not been consulted in the negotiations that led to the treaty. The French believed that England had wished to prevent France from enjoying the fruits of Brazza's exploration, and they were incredulous when Serpa assured them that the first overtures for the treaty had come from Portugal. The French appreciated that Portugal wanted little more than satisfaction for her *amour-propre*, and her claim to sovereignty might be recognized provided there was no opportunity for her to open custom-houses or otherwise interfere with trade or navigation on the river.[54] The Foreign Office suspected a further arrangement by which France, if she took over International Association territory, would occupy the north bank of the Congo and approve of Portuguese occupation of the south.[55] In Berlin Serpa met with no success. He called on Hatzfeldt, the Acting Minister of Foreign Affairs, who assured him he would communicate his remarks to Bismarck. In Germany Serpa found considerable jealousy of Britain. The Netherlands Government assured him it was quite satisfied with the concessions Portugal was ready to make, and quite prepared to come to an agreement. He continued to London, where he had an unexceptional conversation with Granville.[56] He

51 Granville to Petre, 23/6/84, CP 5000, pp. 136–7; Statement in Commons, 26/6/84, pp. 141–2; Granville to Lumley, 3/7/84, 3 Af., CP 5019, p. 4.
52 Petre to Granville, 24/6/84, 71 Af., CP 5000, pp. 142–3; and 29/6/84, 74 Af., CP 5019, p. 6.
53 Petre to Granville, 13/7/84, 79 Af., CP 5019, p. 17.
54 Lyons, Paris, to Granville, 16/7/84, 70 Af., CP 5019, p. 12, CP 5023, p. 4; and 23/7/84, 75 Af., CP 5019, p. 22; Granville to Petre, 6/8/84, 81 A Af., CP 5019, p. 36, CP 5023, p. 16.
55 Anderson, memo., 25/7/84, CP 5019, pp. 22–3.
56 Ampthill to Granville, 25/7/84, 8 Af., CP 5019, p. 23, CP 5023, p. 5; and 31/7/84, 9 Af., p. 26 and p. 5; Granville to Petre 6/8/84, 81 A Af., p. 36 and p. 6.

returned to Berlin, but Hatzfeldt could give him no indication of the views of the German Government, nor was he able to obtain an interview with Bismarck. At his instigation the King of Portugal wrote to the Emperor, requesting him to direct Bismarck to grant Serpa an audience. This finally shattered his hopes of meeting the Chancellor, and he left Berlin defeated.[57] Bocage, however, preferred to believe that Bismarck had not yet made up his mind on African matters, and that he was awaiting word from Nachtigal, on arrival of which he would probably launch a spirited colonial policy in Africa designed to help him in the approaching elections.[58] But that spirited policy had already begun, with the raising of the German flag at Angra Pequena in August, and the declaration that the entire coastline from 26° south to the Portuguese border (with the exclusion of Walvis Bay) was German territory.[59]

Bismarck decided to take from Portugal the initiative in calling a conference on African affairs. He persuaded the French Government to agree. On 8 October 1884 the German minister in London informed Granville that the extension of trade in west Africa had suggested to the German and French Governments that it would be in the mutual interest of all nations engaged in that commerce to regulate it for the common good; it was necessary to establish accord on the liberty of commerce in the Congo basin, and apply to the Congo and the Niger the principles applied by the Congress of Vienna to the Danube; it was also essential to define the formalities to be observed in new occupations. The German Government, in accord with the French, therefore invited representatives of all powers interested in the commerce of Africa to meet in conference in Berlin.[60] The French minister in London confirmed the accord with Germany. The British Government accepted the invitation in principle, but asked for more information.[61] The immediate German response was that if the points in question could be answered by correspondence there would be no object in holding a conference.[62] Portugal accepted her invitation unconditionally, observing that Portugal had already adopted the principle of freedom of navigation of the Congo. In regard to settling the form of future acquisitions, Portugal maintained that this could apply only to the powers—which of course excluded the International Association.[63]

The Foreign Office came to the conclusion that the projected conference might have advantageous results for British trade and colonization, especially if its scope could be extended to include east Africa.[64] Such British gains would, of course, be at the expense of Portugal. A vague statement from the German

---

57 Petre to Granville, 11/9/84, 92 Af., CP 5019, pp. 67–8; Scott to Granville, 30/8/84, 13 Af., p. 63; and 26/9/84, 17 Af., p. 68.
58 Petre to Granville, 2/10/84, 93 Af., CP 5019, p. 69.
59 C 4262, 4265.
60 Plessen to Granville, 8/10/84, CP 5023, p. 8.
61 Granville to J. Walsham 10/10/84, 141 Af., CP 5023, p. 10.
62 Granville to Plessen, 8/10/84, CP 5023, p. 9; Granville to Malet, 11/10/84, 33 Af., p. 10.
63 Petre to Granville, 9/10/84, and 17/10/84, tel., 20/10/84, 99 Af., ibid., pp. 9–10, 24, 39. Dantas and Serpa declined to represent Portugal and the choice lay between Hintze Ribeiro, Min. of Finance, and Visconde de S. Januário, who had been Governor-general of Portuguese India and Minister of Ultramar in the late Progressista ministry.
64 Lister, Anderson, minutes, 14/10/84, CP 5023, pp. 13–14; cf. AWLH, CO, memo., 16/10/84, pp. 42–3; C. L. Hall, memo, 20/10/84, ibid.

minister in no way added to the definition of the scope of the conference. Bismarck declared himself disappointed at Britain's qualified acceptance, hurt at her procrastination, and aggrieved over her attitude to the Angra Pequena affair, so on 23 October the British Government formally accepted the invitation.[65]

Portugal was most anxious to know if she could rely on the full support of Britain at the conference, and though the two governments had resumed full liberty of action, Bocage trusted that Britain would not withdraw her acknowledgment of Portugal's sovereign rights; he reminded Granville that but for the attitude of England she would long since have been in unchallenged possession of the Congo country.[66] The Foreign Office had already done considerable soul-searching as to whether the British Government was committed to the territorial terms of the unratified treaty; Granville had ruled that the Government was neither legally nor morally bound.[67] Anderson, head of the Africa section, now reminded Granville that Portugal had been secretly negotiating with France the previous year, while that year she had been secretly negotiating with Germany. Her hopes were now again pinned on Britain. If her Government thought their game about to be lost, they would bid high for British support. In Delagoa Bay they had an exceptionally powerful bribe. If the French were to acquire the bay Britain would be debarred from the only port from which her squadrons could watch over French vessels in Madagascar and the Comoros. If Germany were to get Delagoa Bay, she would be in close relations with the Transvaal and might even stretch across Africa to join hands with her new settlement at Angra Pequena. Anderson suggested that in return for a promise to support Portuguese claims on the Congo, but excluding the river bank, the Portuguese Government should give a formal engagement that if she ever withdrew from Delagoa Bay Britain should have the reversion.[68] Some at the Foreign Office thought it unreasonable since Britain earlier that year had agreed that Portugal should have both banks as far as Noqui, now to refuse to let her have at least as far as the south bank. Others felt that since there was so much antagonism to Portugal it would be as well to be free from any engagement with so embarrassing an ally. Granville decided it would be inexpedient to introduce the question of Delagoa Bay at that juncture,[69] and the British Government would not go further than undertake to support Portuguese territorial claims in so far as it was possible to induce other powers to accept them; the British attitude would be friendly, but the British representative would assist the Portuguese plenipotentiary only when there was a prospect of his being able usefully to do so; he would avoid doing anything that would put him in direct opposition to the other powers.[70] Sir Edward Malet, the British representative at the

65 Plessen to Granville, 15/10/84, CP 5023, p. 17; Granville to Malet, 19/10/84, 39 B, p. 29; Munster to Granville, 22/10/84, p. 36; Granville to Malet, 23/10/84, 47 tel., p. 38.
66 Petre to Granville, 24/10/84, 102 Af., CP 5019, pp. 72–3, CP 5023, pp. 54–5.
67 Lister, Pauncefote, Granville, minutes, 23/8/84, CP 5019, p. 59. (Lister confirmed that it was only the threat in the Commons that had prevented ratification.)
68 Anderson, memo, 27/10/84, CP 5033, pp. 1–3.
69 Lister, RGWH[erbert], Derby, Anderson, Granville, minutes, 29/10–1/11/84, CP 5033, pp. 2–3.
70 Granville to Petre, 5/11/84, 113 Af., CP 5033, p. 40.

conference, received instructions to follow a policy of freedom of commerce in the Congo basin and of navigation of African rivers. While the opening of Congo markets was to be desired, the welfare of the natives was not to be neglected. But as to the interests of Portugal Malet's instructions said nothing. Granville simply observed that the powers would be able to give and receive assurances as to the existing possessions of Portugal, France and the Association, and it was presumed that a general engagement was desirable to which other powers would be invited to adhere.[71]

Two days before the conference opened an extraordinarily amiable Bismarck invited Malet to call on him, since his understanding with France was wearing thin. Bismarck read Malet his opening address, which was in complete accordance with the views of the British Government. Malet then communicated his instructions. Bismarck approved of them, and suggested that he turn them into a speech which would follow his own at the opening session. Bismarck then intimated that he thought there were matters concerning Africa, not included in the bases of the invitation, which might be usefully decided by Germany, England and France outside the conference. Bismarck added that he was sure he could obtain the assent of Austria-Hungary, Russia, Italy and probably Turkey, to such decisions. The British Government approved these extra-conference discussions between Malet, Bismarck or his representative, and the French Ambassador.[72] Territorial matters were to be decided behind the scenes.

The conference duly opened on 15 November; Bismarck declared its primary aim was to facilitate the access of all commercial nations to the interior of Africa, and Malet added that the British Government wished to see these principles applied also to territory between Gaboon and Angola. At the second meeting Penafiel, the Portuguese plenipotentiary, declared that Portugal had received the invitation to the conference with satisfaction, in view of the wish expressed in her circular despatch on 13 May. He calmly announced that his Government had every intention of admitting the principles of liberty of navigation and commerce in the basin and mouth of the Congo as soon as Portugal established regular administration in the territories between 5° 12' and 8° south, territories which for centuries, Penafiel declared, had been incorporated by incontestable title in the domains of the Crown of Portugal. The Conference then appointed a Commission to define the Congo basin.[73]

In this Commission Serpa, Portugal's second representative, tried to restrict the freedom of commerce to that part of the Congo basin which lay between the sea and Stanley Pool, but he was soon prevailed upon to withdraw this unpopular proposal which would have nullified the work of the Conference.[74] Anderson traced a line on a map which was approved of by Stanley, who was nominally a USA delegate but actually represented Leopold's Association. Malet then asked Stanley to propose this line since it would have greater weight coming from him than from a British delegate. This proposal covered the area

71 Granville to Malet, 7/11/84, 59 Af., CP 5033, pp. 51–3.
72 Malet to Granville, 13/11/84, tels 37 and 38, CP 5033, p. 65; Granville to Malet, 14/11/84, tel., p. 65.
73 *Africa No.* 4 (1885), pp. 1–4, 20–1, 24.
74 Ibid., p. 48.

contained by the coast between Fernão Vaz and Ambriz, and the parallels of these places to the Ogooue and the Congo, thence north and south along the watershed to embrace the whole Congo basin.[75] Kasson, the United States plenipotentiary, declaring that the USA traded with the Congo basin not only from the west but also from the east, then put forward a vast plan to join the Congo basin almost to the Indian Ocean, and included the whole region of the central African lakes, the sources of the Nile, and the lower basin of the Zambezi. The zone would approach the Indian Ocean between 5° north and 18° south, and extend to within a degree of the coast. On the left bank of the Zambezi the line would recommence five miles above the confluence of the Shire, and then follow the watershed west of Lake Nyasa, whence it would follow the watershed between the Zambezi and the Congo. Serpa immediately declared that Portugal's rights of sovereignty in east Africa must be observed. The delegates consulted their governments about these far-reaching proposals.[76]

The British Government considered the United States definition to be inaccurate and unacceptable on geographical and commercial grounds; the proposal went far beyond the original bases of discussion; and the extended area included territory belonging to Portugal and Zanzibar; it instructed Malet to protest. The United States plenipotentiary extended his proposal to reach the coast. The German and French, and even the Portuguese, representatives accepted the new definition. Malet warned Granville that if Britain did not accept she would be isolated; this would be particularly unfortunate when the Niger question came up, "for Bismarck returns blow for blow". Britain agreed to this extension, in so far as it was not inconsistent with sovereign rights.[77]

The French Ambassador refused to allow Gaboon or the Ogooue to be included in the zone, and proposed the parallel of 5° 12′. The Portuguese plenipotentiary proposed the River Massabe in preference, but eventually the line was set at the river which was presumed to flow into the sea at Sette Cama, and from its source a line running eastward along the watershed that divided the Congo basin from those of the Niari, Ogooue, Chari and Nile; it would include Lake Tanganyika, and extend to the Indian Ocean as noted, provided it was endorsed by those states that possessed sovereign rights. After following the watershed between the Zambezi and the Congo, the line returned to the Atlantic at the Loge. The Conference accepted the Commission's report at the end of November.[78]

The Conference next considered the report of another Commission appointed to detail the freedom of trade to be applied in this area. The Portuguese plenipotentiary again expressed his Government's reservations.[79]

Another Commission started drawing up regulations for the navigation

75 Malet to Granville, 21/11/84, tel., 12 Af., ibid., p. 91; 22/11/84, tel., 92 Af., p. 99.
76 Malet to Granville, 22/11/84, tel., 13 Af., ibid., p. 95; Africa No. 4 (1885), p. 50.
77 Granville to Malet, 24/11/84, tel., CP 5033, pp. 103–4; Malet to Granville, 24/11/84, 17 Af., p. 104, and 25/11/84, tel., 18 Af., pp. 112–3, and 25/11/84, tel., 21 Af., p. 113; Granville to Malet, 25/11/84, tel., p. 114; Malet to Granville, 25/11/84, tel., 23 Af., p. 115.
78 Africa No. 4 (1885), pp. 39–47.
79 Ibid., pp. 67–81.

of the Congo and the Niger. Malet suggested to the Portuguese plenipotentiary that it would be a graceful act on the part of Portugal to adhere as far as the Zambezi was concerned to the projected Declaration of Free Navigation, to avoid the appearance of having concurrence forced upon her. But Portugal was not prepared to forego her 3 per cent transit duty; Britain was demanding another concession from Portugal, Penafiel declared, and he suggested that in return Britain no longer oppose Portuguese occupation of the mouth of the Congo. Malet gave him no expectation that the answer would be favourable.[80] At a session of the Conference in mid December, Malet therefore publicly asked whether Portugal would be prepared to introduce the system of free navigation to the Zambezi. Penafiel declared that Portugal had already done so; but the question was outside the programme of the Conference, and the Portuguese Government could not consider discussion of it; his Government, however, reserved its full right to apply to any part of the Portuguese dominions the principles which it judged to be the most suitable according to the circumstances.[81]

The United States plenipotentiary next proposed the neutralization of the Congo zone, which was agreed to.[82]

The Conference, having disposed of the first two bases of the invitation, could easily have settled the third within a few days, and risen before Christmas. But Bismarck was extremely anxious for an arrangement of territorial claims before the Conference dissolved, and it was accordingly adjourned until the new year.[83] Those territorial claims hinged on the recognition to be accorded the International Association.

When the Conference opened it was the opinion of the British Government that the International Association did not present the conditions which constitute a State, though it possessed the elements out of which a State could be created. If its efforts resulted in a political organization possessing a regular government, then the British Government would unite with other governments in recognizing it; but such a result must take time.[84] The Association's diplomatic pressure, and the friendly assistance of Bismarck, reduced that time to a matter of weeks.

The representatives of the Association were very concerned to observe what they considered to be growing solidarity between Portugal and France at the Conference, and there were renewed rumours that they were planning to partition the lower Congo. If Portugal were isolated, it might be possible to come to terms with France. While Strauch and Lambermont, the Belgian minister, who was a confidant of Leopold, had conversations to this effect with Hatzfeldt, Stanley paid a flying visit to England, on 9-10 December.[85] He threatened that if the Association were not given all she asked for, she

---

80 Malet to Granville, 2/12/84, tel., 171 Af., CP 5051, p. 32 and 5/12/84, 47 Af., pp. 22–3.
81 *Africa No.* 4 (1885), pp. 126–51; Malet to Granville, 18/12/84, 73 Af., CP 5051, p. 122.
82 *Africa No.* 4 (1885), pp. 175–86.
83 Malet to Granville, 20/12/84, 261 Af., CP 5051, p. 142.
84 Granville to Malet, 15/11/84, 78 Af., CP 5033, pp. 70–1.
85 Crowe, p. 157.

would be thrown into the arms of France. "In this critical period war might result—everything moves so swiftly to destruction perhaps." England must act with Germany, and save the Association. He got Mackinnon to bring pressure to bear on the Government.[86] It is not known to what other measures he resorted, but overnight he converted Granville into recognizing the Association and throwing overboard the understanding with Portugal.[87]

On 10 December a Foreign Office official put to paper "suggestions for a Proposal . . . for a territorial arrangement"; a document which was approved by Stanley and Mackinnon. France was claiming from Sette Cama to Massabe; Portugal from Massabe to the Loge; the Association from Sette Cama to Massabe, and inland up the Congo. On the Congo France claimed both banks of Stanley Pool, but offered to forego her claim to the left bank if the Association would recognize her claim from Sette Cama to Massabe. The suggestion was that the French claim be admitted southwards to Massabe, thence along a diagonal line to the Djoue River, and as far as she wished to go, marching with the Association's territory. The Association would be recognized to the south of this line, which would give the Association the entire north bank of the Congo estuary to Noqui, whence it would have both banks. Portugal would be allowed to advance from the Loge to the Congo and have the southern bank as far as Noqui. The memorandum added that if Britain negotiated this scheme she would have the credit for supporting French claims, almost in their entirety; the arrangement would allow Portugal to take what no other power had offered her; it would grant the Association access to the sea, and a very large territory, including Vivi, the terminus of the proposed railway.[88]

The essentials of these proposals were put in a despatch the same day and sent by messenger to Berlin[89] while Granville telegraphed the basic plan, to give the Association the north bank and Portugal the south. Granville instructed Malet to see Stanley as soon as he returned, and then Bismarck and endeavour to secure his support. Then, with supreme casuistry, Granville suggested that the proposals had better be made to appear as if they were of German origin.[90]

Hatzfeldt declared to Malet that unless some territorial agreement was reached while the conference was sitting, disputes then smouldering would burst into flame after its close. Bismarck was anxious to avoid this, and had asked Hatzfeldt to submit a plan for a territorial arrangement. When Hatzfeldt produced this, it proved to be identical to the one submitted by the British Government—Strauch had done his duty as successfully in Berlin as Stanley in London. Malet was able to intimate the acquiescence of the British Government. Hatzfeldt and Kusserow, Malet and Anderson, then met to arrange the

---

86 Stanley to Hutton, 10/12/84, CP 5051, p. 65.
87 It is significant that Lord Fitzmaurice's biography of Granville completely ignores this volte face.
88 C. L. Hill, 'Suggestions . . .', 10/12/84, CP 5051, p. 55; and Hill, memo., 3/2/85, CP 5103, pp. 15–6.
89 Granville to Malet 10/12/84, 145 Af.; the despatch was not printed in the confidential print, and I have not traced the original; nor apparently did Miss Crowe, for she did not refer to it in her scrupulously detailed footnotes (p. 160).
90 Granville to Malet, 11/12/84, tel., 29 Af., CP 5051, p. 61.

78

negotiation. It was decided that the proposals about France and the Association had better be made by Germany, while Malet should approach the Portuguese Ambassador. He had also the task of passing on the condition imposed by Bismarck, that Portugal must modify her colonial tariff, and abolish differential rates. Malet approached Serpa, and told him that Granville had approached Germany on the subject of the Portuguese territorial claims, but Germany had shown such an unfriendly feeling towards Portugal that the move had done no good. In spite of that, however, Malet was authorized to make certain propositions, and if the Portuguese Government accepted them he would do his utmost to induce Bismarck to agree. If the Portuguese Government would modify the colonial tariff and abolish differential dues, then the coast from Ambriz to the mouth of the Congo, and up the left bank of the river as far as five miles below the farthest point to which ocean steamers could go, would be acknowledged as Portuguese; the territory would include S. Salvador, and extend as far as 14° east longitude. Serpa agreed to telegraph his government, but his opinion was that the proposal would not be accepted: Portugal insisted on both banks of the river, and the coast northwards as far as the French possessions. Malet remarked that if Portugal did not accept this offer she would get nothing at all. To Granville he suggested that pressure be brought to bear in Lisbon. The eventual reply of the Portuguese Government was that it was not prepared to submit to the Cortes any modification of the colonial tariffs.[91]

Germany made no approach to France. On 14 December Lambermont told Malet he suspected an understanding between Portugal and France; France would hear of the territorial proposal, and object to the other powers negotiating behind her back. Malet saw Kusserow, and urged him to make the communication to France, but he declared he could do nothing without reference to Bismarck, and Bismarck was indisposed. On 16 December Malet and Strauch signed a convention by which the British Government formally recognized the Association. On the 17th Malet saw Bismarck. The Chancellor manifest no enthusiasm for the tripartite territorial arrangement, declaring he thought it better to let France and the Association fight the matter out between themselves. Malet demurred, urging the agreement made with Hatzfeldt. Bismarck admitted he had been mistaken in supposing that the Association claimed the right mouth of the Congo; he now found that it not only had no right to the right bank, but had laid no claim to it. Eventually Malet had his way, and the proposal was made to France. Courcel, the French Ambassador, informed Strauch that France claimed all the territory north of the Congo. Strauch objected to surrendering territory in the Kouilou-Niari valley actually occupied by the Association, and intimated that Leopold would require an indemnity of £200,000.

It was in these circumstances that the Berlin Conference adjourned.[92]

---

91 Malet to Granville, 13/12/84, tel., 61 Af., CP 5051, p. 67; and 13/12/84, 221 Af., pp. 99–100; and 17/12/84, tel., 70 Af., p. 116; and 19/12/84, tel., 74 Af., p. 124; and 20/12/84, 261 Af., p. 142; *Africa No. 4* (1885), pp. 264–6.
92 For summaries of the work of the Conference to date see Hill memo., 23/12/84, CP 5051, pp. 149–51, and Malet to Granville, 23/12/84, 272 Af., pp. 164–6.

Negotiations between France and the Association were resumed in Paris on 31 December. At first France steadfastly refused to pay indemnity, but eventually the French Government agreed to allow a lottery to be held in France to raise the money Leopold demanded. The Association also insisted as a condition of the settlement that France use her good offices to induce Portugal to accept her claims to the north bank. Portugal sent Carlos du Bocage, nephew of the Minister for Foreign Affairs, who was military attaché in Berlin, to Paris, where Ferry, the Prime Minister, kept him informed of the negotiations, and refused to bring pressure to bear on Portugal. The negotiations temporarily broke down.[93] The British Government now intervened. On 3 January 1885 Granville telegraphed Lisbon that Germany was disinclined to admit of any extension of Portuguese territory; but the British Government was anxious to obtain all it could for Portugal and thought it the most friendly course to tell her what was open to negotiation. It was hopeless to obtain German consent to any Portuguese extension north of the Congo. South of the Congo, however, there was some hope for Portugal if she would make commercial concessions in Angola and Moçambique, and abolish differential treatment. The British Government enquired whether Portugal would be prepared, if Britain could obtain Germany's concurrence, to sign simultaneous conventions with England and Germany by which these two powers would recognize her extension of territory to the south bank of the Congo, if Portugal would engage that the navigation of the Zambezi would be free, and that existing tariffs be maintained for a fixed period, and the Ruo be acknowledged as the Portuguese frontier. No time was to be lost, however, for the Conference was to resume on 5 January and if nothing were settled by then all chance of Portugal obtaining additional territory might be lost.[94]

Bocage replied that no Portuguese Government would last a day that voluntarily acceded to an arrangement which involved the surrender of territory regarded in Portugal as being Portuguese. The Portuguese Government had accepted the invitation to the Conference with the express reservation of her sovereign rights. Bismarck had declared at the opening session that questions of sovereignty were implicitly excluded, and would have to be settled by private negotiation. To sign separate conventions with Germany and Britain would give umbrage to France; and he did not see what Germany had to do with the Ruo, he tartly remarked. But Portugal was quite prepared to enter into negotiation with the French Government and the Association for the delimitation of frontiers. Portugal tenaciously insisted that she must possess the south bank of the Congo as far as Noqui, the port of S. Salvador, which was incontestably Portuguese; and she must possess the north bank. But Boma was divided by a creek, on the west side of which were the Portuguese factories, and Portugal was prepared to accept that as the boundary. As for her fiscal policy, Portugal was not prepared to modify that for anybody. Petre on 9

93 Crowe, pp. 164–6, Thomson, *La fondation*, pp. 265–6, E. Banning, *Mémoires politiques et diplomatiques* (Paris, 1927), p. 54.
94 Granville to Petre, 3/1/85, tel., 1 Af., CP 5080, p. 8.

January telegraphed London that he found it useless to press the matter further.[95]

Like reply was made to Paris. When Ferry communicated the Portuguese stand, and intimated that he refused to bring pressure to bear on Portugal, there was a stormy scene, and a temporary breakdown of negotiations between France and the Association.[96] Granville now had qualms of conscience and put in a good word for Portugal, declaring that he saw no danger to free commerce if Portugal were to occupy the north bank to Boma and the south to Noqui; and in fact the usefulness of the international commission would be best secured by the establishment of several civilized riverine stations or colonies on the banks of the Congo.[97] But everything depended on the attitude of Bismarck. Bismarck, who was receiving reports from Nachtigal which revealed how monopolistic was the policy of the Association, saw how he could turn the deadlock to Germany's advantage. Penafiel was asked whether Portugal would be prepared to make commercial concessions to German commerce in return for the consent of Germany to a territorial arrangement which might be acceptable to Portugal.[98] Bismarck followed this up on 17 January with the offer of a German-Portuguese treaty. At a meeting with the Chancellor on 23 January Penafiel expressed a wish that this treaty be as wide as possible. Bismarck objected to its going into details and thought it should be confined to the general bases of a treaty of commerce, peace and friendship, with the most favoured nation clause extended to their respective colonies. Portugal would also be required to concede liberty of transit, with minimum dues, on goods between Lourenço Marques and an area to be occupied by Germany, or placed under German protection, on the Transvaal border, this concession to be subsequently extended to other possessions of the two powers. Bismarck declared that though he had recognized the International Association he had not determined its boundaries, and he assured Portugal of his best offices in this delimitation. He hinted that German capital might be made available for the development of Portuguese territory. The new alliance promised prosperity for Portugal.[99] In these circumstances Portugal refused to surrender at Paris, and gladly assented to the negotiation being transferred to Berlin.

At Berlin the Conference moved into its final phase. It defined the conditions to be observed for new occupations on the coasts of Africa to be accepted as effective. It laid down that any power in future taking possession or assuming a protectorate must notify the other powers; and the powers "recognize the obligation to ensure the establishment of authority in the region occupied by them on the coasts of the African continent sufficient to protect existing rights, and, as the case may be, freedom of trade and of transit under conditions agreed upon."[100]

95 Petre to Granville, 5/1/85, 2 Af., CP 5080, p. 30; and 4/1/85, 3 Af., pp. 47–8; and 9/1/85, tel., p. 30.
96 Lyons to Granville, 14/1/85, 8 Af., CP 5080, p. 53, Crowe, p. 167.
97 Granville to Malet, 15/11/85, 16 Af., p. 57.
98 Petre to Granville, 15/1/85, 8 Af., CP 5080, p. 68, and 9 Af., pp. 68–9.
99 S. Mamede to Min., 27/1/85, 7A, Nec., SPZ 1.
100 General Act, *Africa No.* 4 (1885), p. 312.

As the time approached for the closing of the Conference, the powers, including even Portugal, realized that a territorial settlement was essential. France and the Association came to an agreement, but Ferry still refused to exert pressure on Portugal, while Bismarck, in view of his secret understanding with Portugal, would do no more than express an urgent wish that an arrangement be come to before the close of the Conference. It was Britain that again intervened and on 3 February Malet expressed to the Portuguese plenipotentiary the strong opinion of the British Government in favour of an early agreement. Malet reported that Leopold would not go further than allow the Portuguese to occupy the south bank as far as Noqui, with free commercial access thence to the interior; the Association insisted on the north bank, but gave way to Portugal as regards Cabinda and Malembo. Portugal continued to insist on both banks, the north as far as Boma, and the coastline from the Loge to the French frontier. Malet declared that such demands sacrificed the Association to Portugal: and if the Portuguese demands were met the arrangement would be most distasteful to English commercial circles. He urged the British Government to exert pressure on Portugal.[101] The British Government agreed to do so, on condition that the German and the French did the same. But this neither was prepared to do.[102]

In reality the Portuguese Government was quite prepared to have pressure brought to bear upon it, if the question were to be resolved. The Portuguese plenipotentiary explained to Malet on 4 February that it was impossible for Portugal to come to an agreement with the Association because his Government had not yet recognized the Association; and no power had as yet expressed the slightest wish that Portugal should accept the Association's proposal. It would be impossible for his Government to face the Cortes after making such voluntary concessions to the Association. Penafiel then suggested that Malet and the French Ambassador should come to an agreement with him as to what his Government should yield; they should then present the proposal to him officially, and his Government would then have something to present to the Cortes.[103]

On 5 February France and the Association signed a convention formally recording their agreement,[104] after France at long last had been persuaded to use her influence with Portugal to come to an agreement with the Association.[105] The same day the French Ambassador recommended the Portuguese government to yield.[106] The Portuguese Government, while now consenting to surrender Boma, insisted on the retention of Porto da Lenha, Banana and Cabinda; but it was prepared to have its hand forced.[107] Meanwhile, in Berlin, Penafiel was demanding north of the Congo only territory from south of

101 Malet to Granville, 3/2/85, tel., 22 Af., CP 5103, p. 13.
102 Granville to Malet, 4/2/85, tel., 15 Af., CP 5103, p. 20; Petre to Granville, tel., 6 Af., ibid., p. 30; Malet to Granville, tel., 26 Af., 5/2/85, p. 28.
103 Malet to Granville 4/2/85, 23 Af., CP 5103, pp. 22–3.
104 Hertslet, 1, pp. 409–11.
105 Crowe, p. 169.
106 Malet to Granville, 5/2/85, tel., 26 Af., CP 5103, p. 28.
107 Petre to Granville, 5/2/85, tel., 7 Af., CP 5103, p. 31; and 7/2/85, 18 Af., p. 52.

Cabinda to the French frontier, extending thirty to fifty kilometres inland. Bismarck and the French Ambassador considered this to be reasonable, so on 7 February the German, French and British governments addressed identic notes to Penafiel demanding that Portugal come to an agreement with the Association; the north bank of the Congo would go to the Association, with the exception of Cabinda and Malembo, while Portugal would have the south bank as far as wherever the Association's frontier would be fixed.[108]

On 11 February Penafiel replied that his Government was prepared to consider the advice given, but it insisted on the occupation of Banana. Verbally, however, he declared that his Government did not hold to that point, but it wished the powers to exert greater pressure to strengthen the Government's position in the Cortes; he went so far as to indicate the terms which the reply might take. Bismarck was irritated at having to join in this comedy, and to the reply, drafted by Courcel, he added a tart paragraph declaring that if Portugal did not yield the powers might refuse to acknowledge Portuguese rights to the south bank. This had the desired effect, and Portugal and the Association came to terms. On 15 February Strauch and Penafiel signed a convention which was predated to the previous day.[109] Portugal acknowledged the flag of the Association as that of a friendly government. The Association granted to Portuguese subjects the same privileges as had been granted to subjects of the other powers that had signed conventions with her. The frontiers of Cabinda were defined.[110] South of the Congo the frontier ran from the mouth along the course of that river to the Vango-vango creek, which separated Portuguese and Netherlands factories; along this meridian to the parallel of Noqui and along this parallel to where it intersected the Cuango, thence along the course of the Cuango.[111]

At a session of the Conference on 23 February the powers formally recognized the Association. At the final meeting on 26 February they ratified the General Act of the conference.[112] One article enabled other powers to adhere to its provisions by a separate instrument, which the Association did the same day. The acceptance of this declaration by the conference formally transformed the Association into a sovereign state.[113]

Bocage met a hostile Cortes, but eventually succeeded in winning approval for his actions.[114] In the due course of time all the Powers represented at Berlin ratified the General Act with the exception of the USA.[115]

108 Malet to Granville, 6/2/85, tel., 28 Af., CP 5103., p. 31; and tel., 29 Af., p. 33; Granville to Malet, 6/2/85, tel., 17 Af., p. 34; and 7/2/85, tel., 18 Af., p. 36; Malet to Penafiel, 7/2/85, p. 42; the notes were communicated on 8 February, Malet to Granville, 8/2/85, 31 Af., p. 41.
109 Penafiel to Malet, 11/2/84, CP 5013, p. 61; Malet to Penafiel, 13/2/85, p. 62; Malet to Granville, 14/2/85, 101 Af., pp. 60–2; Malet to Granville, tel., 15/2/85, p. 59; and 16/2/85, tel., 34 Af., p. 65.
110 From C. Lombo, near Ponta Vermelha, the parallel of latitude of this point till it intersected the meridian of the junction of the Culacalla with the Luculla; this meridian to the river Luculla; and the course of the Luculla to its junction with the Chiloango.
111 Africa No. 4 (1885), p. 276.
112 Ibid., pp. 304–13.
113 Ibid., pp. 300–3; Reeve, p. 59; H. E. Yarnall, The great Powers and the Congo Conference in the years 1884 and 1885 (Göttingen, 1934), p. 78.
114 Petre to Granville, 21/2/85, 23 Af., CP 5103, pp. 94–5.
115 Yarnall, The great Powers, p. 78.

5

THE NORTHERN BOUNDARY OF MOÇAMBIQUE 1879-1889

The first test of the Berlin Conference as a means of solving international disputes came over the question of the northern boundary of Moçambique. To most foreign observers the squabble over a few miles of coastline seemed petty, but to the Portuguese Government important questions of principle were at stake.

Portuguese ministers had not ceased to attempt to restore sovereignty over the Bay of Tungue. When however the local Sultan, in 1879, announced that he was prepared to render homage to the Portuguese Government and fly the Portuguese flag the Governor-general was doubtful of his motives and his sincerity.[1] That year the Governor-general visited Zanzibar to negotiate a commercial treaty which would enable the appointment of a Portuguese consul in Zanzibar; when however he demanded recognition of the Rovuma River as frontier, the Sultan would not budge. The treaty was signed on the 25 October 1879; there was delay in ratification mainly because divergencies were found between the Portuguese and the Arabic texts.[2] In 1883 the commander of the Portuguese naval forces in Moçambique was sent to Zanzibar with full powers to ratify the treaty; if possible he was not to alter or amend the treaty. The Sultan refused to re-open discussion on the original bases, and in June ratifications were duly exchanged.[3]

The Sultan acknowledged the Minangani River to be the frontier. Coelho, the Governor-general, recommended that a military post be established on its right bank as an assertion of Portuguese sovereignty at least as far as this river, to prevent any southward march by the Sultan's forces, and to watch Arab commerce.[4] In 1885 Serpa Pinto became Portuguese consul-general in Zanzibar. In November of that year he proposed to the Sultan a boundary treaty; the Sultan acknowledged territory south of the Minangani to be Portuguese, but postponed the discussion pending the signature of a treaty with Germany. When it was known that Germany, England and France were planning to delimit the Sultan's mainland territories, Pinto urged the necessity of occupying at least up to the Minangani River.[5] The Governor-general

---

1 GG to Min., 4/1/79, 2/4, AHU, Moç., 1 Rep., Pasta 1; and termo de ratificação de vassallagem of the chiefs of Umtende, 23/1/79.
2 Kirk to Granville, 23/2/81, CP 4626, pp. 220–1; and 3/7/82, CP 4777, pp. 214–5.
3 O'Neill to Granville, 8/5/83, 8 Af., CP 4914, pp. 43–4; Miles, Zanzibar, to Granville, 22/6/83, 2 Treaty, ibid., pp. 155–6.
4 Coelho to Min., 28/8/82, CP 4914, pp. 25–6.
5 Serpa Pinto, Zanzibar, to Bocage, 16/1/86, Livro Branco, *Negociações com o Zanzibar*, pp. 36–7.

immediately wrote to Palma Velho, the Governor of Cape Delgado, that since the Portuguese flag was not to be seen between Mucimbua and Cape Delgado, there was danger that the delimiting commissioners might regard that territory as being abandoned by Portugal; he instructed the Governor immediately to send a Government yacht to anchor in Tungue Bay as a sign of Portuguese occupation; if resources allowed, he was also to place small detachments on land to the extreme north of the Portuguese dominion. The lieutenant commanding the detachment at Mutamba, in Mucimbua Bay, proceeded to Mocoloe, on the southern side of Tungue Bay. He raised the Portuguese flag, but Arabs promptly threw down the pole; and the local Wali declared that Arab rule extended to Muluri. Palma Velho went to the scene himself, and under the guns of the gun-boat *Quanza* he raised the Portuguese flag on Mocoloe beach. He withdrew that evening, and two days later, on 1 January 1886, he occupied the uninhabited island of Tecamagi, in the mouth of Tungue Bay. Palma Velho asked that the Sultan of Zanzibar give orders to his local governor that no armed forces pass south of the Minangani; and he asked for military reinforcements. The Governor-general telegraphed Serpa Pinto in Zanzibar demanding satisfaction for the occupation of the Minangani. The Sultan promptly sent a vessel ordering the Wali to evacuate Mocoloe, and he assured Portugal that he would dismiss and punish him.[6]

Kirk suspected that Portugal was seeking an occasion to occupy the Bay, while the British, French and German governments feared that the work of the commissioners might be prejudiced. The German and English commissioners were ready to sail to Tungue, but there was delay in the arrival of the French commissioner at Zanzibar.[7] Events at Tungue and the appointment of the international delimitation commission took the Portuguese Government by surprise. It promptly and reasonably requested representation on the Commission during the delimitation of Zanzibar's southern boundary. Penafiel, the Portuguese minister in Berlin, wrongly construed his instructions, and demanded Portuguese participation in all the Commission's work; but none of the Powers would agree to even limited participation.[8] Serpa Pinto urged the Governor-general to occupy the southern shore of Tungue Bay without delay, and demanded of the Sultan that he come to agreement over the boundary. Pinto's draft treaty placed the boundary on Cape Delgado, whence westward to the River Rovuma and the course of that river reserving however to the Sultan coalfields which he had ordered to be surveyed. Pinto acknowledged the Sultan's repugnance to cede Tungue, where he had had his Wali, customs station and troops for many years; he himself wondered whether it was wise to insist on Cape Delgado for this would prejudice the chance of getting the Rovuma acknowledged as the internal boundary.[9]

6 A. J. da Silva Costa, relatório, 28/1/86, *Bol. Off.*, 3/2/86, p. 46; J. R. de Palma Velho, relatório, 28/1/86, ibid., pp. 46–7.
7 J. Walsham, Paris, to Salisbury, 7/1/86, 1 Af., CP 5271, pp. 8–9; Kirk, Zanzibar, to Salisbury, 4 tel., ibid., pp. 9–10; Salisbury to Walsham, 9/1/86, 9 Af., ibid., p. 11.
8 Salisbury to Petre, 9/1/86, 2 Af., CP 5271, pp. 13–4; Petre to Salisbury, 10/1/86, 2 Af., CP 5271, p. 16; Petre to Salisbury, 16/1/86, 10 Af., ibid., p. 49; and 27/1/86, 11 Af., ibid., pp. 57–8.
9 Serpa Pinto to Bocage, 16/1/86, *Neg.*, pp. 36–7; and 17/1/86, p. 39.

On 22 January 1886, at the instigation of Serpa Pinto, a force raised without opposition the Portuguese flag at Minangani on the northern bank of the mouth of that river which had been under the sovereignty of the Sultan for close on forty years. Two days later the warships of the tripartite commission sailed into the Bay.[10] The three commissioners unanimously decided that the Sultan's southern boundary should be the Minangani River for a distance of five miles up-stream, and thence a parallel of latitude to the Rovuma River.[11] The Governor-general without abandoning his claim to land north to the Rovuma, established a military post and a customs station south of the Minangani.[12] The British Government, at Dantas's instance, had asked Kirk to use his good offices with the Sultan in the treaty negotiations, but in view of Serpa Pinto's brusque attitude, and the action at Tungue, this instruction was withdrawn. Diplomatic opinion was that Serpa Pinto had exceeded his instructions, and it was in fact with some relief that the Portuguese Government granted him sick leave to return to Portugal.[13] Great therefore was the surprise of the Portuguese Government when it learnt that Serpa Pinto had precipitated an international crisis.

On 14 April 1886 Pinto telegraphed his minister that the Sultan had violated the existing treaty by placing a Portuguese in irons: the Sultan's reply to the consul's protest had been so insulting that he had lowered the Portuguese flag, and placed the lives and property of Portuguese in the Sultan's dominions under German protection.[14] The incident was slight enough in itself, and certainly insufficient to warrant an ultimatum and the rupture of consular relations. Kirk was convinced that the whole affair was premeditated, since Pinto had failed to secure the desired boundary by normal diplomatic means. Kirk had a suspicion that Pinto was acting in collusion with the German commissioner. As a matter of fact Pinto confided to Kirk that negotiations were on foot in Lisbon for the cession to Germany of certain rights on the east coast of Africa, and hinted that Delagoa Bay, Nyasaland and the Zanzibar coast might be affected. Rosebery, the British Secretary of State for Foreign Affairs, reminded Petre that Portugal was obliged to give Great Britain the first refusal before ceding Delagoa Bay to any other power, and asked him to make enquiries in Lisbon as to whether there was any truth in the rumour.[15] The Portuguese Government was as surprised as the British at the news of the events in Zanzibar for it had been under the impression that Pinto was on his way home.[16] The incident seemed to be closed when the Sultan, nervous lest

10 Palma Velho to GG, [1/86], *Bol. Off.*, 3/2/86, *A tomada do Tungue* . . ., pp. 20–2; Pinto to Bocage, 8/2/86, *Neg.*, pp. 40–1.
11 'Informação sobre a determinação do limite meridional do Sultanado', 19/1/87, *Neg.*, pp. 26–7.
12 Castilho, GG, Portaria 71, 15/2/86, *Bol. Off.*, 20/2/86, p. 77; and 130, 31/3/86, ibid., 3/4/86, pp. 141–2.
13 Pauncefote to Kirk, 19/2/86, 38, CP 5271, p. 83; Rosebery to Petre, 20/2/86, 16, ibid., pp. 87–8; Petre to Rosebery, 5/3/86, 20 Af., ibid., p. 97.
14 Pinto to Gomes, 14/4/86, tel., *Neg.*, p. 41; Gomes to Penafiel, 15/4/86, tel., ibid., p. 41. The exchanges between Pinto and the Sultan, 12–17/4/86, appear in CP 5308, pp. 65–7.
15 Kirk to Rosebery, 15/4/86, 30, tel., CP 5308, p. 28; Rosebery to Petre, 15/4/86, 29 Af., ibid., p. 29; Kirk to Rosebery, 16/4/86, 32, tel., ibid., p. 30.
16 Petre to Rosebery, 16/4/86, tel., CP 5308, p. 31; and 18/4/86, 27 Af., pp. 36–7; Gomes to Dantas, 26/4/86, *Neg.*, p. 43.

Germany support Portugal, paid the allegedly aggrieved Portuguese nation a token sum of 100 dollars, and saluted with 21 guns the Portuguese flag when Pinto re-hoisted it; and he promised to place the frontier question in the course of settlement within six months.[17] But the crucial question remained unresolved. Petre warned Barros Gomes that Serpa Pinto, no matter how bold an African explorer he might be, was no diplomat but a fire-brand, who might seriously embarrass his Government. To Rosebery he added that Pinto had the reputation of being the reverse of truthful; "He is in a way, however, a popular hero and this ostentatious display of vigour under pretext of defending the national interest and honour, thereby causing Portugal to appear as an important Colonial Power to be reckoned with in Africa, flatters the national vanity and no Government here dares run counter to that feeling." Petre invited Gomes to disavow Pinto's action.[18] This he was not prepared to do, but he did telegraph to Pinto, "Incident could have had serious results; I approve happy ending, but recommend moderation. Say when you intend to return to Europe."[19] Petre did not doubt that it was the moral support of the German representative that had caused Pinto to act in such a high-handed and dictatorial fashion, but he was sure that there had been no communication between the Portuguese and the German governments. He was confident that there could be no question of any such understanding, considering with what tenacity the Portuguese Government and nation clung to their colonial possessions. He thought there might be some reference, however, to a negotiation proposed a few months previously by Germany for the delimitation of the southern frontier of Angola: Portugal affirmed the latitude of Cape Frio to be the boundary, but the Germans placed it at 18° south latitude.[20]

In October 1886 Germany and Britain came to an agreement regarding east Africa. Both countries recognized the Sultan's authority over the islands of Zanzibar and Pemba, Mafia and Lamu, and over the coast to a distance of ten miles, from the River Minangani to Kipini, and over certain towns in the north with radii of up to ten miles around each; the remainder of the territory between the Rovuma River and Tana was to be divided into British and German spheres of influence.[21]

This agreement seemed to spell the doom of Portuguese attempts to secure the area from the Minangani to Cape Delgado. But, on 30 December 1886, the German and Portuguese governments came to an agreement over their possessions in southern Africa, by which they recognized the mouth of the Rovuma as the northern limit of Portuguese territory.[22] Since Great Britain and Germany had recognized the Minangani as the southern limit of German

17 Kirk to Rosebery, 17/4/86, 32A, tel., CP 5308, p. 32; Pinto to Gomes, 17/4/86, tel., *Neg.*, p. 42.
18 Petre to Rosebery, 18/4/86, 28 Af., CP 5308, pp. 37–8; and 22/4/86, 30 Af., p. 47.
19 Gomes to Petre, 19/4/86, tel., *Neg.*, p. 42.
20 Petre to Rosebery, 21/4/86, 29 Af., CP 5308, pp. 46–7.
21 Hertslet, II, pp. 615–7; R. Coupland, *The exploitation of East Africa, 1856–1890* (London, 1939), pp. 474–5.
22 CP 5466, pp. 55–6; Hertslet, I, pp. 323–6; Holmwood, Zanzibar, to Salisbury, 25/1/87, 5 tel., CP 5466, p. 33.

territory, Bismarck was asked for an explanation.[23] The German explanation was simple: it was true that the Rovuma was recognized as the line between the German and Portuguese interest: but that in no way interfered with the English and German recognition of the Sultan's territories: it merely provided that Germany would not interfere in any arrangement that Portugal might come to with the Sultan regarding territory beyond the German sphere.[24]

On 5 January 1887 Castilho, the Governor-general, telegraphed to Lisbon urging that advantage be taken of the presence of the corvette *Afonso de Albuquerque* to seize Tungue and fix the boundary definitively at the Rovuma, as was provided for in the German agreement.[25] On 8 January he received instructions to go to Zanzibar to treat with the Sultan. The German Government informed the Portuguese that it was convinced that Castilho would not encounter difficulty in getting the Rovuma recognized as the frontier, but if he did, the German consul there was authorized to lend him moral assistance.[26] The Sultan raised no objection to his coming, in accordance with his promise made in the previous April. On her arrival in Zanzibar the *Afonso de Albuquerque* failed to fire the salute customary and that courtesy demanded.[27] The Sultan, in a huff, refused to treat. On 21 January Castilho succeeded in presenting his respects to the Sultan who, however, still had no desire to discuss the frontier.[28] With knowledge of the moral support of Germany, on 29 January he addressed a sharp letter to the Sultan, declaring that his Government had told him that in the previous April the Sultan had declared his intention of delivering the northern part of Tungue Bay, and Cape Delgado, to Portugal and he had renewed his promise in his telegram to the Portuguese Government agreeing to Castilho's coming. In view of these categorical and solemn promises he demanded that the Sultan give orders for the prompt delivery of the territory in dispute.[29] The astonished Sultan could only reply that he had made no such promise to cede this territory. In April all that he had undertaken to do was to appoint a commission within six months to treat with a Portuguese commissioner—but none had arrived; and this undertaking in any case had become void because the English, German and French governments had agreed to acknowledge the mouth of the Minangani River as belonging to the Sultan, and five miles about it, whence the boundary was the line of latitude that ran to the Rovuma River.[30] He added that he intended retiring

23 Salisbury to Malet, 26/1/87, 17 Af., CP 5466, p. 35.
24 Malet to Salisbury, 28/1/87, 3 Af., CP 5466, p. 36.
25 Castilho to Pereira Coutinho, 5/1/87, tel., *Neg.*, p. 47.
26 Penafiel to Gomes, 15/1/87, *Neg.*, p. 50.
27 Castilho to Min., 4/3/87, 2/4, CP 5466, pp. 117–9.
28 Gomes to Castilho, 27/1/87, tel., CP 5466, pp. 53–4.
29 Castilho to Bargash, 29/1/87, CP 5466, p. 120.
30 Sultan to Castilho [c. 2/2/87], CP 5466, pp. 117–9, 122. The Sultan's undertaking had run as follows, according to a translation made by Dr Gregory and taken to Lisbon by Pinto: "Nous informons Votre Majesté quant à la question de fixer entre nous les limites qui séparent le royaume de Zanzibar de celui de Portugal, que nous somme disposés, après un délai de six mois, d'envoyer, conjointement á un agent de la part de Portugal, un délégué pour que chacun de nous rentre dans ces droits." A later translation by Gregory, made at Castilho's request, ended "que nous attendrons avec cette affaire six mois, qu'après ce temps nous rassemlerons une commission de representents des deux pays sur le lieu et chacun recevra ce que lui est dâ selou le droit." (Castilho to Min., 4/3/87, 2/4/, *Neg.*, pp. 117–9). The Portuguese view was that Gregory's first translation had been "Maliciously false, abusing the confidence of Serpa Pinto" (A. Braz de Sousa, Zanzibar, to Gomes, 14/2/87, *Neg.*, pp. 70–1).

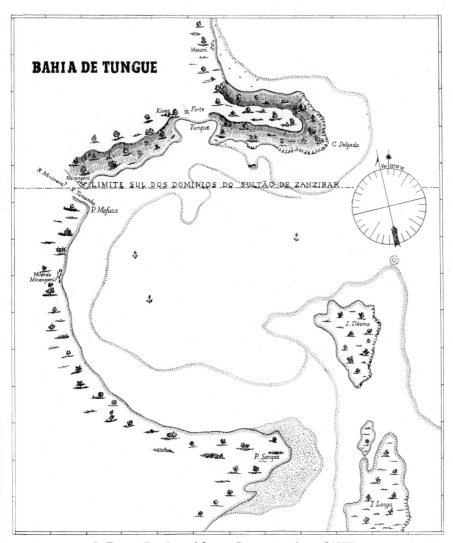

BAHIA DE TUNGUE

Masani

Kivea — Forte

Tungue

C. Delgado

R. Mrinrere

R. Tumumbo

Minangani

Var 12°15'W.

LIMITE SUL DOS DOMINIOS DO SULTÃO DE ZANZIBAR

P. Mofuca

Milende
Minangani?

I. Tikoma

P. Sangas

I. Longa

5   Tungue Bay (traced from a Portuguese chart of 1877)

to his country estate and he could not engage in public negotiation. Castilho, reporting this reply to his Government, urged that Portugal should now take Tungue by force of arms.[31] The Portuguese Government decided that the Sultan's reply had been offensive, and authorized the military occupation of Tungue.[32] Castilho requested the German consul-general again to protect the interest of Portuguese subjects, but he refused to do so until he had received definite authorization from Berlin.[33] As soon as this authority arrived, Castilho presented an ultimatum to the Sultan, on 11 February, again demanding the territory north of the Minangani as far as Cape Delgado; failing a satisfactory answer by midday on 12 February, he would, in compliance with orders of his Government, lower the consular flag, place the interests of Portuguese subjects under German protection, and leave Zanzibar with the two warships which were then at anchor off the town. Even the formal ending of the letter seemed to hold menace: "May God have in his Holy guard the precious life of your Highness."[34]

The British consul reported the ultimatum to his Government and expressed his fear lest Zanzibar be bombarded. Salisbury requested the British minister in Lisbon to express the regrets of the British Government that such action had been taken without prior intimation to it, and the hope that no force would be used until there had been a further opportunity for discussion. He expressed to Dantas his gravest disapproval of Portugal's violent proceedings, and fear of grave complications; he trusted that Bismarck had had no part in these proceedings.[35] But it was now too late to restrain the Portuguese Government, and Castilho. On 12 February the ultimatum expired. Castilho received from the Sultan a dignified letter saying that he would not deign to disturb the definitive settlement of the boundaries delimited by the representatives of England and Germany, or the sovereignty recognized by those powers. The powers had declined to admit either Portugal or Zanzibar to the commission, and if Portugal had not been allowed a voice regarding her claims north of the Minangani, Zanzibar had been equally prevented from establishing her claims to the territory south of that river. Any attempt to interfere with those decisions would be an affront to those powers. At 2.30 p.m. the consular flag was hauled down, and at 3 p.m. Castilho sailed off in the *Afonso de Albuquerque;* the gun-boat *Douro* had already sailed that morning, to shadow a

31 Castilho to Min. Coutinho, 3/2/87, tel., *Neg.*, p. 54.
32 Coutinho and Gomes to Castilho, 3/2/87, tel., *Neg.*, p. 55.
33 Castilho to German Comm. Sec., 7/2/87, tel., *Neg.*, p. 122; Castilho to Coutinho and Gomes, 9/2/87, ibid., pp. 58–9; Gomes to Penafiel, 9/2/87, ibid., p. 57; Penafiel to Gomes, 10/2/87, ibid.
34 Castilho to Bargash, 11/2/87, *Neg.*, pp. 117–9.
35 Holmwood, Zanzibar, to Salisbury, 11/2/87, tel., CP 5466, p. 54; Salisbury to Bonham, tel., 12/2/87, ibid.; Dantas to Gomes, 12/2/87, tel., *Neg.*, pp. 60–1; Salisbury to Malet, 16 and 17 Af., tel., 12/2/87, CP 5466, p. 59; Bonham to Gomes, 12/2/87, *Neg.*, p. 61. Gomes showed Bonham copy of a despatch written to Dantas, declaring that the Government had adopted an insolent attitude, and this affront obliged the Portuguese Government to adopt measures necessary to conserve Portuguese prestige (*Neg.*, pp. 55–8); it had been dated, or pre-dated, 4/2/87; it was read only on 11 February. A FO memo., written by Sir P. Anderson, 11/2/87, stated, "These pretensions on the part of Portugal are monotonous" (CP 5466, p. 54).

ship of the Sultan believed to be bound for Tungue with reinforcements.[36] As soon as Castilho had left Zanzibar he was beyond reach of the telegraph, beyond recall.

The *Afonso de Albuquerque* and the *Douro* anchored off Tungue on 14 February.[37] Already in the harbour was a yacht containing Palma Velho, who had been warned by Castilho as far back as 15 January to be prepared to occupy Tungue; he had sailed from Ibo on 26 January, but had holed his vessel on the way and had arrived off Tungue only on 8 February. After the warships had arrived the Sultan's steamer *Kilwa* entered the harbour with mixed merchandise, including 5 barrels of gunpowder. Palma Velho permitted her commander to off-load the general cargo—but only on condition that it went through the Portuguese custom post; and he was absolutely forbidden to land any arms or ammunition. The captain refused to comply with these demands, and a few days later raised anchor to leave harbour; the Portuguese arrested the ship, and sent her to Moçambique with an urgent request for reinforcements, for it was believed that local tribes were rallying to the assistance of the Arabs, who had 300 men under arms. Actually, the Wali had only thirty soldiers at his disposal.

On 16 February the Governor-general sent a German trader to the Wali with a message to the effect that the Sultan had ceded Tungue to the Portuguese, and demanding that he lower the red flag. He also sent a letter to the traders of Minangani advising them to evacuate the town within twelve hours. The traders, most of whom were British subjects, replied that night that they had too many goods to remove them within so limited a time. On the 18th a deputation went to the Portuguese station south of the creek where it was assured that there would be no damage to the British section of the town. But before the deputation could return, the bombardment started. The *Afonso de Albuquerque* had taken up position in front of Tungue and the *Douro* before the town of Minangani. The bombardment continued for five days. On the afternoon of the 23rd sixty troops and sailors landed, under cover of a Hotchkiss, and occupied Minangani without loss and without resistance. Then, Palma Velho reported, "following the humanitarian and generous ideas of the Portuguese people, preferring material destruction to the shedding of blood, I ordered the town to be destroyed, which was quickly razed and reduced to flames."[38]

At a conference on 26 February the Governor-general determined that no attack on Tungue should be made until the arrival of the gun-boat *Vouga*, and more troops from Moçambique. The next day, however, Palma Velho,

36 Bargash to Castilho, 12/2/87, *Neg.*, pp. 125–6; Castilho to Coutinho and Gomes, 12/2/87, ibid., p. 60; A. B. de Sousa to Gomes, 14/2/87, ibid., pp. 70–2.
37 The *Afonso de Albuquerque* was of 1,100 tons, with 7 guns and a complement of 220; the *Douro* of 587 tons, 2 guns, 100 men (Petre to Salisbury, 25/2/87, 26 Af., PRO, FO 179/253).
38 [Palma Velho], *Tomada . . .*, pp. 40–8, which includes his report of 24/2/87; Military Commander, Bay of Tungue, to Governor, 19/2/87, *Neg.*, pp. 126–7; Holmwood to FO, 21/3/87, CP 5466, p. 176, forwarding abstract of affidavits by British refugees; Clarke, memo., 19/4/88, CP 5673, pp. 9–12; Capello to Gomes, 30/5/87, *Neg.*, pp. 147–8 re the *Kilwa*.

while ostensibly on a reconnaisance with a large force, landed and occupied Tungue, again without resistance and with no casualties, for the Arabs withdrew.[39]

So ended the petty action of Tungue; but not the diplomatic activity. The British Government deplored the Portuguese aggression, and urged resort to the Berlin Act, which provided for mediation by one or more friendly powers before any signatory should appeal to arms.[40] London was greatly concerned about the damage to trade, both directly, from the bombardment, and indirectly —for instance a Zanzibar ship full of British cargo and mails feared to set sail for India lest it suffer the fate of the *Kilwa*.[41] The British Government invited the German Government to exercise strong pressure on Portugal to put an immediate stop to hostilities pending an examination of the question by the German Government, especially in view of the passive attitude of the Sultan, and the injury to international trade.[42] The British and German governments proposed that the Sultan should appoint a commissioner to discuss the border dispute with Portugal; and that Portugal should cease hostilities forthwith and restore the *Kilwa*.[43] On 25 February it was known that the Sultan was prepared to treat for peace.[44] The Portuguese then replied smugly to Petre that it had taken cognizance of Salisbury's wishes for hostilities to cease and orders had accordingly been sent to Tungue to abstain from any further military action.[45] But Portuguese administration became consolidated at Tungue, and the fortification was ordered of the new town of Palma, named in honour of the Governor; two gun-boats remained to support the establishment of the new order, and to help extend authority as far as the Rovuma.[46]

The Sultan appointed General Mathews as his commissioner to negotiate with the Portuguese representative, and formally requested the return of the *Kilwa*. The Portuguese Government undertook to return the vessel without delay.[47] But there was delay in its return—Castilho blandly sent it on another voyage, from Moçambique to Tungue, with instructions and provisions[48]— and the British Government was exasperated both at this, and at news that the natives in the vicinity of Moçambique had taken advantage of the absence of the Governor-general and naval and military forces at Tungue to revolt, so that the houses of several British subjects at Namarral were looted.[49] This

39 [Palma Velho], *Tomada*, pp. 48–61, including his report of 28/2/87; Clarke, memo., 19/4/88, CP 5673, pp. 9–12.
40 e.g. Salisbury to Petre, 16/2/87, 19 and 20 Af., CP 5466, pp. 79–81; Anderson, memo., 18/2/87, ibid., pp. 84–5.
41 FO to Law Officers, 23/2/87, CP 5673, p. 41; Holmwood to Salisbury, tel. 16, CP 5466, p. 95.
42 FO to Malet, 23/2/87, CP 5466, p. 95.
43 Salisbury to Petre, 24/2/87, 10, CP 5466, p. 97.
44 Sousa to Gomes, 25/2/87, tel., *Neg.*, p. 77; Schmidtals to Gomes, 26/2/87, ibid., p. 80.
45 Gomes to Petre, 28/2/87, *Neg.*, pp. 82–3.
46 Castilho to Palma Velho, 1/3/87, and to Coutinho and Gomes, 3/3/87, *Neg.*, pp. 128–31. The fort would mount the Hotchkiss, two bronze pieces brought from Moçambique in the *Kilwa*, and those cannon captured at Minangani and Tungue (one of which bore the date 1578).
47 Petre to Gomes, 4/3/87, *Neg.*, p. 89; Gomes to Petre, 5/3/87, ibid., pp. 90–1; Gomes to Penafiel, 5/3/87, p. 91.
48 Castilho to Coutinho and Gomes, 12/3/87, tel., *Neg.*, p. 93.
49 Dantas to Gomes, 2/3/87, *Neg.*, p. 85; Coutinho and Gomes to Castilho, 8/3/87, p. 92.

exasperation increased. The British consul at Zanzibar reported the arrival there of twenty-three British Indian merchants and their families, refugees from Minangani, who had suffered great loss in the bombardment and severe privation. He estimated their loss at 102,000 dollars, but this amount was trivial compared with the total ruin of the trade which they had been rapidly developing. Moreover three British vessels had arrived in the port but had been unable to off-load their cargoes.[50] A British man-of-war was sent to Tungue to hold enquiry.[51] The Portuguese Government would not consider submitting the frontier dispute to arbitration or to mediation, declaring that this would disagreeably wound public opinion in Portugal as it was already excited by the demand to surrender the *Kilwa;* it appointed Brito Capelo as its commissioner.[52] The German Government concurred with the British suggestion that a Netherlands umpire be appointed should the Portuguese and Zanzibar commissioners fail to agree.[53] Bismarck read with surprise the correspondence between the Portuguese envoy and the Sultan, and declared that Serpa Pinto had entirely misinterpreted the nature of the agreement between Portugal and Germany; the German Government did not consider, however, that the dispute fell within the terms of Chapter III of the Berlin Act which in its opinion applied only to the free trade areas.[54]

Rumours of an Arab attack on the Portuguese at Tungue gave the Governor-general an excuse for sending the *Kilwa* again to the north. The reports were false, but Castilho kept the captured vessel on this run. There were repeated and ever more insistent diplomatic demands for the surrender of the ship. The Portuguese Government was forced to give the most peremptory orders to Castilho to surrender the ship, which he eventually did, on 21 May, to the British and German consuls, and she was returned to the Sultan on the 31st.[55]

The Portuguese Government considered that with the delivery of the *Kilwa* it had reached the limit of concession, and it considered incompatible with national honour any solution of the dispute which did not confer possession of the territory to which, it affirmed, Portugal had always had the right, and which she was now definitely occupying.[56] The Government's instruction to Dantas declared that to Cape Delgado Portugal affirmed a right, to the Rovuma it expressed a desire. Since Tungue was now fortified, Capelo's attitude was to be one of the greatest firmness, yet he was to express his demands moderately. If he was unable to obtain the mouth of the Rovuma, he was to accept Cape Delgado as the boundary; but in the interior, beyond the ten-mile strip which

50 Holmwood to FO, 12, 21/3/87, CP 5466, pp. 130, 176.
51 Salisbury to Petre, 15/3/87, 39 Af., CP 5466, p. 164. The ship was the *Reindeer*.
52 Gomes to Penafiel, 16/3/87, tel., *Neg.*, p. 103; Gomes to Petre, 20/3/87, pp. 105–6.
53 Salisbury to Malet, 21/3/87, 78 A Af., ibid., p. 177.
54 Malet to Salisbury, 26/3/87, 41 Af., PRO, FO 179/250; Salisbury to Malet, 30/3/87, 91 Af., ibid.
55 Castilho to Min., 4/4/87, 2/62, and 20/4/87, 2/76, and 25/5/87, 2/132, AHU, Moç., 2 Rep., Caixa 4; Gomes to Dantas, 15/4/87, tel., *Neg.*, pp. 115–6; Gomes to Castilho, 10/5/87 and 12/5/87, tel., *Neg.*, p. 145; O'Neill to Salisbury, 24/5/87, 35 Af., CP 5536, p. 3, and 3/6/87, 38 Af., ibid., p. 19.
56 Gomes to Dantas, 7/5/87, *Neg.*, pp. 142–4.

the Anglo-German convention left to the Sultan, the boundary was to be the Rovuma.[57]

Castilho returned to Zanzibar to re-open relations with the Sultan, re-establish the consulate, and introduce the commissioner. In a private audience Castilho insisted that the Portuguese flag be saluted when it was raised; the Sultan refused, and started discussing Tungue, which Castilho refused to countenance. Barros Gomes suggested to Castilho that he consult with the other consuls as to whether it might be possible to insist that the flag be saluted when he was received in public audience; if the Sultan refused, he should announce his withdrawal and request a vessel to take him back to Moçambique in an ostentatious telegram. The British and German consuls consulted their governments. These governments both considered that the demand for the salute of the flag was completely unjustifiable for such a salute would imply admission that Portugal had been justified in breaking off relations; in fact, it was the Sultan who had been aggrieved, not the King of Portugal. The Portuguese Minister of Ultramar and Foreign Affairs agreed that a mistake had been made in demanding the salute. Castilho replied that if he could not demand a salute for the flag, he would resign. This offer was not accepted, and the Portuguese Government pointed out that the break of relations had been due to a misunderstanding: that it thought that the Sultan had affronted Portugal by refusing to name a commissioner, whereas he had refused to accede to the demand to cede Tungue; Portugal had avenged herself by taking Tungue and lowering the Sultan's flag; but he had satisfied Portugal by asking for peace, and nominating a commissioner. The imbroglio was resolved by the omission of a word in a telegram. Castilho telegraphed to Moçambique that the flag had not been raised. Exactly the opposite sense was conveyed to Capelo, who was waiting in Moçambique; he sailed to Zanzibar aboard the *Bartolomeu Dias* which raised the Sultan's flag and complimented the ruler with the royal salute. Zanzibar batteries replied, shot by shot in honour of the Portuguese colours and Castilho was satisfied. He presented Capelo in solemn audience, and the consular flag was raised.[58]

It was now Capelo's turn to feel frustrated. He met General Mathews on 19 July and communicated his Government's proposals. He refused to enter into any discussion of the territory occupied by Portugal. The Sultan replied that he had not apprehended so material a revision of his southern boundary so recently delimited by himself, Germany and England; he would have to communicate, as a matter of necessity and courtesy, with the local representatives of the other governments. These of course had no instructions, and they had to communicate with Europe. After ten days Capelo declared to Mathews that his health did not permit him to remain in Zanzibar any longer. In a

57 Gomes to Capello, 14/4/87, *Neg.*, pp. 113–5.
58 Castilho to Gomes, 3/7/87, tel., *Neg.*, p. 155; Gomes to Castilho, 4/7/87, tel., ibid., p. 155; Salisbury to Petre, tel., 5/7/87, 30,31, 32 Af., PRO, FO 179/250; Malet to Salisbury, 6/7/87, 23, 24 Af., ibid.; Gomes to Castilho, 6/7/87, *Neg.*, p. 156, and 7/7/87, ibid., p. 156; Capello to Gomes, 31/7/87, ibid., pp. 169–71; Castilho to Gomes, 11/7/87 and 15/7/87, tel., ibid., p. 157.

note verbale he declared that the Sultan must understand that there was no question of discussing the Minangani as the boundary: the seizure of Tungue Bay was an accomplished fact; the only question was whether Cape Delgado, or better still the River Rovuma, being a natural boundary, should be the common frontier. The Sultan appealed to the British and German governments which expressed themselves to being strongly of the opinion that Portugal and Zanzibar should submit their claims to the arbitration of some impartial sovereign; the King of the Netherlands was suggested, a proposal which the Sultan accepted.[59]

The Portuguese Government, however, feared that arbitration would revolt public opinion: having ceded on the question of the *Kilwa*, it must maintain its position now all the more firmly: it insisted on a direct settlement with the Sultan. It authorized Capelo, nonetheless, to withdraw his demand for the mouth of the Rovuma, and to insist only on Cape Delgado.[60] This the Sultan would not consider. During the resultant deadlock and this period of uncertainty conditions at Tungue deteriorated; its commerce was dead, and in the interest of its inhabitants a speedy settlement was urgent.[61] Gomes then made a proposal that he was ready to consider the matter in Lisbon, conjointly with representatives of Britain and Germany. This was agreed to, and in September the negotiations in Zanzibar were suspended.[62]

The Portuguese Government issued a memorandum re-asserting Portuguese claims to Cape Delgado, dating its arguments back on rather flimsy historical evidence to the days of Vasco da Gama.[63] The British Government refused to admit that the territorial references in the treaty of 1817 did more than roughly sketch a convenient zone in which it was mutually agreed that the provisions of the treaty should apply: there was no intention of recognizing a boundary. From the time of the institution of the Sultanate the River Minangani had been recognized as the boundary, and Britain had acknowledged the Arabs as the actual possessors. Britain could not accept the forcible seizure of the territory of a friendly country while negotiations were still pending. It was with surprise that the Government had learnt that the Portuguese commissioner had no instructions to deal with the matter in dispute, but only requested the Sultan to settle the boundary of the territory seized. In the circumstances the British Government suggested a compromise, by which Portugal should retain possession of the district of Minangani, and Tungue be restored to the Sultan.[64] This suggestion was unacceptable.

---

59 L. W. Mathews to Capello, 19/7/87, *Neg.*, p. 158; Capello to Mathews, 30/7/87, ibid., p. 166; Mathews to Capello, 31/7/87, ibid., pp. 168–9; Sultan to Salisbury, 31/7/87, tel., CP 5536, p. 35; Salisbury to Petre, 7/8/87, 33 Af., PRO, FO 179/250; Dantas to Gomes, 7/8/87. *Neg.*, pp. 173–4; Mathews to Capello, 11/8/87, ibid., p. 176, and 13/8/87, p. 177.

60 Gomes to Penafiel, 11/8/87, *Neg.*, p. 177; Gomes to Capello, 18/8/87, ibid., pp. 177–8.

61 Castilho to Min., 20/8/87, 2/235, and 21/8/87, 2/237, and 21/8/87, 2/238, and 21/8/87, confid. 19, AHU, Moç., 2 Rep., Caixa 4.

62 Gomes to Capello, 5 and 13/9/87, *Neg.*, pp. 189–90.

63 e.g. Gomes to Schmidtals, 20/9/87, *Neg.*, pp. 192–5, and memo., pp. 195–9.

64 Petre to Gomes, 18/11/87, ibid., pp. 208–9.

The Portuguese action in Tungue had revealed to the world that there was a Portuguese understanding with Germany. Moreover it made Great Britain less sympathetic to Portugal's claims in the district of Delagoa Bay, in Gazaland and Manicaland and up the Zambezi and the Shire Rivers. Her gain of a few paltry square miles in the north of the province of Moçambique contributed largely to losing her vast tracts elsewhere in the continent.

6

THE SOUTHERN BOUNDARY OF MOÇAMBIQUE 1879-1889

It will be recalled that President MacMahon in 1875 found in favour of Portugal's claim to the lands of Catembe and Maputo, the Inhaca peninsula, and the Inhaca and Elephant Islands. His award described the lands of Catembe as being bordered on the north by the Rivers Espirito Santo and Lourenço Marques, on the west by the Lebombo range, on the south and east by the River Maputo, and from the mouth of this river to that of the Espirito Santo. Maputo he declared to include the peninsula and Island of Inhaca and Elephant Island; otherwise it was bounded on the north by the shores of Delagoa Bay, on the west by the Maputo River from its mouth to 26° 30′ south latitude, and by this parallel to the sea.[1]

The Portuguese Government repeatedly called on the Governor of Lourenço Marques to exert his authority southwards to 26° 30′, but lack of resources made it impossible for him so much as to show the flag on the south side of Delagoa Bay. As relations between England and Zululand deteriorated Governor Augusto de Castilho in 1878 sent a messenger to Maputo to ask the Paramount Chief his attitude in the event of war; the reply was that he would remain neutral. The Governor then sent an official with presents to the chief, who re-affirmed friendship with Portugal.[2]

When, shortly afterwards, the king died, leaving a minor heir, and events in Zululand were marching to their climax, Castilho took advantage of the visit of a corvette to Lourenço Marques to establish a post on Inhaca Island. Thirty troops and fifteen workmen fortified Black Bluff where, on 14 September, 1878, the Portuguese flag was unfurled. But the Maputo tribesmen objected to this assertion of Portuguese rights; they expelled Portuguese traders from their land, and confiscated their goods. Castilho courageously visited the head kraal. The regent demanded that the Portuguese evacuate Inhaca Island, as a preliminary to discussion. Before Castilho came to a decision all the garrison of the post, bar five or six, fearing attack, fled. Castilho ordered the island to be evacuated. The consequences of this blow to Portuguese prestige, he reported to the Governor-general, might well be grave: Lourenço Marques itself might be attacked; and there was even talk of a general uprising against the whites.[3] The Governor-general begged Lisbon for 500 European troops to supplement the 800 soldiers and policemen in the Province, most of whom were convicts and Indians.[4] Corvo attributed the tribesmen's hostility to their

1 24/7/75, *RSEA* IX, pp. 266–8, The Lourenço Marques river was the lower Umbulusi.
2 GG to Min., 16/4/1878, 85, 2/515, AHU, Moç., 1 Rep., Pasta 2.
3 Castilho to GG, 7/10/1878, 264, AHU, Moç., 1 Rep., Pasta 1; J. L. Raines to Salisbury, 7/10/78, CP 3928, pp. 175–6.
4 GG to Min., 18/11/78, 264, AHU, Moç., 1 Rep., Caixa 1.

being forbidden to buy arms and ammunition.[5]   But their reasons went far deeper.

O'Neill, the British consul in Moçambique, in 1879, visited Maputo ostensibly to ensure that no arms or gunpowder were reaching the Zulus, but doubtless also to enquire into the tribe's attitude to Portugal. North of the MacMahon line he observed numbers of kraals of chieftains who acknowledged allegiance only to the King of the Tongas (as Zulus and English called the members of this tribe); in fact, nowhere south of Inhaca Island did the tribesmen acknowledge Portuguese authority. A garrison had been re-installed on Inhaca Island with Tonga permission after negotiations which had been lubricated with a barrel of rum and three cases of gin supported by four guns and a package of scarves. "But in no part of the country inland to their boundary line do they have the least shadow of jurisdiction".[6]   O'Neill's mission disconcerted the Governor-general,[7] who was even more affronted by an incident that took place a few months later.

O'Neill nominated as honorary vice-consul in Lourenço Marques a local agent, Thompson by name. Thompson visited Maputo, without so much as informing the Governor of Lourenço Marques, and took with him a present from the Governor of Natal to the infant chief Ngwanasi.[8] A few months later he was planning a further visit to the same area, in response to instructions contained in a telegram from O'Neill[9] when the Governor prohibited his journey. The next day troops surrounded the houses of the English residents of Lourenço Marques, and police searched their private papers; two men were arrested, held for a week, and released on bail. These domiciliary visits brought prompt protests from O'Neill to the Governor-general, and from the Secretary of State for Foreign Affairs to the Portuguese Government. The official explanation was that two Englishmen and two Frenchmen had been enticing soldiers to desert and join the Transvaal police force, and the searches were to find incriminating documents. The protests emphasized the sanctity of a home in British and Portuguese law, a sanctity which could be broken only if there were a prima facie case. This incident clouded British-Portuguese relations for months.[10]   Some saw in this diplomatic activity and public

5 Morier to Salisbury, 16/11/78, 50 ST, CP 3928, p. 174; Frere to S of S for Colonies, 29/11/78, 9 ST, PRO, FO 179/215.
6 O'Neill to Salisbury, 20/7/79, 23 ST, PRO, FO 179/215.
7 GG to Min., extra, AHU, Moç., Pasta 32.
8 Castilho to GG, 4/8/79, 5, AHU, Moç., 1 Rep., Pasta 1.
9 The cable reached Lourenço Marques from Natal on 22/9/70; it was opened to Moçambique in August (Castilho to GG, 4/8/79, ibid.).
10 D. B. Thompson to Salisbury, 6/1/80, PRO, FO 179/218, CP 3403, p. 1; J. Pender, Chairman, East and South Africa Telegraph Co., to Salisbury, 7/1/80, ibid.; Salisbury to Morier, 14/1/80, ibid., p. 2; C. L. de Abreu, Lourenço Marques, to Procurador da Coroa, Goa, 3, AHU, Moç., Pasta 32; Morier to Braamcamp, 20/1/80, PRO, FO 179/223; Braamcamp to Morier, 20/1/80, ibid., FO 179/222 (reply the same day, a promptitude "without precedent in the annals of the Portuguese Foreign Office"); Morier to Salisbury, 21/1/80, ibid., FO 179/220; O'Neill to Salisbury, 25/1/80, 7 ST, CP 4303, pp. 7–8; GG to Min., 30/1/80, 18, AHU, Moç., Pasta 32; Salisbury to Morier, 24/3/80, PRO, FO 179/218, CP 4303, p. 16; Morier to Braamcamp, 3/4/80, ibid., pp. 20–1 (O'Neill admitted the "aggressive and arrogant temper of some of those British residents" at Lourenço Marques); Morier to Braamcamp, 3/4/80, ibid., pp. 18–20; Morier to Salisbury, 7/4/80, ibid., pp. 17–8; Braamcamp to Morier, 21/4/80, ibid., pp. 21–2; Morier to Granville, 9/11/80, 137, PRO, FO 179/220 (S. Januário, the new Minister of Foreign Affairs "who both in the matter of intelligence and straightforwardness contrasts most favourably with his colleagues" admitted that the English case was unanswerable).

indignation an attempt to undermine Portuguese authority.[11] The raids probably stemmed from the over-zealous Castilho's wish to lay hands on O'Neill's instructions to Thompson and find out the extent of British intentions in Tongaland.

That these intentions were dishonourable appeared clear from the next incident in which Thompson was involved.

An uncle of the previous king of Maputo fled to Portuguese territory after the accession of Ngwanasi to escape death, it being customary policy for a new chief to exterminate relatives of his predecessor. The regent, Zambili, sent her secretary to Lourenço Marques to request the return of the fugitive, but the Governor confirmed his right of asylum. A few days later Thompson kidnapped the man and set forth with him and the secretary for the Catembe shore. The wind failing, Thompson had to return. The fugitive jumped overboard and swam to safety. The Governor-general declared to his minister that Thompson was anxious to ingratiate himself with the new king, so that the English might establish themselves on the southern shores of the Bay; already the Natal papers were demanding that the Tongas be disarmed on the pretext that they had assisted the Zulus in the recent war.[12] The Portuguese Minister of Foreign Affairs lodged no formal protest but demanded, with reason, that Thompson, who had not received his exequatur, be replaced as vice-consul.[13]

Actually the British Government had no active designs on Tongaland, and had become reconciled to MacMahon's arbitration. But Britain would not countenance any other power acquiring from Portugal rights in the Delagoa Bay area and German action soon gave Britain cause for concern. In 1882 the ex-Portuguese consul in the Transvaal suggested an influx of immigrants from eastern Germany to the hinterland of Lourenço Marques.[14] The next year a German naturalist of distinction applied for a concession of over 500,000 hectares of land on the eastern slopes of the Lebombo range, adjoining the frontier, on both sides of the King George or Komati River, with up to 10,000 hectares at the mouth of the river, this land to be granted as the perpetual property of the German Colonial Society, which was to enjoy full self-government with exemption from military service and various taxes.[15] German

11 Duprat, London, to Sabugosa, Min. of Ultramar, 6/4/80, 19, AHU, Moç., Pasta 32.
12 GG to Min., 30/1/80, 18, AHU, Moç., Pasta 32; Braamcamp to Morier, 3/4/80, PRO, FO 179/222.
13 Morier to Salisbury, 7/4/80, PRO, FO 179/220. Morier urged the appointment of a professional salaried vice-consul, preferably a naval or military officer (Morier to Salisbury, 26/4/80, 35, 36, FO 179/222). Granville ordered his letter of authority to be cancelled (Granville to Morier, 22/10/80, FO 179/219). Another English resident of Lourenço Marques, Menlove, one of those who had been arrested at the time of the domiciliary visits and reckoned by the Governor-general to be a spy, made off with £1,600 of his Company's money (A. Menlove, Durban, to O'Neill, 11/5/81, FO 179/225; GG to Min., 25/6/81, AHU, Moç., Pasta 32; O'Neill to S of S, 26/6/81, 15, FO 179/225; GG to Min., 9/11/81, AHU, Moç., Pasta 32). A long-standing charge against Menlove was re-activated as a result of a curious slip in telegraphic communication, *archivar* being rendered *activar* (Min. Foreign Affairs to Min. Ultramar, 7/8/82, ibid.).
14 Forssman, Bloemfontein, to Min., 6/7/82, Nec., Consulado Português no Transvaal 1. He was ex-, because he had taken the British side in the recent hostilities.
15 Dr J. Laevernick to Min. Ultramar, 10/9/83, AHU, Moç., 2 Rep., Caixa 1, and minutes 15/10/83.

SKETCH MAP
TO SHEW THE VARIOUS
STATES & TRIBES IN S.E. AFRICA
BETWEEN
NATAL AND THE LIMPOPO

Compiled from the best available sources.
1890.

Note: The boundaries on a map of this size can only be accepted as approximate. The positions of Ingadu Beacon and Lake Sibai are doubtful, they are taken from a sketch map by C.R.Saunders, 21st September 1889.

Scale 1/1900800 or 30 miles to 1 inch.

6 Tongaland and neighbouring territories (map in British Command paper 6200)

moves in south-west Africa and Tanganyika advertised Germany's changed attitude towards colonies. A George Baden-Powell told Granville that the recent annexations by Germany had caused consternation amongst Englishmen who looked to east Africa as a new field for English enterprise.[16] Admiral Horsey, who had once been a staff captain on the east African coast, warned the British Government that there were persistent rumours that Germany planned to obtain possession of Delagoa Bay, the only harbour for large ships between the Cape of Good Hope and Moçambique, the key to the south-western Indian Ocean and the Moçambique Channel. "Whilst the late award of Delagoa Bay to Portugal instead of to England was a misfortune, it would in my humble opinion, be a calamity for its possession to fall into the hands of a Power with whom we may some day be at war."[17] A barrister, a one-time intimate of McMurdo, the American citizen who owned the concession to build a railway from Lourenço Marques to the Transvaal border, declared that McMurdo had been invited to Germany where he had met representatives of the principal banks, who had told him with engaging frankness that they needed control of the railway, as the key to South Africa. They intended to bring in German manufactures and German immigrants; and they wanted to purchase the concession—at once. The German Minister of Foreign Affairs requested the German Army to prepare a report on the potentialities of the railway and the area.[18] Cameron, the trans-African traveller, warned the Foreign Office that Germany was acquiring free anchorage in Delagoa Bay, at the mouth of the Usutu River, and was then going to annex the Tongaland coast, from Delagoa Bay to St Lucia, and secure entrance from the coast to the Transvaal.[19] The British annexation of St Lucia Bay debarred the Germans[20] but no sooner was that proclaimed than there were reports that they had secured land on the Limpopo side of Lourenço Marques, up to the Transvaal border.[21] Sir Donald Currie now declared that there was an organized conspiracy to deprive England of her just position in south-central Africa. Delegates of the Transvaal had been in communication with the Koloniale Verrein, he declared, for the entry of German manufactures, free of duty, and German immigrants in exchange for German support of a railway from St Lucia to the Transvaal. The annexation of St Lucia had thwarted these immediate schemes, but Bismarck had issued instructions for the penetration by German traders of Zululand; Swaziland would lose her independence to the Transvaal; and Germany would step in as the protector of the Transvaal. Negotiations were even then in progress for Germany to acquire the Lourenço Marques-Transvaal railway. Portugal, in these circumstances, found that she had more in common with

16 G. Baden-Powell to Granville, 26/12/84, CP 5051, pp. 177–8; he urged the necessity for a political economic report on the east coast, and offered his services.
17 Vice-Adm. A. F. R. de Horsey, Portsmouth, to Sec., Adm. 23/12/84, CP 5080, p. 6.
18 J. Trehane, London, memo., 26/12/84, CP 5080, pp. 34–5. See E. Lewin, *The Germans and Africa* (London, 1939), pp. 93–6.
19 FO to CO, 27/12/84, CP 5051, p. 174.
20 E. A. Walker, *History of South Africa* (London, 1947), pp. 407–10 and N. H. Garson, 'The Swaziland question and a road to the sea', *Archives Year Book for South African History* 20th year, 1957, II, p. 303.
21 Bulwer to Derby, 11/1/85, CP 5080, p. 50.

Britain than she had suspected.[22] The British Government thought it advisable, however, to remind her representatives in Berlin and Lisbon of Portugal's engagement not to cede Delagoa Bay to a third power.[23] The Portuguese Minister of Foreign Affairs, though he spoke warmly of Portugal's relations with Germany, gave an unqualified assurance that Portugal would abide by the 1875 engagement, and declared that no idea of giving up Delagoa Bay was even remotely entertained.[24]

There now came repeated rumours that the Boers of the Transvaal were planning to overrun Swaziland and Tongaland and take Delagoa Bay. They were collecting much revenue from gold-mining, and purchasing great quantities of arms and ammunition. And, warned McMurdo, "I know Portugal and the Portuguese well, they would rather lose Delagoa Bay to the Boers seizing it by conquest than accept any millions for it by sale."[25] The resident magistrate in the north of Natal heard that the Transvaal had sent a secret communication to Bloemfontein, proposing the seizure of Delagoa Bay.[26] The High Commissioner in South Africa reported to London that there were persistent rumours as to Boer designs on Delagoa Bay, assisted perhaps by the Germans.[27] Such designs would never have been permitted by the British Government, which had a policy of deliberately depriving the Boer republics of any seaboard.[28] In reality there were greater prospects of British intervention.

Tongaland, to the farmers of Natal, was a potential source of labour.[29] A Pietermaritzburg firm made arrangements with the Tonga king and his regent mother to supply labourers, and it planned to export them from Inhaca Island. But it refused to pay the high passport charges demanded by the Portuguese authorities; it asked for this to be reduced to a nominal shilling or two shillings a head. When the Governor of Lourenço Marques declared it was not in his power to make such a reduction it appealed to the Governor-general, and threatened to disturb good understanding between Portugal and the adjoining native tribes by telling them that the Portuguese Government was placing obstacles in the way of the tribesmen earning money and the means of livelihood. The threat stiffened Governor-general Castilho in his refusal.[30] The move warned the Portuguese Government of British interest not only in the strategically important Delagoa Bay, but in the thorn-bushed palm-studded sandy plain of Tongaland.

22 Sir D. Currie to Derby, 17/1/85, CP 5103, pp. 9–11.
23 Granville to Malet, 17/1/85, 23 Af., CP 5080, p. 64; Petre to Granville, 18/1/85, 11 Af., ibid., p. 88. The Berlin syndicate planned to issue 'freight coupons' for shareholders which, by an ingenious evasion of the spirit of the concession, would give Germans differential treatment, so that the whole trade and commerce would become a monopoly of Germany. Münster to Granville, 7/2/85 CP African No. 294a.
24 Petre to Iddesleigh, 8/1/87, 4 Af., PRO, FO 179/253.
25 McMurdo, London, to CO, 8/8/87, FO 179/250.
26 C. Manning, Newcastle, to Col. Sec., 13/8/87, FO 179/250.
27 Robinson to Holland, 14/9/87, FO 179/250.
28 D. W. Kruger, ed. of A. J. H. van der Walt *et al. Geschiedenis van Suid-Afrika* (Cape Town, [1965]), p. 368.
29 Saunders, 17/11/87, C 6200. p. 46.
30 Castilho, GG, to Min., 7/3/86, 96, AHU, Moç., 2 Rep., Caixa 4, enclosing Craig Brothers, Pietermaritzburg, to GG, 25/11/85.

The Portuguese consul in the Transvaal warned Castilho and Kruger that Britain intended to take the New Republic in Zululand under its protection, and follow this up by occupying Swaziland.[31] It was as well that he could not hear a proposal that was made to his British opposite number in Pretoria by three men who called on him and commented on the harm that would be done to Natal and Cape ports by the railway that was under construction from Lourenço Marques to the Transvaal. They then made a proposition which the British Agent regarded as almost too astonishing to be credible: "We propose", they said, "to seize Delagoa Bay, which we can easily do. If we do so, will you give a promise that the British Government will back us up. It is a filibustering expedition. If you do not agree we will make our proposition to the Boers." The Agent protested that the British Government was at peace with Portugal. Then Finaughty said, "Well, boys, there is only one man whom we can get to help us, and that is Rhodes."[32]

Rhodes was more interested at the time in buying interests on the Witwatersrand (where gold had been proved in payable reefs in 1886), and his interest in Delagoa Bay was not to be roused for several years. But a scholarly and far-seeing politician in Cape Town correctly assessed the importance of the Bay. Merriman, in September 1887, called Robinson's attention to the possible increase of German influence over the Transvaal, and in particular to the chance of that power becoming possessed of Delagoa Bay.

It is not necessary for me to enlarge upon the value of that port arising out of its geographical position, as well as from the fact that it is the only absolutely secure harbour for vessels of any size on the African coast to the east after leaving Table Bay. As regards South Africa, Delagoa Bay is the nearest and the best outlet for the whole of the fertile eastern tablelands and the route to the interior that passes through and over them. There seems now to be little reason to doubt that in the near future this country, which is at once temperate and well-watered and suited for European occupation, will become one of the great gold-producing countries of the world.

The only possible competition for its trade when the Delagoa Bay-Transvaal railway was complete were ports in Natal and the Cape, handicapped by inferior harbours and distance.

As regards the Empire, Delagoa Bay dominates the Moçambique channel. It is a commodious harbour within easy striking distance of the French possessions in the Eastern ocean and our own colony of Mauritius and it has a coal supply within a few miles inland. Everything points to the fact that the power which holds this harbour, in any future war which compels the traffic to the East and China to go round the Cape, will have a great advantage for attack or defence, quite apart from its internal value

31 Cohen to GG, 30/7/86, 46/1294, Nec., CPT 1.
32 R. C. Williams, Pretoria, to Robinson, 1/6/87, PRO, FO 179/250.

as regards the trade of South Africa. At present this valuable port is held by the Portuguese on the sufferance of their Transvaal neighbours, who are quite aware that a 'commando' of a few Boers could without any difficulty dispossess the present owners, and who know quite enough of the Portuguese army and navy to treat them with entire contempt. They are restrained from carrying this project into execution . . . by the knowledge that any approach to the seaboard on such lines will bring them into contact and conflict with the detested English Government.

* Now, Merriman declared, there was an alternative in the minds of the faction dominant in the Transvaal: the acquisition by Germany of Delagoa Bay; the object

> to interpose a barrier to the spread of English influence, trade and language, which owing to the influx of capital attracted by the goldfields bids fair to sweep away the power and influence of the party to which the Transvaal owes its deliverance from English rule; and by establishing a distinct interest, powerful both on sea and land, to put an end to the prospect of any anglicising of South Africa.

The point of Merriman's letter was to

> submit with respect that the circumstances of the case call for the most serious effort on the part of Her Majesty's Government to acquire this port, an effort which if successful will absolutely restore our prestige and secure our South African possessions.

He recommended purchase for say two million pounds, and a cession or exchange of a British west African possession to soothe Portuguese pride. He was convinced that the Cape Parliament would be prepared to find the purchase price; another course would be to use a chartered company.[33]

The Colonial Office approached the Foreign Office:

> Looking to the great importance of Delagoa Bay to British interests in South Africa, Sir H. T. Holland would suggest for Lord Salisbury's consideration whether the Portuguese Government might not be sounded in such a way as his Lordship may think most convenient, either as to their willingness to dispose of their rights to His Majesty's Government, or as to whether they hold to the undertaking given in 1875 to be still binding upon them and to be such as would prevent them from either ceding or selling the Bay to any other Power, without having first given Her Majesty's Government the opportunity of making a reasonable offer for this acquisition.[34]

The Foreign Office considered such an approach unnecessary in view of the recency of positive Portuguese assurances. If the British Government were

---

33 Merriman to Robinson, 3/9/87, PRO, FO 179/250, CP CO Af., 359, pp. 39–42, and P. Lewsen (ed.), *Selections from the correspondence of J. X. Merriman* (Cape Town, 1960), I, pp. 259–63.
34 CO to FO, 15/10/87, PRO, FO 179/250, CP CO 359, p. 44.

to interfere at all, Salisbury considered, it should be simply to declare to the Portuguese Government that Britain had agreed to arbitration in 1875 because she believed her rights to be incontestable and on the assumption that the only question was whether Portugal or England should hold the Bay: the British Government would have made no such concession had it supposed there to be any possibility that Portugal would alienate the Bay: in the event of any such alienation Britain would resume her rights and occupy the Bay. But there was no danger imminent enough to justify such a step at the moment. Salisbury added, "If the Cape Colony should buy the district it could of course become the Queen's dominions and the colonists' consent would be necessary for any compact with the Boers."[35]

The Colonial Office then enquired whether Salisbury would have any objections to the Cape Government, on its own account and without official authority from the British Government, sounding the Portuguese Government as to its willingness to transfer Delagoa Bay to Britain—and its power to carry such a transfer through the Cortes.[36] Petre, the British minister in Lisbon firmly adhered to his conviction that the Portuguese had no intention whatever of relinquishing their possession of Delagoa Bay by sale, cession or exchange, nor was there any likelihood of any change taking place in the national feeling of repugnance at parting with a single acre of colonial soil. Petre considered that it would be to Portugal's advantage if she were partially to relieve herself of the heavy burden of administering her vast colonial empire; but she clung to it with extraordinary pride and tenacity, and no government would have the courage to face the storm that any such proposal would precipitate. As for Delagoa Bay, great hopes were entertained of its future prosperity, and though the Portuguese might not be able to withstand a filibustering expedition, they would never give the Bay up without a severe struggle. It was naturally in British interests, if Britain were unable to obtain the Bay, for Portugal to continue to hold it. Petre considered it impolitic to seek reassurance on the Portuguese holding to their undertaking, lest this implied some doubt on the subject.[37] Salisbury's ruling was accordingly that no encouragement should be given to the Cape's suggestion; private individuals might act as they thought fit, on their own responsibility, but any person holding office under a colonial government was to a certain extent a representative of Her Majesty's Government and the Portuguese Government, if approached by such a person, would undoubtedly jump to the conclusion that the move was suggested or supported by the British Government.[38] In 1891 the Cape Government was to make such a move. But in the meantime there seemed to be another line of approach:

> The control of Delagoa Bay is necessary to the interests of Great Britain, alike to the preservation of Cape Colony and Natal and in the maintenance of a safe alternative route to India. At all risks that control

35 FO to CO, 28/10/87, FO 179/250.
36 CO to FO, 30/11/87, FO 179/250.
37 Petre to Salisbury, 2/12/87, 140 Af., FO 179/253.
38 FO to CO, 12/12/87, FO 179/250.

must be secured. Fortunately a mode to secure it without violating the law of nations is offered to us. If we assume the protection of Amatongaland and maintain the rights of the Amatongas, Delagoa Bay is practically ours.[39]

Formal relations between the Tongas and Britain began in the middle of 1887, when an embassy consisting of two indunas and Brüheim, a German who had married a daughter of the previous king and had been living in the country for ten years, arrived in Pietermaritzburg. Queen Zambili, the regent, and her tribe were in great distress: Portuguese officials had demanded that they pay taxes, and when they had declined, the kraal of a petty chief had been burnt down; this was followed by a demand not only for taxation but for tribute; unless this was sent within twenty-five days an army would be sent to eat them up; the Governor of Lourenço Marques had gone to Moçambique to get the soldiers. The embassy asked that the Governor of Lourenço Marques be informed that the Tongas had paid tribute to Cetewayo, and since Britain had annexed Zululand they considered themselves to be British subjects. Zambili was agreeable to any dispute between the Tongas and the Portuguese being settled by arbitration—if Britain were the arbitrator. Inhaca Island had been awarded to Portugal without the knowledge of the Tongas; Zambili declared the Portuguese had paid tribute when they first occupied it; but she was willing to allow the Portuguese to retain possession of it and a small strip along the shores of Delagoa Bay, from which she would withdraw her people.[40] Questioning the envoys, Havelock, the Governor of Natal and Zululand, discovered that the Tongas had never been informed of the MacMahon award. He explained the matter to the best of his ability to the messengers, and sent a written communication to Zambili declaring that the British Government could not intervene in regard to events north of the Maputo River and latitude 26° 30' south, for that territory belonged to Portugal, and all that she could do was to withdraw south of that line those of her people who did not wish to live under Portuguese rule. With these reservations, and with the advice that she should not enter into any reckless grant of concessions, he would be happy to enter into an agreement with the Queen.[41]

The purpose of this agreement was ostensibly "that peace and amity shall continue forever between Her Britannic Majesty, Her subjects, and the Tonga people." The Tonga country was defined as lying "to the north of Zululand, and is bounded by the Indian Ocean on the east, by the Portuguese territory of Lourenço Marques on the north, and by the Swazi country on the west." Havelock took advantage of the opportunity to insert a paragraph, ". . . Zambili, Regent and Paramount Chief in and over the Tonga country aforesaid will refrain from entering into any correspondence or treaty with any foreign state or power to sell, alienate or cede, or permit or countenance any sale, alienation

---

39 'A Correspondent', *Morning Post*, 16/1/88, in FO 179/257.
40 Statement by G. Brüheim, Masololo and Umkonko, 17/6/87, C 6200, pp. 13–15.
41 A. E. Havelock, notes on interview, 18/6/87, C 6200, pp. 15–16; Havelock to Robinson, 10/7/87, ibid., pp. 12–13; H. C. Shepstone, SNA, to Zambili, 7/7/87, ibid., pp. 16–17.

or cession of the whole or any part of the aforesaid Tonga country under her Paramount Chieftainship, or upon any other subject, without the previous knowledge and sanction of Her Majesty's High Commissioner in South Africa."[42] Word of this agreement, published in the Natal newspapers, caused consternation in Lourenço Marques. The Governor promptly despatched a trader to Maputo, who had various meetings with the Queen and her councillors; the British protection had been sought, the Governor gathered, because of Brüheim's influence. The Governor urged that a detachment of troops be established on the Catembe frontier.[43] Castilho, now the Governor-general, urged his Government to castigate this insolent chief: it would be a true calamity to Portuguese dominion if the British flag were to be hoisted in that part of the country.[44] When McMurdo reported that a Portuguese military force was preparing to occupy the south side of Delagoa Bay and to assert Portuguese domination over Tongaland, the British Government assumed that this would be only within the limits of the MacMahon award. It thought it advisable, however, for the British minister in Lisbon to enquire, in a "friendly and unofficial way", the scope and objects of the expedition, and to intimate to the Portuguese Government that since the Tonga Queen had repeatedly and recently pressed for British protection, it could not look with indifference on any interference with the neutrality and independence of the Tongas.[45] The minister duly saw the Minister of Foreign Affairs, who declared that the report was pure fabrication. He repeated the assurance that Portugal would steadfastly respect the terms of the arbitration, but, he pointed out, there was nothing in that instrument which precluded Portugal from acquiring territory beyond the boundaries marked out by MacMahon, provided the conditions laid down in the Act of Berlin were observed.[46] Portuguese officials assumed that British interest in Tongaland was quickening because of concessions obtained, or allegedly obtained, by Englishmen; one, for instance, was for mineral and fishing rights and exclusive railway rights. The officials demanded that Maputo be subdued.[47] Queen Zambili ratified the agreement with Britain, denying that she had granted concessions, and again protesting that portion of her country had been given to the Portuguese without her knowledge or consent.[48] A Tonga deputation went to England to beg for a British protectorate to be extended over their country.[49] The Portuguese now very conveniently discovered in the Governor's archives a concession allegedly signed by the previous king of Tongaland in 1881 accepting a Portuguese protectorate over Tongaland. The councillors split into two sections, those in favour of accepting the Portuguese

42 Agreement, Havelock, and Masololo and Umkonko, 6/7/87, C 6200, p. 16; Havelock to Robinson, 9/7/87, ibid., p. 12.
43 Serra, A Gov., Lourenço Marques, to Dir. Geral, 28/7/87, AHU, Moç., 1 Rep., Pasta 2.
44 Castilho, GG, to Min., 11/8/87, 2/223, AHU, Moç., 2 Rep., Caixa 4.
45 CO to FO, 15/8/87, PRO, FO 179/250; Salisbury to Bunsen, 18/8/87, 98, Af., ibid.
46 Bunsen to Salisbury, 31/8/87, 111 Af., FO 179/253.
47 Machado to Dir. Geral, 26/10/87, AHU, Moç., 1 Rep., Pasta 2, enclosing cutting from Empire, 9/9/87.
48 C. R. Saunders, report on mission, 12/11/87, FO 179/257, C 6200, pp. 37–9, and Saunders, report on Tongaland, 17/11/87, ibid. and ibid., pp. 42–50.
49 Annual Register, 1887, p. 346, quoted in Garson, p. 307.

protectorate as the only means of ensuring the unity of the tribe, the other favouring adherence to Britain.[50] Another Portuguese attempt to collect taxes failed. Machado, the Director of Public Works in Portuguese Africa who had a special commission to determine frontiers,[51] visited Zambili and threatened that all her lands would be occupied by Portuguese forces if she did not accept Portuguese dominion and pay tribute. The Governor believed that only war would resolve the question, but Zambili submitted[52] and to preserve the unity of her tribe, sent a deputation to Portugal to request a Portuguese protectorate over the entire area of Tongaland.[53]

Meanwhile, the Colonial Office was considering the advisability of extending a British protectorate over Tongaland south of 26° 30′. The purpose of this was undoubtedly not any altruistic wish to help Zambili and her people, but to prevent the Boers of the South African Republic from reaching the sea by way of Tongaland.[54] When the Government of the Republic protested against the definition of the frontiers of Tongaland contained in the agreement of 1887, declaring that chiefs Zambaan and Umbigesa, who lived on the east of the Lebombo range, were independent of Zambili and in fact wished to become subjects of the Republic,[55] Robinson replied curtly that "the territory described in the Treaty with Zambili is regarded by Her Majesty's Government as exclusively within the sphere of British influence, and it is my duty, therefore, to state frankly to your Honour that I have no expectation that the assent of Her Majesty's Government will be given to the agreements referred to in your letter as they would be considered to be in conflict with the interests of Great Britain and of Her Majesty's possessions in South Africa."[56]

A London periodical advocated a British protectorate over Tongaland with such an air of prescient authority that Dantas enquired at the Foreign Office whether special weight was to be attached to the item. He gave it as his own personal opinion that his Government would have no wish to interfere with British action in Tongaland and added that he would welcome a British protectorate over one side of Delagoa Bay. This was such a remarkable statement that Salisbury instructed his minister in Lisbon to enquire whether there had been any change in the attitude of the Portuguese Government; but the latter promptly declared that Portugal had no intention of abandoning her rights.[57] In view of her repeated assurances, it was confidently anticipated that these would be restricted to the area north of the MacMahon line.[58]

In ignorance of Zambili's change of policy, the Colonial Office decided to extend a British protectorate over Tongaland south of the MacMahon line —if Zambili still desired it. She was to be told that her administration would

50 Drummond, V/Consul, Lourenço Marques, to Havelock, 31/12/87, 53, FO 179/257.
51 Machado, *Questões Africanas*, p. 11.
52 Gov., Lourenço Marques, to Dir. Geral, 19/1/88, 4/5, AHU, Moç., 1 Rep., Pasta 4.
53 *Gazeta de Portugal*, 1/3/90, enclosed in Petre to S of S, 1/3/90, C 6200, p. 254.
54 Garson, 'The Swaziland question', pp. 307–10.
55 W. E. Bok, State Sec., Pretoria, to HC, 30/1/88, C 6200, p. 58.
56 Robinson to State President, 7/2/88, C 6200, pp. 58–9.
57 Salisbury to Petre, 27/1/88, 6, FO 179/257.
58 CO to FO, 9/2/88, and FO to CO, 16/2/88, FO 179/257.

continue; she would be protected from being induced to grant concessions the nature of which she did not fully understand; future concessions would be confirmed by the Governor of Natal or his representative; she would be advised by the Governor of Natal or a resident or visiting officer for whose expenses she would be responsible; and she was to be given clearly to understand that the British Government was not in a position to support any claim to Tonga territory north of the MacMahon line.[59] It was decided to inform the Portuguese Government of the proposed protectorate but no other power; this government would be assured that the MacMahon line would be observed; and it was asked to keep the move strictly confidential for the time being to prevent complication "in other quarters".[60]

Havelock sent a commissioner to Tongaland to convey the British proposals to Zambili. On his arrival he learnt of the Queen's change of attitude. Machado had sailed as far up the Maputo River as he could with two lighters loaded with presents, £1,000 in cash, and building materials. At the royal kraal, some five miles south of the MacMahon line, the Portuguese flag was hoisted. The Queen and her councillors laid hands on the pole and paid homage to Portugal. Other Portuguese flags were raised as far south as the Umkuzi Lake (i.e. St Lucia). On Machado's return to Lourenço Marques there was a brisk interchange of telegrams with Lisbon and his act was disallowed. He had to return to Tongaland and haul down the Portuguese flag.[61] Havelock's commissioner reminded Zambili and her councillors of the agreement of 1887 which bound them not to enter into correspondence or treaty with any foreign power for any cession of territory without the approval of the British Government. The head indunas explained how anxious the tribe was to retain its unity; and with Portuguese protection they would have that unity, westwards to the Lebombos and southwards to the Umkuzi River. If they accepted British protection, with young Ngwanasi as king, the Portuguese, they were convinced, would not accept him north of the dividing line; and though the Portuguese flags had been removed, they were under the impression that the country was still under Portuguese protection. They expressed a wish for a meeting between the British commissioner and a Portuguese representative, when they would hear the whole truth of the matter, before committing themselves.[61a] Two months later the commissioner again visited Zambili; but she and her councillors now definitely refused to have anything to do with the British proposals. Holland, now Lord Knutsford, bitterly regretted Zambili's decision, because he now regarded it as all-important in the interests of Britain that British influence should definitely extend to the MacMahon line.[62] Its control was regarded as essential not only to deprive the Boers of access to

59 CO to FO, 28/1/88, FO 179/257; Holland to Havelock, 9/2/88, ibid., C 6200, p. 54.
60 CO to FO, 6/2/88, FO 179/257; FO to CO, 7/2/88, ibid.; Salisbury to Petre, 7/2/88, 9 Af., FO 179/253; CO to FO, 14/2/88, FO 179/257.
61 Drummond to Salisbury, 14/3/88, 4 Af., FO 179/257; message by Morforbiana and others, 18/5/88, FO 179/258; Shepstone, note, 18/5/88, ibid.; Havelock to Knutsford, 20/5/88, Zululand 44, ibid., and 25/5/88, FO 179/257.
61a R. E. R. Martin to Havelock, 21/7/88, C 6200, p. 86, and 27/5/88, FO 179/258.
62 Martin to Havelock, 19/7/88, and CO to FO, 30/7/88, FO 179/258.

the sea, but to command the approaches to Swaziland. When the South African Republic requested permission to annex the territory of Zambaan and Umbigesa, Havelock stressed to Robinson that such a move would deprive Britain of uncontrolled access to Swaziland.[63] The Secretary of State was more concerned about the possibility that these and other petty chiefs might, under Zambili's influence, accept Portuguese protection; and that Sordwana Bay, reported to possess great potentialities as a harbour, be lost to Britain. But there was an alternative method of extending British influence northwards, and that was by extending the boundaries of Zululand.[64]

While the extension of Zululand northwards was under discussion, another embassy from Queen Zambili arrived in Pietermaritzburg, begging the Governor for redress in the matter of the division of Tongaland; more than half the country had been cut off, and the boundary line ran beside the royal kraal which had been in the centre of the country. "This country and the people occupying it are said to belong to the Portuguese, though we, who own it, never gave it and we know nothing about it. The people in it regard Zambili as their chief and not the Portuguese. Zambili and the indunas do not understand how they can control and rule over people living in a country which is said not to belong to them." The embassy brought also a letter (written by Brüheim) declaring that Zambili and her indunas wished to be released from the treaty of July 1887, and to be free to do as they thought best for their country and their people.[65] The Governor replied that only Queen Victoria could release them from the treaty, and it was very unlikely that she would do so, because she had conquered Cetewayo, to whom they had paid tribute; the treaty moreover was in their interests, because it prevented them from being exploited; as for the division of the country, that had been settled years before, and was beyond revision.[66]

Zambili simultaneously sent envoys to Lourenço Marques, where the Governor received them formally. The British vice-consul objected to such reception. The Governor explained Zambili's intense desire to preserve her kingdom intact under Portuguese protection if not under British.[67] The British minister in Lisbon protested that the Queen had no right to enter into correspondence or negotiation with a foreign state. The Portuguese Minister of Foreign Affairs pointed out that if portion of her territory was under British protection it was equally true that part of her country was under the sovereignty of Portugal. He again undertook that Portugal would not go beyond the MacMahon line.[68]

Zambili maintained that Tongaland used to extend to the Umkuzi River, but Natal officials insisted that the southernmost petty chiefs in the territory

63 Havelock to Robinson, 19/11/88, C 6200, pp. 96–7.
64 Knutsford to Havelock, 21/2/89, C 6200, p. 109, and 5/4/89, ibid., p. 116. On the Mapootaland Syndicate and Sordwana see e.g. C 6200, pp. 122–6, 154–6.
65 Message from Zambili, 24/4/89, and Brüheim to Havelock, 19/4/89, C 6200, p. 166.
66 Message, Gov. to Zambili, 17/5/89, C 6200, pp. 7–8.
67 O. Knee to Salisbury, 15/5/89, C 6200, pp. 168–9.
68 Petre to Salisbury, 26/6/89, C 6200, p. 174.

in dispute had owed allegiance to Cetewayo, and so could be absorbed in Zululand.[69] Zambili protested and

> reserves to herself the right of appealing to the English nation against the act of injustice that this Government, wrongly informed of the facts, contemplate enforcing. She considers this act of injustice if carried out by a great nation like England, the more harsh and cruel, as she entered into a treaty of amity with England.[70]

A visiting commissioner reported that these petty chiefs had not acknowledged the paramountcy of the Tonga king,[71] and their territories were duly incorporated in Zululand.[72]

Other territories in dispute, south-west of Tongaland, were not included in this act, since they were involved in the negotiations between Britain and the South African Republic over the future of Swaziland and the Republic's demand for access to the sea. In May 1889 the President of the Republic proposed a friendly settlement of territories, by which his Government would withdraw its claims to lands northwards and westwards, in return for British support of its claims to the lands of Zambaan and Umbigesa, in Swaziland and Tongaland, including Kosi Bay.[73] Subsequent negotiations led to a Swaziland convention in which the British Government approved of the Republic's acquisition of rights from Umbigesa and Zambili over a strip of land not exceeding three miles in width north of 27° south latitude for the construction of a railway between the frontier of Swaziland and the sea at or near Kosi Bay. The British Government further undertook to use its influence to obtain a cession of land, ten miles in radius, on the coast in Tongaland, "which area of land shall be deemed to be and to form portion of the Territory of the South African Republic."[74] The victim of Portuguese—British—Republican policies, there was no space for a corporate, traditional Tongaland.[75]

Another railway—that projected between Lourenço Marques and the Transvaal—demanded demarcation of frontiers and precipitated diplomatic differences which prejudiced still further relations between Britain and Portugal.

The original surveys for this railway, made by Moodie, Hall and Machado, had provided for the line to cross the Lebombo range by way of the Umbulusi valley, whence it would cross northern Swaziland before reaching the Transvaal. The Government of the South African Republic, once it regained its

69 Message, Gov. of Zululand to Zambili, 11/3/89, C 6200, pp. 128–9; Brüheim to Havelock, 15/2/89, ibid., p. 129; Shepstone, SNA, memo., 24/4/89, ibid., p. 158; Havelock to Osborn, 4/5/89, ibid., p. 159; C. R. Saunders to Res. Commissioner, 19/8/89, ibid., pp. 198–9; Mitchell to Knutsford, 9/9/89, ibid., pp. 200–1.
70 Brüheim to Osborn [8/89], C 6200, pp. 201–2.
71 C. R. Saunders to Res. Commissioner, 10/9/89, C 6200, pp 295–6; Mitchell to Knutsford, 17/9/89, ibid., pp. 204–5; Saunders to Res. Commissioner, 21/9/89, ibid., pp. 212–9, followed by depositions to p. 232. For maps of the area in dispute, see C 6200 facing p. 1 and 205. See Pl. 6, facing p. 98.
72 Government Notice, 15/2/90, C 6200, p. 259.
73 State President, Pretoria, to HC, 3/5/89, C 6200, p. 153.
74 Convention, signed Cape Town, 24/7/90, Pretoria, 2/8/90, C 6217, pp. 8–9; Loch to Knutsford, 13/8/90, for an outline of the negotiations leading to the Convention.
75 Southern Tongaland, and the lands of Zambaan and Umbegisa, were annexed by Britain in 1895. See Garson, 'The Swaziland question', pp. 312–422.

independence in 1881, convinced that the day would come when Swaziland would pass under British domination, required the projected line to be re-aligned so that it would pass directly from Portuguese to Transvaal soil: it would have to cross the frontier north of 26° 30' south latitude. The route provisionally suggested was by way of the headwaters of the Matinga-tinga River, which had cut a *poort* through the Lebombo range;[76] the valley was being used for a road, and in the winter of 1882 upwards of thirty waggons, aided by a recession of the tsetse fly, reached Lourenço Marques, to make the first direct commercial contact with the coast.[77]

The Transvaal Government requested the Portuguese to nominate an engineer who would meet one from the Transvaal at Matalha, on the Matinga-tinga, and decide definitely where the two systems would join. The Portuguese Government sent out Machado who, however, not convinced that the Matinga-tinga was the best pass, and hearing of the advantages of the Komati, did some work in the field before continuing to Pretoria. There, in January 1883, he persuaded the Transvaal Government to accept the Komati route which would make the Portuguese stretch of line somewhat longer (a total of 81·97 km. to the frontier) but which would be much freer of technical difficulties, than any other. Kruger, the vice-president, and his colleagues asked that a mixed commission determine the exact point on the frontier where the lines would meet.[78]

The Portuguese Government granted a concession for the construction of the Lourenço Marques-Transvaal border railway to an American citizen, Edward McMurdo, miner, adventurer, and promoter of fraudulent companies.[79] Pinheiro Chagas, the Minister of Marine and the Colonies, in December 1883 signed a contract with McMurdo, granting him the exclusive right to construct and work the railway from the port of Lourenço Marques to the border: the Government guaranteed not to permit any other railway for one hundred kilometres on either side of this line which might compete with it. The Government would supply the concessionaire with tracings of the survey already carried out and all other particulars: he was then to put in detailed plans for approval by the Government. The line was to be constructed within three years of the approval of the plans, except for some *force majeure*, failing which the Government might confiscate the line and put it up to auction. Ownership

76 J. J. Machado, *Relatório* . . . (Lisbon, 1884), p. 7; and Machado, 'De Lourenço Marques á Pretoria', *Bol. SGL*, 1885, pp. 645–67.

77 GG to Min., 17/7/82, 174, AHU, Moç., 1 Rep., Pasta 1; O'Neill to Granville, 24/7/82, CP 4777, pp. 93–4. The trade was soon extended to the Orange Free State: early in 1886 over 100 wagons reached Lourenço Marques to load principally gin and brandy (Cohen to Min., 5/4/86, 8/850, Nec., CPT 1).

78 Machado, *Relatório*, pp. 5–31; this is followed, pp. 37–87, by a description of conditions in the Transvaal at the time, and the potentialities for commerce.

79 According to W. Dennis (to Salisbury, 11/7/89, CP 5988, pp. 136–7) he had been born in Dakota, with the name MacMurdie. After being connected with abortive schemes in the western states he moved to New York where he floated more companies which failed. He crossed to England and in 1882 floated the South African Syndicate, sold the £24 shares at up to £80, and put the proceeds in his pocket. In June 1883, he registered the Balkis Company; at a meeting of shareholders he was unable to account for £53,790. Also in 1883 he raised £45,425 to buy land at Highlands Creek, Swaziland; in court it emerged that no land had been bought, and the deal had been fraudulent. He had been connected with other bogus schemes.

of the land on which the line stood, and half of a 500 metre strip of land on each side of the line was granted the concessionaire, as also was an area one kilometre square at Lourenço Marques for the construction of wharves and a terminus, and 100,000 hectares of waste-land between Lourenço Marques and Inhambane (with mineral rights), to be chosen by the concessionaire. The concession, which was for 99 years, was to be vested in a company, to be Portuguese "to all intents and purposes", with its seat in Lisbon. The directors of this company were granted the right to fix the tariffs to be charged by the line. In the event of any dispute between the Government and the Company, resort was to be had to arbitration.[80] The Lourenço Marques and Transvaal Railway Joint Stock Co., Ltd came into being, with its seat in Lisbon, and acquired the concession.

Some members of the Portuguese Government must soon have had qualms about McMurdo's standing when he failed to raise in England the capital he required. When in April 1884, Kruger and other ministers from the South African Republic called at Lisbon on their return from signing the London Convention they were disconcerted to read the terms of the contract made with McMurdo. They were planning to give the contract for the construction of the railway from the frontier to Pretoria to a German-Netherlands syndicate; this could begin work only after the construction of the line from the coast to the frontier; and there was danger that it might not be able to agree with McMurdo's company over tariffs.[81] On 17 May 1884 the Portuguese Government came to a secret agreement with Kruger engaging to grant a concession for the construction of a *tramway* [a transparent subterfuge not to break the letter of the McMurdo contract] to connect Lourenço Marques with the frontier for the purpose of conveying railway materials for the Transvaal railway to the company that obtained that concession should the Lourenço Marques Company not complete its line with the necessary despatch: and this tramway could be further used for the conveyance of goods and passengers if the two companies failed to come to an agreement over tariffs.[82]

McMurdo and his agents had received promise of financial support in Germany and the Netherlands, but this support was withheld when rumours began to circulate about the possibility of a rival steam tramway. The Lourenço Marques Company accordingly wrote to the Minister of the Colonies to ask whether there was any truth in these and other reports that its directors did not have the power to fix the tariffs.[83] The minister replied that since the Transvaal application for a railway loan had failed, and the Lourenço Marques Company underlook to complete its line on time, the question of a tramway fell away; and as for the second question, "there cannot be the slightest doubt that the Lourenço Marques and Transvaal Railway Company has the right of fixing its tariffs as it may think fit without interference from the Government

80 Contract, 14/12/83, CP 5988, pp. 29–37.
81 J. van der Poel, *Railway and Customs Policies in South African 1885–1910* (London, 1933), pp. 19–21.
82 Agreement, 17/5/84, CP 5988, p. 43.
83 30/4/85, CP 5988, p. 115.

as expressly stipulated in the Statutes . . .".[84] Armed with this document, and permission from the Government to have only three Portuguese nationals among the seven directors[85] McMurdo persuaded bankers in Brussels to lend him money, but further reports of the tramway concession satisfied the bankers that Portugal was not acting in good faith, and they refused to find the funds.[86] The Company again applied to the minister, who caused a decree to be issued in May 1886: to resolve difficulties which had arisen in the issue of debentures, it declared that the Lourenço Marques and Transvaal Railway "has in virtue of, and in the terms of, Art. 20 of the said contract the exclusive right to the construction and working of the railway from Lourenço Marques to the Transvaal, so that legally the concession to which the contract refers may be understood to be in form. That no other concession exists for the construction and working of any sort of means of communication whatever across the Lourenço Marques district. That no promise of concession of such a nature has been made by the Government of His Majesty by which the terms or conditions can be interpreted as contrary to any of the stipulations of the said contract of the 14th December, 1883."[87]

The Government followed this up by granting the Company an extension of time and by actually starting work on the railway, on 2 June 1886, on behalf of the Company, in the firm expectation that it would be reimbursed.[88] Its faith was rewarded, for on the strength of these favours McMurdo talked a group of Englishmen, under one Magniac, into taking up the concession. Since the construction and operating company had to be Portuguese, a subterfuge was resorted to. The Delagoa Bay and East African Railway Company, Ltd, was formed, and it simply acquired the shares of the Lisbon Company which however remained in being as the nominal owner of the concession. The articles of association included among the objects of the Company the acquisition of the concession, the taking over of the ten miles of line already constructed, and the colonization and development of lands and mines.[89] The Minister of the Colonies declared that the constitution of the new company was perfectly legal, and it might buy up any number of shares it wished in the Portuguese Company, provided the latter did not cease to exist.[90] Pinheiro Chagas became chairman of the board of the Portuguese Company, which, however, was completely dominated from London, by McMurdo.[91]

Through reluctance to spend money and from the incompetence of direction, construction was extremely slow. Pressure from the Transvaal increased; but the frontier still remained undemarcated. In January 1888, the Minister of the Colonies remarked to the Portuguese Company, "The delimitation of the

84 F. J. da Costa e Silva, Dir. Geral, to Directors, Lourenço Marques and Transvaal Railway Company, 5/5/85, CP 5988, p. 37.
85 Articles of Association, 4/12/85, CP 5988, pp. 37–42. One of the Portuguese directors was Serpa Pimentel, late Min. of Foreign Affairs.
86 CP 5988, p.116
87 Decree, 15/7/86, Government Gazette, 16/7/86, CP 5988, p. 43.
88 Bonham to S of S, 2/2/87, 11 Af., PRO, FO 179/253.
89 Memorandum, CP 5988, pp. 43–5, articles of association registered 3/3/87, ibid., pp. 45–61.
90 M. Pacheco, 19/3/87, tel., CP 5988, p. 66.
91 H. Rumbold, Hague, to Salisbury, 123, 7/7/89, CP 5988, p. 134.

frontier being decided, the Government will have no hesitation in a reasonable time being fixed for the conclusion of the line."[92]   But a decree issued in October 1888, ordered the Company to complete the construction of the line by 24 June 1889, or the concession would be forfeited; and an extra eight kilometres were added to the previously approved plans to bring the line to the frontier. The Delagoa Bay Company protested that this demand was quite unreasonable: money had been raised to construct 81 km. of line and there was not the capital available for this extension. The Company contested the arbitrary right of the Government to set a new terminal point until the frontier was resolved. It was prepared to build the extension (and in fact appointed a contractor) but against a new contract. It protested against the arbitrary term of eight months, which in any case was illusory, since no major work was possible during the six months of rainy season. As it happened, there were phenomenal floods that summer, and some 14 km. of existing line were severely damaged; and the pegs marking the extension demanded were submerged by over fifteen feet of water. As June approached and the Government made plain in the Cortes its intention to confiscate the line or sanction the Transvaal tramway the Company again protested against the injustice of such action adding to the objections already noted that the floods had provided a *force majeure;* and any differences between the Government and it should be submitted to arbitration. It appealed to the British Foreign Office to prevent serious loss to British stock and shareholders.[93]

This was an appeal that no Conservative Government could overlook, and when word reached London that railway officials were being sent from Lisbon in readiness to take over the line[94] Salisbury instructed Petre, his minister in Lisbon, to do all he could to obtain an extension of time for completion of the line, with the question of compensation to be settled by arbitration; arbitrary confiscation of British capital would be quite unjustifiable.[95] The Sociedade de Geografia of Lisbon, however, was organizing meetings at which it complained that English had become the language of commerce in Lourenço Marques: Englishmen were claiming that the town of Lourenço Marques (then being transformed by this injection of capital) was being built on Company land. Holding that the Delagoa Bay Company was a menace to Portuguese dominion, it urged that the contract be rescinded, and a stream of Portuguese immigration be directed there.[96]   Magniac stormed into the Foreign Office, declared that Petre was too weak-kneed, announced that the investors would not allow confiscation "without making a tremendous row", and announced himself as being "in favour of taking Delagoa Bay straight off."[97]

The Delagoa Bay Company took legal opinion, and five eminent counsel (including the Attorney-general) were of unanimous opinion that the Portuguese

92 Macedo to Chagas, 30/1/88, CP 5988, pp. 75–6.
93 A. Larcom, FO, statement of facts . . . , 28/5/89, CP 5988, pp. 62–4.
94 Larcom, memo., 31/5/89, CP 5988, p. 65.
95 Salisbury to Petre, 3/6/89, 13 Af., tel., CP 5988, p. 65.
96 *Jornal do Commercio*, 28/5/99, CP 5988, pp. 68–9.
97 Sir T. Sanderson, memo., 11/6/89, CP 5988, p. 74.

Government had no moral or legal right to take possession of the line.[98] The law officers of the Crown found similarly, and advised that the British Government would be justified in intervening diplomatically to prevent confiscation.[99] Salisbury instructed Petre to "press very earnestly" for a three months extension; to refuse such extension, and to refuse to refer the question to arbitration, would be looked upon by the British Government as a very serious step.[100] The United States Government joined in these representations.[101]

A decree signed on 25 June 1889 however rescinded the contract of December 1883.[102] The Portuguese Government accepted the principle of arbitration, but it would not suspend sequestration.[103] The Delagoa Bay Company complained:

> In defiance of all these protests, and without a shadow of justification, the Portuguese Government has summarily forfeited the Concession, a deed to which the modern history of civilized governments affords no parallel. For their action there has been but one motive, viz., the desire on the part of both Portugal and the Transvaal Government to nullify British influence in Delagoa Bay. Because Portugal is a weak Power she relies on the chivalry of two English-speaking Governments, which makes them reluctant to lay a mighty hand on a feeble opponent. It remains for the British people and the British Government to say whether feebleness is to be a protection for fraud and for Great Britain to remain passive while a treacherous and deadly blow is struck at her most valuable political and commercial interests.[104]

There certainly seemed no prospect for passivity when the Admiral, Simonstown, received a telegram from Knee, then acting British vice-consul in Lourenço Marques: "Portuguese Government determined to seize English railway. Send man o' war quick to protect British lives. When may expect?" The Admiral asked for details; he could not conceive of danger of life to English residents under a Portuguese Government; *Stork* was already on her way northward, but he ordered two further gun-boats there, *Bramble* and *Peacock*.[105] On 28 June the vice-consul telegraphed the Governor of Natal, "Portuguese Government seized English railway; men will defend line and works. Hasten gun-boats, serious, *Stork* not here"[106] and on 29 June he cabled the Delagoa Bay Railway Company, which promptly passed the message on to the Foreign Office, "Portuguese Government torn up railway. Head of Police fired on English driver. Liberty and lives in great danger. Station-master terminus and my interpreter arrested. Demand Foreign Office assistance. Consulate crowded. Lawyer cannot get to

98 Horn to Salisbury, 21/6/89, CP 5988, p. 98.
99 Law Officers to Salisbury, 22/6/89, CP 5988, pp. 98–100.
100 Salisbury to Petre, 21/6/89, CP 5988, p. 98; Petre to Barros Gomes, 25/6/89, ibid., pp. 101–2.
101 Petre to Salisbury, 28/6/89, CP 5988, pp. 120–1.
102 Ressano Garcia, report, 25/6/89, *Diario do Governo*, 26/6/89, CP 5988, pp. 107–10, and decree, 25/6/89, ibid., pp. 110–1.
103 Petre to Salisbury, 27/6/89, CP 5988, p. 112.
104 Horn, History of the Delagoa Bay Railway Concession, 27/6/89, CP 5988, pp. 114–20.
105 Rear-Adm. Wells to Admiralty, 24/7/89, CP 5988, p. 162.
106 Smith to Knutsford, 28/6/89, CP 5988, p. 122.

me."[107] Drummond, the vice-consul in Lourenço Marques, who was temporarily in London, assured the Foreign Office that Knee, General Manager of the Delagoa Bay Railway Company in Lourenço Marques, was a cautious man on whose reports reliance could be placed. Drummond gave information about the military strength of the place and thought that since the Portuguese had strong hold over the natives they would have the best of any conflict.[108]

It was decided in cabinet to postpone decision until further information was available.[109] And on 5 July the Admiralty reported a telegram from the commander of *Stork* that everything was quiet in Lourenço Marques.[110] The Governor of Lourenço Marques had sent Knee a copy of the decree rescinding the contract on 26 June but Knee, who had received orders from his Head Office in London to oppose the take-over, told the Governor he would resist. On 29 June the Governor ordered police to take over the station. The station-master persisted in ordering the usual morning train up the line. Police took possession of the engine. The engine driver backed another engine on to the train, blew steam and hot water over the police, and pulled out. The chief of police drew his revolver but did not use it. Knee, fearing arrest, hid in his house and despatched telegrams. The naval officers paid tribute to the reasonableness and courtesy of the Governor (who had served for some years in the British navy). A consular officer sent to Lourenço Marques to report found that Knee had been a more obedient servant of the company than a loyal vice-consul; the fault was Drummond's for having nominated him to act. As it was, it had all been a tempest in a very small teapot. And the legality of the seizure would not be settled in Lourenço Marques.[111]

The law advisers to the Crown declared the Portuguese action to be wrongful: it had violated the clear rights and injured the interests of the English company; the case was so clear that the British Government was entitled to press for compensation; the amount of this compensation might be submitted to arbitration.[112] The lords of the Treasury agreed that there had been "flagrant injustice"; but it would be unwise for the British Government to demand a specific amount.[113] It might also have been embarrassing, for the company was demanding £750,000 for the debenture-holders, and £1 million for the shareholders,[114] while the company had actually spent only £340,000 on the construction of the line.[115] The British Government accordingly demanded that

107 A. Knee to Delagoa Bay Railway Co., 29/6/89, CP 5988, p. 121. "Lawyer" was presumably a telegraphic corruption for Sawyer, the contractor building the extension.
108 H.P.A., memo. of conversation with Drummond, 29/6/89, CP 5988, p. 122.
109 H.P.A., T.H.S., Salisbury, minutes, 29/6/89, CP 5988, p. 122.
110 Admiralty to FO, 5/7/89, CP 5988, p. 129.
111 Knee to Salisbury, 28/6/89, CP 5988, pp. 149–50; and 5/7/89, p. 156A, demanding £10,000 compensation from the Portuguese, enclosing report by the station-master with a like demand; Lt.-Comdr Balfour, *Stork*, to Wells, 5/7/89, ibid., pp. 162–3; statement by Knee, 5/7/89, ibid., pp. 163–4; statement by E. E. Sawyer, 5/7/89, ibid., pp. 164–7; Lt.-Comdr Langdon, *Bramble*, to Wells, 13/7/89, ibid., pp. 168–9; A/Consul Smith to Johnston, 6/8/89, ibid., p. 183.
112 Webster and Clark to Salisbury, CP 5988, pp. 158–60.
113 Treasury to FO, 26/8/89, CP 5988, p. 171.
114 FO to Law Officers, 10/8/89, forwarding Company's memorial, CP 5988, pp. 154–5.
115 Sir F. Fergusson, memo., 3/7/89, CP 5988, p. 128.

the amount of compensation go to arbitration, as its advisers recommended.[116] The arbitration, at Berne, dragged on and on, and it was not until 1898 that the matter was settled.[117]

Under stronger leadership the Delagoa Bay Railway Company might forcibly have resisted sequestration, and bargained from strength, illegal though its action would have been. But the Portuguese Government's confiscation of the line, however strong were its motives, however exasperated it was by the dishonesty, incompetence and obstructionism of the company, was obviously unjust. It was this injustice that rankled in Whitehall, and contributed to the ultimatum of January 1890.

116 Salisbury to Petre, 10/9/89, CP 5988, pp. 178–80.
117 D. J. Coetzee, *Spoorwegontwikkeling in die Suid-Afrikaanse Republiek (1872–1899)* (Cape Town, 1940).

GAZALAND AND MANICA 1879–1889

Competition in Gazaland and Manica also straitened relations between Britain and Portugal.

The Portuguese in both Lourenço Marques and Inhambane remained nervous of Umzila. When in 1879 Chief Závora attacked and subdued tribes in the Inhambane district it was taken for granted that he had been acting under the instructions of Umzila, or at least with his assent. A determined effort would be necessary to restore the coastal tribes to the allegiance they had previously owed to the Portuguese.[1] Since this was impossible, the district remained in revolt.[2]

To complicate matters there came a European contact with Umzila, not from the coast, but from the interior. In 1879 a Jesuit mission left South Africa, to operate in a new Apostolic Prefecture lying between the Limpopo and 10° south latitude, between 22° east longitude and the Portuguese possessions on the east coast. At Bulawayo great festivities were in progress, since Lobengula was about to marry a daughter of Umzila, to cement a new peace between the two tribes. A thousand Gazas waited on the bride, and in conversation with some of their headmen the Jesuits gained the impression that a mission to Gazaland would not be unacceptable. Accordingly, in June 1880, four fathers and brothers set out. Across the Sabi they came to the tribe of Umtasa, who was subject to Umzila. Messengers ordered the party to make for Umtasa's kraal. They were saved from blundering into a belt of tsetse fly, but their apprehensions were aroused, and when one of the fathers wandered off into the veld for silent meditation and failed to return, the others were filled with fear. They abandoned their wagon one night, and back-marched to west of the Sabi. But they persevered in their purpose and eventually reached Umzila's kraal, where the leader of the party, exhausted by his march, fell victim to fever and died. One of the party with an escort supplied by Umzila went to fetch the wagon, with its span of oxen carefully tended by Umtasa. As it was now the rainy season, a withdrawal was impossible. Their possessions were fast dwindling, so the father who had disappeared and had been found and succoured by a Matabele impi and conducted to Umzila's, set out with a brother for Sofala. He died on arrival, but the Governor entertained his companion

---

1 GG to Min., 20/5/79, 2/143, AHU, Moç., 1 Rep., Pasta 1, who declared that after an initial Portuguese success they suffered a reverse; they then collected 8,318 sepoys and on 1 April completely routed the enemy who left 4,000 dead on the field. But this claim was false (GG to Min., 28/4/80, ibid.).
2 GG to Min., 30/1/80, 19, ibid.

well who returned safely with his native porters. The two survivors reached Bulawayo in October 1881.[3] They had been the first Europeans to approach Gazaland from this direction, a precedent which caused the Portuguese considerable concern; they were the first educated Europeans to live in Gazaland, and describe the ways of its chiefs and the customs of its people; and they had provided proof that Umtasa was a subject of Umzila, a simple fact which was soon to become a diplomatic question.

Other foreigners drawn to Gazaland entered from the coast. Numbers were missionaries. One, sent by the American Board of Commissioners for Foreign Missions, died in 1880 on the way, but the next year Rev. E. H. Richards was well received by Umzila.[4] An Italian and a German arrived in Inhambane in the same year with the same destination.[5] But all were not missionaries; the motives of some of the other travellers were definitely suspect.

Captain T. B. Wybrants, having seen service in Gibraltar, Mauritius and South Africa, informed the council of the Royal Geographical Society that he intended to explore the country inland from Sofala, "the supposed realm of the Queen of Sheba", of which there was little or nothing known. The Geographical Society supplied him with instruments and taught him how to use them. His friend Mackinnon, chairman of the British Steam Navigation Company, introduced him to Duprat, Portuguese consul, who gave him letters to the Governor-general, and the Governor of Sofala. The Royal Geographical Society introduced him to Granville; the Foreign Office requested Kirk and O'Neill to give him all assistance while Granville instructed the British Chargé d'Affaires in Lisbon to request the Portuguese Government to give him special facilities for his scientific exploration; the Governor-general was requested to give him every assistance.[6]

Kirk remarked that the expedition was ostensibly for hunting and exploration in Umzila's country; "There is good reason to think, however, that examination of the goldfields known to exist in that region is a principal object of Captain Wybrants and his associates." These associates consisted of an experienced gold-miner, an artisan, and a doctor; an unsavoury Englishman called Mayes picked up in Zanzibar, who had the dubious reputation of being the only European to be lodged in an Arab prison by order of a British court; and sixty Zanzibaris led by Chuma, who had served Thomson on his journey to the lakes.[7] The Governor-general, who conceded him exemption from customs duty for his scientific enterprise, was not taken in. He came immediately to the conclusion that Wybrants's objective was the gold-mines of Manica,

3 Mattheus da Conceiço, A/Gov. Sofala, to Sec. Geral, 31/5/81, with enclosures, Civil 22, ibid., *Proceedings RGS*, 1880, pp. 432–3, 506, 1881, pp. 177, 306–8, 1882, pp. 228–9, 1883, pp. 230–1; A. Weld, *Mission of the Zambezi* (London, [1880]).
4 *Proceedings RGS*, 1882, p. 93; L. H. Bates and M. E. Thompson, *Sketch of the East Central African Mission Gazaland* (Boston, 1903), p. 6.
5 GG to Min., 29/4/81, 2/145, AHU, Moç., 1 Rep., Pasta 1.
6 GG to Granville, 29/4/81, 2/145, AHU, Moç., 1 Rep., Pasta 1.
6 Aberdare, President, RGS, to Granville, 16/6/80, PRO, FO 179/219; Wybrants to Granville, 24/6/80, ibid.; Granville to Vansittart, 30/6/80, 20 ST, CP 4498, p. 168; Vansittart to Braamcamp, 13/7/80, ibid., pp. 169–70; Braamcamp to Vansittart, 6/8/80, ibid., p. 172.
7 Kirk to Granville, 21/9/80, 110, ibid., p. 518; and 10/12/80, CP 4626, p. 170; and 1/4/81, ibid., pp. 243–4.

especially of Inhaoche. He had no doubt that Wybrants's intentions would be detrimental to the interests of Portugal. Wybrants asked for a recommendation to Umzila, which was sent with a present by way of Sena. He and his party left Moçambique in a schooner towed by a British India ship, which, however, soon had to give up the tow because of bad weather. The schooner put back to Moçambique; if the party behaved only half as badly in Gazaland as it did in Moçambique, the Governor-general commented, Umzila would have sufficient reason to assagai the lot.[8]

The Englishmen were given every assistance by the Governor of Sofala. In Chiloane they engaged as guide a servant of an Englishman, Eastcott, who was a trader in Gazaland. The Sabi River was too shallow for their steam-launch, but most of the party found themselves four days' journey short of Umzila's kraal, where they were kept waiting for the potentate's permission to proceed. The rains began. Wybrants died of fever, and was soon followed by his doctor. Most of the survivors extricated themselves, though with difficulty. Mayes, however, continued; he met Umzila, and spent eight months in the country, prospecting; he claimed to have found alluvial gold and gold quartz.[9]

Mayes conducted out of Gazaland two envoys from Umzila who made their way to Natal, where they sought out Shepstone, the Secretary of Native Affairs. Their mission was to ask how the people of the Transvaal and of Zululand now stood towards the British Government; if their relations were friendly, Umzila would have no care; but if not, since he was well disposed towards the British, he would have to keep his eyes open. He sent three tusks as greeting. These the Lieutenant-governor accepted; he sent a return present, and a message to the effect that the Transvaal people were still under the rule of the Queen as Supreme Chief; she had, however, been graciously pleased to allow themselves to manage their own affairs. As for the Zulus, they were the friends of England; the Queen had placed an officer there to counsel the thirteen chiefs. The Governor of Natal remained the friend of Umzila and of his people,[10] but his action in arresting ten of those tribesmen was to cast doubt on this assertion.[10a]

There had been for a long time no official attempt to re-assert Portuguese

---

8 O'Neill to Granville, 17/9/80, 8 Consular, CP 4498, pp. 261–2; A. C. Rodrigues Sarmento to Min., 5/11/80, 234, AHU, Moç., Pasta 32.

9 O'Neill to Granville, 24/11/80, 14, FO 179/224; J. Heathcote, Inhambane, to Capt E. Smith, 16/2/81, ibid.; O'Neill to Granville, 27/2/81, 2 Consular, ibid.; Kirk to Granville, 8/3/81, CP 4626, p. 228, and 1/4/81, pp. 243–4; Milne to Granville, 12/1/82, 8, CP 4777, p. 164; *Proceedings RGS*, 1881, pp. 238–40, 305–6, 1883, pp. 271–4; J. C. de Alegria Rodrigues to Sec. Geral, 27/10/87, 7 Confid., AHU, Moç., 2 Rep., Caixa 5.

10 Statement by Umzungulo, 3/2/82, A/SNA to Lt Gov., 4/2/82, Rodrigues to Sec. Geral, 27/10/87, 7 Confid., AHU, Moç., 2 Rep., Caixa 5; answer to be returned to the deputation, NA, SNA 1/1/52, No. 58; Shepstone to Deputation, 10/2/82, AHU, Moç., 2 Rep., Caixa 5; Shepstone to N. G. Mayes, 16/2/82, ibid., in which he refers to a secret, unspecified, referred to by Mayes. The three tusks fetched £47-8-10. £34-15 was expended on presents: 18 Newmarket rugs, 1 St Leger rug, 5 assorted rugs, 10 shawls, 10 blaize blankets, 7 striped blankets, 1 drab hat, 22 red and 24 blue Maconde beads.

10a The ten men had entered Natal to buy long-hair goat skins and ox tails. They were arrested in Alfred county for not having passes. A white man pocketed 10s.; they refused to pay a further 10s. fine imposed by a magistrate, and demanded to be taken to the colony's capital. Statement by 10 men of Umzila's tribe . . ., 11/2/82, NA, SNA 1/1/52, No. 68.

communication with Gazaland. When this was eventually done it was thanks to the commercial exertions of Paiva de Andrada.

Captain J. C. Paiva de Andrada had been military attaché in Paris. A young man of intelligence and energy, and sincerely patriotic, he determined, like Serpa Pinto, to devote his life to the task of bringing civilization to the interior of the Portuguese territory in south-east Africa by developing mining, commerce, and industry, based on free labour. He persuaded numbers of his friends, in both France and Portugal, to take shares in a company, and at the end of 1878 he obtained a far-reaching concession from the Portuguese Government.[11] This concession granted him the possession of all gold-mines known to exist but not worked, belonging to the State, within a radius of thirty-six leagues from Tete and Zumbo, and including the area enclosed by parallel tangents to these two circles; the exclusive privilege of working, for twenty years, any other gold, iron, copper and other mines within this area; the possession of all coal-mines known to exist but not worked belonging to the State, in the basin of the Zambezi; the exclusive privilege of working, for twenty years, any other coal-mines in this basin; and the exploitation of all timber belonging to the State in Zambezia. Furthermore, the Governor-general of Moçambique was empowered to grant him, and companies organized by him, up to 100,000 hectares of un-developed land in Zambezia. The concession was to be null and void if work had not commenced within twenty-four months from the date of the decree.[12]

Morier's comments were pointed:

> By a strange act of infatuation for which I believe the premier Senhor Fontes is solely responsible a concession of absurd magnitude and amount-ing to a monopoly of all the mines, forests, and other natural resources and all the basin of the Zambezi was made to Captain Paiva de Andrada, Portugal's military attaché at Paris, officially announced in the *Gazette* of the 26th December, i.e. immediately before the meeting of the Cortes. This concession, utterly unmanageable as a practical undertaking and doomed like many similar ones to death from inanition is both in theory and for practical purposes radically vicious for it confers a monopoly thus excluding competition and if it can be worked at all it can only be so by selling it in detail to different companies for the benefit of an individual at the expense of the State. The consultative Colonial Board has pronounced strongly against the monopoly and the Attorney-general was likewise known to have expressed himself unfavourable to it. But Senhor de Andrada was a personal friend of Senhor Fontes, and enjoyed a reputation of being one of his principal wire-pullers and so the concession received the Royal Sanction and was considered for good reason as an act of accessive administrative power on the part of the premier such as in England goes by the name of a gross political job.

11 Morier to Salisbury, 28/7/79, 60 ST, PRO, FO 179/216; draft prospectus, 14/12/78, AHU, Moç., Pasta 31.
12 Government Gazette, 26/12/78; translation in FO 179/216; Morier to Salisbury, 5/2/80, 8, FO 179/220.

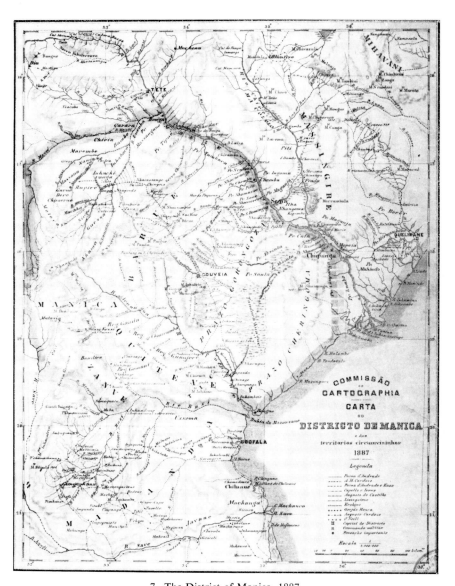

7 The District of Manica, 1887

There were heated public meetings, and a violent debate in the Cortes. The Government faced defeat, and it was saved only by the liberal Corvo, who endorsed the concession rather than lose the Goa and Delagoa Bay treaties.[13] Salisbury deplored the concession,[14] but Morier held out to him the consolation that Andrada would probably fall a victim of fever or to the bullets of the Makololo. Such a fate Morier would regret for he considered Andrada to be going on a humanitarian mission influenced by large and unselfish motives.[15]

The Progressistas who in opposition had vigorously attacked the concession, when they came to power ordered an investigation as to whether the concession was compatible with the law.[16] Based on the Solicitor-general's report, the Government forbad the Governor-general of Moçambique to place Andrada in actual possession of any of the concession until he had proved competence; he was to supply a list of mines belonging to the State and present his plans of exploitation.[17] Andrada was already on his way. He arrived in Moçambique in October 1879, an extraordinary time of the year to begin a journey into the interior. To O'Neill the concession appeared

> chiefly significant as an assertion of the authority of the Portuguese Government over a large area of the country, in the greater part of which they possessed absolutely no power, jurisdiction or influence, carried so far in the southern limits that (with respect to the goldfield) they have conceded important rights in the heart of a country, to the ruler of which they actually pay an annual tribute for the privilege of trading upon its borders, viz. at Sena and Tete, and if my information be correct, to the northwards carried beyond the limits of Portuguese discoverers and former occupations . . .[18]

O'Neill's fears seemed confirmed when there arrived in east Africa the sections of two 90 foot paddle-steamers, each fitted with a machine-gun, and well suited for river service.[19]

Andrada did not leave Quelimane until December, and then he was unable to do more than visit Sena and Tete. His mining engineer died of fever, his doctor had to be invalided out, and his third companion was incapacitated.[20] Despite his curtailed journey and inadequate report, the Government now recognized Andrada's company as legally constituted. It had a registered capital of 1,800 *contos* (£400,000) and it was granted a further eighteen months in which to effect exploration.[21]

13 Morier to Salisbury, 27/1/79, 4 ST, FO 179/216.
14 Salisbury to Morier, 22/2/79, 7 ST, FO 179/215.
15 Morier to Salisbury, 28/7/79, 60 ST, FO 179/216.
16 Morier to Salisbury, 1/9/79, 63 ST, FO 179/216; Salisbury to Morier, 14/10/79, FO 179/215, enquiring whether the concession would interfere with free navigation to Nyasa.
17 J. C. B. da Silva, F. de C. Martens, *parecer*, 4/10/79, FO 179/220; Portaria, *Diario do Governo*, 17/10/79.
18 O'Neill to Salisbury, 14/10/79, FO 179/215.
19 O'Neill to Salisbury, 14/12/79, 61 ST, CP 4498, pp. 205–6.
20 O'Neill to Salisbury, 28/2/80, 10 ST, CP 4498, p. 217.
21 Vansittart to Granville, 26/7/80, 95, FO 179/220, and 2/8/80, 98, ibid.

Andrada returned to the Zambezi in 1881, accompanied by a large party which included three mining engineers (one of whom had had experience in California) and six French and Spanish miners. This time he chose the winter for his travels. He found the Landeens as importunate as ever; they even maintained a permanent detachment at Shupanga, so that the *prazos* on the right bank of the Zambezi were abandoned and those farther afield had to buy freedom from molestation. The Governor of Sofala, from fear of Umzila's subjects, still lived on the island of Chiloane. Andrada went north of the Zambezi. He was forced to turn at Machinga because his porters and escorting soldiers decamped. He tried to examine the valleys of the Luia and Mazoe, but was forced to retreat when sixty miles south-west of Tete, because of the hostility of the natives. He returned to civilization by way of Manicaland, visiting Umtasa and passing the ruins of the seventeenth-century fort at Macequece. He was the first white man to traverse this district for close on sixty years.

On his return to Lisbon, Andrada addressed the Sociedade de Geografia, urging the Society to represent to the Government with the greatest urgency the necessity for sending an emissary to Umzila to settle the questions that were affecting the security of the *prazos* of Sofala and Sena; that a permanent resident should be installed at Umzila's kraal; and that a military command should be established in Manica, with a garrison of sixty European soldiers. These proposals were enthusiastically adopted by the Sociedade de Geografia.[22]

The Portuguese Government decided to send an expedition to Gazaland. The professed object was to acquire detailed information about the country: its natural products, resources and climate, its form of government, its history, and the customs of its people. The expedition was to impress on Umzila that Portugal did not wish to dominate him, but to protect him against internal disturbance or external aggression.[23] The leader of the expedition received complementary confidential instructions. He was to establish whether there was any political relationship between Umzila and the English established on Nyasa and if so its nature and how great was this influence; whether foreigners had established trading stations in Umzila's lands; whether there was any influential party opposed to Umzila, and whether his death would result in internal disturbances; whether the Portuguese Diocleciano das Neves had any influence in Gazaland, and whether Umzila had sent ambassadors to Lourenço Marques; and to report on how Portuguese influence with Umzila could best be fostered.[24]

Lieutenant A. M. Cardoso, first lieutenant of the *Mindello*, who for three years had been Governor of Quelimane and Inhambane, and Franco, the ship's doctor, landed at Inhambane in September—Umzila approved whites coming

22 Andrada, Communição e proposta, 18/2/82, *Bol. SGL*, 1882, pp. 61-4, 67-71; Commissão Africana, SGL, *parecer*, 27/3/82, ibid., pp. 57-60; 'Capt Paiva da Andrada's Zambesi Expedition 1881', *Proceedings RGS*, 1882, pp. 372-4, with map, p. 373, and 'Capt P. de Andrada's Journeys to Maxinga and the Mazoe 1881', pp. 417-20.
23 A. Coelho, GG, Instrucções, 28/8/82, AHU, Moç., 1 Rep., Pasta 3.
24 J. d'Almeida Cunha, Sec. Geral, to Cardozo, 29/9/82, ibid.

to him from Inhambane or Lourenço Marques, but he was hostile to those who approached from Sofala and the Zambezi—and at the end of that month they set out with two officials from Inhambane and two hundred carriers. Their intention was after securing the goodwill of Umzila to pass through Manica country and continue to Nyasa.[25]

Umzila received the Portuguese coldly and they achieved little in Gazaland. The Paramount Chief would not countenance their projected journey; that and the onset of the rainy season caused them to return to the coast. The Governor-general could not conceal from the British consul his dissatisfaction at the failure of the mission.[26]

Andrada floated his Anglo-French Ophir Company, which, by the Lisbon decree of February 1884, was granted the mines of Manica, Quiteve, Bandire and Inhaoche in the Buzi and Aruangua basins. But the conditions were onerous. He was to raise the effective capital of 90,000 milreis within six months; he was not to take possession of the mines until he had deposited 10 per cent of the total capital with the Government; and he was to pay, in addition to the normal mining imposts of Moçambique, 5 per cent of the value of the minerals produced.[26a] In June the establishment of a new administrative district, Manica, was gazetted, primarily to prevent the followers of Umzila from raiding Portuguese *prazos* on the right bank of the lower Zambezi.[27] Andrada contracted to guide an official party to the scene.[28] Andrada failed to raise the £20,000 within the specified time, but being, as Petre declared, "a patriotic visionary rather than an ordinary promoter", the Government was prepared to extend his concession, in either existing or modified form. German financiers were interested in the territory, but the Government would not entertain any concession to them except for some very good equivalent. The Government was more willing to entertain a predominantly English interest in this or a similar scheme. Sir Donald Currie had negotiated a subsidized mail service to Moçambique. Andrada had assisted in this negotiation, and in return Currie undertook to help Andrada find capital. Currie and William Mackinnon formed the Companhia Africana, with a board in London controlling three-quarters of the capital, and a board in Lisbon controlling one-quarter. Currie and Mackinnon subscribed £15,000 between them of the £20,000 initially required. Currie was a director; Mackinnon nominated J. A. Crawford; while the leading director in Lisbon was naturally Andrada. Most of the money subscribed went to Andrada for his previous expenses; there was unissued capital of £80,000. At the end of 1884 Currie insisted that in view of increasing French and German interest in Africa the capital should be doubled or trebled, but Mackinnon had no confidence in a venture so dependent on the goodwill of Portuguese officials and governors. He told the British Government that he would prefer to see a

25 O'Neill to Granville, 4/9/82, 52, CP 4777, p. 101, and 20/11/82, 57, CP 4914, p. 17.
26 O'Neill to Granville, 15/5/83, 10, CP 4915, pp. 44–5; *Proceedings RGS*, 1883, p. 405.
26a Decree, 12/2/84, *Diario do Governo*, 25/2/84.
27 Decree of 16/6/84; J. K. de Moraes Pinto, Vila Gouveia, to Sec., SGL, *Bol. SGL*, 1886, pp. 9–13.
28 Andrada, draft contract, 1/7/84, AHU, Moç., 1 Rep., Pasta 3; for 18 contos.

British company with a royal charter in alliance with another, incorporated in Portugal, with major control in London.[29] Andrada never succeeded in raising the capital which was required.

Andrada returned to Africa. In Quelimane he met the Governor-general, who issued instructions for the establishment of a government in Manica. The *prazo* Gorongosa was attached to the district, but the eventual seat was to be the ancient villa of Manica. Instructions were detailed; for instance, the miserable troops were to wear flannel shirts beneath their uniforms.[30] Andrada proceeded up the Zambezi to confer with Sousa, who was engaged in operations against Inhamissenga, for the *prazos* of the Sena district were verging on revolt. Andrada considered it essential to rely on the military power of Sousa to establish the official administration and his company in Manica, especially since Umzila had died in October 1884, and there was doubt as to the attitude of his successor to the Portuguese.[31]

At the beginning of October 1884, Lima, the newly-appointed Governor of Manica, left Quelimane for the Zambezi by way of Mopeia while Andrada, with equipment for both the Administration and his Ophir Company, left by tug for the Inhamissenga mouth, whence he went up the river by canoe. The expedition waited outside Sena for Sousa's escort, and only in December did it leave for the interior, with four hundred porters. It reached Villa Gouveia on 15 December, where the district headquarters were provisionally established. Andrada visited Revue.[32] The chief miner died on his way to Macequece, but the party gave presents to Umtasa, who declared that the Portuguese were welcome to occupy their old lands. Andrada described Umtasa as a grandee of Gungunhana, Paramount Chief of Gazaland. He intended visiting Gungunhana, to make a treaty with him, in accordance with instructions from the Portuguese Government, but to his intense surprise he heard that the Governor-general had sent a special envoy to Gungunhana. Nor did Andrada wish to leave for Macequece without Sousa's support, and Sousa was away on one of his forays. In the meantime he and the Governor occupied themselves in opening communications with the sea.[33] They reached the Pungue at the point where it was joined by the Mudinguidungue; they confirmed that the Pungue was a splendid natural highway into the interior, navigable with small steamers for fifty or sixty miles, and chose an island for a fortified station which they named Pinheiro Chagas. They were unable to examine the lower course of the river for lack of a boat, but they reported to the Governor-general, who detailed the gun-boat *Quanza* for this service. The ship picked up Moura, the new Governor of Manica, at Quelimane, continued to Chiloane for a pilot, then

29 Petre to Granville, 17/12/84, 115 Af., FO 179/241; W. Mackinnon, memo., 3/1/85, CP 5080, p. 9A.
30 GG, Quelimane, 15/9/84, instrucções, AHU, Moç., 1 Rep., Pasta 3.
31 GG to Min., 24/9/84, ibid., A. Fortunato, A/Gov. Sofala, to Sec. Geral, 1/12/84, ibid.; O'Neill to Granville, 1/12/84, 56 Af., CP 5080, p. 81.
32 Lima to Sec. Geral, 9/2/84, Vila Gouveia, *Bol. SGL*, 1885, pp. 496–500.
33 Andrada, Vila Gouveia, to Dir. Geral, 24/4/85, AHU, Moç., 1 Rep., Pasta 3.

made a detailed survey of the mouth of the Pungue and its lower course.[34] A few months later the Governor-general himself proceeded to the Pungue, and confirmed its use as a port; he visited Gouveia, and observed the security which the military detachments had brought to the *prazos* on the right bank of the lower Zambezi, which were now annexed to the district of Manica.[35]

Castilho saw in the death of Umzila an opportunity to secure advantage for Portugal. Gungunhana, the new Paramount Chief, was apprehensive of attack by one of his brothers, and by Lobengula, his brother-in-law. There was every chance he would welcome foreign aid, which could be given him readily once the district of Manica was established. The Governor-general resolved to send Alegria Rodrigues, who had been director of the recently extinguished custom-house at Angoche, for whom a post had to be found, and who had lived in Sofala and had visited Gazaland. Castilho gave him comprehensive instructions. After complimenting Gungunhana on his succession, he was to remind him that Portuguese links with Gazaland went back to 1861, and if possible make a new treaty. He was to try and persuade the new Paramount Chief to recognize the Inhampura (better known as the Limpopo) as the frontier of the Lourenço Marques district, and to agree to the incorporation of the lands of Závora in the district of Inhambane. Gungunhana was expressly to forbid his subjects to invade Manica and Quiteve; and he was to permit the working of Andrada's mines. In return he would be accepted as a Portuguese authority, and be granted the rank of colonel. He would receive a uniform and be paid a *conto* a year. He would be allowed to fly the Portuguese flag and be aided by a Portuguese resident. Each year he was to hold a court at which chiefs could present their complaints. He was to further agriculture and commerce. Traders were to be given free transit; he was to issue them with licences (in return for two milreis each) to be sealed by a seal supplied to him. His grant, and annual grants to be made to the senior sister of Umzila and her principal sons, would be suspended if there were any unpunished aggression on the Portuguese lands. He was further promised help with troops and munitions against any rebel chief.[36]

Rodrigues, accompanied by J. J. de Almeida, the Secretary-general of the Province, reached Gazaland in the middle of the year, and on 17 June 1885 he raised the Portuguese flag at Gungunhana's kraal. But Gungunhana was reluctant to sign the treaty, and suspicious especially of some of the terms. On the other hand he was alarmed at reports of Warren's march into Bechuanaland (which extended British protection to 22° south latitude), of Boer ambitions in Matebeleland, of Matabele ambitions on his grazing lands, and of various

---

34 Andrada, Vila Gouveia, to Dir. Geral, 17/5/85, ibid., F. G. Moura, 'De Villa Gouveia no Gorongoza ao Rio Pungue', *Bol. SGL*, 1885, pp. 492–6; Castilho to Minister, 16/7/85, 2/208, AHU, Moç., 1 Rep., Pasta 3; Castilho to Min., 23/8/85, ibid., enclosing reports by E. A. Carceres Fronteira, A/Comdr. *Quanza*, Pungue, 8/8/85 and Quelimane 18/8/85; J. P. d'Andrada, *Relatório de uma viagem ás terras de Changamira* (Lisbon, 1886); Andrada, memo. on the history of the Pungue in reply to assertions by Rankin, 26/8/89, Beira, GG 30, Nec., SPZ 2, and *Neg.*, pp. 64–5.
35 Castilho, Sena, to GG, 14/1/85, AHU, Moç., 1 Rep., Pasta 3.
36 GG to Min., 8/2/85, 152, ibid., GG to Rodrigues, instrucções, 8/2/85, ibid.

aggression of Sousa. The fact that the Rodrigues mission was independent of parties of whites seeking concessions from him. He saw some advantage in associating himself with the Portuguese; but he was contemptuous of Portuguese authority in Moçambique. To resolve his doubts he decided to send two envoys to Lisbon. When they arrived in the provincial capital the Governor-general telegraphed his minister, who forbad them to come on to Lisbon. But Castilho persisted, because he had read in the *Natal Mercury* that O'Neill had publicly declared that the death of Umzila would facilitate an English conquest of the gold-mines and a march from the Limpopo to the Zambezi—and there were reports that there was an English party even then in Gazaland. When the envoys arrived in Lisbon the Government appointed Coelho, an ex-Governor-general of Moçambique to treat with them, and on 12 October 1885 they did homage on behalf of their Paramount Chief. Gungunhana was not to consent to the dominion of any other nation over his territory; free transit was limited to Portuguese subjects; and his territories were defined as those over which his father had had dominion, and which had been guaranteed to him on 2 December 1861. Other terms confirmed most of Castilho's instructions to Rodrigues, with the addition that any subject of Gungunhana committing a crime in Portuguese territory was to be judged by Portuguese justice, while any Portuguese committing a crime in Gungunhana's territory was to be handed over to the resident; and, since the primary purpose in establishing a resident in Gazaland was to bring civilization to the country, Gungunhana was to protect schools and missions.[37]

Coelho hailed the treaty as a great step towards bringing security, order and civilization to an area where the Portuguese Government had until then exercised not the slightest sovereignty or protectorate, and whose inhabitants had raided Inhambane, Sofala and the Zambezi districts.[38] Chagas, the Minister of Colonies, issued detailed instructions for the Portuguese residents. They were to stimulate agriculture, commerce and industry, and encourage the chiefs to open roads. They were to take a census of the inhabitants and of their cattle. They were to oppose barbarous punishments, and modify native customs until they approximated to those of civilization. They were to be responsible for education. Above all, they were to be tolerant, and prudent. Rodrigues was appointed chief resident.[39]

Rodrigues and three teachers (two of them women) reached Moçambique early in 1886. The Governor-general had received no instructions regarding them, and since there were widely expressed doubts as to whether the two envoys had really been authorized by Gungunhana to negotiate, he determined to send the Secretary-general, Almeida, to install them.[40] Gungunhana was now having second thoughts about the alliance with Portugal, lest the establishment of the new district restrict his actions, and increase the power and

37 Castilho to Min., 25/7/85, 2/4, AHU, Moç., 1 Rep., Pasta 3; and 20/9/85, 1/266, ibid.; Chagas, 9/10/85, statement, ibid.; Acta de vassalagem, 12/10/85, *Termos*, pp. 33–4; Andrada, 24/4/85, op. cit.; Castilho to Min., 17/10/85, 8, Pasta 2.
38 Coelho to Min., 14/11/85, ibid.
39 Chagas, 12/11/85, instrucções, ibid., repeated in *Bol. Off.* 9/1/86, pp. 10–11, with decree establishing Chief Residency and appointing Rodrigues and school teachers.
40 GG to Min., 6/2/86, 55, AHU, Moç., 1 Rep., Pasta 2; J. de Beires, 5/6/86, memo., ibid.

the Governor of Manica led to confusion and jealousy.[41]   Almeida and Rodrigues proceeded inland with a large party, their goods carried by 600 Tonga porters led by 60 Landeens.   On their arrival at the head kraal, at Mossurize, Gungunhana was persuaded to endorse the action of his envoys in Lisbon; he adhered to the treaty; and Rodrigues was duly installed as chief resident, on 20 May 1886. Gungunhana would not, however, concede a palm of soil; he declared that the *prazos* at the mouth of the Pungue belonged to him; he was overlord of Shupanga on the lower Zambezi; and a recently vassalled chief near Inhambane was tributary to him.   Nor would he allow prospecting in Manica lest the Portuguese establish themselves in that district.[42]

O'Neill, not knowing of these last reservations, reported the installation of the resident as the most successful of all recent efforts by the Portuguese to strengthen their claim over lands in the interior. He declared to Rosebery,

> Portugal must be reckoned with in the future in the questions that would arise out of the advance of English miners and settlers northwards from the Transvaal and eastwards from our Bechuanaland Protectorate— questions that will arise all the sooner from the two facts that the wealth of this country in gold being now known, prospecting for it will soon commence, and that the interior frontier of the Gaza country is nowhere fixed except where it abuts upon the Transvaal, and no doubt it is capable of some expansion.[43]

There would have been an immediate influx of English miners into Gaza- land had Andrada not bought the extraordinary story of Mayes, survivor of the Wybrants expedition.[44]

Gungunhana's doubts were doubtless prompted by word of aggressive Portuguese action in Rupire. Castilho, who had visited Gouveia in November 1885, heard that Andrada had been robbed in the land of Bire and a European killed.   He authorized a punitive campaign, using Sousa's forces.   Sousa assembled 2,300 men, with Moura in nominal command; the force accepted the vassalage of four chiefs, and after an engagement in which Moura claimed the deaths of 1,800 natives, it occupied the lands of Rupire and Massaua. Moura, proudly reporting this to the Governor-general, declared that the insult to Portugal had been avenged, and the campaign once again showed the civilized world that Portugal could comply in a dignified manner with the obligations of a colonial power.[45]

41 Moura, Gouveia, to GG, 9/3/86, 13, ibid.
42 Termo de posse, 20/5/86, *Bol. Off.*, 26/6/86, p. 313, CP 5459, pp. 258–9; Almeida, Mos- surize, to GG, 6/6/86, AHU, Moç., 1 Rep., Pasta 2, and 22/7/86, 70, ibid.
43 O'Neill to Rosebery, 4/7/86, 18 Af., CP 4589, pp. 256–8.
44 Andrada to Sec. geral, 5/7/86, AHU, Moç., 2 Rep., Caixa 3.
45 Castilho, Sena, to Moura, 13/11/85, instrucções, *Bol. Off.*, 24/7/86, pp. 371–2; Moura, 3/7/86, report, ibid., pp. 372–8. Termo de posse, 13/5/86, ibid., p. 378 and *Termos de Vassallagem*, pp. 41–2, of Rupire, mambo Inhampuno, lands between rivers Inhames- sanzara, Aruanha [Ruenya] and Musé [Mazoe], and lands of Massaua and Chiune. Termo de posse, 15/5/86, ibid., p. 378, of Massaua, mambo Inhantare, between rivers Musé, Inhamessanzara, lands of Chidima, lands of Beza. Termo de vassalagem, 30/5/86, ibid., p. 378, and *Termos*, p. 42, of Gosi on behalf of his father Chideu, as soon as a military post was established in Rupire or Massaua. Vassalage, 30/5/86, of Inhamaringa, ibid., pp. 378–9, Caterere and Chiune, ibid., p. 379. Castilho, 23/7/86, Portaria 306, ibid., pp. 365–6; Castilho to Minister, 23/7/87, 18, AHU, Moç., 1 Rep., Pasta 2; Moura, Gouveia, to Sec., Junta da Fazenda, 21/8/86, demanding reward.

Castilho, passing on word of these happenings to his minister, pointed out that the main advantage of these acquisitions lay in the fact that they anticipated any extension of English or Boer influence into Matabeleland or Mashonaland, whither travellers and prospectors had been flocking since Mauch had proved the presence of gold.[46] Rupire was won; but at the cost of Gungunhana's goodwill.

This was unfortunate for Andrada, who returned to Gazaland with Mayes. Mayes had declared that Umzila had granted him a concession of all the mines in Gazaland, and he had entered into a contract with Andrada to guide the Portuguese to one particularly rich deposit of silver near the junction of the Sabi and the Lundi Rivers. But Gungunhana refused to receive Mayes, and refused Andrada permission even to prospect for minerals in his domain.[47]

Jealousies between Moura and Rodrigues persisted. Moura forwarded to Moçambique a report which reflected gravely on Portuguese administration in Gazaland, and when Gungunhana blocked Andrada's plans, the Governor-general thought it advisable to send a mission, headed by Almeida, supported by Fornesini, the *Capitão-mor* of Inhambane. Almeida was to arrange a conference in Mossurize of Moura, Rodrigues, Gungunhana and himself, at which Gungunhana was to be assured of the good faith of Portugal, even to the abandonment by Portugal of various chiefs in the Inhambane and the Lourenço Marques area whom Gungunhana claimed to be tributary to himself.[48] He was to remind him that Portugal could be firm when events demanded, as had been manifest in the Rupire area. Almeida was to urge Gungunhana to agree to the exploitation of the gold-mines of Manica, Quiteve, Inhaoche, etc., which would add greatly to the prosperity of Gungunhana's dominions. He was to explain to Gungunhana the purpose of Andrada's visit, and how remiss the chief had been in his treatment of Andrada. He was to urge Moura and Fornesini not

46 Castilho to Min., 25/7/86, 1/243, AHU, Moç., 1 Rep., Pasta 3.
47 William Mayes had returned from the Wybrants expedition with samples of a mineral he alleged to be muriate of silver. These came into the possession of a reputable firm in London, and later were brought to the attention of Sir Donald Currie. A group was in process of formation to exploit the find when O'Neill advised them that since the locality was in territory claimed by Portugal it would be necessary to ensure the collaboration of Portugal. The Ophir Company accordingly organized a syndicate to prove the silver. A preliminary expedition, it was estimated, would cost only £2,000, but it failed to raise this amount. (Andrada to Min., 19/5/86, AHU, Moç., 2 Rep., Caixa 3.) The Portuguese Government therefore voted the necessary sum (Decree, 18/6/86, ibid.) and Andrada entered into a contract with Mayes to guide a party to the spot, in return for £300 for expenses and 20% of the net profits resulting from the discovery (agreement, London, 29/6/86, ibid.). A few days later a jubilant Andrada reported to Lisbon that Mayes had divulged the location of the deposits, which were close to stone walling near the junction of the Sabi and Lundi Rivers (Andrada to Sec. Geral, 5/7/86, ibid.; he attached a sketch map to show the exact location). Mayes and Andrada, after repeated differences of opinion, reached Mussurize, where Rodrigues organized a meeting of the councillors, at which Mayes brusquely declared that Umzila had granted him a concession of all gold and other mines in Gazaland. Gungunhana refused to receive him. Mayes then suggested to Rodrigues that he tear up the agreement with Andrada, and he and Rodrigues should then exploit the mines. Gungunhana, doubtless at Rodrigues's instigation, ordered him out of the country. (Rodrigues to Sec. Geral, 24/9/86, 75, AHU, Moç., 1 Rep., Pasta 2)
48 Binguana, Masiva, Muabege and Milancula in the Inhambane area, and Maguel in the district of Lourenço Marques.

to listen to falsehoods which would jeopardize the good relations between the Portuguese and Gungunhana.[49]

But these instructions were not to be immediately executed. Four days after the Governor-general put his signature to them, Gungunhana despatched a large impi to bring to his obedience chiefs on the borders of Inhambane who had become Portuguese vassals, and who had supported the *Capitão-mor* of Inhambane in raids on lands which were definitely subject to Gungunhana. Rodrigues borrowed two men from Andrada, who had arrived a few days before, and sent them post haste to Chiloane, from there to catch the southward packet and warn Inhambane.[50] Castilho hurried southwards himself, with such few reinforcements, some fifty in number, as could be spared from the capital. He reported to Lisbon that 30,000 Landeens had invaded the Inhambane district; they had defeated tribesmen loyal to Portugal, until on 23 October the Portuguese had driven off the impi. But danger persisted; he declared a state of war; and he cabled urgently for arms, especially machine-guns, men and money, to safeguard not only Inhambane but Lourenço Marques and Sofala. In the circumstances, Almeida naturally did not leave for Gazaland.[51]

Gungunhana, after the defeat of his forces, decided that it would be as well to come to terms with the Portuguese. He told Andrada and Rodrigues that he would send two envoys to the Governor-general to assure him that he had had no intention of attacking the Portuguese settlement of Inhambane, and to protest his loyalty; to Andrada he repeated his submission to the King of Portugal. He declared he would be happy to receive the projected mission. The Governor-general again despatched Almeida.[52] Moura had reached the neighbourhood of Mossurize on 8 December 1886, but he pettishly refused to see Rodrigues, whose residence was only two hours' journey away. Gungunhana requested Moura to come to his head kraal, but Moura persisted in his refusal to meet Rodrigues; he refused to await the arrival of Almeida, and returned to Manica. In view of his insubordination, and the embarrassing situation caused by it, the Governor-general subsequently transferred him to Cape Delgado.[53] Gungunhana continued to insist on his rights to punish tribes in the Bilene area who had aided Portuguese subjects; the Governor-general was now equally resolved to retain their vassalage.[54]

There was accordingly much ground for discussion when Almeida eventually reached Mossurize, and on 14 February 1887 met Gungunhana, Rodrigues,

49 Castilho, GG, to J. J. Almeida, instructions, 19/9/86, AHU, Moç., 1 Rep., Pasta 3.
50 Rodrigues to GG, 24/9/86, 70, AHU, Moç., 1 Rep., Pasta 2; Andrada, Mussurize, to Dir. Geral, 26/9/86, Expedição de Sofala 9, ibid.
51 GG to Min., 16/10/86, tel., AHU, Moç., 1 Rep., O'Neill to Iddesleigh, 12/11/86, 43 Af., FO 179/250; Conselho do Governo, acta. 13/11/86, AHU, Moç., 1 Rep., Pasta 2; GG to Min., 15/11/86, 2/302, ibid. GG, portaria 506, 1/12/86, *Bol. Off.*, 4/12/86, p. 609; T.A. de Carvalho, memo., 4/12/86, ibid.; GG to Min., 12/12/86, 2/307, ibid.; GG to Min., 27/12/86, 2/319, ibid.
52 Andrada, at Gungunhana's request, sent off a telegram from Lourenço Marques: "Esperando commissão nomeada pera reunir no Mossurise beijo humildemente a mão do meu Rei." (Andrada, Mussurize, to Sec. Geral, 11/12/86) Exped. de Sofala 16, AHU, Moç., 1 Rep., Pasta 2; Andrada, instructions, 13/12/86, ibid.
53 Rodriques to Sec. Geral, 16/12/86, 118, ibid., GG to Min., 11/1/87, 2/15, ibid.
54 GG to Min., 23/12/86, 317, ibid., and detailed report, 27/12/86, 2/319, ibid.

Andrada, and the Acting Governor of Manica. The conference cleared up many points at issue, and Gungunhana undertook to send another two emissaries to Portugal to protest his friendship. But he still persisted in his claims of over-lordship over the chiefs on the borders of Inhambane and between the Pungue and the Zambezi.[55] Andrada urged that these emissaries be told unequivocally in Lisbon that Gungunhana's claims could not be recognized north of the Pungue River.[56]

As an act of insurance Gungunhana had also sent messengers to Natal, asking for a letter declaring that he was the rightful chief, and for guidance from the Natal Administration. He sent a large tusk of ivory by way of greeting, and asked for a tent in return. The tusk was too heavy for the two messengers, who left it on the way. The Lieutenant-governor replied brusquely that since the tusk had not arrived he was unable to send the tent. He had heard more-over that the chief and his tribe paid tribute to the Portuguese and now had a Portuguese resident: "This being so, the Governor trusts that any messages sent to him are sent with the knowledge and concurrence of that official."[57] The messengers received a very different message, however, from a "leading columnist":

> Tell your King he is strong and can therefore afford to act prudently. Tell him that though the Portuguese who molest him are black and de-generate, they are the representatives of white European Power, a weak Power, but still a white people. Tell him they will never overrun his country, because they are not a colonizing, industrious people. Tell him, however, that he is right to resent any inroad in his own territory, or attacks on his people, and tell him his best plan is to send a definite message to Portuguese officials, telling them that he is wishful to be at peace with them as his and their fathers were before, the country is his for his people, that so long as they merely use the sea ports for trading and come and go among the people for trading he is willing they should remain, though they must control their people at the sea ports from molesting or worrying his the King's people.[58]

Gungunhana remained suspicious, with reason, of Portuguese intentions in Manica.[59] His fears would not have been allayed could he have seen the instructions given to the new Governor of the district, Major C. M. de S. Ferreira Simões. Castilho surveyed the growth of the district; originally it had comprised no more than the *prazo* Gorongosa, then it had marched to the Zambezi, and even across it to the Ziu-ziu and Shire, and now Rupire and

55 Acta da reunião . . ., 14/2/87, ibid.
56 Andrada, Manchanrene, to Sec. Geral, 5/3/87, Exped. Sofala 29, ibid.
57 W. H. Acutt, statement of Umzungulu . . ., 28/2/87, CP 6495, p. 217; H. C. Shepstone, SNA, message to Umdungazwe, ibid., pp. 217–8; Rodrigues to Sec. Geral, 27/10/87, 7 Confid., AHU, Moç., 2 Rep., Caixa 5.
58 Mathers, *Zambesia*, pp. 408–9; and GG to Min., 22/12/87, extra 62, AHU, Moç., 2 Rep., Caixa 5.
59 Especially after the death of his mother, who had been a staunch protagonist of the Portuguese. (GG to Min., 27/6/87, 2/191, AHU, Moç., 1 Rep., Pasta 2.)

Massaua lands had been added to it; but it was still impossible to trace the exact boundaries. The new Governor was simply enjoined gradually to consolidate the sovereignty of the Portuguese Government. As soon as practicable the capital of the district was to be transferred from Gouveia to Macequece, the seat of the old fair and Vila. Communications were to be improved, by way of the Pungue. It was hoped soon to introduce steam navigation on this river. He was to occupy the line of the Pungue, and prevent Landeen raids across it to the Zambezi. He was to have a special care in his relations with Antonio de Sousa, who was to be treated with consideration, for the Portuguese still had need of the forces that he could put in the field; but he was not to become dependent on him. He was to consider the possibility of extending Portuguese control over Barue, which Sousa, who had married a daughter of Chief Macombe, had conquered by force of arms; he was to sound Sousa carefully on the subject of the possibility of Sousa surrendering his autonomy in return for a financial grant. He was to co-operate with Sousa in destroying Massangano and the successor of Bonga (of whom more in the next chapter). *Prazos*, Castilho added, yielded virtually nothing to the State, but the so-called lessees were scandalously rich; the Governor was to try all he could to extend Portuguese control over them. And he was to use the *prazos* as reservoirs for sepoys who, it was hoped, would come to obey not the lessees but the State.[60]

There was some conflict of interest between the districts of Manica and Sofala, and it soon became advisable for the military command of Aruangua (i.e. the lower Pungue) to be transferred to the control of the Governor of Sofala.[61] The Governor of Sofala continued in Chiloane—the fortress of Sofala was now verging on destruction.[62] Operations were duly mounted against Massangano, during which the Governor died of fever.[63] The Governor-general redefined for the benefit of his successor the western and the northern boundaries of Manica, describing them as the Zambezi from Massangano, at the junction of the Ruenha, to the junction of the Mazoe, and up these tributaries to their sources, as indicated on a map recently published in Lisbon.[64] With the establishment of a military command at Aruangua that of Shupanga was closed.[65] Early in 1889 Gungunhana agreed to the erection of a residence in Mashonaland, and in Chegualaguala. Since the British claimed a supervisory right over Mashonaland, the minister decided that the first of these extra residences should be at Mogougou on the Mashonaland border, which was undoubtedly under the control of Gungunhana.[66]

60 GG, instructions 17/3/87, ibid.
61 GG, Portaria 303, 22/7/87, *Bol. Off.* 23/7/87, pp. 330–1.
62 J. C. P. de Moraes Sarmento, relatório, 8/8/87, Chiloane, *Bol. Off.* 1887, pp. 437–40. The terrace of the fortress had fallen, and the foundations on the south and east had become exposed. The place was so ruinous that it was not safe for the garrison to live in it. The garrison (1 sergeant, 4 cabos, 1 cornet, 22 men) received no wages, only a ration of maize or rice, and no clothing; there was virtually no discipline, and they were often drunk. In Chiloane there were an officer, 2 sergeants, 3 cabos, 1 cornet and 53 men.
63 Andrada, Pindirire, to A/Gov. Manica, 7/9/87, AHU, Moç., 1 Rep., Pasta 4.
64 Castilho, Portaria 426, 14/10/87, *Bol. Off.* 1887, p. 475. See Pl. 7, facing p. 120.
65 Anon., *O. Território de Manica e Sofala e a Administração da Companhia de Moçambique (1892–1900)* (Lisbon, 1902), p.131.
66 GG, Portaria 37, 17/1/89, *Bol. Off.* 19/1/89, pp. 29–30; GG to Min., 4/2/89, 3/26, AHU, Moç., 1 Rep., Pasta 3, and minutes of Min., 11/4/89.

The main purpose in erecting the district of Manica was the extraction of gold, and this depended almost exclusively on the success or failure of Andrada and his ventures. Andrada was indefatigable in his quest. One journey made a particularly notable contribution to physical and human geography; on it he traversed Mashonaland, from the Mazoe River near its junction with the Gaeresi, to Chicoa, and on to Missanga. He was accompanied by Sousa, who distributed Portuguese flags on the way, and who joined him in urging the foundation of a villa on the upper Mazoe, to be called Principe D. Carlos.[67]

Much depended on the attitude of Umtasa, the most important chief in Manica, whom Gungunhana maintained to be a vassal. In May 1888, however, two sons of Umtasa and four of his councillors arrived at the headquarters of the Acting Governor of Manica, and told him that Umtasa had a considerable time before delivered his lands to the Portuguese—the resident chief of Gaza-land had sent him a Portuguese flag—and he asked the Portuguese to establish themselves at his head kraal. The Acting Governor replied that he could not visit Umtasa's lands without the authority of the Governor-general, and he certainly could not move the capital of the district there because of its distance from the sea and problems of communication; but Andrada would shortly be returning to Africa with some Europeans, who would make their way to Manica; in the meantime, the Portuguese flag would serve as proof of Portugal's friendliness. The Governor-general, so far from leaping at this opportunity to extend Portuguese sovereignty over Umtasa's territory, questioned the sincerity of the mission; he declared to his minister that envoys had been sent to Goron-gosa in 1886, but these, it was later learnt, had not been authorized by the chief.[68] In this the Governor-general was repeating the scepticism of Rodrigues,[69] who had interested motives in resisting the adhesion of Umtasa to Manica. And Gungunhana, of course, was not only adamant in his refusal to give up a vassal, but continued to be apprehensive of the link between Sousa and the Government of Manica, especially after young Macombe of Barue sent envoys requesting Landeen aid to expel the Portuguese from Barue, Rupire and Massangano.[70]

In the middle of 1888 Petre, the British minister in Lisbon, received from an anonymous correspondent an offer to reveal—for a large sum of money—a scheme which the Portuguese Government, rendered nervous by the organiza-tion of the British East Africa Company, had entrusted to Andrada to forestall British expansion into the Zambezia region, and so deprive the British Crown of very extensive territories which might otherwise become its property when frontiers should eventually be delimited. Petre thought it as well for Andrada, who had already left on his return to Africa, to be watched; the Government had great confidence in him, and was fully aware of his energy and his great influence with the natives; Petre thought it not at all improbable

67 Andrada Missanga, to Sec. Geral, 6, 10 and 11/6/87, 35, 36, 37, ibid., Pasta 2.
68 Ferreira to Sec. Geral, 1/6/88, 28, AHU, Moç., 2 Rep., Caixa 5; GG to Min., 18/7/88, and 21/7/88, 2/236, ibid.
69 Rodrigues to Sec. Geral, 18/7/88, AHU, Moç., 1 Rep., Pasta 3.
70 Almeida to Min., 22/7/88, 2/240, ibid., Pasta 4.

that he had been charged to extend Portuguese influence in the region.[71] The Foreign Office promptly warned O'Neill (and Drummond and Buchanan) to keep watch on his movements and report on his actions.[72] Particulars of the enterprise were soon to be divulged. In a debate in the Cortes early in July on colonial expenditure reference was made to the great utility of expeditions for the exploration of the interior of Africa, and Serpa Pinto stated that he knew the secret of Andrada's expedition and could bear witness to its great importance.[73] The press proceeded to dispel what remained of the secrecy. One paper said that the object of Andrada's expedition was to extend, consolidate, and secure Portuguese occupation in the valley of the Zambezi as far as Zumbo and beyond, and then descend southwards by one of the tributaries of the Zambezi. Another confirmed that Portuguese control was to be consolidated as far as Zumbo, as well as inland of Sofala, while A. M. Cardoso was to lead another expedition north of the Zambezi. That these reports were true was confirmed when Serpa Pinto demanded in the House of Deputies that those guilty of such indiscretions be punished, and a minister admitted that the publication amounted almost to treason.[74]

Newspapers soon divulged the creation of the Moçambique Company. Andrada, in the middle of 1888, had succeeded in floating this company, which acquired the mineral rights of the Manica Ophir Mining Co., Ltd, and of the Sabi Ophir Co., Ltd (offshoots of the Ophir Concessions Ltd, of London) in return for 10 per cent of the net profits.[75] The Moçambique Company had a provisional capital of only £40,000, but it was more than a mere gold-seeking concern: its stated objects were

> to acquire by concession, purchase, or any other form, from the State, corporate bodies, or private individuals, mineral, agricultural, or any other property in the province of Moçambique, to execute, with a guarantee of the Government or without it, works of public utility, such as roads, railways, canals, wharves, and any other description of service, either in that portion of the Province which is actively occupied, or in the interior which belongs to the Crown of Portugal, to organize transport communication of any kind whatever, by sea and land, to promote and direct colonization of the lands of the Company or of any other part of the Province, and to undertake any form of enterprise whatsoever, mineral, agricultural, industrial or commercial, which shall directly or indirectly conduce to the above indicated ends, and for this purpose the Company is also permitted to associate itself with any commercial firm or other enterprise already in existence.[76]

A provincial decree soon confirmed the right of the company to lease out

71 Petre to Salisbury, 12/6/88, 48 Af., CP 5727, p. 61.
72 FO to O'Neill, etc., 27/6/88, 20, CP 5727, p. 62.
73 Bonham to Salisbury, 7/7/88, 66 Af., CP 5727, p. 64.
74 Bonham to Salisbury, 12/7/88, 69 Af., CP 5727, pp. 65–6.
75 A. H. B. Greenwood, Sec., Ophir Concession Ltd, 21/8/89, to Ed., *Weekly Bulletin*, 31/8/89.
76 O'Neill to Salisbury, 7/9/88, 48 Af., CP 5727, pp. 118–9.

mining concessions, on condition that these were for not more than ten years, and that the Moçambique Company retained legal title to the land. The Moçambique Company was to pay the Government 5 per cent of the net proceeds of the mines, and 5 per cent of the profits of the sub-contractors. In addition, the Company engaged to build, within two years, a light railway from Aruangua, or the limit of navigation on the Pungue, to Macequece.[77]

The British consul in Moçambique, and the vice-consuls in Lourenço Marques and Quelimane, filled in gaps in the newspaper reports of the movements of Andrada's expedition. He chartered the small steamer *Lion* from Natal, and used her to transport 300 tons of stores, trans-shipped from the mailship at Chiloane, to Beira, at the mouth of the Pungue. These stores, which included 2,000 rifles, and a number of prospectors (mainly Irishmen, in the first place, from Barberton, for a Barberton concern had acquired a sub-concession from Andrada) were transported up the river to the limit of navigation and thence by road to Manica. A steam-launch, constructed at Yarrow, arrived for the navigation of the river; close on 60 foot long, equipped with paddles, and drawing only twelve inches, she was admirably designed for such navigation. She mounted a Gatling or Hotchkiss gun on the bow, and was only the first of nine such craft on order. In view of the limited capital of the company of Moçambique, it was clear that these were being paid for by the Government of Portugal; the ultimate destination of most of these was the Zambezi. Before long there were thirty prospectors in Manica.[78] No legal title had yet been granted. Almeida, the Secretary-general of the Province, had again visited Mossurize, but he had been completely unsuccessful in his mission, to persuade Gungunhana to accept the Pungue as the northern limit of his lands, and to permit the restoration of Manica to the Portuguese. The most Gungunhana would concede was the right to prospect for gold in Manica; but Almeida was not authorized to accept such a restricted concession, and he asked Gungunhana to send one of his men to Moçambique to hear the Governor-general's verdict.[79] Gungunhana's attitude remained so uncertain that when he assembled a great impi there was considerable alarm among the Portuguese lest this be directed against Manica or Inhambane or Sofala; there was positive relief when it was learnt that it was being sent against Umtasa presumably to punish him for his

77 Portaria, 7/11/89, *Bol. Off.*, 11/11/89.
78 One of these, J. Heathcote, a British subject, resident in Inhambane, had discovered gold (near the mountain Gundi Inyanga, lat. 19° 45′ S., 32° 45′ E.); he had registered his discovery on 1/2/87 and been promised title; but in 4/88 was told that title was impossible until there was an understanding with Gungunhana (Bonham to Gomes, 19/9/88, FO 179/260). Salisbury instructed that his minister in Lisbon, when forwarding Heathcote's petition, should add a reserving clause that this was not to be taken as an admission by Britain that the land was within the Portuguese boundary (Salisbury to Petre, 14/11/88, 141 Af., PRO, FO 179/258). Heathcote was not a filibuster but an upright law-abider (Churchill to Salisbury, 28/8/89, 2 Commercial, FO 179/266, Petre to Gomes, 12/11/89, FO 179/270). Heathcote's death ended the matter (Churchill to Salisbury, 27/12/89, 8 Commercial, FO 179/276).
79 Bonham to Salisbury, 12/7/88, 70 Af., CP 5727, p. 66; Drummond, Lourenço Marques, to Salisbury, 6/8/88, 10 Af., ibid., pp. 93–4; O'Neill to Salisbury, 10/8/88, 45 Af., ibid., p. 102*; Geraldes, Mossurize, to Sec. Geral, 7/9/88, AHU, Moç., 1 Rep., Pasta 3; O'Neill to Salisbury, 15/10/88, 56 Af., CP 5727, pp. 129–30; Almeida, Sec. Geral, to Min., 12/11/88, 2/347, AHU, Moç., 1 Rep., Pasta 3.

overtures to the Portuguese; Umtasa suffered deeply at the hands of his over-lord.[80]

But Gungunhana could see the writing on the wall. There was a constantly increasing influx of whites to his lands, who were obviously after much more than the few tusks of ivory which had satisfied Reuben Beningfield.[81] More Englishmen arrived—one touched Andrada for a £20 loan, while another was accompanied by two white women—all demanding the right to prospect. Some Germans arrived. And even some Americans arrived, with a particularly suspicious request, declaring that they had been sent by God to teach Gungun-hana's followers to read and write. But by now the Portuguese teachers were meeting with a certain amount of success; though one was dismissed for lack of professional ability, and her morals left much to be desired, two of Gungun-hana's sons by now were proficient in Portuguese. The chief resident, who had insisted on being present whenever Gungunhana received foreigners, informed them that their presence was unnecessary, irregular and unwelcome, while Gungunhana assured them (as he had assured the Portuguese) that there were no mines in his territory.[82]

But Andrada and 200 prospectors in Manica (working under sub-conces-sions from the Ophir Concessions, Ltd)[83] could not be wrong; and Gungunhana knew it. However much he might still insist on his rights to the left bank of the Pungue, and deny Portuguese rights over Manica,[84] he must have realized that he could not hope to continue his paramountcy over Manica; and he feared attack from Gouveia. He suddenly decided, in the middle of 1889, to move his head kraal, and the bulk of his tribe, from the head-waters of the Buzi, southwards, to an area with its centre some eighty miles north of the mouth of the Limpopo. The misery and fatality occasioned to the tens of thousands of men, women and children of his tribe meant nothing to the potentate; still less did he worry about the tribes and clans that were displaced. His destination was in Chopi territory, and Bilene and other chiefs had paid tribute to the Portuguese and accepted Portuguese flags.[85] Gungunhana's move may, in fact, have been partly influenced by his desire to overawe Lourenço Marques and Inhambane. The *Capitão-mor* of Inhambane and a Major Swart planned to attack the tribe as it passed that town but the chief resident sent urgently to the Governor of the district telling him that Gungunhana had

80 J. J. Ferreira, Gov. Manica, to Sec. Geral, 8/2/89, *Bol. Off.*, 23/3/89.
81 But what tusks! He once brought down a pair weighing 196 and 170 lbs: G. Lacy, 'South African exploration', *South Africa* (London), 29/5/1915, p. 386.
82 Rodrigues to Sec. Geral, 21/7/87, 3, AHU, Moç., 2 Rep., Caixa 4; Sarmento to Sec. Geral, 5/9/88, 95, AHU, Moç., 1 Rep., Pasta 3; Geraldes, A/Resident, to Sec. Geral, 6/9/88, 143, ibid., and 10/9/88, 146, ibid.; and 2/11/88, 178, ibid.; Geraldes, auto., 22/9/88, ibid.; Geraldes to Sec. Geral, 23/8/88, 149, ibid.; Ignazio, Chiloane, to Sec. Geral, 12/6/89, *Bol. Off.*, 22/6/89, p. 397. Geraldes showed Gungunhana a packet of mail that had arrived for the Americans from Chiloane, consisting of seven letters, two periodicals, and some books; he declared that no honest man would receive so much correspondence: they must be receiving secret and malevolent instructions.
83 Ophir Concession Co. to Salisbury, 21/1/91, CP 6086, p. 51.
84 F. A. M. Geraldes, 'Relatório de Gaza', 1/1/89, *Bol. Off.*, 18/5/89, pp. 318–22; Castilho to Min., 24/1/89, 2/24, AHU, Moç., 1 Rep., Pasta 3.
85 Gov. to Min., 3/7/88, tel., Nec., SPZ 1; A/GG to Min., 27/5/89, 2/151, AHU, Moç., 1 Rep., Pasta 5.

warned his warriors not to attack the Portuguese, and begged him not to precipitate a conflict. The chief resident correctly appreciated the significance of the move, which reduced the influence of the Paramount Chief over his north-western marches, where two Portuguese residents had been newly appointed.[86] The move brought Gungunhana closer to the sea and to maritime influences. The chief resident urged that custom posts be established at the mouths of the Buzi, Guvuru and Sabi Rivers to help prevent foreign intervention.[87] The Portuguese refused passage to further concession hunters and arrested those who persisted.[88]

This influx of foreigners, and the growing interest of Rhodes in the area, disturbed Andrada in particular, who realized that he must make haste lest he find himself forestalled and his country debarred from her birthright. Andrada had returned to Beira at the end of 1888. Though ill with fever he had remained less than a week before returning to the interior.[89] He consolidated Portuguese authority in Manica, and moving westward raised the Portuguese flag in Makone. He planned to extend Portuguese influence beyond Bire to the Mazoe and Hunyani, while another expedition under Cordon proceeded up the Zambezi and the Sanyati.[90] But first he returned to the coast, arriving in November,[91] from where he made his way to Moçambique for discussions with the Governor-general. He left Moçambique in a gun-boat, which advertised the intimate connection of the Government with his plans. He returned to Beira; the channel by now had been buoyed, and the port was already the main port of entry to the interior, so much so that Andrada was urging the immediate construction of a railway to the Manica gold-fields. He made final preparations for his expedition.[92] But Andrada's carefully prepared plans were blasted by a diplomatic bomb-shell—the ultimatum of 11 January 1890.

86 Oneat Chegualaguala on the frontier between Gazaland and the Makalakas, the other with the last chief of the Duma tribe, presumably the Amaduma of the 1889 Carta de Moçambique, located between the lower Nuantesi and the Lundi.
87 J. C. de Alegria Rodrigues to Sec. Geral, 18/11/89, AHU, Moç., 1 Rep., Pasta 3 — a 28 folio letter.
88 Notably Frank Colquhoun and William Churchill to Salisbury, 14/9/89, C 5904, p. 148; Petre to Gomes, 11/11/89, PRO, FO 179/270; Petre to Salisbury, 14/11/89, 155 Af., CP 5970, p. 254.
89 Ignacio to Sec. Geral, 4/1/89, *Bol. Off.*, 23/2/89.
90 Andrada, Caureze, to Min., 1/7/89, tel. via Lourenço Marques, *Neg.* (1890), p. 65; and 18/8/89, ibid., p. 69; and 6/10/89, Nec., SPZ 2.
91 Ignacio, 1/2/89, Aruangua, *Bol. Off.*, 11/1/90, p. 14.
92 Andrada, from Quelimane, to Dir. Geral, 27/12/89, AHU, Moç., 2 Rep., Caixa 6.

8

ZAMBEZIA 1879–1889

Events in Zambezia also contributed to the ultimatum of 1890. There Portugal, so far from extending the frontiers of her authority, had for long remained on the defensive. Her prestige remained low from memory of the reverses inflicted by Bonga, and from constant humiliations by the Landeens; there was also some apprehension as to the attitude of the Makololo, supported as they now were by British missionaries and traders. The residents of Sena, in particular, felt themselves to be constantly menaced.

Violence burst in a short but sharp uprising on the *prazos* down-stream from Sena. Revolting *colonos* around Mazaro and Mopeia, in 1878, razed plantations, sacked houses and stores, interrupted commerce. Some of the inhabitants of Quelimane planned to make a last ditch stand in the government buildings covered by the only four cannon available, while others asked the British vice-consul for his protection. This proved to be unnecessary, for the Governor-general rushed down to co-ordinate the defence; eighty troops sent aboard a tug (the only warship in Moçambique could not sail because she had no engineer) joined 1,100 sepoys contributed by more fortunate *prazo*-holders. The basic reason for the uprising, according to the British vice-consul, was the harsh treatment by *prazo*-holders of their negroes; it was precipitated by a census, taken by troops, which was essentially for poll-tax purposes but which would, the *colonos* feared, be only a preliminary step towards enslavement or forcible enlistment. Two educated Indian mulattoes fanned the embers. The uprising was soon suppressed, but the Governor-general commented bitterly on the degradation it had revealed in Portuguese authority in Moçambique. Practically the only troops he had at his disposal were black, from either Africa or India; he urged on his minister the necessity for 500 European soldiers, armed with machine-guns, and for an effective gun-boat to show the flag. As conditions were, he had been forced to rely again on *prazo*-holders and their armed retainers. Kirk, from his observation post at Zanzibar, remarked to the British Secretary of State that these *prazo*-holders and their followers were little better than bandits, as liable to defy the Government as to support it.[1]

Rumours that the notorious Bonga was again raising stockades, sending out his sepoys on raids, and threatening to close the Zambezi, caused renewed despondency in administrative and commercial circles. The reports may have

1 A. M. Cardozo to GG, 23/10/78, AHU, Moç., 1 Rep. Pasta 1; GG to Min., 24/10/78, 450, AHU, Moç., Pasta 31; 6/11/78, 1 Rep. Pasta 1; 19/11/78, 265, ibid.; 8/12/78, 287, ibid.; 3/2/79, 2/43, ibid.; 26/2/79, 2/53, Relatório, ibid.; G. Hölm, A/Brit. Consul, Moçambique, to S of S, 25/11/78 FO 179/215; Kirk to Salisbury, 10/12/78, ibid.

been exaggerated; but he was still proudly exhibiting the skulls of the unfortunate Portuguese officers killed by his forces, and there was no knowing when he might seek to add to his trophies. There was jubilation in Sena and Tete and Quelimane when Bonga died. But such was the awe of his name and fear of his family that the Governor of Tete sent a detachment to give military honours to the body of this unrepentant rebel.[2] A brother, Inhamissenga, for long a refugee in Barue, declared himself the successor. Another brother, Morima, and several nephews, opposed this claim. Traders fled to avoid the war which appeared inevitable. Morima prevailed; and though he was a matricide the Governor of Tete promptly appointed him *capitão-mor*,[3] so that there should be at least the semblance of authority in those parts—and lest the British acquire the *prazo* of Massingire.[4]

Macombe, the king of the Barue, was an independent potentate to whom the Portuguese used to give presents in the hope of maintaining friendly relations. Whenever the gifts fell into arrear the chief expressed his contempt for the authorities of Sena, and disrespect even for Manoel António da Sousa. His support was essential for the re-occupation of the fairs of Manica and Quiteve.[5] The Governor-general was very disturbed when a passing Englishman taught him the secret of making gunpowder; he feared that the natives might at any time destroy themselves—"and us".[6]

The Governor-general, in view of these dangers, in 1880 appreciated that the time had come to put into effect the decree of 1854 abolishing *prazos*. Holders of *prazos* were invited to present to the secretary of the Junta da Fazenda within 180 days documents to prove their title and the number of lives for which each estate had been granted: a tribunal would then judge the indemnity to be paid.[7] The Governors of Quelimane and Tete were required to report which *prazos* could be grouped together for administrative and ecclesiastical purposes, each under a commissioner who would have the powers of a district judge; as far as possible each group should be roughly equal in population, homogeneous, with common customs, and served by communications.[8] O'Neill considered the organization envisaged most excellent on paper; it would be an important step in the breakdown of slavery and the feudal system in Zambezia. But there was little prospect that it would ever be put into effect: the most powerful landowners would doubtless be left in peaceful possession of their estates. There might, however, be some extension of authority over districts where Portuguese authority was purely nominal, and in the hands of

2 GG to Min., 2/1/79, 2/1, AHU, Moç., 1 Rep. Pasta 1; and 26/2/79, 2/53, ibid.; and 17/9/80, 2/232 ibid.; Bayão, Gov., Tete, to Sec. Geral, 28/2/81, Civil 18, ibid.
3 GG to Min., 15/10/79, AHU, Moç., 1 Rep. Pasta 1.
4 GG to Min., 20/11/79, 305, AHU, Moç., Pasta 32; A. M. Cardozo to GG, 3/10/79, ibid.
5 GG to Min., 20/11/79, 305, AHU, Moç., Pasta 32; A. M. Cardozo to GG, 1/11/79, ibid.
6 GG to Min., 17/9/80, 2/202, AHU, Moç., 1 Rep. Pasta 1.
7 F. M. da Cunha, GG, portaria 28, 10/2/80, *Bol. Off.*, 16/2/80.
8 GG, portaria, 29, 10/2/80, ibid.

8 Paiva de Andrada, Serpa Pinto, A. M. Cardoso, Vitor Cordon, Azevedo Coutinho (from J.C., 'A questão Luso-Britannica de Machona e de Nhassa, Chire e Makololos [1890], a sheet published by the *Diário Illustrado*, Lisbon)

PAIVA DE ANDRADA

SERPA PINTO

ANTONIO MARIA CARDOSO

VICTOR CORDON

AZEVEDO COUTINHO

irresponsible officials (commonly half-castes and natives) who had been guilty of the worst abuses. If the provisions were put into effect, O'Neill saw the prospect of some increase in revenue, of perhaps £5,000 per annum, which would permit the payment of officials.[9]

The most frank opinions about the position in Zambezia were expressed by a new Governor, Major Francisco Pinheiro Baião.[10] Baião promptly reported that the lords of the *prazos* were living in a state of almost complete independence. To maintain the peace at Sena it had been necessary to appoint as *capitão-mor* one Ferrão, "chief of the highwaymen", who had murdered his predecessor; as adjutant, one António, lover of a certain Ana Cativa, who had murdered three previous lovers. It was also necessary to tolerate war on the king of Barue by António de Sousa, who dominated Sena and the interior by terror. He recalled the death of Bonga and the succession of Morima. Baião protested against these dishonours to the Portuguese nation: "All the robbers around here," he exclaimed, "are appointed *capitães-mores*".[11]

The longer Baião stayed in Zambezia the greater appeared to him to be the fiction of Portuguese power: such power as there was lay with the lords of the *prazos*, supported by their private armies and their slaves—for the abolition of slavery had never been proclaimed up the Zambezi. The Government granted concessions for the exploitation of mines, but the inhabitants refused to reveal them, and the Government did not have the means to oblige them. It conceded forests, but they were burnt each year. It conceded lands, but these lands it did not possess. "The land and power and sovereignty are divided among the lessees of the *prazos*, the *capitães-mores*, the white kafirs and the black kafirs, who have kept this country in a completely primitive and savage state." There was no security for the resident or the traveller. At rumours of wars the soldiers fled; but this was not surprising, for most had been snatched from the streets of Luanda and were usually unpaid and starving. To expel the battalion and return it to the coast did not solve the Governor's problem. Most power in the district still rested with the Bonga family. The *capitão-mor* of Guengue, D. Luiza's lover, had recently died; D. Luiza, sister of Bonga, would not accept a new delegation of the Government. Bonga himself was restoring his stockades and already demanding gifts from travellers ascending the Zambezi. Chief Zuda, a descendant of Monomotapa, was re-occupying lands on the way to Zumbo, once under governmental control. In Zumbo there was anarchy: it had no garrison, and "the *capitão-mor* and the *sargento-mor* are two kafirs." Anybody wishing to go to Manica had to have recourse to the protection of António de Sousa, "an Indian Kafir" chief, "chief of the bandits"—and *capitão-mor*. In short, Zambezia presented "the saddest example that the government of a country can reach." So serious did the situation appear, with the possibility of war on the two fronts of Bonga and Zuda, and so likely the cutting of

9 O'Neill to Salisbury, 13/4/80, ST 30, CP 4498, p. 227.
10 GG to Min., 2/11/80, 2/224, AHU, Moç., 1 Rep. Pasta 1 protesting against his appointment (from being Governor of Angoche) because of his odd ideas which at times were almost subversive.
11 Bayão to Sec. Geral, 28/2/81, Civil 18, AHU, Moç., 1 Rep. Pasta 1.

navigation on the Zambezi, that Baião even contemplated retreating to the British missions in Nyasaland, going so far as to send an officer there to carry out a reconnaissance. Baião urged that an enquiry be held into the critical situation on the Zambezi; he proposed, as a matter of urgency, the establishment of Portuguese river-steamers on the Zambezi, with service to Zumbo and even beyond, the definition of boundaries, and the re-assertion of Portuguese authority.[12]

The Governor-general dismissed Baião for "mental derangement" and insubordination. But to his minister he had to admit the truth of Baião's accusations: because of lack of men and of means there had indeed been a shameful policy of appeasement and concession on the Zambezi; the situation was as Baião had portrayed it: and he supported Baião's demand for men and money, and an enquiry.[13]

In the Ministry of Ultramar, too, it was recognized that Baião was speaking the truth.[14] The Governor-general accordingly instructed his Secretary-general to go to Tete and hold an enquiry. He was to enquire into the state of the district, especially as to government and administration; he was to check on the *capitães-mores;* he was to inspect the forces and finances; he was to examine municipal and ecclesiastical administration and justice; he was to assess the strength of the *prazos;* he was to investigate foreign commerce. He was then, if possible, to travel up the Shire River, and report on the Makololo. He was to visit Blantyre; while assuring the missionaries of the Government's interest in their welfare, he was to observe their activities and report on whether it would be advantageous to take them under Portuguese dominion, or how else their influence could be combated.[15] But the Secretary-general was too attached to life to carry out this programme. The day he left Sena for Tete he diplomatically developed fever; in Tete he had to lie prostrate, too ill to ask a single question; and the fever did not leave him until he set foot on the ship which carried him away from the Zambezi.[16]

The new Governor of Tete had again to resort to alliance with the most powerful *prazo*-holders. Of these, António de Sousa was more than ever pre-eminent. Any day he could put 10,000 or 12,000 men into the field. He had married a daughter of the king of Barue, and when Macombe died, and he governed the tribe in the name of his son, he could command tens of thousands of warriors. The Governor-general described him as indeed an enemy to be feared—or a friend to be cherished. Andrada, whose plans depended largely on Sousa, declared that if 30 or 40 *contos* could be spent in the right quarter, any campaign in the Zambezi valley would be successful. The Governor-general appreciated the logic; he invited Sousa to Moçambique, where every courtesy

12 Bayão to Sec. Geral, 15/7/81, Civil 50, AHU, Moç., 1 Rep. Pasta 1; do. 21/7/81, Civil 52, ibid.; do. 21/7/81, Civil 53, ibid.; Camara Municipal, Tete, to GG, 23/7/81, ibid.; Bayão to Sec. Geral 31/7/81, 56, ibid.; do. 11/8/81, Milit, 18, ibid.; do. 22/9/81, Milit. 33, ibid.
13 GG to Min., 2/1/82, 3/4, ibid.; and 7/1/82, 2/25, ibid.; and 28/4/81, 2/142, ibid.; and 14/9/81, 2/260, ibid.; and 18/9/81, 2/277, ibid.
14 Costa F., memo., 9/11/81, and minute, 19/11/81, ibid.
15 GG Paço d'Arcos, instrucções, 11/12/81, to Sec. Geral, Almeida da Cunha, ibid.
16 Almeida da Cunha to GG., 5/12/82, ibid.

was extended to him. He received an undertaking that his children (aged seven and five) by his Baruean wife would be educated in Lisbon, and the heir guaranteed his seat on the tribal throne. The Governor-general further urged that the King of Portugal honour him.[17]

Sousa's rule of Barue was far from popular, and the disaffected found alliance with Victorino Vicente da Cruz, Inhamissenga, the successor to Morima. Hostilities between Sousa and Cruz were almost endemic. The Government's alliance with Sousa—though many regarded him as big a villian as Bonga—paid dividends, and in 1883 the Governor of Quelimane was able to take possession of Massingire, the *prazo* which was the key to the Shire valley, and where the Governor-general ordered a military command to be established.[18]

Farther up the Zambezi, too, circumstances changed to Portugal's benefit. A chief Capuianhica, resident some 50 miles south of the Zambezi, overran the Dande, collecting slaves and tribute from six different *prazos*. But the *capitão-mor* of Zumbo assembled 1,500 sepoys (half of them armed with muskets) at the mouth of the Umsengedsi and defeated him. A number of chiefs were brought back to allegiance and the *prazos*, after a pretence at auction, were again leased to the conquerors.[19] From Tete to Zumbo the only lands not now subject to the Portuguese were those of Zuda, on the right bank of the Quebrabasa rapids, and of Senga, on the left bank above Quebrabasa.[20]

Before long Portuguese authority extended above Zumbo, up the Luangwa[21] and up the Zambezi. Especially significant was the conquest of Bruma:[22] but even above Bruma another *prazo* was leased, 60 miles from Zumbo.[23]

On the lower Zambezi the Portuguese hold was more precarious. Massingire was once more swept by disorders, but these were instigated by the Makololo, and so will be referred to in the next chapter.[24] A column soon smothered the revolt and re-opened the Zambezi to navigation.

The success of these operations encouraged António de Sousa to plan the final liquidation of his arch enemy, "the accursed Bonga". He proposed to Governor-general Coelho a campaign, the pretext for which would be the private

17 GG to Min., 3/12/81, 2/317, ibid.; and 10/10/82, 2/237, ibid.; including reciept by the Director of the Escola Academica for the children, 23/12/82.
18 GG Coelho to Min., 18/5/83, 2/154, AHU, Moç., 1 Rep. Pasta 3; Nunes to Kirk, 3/9/83, CP 4914, p. 202; GG to Min., 7/9/83, 2/260, AHU, Moç., 1 Rep. Pasta 3; do. 12/9/83, 2/268, ibid.; GG to Min. 14/11/83, 2/327, ibid.
19 [José Luis] to Sec. Geral, 24/9/83, ibid.; José Luis and others to Sec. Geral, Umsengedzi, 26/10/83, ibid.; GG to Min., 9/1/84, 2/20, ibid.; and 24/1/84, 2/32, ibid., reporting possession of the lands of Capuianhaca Chingudue, Cambango, and Caroeira; Termo de vassalagem, 26/2/84, *Termos*, pp. 25–6, of Mucumbue (Moraes de Almeida, the only bidder, got the *prazo* for 45 milreis a year for 3 years; he was to develop civilization, collect a reasonable tribute, treat the coloureds humanely and improve communications.)
20 GG to Min., 29/6/84, 212, AHU, Moç., 1 Rep. Pasta 3. For reports of travel on the Zambezi at this period see V. C. Courtois, *Relação* . . . 8/7/84, *Bol. Off.*, 8/11/84, pp. 209–11, and 'Viagem as Terras de Makanga' . . . 18/8/85, *Bol. Off.*, 17/7/86, pp. 358–61, and *Bol. SGL*, 1885, pp. 502–20.
21 e.g. Luango, 70 Km above Zumbo, Termo de vassalagem, 26/3/85, *Termos*, pp. 31–2, and Hilara, 25/10/85, ibid., pp. 34–5.
22 Termo de vassalagem, 30/6/85, ibid., pp. 32–3.
23 Termo de vassalagem, Pancha, 27/12/85, pp. 38–9.
24 See pp. 163–6.

differences between the two *prazo*-holders; all that he asked for from the Government was a grant of 30 *contos* for arms and ammunition, and permission for them to be imported into Zambezia free of customs duties.[25] Augusto de Castilho, whose acquaintance with the Zambezi—and the Bonga family—extended back to 1874,[26] succeeded Coelho. Castilho, on his way to Moçambique to assume office, called at Quelimane, where Sousa visited him and repeated his plans. Castilho gained the impression of a man of rare energy; he quite appreciated why Sousa should be so feared in Zambezia; but he was convinced that the Government could trust completely in Sousa's loyalty. Since the Government did not have the force to carry out a campaign of its own, it was better for it to support this expedition than allow chronic exactions from traders using the Zambezi, and perpetual threats of the complete closure of communication. Castilho therefore decided to accept Sousa's offer, except for the waiver of duties.[27]

While plans for the projected campaign were maturing something approaching prosperity came to the Zambezi, with popularization of the Inhamissengo mouth of the Zambezi, which now boasted a lighthouse. Some fifteen miles up the river there was laid out on the muddy mangroved banks the new town of Conceicão, where a Netherlands trading house established a base, soon to be followed by the African Lakes Company and other concerns. Quelimane fell into disuse as a port of entry and Mopeia, at the end of the portage from the Cuacua, with its stone-bastioned timber stockade, was deserted. Shupanga was defended by a bastioned wall, but it was confidently anticipated that Landeen attacks would become a thing of the past with settlement on the Pungue. But Chimoara, the custom post at the junction of the Shire and Zambezi, needed defence.[28]

The Governor of Tete found it expedient to continue to send presents to the Bonga. When Victorino Vicente Cruz died suddenly, there were rumours that he had been poisoned, and Portuguese settlers feared attack, but his successor, António Vicente Cruz, better known as Chatara, sent an embassy which paid his homage. The situation remained critical, however, because Sousa was making no secret of the proposed campaign, while the Governor of Tete was announcing that he had no confidence in Sousa.[29] Sousa meanwhile was putting forward his detailed plans for the expedition, which would be mounted by 5,000 men armed with fire-arms, supported by a further 2,000 warriors who would construct stockades and other fortifications.[30] Chatara adopted a provocative attitude, but Castilho waited in vain for a cable from Lisbon authorizing the war. In a repeated request for authority to wage immediate war he urged also the necessity for two shallow-draught river

25 Antonio de Sousa to Gov., Quelimane, 13/6/85, AHU, Moç., 1 Rep. Pasta 3.
26 Augusto de Castilho, *Relatório da Guerra da Zambesia em 1888* (Lisbon, 1891), pp. 8–9.
27 Castilho, GG, to Min., 18/7/85, 1/–, AHU, Moç., 1 Rep. Pasta 3.
28 GG to Min., 14/12/85, –/396, ibid.
29 Ibid., 21/9/85, 4 Confid., ibid. Across the top of the letter is a minute, presumably by Chagas, dated 9/11/85: "I do not comment on the part of this letter that refers to Manuel Antonio de Souza!!"
30 Sousa to GG, 23/9/85, ibid., GG to Min., 17/10/85, 1/7, ibid., approved by Chagas 1/12/85.

gun-boats, each mounting a Hotchkiss and a battery of rockets, which would help restore Portuguese authority on the Zambezi as far as the Quebrabasa rapids and up the Shire River to the Murchison Falls.[31]

Chatara raided outwards from Massangano.[32] But it was an event farther in the interior which gave the pretext for immediate action. Rupire had been garrisoned by sepoys of Sousa, with outlying stockades as far as the Mazoe. Chief Mtoko, a nominal vassal of Portugal, raided into this area. Sousa marched to castigate this chief, in March 1887, and though he defeated a force which he claimed to total 5,000, on the night of the decisive battle all his levies fled, save two or three hundred. He fell back on Rupire, and was planning a new campaign against Mtoko with Ferreira Simões, Governor of Manica, and Andrada, when he learnt that Chatara, at the request of Mtoko, was preparing to attack Portuguese stockades on the Mazoe. It was then decided to concentrate forces not against Mtoko, but against Chatara. Castilho authorized four columns to take the field. One, from Tete, was directed against stockades erected by Chatara in the direction of that town; one, under the *capitão-mor* of Chicoa, against Chatara's stockades on the lower Mazoe; one, from Sena, against stockades on the Muira; and the main body, consisting of 4,000 of Sousa's sepoys and a force from Manica, of thirteen white soldiers and three pieces of artillery, against Chatara's main stockade at Massangano. The Manica detachment was under the particular direction of Andrada, while Major Ferreira Simões commanded the entire campaign. On 5 September 1887 an attack went in against the outlying stockade of Pindirire, on the Luenha River; after dark the defenders withdrew. On 13 September the main force faced Massangano; that night Chatara and his followers fled. His brother Motontora betrayed him, and surrendered him bound to the Portuguese authorities at Tete. Chatara's stockades were destroyed. But the Portuguese jubilation was marred by the fate of Ferreira Simões, who in a delirium of fever thought he was under attack, and shot three inoffensive tribesmen before turning his fire-arm on himself.[33]

In any case the rejoicings were premature. Andrada had not thought it necessary to garrison Massangano, and before long Motontora started reorganizing opposition to Portuguese traders and authority. To begin with he confined his activities to the north bank of the Zambezi, but early in 1888, after invoking the spirits of his ancestors, he formally refused to pay tribute and began to collect his forces, while in May he was strong enough to rob merchants on their way up the Zambezi, and to attack two posts of Sousa's south of the Zambezi. He rebuilt the stockade at Massangano. Navigation on

31 GG to Min., 5/3/86, –/3, ibid. For description of the lower Zambezi at this time see M. R. Pereira de Carvalho, 'Relatório', *Bol. Off.*, 6/11/86, pp. 547–50.
32 GG to Min., 17/3/87, 2/46, AHU, Moç., 1 Rep. Pasta 2; A. C. d'Oliveira Gomes, Gov., Tete, Relatório, 28/3/87, *Bol. Off.*, 9/7/87, pp. 302–6.
33 Castilho, *Relatório*, pp. 37–8, 57; Paiva da Andrada to Dir. Geral of Ultramar 12/6/87, 38, AHU, Moç., 1 Rep. Pasta 2 (a very valuable report of 35 pages, incorporating much information about the tribes of Zambezia) and 10/7/87, 41, ibid., 9/8/87, 44, ibid.; GG, portaria 419, 14/10/87, *Bol. Off.*, 15/10/87, p. 474, praising operations by Andrada, which are summarized; GG to Min., 14/10/87, 2/302, AHU, Moç., 1 Rep. Pasta 2; Andrada, 'Campanhas da Zambezia', *Bol. SGL*, 1887, pp. 715–38; GG to Min., 26/1/88, 2/31, AHU, Moç., 1 Rep. Pasta 4 summarizing campaigns against Bonga; Teixeira Botelho, II, pp. 252–8.

the Zambezi was again closed.[34] The Governor of Tete organized a force to castigate the rebel. One column built stockades on the lower Luenha to contain the enemy, while another attacked the stockade at Pindirire, capturing it on 13 June. Seven hundred men then moved against Massangano. Three hours after they arrived in front of this stockade the enemy made a surprise attack, and the Portuguese forces fled in disorder.[35] A cordon of stockades contained the rebels. But since the destruction of Bonga's power had been triumphantly proclaimed only the previous year, Castilho appreciated that stronger measures were necessary to restore Portuguese prestige. Such action was particularly necessary since it was already being declared in the chancelleries of Europe that Portugal was incapable of preserving order on her ancient trade route, the Zambezi, let alone governing vaster areas of Africa: it was essential to exercise effective occupation in the sense required by the Act of Berlin.[36]

Castilho reached Quelimane on 7 July. He learnt that this was no mere local rising but a widespread movement against Portuguese dominion. The Bonga brothers had been joined by the chiefs and tribesmen of Macanga and Rupire, and numbers of the elders of Barue had taken advantage of Sousa's absence in Portugal to join the alliance.[37] Sousa, who had been feted in Lisbon, returned to the Zambezi in August. Motontora sent an embassy to Tete which returned the Portuguese flag lost on 21 June, and declared that if the Portuguese forces would disperse he would demolish his Massangano stockade and make submission. The Portuguese authorities threw the ambassadors into prison except for one who was allowed to return with the message that if Motontora really wanted peace he must come in person to Tete. A force of 3,000 sepoys arrived from Manica and built a stockade, which mounted a Hotchkiss gun, facing Massangano. A few nights later this force advanced, and built another stockade only a few hundred yards short of the enemy. Forces from Tete, their morale now recovered, crossed the Luenha and also built a stockade to help confine the enemy. On 3 October the Portuguese attacked a hill which overlooked Massangano. As General Teixeira Botelho has remarked,[38] one piece of artillery in action there, and a few hundred fire-arms, would soon have forced the surrender of Massangano. But the Portuguese allowed themselves to be pushed off the hill, and another attack on it on 6 October proved abortive. It was decided to weaken the defenders by starvation. Patrols on the opposite bank of the Zambezi blockaded the stockade from receiving provisions from that side, while a fortified post on an island denied the defenders access to fresh water. Motontora's followers were close to starvation when Castilho ordered

34 C. J. D. de Castro to Gov., Quelimane, 5/6/88, AHU, Moç., 1 Rep. Pasta 4; GG to Min., 23/6/88, 2/191, ibid.; J. J. Ferreira, A/Gov., Manica, to Sec. Geral, 25/6/88, 35, ibid.; GG to Min., 3/7/88, tel., Nec., Soberania Portuguesa em Zambesia, 1; A/Sec. Geral. to Min., 7/7/88, 2/219, AHU, Moç., 1 Rep. Pasta 4.
35 J. Hiller, vicar, Tete, to GG, 28/11/88; Castilho, Relatório, pp. 85-9; J. de Carvalho to Sec. Geral, 15/6/88, ibid., pp. 91-5; Oliveira Gomes, Gov., Tete, to Sec. Geral, 22/6/88., pp. 97-8; G. Duarte, A/Gov. Quelimane to Dir. Geral, 27/7/88, Extra, AHU, Moç., 1 Rep. Pasta 4.
36 Castilho, Relatório, p. 60.
37 GG to Min., 7/7/88, AHU, Moç., 1 Rep. Pasta 4.
38 Teixeira Botelho, II, p. 260.

a general attack on 27 November. The hill was re-occupied, and the force from Tete adopted a more advanced post. Artillery fire, from an eight-centimetre piece, and Hotchkiss and small-arms fire continued all that day and through 28 November. That night the defenders fled.[39]

The Portuguese took possession of Massangano, and it was announced that a fort would be erected there, to be named after Princeza Amelia.[40] But before this could be done, there was a renewed crisis in Zambezia. Tribesmen attacked the seventy-five-man strong Portuguese garrison at Macanga. One officer committed suicide; two other officers and twenty soldiers were killed; the survivors fled in disorder to Tete, where there was great panic, lest the town be attacked. The Acting Governor told the townsmen that the Government had no means of assisting them, and that if they were attacked it was a case of every man for himself. The garrison at Massangano was attacked, and held its own only with difficulty. It was clear that the Bonga power was not yet broken, the lower Zambezi valley not yet pacified,[41] and a considerable campaign would have to be mounted finally to impose peace and authority.[42]

The basic cause for these uprisings was clear to Castilho, who urged the Government to reconsider the whole matter of *prazos*. All honest and patriotic Portuguese with knowledge of the region agreed that the whole *prazo* system and the custom of granting the holders nominal titles of *capitão-mor* and *sargento-mor* was a public calamity.[43] The office of *capitão-mor* should be abolished for it went only to powerful individuals with large armies, which existed primarily for the sake of pillage and to enslave the blacks. Only by the Government assuming direct, sovereign authority, Castilho insisted, would it be possible to raise the bulk of the inhabitants from their servile condition and make effective the decree of April 1875. Only by such direct administration would it be possible for the Government to obtain worthwhile revenues, which still went into the pockets of a few sybaritic potentates; commerce would prosper; and the manifestation of strong government would silence criticisms by foreigners. The necessity had been proved for a river gun-boat. The telegraph should be extended as rapidly as possible from Mopeia, its then limit, up the Zambezi. He recommended further a programme of road and railway construction. At Massangano the bones of the Cruz family should be exhumed,

39 O'Neill to Salisbury, 4/1/89, 3, CP 5970, pp. 20–1; J. Ferreira, A/Gov. Manica to Gov. Quelimane, 11/7/88, AHU, Moç., 1 Rep. Pasta 4; A. C. de O. Gomes, Gov. Tete to Sec. Geral, 14/7/88, Civil 49, *Bol. Off.*, 26/1/89, pp. 50–2; GG to Min., 19/7/88, Extra 7, AHU, Moç., 1 Rep. Pasta 4; and 20/7/88, 2/231, ibid.; and 30/7/88, Extra 18, ibid.; GG to Gov. Manica, 31/7/88, 19, ibid.; GG to Min., 31/7/88, Extra 20, ibid.; and 6/8/88, Extra 22, ibid.; and 17/8/88, Extra 26, ibid.; Sec. Geral Almeida to Min., 18/8/88, 2/258, ibid.; GG to Min., 28/8/88, Extra 37, ibid.; do., 3/10/88, Extra 61, ibid.; do., 2/11/88, Extra 86, ibid.; Sec. Geral to Min., 12/11/88, 2/246, ibid.; Termo, 29/11/88, *Bol. Off.*, 2/2/89, pp. 93–4; Castilho, *Relatório*, pp. 60–74; Teixeira Botelho, II, pp. 260–2.
40 Termo, 29/11/88, *Bol. Off.*, 2/2/89, pp. 73–4.
41 GG to Min., 28/5/88, 2/189, AHU, Moç., 1 Rep. Pasta 4; A. C. de O. Gomes to GG, 26/10/88, 50, ibid.; GG to Min., 30/10/88, 2/84, ibid.; and 2/11/88, 2/85, ibid.; O'Neill to Salisbury, 6/12/88, 61 Af., FO 179/263; Sec. Geral to Min., 9/12/88, 3/190, AHU, Moç., 1 Rep. Pasta 4; O'Neill to Salisbury, 4/1/89, 3, CP 5970, pp. 20–1.
42 A. de C. M. Pimentel to Sec. Geral, 30/11/88, *Bol. Off.*, 13/1/89, p. 21.
43 M. H. Maas, 12/88, 'Duas palavras acerca dos prazos de coroa de Quelimane', *Bol. Off.*, 5/1/89, pp. 10–12; Gomes, Gov., Tete, 22/2/89, 'Relatório,' *Bol. Off.*, 6/7/89, pp. 413–9.

and a strong fort completed. The duty on arms and powder should be increased; it would be better still, he added, if the sale of powder were made a government monopoly, like that of tobacco. A military command should secure the Quebrabasa portage, while above the rapids more steam-launches should be placed on the river. He urged the introduction of white couples from Madeira and the Açores, and their establishment on elevated territory in the Macanga and Zumbo areas. He urged too the establishment of a district governorship based on Zumbo to serve the upper Zambezi. Moçambique was the richest province belonging to the Portuguese Crown; but it needed, urgently, to be directly administered, civilized and developed.[44]

But the Government was not prepared to advance along the path of direct control. Castilho forwarded to Lisbon a report by an inspector of *prazos*, which declared unequivocally that slavery and injustice were still common on the *prazos*, citing specifically conditions at Guengue and Goma. Castilho again demanded authority to take measures to strengthen governmental authority and extend the rule of law.[45] When he received no reply to his representations he threatened to resign.[46] A curt telegram from the minister to Castilho in February 1889, declared, "Accepting the divergence on the question of *prazos*, the Government has resolved to accept your resignation."[47]

The Portuguese Government even though it did not agree with Castilho's *prazo* policy admitted the necessity for doing something to develop Zambezia. It approved, for instance, a survey for a railway line from Quelimane to Sena,[48] and of a road from Tete to Cachombo, so by-passing the Quebrabasa rapids. To assist in these enterprises the Government sent out about thirty Portuguese, some of them accompanied by their wives, and an engineer, Vitor Cordon.[49] It was this same Cordon who, sent on a mission to Mashonaland, threatened to baulk Rhodes and the British South Africa Company of the fruits of their efforts, and so helped precipitate the crisis with Britain.

British travellers had for long been visiting to the area north of the Limpopo River.[50] Subsequent travellers owed much to Robert Moffat, whose mission station at Kuruman proved so valuable a base, and whose remarkable friendship with the king of the Matabele, dating to the days when that tribe had been established in the Transvaal,[51] greatly facilitated visits by his countrymen who were traders, ivory hunters and sportsmen in the first instance, and rendered possible the establishment of a London Missionary Society station at Inyati in 1859.[52] British interest in the area increased greatly after reports by Hartley of ancient mine-workings and Mauch's discovery of gold on the Tati and in

44 Castilho, *Relatório*, 14/4/89, pp. 77–82.
45 GG to Min., 24/6/88, 2/200, AHU, Moç., 2 Rep., Caixa 5.
46 GG to Min., 1/10/88, Extra 59, ibid.
47 Min. to GG, tel. 23/2/89, tel., *Bol. Off.*, 2/3/89, p. 149.
48 Petre to FO, 25/9/88, CP 5727, p. 110.
49 O'Neill to Salisbury, 13/9/88, 50, CP 5727, p. 119; ALC to Salisbury, 26/10/88, CP 5896, pp. 106–7.
50 See E.C. Tabler, *The far interior* (Cape Town, 1955).
51 See J.P.R. Wallis (ed.) *The Matabele journals of Robert Moffat* (London, 1945), 2 vols.
52 See J. P. R. Wallis (ed.) *The Matabele mission of J. S. & E. Moffat* (London, 1945).

Mashonaland in 1866.[53] There was great excitement when the London *Times* published an assay of 1,185 oz. of gold and 60 of silver to the ton from one sample.[54] In 1868 a group of London financiers sent out a party headed by that great traveller and artist Thomas Baines,[55] to prospect between the Limpopo and the Zambezi and Lobengula, the new king of the Matabele, in 1870 gave him a verbal concession which was confirmed in writing on 29 August 1871; it granted Baines, on behalf of the South African Gold Fields Exploration Company "full permission to explore, prospect, and dig or mine for gold in all that country lying between the Gwailo [Gwaai] River on the south-west and the Ganyana [Hunyani] on the north-east"; but, added Lobengula, "In making this grant I do not alienate from my kingdom this or any other portion of it; but reserve intact the sovereignty of my dominion." A sample of quartz assayed 60 oz. of gold and 17 of silver to the ton.[56] But no exploitation ensued, even after the publication of the discovery of the Zimbabwe ruins[57] focussed still more attention on the far interior. In 1872 Lobengula granted a concession to Swinbourne, of the London and Limpopo Company, to mine in the Tati area,[58] near the limits of Lobengula's authority on the borders of Bechuanaland.

By the London Convention of 1884 the South African Republic was forbidden to conclude any treaty with any state other than the Orange Free State, or with any tribes to the east or west, except with the approval of the British High Commissioner.[59] The Republic's attempt to absorb the petty republics of Stellaland and Goshen, which lay across the road to the north,[60] and Germany's action in south-west Africa, provoked the Warren expedition. Bechuanaland south of the Molopo River became a British colony, while the area northwards as far as 22° south latitude and westwards to 20° east longitude was declared under British protection.[61] That year, 1886, gold was proved on the Witwatersrand, and Rhodes in 1887, with the assistance of Rudd, an Oxford friend and business associate, formed the Goldfields of South Africa. The deed of trust of the company authorized revenue to be used for enterprises in the north.[62] But most of Rhodes's energies in 1886 and 1887 were devoted towards amalgamating the various diamond interests of Kimberley, with the deliberate intention of gaining sufficient wealth and power to carry the Union Jack northwards. Barnato, Rhodes's most serious rival, for long held out against such departure from purely business ends, but early in 1888 he threw in his hand, and De Beers Consolidated Mines came into existence. The trust deed

53 Tabler, pp. 273–4 and Mathers, *Zambesia*, pp. 203–10.
54 H. M. Hole, *The passing of the black kings* (London, 1932), p. 4.
55 J. P. R. Wallis, *Thomas Baines of King's Lynn* (London, 1941).
56 T. Baines, *The gold regions of South Eastern Africa* (London, 1877), pp. 12–31, and Mathers, *Zambesia*, pp. 229–32, 264–5.
57 Carl Mauch's Reisen im inneren von Süd-Afrika 1865–1872, Petermann's *geographischen Mittheilungen* (Gotha, 1874), VIII, No. 37.
58 Mathers, p. 265.
59 C 3947, 1884, p. 40.
60 J. A. I. Agar-Hamilton, *Road to the North* (London, 1937), p. 271; Lovell, pp. 46, 63.
61 C 4588, 1885, pp. 57, 81, 117; Lockhart and Woodhouse, pp. 101–5; W. W. Williams, *Life of General Sir Charles Warren* (Oxford, 1941), pp. 48–81; Agar-Hamilton, *Road to the North*, pp. 383–7.
62 Lockhart and Woodhouse, p. 130 etc.

conferred on the life-governors the widest powers. Dissentient shareholders in Barnato's Central Company appealed to the Supreme Court of the Cape Colony. J. Rose-Innes, their counsel, was reading from the trust deed the objects of the new company when the judge interrupted, remarking, "It would be far shorter to tell us what the company may not do." Rose-Innes continued, "they can do anything, and everything, my lord. I suppose since the time of the East India Company, no company has had such power as this. They are not confined to Africa, and they are even authorized to take steps for the good government of any territory; so that, if they obtain a Charter in accordance with their trust deed from the Secretary of State, they would be empowered to annex a portion of territory in Central Africa, raise and maintain a standing army, and undertake warlike operations."[63]

Rhodes's plans for northward expansion had suffered a setback when, early in 1887, his agent Fry failed to obtain a concession from Lobengula,[64] and they were positively prejudiced, when, in July 1887, the Grobler brothers persuaded Lobengula, now distracted by an ever-increasing number of concession-hunters, to renew an old alliance with the South African Republic. But the document on which he was induced to make his mark went beyond this purpose. The first two paragraphs, it is true, declared Lobengula to be an independent chief, an ally of the Republic, and proclaimed perpetual peace and friendship; but the third bound Lobengula "at all times, whenever he is called upon by the government . . . to grant any assistance, either by troops or otherwise . . ." while the sixth provided for the appointment at Lobengula's head kraal of consuls "who shall have civil and criminal jurisdiction over all subjects of the South African Republic."[65] By the London Convention there could be no legal grounds for protest by Britain unless the treaty could be proved to be fraudulent.[66] Rhodes appreciated that if foreign competition were to be eliminated he must have the assistance of the Imperial authorities. He sought out Hercules Robinson, the High Commissioner, in his Christmas retreat, and persuaded him of the urgency of the occasion. Rhodes could not induce him to take any very positive action, but suggested what amounted to an option over Lobengula's lands.[67] Robinson had already appointed the ex-missionary and magistrate, John Moffat, to be assistant commissioner for the Bechuanaland Protectorate and had envisaged the possible extension of that Protectorate northwards to the Zambezi.[68]

Moffat, when he received Robinson's instructions, was on a goodwill visit to Bulawayo. Lobengula hilariously repudiated rumours that he had agreed to a Transvaal Protectorate, declaring it "to be the best joke of the season, at which he never fails to laugh until his chair threatens to collapse under him."[69]

63 H. Raymond, *B. I. Barnato* (London, 1897), pp. 43–4; H. A. Chilvers, *Story of De Beers* (London, 1940), pp. 65–6; etc.
64 C 5237, p. 22.
65 C 5524, p. 2, C 5918, p. 149; M. J. Conchar, 'The Rudd Concession and Royal Charter', p. 77.
66 Conchar, pp. 8–9.
67 Fuller, p. 57, 65; Williams, pp. 120–1.
68 Robinson to Administrator, 28/7/87, C 5237, pp. 33–4, Robinson, commission to J. S. Moffat, 1/7/87, ibid., pp. 34–5.
69 J. S. Moffat to Shippard, 12/12/87, CO 5/89, pp. 1–4.

But he was concerned about prospectors and concession-hunters. The king had given Johnson, an ex-member of the Bechuanaland Border Police, a verbal authority to prospect between the Hunyani and Mazoe Rivers, in return for £100, and £200 a year if payable gold were found. He reported Mashonaland to be devastated and depopulated by Matabele raids. He penetrated to a point on the Mazoe reached by Portuguese traders. And he found gold in 124 places. On his return the King and his councillors, much disturbed because of unauthorized prospecting by other parties, fined him and expelled him from the country. He had proved the presence of payable gold, but "in its present state the country can never be developed, as there is not the very slightest security for investment of capital."[70]

Moffat resolved Lobengula's doubts and persuaded him to put his mark, on 11 February 1888, to a treaty in which he was declared to be "Ruler of the tribe known as the Amandebele, together with the Mashuna and Makalaka, tributaries of the same." Peace and amity were to continue for ever between the British and the Matabele people. "It is hereby further agreed to by Lo Bengula, chief in and over the Amandebele country with its dependencies as aforesaid, on behalf of himself and people, that he will refrain from entering into any correspondence or treaty with any foreign State or Power to sell, alienate, or cede, or permit or countenance any sale, alienation or cession of the whole or any part of the said Amandebele country under his chieftainship, or upon any other subject without the previous knowledge and sanction of Her Majesty's High Commissioner for South Africa."[71]

Shippard, the Administrator of Bechuanaland, regarded the agreement as no more than a gratuitous promise by the chief as an individual, and he criticized it for bearing the signatures of two Bechuanaland policemen in authentication of Lobengula's cross; he would have preferred the signatures of the principal councillors to be appended, or a more formal instrument to be negotiated.[72] Knutsford, the Secretary of State for the Colonies, was also dubious about the agreement, especially since he had reason to believe that the *indunas* were opposed to it, and acceptance of it would involve Britain in responsibility for Lobengula's territory.[73] But Robinson declared the agreement to be valid: three *indunas* had been present at the discussions and were consenting parties; it was not the custom of the country for *indunas* to sign such documents; and Lobengula would resent any suggestion as to the inadequacy of his signature. Lobengula was being urged on many sides to make alliances and grant concessions: the agreement would help him reply to such applications; it should be ratified.[74] Knutsford observed that the agreement did not confer British

---

70 F. Johnson to Sec. to Administrator, 17/11/87, C 5363, pp. 40–2.
71 Treaty, C 5524, p. 13.
72 Shippard to Robinson, 9/3/88, CP 5727, pp. 22–3. He recalled that the German commissioners on the Angra Pequena Commission maintained that their government would not recognize the validity of any document purporting to bear the mark of a chief unless his mark was attested to by independent European witnesses; and the document, if professedly for sale, grant, lease or concession must have the approval of the tribe and bear the marks of the principal councillors.
73 Knutsford to Robinson, 29/3/88, CP 5727, p. 21.
74 Robinson to Knutsford, /3/3188, CP 5727, p. 22.

protection over Lobengula's territory but presumed that such a protectorate could be declared without consulting the South African Republic.[75] Salisbury had been quite prepared to denounce any Republican protectorate over Matabeleland on the pretext that the Matabele were not a tribe but a nation, and any agreement with them was limited by the London Convention.[76] The British Government ratified the Moffat treaty.[77] Transvaal interests were still planning a trek north of the Limpopo and Piet Grobler returned to Bulawayo to take up his consular duties. Returning to the Transvaal across a strip of territory in dispute between Khama and Lobengula he was attacked and fatally injured by Bechuana tribesmen.[78] The South African Republic was finally debarred from expansion northwards by a British proclamation declaring the country north of Bechuanaland and the Transvaal, south of the Zambezi, and between 20° east longitude and the Portuguese Province of Sofala as being within the sphere of British influence.[79]

Cawston, a London financier, decided to profit by the occasion and with financial support from the shareholders of the Bechuanaland Company, planned to send out Maund, who had served under Warren and was well known to Lobengula.[80] Rhodes on a visit to London heard of Cawston's plans;[81] urgent action was necessary. He hurried back to South Africa, and in August 1888 despatched from Kimberley a party consisting of Rudd, Maguire, a barrister by training, and Thompson, expert in native languages.[82] They reached Bulawayo on 21 September 1888 and had profitable talks with the King, thanks to the good offices of the missionary Helm. Maund arrived on 10 October, followed shortly afterwards by Renny Tailyour, the agent of the German SAR financier Lippert. But by then Rudd, who had presented a letter of commendation from the High Commissioner, had made considerable impression on Lobengula, and Shippard visited Bulawayo and gave further backing to Rudd's suit. On 30 October Lobengula put his mark to a document by which, in return for 1,000 Martini-Henry breech-loading rifles, 100,000 rounds of ammunition, a steam-boat on the Zambezi, and £100 per month,

> I Lobengula King of Matabeleland Mashonaland and certain adjoining territories in the exercise of my sovereign powers and in the presence and with the consent of my council of Indunas do hereby grant and assign unto the said grantees their heirs representatives and assigns jointly and severally the complete and exclusive charge over all metals and minerals situated and contained in my Kingdoms, Principalities, and dominions

---

75 CO to FO, 7/4/88 and FO to CO concurring, 20/4/88, ibid., pp. 21, 26.
76 FO to CO 28/3/88, CO 5/89, p. 14.
77 CO to FO 7/4/88, CO 5/89, p. 16; FO to CO, 20/4, p. 18.
78 For the lengthy enquiry conducted by Shippard see C 5918; R. C. Williams to Robinson, 18/5/88, CO 5/89, pp. 33–4.
79 Robinson, Knutsford, 20/6/88, CO 5/89, p. 40; CO to FO 19/7/88 ibid., pp. 49–50; FO to CO, 23/7/88, ibid., p. 50; Knutsford to Robinson, 24/7/88, tel., ibid., p. 51.
80 G. Cawston to CO, 30/5/88, CO 5/89, p. 31 and CO to Cawston, 4/6/88, p. 32.
81 Williams, p. 123.
82 C. E. Fripp and V. W. Hiller (eds.), *Gold and the Gospel in Mashonaland 1888* (London, 1949), pp. 150–1.

together with full power to do all things that they may deem necessary to win and procure the same.

Lobengula undertook to make no concession of land or mining rights from that date without the consent of the grantees.[83] Rudd and his companions promised Lobengula that "they would not bring more than ten white men to work in his country, that they would not dig anywhere near towns etc. and that they and their people would abide by the laws of his country and in fact be as his people." But these promises were not put in the concession.[84]

The terms of the concession were denounced by Bishop Knight-Bruce of Bloemfontein, who had reconnoitred Mashonaland in 1888 as a field for missionary enterprise, and who himself had advocated extension of the British protectorate to the Zambezi.[85] "Such a piece of devilry and brutality as a consignment of rifles to the Matabele cannot be surpassed," he declared.[86] He also denied Lobengula's right to make any concession relating to Mashonaland: "I contend that though it is necessary to ask permission from the Matabele to go into Mashonaland it could fairly be argued that Mashonaland does not properly belong to Matabeleland. A chief does not make war on his own subjects and devastate whole regions."[87]

Shippard, admirer of Rhodes, indignantly contradicted both statements: to arm the Matabele with rifles was a piece of humanitarianism; and Mashonaland belonged to the Matabele by right of conquest: "Does a white farmer forfeit his pigs because he kills a few at certain seasons?" he asked. "It is perfectly certain that Mashonaland is an integral part of the Matabele kingdom and must be dealt with accordingly."[88]

Maund, disappointed but not despairing, worked on Lobengula and obtained a concession of mineral rights in the Mazoe valley, which indicated that Lobengula regarded this area as outside his domain, or that he had not appreciated the monopolistic implications of the Rudd concession—or that he repudiated the Rudd concession. When it was suggested to the king that he had signed away his birthright, he decided to send two *indunas* to seek out the Queen. "Lobengula desires, if there is a Queen, to ask her to advise and help him, as he is much troubled by white men who come into his country and ask to dig gold. There is no one with him he can trust and he asks that the Queen will send someone from herself."[89] The deputation had the particular task of declaring that Rudd's concession was "not genuine". Maund conducted the deputation through the Transvaal, to avoid the Administrator of the Protectorate, and planned to keep the mission secret from the High Commissioner.[90]

83 For Rudd's diary see *Gold and the Gospel*, pp. 155–217, and for the concession, pp. 219–20.
84 C. D. Helm to London Missionary Society, 29/3/1889, *Gold and the Gospel*, p. 227.
85 *Gold and the Gospel*, introduction to Knight-Bruce's diary by C. E. Fripp, pp. 6–7.
86 Speech, 8/12/1888, *Gold and the Gospel*, pp. 137–8.
87 Knight-Bruce to Shippard, 7/12/88, CO 5/89, pp. 95–7.
88 Shippard, minute, CO 5/89, p. 98.
89 C 20/11/89, C 5918, p. 162.
90 E. A. Maund to Gifford, [12/88], received 21/12/88, CP 5727, p. 141; Gifford (Chairman, The Exploring Company), to FO, 27/12/88, ibid., p. 143; CO to FO, 10/1/89, CP 5970, p. 7; CO to FO 13/1/89, ibid., p. 8.

Gifford, chairman of the Exploring company, reported to the Colonial Office that there was every prospect of his company obtaining in Matabeleland the same rights as the Bechuanaland Exploration Company had obtained in Bechuanaland; there was a plan to build a railway through Bechuanaland; and he asked the Colonial Office whether it would approve the granting of a royal charter to his company, which would merge with others, for "settling, developing and trading" the area. The Colonial Office could not entertain such a proposal without report from the High Commissioner in South Africa;[91] that meant the end of Gifford's dreams of personal empire, for there was no secret as to where that official's sympathies lay: he promptly condemned Maund's proceedings as "embarrassing and improper".[92] Maund had to pass through Kimberley, where Rhodes tried to buy him.[93] The *indunas* saw the Queen, whose Secretary of State sent back to Lobengula an honest opinion:

> The Queen advised Lobengula not to grant hastily concessions of land, or leave to dig, but to consider all applications very carefully. It is not wise to put too much power into the hands of the men who come first and to exclude other deserving men. A king gives a stranger an ox, not his whole herd of cattle, otherwise what is there for other strangers coming to eat?"[94]

But little was said about the Rudd concession in London because Rhodes and his collaborator Beit, alarmed at Maund's mission, and at criticism of the Rudd concession in the House of Commons,[95] had hurried to England, and come to an agreement with Gifford and Cawston which amalgamated the several concerns in an association, the objects of which were to extend northwards, in the direction of the Zambezi, the railway and the telegraph; to encourage emigration and colonization; to promote trade and commerce; and to exploit the mineral resources of the region;[96] a royal charter was requested. The Colonial Office would not commit itself before it had seen the draft charter, the names of the directors, the provisions for securing the rights and interests of both Europeans and natives; "nor can the question whether such a scheme would be acceptable or otherwise to Lobengula be left out of consideration."[97] Lobengula was protesting that he had done no more than grant *a* place in which to dig for gold.[98] But his protests went unheeded, with the High Commissioner strongly supporting the proposed charter-company, which, with the

91 Gifford to CO 3/1/89, CP 5970, p. 91; CO to Gifford, 10/1/89, ibid., p. 92; Robinson and Gallagher, pp. 234–5.
92 Robinson to Knutsford, 12/1/89, CP 5970, p. 30, tel.
93 Lochhart and Woodhouse, pp. 149–50.
94 Knutsford to Lo Bengula, 26/3/89 C 5918, p. 164; CO to FO, 22/3/89, CP 5970, p. 40.
95 Bradlaugh quoted CO to G. Cawston, 14/5/88 (C 5524, p. 23), "Her Majesty's Government would give no countenance to any concession or agreement unless it were concluded with the knowledge of, and approved by, the High Commissioner." Baron H. de Worms replied that the High Commissioner regarded the Rudd Concession as "an advantageous arrangement on grounds of public policy" (*Neg.*, 1890, p. 10).
96 Gifford to Knutsford, 30/4/89, CP 5970, p. 90, and Rhodes, Beit and Rudd to Knutsford, 30/4/89, ibid., p. 91.
97 CO to Gifford, 16/5/89, CP 5970, p. 92.
98 Lo Bengula to Queen Victoria, 23/4/89, C 5918, p. 201.

financial support of De Beers and Goldfields behind it, could extend British influence without costing the British tax-payer a penny; through a royal charter, the Colonial Office felt, the British Government could then better control its activities, whereas a simple joint stock company might adopt a line of policy which could lead to complications involving perhaps even military operations.[100] The Colonial Office approved the draft of the charter which would empower the company to trade and work various concessions, and, when it acquired from chiefs grants of territory or powers of government, to assume such functions of government as the British Government thought fit. Its area of operation caused considerable discussion. The original draft referred to operations "in that region of territory of South Africa not belonging to any civilized Power, lying to the north of Bechuanaland, and to the west of Portuguese east Africa and in the basin and watersheds of the Zambezi to the north and south of that river." This definition, which would include Lake Nyasa (for Rhodes and Cawston were buying out the African Lakes Company) seemed to the Foreign Office to cover both immediate and future fields of activity;[101] on second thoughts, however, Salisbury decided to concur with Knutsford that the field should be described as "in the region of South Africa, south of the Zambezi, lying to the north of Bechuanaland, and to the west of the Portuguese possessions."[102] Rhodes wished to introduce some reference to the South African Republic, to dispel apprehensions there, and Knutsford was anxious to describe Bechuanaland as British Bechuanaland, to avoid ambiguity over the Protectorate. The next draft accordingly described the field as "north of British Bechuanaland and north and west of the South African Republic." The Colonial Office next enquired of the Foreign Office whether there should be any reference to the Portuguese possessions; and whether the company's activities should be confined to the south of the Zambezi.[103] There were proposals to operate not only in the Matabeleland and Nyasa area but also in Barotseland.[104] Lobengula wrote to the Queen assuring her again that he had not given away his country[105] but his letter was deliberately delayed by officials in South Africa, so that it took not a possible 49 but 110 days to reach London.[106] The Acting High Commissioner recommended that Lobengula be assured that by the proposed charter the company could explore his country, but there was no intention of interfering with his independence or his rights of sovereignty.[107] But his letter arrived too late for any such guarantee to be written into the charter.

100 CO to FO, 16/5/89. CP 5970, pp. 89–90, 28/6/89, ibid., 122–3; Robinson to CO, 18/10/89, ibid., p. 228–30.
101 CO to FO, 28/6/89, CP 5970, pp. 122–3 — encl. with minutes by HPA, 2/7/89, TVL 2/7/89 and Salisbury; Rhodes and Cawston to Ewing of ALC, 5/6/89, ibid., pp. 233–4; Cawston to Herbert, 1/7/89, ibid., pp. 128–30.
102 FO to CO, 5/7/89, CP 5970, p. 132.
103 CO to FO, 15/8/89, CP 5970, pp. 151–2.
104 J. Denoon Duncan to Salisbury, 6/7/89, CP 5970, pp. 140–1 re H. F. Julian concession; CO to FO, 30/8/89, ibid., p. 184.
105 Lo Bengula to Victoria, 10/8/89, CP 5918, p. 235, and CP 5970, p. 260 C.
106 Conchar, p. 62.
107 Smyth to Knutsford, 25/10/89, CP 5970, p. 260 B.

The British South African Company's charter was sealed on 29 October 1889. The principal field of operations was described as "the region of South Africa lying immediately to the north of British Bechuanaland, and to the north and west of the South African Republic and to the west of the Portuguese Dominions"; it set no northern limit. The company was empowered to negotiate for concessions granting "all or any rights, interests, authorities, jurisdictions and powers of any kind or nature whatever, including the powers necessary for the purposes of government and the preservation of public order." To preserve peace and good order the company was to establish a police force. Other clauses authorized the company "to settle any such territories and lands afore-said, and to aid and promote immigration. To grant land in terms of years or in perpetuity, and either absolutely or by way of mortgage or otherwise." The Secretary of State was required to approve the concessions, agreements, grants and treaties; and any difference between the company and any chief or tribe was to be submitted to him if he so required. But no machinery was established to ensure report and observation.[108]

The BSA Company's existence was based on a dubious concession to dig for gold. A message from the Queen assured Lobengula that the men sent by the company to dig for gold would recognize him as the king of the country, and they would exercise such powers as he entrusted to them.[109] But this was not Rhodes's intention. His immediate plan was the exploitation of the gold-fields of Mashonaland; and exploitation involved occupation. It seemed, however, as if the BSA Company might be anticipated in this area by the Portuguese.

The Portuguese base for penetration into Mashonaland was now Zumbo. Several Portuguese traders had established themselves there and in its neigh-bourhood,[110] so that when Knight-Bruce visited the place in 1888 it boasted eight houses,[111] and a Portuguese trader was established twelve days' journey above Zumbo, on Kasoko Island.[112] An increasing number of native chiefs paid homage to Portugal[113] but at times there were revolts; particularly to be feared was attack by Bruma, the most powerful chief in the area.[114] The middle Zambezi could be developed and a firm administration established at Zumbo only if communications were improved and this involved in particular a road or a railway past the Quebrabasa rapids. First the Massangano operations delayed Vitor Cordon, the engineer designated for this work, and then the revolt

108 Charter, 29/10/89, e.g. Neg., 1890, pp. 70–7.
109 Knutsford to Loch, 5/11/89, CP 5970, p. 260A.
110 e.g. J. de Araujo Lobo on the Panhame (Hunyani), GG, portaria 224, 23/5/87, Bol. Off., 28/5/87, p. 231.
111 Fripp and Hiller, p. 47.
112 A. Carnegie Ross, V/Consul, Quelimane, to Drummond, 21/8/88, CP 5727, p. 115.
113 Vieira Braga, Gov. Tete, 'Relatório', 1885, Bol. Off., 2/10/86, pp. 490–4. Vassalagem of prazo Pimbe, 15/7/86, Bol. Off., 20/11/86, p. 591 and Termos, p. 43; of Inhacoe, 18/8/86, Bol. Off., 20/11/86, p. 591, Termos, p. 44; of Chirenga, 16/12/86, Bol. Off., 26/3/87, p. 122 and Termos, p. 44; of Moringuge, 8/4/87, Termos, p. 45; of Moringuge, 27/7/87, Bol. Off., 30/7/87, p. 339; Bonham to Salisbury, 3/8/88, 77 Af., CP 5727, pp. 74–5.
114 GG Portaria, 91, 15/3/87, Bol. Off., 19/3/87, p. 105; A. Carlos, Relatório, 15/10/88, Bol. Off., 9/3/89, pp. 167–73.

of Bruma and tribes in the Dande,[115] but in the middle of 1889 Cordon, accompanied by the *capitão-mor* of Zumbo, was able to continue up-stream from Cachombo. Above the Kariba gorge and about the lower reaches of the Sanyati he obtained the vassalage of a number of local chiefs, obliging them to give any assistance necessary to Portuguese travellers; to send envoys to Zumbo to confirm their allegiance; and to obey all instructions emanating from the King of Portugal.[116] Some chiefs added that the Portuguese were the only white men they knew and with whom they had always had bonds of friendship and trade;[117] another declared he had always obeyed the King of Portugal.[118] Another chief established himself alongside Cordon's stockade at the junction of the Sanyati and Umfuli Rivers, called after Luciano Cordeiro, for defence against raiding Matabele[119] while others made no bones about it that they were accepting the Portuguese flag for the sake of the protection it would give them against Lobengula's impis.[120] Failing to meet Andrada, as planned, on the upper Sanyati, Cordon returned to Zumbo[121] (where he met an officer on his way to Mcheza's, ignorant of the diplomatic flurries that his achievements had occasioned.

A decree signed in Lisbon on 7 November 1889 and published on the 9th declared:

> Considering how important to the interests of the Portuguese nation it is to consolidate the dominion and sovereignty which it already exercises in the interior of the African continent and cause it to radiate out to various points (where its influence preponderates) in such a way as to ensure the greatest success for its humanitarian work in African civilization, in which for a long time the country has been employed; considering that for that end it becomes necessary to establish centres of force and official activity which can grant to legitimate commerce the protection it deserves in this

115 Vitor Cordon to GG, 14/11/88, 8, from Guengue, AHM, GG Avulsos, Caixa 8 (3); Ross to O'Neill, 31/12/88, CP 5970, pp. 22–3; Gomes, Tete, to Sec. Geral., 31/1/89, *Bol. Off.*, 31/3/89, p. 215; Jesus Xavier to Sec. Geral, 31/1/89, *Bol. Off.*, 25/5/89, p. 336; Cordon patriotically offered to lead the primitive expedition against Bruma: A. Carlos to Sec. Geral, 2/4/89, *Bol. Off.*, 25/5/89, p. 338; Milit. Commander, Zumbo, instruções to column, 16/4/89, AHU, Moç., 1 Rep. Pasta 5; Carlos and others, Termo de reunião, 16/4/89, ibid., Carlos to Gov. Tete, 1/5/89, 8, ibid. The Gov. of Tete was sceptical about the revolt and considered it existed mainly in the mind of the military commander. Leite Peixoto to Chefe, Repartição Militar, 19/6/89, Sec. Mil. 29, ibid. Pasta 4.
116 A. Carlos to Gov., Tete, 14/6/89, 62, ibid., Pasta 5; Termo de Vassalagem, Inhamaconde, 2/7/89, *Bol. Off.*, 14/9/89, pp. 56–7, *Termos*, pp. 67–8.
117 Termo, 9/7/89, Mudjinga, *Bol. Off.*, 14/9/89, p. 568. Termo, Chipuriru, 19/6/89, *Termos*, pp. 66–7.
118 Termo, 6/7/89, *Bol. Off.*, 14/9/89, p. 568, *Termos*, p. 68.
119 Acta, 12/8/89, Inhapunga, *Bol. Off.*, 31/12/89, pp. 721–2.
120 Acta, 15/8/89, Muiaforo of the Tongas, *Bol. Off.*, 21/12/89, p. 722, *Termos*, p. 71; Acta, 31/8/89, Tambo of the Tongas, ibid., p. 722 and *Termos*, pp. 74–75; Acta, 31/8/89, Monga, *Bol. Off.*, 21/12/89, p. 722, *Termos*, p. 73; Acta, 31/8/89, Sicauenga, *Bol. Off.*, p. 730, *Termos*, pp. 73–4; Acta, 31/8/89, Sechirombe, ibid., p. 730, ibid., p. 74; Acta, 5/9/89, Chissondele, ibid., p. 730 and p. 75; Acta, 12/9/89, Catecula, *Bol. Off.*, 14/12/89, p. 706; Acta, 12/9/89, *Bol. Off.*, 21/12/89, p. 721, *Termos*, p. 77.
121 Cordon to GG, 19/6/89, Inhapanje, 17, AHM, GG Avulsos, Caixa 8 (3); 2/7/89, Inhamaconde, 21, ibid.; 9/7/89, Luambe, 24, ibid.; 19/7/89, Aringa Luciano Cordeiro, 25, ibid., Carlos, Lumbi to Sec. Geral., 30/9/89, *Bol. Off.*, 21/12/89, p. 725; Peixoto, Tete, to Sec. Geral., 30/10/89, *Bol. Off.*, 30/12/89, p. 732 and 30/11/89, *Bol. Off.*, 15/2/90, p. 85.

development and at the same time to combat measures of enslavement and slavery which are yet in practice among the heathen and barbarous peoples of the interior; and considering how the ancient villa of Zumbo, on the left bank of the Zambezi, not only from the benignity of its climate and the fertility and richness of the territories which it dominates, and the extensive network of navigable rivers of which it is the centre,

the Government decided to establish a new district of Zumbo, with its capital in that town. Its boundaries were described as running from the junction of the Luangwa and Bissombo Rivers to the sources of the Luangwa, down the Luangwa to the Zambezi, along the Zambezi to its junction with the Umsengedsi, up the Umsengedsi to its source, and along the watershed above the sources of the Hunyani, Mazoe and Luia to a junction with the boundaries of the district of Manica. From there they ran along the sources of the Umfuli and along the Umfuli and Sanyati to the Zambezi, whence westwards. The district was to have a governor and a *capitão-mor*, and two military commanders, one at the junction of the Kafue and the Zambezi, the other at Mcheza's. There was to be a chaplain and a physician, and a superintendent of river services. There was to be at least one steam-launch, duly armed and equipped, and four Hotchkiss guns.[122]

A few days later J. J. Machado, the energetic and capable director of public works of the Province of Moçambique, addressed a meeting of the Sociedade de Geografia of Lisbon, which enthusiastically welcomed the provisions of the decree. He advocated the improvement of communication, and especially the construction of a railway line from Beira to the plateau of the upper Sanyati, which, he declared, was admirably suited for white colonization and the promotion of emigration from Portugal.[123]

Simultaneously, the Governor-general of Moçambique was putting his signature to a set of instructions for a Portuguese expedition to the upper Zambezi, to Barotseland. The object of the mission was

especially to call the chief of Barotseland to our dominion and sovereignty, trying by all persuasive means to achieve that those potentates beg for Portuguese protection and pay obedience and vassalage to His Majesty the King of Portugal with the greatest possible solemnity and publicity.[124]

But there had already been too much publicity about Portuguese achievements and intentions in south-central Africa for the peace of mind of the most resolute of Portugal's competitors. Events in Zambezia, coupled with those in Nyasaland, propelled them into action.

---

122 Rei, decree, 7/11/89, *Diaro do Governo*, 9/11/89, *Neg.*, 1890, pp. 85–7; Petre to Salisbury, 11/11/89, 148, CP 5970, pp. 251–2. The Governor's salary was to be £444; the total expenses £4,000 p.a. exclusive of officers' pay.
123 J. Machado, Questões Africanas: Fornecimento d'armas aos Matabelles . . ., *Bol. SGL*, 1889, pp. 18–9.
124 GG, instruções, to Henrique Carlo Lima, 9/11/89, with additions 16/11/89, AHU, Moç., 1 Rep. Pasta 6.

156

9

NYASALAND 1879–1889

The presence of the Protestant mission stations in the interior, that of the Church of Scotland at Blantyre, and of the Free Church at Livingstonia, had continued to be a cause of concern to the Portuguese authorities, especially from their double role: they were intended not only as centres for evangelization, but as industrial settlements. Applications for exemption from customs duties on goods landed at Portuguese ports caused embarrassment; but of more consequence was an assertion of civil jurisdiction by the missionaries within territory which the Portuguese regarded as being reserved for Portuguese activity and expansion.

Henderson, the first leader of the Blantyre party, had instructions from his Church "to act as the General Director and Christian Magistrate of the Settlement, having the Minister and the Doctor as assessors," it was his "duty to frame laws and regulations to extend the Settlement, and to keep out from it all traders who were attempting to bring liquor among the natives." The mission bought land from the nearby chief; it gave sanctuary to escaped slaves, and before long it controlled a belt thirty-five miles long, and seven villages. Henderson considered, "If we had nothing else but evangelistic and educational work, we could carry it on in this country without ourselves inflicting punishment beyond what is necessary for school discipline, but our position as a large industrial Settlement with considerable property of various descriptions, and our having now a number of people living round us who look to us as being in the place of chief, seems to necessitate the exercising of a certain amount of police power."[1]

Henderson thoroughly appreciated his lack of qualification for leadership and availed himself of the proximity of Cape Maclear to seek the advice of the Livingstonia leaders. Dr James Stewart returned to Lovedale at the end of 1877, and though he remained the nominal head of the mission, Dr Laws was actually in charge of it, helped especially by a volunteer worker, a cousin of the medical missionary, also called James Stewart. This Stewart, who was a civil engineer on leave from India, gave much material assistance to the Blantyre mission.[2] But one of his acts at least was unfortunate. In February 1878, he sentenced a man caught stealing, a subject of a Makololo chief, to five dozen lashes. Salt was rubbed in the man's back to harden it, and two days later he received a further ninety lashes, this time with a heavier whip. This incident set

1 Evidence taken before the Blantyre Commission: Evidence of Henry Henderson, CP 4437, pp. 31–2.
2 W. P. Livingstone, *Laws of Livingstonia* (London [1921]), pp. 105–7, 131.

a precedent for the Blantyre mission.[3] Rev. Duff MacDonald, its first clergy-man, reached Blantyre in July 1878; he relied heavily on the advice of the members of the mission who were more experienced than he in local ways.

Early in 1879 the body of a woman was found in the stream that ran past the Blantyre station; she had been murdered. Some weeks later there were rumours that two tribesmen, who had been trained as carpenters, had been responsible. They were required to make stocks for two, in which they were then placed. The Europeans and two headmen of the station then tried them in a travesty of a trial; it was considered sufficient that they could not prove an alibi, and they were sentenced to death. Rats ate holes in their feet, but one succeeded in escaping. The other, on 20 February 1879, was marched to his execution. A witness wrote, "Manga was placed at the head of his grave in a kneeling position, his hands and feet being tied. Eight shots were fired simul-taneously. Three bullets made flesh wounds in the arms, legs and sides. The others missed. Manga then rolled into his grave and stood erect. Another shot was fired which pierced his lung. Dr Macklin then ordered the man to be pushed into a lying position in his grave and to get another shot. I gave my gun to Kumalombe who blew out the man's brains."[4]

Flogging had continued. Several lads, for instance, had received up to ninety lashes for fornication, a punishment supervised by Buchanan, the gar-dener. Another case concerned a porter who delivered in Blantyre a case which had been opened, from which a packet of beads was missing. His guilt was immediately assumed, and Buchanan supervised the flogging. After he had received over one hundred lashes he was required to confess, which he did; but he could not lead his captors to where he had hidden the beads, so he was flogged again. He was marched out to witness the execution of Manga, and fully expected a like fate. Instead, he was flogged again at the graveside, and released. It subsequently emerged that he had been perfectly innocent: John Moir of the Trading Company had himself removed the beads and omitted to alter the invoice. But there was a still more serious case. Another porter was accused of stealing a box which had been entrusted to him. An artisan gave him seventy lashes. Buchanan then intervened, declaring that the man had "not had half enough"; he then ordered three native workers to continue, threatening to dock their pay if they desisted. Twice the man fainted, and was revived. After receiving a total of 270 lashes he was carried to a store where, a few hours later, he died. Buchanan, who for part of this period was seconded to the Trading Company, started a substation at Mount Zomba. A party of carriers on their way to Zomba was robbed. MacDonald assumed the nearest chief to be responsible, and in September 1879 led a punitive party against him. As the party approached the village in the early hours of one morning exchange of fire began; a running fight ensued. Some days later MacDonald sent a party

3 Evidence of John Walker, CP 4337; Hanna, *Beginnings*, pp. 26–7.
4 Evidence of R. Henderson, CP 4437, p. 32; Evidence of G. R. Fenwick ibid., pp. 33–5; A. Pringle, 'Some notes for the use of Capt. O'Neill, RN . . .', ibid., p. 81.

to burn down the offending village. In these two engagements several lives were lost and men were wounded.[5]

Events at Blantyre became common knowledge down the Shire and on the lower Zambezi. MacDonald himself reported to the vice-consul in Quelimane something of what had taken place. When O'Neill received word of this he wrote to the Governor-general mentioning that the missionaries did not anticipate attack, provided the tribesmen were prevented from obtaining powder and bullets from Quelimane. But O'Neill could not forget that the Yao were a powerful tribe.

> I am therefore under the necessity of asking if, in the event of hostilities arising between the natives and one or both these English [sic] Mission stations, your Excellency would consider it as coming within your obligations to take part in the settlement of the difficulty, or whether, regarding this to be a Portuguese jurisdiction as occupying isolated points in a barbarous country, they should be prepared to treat solely and directly with the native rulers, taking the risks incidental to such a position and being responsible for their acts only to their own Government.[6]

The Governor-general assured O'Neill that the missions need have no fear of attack, for orders had already been sent to Quelimane to prevent the sale of ammunition to natives.

> I beg also that your Excellency will assure the Chief of that Mission and of other British subjects residing in those latitudes (as subject to the Portuguese Crown), that they will always receive from the Portuguese Government the frank and faithful protection which such humanitarian and civilizing Missions deserve.

He added that though the vice-consul had refused offers of assistance from the Governor of Quelimane, he would issue orders for the proper protection of the Mission: to provide security for their lives and the legitimate interests of a friendly and allied nation "living in our territories between the upper Shire and Lake Shirwa, and other districts, subordinate also to the Portuguese jurisdiction."[7] O'Neill reminded Salisbury that Moçambique's internal boundaries had not been defined, and there was uncertainty as to whether Portugal claimed jurisdiction over the mission stations or not. The Governor-general's reply indicated a claim to the Blantyre highlands, but left open the question of jurisdiction over the southern shores of Nyasa. O'Neill could not see how, because of local difficulties and the lack of finance, troops could be sent to even Blantyre.[8] Salisbury was appalled at O'Neill's action. The Under-secretary wrote to him,

5 Evidence of R. Henderson, CP 4437, p. 32; Pringle, pp. 82–30.
6 Duff MacDonald, Blantyre, to Vice/consul Nunes, Quelimane, 30/9/79, PRO, FO 179/219; O'Neill to Salisbury, 6/11/79, 49 ST, ibid., O'Neill to da Cunha, 7/11/79, ibid., CP 4498, pp. 193–4 by A. Chirnside, who was an Australian.
7 Cunha to O'Neill, 12/11/79, FO 179/219, CP 4498, p. 194.
8 O'Neill to Salisbury 24/11/79, 53 ST, FO 179/219, CP 4498, p. 193; 5/12/79, 58 ST, ibid., pp. 202–3 which also reported the accidental death of Herbert Rhodes; and 13/12/79, 60 ST, ibid., pp. 204–5, reporting continued slave-trade between Nyasa and the coast.

I am to state to you that your letter to the Governor-general of Moçambique . . . was injudicious, and is to be regretted as indirectly encouraging the Portuguese authorities to claim territories where they have never penetrated, and where British subjects are already established and are carrying on a trade with the natives, and where, moreover, the Portuguese are incapable, however willing they may be, to afford efficient protection. An attempt also on the part of the Portuguese to send an armed force into the interior would introduce a disturbing element into the country, likely to lead to hostilities, and to make the position not only of the missionaries established at Blantyre and on the Lake Nyasa, but also of all European travellers, most dangerous.[9]

Within a few days of this rebuke being penned, two sportsmen, returning from Nyasaland, called on O'Neill with a series of accusations against the missionaries at Blantyre which he regarded as incredible until he obtained confirmation from Nunes, his vice-consul at Quelimane. "If there be truth in what we hear of the harsh and inhuman treatment of natives," he wrote to Lord Salisbury,

it should be stopped before the Portuguese authorities hear of it and institute enquiries, which will bring a storm of abuse upon the whole Mission, throw discredit upon all our mission work, and give occasion for abundant sneering in the Portuguese press, which they will not be slow to indulge in with respect to our humanitarian policy in East Africa and on the coast.[10]

But it was impossible to keep the incidents hushed up; one of the sportsmen, on his return to England, published a pamphlet, *The Blantyre Missionaries: Discreditable Disclosures.*[11] The Church of Scotland appointed a commission to investigate the charges. The Foreign Office was of opinion that O'Neill should join the commission "lest our inactivity may damage us in the estimation of the Portuguese of Moçambique, who know all about it." Fever prevented O'Neill from joining the commission. The Church of Scotland dismissed MacDonald and several of its agents who had been implicated and the new clergyman received instructions, "You must always keep in view the fact that you are labouring to found and build up a Christian church, and not laying the foundations of a British Colony or of a small State . . . Carefully avoid every temptation to act as judges or rulers in the land."[12]

9 Pauncefote to O'Neill, 24/1/80, 4 ST, FO 179/219, CP 4498, pp. 203–4; O'Neill to Salisbury, 11/3/80, 19 ST, ibid., pp. 221–2 for his defence.
10 O'Neill to Salisbury 3/2/80, 11 ST, CP 4437, p. 1.
11 Livingstone, *Laws*, p. 167.
12 Hanna, *Beginnings*, p. 41.

---

9 Sena, seen from the crest of Balamuana hill (from A. de Castilho, *Relatório da Guerra da Zambezia em 1888*. Lisbon, 1889)

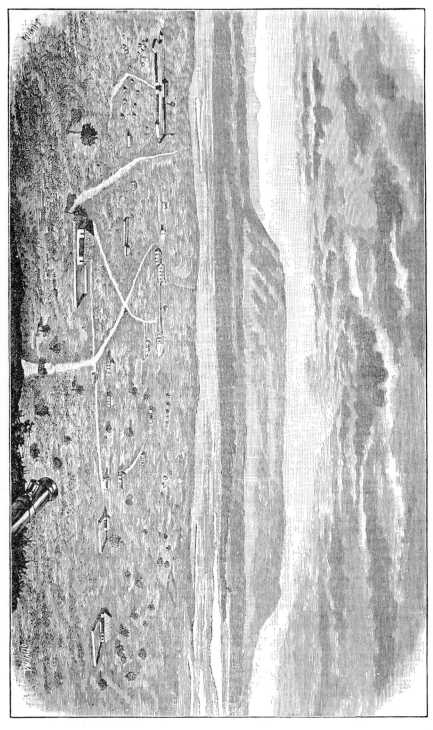

VISTA TIRADA DO ALTO DA SERRA BARAMOANA

Missionary influence, meanwhile, was extending up Nyasa. Members of the Livingstonia Mission further explored the shores of the lake,[13] and visited the Paramount Chief of the Ngoni people inland from Bandawe.[14] It was decided to abandon Cape Maclear, partly because of the limited extent of the peninsula, partly because of its unhealthiness, but more particularly because of the appearance of tsetse fly.[15] In March 1881 the Mission received authority to move to Bandawe, and by October of that year the transfer was complete; only a native teacher was left at Cape Maclear.[16]

At Bandawe the missionaries, and their supporting company, were within easy reach of the northern end of Nyasa. Territory between them and the coast had already been explored by British travellers.[17] The London Missionary Society sent expeditions inland from the coast facing Zanzibar, one of which reached Lake' Tanganyika in 1878.[18] Owing to the difficulties and overland length of this journey, and the discovery of a comparatively easy and healthy route between Tanganyika and Nyasa,[19] James Stevenson, the founder of the Livingstonia Central Africa Company, proposed the construction of a road from Karonga, at the northern end of Nyasa, to Tanganyika, so that the LMS stations might be supplied by the Zambezi-Shire route; James Stewart was commissioned to build this Stevenson road.[20]

As a result of the publicity given to the *Discreditable Disclosures* about Blantyre, and the rejoinders,[21] and the extension of British missionary and geographic enterprise, there was growing interest in Britain about the interior of south-eastern Africa. In 1880 the Livingstonia Mission urged that a British consular officer be appointed on Nyasa.[22] Increasing Portuguese interest in the area caused foreboding in missionary and certain political and official circles. There were rumours of plans to build railway lines up the Zambezi and Shire valleys.[23] When the nervous Baião sent a special commissioner to visit Blantyre there was renewed alarm as to his intentions; the main purpose was actually to reconnoitre the route; and whilst the commissioner reported, with reason, adversely on the Makololo, he formed a most favourable opinion of Blantyre, which was a garden, he exclaimed ecstatically, listing the flowers that grew around the house in which he was lodged.[24] A few months later Nunes, the

13 R. Laws, 'Journey along the western side of Lake Nyassa, in 1878', *Proceedings RGS*, 1879, pp. 315–21; J. Stewart, 'The second circumnavigation of Lake Nyassa', *Proceedings RGS*, 1879, pp. 289–304; Livingstone, *Laws*, pp. 75–80.
14 Ibid., pp. 146–63.
15 Ibid., pp. 116–7.
16 Ibid., pp. 183–91.
17 H. B. Cotterill, 'On the Nyassa and a journey from the north end to Zanzibar', *Proceedings RGS*, 1878, pp. 200–51; K. Johnston, 'Native routes in East Africa, from Dar-es-Salaam towards Lake Nyassa', *Proceedings RGS*, 1879, pp. 417–22; J. Thomson, *To the Central African lakes and back* (London, 1881), I, VII.
18 Coupland, *Exploitation*, pp. 362–3.
19 Hanna, *Beginnings*, p. 45.
20 Livingstone, *Laws*, p. 183.
21 e.g. A. Riddel, *A reply to "The Blantyre Missionaries: Discreditable Disclosures"*; 2 ed. (Edinburgh, 1880).
22 Granville to Morier, 18/8/80, 26 ST, FO 179/216.
23 Herbert to Pauncefote, 16/3/80, CP 4302, p. 140.
24 A. d'Oliveira Barreto, Tete, 16/5/81, Relatório . . . AHU, Moç., 1 Rep. Pasta 3.

vice-consul at Quelimane, warned Scott, the new clergyman at Blantyre, that he had heard rumours to the effect that the Governor-general intended to place an officer and a detachment of troops at Blantyre in order to assert Portuguese jurisdiction.[25] Soon afterwards the British consul at Zanzibar telegraphed London that Portugal intended taking possession of the country as far as Blantyre, and had ordered a company of troops there; he detained the south-ward-bound mailship pending instructions. The Foreign Office promptly telegraphed, "Take no steps re occupation Blantyre", and warned him not to detain Portuguese vessels carrying Portuguese mails.[26] A despatch added that Her Majesty's Government were not "at present" prepared to take any steps in the matter.[27] O'Neill accepted the reports, but he thought Portugal's difficulties on the Zambezi were such that the intention could not be implemented.[28] When, however, the British and Foreign Anti-Slavery Society quoted the rumours and added its pressure, Granville instructed his minister in Lisbon to enquire whether there was any truth in them. The Portuguese Government denied the report: only two missionaries were on their way to the area, one Portuguese and one French.[29] O'Neill was soon in a position to tell London of the visit to be paid by Cunha, the secretary-general, to the Zambezi: after investigating conditions at Tete he was to visit Blantyre and report on the native tribes in that locality, and the feasibility of establishing Portuguese missions among them; he guessed that Cunha would have private instructions to seek a healthy site in the highlands for the establishment of a military post and a sanatorium, which would doubtless lead to a declaration of Portuguese authority over the area.[30] O'Neill urged that he be allowed to undertake a journey through the Nyasa area, but this the Foreign Office refused to countenance, on the grounds that there were no funds for journeys by consuls outside their consular districts; there were dangers from the climate and from natives; any conflict would give rise to complications; and the Portuguese Government might construe the journey to mean that his consular district (and hence Portu-guese jurisdiction) extended throughout the areas he intended to visit.[31] O'Neill was soon able to inform the Foreign Office that Cunha had been unable to reach Blantyre.[32] But Portugal extended her authority to the base of the high-lands when, in 1882, she re-occupied the *prazo* of Massingire, which brought her up to the lands of Chipatula.[33] The prospects of a clash were greatly increased especially by the ambitions of António da Sousa, who had killed all the elephants in the area which he controlled, between Sofala and Gorongosa and the Zambezi, and could, he boasted, put five or six thousand men in the

25 Nunes to Scott, 28/10/81, FO 179/230.
26 Miles to Granville, tel., 15/11/81, CP 4626, p. 358; Lister to Miles, 17/11/81, tel., ibid., Granville to Miles, 18/11/81, tel., ibid.; Miles to Granville, 18/11/81, ibid., p. 373.
27 Lister to Miles, 24/11/81, 56, ibid., p. 361.
28 O'Neill to Granville, 12/12/81, 28 ST., FO 179/230.
29 Granville to Saurin, 24/12/81, 50, ibid., pp. 53–4; Saurin to Granville, 18/1/82, 2, CP 4777, p. 37.
30 O'Neill to Granville, 25/1/82, 9, ibid., pp. 64–5.
31 O'Neill to Granville, 10/1/82, 4, ibid., pp. 61–2, Lister to O'Neill, 30/3/82, 6, ibid., p. 66.
32 O'Neill to Granville, 27/4/82, 25, ibid., p. 80.
33 Auto da posse, 12/8/82, *Termos de Vassallagem*, pp. 23–4.

field, apart from his 600 elephant hunters. Chipatula was disliked by his fellow Makololo chiefs, with whom he was sometimes at war; but it was probable that they would unite against a common enemy. The missionaries and the African Lakes Company could not join in such a war; but they would be the sufferers from the closure of the Shire and the lower Zambezi.[34] Such a war would have its effect on the slave-trade. Humanitarian sentiments in Britain were very strong, and there was a genuine desire to take active steps to curtail the traffic. The growth of legitimate commerce was, ironically, leading to an increased demand for slave labour.[35] When O'Neill repeated his request for permission to travel in the interior, his purpose to investigate the interior slave-trade, and utilizing a period of home leave due to him, the Foreign Office approved, on condition that he travelled in a private capacity.[36] It seemed as well, too, to investigate the position on the Shire, for the proclaimed boundaries of the newly annexed—or rather re-annexed—Massingire included land claimed by Chipatula; and the annexation threw into chaos the regulations which affected transit traffic, for the territory lay beyond the interior custom-post at the junction of the Shire and Zambezi, and goods sold there (mainly by the African Lakes Company) would probably have to pay full duty. O'Neill considered, probably correctly, that the annexation had been carried out not on orders of the Lisbon Government, but on the initiative of the patriotic and energetic Governor Avila of Quelimane, under the inspiration of a powerful party in Portugal, strongly represented in Moçambique, which held Nyasa to be Portuguese territory, with the aim of compelling the Government eventually to advance in the direction of the lake.[37] In view of disorders on the Shire, O'Neill travelled inland from the Moçambique coast; he explored the area around Lakes Shirwa, Chiuta and Amaramba and reported a considerable trade in slaves brought by Portuguese mulattoes for guns and gunpowder.[38]

The disorders on the Shire were provoked by Chipatula. One of his wives fled to Massingire; he sent two tusks to induce the Portuguese authorities to return her, and when they rejected the ivory he raided into the *prazo*. The Governor of Quelimane protested to the vice-consul of Britain and announced that Portugal would not be responsible for any losses that the missions might experience.[39] The African Lakes Company promptly denied any association with Chipatula, declaring that he often interfered with goods passing his villages, and recalling that he had once fired across the bows of their steam-launch.[40] O'Neill declared to London that Portuguese officials were using this "so-called invasion" by Chipatula as a pretext for a further advance up the Shire: the Governor-general had already announced that there was no prospect

34 F. Moir to O'Neill, 15/9/82, FO 179/235 and CP 4914, pp. 23–4.
35 Hanna, *Beginnings*, pp. 58–9.
36 O'Neill to Granville, 22/11/82, 58, CP 4914, pp. 18–9; and FO minute, 31/1/83, FO 179/235.
37 O'Neill to Granville, 30/11/82, 62, CP 4914, pp. 21–2.
38 O'Neill to Granville, 6 confid, 20/2/84, FO 84/167.
39 Governor of Quelimane to Nunes, 2/5/83, CP 4914, pp. 46–8.
40 F. L. Moir, Quelimane, to Nunes, 3/5/83, CP 4914, p. 48.

for a peaceful settlement.[41] The British Secretary of State for Foreign Affairs called on the Portuguese Government to desist from offensive operations up the Shire River.[42] Avila reported that his firm measures had stopped Chipatula from invading Portuguese soil;[43] in reality he was most relieved at the end of this "imaginary war", as the vice-consul called it, for in place of the 6,000 militia he had called up he was actually able to assemble only 60. Chipatula's main grievance, it emerged, was that he was forbidden to buy guns and gun-powder, while his neighbours, competitors and enemies were under no such prohibition.[44]

In view of these uncertain conditions on the Shire and Nyasa,[45] and reports of an increase in the interior slave-trade, the British Government decided to appoint a consul "in the territories of the African kings and chiefs in the districts adjacent to Lake Nyasa." His primary object was the suppression of the slave-trade. He was instructed to avoid any steps that might bring him into armed collision with natives or Arabs, which might endanger his life or the lives of the Europeans residing at Nyasa. He was rather to use every legitimate means to gain their confidence, and impress on them the ruinous nature of the slave-trade and the advantages of legitimate commerce. He was to do his utmost to develop such commerce, and civilization generally.[46] Captain Foot, RN, who had commanded a cruiser on anti-slave-trade patrol on the east coast, received the commission. The British Government informed the Portuguese that the appointment indicated the British desire to co-operate actively, on land as well as at sea, in checking the slave-trade, and in encouraging the growth of legitimate commerce and consequently of civilization; it requested an assurance that the authorities in Moçambique be instructed to reciprocate in the consul's efforts; and it demanded that his luggage and goods be passed freely and promptly through the Portuguese customs.[47] The Portuguese Government granted him exemption from customs duties, but sought—unsuccessfully—clarification as to the nature of his mission, the extent of his jurisdiction, and the names of the tribes with which he would treat; it again asserted the rights of the Portuguese Crown over territory which it had always regarded as being Portuguese.[48]

Foot confirmed that the Ruo could be regarded as the southern boundary of the Makololo lands, but Chipatula had his principal stockade on the bank of that river at its confluence with the Shire, and he often raided southwards.[49] But his hostilities soon came to a sudden end. He asked Fenwick, an artisan who had been discharged from the Blantyre Mission, and subsequently from

41 O'Neill to Granville, 18/5/83, tel., and 12 Af., CP 4914, pp. 45–6.
42 Granville to Wyke, 21/5/83, tel. 19 Af., FO 179/235: Wyke to A Min. For. Affairs, Nec., SPZ 1, Neg., p. 3; Baring to Min. of For. Affs. 14/7/83, ibid., Neg., pp. 4–5.
43 GG to Min., 16/7/83, 2/209, AHU, Moç., 1 Rep. Pasta 3.
44 Nunes to Kirk, 3/9/83, CP 4914, pp. 202–3.
45 O'Neill to Granville, 5/6/83, 15 Af., CP 4914, p. 50.
46 Lister to Foot, 1/10/83, 1 Af., CP 4914, p. 10; all this for £500 p.a., plus £170 fitting-out allowance and £100 for expenses.
47 Granville to Baring, 23/10/83, 41 Af., CP 4914, p. 14.
48 Bocage to Baring, 8/11/83, Neç., SPZ 1, Neg., pp. 6–7, CP 4914, p. 16.
49 Foot, Mandala, to Granville, 18/1/84, 1 Af., CP 5366, pp. 73–4.

the African Lakes Company, to sell some hippo teeth and grain. When Fenwick returned and gave him three guns and three kegs of powder, an argument developed over whether these were the proceeds of the sale or a present. The wrangling, which lasted for a day and a night, was cut short by a shot which ended Chipatula's life. Fenwick escaped across the river, only to be pursued and despatched.[50] Great alarm ensued among the twenty-two white men, seven women and three children who were in the Blantyre and Nyasa area. Chikuse, eldest son of Chipatula, became chief of the southern Makololo. He expressed himself as being not averse to fighting the British, and Foot asked for a party of bluejackets to be sent to the scene, but the elderly Ramukakan, who exercised something of a paramountcy, declared that the enmity of the tribe was directed only against the African Lakes Company.[51]

Coelho, the Governor-general, ordered the Governor of Quelimane to lead to Massingire forces which would prevent possible attack on the *prazo* and then take advantage of the opportunity to re-establish Portuguese authority over Makololo lands. The Governor approached the Ruo; but the spokesmen of Chikuse were arrogant, declaring that the Makololo would not countenance any whites from any nation, and the Governor could make war on them if he so desired. When a few shots were discharged in the direction of the Governor's camp he decided that he could direct operations better from the Zambezi. The Governor-general reported to his minister that the Makololo were well armed with fire-arms which had been bought from the English, partly in the normal course of commerce, partly in anticipation of being used against the Portuguese.[52] They soon pointed these guns against the suppliers.

The African Lakes Company sent the *Lady Nyasa* up the Shire. The decison was premature. As soon as she reached Makololo country tribesmen boarded and plundered her; they released most of the crew, after stripping them, but they held the captain prisoner. British opinions differed as to the course of action. Foot favoured recruiting reinforcements in Zanzibar and defeating the Makololo, but O'Neill, consulted on his journey, was emphatic that the only way to save the lives of the captain and the other British subjects in Nyasaland, and to restore amicable and commercial relations with the Makololo, was to pay an indemnity for the murder of Chipatula.[53] The captain was soon released—wearing little more than a fig-leaf[54]—but the main threat remained. The Portuguese authorities announced their intention of coming to the assistance of their beleaguered fellow-citizens. The British Government held that such action would only further endanger the lives of the missionaries,[55] and before the Portuguese could move north of the Ruo they found themselves on the defensive south of that river.

50 Likino, statement, 26/2/84, CP 5366, p. 80; he was emphatic that there was only one shot. Moir asserted that Chitapula fired first (Moir to Foot, 20/2/84, ibid., pp. 79–80).
51 Foot to Granville, 8/3/84, 6 Af., CP 5366, p. 77, and 19/3/84, ibid., p. 78.
52 Coelho, GG, to Chagas, Min., 27/5/84, extra and 2/157, AHU, Moç., 2 Rep. Caixa 1, and Neç., SPZ 1; extract only in *Neg.*, pp. 10–11.
53 O'Neill, Maruro, to Serra, A Gov., Quelimane, 25/4/84, AHU, Moç., 2 Rep. Caixa 7.
54 D. J. Rankin, *The Zambesi basin and Nyassaland* (Edinburgh, 1893), p. 83.
55 Petre to Bocage, 11/6/84, Neç., SPZ 1, *Neg.*, pp. 7–8.

The first year that the Portuguese re-occupied Massingire they levied no tax. The second year they collected tax where there was no opposition. Now, with a stockade and a garrison to support their demands, they sought to levy poll-tax not only on men and women, but on boys and girls; those who refused were drafted to forced labour. When Chief Vingwe protested he was arrested; on his way to the Zambezi he escaped and he raised the land against the Portuguese, in July 1884. His followers attacked Chironge and Mpassa's. At the former stockade they killed the commandant and the garrison, and destroyed goods belonging to the African Lakes Company; at the latter place they killed a Portuguese trader. Storming southwards, they pillaged and burnt a wooding and trading station of the company below Morrumbala. At Shamo they killed another Portuguese trader. At Chimoara they destroyed the frontier post and looted a French factory and several Netherlands barges. The local natives joined the insurgents. Most of the Portuguese at Mopeia fled, and panic spread to Quelimane. The Governor sent off the only troops available, fifteen in number, under two officers, and called a conference which after hours of debate came to no decision. Agents of the foreign firms decided to form a volunteer company; they elected J. Moir as commandant, and six Englishmen, four Frenchmen, three Netherlanders and a German sallied out, at the head of one hundred armed natives. The volunteer company reached Mopeia as it was in the final throes of attack; the three surviving Europeans were piling gunpowder in the centre of the store of the opium factory preliminary to blowing themselves up when they heard the volleys of the relieving force. The volunteers saved not only Mopeia but possibly Quelimane. The Governor-general came to Quelimane; he accepted the resignation of the local governor, and with 130 Angolans, and levies from the *prazos* south of the Zambezi, the situation was soon restored—except that with the destruction of the custom station the African Lakes Company could no longer obtain a rebate of duty on goods in transit.[55a]

In fact, a larger force was assembled than was necessary simply to restore the situation. Three thousand sepoys concentrated at Chironge and Mpassa.[56] When Serpa Pinto called at Moçambique with eighty Landeens, with the expressed intention of exploring inland to Nyasa and thence northwards, O'Neill correctly reported to Britain that a determined effort was about to be made to enforce Portuguese claims to Nyasa and to the region of the central African lakes.[57] The Church of Scotland reacted strongly to the threat.[58] But her alarm was premature. Serpa Pinto fell ill, and had to hand over command to his lieutenant, Augusto Cardoso. The expedition reached Nyasa,[59] but it lacked the strength to extend Portuguese influence or prestige.

From Nyasaland, Foot was urging that chiefs be subsidized by Britain in return for keeping the river route open. O'Neill held that this would be setting

55a J. Moir to O'Neill, 27/9/84, CP 5366, pp. 68–9.
56 O'Neill to Granville, c. 20/9/84, CP 5366, pp. 62–3.
57 O'Neill to Granville, 20/9/84, 34 Af., CP 5366, pp. 63–4.
58 Foreign Missions Committee, Edinburgh, to Granville, 25/10/84, CP 5023, pp. 47–8.
59 Amadeu Cunha, *Serpa Pinto e o Apelo de Africa* (Lisbon, 1946), p. 58.

a dangerous precedent;[60] and Foot died before 1884 was out.[61] Ngoni raids devastated the Blantyre highlands and threatened the missions,[62] but the Scots regarded the Portuguese as the greater menace. The continual refusal to rebuild the frontier post at Chimoara seemed a deliberate attempt to exact duties on goods in transit; when plans were proposed for a post to be built at Mpassa's, close to the confluence of the Ruo, this was seen as a deliberate step towards Nyasa; the Makololo were to be punished for harbouring rebels from Massingire; and Andrada's concession, it was rumoured, included the Blantyre highlands. Actually Portuguese hold even on the coast was thin: the Governor-general complained that even from the windows of his palace on the island of Moçambique he looked out over territories which were absolutely beyond Portuguese jurisdiction.[63] As a result, there could be little extension of Portuguese jurisdiction in the interior.

Using, however, the threat of a Portuguese advance the Moirs persuaded a number of chiefs to put their marks on documents which requested the British Government to declare a Protectorate over the area, and immediately ceded their territories and their rights to the African Lakes Company. When Hawes, Foot's successor, enquired into these treaties, the chiefs denied that they had disposed of any sovereignty. Petre, the British minister in Lisbon, also advocated the declaration of a British protectorate over the Shire highlands, but the British Government rejected the suggestion. When it appreciated the inadequacies of the African Lakes Company, it favoured freedom of commerce.[64]

Augusto de Melo Pinto Cardoso, on the shores of Nyasa, persuaded Cuirassia Checapoto to accept a Portuguese flag. The chief undertook, in what became a *pro forma* for such instruments, to give any assistance that might be required by any Portuguese traveller; to send an ambassador to Quelimane to confirm the act of vassalage; and to obey any orders that he might receive from the King of Portugal.[65] Cardoso's expedition, reduced to desperate straits, was succoured by Last, a traveller sent out by the Royal Geographical Society to journey inland from Lindi, ascend the Rovuma and Lokuga and make observations in the vicinity of the Namuli hills east of Lake Shirwa. Last found frequent evidence of the slave-trade.[66] Even Ramukakan, also known as Kasisi, had been indulging in this trade.[67]

Hawes took over some of Last's efficient Swahili porters and set out on a journey of his own. Mponda, close to where the Shire issued from Nyasa, assured him that of course he sold slaves—how else could he obtain cloth?

60 O'Neill to Granville, 3/10/84, 41 Af., CP 5366, pp. 66–7.
61 O'Neill to Granville, 1/10/84, 35 Af., CP 5366, pp. 64–6.
62 O'Neill to Granville, 3/10/84, 40 Af., CP 5366, pp. 65–6.
63 J. Stevenson to Granville, 10/11/84, CP 5033, p. 58; O'Neill to Granville, 14/11/84, 48 Af, CP 5051, pp. 155–6; 11/12/84, 59 Af., CP 5080, p. 82; and 27/12/84, 62 Af., CP 5103, pp. 2–3.
64 Hanna, *Beginnings*, pp. 72, 83, 126–7.
65 Termo de Vassalagem, 20/1/86, *Bol. Off.*, 26/6/86, p. 314. Hawes refused to believe the report (Hawes to S of S, 1/11/86, FO 179/250).
66 Kirk to Rosebery, 12/3/86, 26, CP 4549, pp. 305–6; Hawes to S of S, 10/2/86, 5 Af., CP 5459, p. 62 and 28/3/86, 12 Af., FO 179/248.
67 Hawes to Salisbury, 27/1/86, 1 Confid, CP 5459, pp. 60–1 and 25/4/86, 3 Af., ibid., p. 65.

Hawes was confident that many of the slaves ended up on Portuguese *prazos*. The chief informed Hawes that the Portuguese had sent a message the previous year to his father announcing that the country was about to be placed under Portuguese control but his father adopted a hostile attitude. Mponda was virtually a tributary of the Ngoni people. Hawes visited the Ngoni king and obtained a pledge from him to discontinue raids in the direction of Zomba, where Buchanan was now growing coffee, and Blantyre.[68] Hawes urged that a road be constructed between Blantyre and Zomba, to encourage the natives to grow coffee for export as a substitute for slaves, but the Foreign Office was compelled to reply that no funds were available for such purposes.[69]

Makololos killed Hinkleman, an Austrian trader, in the lands of Chikuse. Kasisi appreciated the likely consequences of the murder, and moved to castigate the chief before outsiders could act. In the consequent disorders ALC stores were broken into, guns and ammunition stolen. The Europeans resident in Nyasaland urged the necessity for force to protect their goods and their lives, and enquired whether the British Government would approve the establishment of a military police force.[70] When the military commander at Sena heard that the Makololo had murdered also a Portuguese trader and four of his men, and had raided on to the *prazos* of Ingoma and Guengue, he determined to assemble an expedition which after castigating the chief would occupy Makololo lands north of the Ruo, but before launching the expedition thought it as well to report his plans to the Governor-general.[71] Hawes hearing of these intentions sent messages to the vice-consul in Quelimane and to O'Neill urging them to dissuade the Governor and the Governor-general from countenancing such plans, while he urged diplomatic pressure on the Portuguese Government to prevent the annexation of what was practically an English colony.[72] Kasisi rapidly got the better of his opponent. He planned, as soon as he captured him, to send Chikuse down-stream and hand him over to the Portuguese authorities.[73] Hawes was shocked at the proposal, for such action would be tantamount to acknowledging Portuguese sovereignty over the Makololo. The Governor-general, meanwhile, was writing instructions for the military commander of Sena to prepare for operations against the Makololo of the upper Shire; he was to organize a column of irregulars from the *prazos* around Sena and from Manuel António de Sousa, to be supported by one or two Hotchkiss guns and some troops from Manica. The principal object of the campaign was the arrest of Chikuse and allied chiefs and headmen. Then, if his forces were adequate, the commander was definitely to occupy, under the shade of the Portuguese flag, points of strategic importance to ensure communication between them and Sena. Any white adventurers who had been sowing malevolence

68 Hawes to Rosebery, 3/6/86, 19 CA, CP 5459, pp. 66–8, 1/7/86, 20 CA, ibid., pp. 69–70; and 7/7/86, 21 CA, ibid., pp. 72–74.
69 Lister to Hawes, 22/9/86, 16, CP 5459, pp. 71–2.
70 A. C. Ross, to v/consul Quelimane, Hawes to S of S, 19/11/86, CA 43, ibid.
71 J. J. Ferreira to Sec. Geral, 23/11/86, 127, AHU, Moç., 1 Rep. Pasta 2; J. M. Guerreiro Amosim to Sec. Geral, 6/12/86, 176, ibid.
72 Hawes to S of S, 28/11/86, CA 44, FO 179/250, 29/11/86, CA 45, ibid.
73 Hawes to S of S, 2/12/86, FO 179/250.

against the Portuguese and generally agitating the tribes were to be arrested and sent to Quelimane and Moçambique for trial. Other whites were to be assured that there would be free commerce for all nations under the protection of the Portuguese flag.[74] The British Government was fully aware of the situation: "Unless the English settlers have sufficient influence to cause murderers of whites and thefts of their property to be punished, it will be impossible for Her Majesty's Government to resist the offers of the Portuguese Government to chastise offenders even if by so doing should lead to the ultimate occupation of the country."[75] Great was the relief of Hawes and the missionaries when they heard that Kasisi had captured Chikuse with three of his headmen and had put him to death.[76]

Great was the chagrin of the Governor-general that his expedition had been deprived of its primary purpose; but he found consolation in the fact that there must be other headmen and councillors of Chikuse that needed chastising.[77] The Foreign Office warned Hawes not to do anything that would place him in antagonism with the officials of a friendly power;[78] at the same time it exerted pressure to have the custom post rebuilt at the junction of the Shire and the Zambezi, and not higher up the river.[79] But the British minister in Lisbon was confident that Portugal would be incapable of extending her authority over bordering territories, from lack of resources: the colonial burden was already pressing heavily on the finances of the mother country.[80] And so it proved. Portugal re-established a military command at Massingire,[81] and set up others at Macanga[82] and Boror,[83] but no advance was made into Makololo lands. Salisbury warned Hawes—unnecessarily—not to call on the Portuguese for aid for that would invite a Portuguese advance; nor could he seek material support from Britain; to check the slave-trade, restrain lawlessness and assist the British settlers, and extend civilization, he could rely only on his moral influence.[84]

Hawes had already embarked on a deliberate policy to increase this influence: he had set out on a series of journeys to visit the chiefs who surrounded the Blantyre highlands. He directed his feet first to the Mlanje area, where there was particularly bad feeling against the missionaries for harbouring slaves,[85] and where some of Hawes's deserting Zanzibar porters had set themselves up, after the Makololo example, as brigands. Matapwira, the Paramount

74 GG, instruções, c. 11/12/86, AHU, Moç., 1 Rep., Pasta 2; GG to Min., 12/12/86, 2/308, ibid., confirming tel. of 10/12/86 and enclosing instructions.
75 Iddesleigh to Hawes, 31/12/86, FO 179/250.
76 Hawes to Iddesleigh, 8/12/86, 47, CP 5616, p. 1.
77 GG to Min., 9/1/87, 2/10, AHU, Moç., 1 Rep., Pasta 2.
78 FO to Hawes, 9/2/87, 4, FO 179/250.
79 Petre to Barros Gomes, 14/12/86, Nec., SPZ 1, *Neg.*, pp. 11–12; Salisbury to Petre, 27/6/87, 77 Af., FO 179/250; W. Ewing, Sec. ALC to Salisbury, 14/11/87, ibid.
80 Petre to Salisbury, 14/7/87, 93 Af, FO 179/253.
81 Portaria 181, 29/4/87, *Bol. Off.*, 30/4/87.
82 Auto, 19/4/87, *Bol. Off.*, 11/6/87, p. 261; Oliveira Gomes, Gov. Tete, to Sec. Geral, 30/4/87, *Bol Off.*, 4/6/87, p. 249.
83 Portaria 435, 21/10/87, *Bol. Off.*, 22/10/87, pp. 484–5.
84 FO to Hawes, 22/10/87, 22, CP 5616, p. 16.
85 Hawes to Iddesleigh, 11/12/86, 48, CP 5616, pp. 2–3.

Chief of the area around Lake Shirwa, and whose town was an important centre on the caravan route to Quelimane, refused to receive him, though he welcomed Portuguese traders, and had in fact himself visited Quelimane. Having heard that Cuirassia was seeking Matapwira's aid to free himself from Portuguese vassalage,[86] Hawes determined to visit him and his superior, Makanjila. Makanjila received Hawes amiably, despite his Arab councillors, and his courtesy even survived a homily by Hawes on the evils of the slave-trade and in praise of legitimate commerce. Councillors assured Hawes that Cuirassia was not an independent chief: he did not have the authority to enter into any treaty; and they declared he was not even a member of their Machinga tribe, but had been granted land when he arrived years before as a refugee. But Hawes heard another report to the effect that he was the son of a previous chief of the Machinga tribe; there had been dynastic differences; and Matapwira was hostile to Cuirassia for allowing Cardoso to depart without directing him to the Paramount Chief's town.[87]

Hawes continued to Cuirassia's. The chief and most of his people had removed some thirty miles inland, but from an old headman he heard how they had befriended Cardoso. Cardoso in return had asked Cuirassia to accept a flag, and raise it to attract attention whenever a steamer passed: and he left a letter which, he said, would secure the friendship of any white people; no one knew the contents of the letter, which had not been read or explained to them. When Hawes asked whether the flag had been raised and ceremoniously saluted there were indignant denials. The headman pressed Hawes to stay until a runner could fetch the flag and the letter; both could be acquired for a little cloth. But the consul was availing himself of the services of a Universities' Mission launch, and could not linger.[88] He had to abandon his intention of visiting tribes at the north-eastern end of Nyasa because of the desertion of his porters,[89] but on his return to the southern end he visited Cuirassia, in whose village he learnt little to his comfort. His interpreter, in conversation with headmen, learnt that Cuirassia had indeed given his lake-side village to the Portuguese; Cardoso drew up two papers, on both of which the chief made his mark, Cardoso keeping one, Cuirassia the other, until Arabs explained the significance of the contents, when he threw it away. Arabs of Mponda confirmed the contents of the letter. Hawes was forced to accept that Cardoso had succeeded in making a treaty; but, Hawes insisted, Cuirassia had no right to alienate any portion of Makanjila's territory. He was confident that the Portuguese would never be able to carry out the treaty without resort to arms.[90]

The next embarrassment to British enterprise in the interior came not from Portuguese interference, but Arab. From 1883 there was a remarkable growth of Arab power in central Africa, in consequence, according to some who knew the region well, of the withdrawal of British cruisers from the Zanzibar coast.

86 Hawes to Salisbury, 25/2/87, J, CP 5616, pp. 4–6; and 4/7/87, 29, ibid., p. 14.
87 Hawes to Salisbury, 26/3/87, 84, CP 5616, pp. 7–8; and 8/4/87, ibid., pp. 8–9.
88 Hawes to Salisbury, 22/4/87, 19, CP 5616, pp. 10–11.
89 Hawes to Salisbury, 27/8/87, 39, CP 5616, pp. 16–16A, and 16/11/87, 45, CP 5896, pp. 1–3.
90 Hawes to Salisbury, 16/11/87, 46, Confid., FO 179/257.

Slavers, usually half-caste, ranged far into the interior. Unable to penetrate the Congo, they concentrated in the area west and south-west of Tanganyika, and then at the northern end of Nyasa. Here lived the Konde people on well-watered, fertile lands, which carried large numbers of cattle and of sheep. Arabs bought land and increased their hold to such an extent that Mlozi, their leader, even asserted that he was sultan of Konde. In July 1887, an argument took place between a follower of Mlozi and Kasote, the Konde chief; the Arab shot Kasote dead. The tribesmen gathered their forces and prepared to attack the Arab village of Mirambo. The African Lakes Company agent at Karonga, at the beginning of the Stevenson road to Tanganyika, acted as mediator, and persuaded the Arabs to buy peace with cloth. But six weeks later another quarrel flared up when a Makonde seized a slave of an Arab; the owner gave cloth to redeem the slave, but the slave was not released. Friends of the slave then shot the native dead. This incident precipitated war. Arabs fired the villages, and the Konde fled northwards. Mlozi declared that he had no quarrel with Karonga, but the ALC agent, fearing attack, sent to Livingstonia for aid.

O'Neill, on leave, with a companion, arrived at Livingstonia at the end of October, and hearing of the situation at Karonga, he immediately responded to the call. The *Ilala* headed northwards, picking up Sharpe, a sportsman, on the way. The party arrived at Karonga on the evening of 11 November, to be told that the Arabs had demonstrated against the station that afternoon. The *Ilala* promptly returned southwards in search of reinforcements. On 19 November a thousand Konde returned, and looked to the whites for protection. That afternoon the Arabs formally declared war on the station. The defenders heightened the wall round the station and built a stockade to house the refugees.

On 23 November Arabs fired several volleys into the station, but retired when the defenders opened fire. An ALC employee was sent to the Mwamba tribe, north of Nyasa, who had volunteered assistance. The next day some 500 men with guns attacked Karonga. The defenders numbered six Britons, and forty-five other armed men. Their ammunition was desperately short, and for the sixteen Chassêpots they had only eight rounds a carbine. The Arabs built a stockade and from the roof of a nearby store fired down into the fortified camp. O'Neill led a party which sallied out and burnt the store. For five days shooting continued, but on 28 November the enemy stockades were found to be deserted; the reason became clear when 5,000 Mwamba appeared in sight. The enemy stockades, and Mirambo village, were fired. When the Mwamba warriors, disappointed at the lack of loot, announced their intention of returning home, and that the Konde intended to accompany them, the Europeans, considering the shortage of ammunition, and the insanitary nature of the stockade, decided to abandon Karonga and take to the field.

When Hawes arrived on 9 December he found Karonga in ruins and deserted. He encountered the Europeans eight miles north of the station. The number of whites was now increased to twelve, but powder and balls had been accidentally off-loaded at Bandawe. Hearing that the Arabs had sent for reinforcements Hawes sought more assistance from the Mwamba, and on 23 December seven Europeans, fifty-two natives armed with breech-loading rifles and forty-four with muzzle-loaders, and some 4,000 warriors, stormed Mlozi's stockade. The allies promptly decamped with their loot, and rain hampered the firing of the village, but this incomplete victory persuaded many of Mlozi's supporters to desert and it secured the Europeans from immediate attack. Because of continued shortage of ammunition and supplies, however, Hawes advised them to withdraw to the southern end of the lake. At a meeting it was decided that it would be impolitic to withdraw entirely from the area, for then the Arabs would undoubtedly attack the Konde and Mwamba who would reproach the British for breaking faith; two of the ALC men would establish themselves at nearby Mwini-manda with the doctor of the Free Church of Scotland, while the rest of the party would withdraw to the south end of the lake. The Moirs undertook to send to Karonga within three months a force of at least 150 men with breech-loading rifles and at least 100 rounds of ammunition per man, as much ammunition for the muzzle-loaders as they could get, and other munitions if possible, including rockets and dynamite. These forces, to be organized by the ALC, would drive the Arabs completely from the district. Hawes warned the ALC to confine its action to hostile Arabs only. To Salisbury he declared that Mlozi and his followers had for some time premeditated the conquest of the Konde, and this formed only part of a larger scheme for the extension of Arab power over the whole of the western side of Nyasa. He had already seen evidence of the extension of this power over the eastern and southern end of Nyasa. The real question, one of his companions declared in a letter to the *Manchester Guardian*, was not whether England or some other nation should occupy the area, but whether European and Christian, or Arab and Muslim, influence should prevail.[91]

Hawes's doubts about the ALC's proposed venture were deepened by incidents on the voyage southwards, when Moir, hearing of Arab caravans in villages near the shore, twice proposed surprise attacks on them, and the looting of their contents. Hawes felt that such attempts, since there was nothing to link the caravans with Mlozi, would be nothing else but piracy. He urged on Salisbury that nothing but a disciplined force, under a trustworthy commander, be allowed on such an operation, else the whole of the Nyasa area would rise against the European settlers. His preference was for conciliatory measures directed towards a peaceful solution.[92] Hawes formally protested to the ALC against its proposed campaign, and great was his indignation when he discovered that O'Neill was planning to take extra leave and join the expedition. A bitter exchange of letters took place between Hawes and Moir and O'Neill. As a consequence O'Neill cancelled his application to extend his leave and the Moirs abandoned their plans to re-open the Stevenson road, declaring that they

91 Fotheringham to Hawes, 10/10/87, CP 5896, pp. 3–5; Fotheringham to Bain, diary 17/10–4/12/87, ibid., p. 34 ff. W. Howat to Hawes, 25/10/87, p. 7; O'Neill to Salisbury, 31/10/87, 57, pp. 64–5; Hawes to Salisbury, 16/11/87, 47 Af., p. 3; A correspondent, 10/12/87 *Manchester Guardian*, 25/2/88, pp. 8–12; Another correspondent, 10/12/67, ibid., pp. 12–14; Hawes to Salisbury, 10/12/87, 49 Af., pp. 7–8; Hawes to Salisbury, 11/1/88 1 Af., p. 23; Tamory to Hawes, 14/1/88, pp. 38–40; Hawes to Salisbury, 16/1/88, 3 Af., pp. 27–32.
92 Hawes to Salisbury, 28/1/88, 5 CA, CP 5896, p. 41, and 4/2/88, 13 CA, pp. 42–3.

would content themselves with re-occupying Karonga peacefully. Having handed over to Buchanan as vice-consul, Hawes set out on leave for England, much relieved to hear that the Moirs had given an undertaking not even to re-occupy Karonga until Buchanan had first been given the opportunity of treating with Mlozi.[93]

The warlike activities of the ALC gave rise to great concern in Portuguese official circles, especially when the ALC began to demand the entry, through Portuguese ports, of additional and heavier weapons. The Moirs were anxious to arm the ALC launches and stations with machine-guns, but they appreciated that without official backing from the British Government they would be refused permission to import them through Portuguese territory. Hawes admitted to his Secretary of State that while the possession of such weapons would be salutary, some guarantee would be necessary to ensure that only responsible persons were placed in charge of them, else they might be used for illegal purposes.[94] But he did make available to the ALC a few rockets which were the property of the consulate,[95] and when passing through Quelimane he persuaded the Governor to release, as a matter of urgency, nineteen boxes of arms which he declared belonged to the British Government. The Governor expressed himself forcibly on the subject of the ALC's proceedings; he was convinced that its military operations would adversely affect general commerce.[96] The Governor-general cabled the gist of this report to Lisbon, and the Portuguese Government called on Britain, as a matter of urgency, to cease a war which was harming the commerce of Quelimane.[97]

Castilho declared to his minister, "In my opinion the territory adjacent to the Zambezi, to the Shire, and at least to the south of Nyasa, and far into the interior, should be considered as ours"; the British were provoking differences, and bringing about a state of affairs which was greatly to the prejudice of Portugal; the Governor of Quelimane had the right, since 1885, to prohibit the entry of arms and ammunition if they contributed to an abnormal state of affairs, and he felt that this measure should again be invoked.[98]

There was another way by which pressure could be brought to bear on the ALC. Articles 136 and 137 of port regulations issued in 1887 forbad foreigners to own vessels plying on the waters of the ports and rivers of the province of Moçambique. The *James Stevenson* was arrested and released only on condition that she abandon her British nationality and that she be registered in the name of a Portuguese, with Portuguese ship's articles and with a Portuguese

93 O'Neill to Salisbury, 3/2/88, 2 Af., CP 5896, pp. 608–10; Hawes to ALC, 8/2/88, ibid., p. 44; Hawes to O'Neill, 8/2/88, p. 45; J. W. Moir to Hawes, 8/2/88, p. 45; Moir to Hawes, 8/2/88, p. 46; Hawes to Moir, 8/2/88, p. 47; ALC to Hawes, 8/2/88, pp. 47–8; O'Neill to Hawes, 9/2/88, pp. 50–1; Hawes to ALC, 9/2/88, pp. 48–9; O'Neill to Salisbury, 10/2/88, 3, pp. 610–1; ALC to Hawes, 10/2/88, p. 50; J. Buchanan to Hawes, 15/2/88, 12 ACA, p. 52; Buchanan to Hawes, 16/2/88, 13 ACA, p. 53; Hawes to Salisbury, 18/2/88, 14 CA, pp. 43–4; Buchanan to Hawes, 18/2/88, 14 ACA, p. 56; Buchanan to Hawes, 23/2/88, p. 62.
94 F. Moir to Hawes, 26/1/88, CP 5896, p. 51; Hawes to Moir, 21/2/88, ibid., p. 51.
95 Buchanan to Hawes, 11/5/88, 25, CP 5896, pp. 83–4.
96 J. M. G. Amorim to Sec. Geral, 25/2/88, Civil 19, AHU, Moç., 2 Rep. Caixa 5.
97 Min. of Ultramar to Min. of Negocios Externos, 2/3/88, Nec., SPZ 1.
98 Castilho to Minister, 3/3/88, 2/82, AHU, Moç., 2 Rep. Caixa 5.

captain and a required Portuguese proportion of her crew, within four months.[99] The directors of the African Lakes Company called for the intervention of the British Government. They deplored a statement in the Commons by the Under-secretary for Foreign Affairs that "Her Majesty's Government could not under-take responsibilities in connection with settlements established without their concurrence." They tried to prove that the ALC was a natural development from the appointment of Livingstone as consul to central Africa in 1858; and they condemned Portuguese interference with their steamer traffic as being entirely at variance with the spirit and the promise of more recent Portuguese legislation.[100] The Foreign Office replied that it had never accepted any obliga-tion to defend the settlements of Nyasa.[101] But it took up with the Portuguese Government the question of the navigation of the Zambezi and the Shire. The Lisbon attitude was that the Moçambique authorities were entirely justified in their action since the Portuguese representative at Berlin had specifically reserved Portuguese rights. Petre, the British minister, explained to the Minister of Foreign Affairs that he was extremely surprised to hear that the Portuguese Government regarded an arterial African waterway as if it were the Tagus or Douro, and such an intention was certainly contrary to the spirit of the Act of Berlin.[102] As recently as 1885 a Portuguese decree had thrown open the whole coast of the province of Moçambique to the flags of all nations, without re-serve.[103] The British Secretary of State for Foreign Affairs called on Sir E. Hertslet, the Office's librarian, to write a memorandum "on the right of a Power holding possession of the mouth of a river (both banks) to stop the passage of merchant ships,"[104] whilst to Petre he expressed the surprise of the British Government at the Portuguese attitude. He did not dispute that the navigation of the Zambezi was not directly dealt with at Berlin, or that Portugal had reserved her rights; but it was equally undisputed that the Portuguese pleni-potentiary had committed his country to the fullest recognition of the principles of commercial liberty in the region—he recalled Serpa Pinto's protestations when adhering to Protocol 3; it was hardly credible to him that a power which then publicly expressed such liberal sentiments should now be deliberately adopting a policy of excluding foreign vessels from navigating her rivers and interfering with transit traffic. If Portugal persisted in her determination, Britain would have to consider inviting the other powers who had signed the Act of Berlin to consider whether the Portuguese position was justified.[105] In Lisbon it was now admitted that the Governor-general of Moçambique had not had the right to suspend transit traffic except in arms and ammunition.[106]

99 O'Neill to Salisbury, 2/3/88, tel., CP 5727, p. 13; Salisbury to Petre, 6/3/88, tel., FO 179/251; GG to Min., 8/3/88, tel., Nec., SPZ 1; O'Neill to Salisbury, 10/3/88, tel., CP 5727, p. 14; Dir. Geral to Sec. Geral, 12/3/88, tel., Nec., SPZ 1; O'Neill to Salisbury, 12/3/88, 10, CP 5727, pp. 30–1.
100 ALC, Glasgow, to Salisbury, 10/3/88, CP 5896, pp. 24–5.
101 FO to ALC, 21/3/88, CP 5895, p. 40.
102 Petre to Salisbury, 12/3/88, 11 Af., CP 2727, p. 15.
103 O'Neill to Salisbury, 24/3/88, 17, CP 2727, pp. 34–5.
104 c. 28/3/88, CP 2727, pp. 16–18.
105 Salisbury to Petre, 29/3/88, 28 Af., CP 2727, pp. 18–19.
106 Minute, 17/5/88, on Castilho to Minister, 2/4/88, 2/104, AHU, Moç., 2 Rep. Caixa 5.

Quotation of Serpa Pinto's speech at Berlin had a pronounced effect on the Portuguese Minister of Foreign Affairs, but Serpa Pinto was even then stirring up the Chamber of Deputies into taking a greater interest in Africa, and exhorting it to protect Portuguese territory from attack by the British. The Government postponed the nationalization of the *James Stevenson;* but further than that it dared not go while the Chamber of Deputies was in session.[107] When it decided that vessels then navigating the Zambezi might continue to do so undisturbed, and the new regulations would be applied only to new registrations, Salisbury demanded the entire abandonment of all interference with free navigation, in accordance with the practice in other countries where a waterway passed through more than one territory. Barros Gomes refused to abandon the indisputable rights of Portugal—without at least an equivalent advantage being granted to Portugal; he suggested an agreement analogous to the German-Portuguese convention. Petre quickly disabused his mind that the British Government would ever recognize as exclusively within Portuguese influence or protectorate a vast zone stretching across Africa. Petre was convinced that Portugal would never voluntarily and officially recognize the free navigation of the Zambezi; but he thought that practical navigation would continue.[108] Sir P. Anderson correctly minuted that the real reason why Portugal refused to re-open the custom-house on the Shire and abolished transit duties was that she did not wish to be committed to an interior frontier, which was inconsistent with her plan for trans-continental expansion; he recommended that the other signatory powers to the Act of Berlin bring pressure to bear on Portugal. But Salisbury decided first to fight on the nationalization question.[109] The Portuguese Government was accordingly informed that the British Government did not recognize the right of Portugal to close the Zambezi to British ships seeking to pass beyond Portuguese dominion.[110] Portugal continued to angle for some equivalent. Petre, after conversations with Barros Gomes, became convinced that he could obtain without difficulty important concessions over transit duties and facilities for intercourse and trade with the lakes, provided that Britain acknowledge the Zambezi as her northern boundary and as the southern boundary of Portuguese influence, as far as the Victoria Falls.[111]

Salisbury, in the meanwhile, had been considering the whole matter of the British settlements in Nyasaland and in particular whether he should approve the recent conduct of consul Hawes. Salisbury now decided,

> His personal action merits every sympathy, and, so far as it can be separated from the question of policy, deserves our high approval. He has been courageous, prudent and clearsighted. But I cannot render to myself any account of the policy which he is supposed to represent. What is he

107 Petre, memorandum and aide-memoire, 17/4/88, Nec., SPZ 1, *Neg.*, pp. 20, 21; Petre to Salisbury, 17/4/88, 22 Af., CP 5727, p. 26; Precis of Proceedings, Chamber of Deputies, 17/4/88, ibid., pp. 277–8; Petre to Salisbury, 26 Af., ibid., pp. 31–2.
108 Salisbury to Petre, 24/4/88, tel., 6 Af., CP 5727, p. 29; Petre to Salisbury, 25/4/88, 27 Af., ibid., pp. 32–3.
109 P. Anderson, memo., 26/4/88, CP 5727, pp. 29–30; minute by Salisbury, 27/4/88, ibid.
110 Salisbury to Petre, 28/4/88, 37 Af., CP 5727, p. 32.
111 Petre to Salisbury, 2/5/88, 30 Af., CP 5727, pp. 35–6.

doing? Nyasa is not a centre of trade. He can perform none of the ordinary duties of a Consul. The number of Her Majesty's subjects is very small. If there were no disturbance in the country, he would have absolutely nothing to do. But is a Consul the proper agent with which to deal with disturbance, if we mean to meddle with it? What weapons has he got? Or why, being without weapons, does he interfere in quarrels where he may involve Her Majesty's Government, but where he can produce no durable effect? I feel that he represents a compromise between the desire of the missionaries to obtain protection and the desire of the Home Government not to be involved in expensive operations. To please the missionaries, we send a Representative of the Government; to spare the taxpayers, we make him understand that he will in no case be supported by an armed force. The only weapon left him is bluster, for it is absurd to suppose that exhortation can have an influence on men like the Arab slave-hunters. I distrust bluster very much as a weapon. It is apt to end either in discredit or a deferred engagement for material action which cannot be honoured.[112]

Anderson considered that the original intention had been reasonable, but the advance of the Arabs and the determination of the British settlers to resist them by force had paralyzed the original peaceful intentions. Consequently, no result could be expected from the consul's influence over the chiefs.

This being so, his presence is positively mischievous. He has no power; his advice is turned against him; and yet he is a Representative, if only a dummy Representative, of British Government, and if the Government wishes to put a weapon in his hand he could not use it for British forces cannot be sent to Nyasa without leave from Lisbon. Force is out of the question.

Anderson's deduction was that the consulate should be withdrawn. If the steps were taken hastily, it would produce a bad impression in Scotland; and if the result of the struggle was to be the defeat of the Arabs or their retirement, moral influence over the chiefs might again be exercised. Lister agreed that the consulate was a mischievous institution; even if peace and prosperity were re-established, Hawes should not be sent back, but the post should be abolished.[113] The Foreign Office accordingly approved Hawes "courageous and prudent action." It instructed his substitute to confine himself to non-political duties of a strictly consular action; he was not to interfere, by action or advice, in any warlike operations; his position was to be confined to the charge of the archives of the consulate; but he was to report current events.[114] There was much to report; for he, the representative of the British Government, had been humiliated, and the African Lakes Company had resumed warlike operations.

Buchanan had proceeded to Karonga, and in its area had met Mlozi and his allies Kopa-Kopa and Msalema. These expressed themselves as desiring

112 Salisbury, minute 15/5/88, CP 5896, p. 59.
113 Anderson, minute, 16/5/88, CP 5896, pp. 59–60 and T. V. Lister, minute, 17/5/88, ibid., p. 60.
114 FO to Buchanan, 18/5/88, 2, ibid., pp. 62–3; FO to Hawes, 19/5/88, p. 63.

peace, but as soon as Buchanan announced his conditions, starting with the banishment of the three of them from Nyasa and the destruction of their stockades, negotiations broke down.[115] During his return to the south end of the lake "a most horrible scene was enacted". He landed at Makanjila's, but the tribesmen, taking exception to his consular flag and to a homily about the misdeeds of Mlozi, stripped him and kept him prisoner overnight, to be released on payment of several drums of paint and oil and several pieces of cloth and handkerchiefs. "A more dastardly act could hardly be perpetrated," he exclaimed and demanded that it be not allowed to pass unpunished, or the lives of Europeans would be endangered.[116] But only the ALC could mount a punitive expedition, and its agents were becoming increasingly involved at Karonga.

Early in May the ALC, without waiting for reinforcements which were on their way, attacked an Arab village. F. Moir was wounded before he could give the command to fire, and thirty native supporters also became casualties. ALC prospects brightened with the arrival on Nyasa of half a dozen mercenaries from Natal, and most of all with the arrival of Captain F. J. D. Lugard, who, boarded out of the Norfolk Regiment because he was "suffering from mental depression to a serious extent," and told on leave by O'Neill of the difficulties at the north end of Nyasa and the importance of upholding British authority, had responded to the consul's call. He was offered command of the expedition, and accepted it with the blessing of Buchanan (who shortly afterwards received an injunction from the Foreign Office, "Avoid any participation in warlike proceedings against Arabs"). He arrived at Karonga at the end of May. Sharpe soon joined him, having travelled overland from Bandawe with a number of Tonga he had enlisted, bringing the strength to twenty-four British (twelve employees of the Company, nine mercenaries from Natal, a medical missionary, Lugard and Sharpe) and 340 natives; the force had at its dispersal 100 Sniders and Martinis, and 160 muzzle-loaders, apart from sporting rifles. At first light on 16 June the force attacked the enemy stockade. There had been inadequate reconnaissance, and the attackers were completely unprepared to find that the stockade comprised a six-foot high loopholed mud-wall, surmounted by five or six feet of thorn branches. Ten natives were killed and three Europeans including Lugard wounded, one mortally. It was decided that the stockade was impregnable without the aid of artillery, and the force retired. A boat party, towed by a steam-launch, was sent to attack an Arab settlement at Deep Bay. Sparks exploded powder bags worn by the men, seventeen of whom were wounded; two died. This incident still further dejected the ALC and its supporters. A council meeting decided that further offensive operations would be futile without artillery support.[117]

115 Buchanan to Hawes, 12/7/88, 17 CA, CP 5896, pp. 65–71 and enclosures pp. 71–3.
116 Buchanan to Hawes, 12/4/88, 18, CP 5896, pp. 76–7.
117 Buchanan to Hawes, 24/4/88, 20, CP 5896, pp. 79–80; and 8/5/88, 23, ibid., pp. 80–1;
     J. W. Moir to Buchanan, 10/5/88, ibid., p. 84; Lugard to Buchanan, 12/5/88, ibid., pp. 86–
     7; and 16/5/88, ibid., pp. 87–88 A; D. C. Scott et al. to Buchanan, 17/5/88, ibid., p. 88 B;
     Buchanan to Hawes, 20/5/88, 26, ibid., pp. 85–6; FO to Buchanan, 26/5/88, tel., ibid.,
     p. 64;* ALC to FO, 28/5/88, tel., ibid., p. 65; Buchanan to Salisbury, 13/7/88, 36 Af.,
     ibid., p. 99; Anderson, memo, 3/8/88, ibid., p. 88 D; FO to Buchanan, 9/8/88, ibid.,
     p. 88 E; War Office to FO, 23/8/88, ibid., p. 83; Lugard to Buchanan, 10/9/88, ibid.,
     p. 108 A–C; M. F. Perham, *Lugard* (London, 1956), pp. 111–26.

The African Lakes Company accordingly demanded that it be allowed to import artillery to the area equally with small arms and ammunition. Its directors, with a naive disregard for history, told Salisbury that it was Livingstone who had discovered the Zambezi, British enterprise and energy that had exploited it. Portugal had done virtually nothing towards that end; her authority was a shadow, and it was preposterous that she should presume to sit at the gateway and levy toll on British industry and commerce. They demanded the right to import goods for Nyasaland by way of the Zambezi free of duty and molestation. As for the importation of ammunition with which to oppose the slave-traders, this was "not a personal but a European claim, nay more a claim of common humanity"; they accordingly demanded the right to import ammunition and supplies on both international and humanitarian grounds.[118] There were those who felt that "surely for the advantage of a small trading house like the African Lakes Company Her Majesty's Government would never involve the country in difficulties with Portugal,"[119] and that the Company was greatly exaggerating the differences at Karonga which in any case were caused by the overbearing manner of its managers.[120] But the British Government agreed to bring pressure to bear in Lisbon to obtain the removal of restrictions on transit trade and the admission of necessary ammunition at least.[121] An announcement to this effect in the Commons prompted the Portuguese Government, already worried by the mounting tide of newspaper hostility to Portugal, to protest against the British attitude, and again assert Portuguese claims to central Africa.[122] It notified the British Government that Portugal was prepared to bring her legislation affecting navigation and commerce on the Zambezi into harmony with the views of the British Government—provided that her territorial rights and interests in that area were secured by an arrangement with Britain.[123] Salisbury rejected territorial claims resting on ancient historic rights and recalled that at the Berlin Conference the Portuguese representative declared that she had adopted a system of free navigation on the Zambezi; and she was a party to Article 1 of the Act which bound the powers to facilitate and promote freedom of transit through existing sovereign territories. Even if she had not given any such pledge Britain would not admit her right to exclude from her waters British ships passing beyond those waters.[124] The Portuguese point of view was that all trade in arms and ammunition had

118 ALC to Salisbury 23/5/88, CP 5896, pp. 63–4; British and Foreign Anti-Slavery Society to Salisbury, 24/5/88, ibid., pp. 64–5.
119 S. W. Black to FO, 23/4/88, CP 5896, p. 57.
120 J. G. Farquharson to FO, 23/4/88, CP 5896, p. 57.
121 FO to ALC, 30/5/88, CP 5896, p. 65.
122 Barros Gomes to Henrique de Macedo, 12/4/88, Nec., SPZ 1; Gomes to Dantas, 28/5/88, CP 5727, pp. 52–8; Petre to Salisbury, 6/6/88, 41 Af., ibid., p. 59; Salisbury to Petre, 28/5/88, 50 Af., ibid., pp. 48–9.
123 Petre to Salisbury, 7/6/88, 45 Af., CP 5727, p. 59.
124 Salisbury to Petre, 25/6/88, 67 Af., CP 5727, pp. 61–2.

been prohibited to confine the state of war in the interior; Portugal claimed jurisdiction over this interior; and the Moçambique Government was both able and willing to go to the assistance of the British settlements and protect them. The ALC was a trading company, and it had incited wars among native tribes in order to divert trade into its own hands. And there was always the danger of these goods finding their way into the hands of rebels against Portuguese authority.[125] The Portuguese Government, however, out of deference to British wishes, overruled the prohibition imposed in Moçambique, and authorized the importation of arms and ammunition required by the missionaries; it required, however, to know the exact quantities required.[126]

Whilst the Foreign Office was obtaining information as to these quantities it heard that Cuirassia had sent his sons to Ibo to confirm, before the Governor there, the vassalage he had paid two years before.[127] Lisbon was informed that Cuirassia had been a vassal of Makanjila, who had expelled him, and Makanjila would undoubtedly resist by force of arms any Portuguese attempt to claim territory founded on a treaty with Cuirassia.[128] Salisbury, in fact, now asserted that Portugal had no rights north of the junction of the Shire and the Zambezi.[129]

It was at this juncture that the ALC heard of the rebuff to the forces commanded by Lugard. It promptly asked the War Office to lend it one or two light mountain guns, and the services of some officers of the British Army.[130] To Salisbury it complained of the unlimited supply of arms which the Arab "banditti" were obtaining from the "convict" population of Quelimane; and it urged the necessity for coming to an agreement with Germany lest, after further expensive operations, it find itself forestalled by German penetration. It requested him to obtain Portuguese permission to pass a Hotchkiss quick-firing gun (a three- or six-pounder), also about two light mountain guns, possibly nine-pounders, and ammunition for them.[131] But the Foreign Office received new light on events when a convalescent F. Moir, visited Whitehall, and revealed that since the outbreak of hostilities the ALC had received, through Quelimane, no less than 400 Sniders and 40,000 cartridges.[132] Salisbury decided, however, not to object to officers volunteering for service with the ALC, and he passed on the request regarding the artillery to Lisbon, with the proviso,

---

125 Petre to Salisbury, 27/6/88, 57 Af., CP 5896, pp. 624–5; Sir G. Bonham to Salisbury, 3/7/88, 59 Af., ibid., p. 626; Castilho to Min., 10/7/88, 2/220, AHU, Moç., 2 Rep. Caixa 5.

126 Bonham to Salisbury, 4/7/88, 6 Af., tel, CP 5896, p. 625, and 5/7/88, 62 Af., ibid., pp. 627–8; FO to ALC, 7/7/88, ibid., p. 82.

127 Termo de ratificação de Vassalagem . . ., 13/5/88, Bol. Off., 26/5/88.

128 Salisbury to Bonham, 28/7/88, 81 Af., CP 5727, pp. 71–2; Bonham to Salisbury, 6/8/88, 79 Af., p. 76.

129 Bonham to Salisbury, 9/7/88, 68 Af., CP 5727, pp. 64–5; Bonham to Gomes, 1/8/88, Nec., SPZ 1, Neg., pp. 70–1.

130 ALC to War Office, 8/8/88, CP 5896, pp. 88F–90.

131 ALC to Salisbury 11/8/88, CP 5896, p. 90; and 13/8/88, p. 91.

132 C. Hill, memo., 10/8/88, CP 5896, p. 89.

however, that the Company pay for the guns.[133] The overtures in Lisbon brought repeated assertions of rights by Portugal to the Nyasa area, while continued disturbances on the lower Zambezi made the authorities unwilling to allow the entry of artillery lest it fall into rebel hands.[134] Salisbury described the Portuguese refusal to allow passage of the guns as an unfriendly act; but just at the time when the Portuguese cabinet was reconsidering the matter, an article in *The Times*, suggesting that Delagoa Bay might fall into British hands, re-awakened Portuguese suspicions of British intentions; the cabinet, while it sanctioned the passage of arms, refused to consider the admitting of artillery for the use of a private company, lest it fall into the hands of elements hostile to the Portuguese Government; such permission could not be granted to a Portuguese, not even to Manuel António de Sousa, exclaimed the Minister of Foreign Affairs. Sir G. Bonham, the British Chargé d'Affairs in Lisbon, appealed to Luciano de Castro, the Prime Minister; he denied that Britain had territorial ambitions in the area, pointing out that Britain had declined to protect the mission stations, and declared that Britain demanded only commercial facilities. Castro could hold out only some prospect for a more liberal commercial policy by his Government. Bonham proposed to his Government that Britain give an undertaking that the artillery would not fall into the hands of Portugal's enemies; but, he pointed out, this would entail assuming the responsibility of a protectorate.[135] Salisbury instructed Bonham to press the Portuguese Government to reconsider its decision; if lives were lost fighting the slave-traders, the British people would hold the Portuguese Government responsible; the ALC gave assurances that neither the guns nor the ammunition would be ever given or sold to Arabs or natives, so the British Government gave the Portuguese an engagement to this effect.[136]

But now permanent officials in the Foreign Office began to realize the implication of Salisbury's stand. Lister pointed out that a State possessing the whole course of a river and its tributaries could, failing treaties to the contrary, forbid the navigation of such rivers to foreigners; there could be no question of transit. But where the upper waters or affluents belonged to other states, the question of transit immediately arose. The Niger Company, for instance, had the right to levy customs duties, not transit dues; the Germans to evade these duties were trying to persuade the chiefs of the upper waters to declare themselves independent of the Niger Company. The Portuguese claimed the Shire and the country bordering on Nyasa, and so denied that there was any question of transit, and that they had the right to regulate or forbid the importation of arms into their territory. In fact, the whole question at issue was basically a

---

133 Salisbury to Bonham, 17/8/88, 88 Af., CP 5896, p. 636; FO to WO, 18/8/88, ibid., p. 91.
134 Bonham to Salisbury, 18/8/88, 82, CP 5896, p. 636; and 20/8/88, 83 Af., CP 5727, p. 82; and 22/8/88, 84 Af., ibid., pp. 86–7; and 23/8/88, 85 Af., CP 5896, pp. 639–40.
135 Salisbury to Bonham, 29/8/88, 93 Af., CP 5896, p. 640; Bonham to Salisbury, 29/8/88, 87 Af., ibid., pp. 641–2, and 4/9/88, 95 Af., ibid., pp. 640–1; and 5/9/88, 98 Af., ibid., pp. 644–5; and 6/9/88, 100 Af., ibid., p. 642.
136 Salisbury to Bonham, 6/9/88, 97 Af., CP 5896, p. 643; and 7/9/88, 101, ibid., p. 643; Bonham to Gomes, 8/9/88, ibid., pp. 645–7, Nec., SPZ 1, and *Neg.*, pp. 57–9; Salisbury to Bonham, 20/9/88, 107 Af., CP 5896, p. 649.

matter of territorial claims. Hertslet's memorandum showed how weak were the British claims. If the Zambezi and its affluents were indeed Portuguese, Britain could ask permission to navigate it, or claim the right to do so. If the upper waters were beyond Portuguese limits, Britain could ask permission for transit, or claim the right to do so. The first alternatives were very mild; the second were not supported by international law or by the Berlin agreement, Lister concluded, but he gathered that that was what Britain was demanding. Salisbury minuted that he and Lister were entirely at cross purposes: he imagined the request of the ALC to be for permission to carry the gun across what was undoubtedly Portuguese territory; the custom-house was at Quelimane, and a land portage of half a mile was necessary from the head of the Cuacua to the Zambezi, for the Congone mouth of the Zambezi was too shallow for ocean-going ships. Salisbury did not dispute the right of Portugal to bar transport of the gun across Portuguese soil; but there was no indisputable right to bar passage up a navigable river to territory beyond that State's control; Portuguese claims to the banks of the Zambezi were of a very shadowy nature, Salisbury held; and if the ALC decided that it could introduce the gun by way of the Congone mouth, Britain would see that no one stopped it. But on the Zambezi itself, owing to the shallowness of the water, Britain had no *de facto* power.[137]

The ALC sent to South Africa a seven-pounder muzzle-loading mountain gun, and in Natal purchased a twelve-pounder breech-loading gun.[138] Bonham was required to ask for further transit rights for the second gun and more ammunition. Barros Gomes, the Minister of Foreign Affairs, insisted that it was still the principle that was at stake, irrespective of the number of guns; the ALC repudiated Portuguese sovereignty in the area. English newspapers and periodicals were waging a campaign against Portuguese rights in south-east Africa, and Barros Gomes repeated a request he had previously made for delimitation of the Portuguese-British frontier south of the Zambezi.[139] Under pressure from Bonham the Portuguese cabinet reconsidered the matter of the artillery. It appreciated the guarantees offered, but pointed out that it could not provide for the possible eventuality of the guns being taken by the Arabs and used against the Portuguese. It admitted that to avoid loss of life immediate action was necessary. The Portuguese Government was willing to send orders to Moçambique to intervene and if possible end the hostility by peaceful means, and if those failed, actively to support the British efforts.[140] Barros Gomes elaborated his Government's point of view in a letter to the Sociedade de Geografia, which had staged a monster demonstration in support of Portuguese rights in Africa after disturbances in Lourenço Marques. It quite appreciated the paramount importance of developing use of the great waterways of the Zambezi and the Shire as routes into the interior; and these would soon be

137 T. V. Lister and Salisbury, minutes, 11–13/9/88, CP 5727, p. 95; FO to ALC, 30/9/88, CP 5896, p. 105.
138 ALC to Salisbury, 3 and 13/9/88, CP 5896, pp. 99–100, 101–2.
139 Bonham to Salisbury, 12/9/88, 104, CP 5727, p. 98.
140 Barros Gomes to Bonham 14/9/88, CP 5896, pp. 650–2; Bonham to Salisbury, 17/9/88, tel., 12 Af., CP 5896, p. 648, CP 5727, p. 99, and 17/9/88, 110 Af., pp. 649 and 99–100; and 19/9/88, 114 Af., CP 5896, pp. 652–3.

supplemented by a railway from Quelimane to the junction of the Shire, later to be extended up the Shire, and past the Quebrabasa rapids. Moderate transit dues and a more liberal policy would open up the vast mineral resources of the interior. But it was an indispensable condition that facilities thus granted to the commerce of the world should not be turned into the means of opposition to Portuguese political supremacy. It was essential for the frontiers of Portugal to be delimited.[141]

Salisbury reminded Barros Gomes that Britain had never admitted the claims of Portugal to the Nyasa valley.[142] *The Times* pointed out that Portugal had never claimed the north end of the lake, where the Karonga operations were taking place. Opinion in Britain hardened against Portugal, and Salisbury required Bonham to bring further pressure to bear on the Portuguese Government to admit the artillery—one gun had reached Quelimane, and a third was being bought in Natal—without accepting the Portuguese offer of assistance which in any case was rather empty, considering her difficulties on the lower Zambezi and that there were no Portuguese vessels on Nyasa. Bonham prepared a memorandum which stressed that the arms were required in an area far beyond the limits claimed by Portugal and beyond where they were in a position to send assistance. His arguments told with the Council of Ministers which eventually granted the permission required. But Bonham stressed to Salisbury that the basic difference would continue until the Portuguese frontier had been defined.[143] The arrival of a second gun and more ammunition at Quelimane resulted in new difficulties, the Portuguese Government being afraid of renewed hostile comment in the press and the Cortes. When reminded that the principle had been settled, and that permission had been sought for the entry of three guns it gave way.[144] When, however, Britain called for an international blockade of the north Moçambique coast to prevent the importation of arms for the slave-traders and the export of slaves, Portugal agreed to this only on condition that it be by her own naval forces; to make it effective, she would increase her number of naval units on the coast.[145] When the ALC requested permission to import a machine-gun, the Portuguese authorities were able to declare that this was incompatible with the blockade; and when a missionary landed at Quelimane, his revolver for personal defence and a pocket full of ammunition were confiscated.[146] The Sultan of Zanzibar sent an envoy to the

141 Bonham to Salisbury, 18/9/88, 112 Af., CP 5727, p. 104.
142 Salisbury to Bonham, 3/10/88, 116 Af., CP 5727, p. 114; Bonham to Barros Gomes, 9/10/88, ibid., p. 116.
143 ALC to Salisbury, 13/10/88, CP 5896, pp. 105–6; Bonham to Salisbury, 14/10/88, tel., 14 Af., and 126 Af., ibid., pp. 653–655; Salisbury to Bonham, 16/10/88, tel., 16 Af., ibid., p. 654; Bonham, memo., 17/10/88, Nec., SPZ 1, *Neg.*, pp. 62–3; Bonham to Salisbury, 18/10/88, tel., 15 Af., and 128 Af., 1 CP 5896, pp. 653, 660–1; Salisbury to Bonham, 18/10/88, tel., 17 Af., ibid., p. 654; Bonham to Salisbury, 19/10/88, tel., 16 Af., ibid., p. 656 and 133 Af., pp. 662–3; and 20/10/88, 136, Af., p. 657.
144 Petre to Salisbury, 12/11/88, 152 Af., CP 5896, p. 666; and 13/11/88, 153 Af., ibid., p. 668; Salisbury to Petre, 14/11/88, 146 Af., ibid., p. 667. Petre to Salisbury, 15/11/88, 158 Af., ibid., p. 668.
145 Petre to Gomes, 16/11/88, CP 5770, p. 175; Petre to Salisbury, 17/11/88, 24 Af., p. 138; Gomes to Petre 18/11/88, ibid., p. 245; Salisbury to Malet, 27/11/88, 264 Af., ibid., p. 291.
146 Gomes to Dantas, 7/1/89, tel., *Neg.*, p. 7; Ross to British consul, Moçambique, 8/3/89, FO 179/264.

Karonga area to try and persuade the Arabs to make peace, but fifty days of negotiation failed to produce result, and fighting again flared up.[147] The ALC requested additional shells for its mountain gun, 100 more Snider rifles, and 50,000 rounds of ammunition. The Portuguese authorities again referred to the state of blockade, and decrees which carried five years' imprisonment for trading in arms and ammunitions. But they could and did grant exemptions to individuals; and made presents themselves of arms and powder to chiefs which were all the more appreciated in view of the growing shortage.[148]

Portuguese influence in the Nyasa area was increasing, thanks especially to the efforts of the Cardosos. In July 1888, the King had put his signature to confidential instructions to António Maria Cardoso, a first lieutenant of the Navy. Cardoso was to establish a mission on Nyasa which would serve as a centre from which Portugal would enlarge her influence in the area, taking advantage of the respect that the people of those regions had for the Portuguese and the repugnance with which some of them regarded the English. He was to establish the mission in the territory of Chief Cuirassia, taking advantage of the vassalage he had paid in 1886 to Augusto de Melo Cardoso; this site, on the south-east of the lake, would be conducive to the comfort and security of the personnel of the mission; and it was well situated as a base for possible future operations; Cuirassia and the neighbouring chiefs were to be well treated; in fact, no hostility was to be shown to either foreigners established in those parts or native tribes; the latter were to be persuaded by words and by deeds that Portugal had no desire to conquer them, but only to protect them, and provide them with the means of increasing their commerce. The Government intended to place steam-boats on the Shire and Nyasa, so Cardoso was to report on the means of communication. He received a grant of twenty-five thousand milreis for his mission.[149]

But unfortunately for Portugal Cuirassia had been a tributary of Makanjila, and Makanjila had already driven Cuirassia from his land. Makanjila was in alliance with Mponda, who controlled the entrance to the lake, so only by force of arms could Portugal hope to found her proposed settlement. The British consul in Nyasaland admitted to Salisbury that if a troublesome chief like Makanjila could be completely subjugated the slave-trade would receive a considerable check, and the moral effect on other chiefs would be of immense advantage to white settlement generally.[150] On his arrival at the mouth of the Zambezi Cardoso was shown a telegram from his minister inviting him to give assistance to the British mission on Nyasa. He entered the Chinde mouth, and engaged close on 300 hunters from the Marral *prazo* and 250 sepoys from Maganja; a number of Landeens also accompanied the expedition, the total strength of which was about 1,200 men armed with Sniders, Enfields and Chapupats and supported by machine-guns and two Hotchkiss guns, while there

147 M. F. Perham, *Lugard* (London, 1956), 1, pp. 137–8.
148 ALC to Salisbury, 15/4/89, CP 5970, p. 58 which makes reference to 400 rounds of shell for the 7 pr mountain gun; it is not clear whether two guns were referred to. J. Stevenson to *Times*, 28/4/89, *Neg.*, p. 33; Ross to Smith, 3/5/89, ibid., p. 118; Buchanan to Salisbury, 23/5/89, 19 CA, ibid., p. 139.
149 Rei, instruction, 5/7/88, Nec., SPZ 1.
150 Hawes to Salisbury, 23/7/88, CP 5727, pp. 69–70.

were over 2,000 carriers. Cardoso was understandably in no fear of hostility from the natives, but drought and famine might embarrass the expedition. The expedition crossed the slopes of Mlanje, finding an abundance of water, and passed up the west side of Lake Shirwa, shadowed by Buchanan's spies. A handsome present made its way to Mponda, with a request for an interview, but the chief refused to see Cardoso, who accordingly kept to the east.[151] The expedition reached its goal on 12 December 1888 when Cardoso confirmed that Cuirassia had indeed been driven out from his lake-side position by Makanjila, and was leading a precarious existence in the hills in the interior, in latitude 13° 38' south. Cuirassia agreed to the establishment of the mission—and in fact welcomed it—but the site was useless from the Portuguese point of view and there was constant threat of attack from Makanjila. Cardoso reported to his superiors that it was absolutely impossible for him to comply with his instructions, and he requested new orders to be telegraphed him as far as possible.[152] The Portuguese Government had already ordered a supporting expedition to be organized, with some 300 Landeens under the command of Augusto Cardoso. It urged Maria Cardoso to remain active in the area, trying especially to secure the vassalage of Makanjila, until the relief expedition could arrive. But Augusto Cardoso refused to command the relief column, alleging ill health, and Geraldes also declined. Eventually Serpa Pinto undertook to command the expedition. But whilst Serpa Pinto was on his way from Portugal to South Africa such good news arrived from Nyasa that orders for the relief expedition were countermanded.[153]

Cardoso had been spending his time to good advantage pending authority to retire, and he succeeded in gaining the vassalage of a considerable number of chiefs at the south-eastern corner of Nyasa, mainly between latitudes 12° and 13° south. They signed the standard form of treaty, by which they declared themselves vassals of the King of Portugal, begged for a Portuguese flag, promised to help any Portuguese traveller, send an embassy to Quelimane to renew this vassalage before the Governor, obey the orders of the King of Portugal, and defend and honour the flag. Cardoso even succeeded in persuading Mponda and Matapwira to put their marks to such treaties.[154] No

151 O'Neill to Salisbury, 13/9/88, 50, CP 5727, p. 119; A. M. Cardoso to Dir. Geral, 16/10/88, 19 Confid., AHU, Moç., 2 Rep., Caixa 5; O'Neill to Salisbury, 8/11/88, tel., CP 5896, p. 665, CP 5727, p. 124.
152 Buchanan to Salisbury, 27/11/88, 48, CP 5970, p. 11; and 1/12/88, 50, ibid., p. 19; Petre to Salisbury, 21/1/89, 8 Af., ibid., p. 13; Buchanan to Salisbury, 28/1/89, 8 CA, ibid., p. 59; Cardoso to Dir. Geral, 31/1/89, tel., Neg., p. 7, Petre to Salisbury, 13/3/89, 23 Af., CP 5970, pp. 37–8; and 14/3/89, 24 Af., ibid., p. 38.
153 Min. to GG, 2/2/89, tel., Neg., pp. 7–8; and 3/2/89; ibid., p. 8; Min to Gov., L.M., 7/3/89, tel., Neg., p. 13; Gov. L.M. to GG, 8/3/89, tel., ibid., p. 13; GG to Dir. Geral. 15/3/89, Neç., SPZ 2, Neg., p. 13. Petre to Salisbury, 17/3/89, 25 Af., CP 5970, p. 39; Petre to Salisbury, 42, ibid., p. 60.
154 Termo de Vassallagem, Carange bin Kintira Macanga, 17/1/89, Bol. Off., 30/3/89, p. 211, and Termos, pp. 46–7; Meponda Mucuata, 11/2/89, ibid., pp. 211 and 48; Kabuto Messaco, 25/2/89, ibid., pp. 211 and 49; Nametungue bin Mutuana, 6/3/89, Termos, pp. 49–50. Muita bin Capambala, 6/3/89, ibid., p. 50; Maniamba bin Mucondora, 6/3/89, ibid., p. 51, confirmed, Quelimane, 15/6/89, pp. 51–2; Quingomage bin Maponda, 6/3/89, ibid., p. 52, confirmed, Quelimane, 15/6/89, pp. 52–3; Massange bin Capirula, 6/3/89, ibid., p. 54, confirmed, Quelimane, 15/6/89, pp. 53–5; Maendaenda, 6/3/89, ibid., p. 56, confirmed, Quelimane, 6/4/89, pp. 56–7; Mapunda bin Quiçolola, 6/3/89, ibid., p. 58; Chitesse bin Metepereira, 6/3/89, ibid., p. 58; Maniamba bin Chipaniro, 7/3/89, ibid., pp. 55–6; Matapire Macinda, 20/3/89, ibid., p. 59; and Bol. Off., 4/5/89, pp. 291–2 for further ratifications.

matter how much Buchanan might scoff at these treaties, declaring that any chief would put his mark on anything in return for an express rifle, a few hundred yards of cloth, and promises of powder, and Ross, the vice-consul in Quelimane, might describe the confirmation ceremonies as "just the sort of thing any one in authority could get an ignorant native to do for a few pieces of cotton and a gaudy flag",[155] Cardoso's treaties presented Portugal with a spectacular triumph. He left a lieutenant in the Nyasa area, and returned to the coast, to be greeted with cables of the warmest and most fulsome praise from his minister.[156]

The Portuguese Government had arranged for the strongest spiritual support for the new mission. Cardinal Lavigerie, founder in Algeria of the near-militant missionary order Société de Notre-Dame d'Afrique, had worked out plans for a central African mission, and had already sent some of his White Fathers to east Africa, to territories bordering on Lakes Tanganyika and Victoria. In 1888 he toured Europe, preaching a crusade against slavery, and adding to his reputation as an authority on Africa.[157] Barros Gomes enlisted Lavigerie's aid in the Cardoso mission. Through Martens, the Portuguese ambassador in Rome, he settled the details by which Lavigerie and his Order were to co-operate in the foundation of this Portuguese Catholic mission in the region south-east of Nyasa. The mission was to be considered Portuguese. The Cardinal undertook to send out five missionaries, to propagate the Catholic faith, found churches, chapels and schools, suppress the slave traffic, etc. In the schools the natives were to be taught through the Portuguese medium. The Portuguese Government undertook to give the mission free passage, and all protection. It made available 9,000 milreis for the initial establishment, and an annual subsidy of 3,600 milreis.[158]

When it learnt that the Cardoso expedition was giving promise of success, and that Lavigerie's influential support had been pledged to it, the British Government saw advantages in coming to an agreement with Portugal over the territorial claims of the two countries.

155 Buchanan to Salisbury, 8/3/89, CP 5970, pp. 85–6; Ross to Smith, 24/4/89, ibid., pp. 109–10.
156 J. J. Almeida to Min., 29/3/89, tel., *Neg.*, p. 16; Cardoso to Min., 10/4/89, tel., ibid., p. 19; Min. to GG, 21/4/89, tel., ibid., p. 21. Further acts or ratifications were of Mutomanga Mucuate, 11/4/89, *Termos*, pp. 60–1; Malemia Mucoola of the lands of Zomba etc., ibid., pp. 61–2; Kauvinga, 27/5/89, ibid., p. 62.
157 R. Oliver, *The missionary factory in East Africa* (London, 1952), pp. 45–9; G. Goyau, *Un grand missionaire le cardinal Lavigerie* (Paris, 1925).
158 Gomes to Martens, 10/11/88, *Neg.*, 1891, pp. 243–5; Martens to Gomes, 23/11/88, Nec., SPZ 2 and *Neg.*, pp. 245–7; Lavigerie to Martens, 26/11/88, ibid., p. 247; Gomes to Martens, 4/12/88, Nec., SPZ 1, and *Neg.*, pp. 248–50; Martens to Lavigerie, 14/12/88, Nec., SPZ 1; Lavigerie to Gomes, 3/2/89, *Neg.*, p. 251; and 25/5/89, ibid., pp. 254–6; Gomes to Lavigerie, 27/5/89, with draft convention, ibid., p. 256.

10

DIPLOMACY

Portugal had for long been worried about foreign competition not only in Nyasaland but in Mashonaland. Her Government knew that the latter country was rich in mineral wealth and it thoroughly appreciated that the plateau was ideally suited for white colonization. Its most likely fate, it was felt in the middle 1880's, was to fall under the heel of adventurers from the South African Republic[1]—unless, of course, Portugal could make effective her occupation of the area which she regarded as being reserved to her by historic right. There seemed to be more prospect of such a possibility after her diplomatic successes of 1886.

In May 1886 a convention between Portugal and France defined the common boundaries of their territories in Africa. An article added:

> The Government of the French Republic recognises the right of His Most Faithful Majesty to exercise his sovereign and civilising influence in the territories which separate the Portuguese possessions of Angola and Moçambique, reserving rights already acquired by other Powers, and binds itself on its side to abstain from all occupation there.

This was followed by a treaty between Portugal and Germany, signed in December 1886, which declared "certain boundaries, within which each of the two Powers shall keep their freedom of action for their colonizing activity." In south-east Africa the line ran from the mouth of the Cunene River to the Ruacana falls, thence along the line of latitude to the River Cubango, up that river to the village Andara, and from there due east to the Katima rapids on the Zambezi. In south-east Africa the line ran from the mouth of the Rovuma River to its confluence with the Msinje, and thence along the line of latitude to the shores of Nyasa. And

> His Majesty the German Emperor recognises the right of His Majesty the King of Portugal to exercise his influence of sovereignty and civilisation in the territories which separate the Portuguese possessions of Angola and Moçambique without prejudice to the rights which other Powers may have acquired there up to now of exercising their sovereign and civilising influence.

The Portuguese Government published a white book which contained the

---

1 Min., London, to Min., 4/10/84, 138A, Nec., SPZ 1, enclosing cutting from *Daily News*, 2/10/84.

treaty, annexed to which was a map which indicated the belt claimed by Portugal for the exercise of her influence.[2]

On the publication of these treaties with France and Germany, Britain promptly protested to the Portuguese Government. Especially did the British Government object to the "immense field" which Portugal reserved to her enterprise:

> In the districts to which Portugal thus appears to lay a preferential claim, and in which, except near the sea-coast and on portions of the Zambezi River, there is not a sign of Portuguese jurisdiction or authority, there are countries in which there are British Settlements, in which Great Britain takes an exceptional interest . . . Great Britain considers that it has now been admitted in principle by all parties to the Act of Berlin that a claim of sovereignty in Africa can only be maintained by real occupation of the territory claimed . . .

The British protest applied in particular to the districts of Nyasa occupied by British traders and missionaries, and to Matabeleland; it further pointed out that Portugal was debarred from expanding southwards of the 26° 30′ south line of latitude.[3]

The reply of the Portuguese Minister of Foreign Affairs was that while the occupation articles of the Act of Berlin applied only to the coast and not to the interior, Portugal had no wish to dispute the sovereign rights of other powers where they could be shown to exist; she certainly had no intention of extending her dominion south of 26° 30′ south; and in fact Portugal was most anxious to arrive at an understanding with Britain similar to her agreements with France and Germany, to define with precision the respective spheres of influence in southern Africa; Barros Gomes added that he looked forward eagerly to the time when negotiations with this end in view could be set on foot in Lisbon.[4] He followed this up by a memorandum elaborating the Portuguese argument, quoting back to the 1629 treaty with Monomotapa, and arguing that the British protest was void of foundation.[5] Holland, the Secretary of State for the Colonies, considered that defining British and Portuguese spheres of influence would not be to the advantage of the British colonies in South Africa; he sought their opinion, and months passed without reply being made to the Portuguese proposal.[6]

The Moffat treaty revealed the Cape Colony as a greater menace to Portuguese claims than the Transvaal. Carvalho, the Portuguese consul in Cape Town, without waiting for instruction from Lisbon, promptly protested to the High Commissioner, declaring that the Crown of Portugal claimed sovereignty

2 Hertslet, *Map*, pp. 298–300, 323–6. Carta da Africa Meridional Portuguese 1886. Pl. 10.
3 FO to CO, 13/7/87, CP 5727, p. 5, CP CO Af. No. 359, pp. 5–6; CO to FO, 27/7/87, CP 5727, pp. 5–6, Af. No. 359, p. 16; Salisbury to Petre, 2/8/87, 89 Af., CP 5727, p. 6, Af. No. 359, pp. 18–9, Hertslet, *Map*, pp. 325–6.
4 Bunsen to Salisbury, 17/8/87, 106 Af., CP 5727, pp. 7–8, Af. No. 359, pp. 21–2.
5 Barros Gomes to Bunsen, 19/8/87, CP 5727, pp. 9–11, Af., No. 359, pp. 50–2.
6 CO to FO, 2/12/87, CP 5727, p. 12, Af. No. 359, p. 76; FO to CO, 13/12/87, CP 5727, pp. 12–3, Af. No. 359, p. 79.

over Mashonaland by rights of conquest and cession.[7] To his amazement, Robinson accepted his protest. Carvalho correctly saw that the British assertion of Lobengula's rights over the Shona was a preliminary act to future British annexation northwards, and he regretted that his advice had not been followed to send an ambassador to Lobengula and to define the western boundary of the province of Moçambique.[8] The Portuguese Government instructed its minister in London to protest to the British Government, adding that it trusted that Britain would act in this matter with the same loyalty to its ancient ally as Portugal had to Britain over the matter of Tongaland.[9] Dantas averred to Salisbury that British maps showed the Shona and Kalakas as under the direct influence—and even the effective occupation—of Portugal, and he left with the Foreign Office a memorandum giving the Portuguese point of view.[10]

But the Foreign Office was not converted. A Government statement in the House of Commons brusquely announced that the Government did not recognize the unlimited claims of Portugal in the interior of Africa. Her influence was acknowledged where settlement had taken place and she possessed the means to maintain order, protect foreigners and control the natives. Portugal had made no advance in settling the interior, she had not attained a position which rendered her capable of fulfilling international duties.[11] The statement inflamed public opinion in Portugal, and led to another visit by Dantas to the Foreign Office. Salisbury tartly recalled Portuguese action at Tungue.[12] And unfortunately for Portugal the annexure to the treaty with Germany marked the Shona and Kalakas as being within the boundaries of Matabeleland.[13]

Petre, after a conversation with Barros Gomes, reported that he did not think that Portugal would give practical effect to her claim to close the Zambezi to free navigation; but she would not forego that claim without an equivalent. What the Portuguese Government desired above all else, to obtain which she would make any sacrifice short of ceding territory, was to obtain recognition of the Zambezi as the southern boundary of the Portuguese sphere of influence. Petre declared that this would shut the door against future expansion northwards of British colonies in South Africa. Barros Gomes replied that the door would be an open one and ample provision would be made for transit and commerce.[14]

Holland, now Lord Knutsford, was prepared to accept the Zambezi as the southern limit of Portuguese influence, leaving Portugal free to expand northwards and westwards, provided free trade along that river were indeed

7 E. A. de Carvalho to Robinson, 27/4/88, *Negocios Externos: Documentos apresentados ás Cortes . . . 1890 . . . Negocios da Africa Oriental e Central . . . 1890*, p. 109.
8 Carvalho to Min., 1/5/88, 14, Nec., SPZ 1.
9 Barros Gomes to Dantas, 29/4/88, tel., ibid.
10 Dantas to Salisbury, 1/5/88, CP 5727, p. 33; Petre to Salisbury, 2/5/88, 30 Af., ibid., pp. 35–6.
11 Sir J. Fergusson, 17/5/88, CP 5727, p. 42; Petre to Salisbury, 20/5/88, 37 Af., ibid., pp. 44–5.
12 Pauncefote, memo., 23/5/88 and minutes by H.P.A. and Salisbury, 23/5/, ibid., pp. 41–3. The Portuguese point of view was well expressed by 'A Portuguese' in *The Morning Post*, 20/6/88, Nec., SPZ 1.
13 Carta da Africa Meridional Portugueza, 1886.
14 Petre to Salisbury, 2/5/88., 30 Af., CP 5727, pp. 35–6.

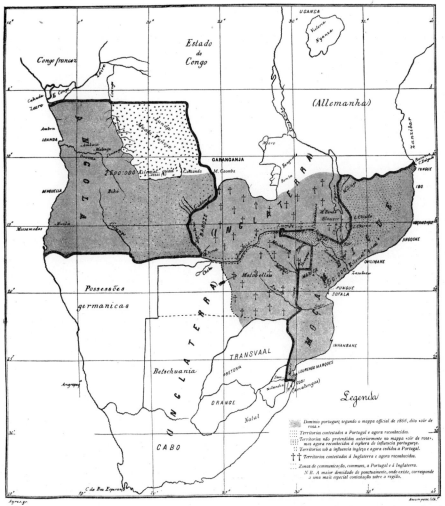

10 Sketch-map of southern Africa to show the area (shaded) claimed by Portugal as reserved
for Portuguese influence in the map annexed to the Portuguese-German Treaty of 1886
(from J. de Almada, *Tratados aplicaveis ao Ultramar*. Mapas apensos ao Volume V,
Lisbon, 1943, No. LXXIII)

confirmed. Anderson welcomed this opinion, for on this basis an agreement might be negotiated:

> The vanity of the Portuguese, though nearly insatiable, would for the present be satisfied with recognition of a sphere of influence between their westward colony of Angola, and their eastern of Moçambique, by which the Zambezi would be the southern boundary. To secure this they would give substantial concessions.

The British colonies would free themselves of Portuguese claims to Mashonaland, and would lose nothing by agreeing to such a sphere of influence. He agreed that freedom of navigation on the Zambezi would have to be guaranteed. Portugal, moreover, should be required to undertake not to occupy the Nyasa area without the assent of Britain; this was all that the traders and missionaries wanted, and at the same time it would "get rid of the impracticable idea of a British Protectorate." There must be fixed transit dues and commercial facilities for the Nyasa area and transit and other facilities from Delagoa Bay. There would have to be a fixed line, perhaps a line of longitude, to hedge in the Portuguese between Delagoa Bay and the Zambezi. Salisbury approved that the proposal be put to the Colonial Office; he only hoped that the Colonial Office would not consult the colonies, which would mean a delay until the Greek Kalends.[15] Salisbury accordingly instructed Petre, "It is not my wish that you should make at present any further request for the definition of the Portuguese claims in regard to the countries south of the Zambezi."[16] But the Portuguese proposal was put formally to the Colonial Office.[17] Petre was now receiving word, through an anonymous paid informant (whom he believed to be an official in Barros Gomes's own office) "of a plan, which has been cleverly drawn up, for the purpose of depriving the British Crown of a most important part of territories which might hereafter become its property when a delimitation of frontiers will, at some future time, have to be discussed."[17a] In July 1888, the two Cardosos, Andrada and Cordon, left Lisbon for Africa.[18]

Robinson proposed that the British Government should declare to the governments of Portugal and Germany and the South African Republic a British

---

15 Minutes by H.P.A., 8/6/88, J.F., 8/6/88, Salisbury, 10/6/88, CP 5727, pp. 39–41.
16 Salisbury to Petre, 58 Af., 11/6/88, Af. No. 358, pp. 32–3.
17 FO to CO, 20/6/88, p. 37, and CP 5727, p. 60: "It appears to His Lordship that if the principle were adopted with the assent of the South African Colonies, that there would be no objection to conceding to Portugal a sphere of influence to the north of the Zambezi between the Colonies of Angola and Moçambique, on her assenting as far as she is concerned, to an exclusive British sphere of influence in all the territories to the south of that river, not at present comprised in the Moçambique Colony, it might be possible to endeavour to negotiate an arrangement under which the respective spheres of influence should be thus delimited in return for stipulations for the free navigation of the Zambezi, and neutralization of the Nyasa districts with fixed transit dues and commercial facilities, and of guarantee of most-favoured nation treatment in Moçambique for British trade which would secure equality of our commerce in the Delagoa Bay districts. Such an arrangement would, of necessity, involve some delimitation of the interior of the frontier of Moçambique, north and south of the Zambezi."
17a Petre to Salisbury, 12/6/68, Af. No. 358, p. 39; FO to CO, 28/6/88, ibid., p. 38; Petre to Salisbury, 18/3/89, Af. 21, FO 179/269.
18 Bonham to Cardozo, 12/7/88, 70 Af., Af. No. 358, p. 49.

sphere of influence over the country between the Zambezi and the Bechuana-land Protectorate and the Transvaal, east of 20° east longitude and west of the Portuguese province of Sofala.[19] The Colonial Office concurred, and recommended that the South African Republic be notified immediately, since Grobler was on his way to Matabeleland.[20] Grobler's death[21] made this communication less urgent. Knutsford declared to Robinson that the delimitation of the Portuguese sphere of influence in South Africa seemed to him "well calculated to secure in the best practicable manner substantial advantages to British trade and British interests generally."[22] Salisbury considered that it was essential to announce to Portugal the British sphere to forestall action by the Portuguese explorers then on their way to the Zambezi.[23] The Portuguese Minister of Foreign Affairs welcomed the invitation to delimit the frontier. Informed of the proposed British sphere, Barros Gomes reminded the British Government that Portugal had exercised influence south of the Zambezi for three hundred years, and declared that much of that area was in actual occupation by Portugal, her influence extending as far west as the Sanyati River; nearer the coast, *prazos* were under Portuguese authority; and Gungunhana was under Portuguese protection.[24] The British Government chose this moment to declare as being valueless Portugal's treaty with Cuirassia. The Portuguese Government's reply was to call on Andrada and Cardoso to act with still greater energy—but with all prudence.[25]

The High Commissioner, after duly proclaiming as being within the British sphere of influence all territories northwards to the Zambezi, between 20° east and the Portuguese possessions, reported, "If the Cis-Zambezi territory so defined should prove as rich in gold as it is supposed to be, it seems possible that it may, either as a part of the Cape Colony or as a separate dependency, eventually become a portion of Her Majesty's dominions."[26] But where was the eastern boundary to be drawn? Gifford complained that the Compagnie de Moçambique was granting concessions in the Mazoe valley—one concessionaire had been granted the sole right to prospect over 3,600 square miles—and this was in the area reserved for British influence. Gifford's solution was simple: the Portuguese "ought to be got rid of if possible." Gifford was also looking across the Zambezi to Barotseland, "a valuable tract of country", where he was prepared to put British capital to work. But the Colonial Office

19 Robinson to Knutsford, 20/6/88, received 12/7/88, 249, CP 5727, p. 40.
20 CO to FO, 19/7/88, CP 5727, p. 87.
21 Carvalho to Min., 31/7/88, 35, Nec., SPZ 1. With further warnings of the machinations of Portugal's enemies.
22 28/6/88, Af. No. 358, p. 38.
23 FO to CO, 23/7/88, Af. No. 358, p. 50, CP 5727, p. 69.
24 Salisbury to Bonham, 24/7/88, 80 Af., CP 5727, pp. 70–1; Bonham to Barros Gomes, 2/8/88, CP 5727, p. 75; Gomes to Bonham, 6/8/88, ibid., pp. 78–9 and Af. No. 358, p. 57. For a summary of Portuguese claims in Africa by 'P', presumed by Bonham to be Serpa Pinto, see Bonham to Salisbury, 3/8/88, 77 Af., Af. No. 358, p. 53.
25 Min. to GG, 7/8/88, tel., Neg., p. 6.
26 Robinson to Knutsford, 8/8/88, Af. No. 358, p. 59.

declared it could not consider taking a chief on that side of the river under British protection.[27]

Barros Gomes became still more apprehensive of Cape intentions when a blue book appeared containing a map marking Mashonaland as reserved for British influence. The minister again quoted the Portuguese-German agreement of 1886, and suggested that the German Government be invited to join in the settlement of the Portuguese and British spheres of influence.[28] The Portuguese Government had for long convinced itself that there was a community of interests between Portugal and Germany,[29] and it had been keeping the German Government informed of the British moves and declaring that British designs in Mashonaland were contrary to the British-German agreement which had fixed the line of 22° south latitude as the northern limit of expansion of the British colonies.[30] The Colonial Office had favoured informing Germany of the proclamation of the British sphere, but Salisbury had declined lest Germany come to think that she had a right to be consulted in such matters.[31] A visit by the King of Portugal to Germany afforded opportunity for discussions of common problems; the Portuguese Government and press felt that it was only from Germany that Portugal could look for assistance against the aggressive designs of Britain, while some optimists hoped for a conflict between Britain and Germany which would reduce British pressure on Portuguese territory.[32] The German Government asked Salisbury if it were true that Britain had notified Portugal and the South African Republic of a sphere of influence.[33] On receiving answer in the affirmative, the German Minister of Foreign Affairs expressed his surprise that Britain should make such a declaration without previous understanding with the German Government. The German-Portuguese agreement defined their boundary to the Katima rapids on the Zambezi, and thus secured German influence in territory north of Bechuanaland which the British Government had now described as being exclusively within the British sphere. A conflict of interests could lead to unfortunate results if either power took steps to realize its claims. To prevent any misunderstanding, Hatzfeldt accordingly declared that the German Government would not admit any exclusive claim by Britain to territory east of longitude 20° east and north of latitude 22° south; but Germany was prepared to open negotiations for a delimitation of the German and British spheres in south Africa.[34] Salisbury, in his reply, declared that the British Government was aware that in virtue of her agreement with Germany, Portugal had debarred herself from attempting to extend her influence over certain districts of the upper Zambezi, and that Germany had

---

27 FO to CO, 12/9/88, Af. No. 358, p. 61; Gifford to FO, CP 5727, p. 97; CO to FO, 15/9/88, Af. No. 358, p. 62; CO to FO, 24/9/88, ibid., p. 65; Gifford to FO, 24/9/88, CP 5727, pp. 109–10. The concession was between 16° and 18° south lat., and 32° and 34° east long., between the mouth of the Mazoe and the source of the Gourampoutse.
28 Gomes to Bonham, 14/9/88, Af. No. 358, p. 68.
29 Min. to Min. in Berlin, 30/4/88, Nec., SPZ 1.
30 Penafiel, Berlin, to Min., 5/5/88, A 25, ibid., Min. to Min., Berlin 9/7/88, 4, ibid.
31 FO to CO, 23/7/88, CP 5727, p. 69.
32 Bonham to Salisbury, 31/7/88, 74 Af., CP 5727, p. 72.
33 Salisbury to Scott, 17/9/88, Af., CP 5727, pp. 100–1.
34 Leyden, note verbale, 2/10/88, CP 5727, p. 111.

had an interest in so excluding her. But Britain had not been a party to this agreement, which could not affect her rights to extend operations over such territory unless either power had obtained priority by previous engagement or treaty with native chiefs; and the British Government was not aware of any such engagements. But to avoid any possible conflict of interests, the British Government readily accepted the German Government's invitation to delimit spheres of influence in south-west Africa.[35] A year was to pass before this delimitation was carried any further.

British resentment against the Portuguese increased with reports of intensified slave-trading in south-east Africa, and the restriction imposed on the importation of arms by the African Lakes Company. These strained relations would have been eased had boundaries been delimited and Barros Gomes in September 1888 complained about the British delay in replying to his overture. The British minister in Lisbon solemnly assured him that Britain wanted not an extension of territory, but facilities for commerce. Barros Gomes retorted that Portugal could not give facilities for Englishmen to found settlements in the interior if they then turned round and denied the claims of Portugal; such action would lead to the Portuguese possessions being reduced to the same status as those of the Sultan of Zanzibar. He could not understand how the Congo State could be granted international sovereignty over vast and shadowy dominions whilst Portugal, with superior claims based not only on discovery but on experienced intercourse with the natives, was denied her rights.[36] The Portuguese Government again turned to Germany and sought to initiate negotiations by which Germany would acknowledge her rights; but the German Government replied curtly that such proposals could not be entertained unless made jointly by Portugal and Britain.[37] Britain refused to consider admitting Germany to such negotiations, for Germany had no interest in Matabeleland or the lower Zambezi.

The British Government at the end of October 1888 tried to find a general basis for agreement with Portugal. Petre repeated to Barros Gomes that the British Government did not recognize Portuguese jurisdiction or sovereignty beyond the Ruo. Unless forced to do so by circumstances it did not wish to create jurisdiction itself in the Nyasa area, but it insisted that the British settlements be not interfered with, and that the settlers be able to import and export without hindrance, subject to payment of reasonable transit duties. Whatever belonged genuinely to Matabeleland the British Government would desire to retain within the boundaries of the British sphere, which might run from the north-eastern apex of Matabeleland to the Zambezi at Zumbo. With free navigation on the Zambezi and facilities of transit across it to central Africa, the British Government would not object to recognizing the territory north of the river as being exclusively within the Portuguese sphere. Barros Gomes listened without remark and apparently unmoved to Petre's exposition. He

35 Salisbury to Malet, 19/11/88, 251 Af., CP 5727, pp. 125–6.
36 Bonham to Salisbury, 12/9/88, 104 Af., CP 5727, pp. 98–9, CP 5896, pp. 647–8.
37 Malet to Salisbury, 26/12/88, 38 Af., tel., CP 5727, pp. 140–1.

then declared that an agreement which did not acknowledge Portuguese sovereignty over the eastern area in question would not have the remotest chance of being ratified by the Cortes; but that such recognition would meet British wishes for free navigation of the Zambezi and moderate transit dues. He added that the Portuguese claimed the Sanyati as far as its confluence with the Zambezi as the interior limit of Moçambique.[38] It was clear that Barros Gomes's anxiety for negotiation had cooled, that even the leverage of allowing Portugal a free hand to expand across the continent north of the Zambezi had lost its potency. Portugal was now more interested in the possibility of development in Nyasaland and the basin of the lower Zambezi, Petre considered.

> The extraordinary delusions which the Portuguese are under, or seem to be under, in regard to the ubiquity and strength of Portuguese influence in parts where it is notorious that they have none whatever, appear to blind them to the material difficulties confronting them in every direction in their attempts to consolidate Portuguese rule over a mere fraction of the territories which they claim or covet.

Barros Gomes admitted that Portugal hoped to gain more by direct action than would be possible by diplomatic negotiation.[39] Portugal was still hoping, too, for German support. Barros Gomes had sent Batalha Reis on a secret mission to Berlin. Batalha Reis was exerting pressure in official quarters and making general propaganda for Portugal; he recommended that complete secrecy be observed about the Portuguese expeditions to Africa, and especially about Cardinal Lavigerie's participation.[40]

In November 1888 London received confirmation of the despatch of the Nyasa expedition. Salisbury promptly denied that Portugal had any rights over any part of Nyasaland, while the High Commissioner was instructed to keep watch over Portuguese action in Mashonaland and Matabeleland.[41]

The Portuguese consul in Cape Town, on instructions from Lisbon, denounced the Rudd concession, declaring "His Most Faithful Majesty's Government do not recognise the pretended rights of Lobengula to Mashonaland and adjacent territories over which the Crown of Portugal claims sovereignty,"[42] and the minister in London protested to Salisbury. The High Commissioner denied that there was any substance in Portugal's claim to sovereignty over Mashonaland: for years the Matabele had exercised undisputed authority over the whole of Mashonaland and had literally exterminated those tribes which presumed to question that authority; no Portuguese official had ever resided in the country; and there had been no attempt to enforce the rights or discharge

---

38 Petre to Salisbury, 30/10/88, 145 Af., Af. No. 358, pp. 78–80.
39 Petre to Salisbury, 31/10/88, 147 Af., Af. No. 358, p. 77.
40 J. Batalha Reis to Barros Gomes, 9/9/88, J. de Almada, *A Aliança Inglesa* (Lisbon, III, 1949), pp. 406, 411–2.
41 Salisbury to Petre, 14/11/88, 144 Af., CP 5727, pp. 124–5; FO to CO, 19/11/88, ibid., p. 126; Petre to Gomes, 14/11/88, ibid., p. 125*; Knutsford to Robinson, 22/11/88, ibid., p. 129.
42 Carvalho, notice, 3/12/88, CP 5970, pp. 3–4; Dantas to Salisbury, 10/12/88, CP 5927, pp. 131–2.

the duties of sovereignty.[43] Missionary circles protested to Salisbury about the reported invasion of Nyasaland and the financiers behind the Rudd concession also brought their pressure to bear.[44]

When word of the Batalha Reis negotiations reached London, Salisbury reacted sharply. On his telegraphed instructions Malet, the British Ambassador in Berlin, expressed to Bismarck the British hope that Germany would avoid entering into any engagements which affected any British rights. He reported that British relations with Portugal were strained, for "a powerful expedition has been secretly despatched to Lake Nyasa, where we have rights." It was impossible to abandon the missionaries there to the Portuguese, especially since the Government had been accused of sacrificing British missionaries farther north to the Germans. "Lord Salisbury adds that if Portugal interferes with the Lake Nyasa region we should be forced to take some one of the Portuguese possessions in India or the Atlantic coast as a material guarantee."[45] Bismarck denied that there were any negotiations in progress: there had been only a Portuguese approach in September. He regretted the British-Portuguese tension, especially since the three powers were now uniting in a concerted effort to put down the slave-trade on the east coast of Africa.[46] Petre did not contribute to any easing of the tension when he accused Barros Gomes of lack of candour and of reducing the proposed negotiations to a comedy.[47]

As soon as he was assured that there was no German complicity in the Portuguese action Salisbury summoned Dantas to him. After recalling the bombardment of British subjects and property at Tungue, and difficulties of getting arms to Britons beset by slave hunters on Nyasa, Salisbury denounced the expedition to Nyasa which, he had ground to believe, was directed against British missionary and trading stations on Nyasa. He solemnly warned Dantas that good relations between the two countries could not stand such strains.[48] He followed this up a few days later by declaring that Lobengula was the undisputed ruler of Mashonaland; he was confident that Lobengula had no idea of the Portuguese claims to Mashonaland, and that if he did he would reject them: "Mashonaland is distinctly and unquestionably part of the territory ruled by Lobengula, and, as such, under British influence."[49] In vain did Barros Gomes try to explain the realities of the situation, and declare that Matabele raids did not confer sovereignty. Petre was disconcerted when a British traveller, who had entered Mashonaland from the Portuguese side, certified to the lack of Matabele authority and supported Portuguese claims. The Portuguese expeditions falling short of expectations, however, Barros Gomes, early

43 Robinson to Knutsford, 5/12/88, CP 5970, p. 3.
44 e.g. M'Murtrie to FO, 22/12/88, CP 5727, p. 136; Balfour to Salisbury, 22/12/88, ibid., p. 138; J. Fergusson, 24/12/88, memo. on deputation, ibid., pp. 137–8.
45 Malet to Bismarck, 23/12/88, CP 5727, p. 144.
46 Malet to Salisbury, 26/12/88, 38 Af., CP 5727, pp. 140–1; Gomes to German Min., Lisbon, 16/11/88, CP 5770, p. 193.
47 Petre to Salisbury, 26/12/88, 184 Af., CP 5770, p. 140.
48 Salisbury to Petre, 5/1/89, 6 Af., CP 5970, p. 4; Dantas to Gomes, 5/1/89, tel., Neg., p. 6–7; Dantas to Gomes, 6/1/89, A1, Nec., SPZ 2.
49 Salisbury to Dantas, 15/1/89, CP 5970, p. 9; Salisbury to Petre 28/1/89, Af. No. 358, pp. 90–1; Petre to Gomes, 4/2/89, CP 5970, p. 18, Nec., SPZ 2.

in 1889, expressed a desire for a general territorial understanding between Portugal and Britain; but he wished this understanding not to be limited to Portugal and Britain, but to all governments interested in the region.[50]

British missionaries and their societies, traders and financiers maintained constant pressure on the Government by means of public meetings, articles in the press, deputations, and questions in the House of Commons, to push the British boundary northwards to the Zambezi. This agitation increased when there were rumours of a Boer trek to Mashonaland, "a veritable land of Ophir". Lister was moved to comment after receiving one Church of Scotland deputation, "All these Scotch people talk as if the Portuguese were Mahdists."[51] But this constant pressure stiffened Salisbury's attitude; he declared to Petre that Portugal's despatch of secret expeditions had entirely changed the situation, and until the results of these expeditions were known, and their effect on British interests, negotiation was out of the question.[52] But then Salisbury, in a sudden decision that surprised the Foreign Office, decided to send a junior consul to Lisbon to hold discussions with members of the Portuguese Government.

H. H. Johnston, an artist by training, had travelled in Tunisia and Angola and on the Congo. He had leased land on the slopes of Mount Kilimanjaro, and made spirited attempts to persuade the British Government to take the area under its protection. He had held a consular post in the Niger delta. A three-column article by him, under the *nom de plume* 'African Explorer', in *The Times* in August 1888, entitled "Great Britain's policy in Africa", urged Britain to assert herself in the partition of the continent. In east Africa the coast between the Tana and the Umba had been secured, with a wedge stretching inland to Victoria Nyanza. The eastern shore of Tanganyika, frequented by British missionaries and traders, should be obtained. From

> the western shore of Lake Nyasa, along the course of the Luangwa River, through a country rich in gold, tin and iron, we may eventually extend our rule over the relatively short distance which at present separates our recently acquired protectorate over the middle Zambezi from the British settlements on Lake Nyasa. Thus, if our Government only grants some measure of support to the British agencies, commercial and evangelical, which have obtained such footing in the Lake region, our possessions in South Africa may be linked some day to our sphere of influence in eastern Africa and the Egyptian Sudan by a continuous band of British dominion.[53]

In January 1889 Salisbury appointed Johnston consul at Moçambique, an appointment which appealed to Dantas, "for he has expressed himself more

50 Petre to Salisbury, 25/1/89, 9 Af., CP 5970, p. 15; and 7/2/89, 14 Af., ibid., p. 25; and 7/2/89, 15 Af., ibid., p. 26; Gomes to Petre, 20/2/89, draft, Nec., SPZ 2, CP 5970, pp. 31–2.
51 Dantas to Gomes, 2/3/89, 22A, Nec., SPZ 2, enclosing cutting from *Times* describing a meeting in Eaton Hall presided over by the Archbishop of Canterbury; and 7/3/89, ibid., with a cutting from the *Telegraph* of 7/3/89; minutes by T.V. Lister, etc., 23/3/89, CP 5970, pp. 42–3.
52 Salisbury to Petre, 9/3/89, 42 Af., CP 5970, pp. 32–3, Af. No. 358, p. 100; Gomes to Dantas, 20/3/89, tel., *Neg.*, p. 15; Petre to Salisbury, 21/3/89, 26 Af., CP 5970, p. 44.
53 Oliver, *Johnston*, p. 143.

than once in sentiments favourable to Portugal and the Portuguese, as can be seen in his book published on the Congo."[54] The Colonial Office suggested that Johnston, on his arrival in his area, write a comprehensive report on Portuguese power on the Zambezi.[55] Dantas told Salisbury that his Government would be glad if Johnston were to visit Lisbon before his departure for Moçambique, and make himself acquainted, by personal conference, with the views of the cabinet on the many questions that were of common interest to Portugal and to Britain. The day after Dantas's interview Johnston called at the Foreign Office preliminary to leaving for Moçambique; Salisbury instructed him to visit Lisbon.[56] Salisbury, impressed by Johnston's plans to colour the map red from the Cape to Cairo, and fully aware of the menace to British interests from the Cardoso, Andrada and Serpa Pinto expeditions, hoped that Johnston would find the basis for an understanding with Barros Gomes which would keep Portugal out of the Shire highlands and central Zambezi.[57]

Petre, no matter how hurt he must have felt at this extraordinary mission, gave Johnston every assistance both officially and socially. To such good effect did Johnston apply his charms[58] that he was quickly able to find the basis of agreement. The arrangement, he explained to Salisbury, had to be acceptable to Portuguese vanity and yet not utterly displeasing to British colonists in south Africa and the missionaries and traders of Nyasa. His primary concern was to induce Portugal to give up her ancient dream of a Portuguese belt across Africa, and to leave the map clear for British expansion northwards; his second was to secure British domination on the middle Zambezi: "I cannot bear the idea of making the Zambezi a hard and fast limit to British enterprise in southern Africa and wilfully and almost carelessly chucking away our last chance of securing to our grandchildren an open way between Tanganyika and the South African colonies which shall some day serve as a link between Egypt and the Cape." For this there had to be British concessions. The Nyasa settlements were entirely dependent for communication with the outside world on the lower Zambezi and the transit of territory that was indubitably Portuguese; to insist on this transit in opposition to Portuguese laws and regulations and in defiance of Portuguese authority would involve going to war with Portugal. Since Britain was not prepared for such a war, it was better to come to terms with Portugal, Johnston declared.[59]

54 Dantas to Gomes, 16/1/89, A 10, Nec., SPZ 2.
55 CO to FO, 22/1/89, CP 5970, p. 12.
56 Salisbury to Petre, 16/3/89, CP 5970, p. 46, Af., ibid., p. 37.
57 Oliver, *Johnston*, p. 147.
58 "As to my amiability here, it knows no bounds, and I ought to get a special allowance for such expenditure of sweetness from the Chief Clerk. I smile widely on an average for eight hours a day, so that I have lost all control over the muscles at the corners of my mouth. I extol everything Portuguese—the sky, the public gardens, the local opera, the hotels, the wines, the recent realistic fiction, the Colonial Administration, the language, the history, the army, navy and police, and anything else Lusitanian on which my opinion is asked. I also paint Lord Salisbury as a raging lion where his least little tiny bit of British interest is concerned. The joint effect of these two phases seems to have made a good impression on the Portuguese." (Johnston to Lister, 4/4/89, CP 5970, p. 50, and Oliver, *Johnston*, p. 148).
59 Johnston to Lister, 4/4/89, CP 5970, pp. 49–51.

Johnston accordingly persuaded Barros Gomes to abandon the idea of a continuous band of territory across the continent uniting Moçambique and Angola, and to accept the idea of British possessions and protectorates sweeping not only to the Zambezi, but of uninterrupted territory north of the Zambezi reserved for Britain's exclusive political influence. Johnston agreed that parts of the Nyasa area should become Portuguese; but Barros Gomes undertook that if Britain agreed to this Portugal would guarantee the free navigation of the Zambezi, and the transit of arms and ammunition under reasonable conditions; Portugal would not admit free transit of goods, but agreed that the rates would not exceed 3 per cent and that the regulations would apply only to certain routes. Johnston requested a treaty which would perpetually limit the tariff to a moderate percentage, but Barros Gomes insisted on drawing a distinction between parts of Moçambique traditionally Portuguese, and parts that would only now be acknowledged as Portuguese. Such concessions, and freedom of religion, could be granted only in the newly acquired territory. In the delimitation of spheres of influence, Portugal refused to accept the Shire as the boundary, and demanded the western shore of Nyasa as far as 12° south latitude, thence along that parallel to the Luangwa. Johnston was reluctant to yield north of the mouth of the Bua, in about 13° south, in view of the proximity of Bandawe, thence up the Buareze and Lukushwa to the Luangwa, but he persuaded Barros Gomes to accept Lukoma Island as being within the British sphere, despite its proximity to the eastern shore of Nyasa, because of its Universities' Mission station. The line would follow the Luangwa to the Zambezi. Portugal insisted on the junction of the Sanyati and the Zambezi as their western limit. Johnston told Barros Gomes that in view of British engagements to Lobengula the farthest line that Britain would admit would run from the confluence of the Bakedi and the Zambezi in Bruma's area, thence southeast to the Hunyani, up this river and its tributary the Mutiki to its source, thence skirting Mashonaland, roughly on the watershed, and southwards to the Limpopo. In the west, the boundary agreed upon was the Kabompo River, thence down the Zambezi to the Chobe, and up the Chobe to the Angolan-German boundary. Britain would also recognize a Portuguese protectorate over the kingdom of Muata Yanvo, to soften disapproval over the loss of the trans-African belt. And Britain would also use her influence with the Sultan of Zanzibar to effect a solution of the Tungue question that would favour the pretensions of Portugal.[60]

The Portuguese Government was most anxious to come to agreement with Britain as speedily as possible: the Cortes was due to rise in June, and would not meet again until the new year; and in the interval there was to be a general election. The opposition was strongly opposed to any agreement that did not grant Portugal a transcontinental belt. "The Portuguese care more about sustaining their national prestige than utilizing the natural wealth and developing the splendid resources. They are content to hand over to Englishmen (for

60 Johnston to Petre, 8/4/89, CP 5970, pp. 52–6; one proposition, the third, is missing in the CP.

preference) the exploitation of these territories in a commercial sense. If we do not come to terms with them about their political rights they will favour (out of pique) subjects of other European powers,"[61] was Johnston's opinion.

Petre commented that the arrangement involved surrendering much which his instructions had precluded him from yielding, "but in my humble opinion the practical benefits amply justify any such surrender by Her Majesty's Government, and I hope that in its main features at least it will be ultimately approved." The only insurmountable obstacle to an understanding had been the Blantyre settlement; how much importance Portugal attached to that area was indicated by her abandonment of her cherished transcontinental schemes.[62]

Lister advised Salisbury to accept the plan: "I am convinced that the plan proposed offers a very good basis for a settlement of our dispute with Portugal in Africa and that it would be a great pity to reject it in order to please one very shaky company and a few missionaries." He reminded Salisbury that the Portuguese had an expedition on the spot: "They can take all they want, the Company and the missionaries would be at their mercy, and we cannot send a man to defend them, nor plead the slightest claim to any territory."[63]

But Salisbury was not impressed—as Professor Oliver remarks, "he knew very well that he would rather face the wrath of Portugal than of Scotland."[64] "I think we gain nothing by the suggested terms," Salisbury minuted.

> The free passage along the Zambezi we can take for ourselves whenever the Zambezi becomes physically accessible from the sea; and until it does, the admission of a free passage will be of no use. The same can be said of the territory to the west of the Luangwa; it is of little value, as is the northwest shore of Nyasa. In exchange for these concessions, which Portugal is not in a condition to give or refuse, we stop ourselves from ever claiming the south-western and southern shores of Nyasa, the banks of the Shire, and the banks of the Zambezi above Tete. We also made concessions in Mashonaland which would be at variance with our recent proceedings.

The only counter-advantage was the low tariff; but this was limited to a term of years. The traders and missionaries were opposed to the plan; and the suggestion that Britain should retract her language over Tungue was completely unacceptable.[65]

Lister complained that Salisbury was unfair to the scheme; Lister, from a long acquaintance with the subject, was

> convinced that the terms offered are far more favourable than we had any right to expect, or than any Arbitration would give us, and that the rejection of this may lead to a long enmity between England and Portugal, and the ruin of present and prospective British interests in south-east Africa, and to the closing up of that northern outlet for our Cape Colonies.

61 Johnston to Salisbury, 16/4/89, CP 5970, p. 61; and 22/4/89, ibid., pp. 63–4.
62 Petre to Salisbury, 9/4/89, 39 Af., CP 5970, p. 52.
63 Lister, minute on Johnston, 8/4/89, CP 5970, p. 56.
64 Oliver, *Johnston*, p. 150.
65 Salisbury, minute, 26/4/89, CP 5970, p. 66.

It was not his business to advise on policy but, Lister courageously declared, it was his duty to see that the facts were correctly placed before the Secretary of State. Free navigation could, of course, be taken by force, but it would not be justifiable to take by war what had been offered in peace; the recent discovery of a new navigable mouth gave the Zambezi added value. The country west of the Luangwa, so far from being of little value, was rich in gold and other minerals. The north-western shores of Nyasa were the most valuable areas bordering on the lake: most of the missionaries and traders were stationed there, and there was no British settlement on the east side. Navigation of the Shire was of little value because of the rapids and recent decline in the flow of water. Concerning customs duties, no Portuguese Government could vote a tariff in perpetuity. As for Scottish opposition, Johnston was convinced that he could convert the missionaries in a few days, and he, Lister, was sure that he could talk the African Lakes Company into accepting the agreement. He knew of no grounds for accusing Portugal of bad faith. And the Portuguese had a right to the lower Zambezi: they had been on the river for three hundred years. Since the Colonial Office was interested in the matter, Lister proposed a conference at which Salisbury would preside, and which would be attended by Knutsford, Herbert, Johnston and himself.

But Salisbury would have none of it. He agreed that the assent of the ALC and the missionaries would make a difference. But

> my main objection is this: that I am asked to hand over to Portugal settlements occupied by British subjects who are in actual possession and who object very strongly to being transferred to Portugal. I should require some very plain and substantial concession on the part of Portugal to justify such a step; and the concessions proposed appear to me to be in the main speculative and problematical. The free navigation of the Zambezi is no concession, for Portugal has no right to exclude any nation from it.[66]

When word of the proposed agreement reached Scotland the storm broke. At the end of March Dr Rankin, the commissioner who had investigated the affairs of Blantyre, who had an intimate knowledge of the situation, and who was a member of the Church of Scotland Colonial Missions committee, and represented Buchanan in the United Kingdom, had been perfectly prepared to accept the transfer of the Nyasa area to Portugal, under certain conditions.[67] But by the end of April close on 11,000 ministers and elders of the three Presbyterian churches had signed an anti-Portuguese petition.[68] The Foreign Missions committee of the Free Church of Scotland remained prepared to accept the Johnston agreement,[69] and Johnston was of opinion that even the Established Church was favourable to his plan at heart.[70] But the Universities' Mission

---

66 Minutes, Lister, 28/4/89, and Salisbury, 29/4/89, CP 5970, p. 67.
67 J. Rankin to FO, 30/3/89, CP 5970, p. 46. The conditions were recognition by Portugal of titles to property; freedom of worship; freedom to navigation of the Zambezi and Shire; limited tariffs; and efficient control of the trade in guns, ammunition and spirits.
68 Balfour to FO, 5/1/89, CP 5970, p. 76.
69 Foreign Missions Committee of the Free Church to FO, 23/5/89, CP 5970, p. 78; the conditions were similar to those postulated by J. Rankin.
70 T.V.L., memo., 29/5/89, CP 5970, p. 104.

petitioned against it, and so did the royal and parliamentary boroughs of Scotland;[71] there was an ever-increasing body of extremely vocal opposition, expressed at public meetings, in the press, and in the House of Commons. The question of the supply of arms to the African Lakes Company continued further to complicate the situation, especially after the arrest of the British vice-consul in Quelimane after he had applied openly for permission to import twenty-five seven-pound rockets, and his removal to Moçambique to stand trial on a charge of "smuggling arms".[72] When Bishop Smythies wished to travel inland from Tungue Bay and it was understood that the Portuguese would refuse him permission to land arms for his personal defence, Salisbury declared that he was willing to send a warship to superintend the landing of any arms that he might require.[73] Dantas correctly saw in this bluster Salisbury's desire to render the Johnston negotiations abortive,[74] and when the petition from the Scottish churches was presented Salisbury had no hesitation in declaring the Nyasa missions to be "British territory". Salisbury was strengthened in his attitude not only by the attitude of the Scots, but by a new cordiality between Britain and Germany.[75] As a result, when a questioner in the House of Commons asked in June 1889 for information about the negotiations with Portugal, a Government spokesman announced curtly, "There are no negotiations at present with the Portuguese Government."[76] In Portugal feelings had been inflamed by British comment.[77] The Chamber of Peers unanimously approved a motion affirming once again the rights of Portugal in east and central Africa, based on discovery, conquest and effective occupation and calling on the Government to maintain with firmness those rights, which had been solemnly acknowledged by the governments of France and Germany.[78] Diplomacy was dead: Britain and Portugal were now set on a collision course in southern central Africa.

71 Convention of royal and parliamentary boroughs of Scotland, 7/5/89, CP 5970, p. 82; University Mission to Salisbury, 13/5/89, ibid., p. 85; Balfour to Salisbury, 17/5/89, ibid., p. 93; U/S of S for FA, House of Commons, 7/5/89, ibid., p. 78; Petre to Gomes, 14/5/89, ibid., pp. 95–6, *Neg.*, pp. 34–5; Petre to Salisbury, 14/5/89, 66 Af., FO 179/264; Salisbury to Petre, 24/5/89, 90 Af., CP 5970, p. 100; GG to Min., 29/5/89, tel., *Neg.*, p. 44; Petre to Salisbury, 30/5/89, 76 Af., CP 5970, p. 108; Petre to Salisbury, 18/7/89, 114 Af., p. 137.
72 Dantas to Gomes, 2/5/89, tel., Nec., SPZ 2, *Neg.*, p. 24; Gomes to Dantas, 3/5/89, tel., *Neg.*, pp. 24–5; Petre to Salisbury, 28/4/89, 49 Af., CP 5970, p. 65; Salisbury to Petre, 30/4/89, 72 Af., ibid., p. 69; Petre to Salisbury, 9/5/89, 60 Af., ibid., p. 87; Buchanan to Salisbury, 10/5/89, 18 CA, ibid., p. 121.
73 FO to Portal, Zanzibar, 11/5/89, tel., 160, FO 179/264; Salisbury to Petre, 20/5/89, 86 Af., ibid.
74 *Standard*, 15/5/89, *Neg.*, pp. 38–40; Dantas to Barros Gomes, 18/5/89, tel., ibid., p. 37.
75 Malet, Berlin to Salisbury, 25/5/89, 174, FO 64/1212. Bismarck called in person at the British Embassy on the occasion of the Queen's birthday, writing on his card. "God save the Queen"; the Emperor followed him.
76 27/6/89, CP 5970, p. 120.
77 e.g. *Pall Mall Gazette*, 29/5/89, *Neg.*, pp. 48–50, *Times*, 19/4/89 and 29/5/89.
78 Dantas was under the impression that the negotiations were not broken, but only interrupted; Johnston would probably return in the autumn. (Dantas to Gomes, 27/5/89, tel., *Neg.*, p. 43.) It was possible that in the meantime the British Minister in Lisbon might resume the negotiations. (Dantas to Gomes, 28/5/89, tel., *Neg.*, p. 43.)

11

THE ULTIMATUM

Johnston, as soon as he heard that he had been appointed consul at Moçambique, proposed to Salisbury that on taking up his post he should proceed to the Zambezi and prepare a confidential report on the exact condition and extent of Portuguese rule. He would penetrate as far as Zumbo, in mid-year, when the river was at its highest and the adjacent territory at its healthiest. It was essential that the Portuguese should know nothing of his plans lest they place obstacles in his way, so he would simply announce that he was about to inspect his new consular district. He assured Salisbury that he would do nothing rash; he would not embarrass Her Majesty's Government. He was sure that he would get on easily with the Portuguese, "who are usually most kind-hearted hospitable folk, easily won over by a little flattery and the lengthy compliments of their own language."[1] The Foreign Office approved his mission, on condition that he entered the Zambezi by the Congone or some other true mouth, and established to what extent the river was navigable.[2]

On the eve of his departure from London for Moçambique and the Zambezi, in May 1889, Johnston met Cecil Rhodes. They talked through the night, and at the breakfast table Rhodes wrote Johnston a cheque for £2,000 to finance what would be essentially a treaty-making expedition[3] north of the Zambezi. These treaties, Johnston assured Salisbury, would be made with chiefs not subject to Portuguese authority; while not committing the British Government to granting protection, they would formally preclude any subsequent attempt by Portuguese emissaries from bringing those particular districts under Portuguese sovereignty. The treaties should be kept confidential, and the British Government could always disallow them if they were regarded as inconvenient or inopportune. But they would enable Britain finally to dispose of Portugal's claim to a belt of territory across Africa, Johnston insisted.[4] Salisbury decided that while the charter of the British South Africa Company would refer in the first instance to territory south of the Zambezi, the Government would be entitled to add to the bounds of territory allotted the company by simple licence.[5] He approved of Johnston's suggestion for the informal negotiation of

1 H. H. Johnston to Salisbury, 2/2/89, CP 5970, pp. 16–7.
2 FO to Johnston, 13/2/89, CP 5970, p. 24.
3 Oliver, *Johnston*, pp. 152–3.
4 Johnston to Salisbury, 27/5/89, CP 5970, pp. 102–3.
5 FO to CO, 27/5/89, CP 5970, pp. 101–2.

conditional treaties[6] and supplied him with blank forms.[7] To conceal from the Portuguese the main purpose of his expedition, Johnston asked that the Portuguese Government be told that the aim of his journey was to report on the condition of the British subjects in the interior, and if possible conclude peace between them and the Arabs; he asked that Portuguese officials be required to grant him all possible facilities for crossing Portuguese territory and the transport of such arms and ammunition as he required for himself and his escort. He also asked that Buchanan, the acting consul in Nyasaland, be instructed to give him every assistance.[8]

Salisbury determined that Johnston should enter the Zambezi by gun-boat, and so establish the freedom of navigation of the river.[9] There had been much debate on this subject in the Foreign Office. In April Salisbury had told the Admiralty that an attempt might be made by British traders to introduce goods on to the Zambezi by way of the Congone mouth; he asked for naval protection.[10] At the end of that month a report appeared in *The Times* that D. J. Rankin had discovered a new entrance to the Zambezi, 300 yards wide, with a minimum depth of three fathoms.[11] Questioners in the House of Commons demanded that Britain insist on the opening of this Chinde mouth to the flags

6 FO to Johnston, 30/5/89, CP 5970, p. 105.
7 FO to Johnston, 31/5/89, CP 5970, p. 106.

Form of Treaty

Treaty made on   , in
this   day of   in the year 18   , between
                         for and on behalf of Her Majesty the Queen of Great Britain and
Ireland, Empress of India etc., her heirs and successors on the one part, and the Undersigned,
for heirs and successors, on the other part
                                    , the Undersigned,   do in the presence of
Headmen and people assembled at this place hereby promise:—
1st that there shall be peace between the subjects of the Queen of England and subjects
2nd that British subjects shall have free access to all parts of
and shall have the right to build houses and possess property according to the laws in force in this country; that they shall have full liberty to carry on such trade or manufacture as may be approved by Her Majesty; and should any difference arise between the aforesaid British subjects and   the said
as to the duties or customs to be paid to   the said
or the Headmen of the town in country of such British subjects or as to any other matter, that the dispute shall be referred to a duly authorised Representative of
will not extend the rights thus guaranteed to British subjects to any other persons without the knowledge and consent of such Representative;
3rd   the said   will at no time whatever cede
any of   territory to any other Power, or enter into any agreement, Treaty, or arrangement with any foreign Government except through and with the consent of the Government of Her Majesty the Queen of England.
       Done at   this   day of   , 18
       Signed in the presence of
       We, the Undersigned, do swear that we have truly and honestly interpreted the terms of the foregoing Agreement to the Contractors Parties, in the   language.
       Witness to signatures:

8 Johnston to Salisbury, 30/5/89, CP 5970, p. 105.
9 FO to Johnston, 27/5/89, CP 5970, p. 101.
10 FO to Admiralty, 12/4/89, CP 5970, p. 51.
11 D. J. Rankin, to acting consul Smith, 14/3/89, CP 5970, pp. 12–13; *Times*, 29/4/89. This Rankin, not to be confused with the missionary director, was seeking a British consular appointment.

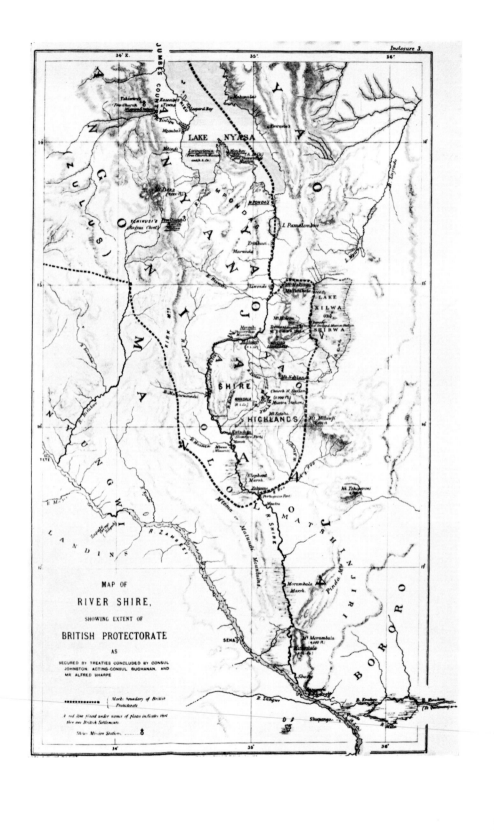

Inclosure 3.

MAP OF
RIVER SHIRE,
SHOWING EXTENT OF
BRITISH PROTECTORATE
AS
SECURED BY TREATIES CONCLUDED BY CONSUL
JOHNSTON, ACTING-CONSUL BUCHANAN, AND
MR. ALFRED SHARPE

of all nations,[12] to the indignation of the Portuguese who pointed out that the mouth had long been known to them and had in fact been shown on Sarmento's charts of 1877-80, under the name of Inhaombe, a river which entered the same estuary, or Mitaone, the name of the island which faced the mouth; Andrada had a share in a property on the Chinde River, he had taken steps to survey the bar, and it was he who had told Rankin of its existence.[13]

The significance of the Chinde River was that it communicated directly with the main stream of the Zambezi: with Salisbury's insistence that the Zambezi was a free international highway it was possible for goods and passengers to enter the Zambezi without touching Portuguese soil.[14] But the Foreign Office now began to question the exact meaning of "freedom of navigation," a term which Lister considered open to many interpretations except the one popularly attributed to it; he called on Hertslet to define the expression. Hertslet reported that the nations had been unable to agree to the interpretation to be attached to it on the Rhine. A treaty for the Po ended transit duties, but ships had to stop at the entrance, on leaving, and at three other places, and make declarations at the extreme custom-houses. Salisbury declared he would be happy to see the Zambezi treated like the Po, but Lister pointed out that because the riverine states had signed a treaty it could be inferred that free navigation did not exist *jure gentium* before that date.[15] Barros Gomes asserted in the Chamber of Deputies Portugal's right to control the navigation of the Zambezi and to extend her influence over territories which lay inland from her coastal possessions: those rights had been acknowledged by the Berlin Conference and by two great powers. He announced that Portugal was going to exploit Cardoso's success; Leal would remain near the lake and build a residence, while another expedition would shortly return to Nyasa accompanied by a religious mission.[16] The British Government did not dispute the right of Portugal to "control" the navigation of the waters of her territory, but it claimed for British vessels the right to navigate the Zambezi as far as it was navigable; nor did it deny the right of Portugal to extend inland the area of her settlement and government, but claimed that the British settlements should not be disturbed by any act of the Portuguese in regions over which she had not previously exercised sovereignty or protectorate.[17] The African Lakes Company promptly announced to Salisbury its intention of running a small steamer straight into

---

12 Question and answer, 3/5/89, *Neg.*, 1890, pp. 25–8.
13 Petre to Salisbury, 4/5/89, 56 Africa, CP 5870, p. 71, enclosing cutting from *Novidades*, 3/5/89; *Times*, 4/5/89, *Neg.*, pp. 28–9; Andrada to Director-geral, 28/6/89, *Neg.*, pp. 59–60 and dd 28/7/89, Nec., SPZ 2; Rankin, 'The Zambezi Delta', 15/8/89, CP 5970, pp. 156–62. For the latest description of the bars of the Zambezi see J. A. Barrahona Fernandes, 'Barras do rio Zambeze', *Garcia de Orta*, 1958, pp. 301–44.
14 V. L. Cameron to Ed., *Times*, 30/4/89, *Neg.*, p. 24.
15 Minutes, 3–9/5/89, CP 5970, pp. 79–80.
16 *Times*, 5/5/89, *Neg.*, p. 29.
17 J. Fergusson, reply in Commons, 8/5/89, *Times*, 9/5/89, *Neg.*, p. 32, CP 5970, p. 83.

---

11 Map of River Shire, showing extent of British Protectorate secured by treaties concluded by Consul Johnston, Acting-Consul Buchanan, and Mr Alfred Sharpe [1890] (from British Foreign Office Confidential Print, PRO, FO, 403/127)

the Zambezi, transhipping her cargo into the company's shallow-draft steamer and taking it up the Zambezi and Shire and so establishing the question of free navigation. The only question had been whether the cargo should consist only of ordinary merchandise, or whether it might include guns and powder for the fighting at the northern end of Nyasa. The lives of Englishmen and Scotsmen were in jeopardy, it declared; but in view of the convention which set up the blockade it wished to avoid incidents which might prejudice Britain's position.[18] Hertslet reminded Salisbury that the Portuguese decree of December 1888, banning the sale of arms and ammunition, had been issued at the request of the British and German Governments for the suppression of the slave-trade; Portugal would therefore be justified in preventing any ships from entering the Zambezi with material of war on board, and in view of the proclaimed blockade she would be justified in stopping them in any bay or roadstead before they entered the river. A riverine power was not entitled to levy custom duties on goods passing through the territory of another power; but naturally she was entitled to ensure that goods were not discharged in her own territory; and rivers were thrown open to free navigation only on certain conditions and regulations. Hertslet quoted the opinion of the Queen's Advocate in 1861,

> where one nation was in possession of both banks of a river at the mouth, and commanded the navigable channel, which nation had *not* conceded the right of free navigation, and where there existed no recognized riparian state higher up the river, there was no sufficient authority for maintaining for any other nation quite irrespective of Treaty or usage lawfully enforce the right of navigation above its mouth, and beyond the territorial limits of the state owning both banks.

Portugal had issued no decree throwing open the river to free navigation, and there had been only the verbal statement of the Portuguese representative at Berlin to the effect that it had introduced a system of free navigation.[19] But Salisbury refused to accept this restraining opinion and he ordered reply to be made to the ALC that in the judgment of the British Government the Zambezi was a free navigable river, "and no Government has the right to prevent its being navigated by your vessels or the vessels belonging to any other person, or to interfere with the cargo which those vessels may contain." The blockade did not limit this right, but to avoid any misunderstanding with the German Government it would be as well to apply to the consul-general in Zanzibar for a permit to import munitions of war.[20]

But it was to be Johnston who was first to assert these claims. Johnston, on his arrival in Moçambique, was disconcerted to find that British travellers leaving for the interior were required to take out tickets of residence; for a traveller to comply was equivalent to admitting the Portuguese claims to the interior.[21] It also worried him to learn that the Makololo had recently fired on

18 ALC to Salisbury, 14/6/89, CP 5970, pp. 111–2.
19 E. Hertslet, 21/6/89, CP 5970, pp. 112–3.
20 FO to ALC, 24/6/89, CP 5970, p. 114.
21 Johnston to Salisbury, 19/7/89, 6 Af., CP 5970, p. 170.

an ALC vessel, and had closed the Shire; the ALC agent had called on the Portuguese for assistance.[22] José Cardoso, the military commander of Massingire, visited Mpassa, where he found that the shots had been directed not at Portuguese authority but at the ALC, for Moir, trying to acquire Katunga, had been guilty of actions of which the Makololo strongly disapproved. Cardoso proposed that the vessel embark a dozen or so of his troops and ensure the vessel's arrival at Katunga. The six British subjects aboard the vessel agreed, but in the meantime the cautious Cardoso telegraphed his Governor for authority. Pending its arrival, he sent a hoe ahead as a sign of peace; but if war came, two or three thousand men, he was convinced, would be more than sufficient to discipline the Makololo. The Governor of Quelimane exhorted him to use the greatest caution and to settle the matter amicably.[23] Moir wrote to Cardoso to assure him that Portuguese intervention was unnecessary; Moir himself was actually planning an attack on Mlauri.[24] Learning of a concentration of whites on the next steamer to pass, Mlauri did not attack it.[25]

Meanwhile, Serpa Pinto had reached the Zambezi. He had been appointed to command a third expedition to Nyasa.[26] Accompanying him were two engineers, Pereira Ferraz and Amaral Themudo, with the specific task of surveying a railway line to bypass the rapids on the Shire River.[27] To support the expedition the Government ordered two armed and armoured steam-launches.[28] Castilho, the retiring Governor-general, made no secret of his hope that Serpa Pinto would join Cardoso in the expedition which would make effective Portugal's occupation of the southern portion of Nyasa.[29] The Portuguese Government then ruled that Serpa Pinto might accompany the engineers and give them the benefit of his experience; but his primary purpose was to advance northwards from Zumbo, up the Luangwa River. Cardoso was not to return to Portugal but recuperate at the Cape of Good Hope, and then conduct the missionaries to Nyasa.[30] Learning that the *prazo* Massingire was simmering with revolt, and that it was inadvisable to cross it to reach the Shire and Nyasa, he appreciated his amended instructions to make for Zumbo, proceed up the Luangwa River, and reach Nyasa from the west. But he had gone no farther than Mopeia when he fell ill with pneumonia, and his engineer, Ferraz, with fever. There he learnt of the ALC request for help. This determined him to modify his plans. When the expedition reached the mouth of the

22 José Cardoso, Massingire, to Governor, Quelimane, 10/6/89, tel., *Neg.*, p. 222.
23 Cardoso, Massingire, to Gov., Quelimane, 12/6/89, tel., *Neg.*, p. 223; and 12/6/89, 74; ibid., p. 222. Ribeiro, Gov., Quelimane, to Pinto, 15/6/89, tel., p. 224.
24 Moir to Cardoso, 13/6/89, *Neg.*, p. 224, saying that Portuguese assistance was unnecessary; Cardoso, Massingire, to Gov., 15/6/89, *Neg.*, p. 223; Pinto to Gov., Quelimane, 21/6/89, ibid., p. 225; Ribeiro to Military Governor, Massingire, 9, 15/7/89, ibid., p. 226.
25 Cardoso to Gov., 23, 24/6/89, *Neg.*, p. 225; Buchanan to Salisbury, 4/7/89, 23 CA, CP 5970, pp. 196–7.
26 Min. to GG, 1/4/89, tel., *Neg.*, pp. 18–9.
27 Min., F. Ressano Garcia, portaria, 30/3/89, Nec., SPZ 2, *Neg.*, p. 139.
28 Min. to GG, 8/4/89, tel., *Neg.*, p. 19; Ross to Smith, 26/5/89, CP 5970, p. 140. The larger with loopholed armoured plate breast-high, carried seven guns, the smaller two guns.
29 Hawes, Zanzibar, to Salisbury, 8/4/89, 190, CP 5970, pp. 70–1.
30 F. J. da Costa e Silva, Dir. geral, instruções, 15/4/89, Nec., SPZ 2, *Neg.*, pp. 139–41; Min. to Gov., Lourenço Marques, 21/4/89, tel., *Neg.*, p. 21.

Ziu-ziu he left it, and made his way to Massingire, to confer with José Cardoso. The sons of the dead Kasisi wanted to expel Mlauri and subject themselves to Portugal. There would be nothing to stop Serpa Pinto and his expedition, Cardoso was convinced, if he were to march up the Shire to Nyasa. But the Governor of Quelimane refused to sanction this advance. Serpa Pinto stopped at Massange, 15 miles south of Mpassa, early in August. Mlauri consolidated his position and refused to allow provisions to reach the Portuguese camp, nor would his tribesmen allow an ambassador to pass through to him, despite a generous present. Tribesmen opened desultory fire on the camp.[31] It was at this stage, on 15 August, that the *James Stevenson* arrived, with Johnston aboard her.

H.M.S. *Stork* had examined the Chinde bar and found a minimum depth of seven feet at low water, with a rise of twelve feet. These figures had been confirmed by the crew of a Portuguese gun-boat which had been surveying the entrance for a fortnight.[32] *Stork's* commander accordingly reported to Johnston in Moçambique that the entrance was perfectly feasible. Johnston cabled to the Foreign Office for official confirmation that he should force the entrance, and on 28 July 1889 *Stork* conveyed him over the bar. The Portuguese gun-boat was in Quelimane refitting; the only assertion of Portuguese authority was by a detachment on Mitaone Island which struggled not very successfully to hoist the national flag. *Stork* did not stop, but steamed up the winding Chinde creek which, Johnston was forced to admit, was well known to the Portuguese, because it bore the name Santa Maria; and before long he passed Andrada's plantation. At the entrance to the Zambezi was a sandbank with a least depth of twelve feet. *Stork* proceeded five or six miles up the main stream then, coming to an expanse of shallow water, since the level of the river was dropping, she anchored. Her commander and Johnston continued in the ship's steam pinnace which towed a cutter, while two other boats followed under sail and oars with Johnston's Zanzibari followers and the bulk of his baggage. At Vicente the Portuguese were considerably perturbed by the sight of bluejackets and the white ensign. The other vessels turned up the Shire; they passed several trading stations, and considerable cultivation; there were two Netherlands posts, and numbers of Polish planters and hunters. At Morrumbala the pinnace caught up with the *James Stevenson* and Johnston transferred to the ALC steamer.[33]

On his way up-stream, and at anchor off the Ruo, Johnston learnt more about the situation on the Shire. The Makololo, of whom no more than twenty or thirty survived, wanted neither Portuguese nor British to be masters of their land: foreign administration would deprive them of their control over the

---

31 Pinto to Min., 27/5/89, tel., *Neg.*, p. 43; A. A. da Rocha Serpa Pinto, 'Relatório . . .' *Neg.*, pp. 211–2; Cardoso to Gov., Quelimane, 18/7/89, tel., *Neg.*, pp. 226–7; Ribeira to Cardoso, 19/7/89, ibid., p. 227.
32 Lt. Comdr Balfour, Moçambique, to Adm., 22/7/89, CP 5970, pp. 203–4; for a general report on the Zambezi at this time see L. P. Bowler to Salisbury, 20/6/89, ibid., pp. 134–6.
33 Johnston, Morumbala, to Salisbury, 4/8/89, 7 Af., CP 5970, pp. 206–8; Balfour, *Stork*, Zanzibar, to Adm., 27/8/89, ibid., pp. 211–3; *Report of Mr. H. H. Johnston . . . on the Nyasa — Tanganyika Expedition* 1889–90, PRO, FO 403/127, pp. 1–5; GG to Minister, 17/8/89, tel., *Neg.*, p. 63; *Novidades*, 30/10/89, CP 5970, p. 231.

dependent tribesmen, and especially of their 50 per cent levy on ivory which brought them comparative wealth. But most of the old chiefs had died off, and the new generation were largely a bunch of "rapacious young ruffians, reactionaries against Christianity," so that navigation could be stopped at any time "by the drunken caprice of these wretched little tyrants." The only reason why the Makololo had not gone to war against England was because they disliked Portugal even more, and the British served as some sort of barrier. Mlauri was alarmed at the approach of Serpa Pinto's expedition. Johnston received a peremptory message to visit the chief, which he did with some trepidation, making his way through groups of insolent warriors. But the chief, wearing a white chimney-pot hat, received him affably. He expressed indignation at the Portuguese advance, and hinted he might place his country under British protection. Johnston spoke sharply to him on the subject of his tribesmen's unfriendly acts against the British, and persuaded him to promise not to attack the Portuguese; but he refused to sign the treaty Johnston produced from his satchel.[34] Johnston did not linger, for he knew of Serpa Pinto's approach. He met with some success at Katunga, however.[35] And he vowed that if Blantyre were ever threatened by a Portuguese expedition he would run up the British flag—or, preferably, induce Buchanan to do so. He had last minute qualms of conscience, and wrote to Salisbury that he thought it only fair if the Portuguese Government were informed of the area he intended to take under British protection; and, he added, Portugal should be warned that armed intervention in that area would not be tolerated.[36]

Serpa Pinto's problems had been mounting,[37] and, according to a report by Johnston, messengers reached him from Serpa Pinto, who asked him to return down-stream for a conference. After compliments had been exchanged, Serpa Pinto stressed the scientific nature of his expedition to Nyasaland; but the Makololo chiefs, instigated by John Moir, refused to allow him to pass. If war came, no chief would stop him and his 731 armed men. Serpa Pinto wished Johnston to reason with the chiefs and induce them to withdraw their opposition, or there would be war. Johnston assured him that the Makololo would never consent to the passage of such an armed expedition, for they suspected the Portuguese had political designs on their country; and he warned that such a war would close the Shire, jeopardize British lives and strain relations between Portugal and Britain. Johnston added that Barros Gomes had solemnly assured him and Petre that the expedition would go not to Nyasa but to the Luangwa. Serpa Pinto admitted that his ultimate destination was the Luangwa, where, he added ingenuously, his intention was to make treaties which would extend Portuguese influence towards Lake Bengweolu and to the west. Johnston advised him, if his immediate intention was to reach Mponda's, to take a more easterly route, via Lake Shirwa, and avoid the Shire. Serpa Pinto was reluctant to do this, and asked permission for two of his officers to sail aboard the

34 *Report of Mr. H. H. Johnston*, pp. 5–6.
35 Treaty, 14/8/89, CP 5970, p. 243.
36 Johnston to Salisbury, 9/8/89, 8 Af., CP 5970, pp. 208–9.
37 Pinto, Relatório, *Neg.*, pp.212–3.

Stevenson and present their case to the Makololo chiefs. Johnston refused, and undertook himself to represent Serpa Pinto. Serpa Pinto could not have had a more dishonest ambassador. Johnston proceeded up the Shire. He landed at Katunga, the port of Blantyre, where he met Buchanan. Buchanan, after a few days, at Johnston's direction, and with the disbursal of £4 in presents, concluded treaties with two near-by chiefs, though Mlauri still stood out. At Blantyre—"a pleasing English Arcadia"—Johnston signed treaties with two Yao chiefs. Buchanan continued the anti-Portuguese mission, while to forestall Serpa Pinto on the Luangwa, Johnston despatched Alfred Sharpe, with £100 in presents and a wad of treaty-blanks.[38]

Johnston himself journeyed northwards, continuing his treaty-making with vigour.[39] At Kota-Kota he made a treaty which, he admitted to Salisbury, somewhat exceeded his instructions. By the first paragraphs Jumbe, sultan of Marimba, undertook to place himself, his people and his dominions under the protection of the Queen. In subsequent paragraphs he pledged himself to follow the advice of the Queen's representative; and to deal only through that representative in relations with all foreign powers. Johnston took this unauthorized step because of Jumbe's importance: he was a Swahili, representative of the Sultan of Zanzibar in the Nyasa area, lord of the southern half of the western shores of Nyasa and the most enlightened of the Arab chieftains; but the irresponsible actions of the ALC had brought him close to war against Britain, Johnston complained.[40] Jumbe's help, and a letter from the Sultan of Zanzibar, proved invaluable at Karonga, and after only a week of negotiation Johnston signed a treaty of peace with the four leading Arabs in that area. Further treaties with other chiefs reserved the whole of the western and northern end of Nyasa to British influence. He carefully avoided the eastern shores of Nyasa; at the southern end the chiefs were pro-Portuguese, while farther north the Germans had aspirations.[41] He extended his treaty-making northwards in the basin of Lake Rukwa and to the shores of Tanganyika. His mission was interrupted by the arrival of a runner from Blantyre, who reported a crisis in British-Portuguese relations on the Ruo. He returned forthwith.[42]

On 15 August 1889, the day when Johnston had met Serpa Pinto, J. Buchanan, the acting British consul, had called a meeting of Britons at Blantyre. He and his brother, J. Moir of the ALC, and Scott of the Church of Scotland mission, "representing British interests in these parts, having heard of the rumoured Portuguese advance upon the Makololo, do hereby most strongly protest that such action is not only absolutely uncalled for, but that it would

---

38 Johnston, Mandala, to Salisbury, 26/8/89, 9 Af., CP 5970, pp. 241–3; Pinto to Min., 15/8/89, tel., *Neg.*, p. 63; Pinto, 'Relatório', pp. 212–3.
39 Johnston to Salisbury, 18/9/89, 10, CP 6061, p. 38 enclosing treaties of 3, 5 and 6/9/89, to p. 40.
40 Treaty, 22/9/89, CP 6061, pp. 155–6; Agreement between Jumbe and ALC, 22/9/89, ibid., by which the ALC undertook to pay Jumbe 3,000 rupees a year; Johnston to Salisbury, 16/10/89, ibid., pp. 154–5.
41 Treaty, 22/10/89, CP 6061, pp. 160–1; 8 further treaties, pp. 161–9; and Johnston, Karonga, to Salisbury, 26/10/89, ibid., pp. 159–60
42 *Report of Mr. H. H. Johnston*, pp. 27–34, with an interesting tribute, pp. 36–9, to the Arabs of central Africa; Oliver, *Johnston*, pp. 165–9.

seriously endanger the lives and property of British subjects on the River Shire and in the Shire highlands and that it would cut the line of communication of Lake Nyasa and the surrounding districts".[43] On 19 August, J. Buchanan, on instructions left by Johnston, directed to Serpa Pinto a declaration that the Makololo country and the Shire hills, north of the Ruo River, had been placed under the protection of the Queen,

> and now beg you to desist from your purpose to march through this country with an armed force of Zulus, as should you do so in the face of this intimation I should not hold myself responsible for the consequences, and it would be a serious matter should you by advancing upon the Makololo country disturb the peaceful and friendly relations that have for so long existed between the Governments of His Most Faithful Majesty the King of Portugal and Her Most Gracious Majesty the Queen of Great Britain and Ireland, Empress of India, etc.
>
> It has been represented to me that you intended marching upon the Makololo country in order to punish the Makololo men, whose chief, through a misunderstanding and while under the influence of drink, fired upon a British steamer.
>
> I have the honour to enclose you a copy of a Protest against any such action on your part from the leading representatives of British interests here; and I trust that you will not fail to see the gravity of the situation and how serious may be the consequences should you disregard the terms of the letter.
>
> If in any way I can render you any assistance I should be only too happy to do so.[44]

The last paragraph was probably a reference to the occasional shots which, at Buchanan's instigation, were being directed on the expedition's camp at Mpassa.[45]

Serpa Pinto and his fellow officers counter-protested. They declared that their mission was purely scientific; and particularly did they protest against the manoeuvring and intriguing of the British at Blantyre, who excited the Makololo against the expedition, and who alone would be responsible for any consequences that might befall them if the expedition were attacked and the Portuguese forced to defend themselves.[46] Serpa Pinto assured Buchanan, as he had already assured Johnston, that he had no intention of punishing any Makololo chief; he repeated that his mission was peaceful; "and if I take with me some armed Zulu, it is in order that the work of this mission shall not be hindered by ignorant people"; he could take orders only from the Portuguese Government, and in the absence of instructions to the contrary, "I shall prosecute tenaciously

---

43 Nec., SPZ 2, *Neg.*, p. 148.
44 Buchanan to Serpa Pinto, 19/8/89, Nec., SPZ 2, *Neg.*, p. 147, CP 5970, pp. 224–5. Buchanan admitted that the arrival of Serpa Pinto "has very materially changed the position of affairs here".
45 Pinto, 'Relatório', p. 213.
46 Pinto, Pereira Ferraz, Themudo, José Cardoso, at Messange, 20/8/89, *Neg.*, p. 150, and CP 5970, p. 265.

and peacefully my journey, carrying ahead a flag of peace, but ready to repel with all energy whatever motiveless aggression can be made against me." He found it difficult to believe that the Makololo were under the protection of the Queen, knowing how the Makololo had treated British subjects. But if it were true, the Makololo should readily admit a scientific expedition belonging to an ally of Britain. If the Makololo attacked him, he would have to take the offensive, and finally bring peace to the Shire. In the absence of instructions to the contrary from his Government he would pursue his journey.[47]

These were brave words; but the expedition did not stir from camp. Buchanan instigated the Makololo to intensify their fire on Mpassa; and a British subject was found smuggling gunpowder to them through the Portuguese blockade.[48] Serpa Pinto ordered the balance of the expedition forward to Mpassa, less a detachment which was to advance up the west bank of the Shire. Then he descended the Shire and the Zambezi to confer with the Governor-general, who cabled urgently to his minister for instructions.[49]

Ferraz advanced up the west bank of the Shire with 200 men. He halted a few hundred yards short of the Makololo stockade-village of Balalika, opposite Mpassa. His men spread out in firing order while he advanced with four companions. As soon as the party came within range muskets fired on it. The Portuguese force advanced and occupied the village, killing six tribesmen in the process. Landeens set fire to the huts; the flames exploded twelve kegs of powder. Then, receiving an urgent call to assist Mpassa, which was being attacked by followers of Mlauri, the detachment crossed the Shire and joined the main body. The defences of Mpassa were improved, and the cutting of grass and bushes improved the field of fire. But at intervals Makololo continued to fire on the encampment, and to shout taunts at the Portuguese.[50]

The minister's instructions, when they arrived, demanded that the missionaries be escorted to Nyasa; the Governor-general was to employ force if necessary to ensure their passage and their protection; but this was Cardoso's responsibility, and Serpa Pinto should already have left for Zumbo and the Luangwa in accordance with his instructions. If Ferraz were able to start a survey of the Shire, he was to transfer to the Cardoso expedition; otherwise, he was to survey a route for a railway past the Quebrabasa rapids.[51] But Serpa Pinto refused to withdraw from the Shire, insisting that this would result in the revolt of Massingire and Manganja; he demanded the support and complete confidence of the Government and arms, especially a machine-gun. The Governor-general supported Serpa Pinto.[52] The Government could not understand why its policies and decisions were being abandoned. The minister

47 Pinto, Messange, to Buchanan, 21/8/89, *Neg.*, pp. 148–9, CP 5970, pp. 264–5.
48 [Pinto], Messange, to Military Commander, Messangire, 23/8/89, 6 Extra, *Neg.*, pp. 227–8.
49 Pinto to GG, tel., 29/8/89, *Neg.*, p. 65; GG to Min., 30/8/89 ibid.; Castellões, Mpassa, to Pinto, Quelimane, 31/8/89, tel., *Neg.*, p. 227.
50 A. de C. Araujo Ferraz, Mpassa, to Dir. geral, 8/9/89, *Nec.*, SPZ 2, *Neg.*, pp. 141–3; statement by H. Pettit, [9/89], CP 5970, p. 268; Buchanan to Salisbury, 17/9/89, 32 CA, ibid., p. 268.
51 Min. to GG., 2/9/89, Tel., *Neg.*, p. 66; and he authorized the expenses of an expedition to M'Cheza's, and a journey to Umtasa.
52 Pinto to Min., tel., 5/9/89, *Neg.*, p. 67; GG to Min., tel., 5/9/89, ibid.

exhorted that chiefs were to be persuaded to accept vassalage by all means short of war; and it instructed the Governor-general to proceed to Quelimane, if necessary to Massingire, and there take decision.[53]

Decisions were certainly necessary, for the crisis could only worsen as long as the expedition remained at Mpassa; and the prestige of Portugal would suffer unless it advanced. Buchanan rejected Serpa Pinto's counter-protest, and further protested against the burning of Balalika's village[54]—though Simpson, agent of the ALC, thanked the Portuguese for their action and for re-opening the Shire to navigation.[55] Buchanan now published the declaration announcing that the Makololo, Yao and Machinga countries had been placed under the protection of the British Queen. The area covered as far as possible the territories of chiefs with whom treaties had been signed, but Mlauri still refused to fly the British flag, of which he had a "superstitious dread" according to Buchanan.[56] A few days later Buchanan claimed to have signed a treaty with him, but, it emerged, he had not signed the treaty, because "Mlauri had a superstitious dread of putting his hand to the paper."[57] Even if it were authentic the treaty was of little account since the Ruo people were in revolt against Mlauri. Persuaded that the Portuguese were about to advance, Mlauri eventually accepted a British flag. Buchanan instructed him to raise it at Balalika's village, in sight of the Portuguese camp at Mpassa,[58] which was duly done, to the indignation of the Portuguese.[59] But the flag was left flying at night, unprotected, with the not unnatural consequence that a party from the Portuguese camp crossed the river and stole it. Buchanan engaged the ladies of the highlands to make flags, one to replace the stolen emblem, the other for Mlauri to fly at Mebeu. But Mlauri refused to accept another flag, declaring that he had been led astray by Buchanan's promises, while Moir's proceedings at Mebeu in June still rankled. Mlauri prepared for war against the Portuguese,[60] while Buchanan made further

53 Min. to GG. 7/9/89, tel., *Neg.*, p. 68.
54 Buchanan, Mudi, to Pinto, 10/9/89, CP 5970, pp. 265–6.
55 A. Simpson, Mpassa, to Ferraz, 22/9/89, *Neg.*, p. 231.
56 Declaration, Mlomba, 21/9/89, *Neg.*, p. 271. The boundaries ran from the confluence of the Shire and the Ruo up the Ruo to its source in the Mlanje mountains; along these mountains to the most southerly point of L. Shirwa; along its eastern shores, including the northern slopes of the Zomba and Malosa mountains, to the upper Shire; and on the right bank of the Shire, from the lowest point of the Makololo country, then opposite to Mpassa's (subject to rearrangement by the British Government), up a line 50 miles west of the Shire to the Lisungwi river (Buchanan to Pinto, 21/9/89, ibid., pp. 270–1; Buchanan to Salisbury, 25/9/89, 33 CA, ibid., pp. 269–70). Treaties had been signed with various Yao chiefs on 3/8/89, CP 6061, pp. 41–2, Machinga chiefs on 2/9/89, ibid., pp. 43–4. One of the latter treaties, with Chitaungo, was bogus according to Pinto ('Relatório', p. 416).
57 Treaty, 30/9/89, CP 5970, pp. 248–9; Buchanan to Salisbury, 26/9/89, 34 CA, ibid., pp. 271–2.
58 Buchanan to Salisbury, 7/10/89, 38 CA, CP 5970, pp. 273–4.
59 A. A. de R. Pinto, Megurrumba, to Gov., Quelimane, 15/10/89, Nec., SPZ 2, *Neg.*, pp. 144, 232. The GG instructed that those who had raised the flags would be invited to lower them; if they declined, all due honours were to be paid, and the flags were to be guarded with due care and sent to Quelimane, where they could be claimed by the Consul (GG to Gov., Quelimane, 9/11/89, *Neg.*, p. 144).
60 Buchanan to Salisbury, 8/11/89, 42 CA, CP 6061, pp. 45–8. J. Moir, hearing of the BSA Company's assumption of control of the ALC, urged his new masters to deal very cautiously with Mlauri, and purchase from him only such powers as were absolutely necessary, such as the right to levy duties and the regulation of the entry of arms and spirits; he should be left in possession of territorial rights (Moir, Mandala, to directors BSA and ALC, 9/10/89, CP 5970, pp. 324–6).

treaty-making journeys.[61]   The Portuguese at Mpassa remained completely passive, awaiting the return of Serpa Pinto and the arrival of reinforcements, including a second and third armoured steam-launch.[62]

Early in November an ALC vessel on her way up the river anchored off Mpassa. Serpa Pinto gave the company's agent a letter declaring that he was obliged to castigate the Makololo, and requesting all foreigners in the Makololo country to place themselves under Portuguese protection, failing which he would not hold himself responsible for any damage which might result to their property. The *James Stevenson* soon returned at speed down the river, having met bands of Mlauri's warriors who had been incited to attack the Portuguese before reinforcements could arrive.   The vessel stopped 12 miles below Mpassa's; the agent made haste to send Serpa Pinto a letter listing the company's property, which totalled only £1,123 in value.[63] As the Governor-general remarked to his minister, if the ALC had to be indemnified for its pretensions to sovereign rights, payment, in the light of this document, would be insignificant.[64]

Serpa Pinto refused to believe that Mlauri would attack him in his encampment 25 miles south of the Ruo, but as a precaution he ordered his men to be vigilant. At 4 a.m. on 8 November fire opened both on his camp and on that of Piri-piri across the river. When dawn came the Makololo force could be seen flying a red ensign; and since some bullets were carrying 1,500 yards, it was obvious that Mlauri had been armed with rifles supplied, in all probability, by the ALC. The attack lasted for over an hour. But the attackers, numerous though they were, could not prevail against fortified positions covered by fire from Kropatcheks and Martinis and a Nordenfeldt. The tribesmen lost at least 72 killed. There were no Portuguese casualties. A body of Landeens counterattacked, and put the Makololo to flight. Prisoners revealed that John Moir and the commander of the *Lady Nyasa* had persuaded Mlauri to attack, and had supplied the warriors with the British flag.[65]

---

61 Buchanan to Salisbury, 21/10/89, 40 and 41 CA, CP 6061, pp. 40–1 and 45; treaty with further Yao chiefs, 3 and 12/10/89, ibid., pp. 42–4.

62 José Cardoso, Massingire, to Sec. Geral, 2/11/89, *Bol. Off.*, 30/12/89, pp. 732–3. The launches, *Cuama, Cherim* and *Maravi*, were 74 feet long, stern-wheeled, armour plated to a height of 3 feet, equipped with machine-guns of the Hotchkiss pattern and each with a crew of 2 officers, 3 sailors, a mechanic, 3 firemen, and a number of natives (Ross, Quelimane, to Churchill, c. 10/89, CP 5970, p. 251; Churchill to Salisbury, 4/10/89, 5 Af., ibid., p. 250).

63 Pinto, 'Relatório', p. 214; A. Simpson, Misanje, to Pinto, 7/11/89, *Neg.*, p. 240; C. P. Ferraz, declaration, 26/10/89, CP 6061, p. 51.

64 GG to Min., 17/11/89, tel., Nec., SPZ 2, *Neg.*, p. 85.

65 Pinto, 'Relatório', pp. 214–5; Cardoso and Pinto to Gov., Quelimane, 9/11/89, tels, *Neg.*, p. 229; Pinto to Gov., Quelimane, 12/11/89, tel., ibid., p. 230. Ross to Churchill, 2/12/89, CP 6061, p. 58, gave 120 men killed according to reports that reached Blantyre. Compare the version in G. Cecil, *Life of Robert Marquis of Salisbury* (London, 1932), 4, p. 261: "But the culminating achievement which stirred Portugal to exultant enthusiasm and roused corresponding fury in England was . . . News reached England in December that Major Serpa Pinto, an officer in the Portuguese army, and a typically irresponsible African adventurer, had marched into the Shire highlands at the head of 700 armed Arabs; had demanded in the teeth of Mr. Johnston's protests, the submission of the Makololo tribe which was under British protection, and had shot them down with Gatling guns when they refused."

On the afternoon of the engagement Portuguese reinforcements began to arrive, and on 12 November the two armoured launches, the *Cherim* and *Maravi*. On 15 November Serpa Pinto started advancing northwards, he and the main body still on the east bank, a force under Ferrão on the right bank, and on the river the three launches and some fifty smaller craft. Two days' march brought the expedition to the Ruo. Serpa Pinto sent Coutinho in the *Cherim* to reconnoitre the fortified village of Chilomo as a preliminary to attack the next day. The vessel did not return. Early the next morning the main body advanced, and the other two vessels. The Portuguese flag was flying from Chilomo. Coutinho had been shot at from the village. He had opened fire with Hotchkiss and machine-guns. The tribesmen had withdrawn. He had landed with some seamen and natives, and occupied the place.[66]

Serpa Pinto fortified Chilomo, which he renamed Vila Coutinho. During the two days he was in the village he heard that the *Lady Nyasa* was descending the Shire and flying the British flag. He sent Coutinho to board her and inform her master that he was navigating Portuguese waters, and could no more fly a foreign flag than if he were on the lower Zambezi. The flag was duly lowered. Trivier, the French traveller and journalist, who was completing a crossing of the continent, observed and reported the incident.[67] The next day Serpa Pinto fell seriously ill. He ordered the columns to combine and advance up the west bank of the Shire under the command of Coutinho, whom the Governor of Quelimane nominated Military Governor of the Shire. Coutinho, in a rapid march, occupied Mebeu; Mlauri withdrew into the hills. On 18 December he occupied Mlomba, Masea's village; headmen presented him with a tusk of ivory as token of vassalage, and the Portuguese flag was raised. He occupied Katunga, the limit of navigation and the port of Blantyre. Each of these villages was fortified and garrisoned. At Mebeu, now renamed Vila Neves Ferreira, Mlauri's senior son formally declared that the Makololo had at heart always considered themselves as Portuguese subjects, from the days when Livingstone had abandoned them at Tete; they had been instigated to revolt by the ALC; they repented of their errors; and he paid vassalage on their behalf. Similar acts of homage were performed by chiefs Masea and Katunga.[68]

Serpa Pinto was borne to the coast by eight unarmed machila-bearers. On 26 December he was able to cable proudly from Moçambique to Lisbon that the Shire had been occupied; the area had been pacified; the Makololo had made submission; they had denounced their treaties with Johnston; the rule of law had been extended, so that slavery and savagery had been abolished; Portuguese authority had been established; and the route to the lake now stood wide open for the commerce of the world.[69]

66 Pinto, 'Relatório', pp. 215–6.
67 Ibid., p. 217.
68 Ibid., p. 216; termo de revindicação de direitos, 8/12/89, Mebeu, *Neg.*, p. 228; Pinto, Chilomo, to Gov., Quelimane, 8/12/89, ibid.; Buchanan to Salisbury, 23/12/89, 50 CA, CP 6061, pp. 230–1; Teixeira Botelho, II, pp. 349–50. The fort at the Ruo junction was being made of earth and adobe bricks; the walls were not strong enough to support the two guns, a 7-pr and a 9-pr; in the meantime, defence rested principally on a stockade (Buchanan to Salisbury, 24/12/89, 51 CA, CP 6061, pp. 232–3).
69 Pinto to Min., 26/12/89, tel., *Neg.*, p. 157.

About the southern end of the lake an increasing number of chiefs, including Cuirassia, Makanjila and Matapwira, adhered to Portugal, or re-affirmed their vassalage, their representatives proceeding to the district capital for this purpose.[70] The lands of the new chief Mponda, however, remained in a state of unrest from a dispute over the succession;[71] the disturbances threatened the launching of the Portuguese mission.

The Portuguese Government had come to a firm agreement with Cardinal Lavigerie in the middle of 1889, by which it entrusted to missionaries of *Notre Dame d'Afrique* the mission to be established on Nyasa. The mission, which was to be centred on Mponda's, was to operate north of the Ruo, and south of the sixteenth line of latitude and the German sphere of influence. Its eastern boundary was the 36° east parallel of longitude. The western limits were not fixed, but it might operate indefinitely in this direction north of latitude 15° south. The mission was to be regarded as Portuguese, but the missionaries need not renounce their nationality, nor were they to be answerable to any Portuguese prelate, only to their own religious superiors.[72] One missionary died on the voyage from Europe but three assembled in Quelimane waiting to be escorted to Mponda's. Cardoso was reluctant to conduct the party, which left Quelimane without him on 27 November 1889.[73] Its way seemed clear, thanks to Serpa Pinto and Coutinho. But before it could reach its objective the diplomatic bomb-shell burst.

Petre, the British minister in Lisbon, had kept his Government informed of the Serpa Pinto expedition from the time of its inception; its purpose, he reported, was to relieve the second Nyasa party, establish a mission at Mponda's, and then operate in the valley of the Luangwa, southwards to the Zambezi.[74] Salisbury received more detailed, if more tendentious, stories about Portuguese activities from his acting consul in Nyasaland. Buchanan reported, for instance, that Portuguese officials were making presents of arms and ammunition, and of Portuguese flags, to various chiefs. Salisbury commented that the former broke the declaration of blockade, while as for the latter, Britain would refuse to acknowledge any claim of Portugal to sovereignty in the Nyasa area "based upon the distribution of flags to the ignorant native chiefs." When

70 Cuirassia termo, 11/6/89, *Termos*, pp. 65–6, ratified in Ibo 19/9/89, ibid., pp. 65–6; Makanjila, 8/10/89, ibid., pp. 78–9; Chiuta, 30/10/89, ibid., pp. 79–80; Mulamira bin Chicunge, 30/8/89, ibid., pp. 72–3; Mussussa bin Mucunguta, 5/9/89, ibid., p. 76; Chivala bin Marira, 12/8/89, ibid., pp. 69–70; Licole Massuse, 19/8/89, ibid., pp. 71–2; Chicoja, 15/11/89, ibid., p. 80; Chicoata, 19/11/89, ibid., p. 81; Cardoso to Min., 81, Nec., SPZ 2, *Neg.*, p. 85; *Novidades*, 19/11/89, CP 5970, pp. 260, 260E; Ross to Churchill, 2/12/89, CP 6061, p. 58; GG to Min., 7/12/89, tel., Nec., SPZ 2.
71 Buchanan to Salisbury, 29/7/89, 25 CA., CP 5970, pp. 221–2; Buchanan to Pinto, 10/12/89, CP 6061, p. 171.
72 Draft convention, 31/5/89, *Neg.*, pp. 260–1; Lavigerie, Algiers, to Gomes, 1/6/89, ibid., pp. 258–60; Convention, Lavigerie and Portuguese Consul-General, Algiers, 17/6/89, ibid., pp. 262–3. Lavigerie was made a Grand Knight of the Order of Christ (Gosselin, Brussels, to Salisbury, 26/7/89, 60 Af., CP 5970, pp. 143–4).
73 Ross, Quelimane, to Salisbury, 23/8/89, 50, CP 5970, pp. 209–10; GG to Min., 24/8/89 and 3/9/89, tels., *Neg.*, pp. 64, 67; Cardoso to Min., 27/9/89, tel., *Neg.*, p. 69; GG to Min., 7/10/89, Nec., SPZ 2, *Neg.*, pp. 69–70; Cardoso to Min., 15/12/89, tel., *Neg.*, p. 131.
74 Petre to Salisbury, 21/3/89, 27 Af., CP 5970, pp. 44–5 and 29/3/89, 35 Af., ibid., p. 48; and 20/8/89, 125 Af., ibid., p. 172.

Petre read this despatch to the Minister of Foreign Affairs, Barros Gomes could not but exclaim on the unfriendly attitude of Salisbury's informants in the area, and especially of the acting consul; the information was often inaccurate; and the chiefs often confirmed their vassalage at subsequent formal ceremonies.[75]

In August 1889 the British Foreign Office heard of the projected strengthening of administration up the Zambezi, notably at Zumbo, and the establishment of a post at the mouth of the Kafue.[76] Bishop Smythies transmitted a report that Serpa Pinto had arrived at the junction of the Umfuli and Umniati Rivers with 3,000 men—he was presumably confusing the Pinto and the Cordon expeditions. The Colonial Office promptly remarked that the Portuguese were encroaching on the territories of Lobengula.[77] The move to take over the ALC by the British South Africa Company united the interests of British and South African financiers in Mashonaland and Nyasaland.[78] Reports that travellers proceeding from the coast to the interior were being required to take out cards of residence prompted suspicion that these areas were to be regarded as within the Portuguese province.[79]

What alerted Salisbury most to Portuguese intentions in the interior was a series of telegrams and despatches from Churchill, whom Johnston had left as his deputy at Moçambique. Churchill reported on the Serpa Pinto expedition, and that Andrada was leading an expedition into Manicaland, the object of which was not only to prospect for gold but to extend Portuguese sovereignty over Gungunhana's country. Gungunhana, Churchill declared, would be happy to accept British protection.[80] Churchill considered the Portuguese plans to punish Mlauri for firing on the ALC so trivial a matter that he saw no reason for bothering the Secretary of State with it,[81] but Buchanan's letters were more emotional and he talked of a critical situation developing.[82]

Towards the end of September unofficial pressure began to be exerted on the Portuguese Government, judging by a cable which it sent the Governor-general of Moçambique, requesting information on the conflict on the Shire and on the difficulties of the British consul there.[83] Churchill reported that the Makololo were prohibiting the advance of Serpa Pinto, who had returned to Moçambique for instructions,[84] but it was not until mid October that Salisbury asked Petre to enquire in Lisbon for further information.[85] Barros Gomes gave the frankest statement on the situation. Petre warned him that Serpa Pinto's

75 Salisbury to Petre, 2/8/89, 136 Af., CP 5970, p. 145 A; Petre to Salisbury, 15/8/89, 123 Af., ibid., pp. 155–6.
76 Petre to Salisbury, 13/8/89, 122 Af., CP 5970, p. 154.
77 CO to FO, 16/8/89, CP 5970, p. 153.
78 W. Ewing to Rhodes and Cawston, 14/8/89, CP 5970, p. 233.
79 Church of Scotland Foreign Missions Committee to Salisbury, 28/8/89, CP 5970, p. 177; Petre to Salisbury, 2/10/89, 137, ibid., p. 214.
80 Churchill to Salisbury, 4/9/89, 1 Af., CP 5970, p. 216.
81 Churchill to Salisbury 14/9/89, 3 Af., CP 5970, p. 217.
82 Buchanan to Salisbury 10/9/89, 30, CP 5970, pp. 262–4.
83 Min. to GG, 21/9/89, tel., Neg., p. 68.
84 Churchill to Salisbury, 8/10/89, 4 Af., CP 5970, pp. 248–50, recording a telegram of 22/9/89.
85 Salisbury to Petre, 17/10/89, 173, CP 5970, p. 215; memo, 23/10/89, Nec., SPZ 2, Neg., p. 70.

proceedings, supported as they were by the colonial authorities, could lead to very serious consequences; the Makololo utterly repudiated Portuguese claims to jurisdiction over them and were perfectly justified in resisting invasion. He added that the British Government would firmly resist any Portuguese action based on an assumption of jurisdiction which was injurious to the interests of British subjects.[86] The ALC now revived the plan to run a steamer loaded with arms and ammunition into the Zambezi. The earlier plan had been dropped when Salisbury had told Rhodes that the time was not opportune. But the Foreign Office would not commit itself on the question of whether the time was yet ripe.[87]

A consular cable of 8 November 1889 told the Foreign Office of the departure of Serpa Pinto for Nyasa with 1,200 armed men and over 2,000 followers; it added that the presence of such a force would be misinterpreted by the natives and unsettle the country.[88] On 12 November Salisbury telegraphed Petre to enquire of Barros Gomes the destination and the objects of the expedition, which was now said to total 6,000 men and to be supported by two river-steamers.[89] Barros Gomes explained that the men were escorting the expedition which was surveying the country bordering on the Shire; especially were they to protect it from the Makololo should the Makololo attack it. Petre accused him of preparing to wage war on the Makololo, to wring submission from them by force. Barros Gomes assured him that the expedition would attack the Makololo only if the Makololo attacked the expedition. With some warmth he declared that Britain was continually spurning the rights of Portugal. He referred to reports appearing in *The Times* and other British newspapers, and to the charter of the British South Africa Company. He expressed emphatically the great desire of the Portuguese Government to come to an amicable arrangement with Britain over boundaries and spheres of influence; such agreement would be greatly to the mutual advantage of the two countries.[90]

An alarmist—and false—cable from Churchill alleged that the Makololo were plundering an ALC steamer and imprisoning two Britons; it ended, "Life and property will be in great danger while Portuguese unchecked."[91] The Colonial Office, receiving reports of Portuguese movements in Mashonaland and of the creation of the new district of Zumbo, raised with the Foreign Office the advisability of making representations to Portugal.[92] The Foreign Office, as soon as it received details of the boundaries of the new district, responded promptly. Petre was required to remind the Portuguese Government that Mashonaland was under British influence, and that the British Government would not recognize the claims of Portugal north of the Zambezi within the boundaries as defined: on the banks of the Luangwa were tribes which had signed treaties with the British Government; and on the Shire River and the

86 Petre to Salisbury, 23/10/89, 141 Af., CP 5970, pp. 219–20.
87 Anderson, memo., 25/10/89, CP 5970, p. 219.
88 O'Neill to Salisbury, 8/11/88, tel., CP 5727, p. 124; and 8/11/88, 88 Af., ibid., pp. 133–4.
89 Salisbury to Petre, 12/11/89, tel. 195, CP 5970, p. 238.
90 Petre to Salisbury, 13/11/89, 154 Af., CP 5970, p. 253.
91 Churchill to Salisbury, 17/11/89, tel., CP 5970, p. 252*.
92 FO to CO, 19/11/89, CP 5970, p. 255.

shores of Nyasa were British settlements. The decree asserted Portuguese rights over vast territories which were still unoccupied and knowledge about which was due principally to British explorers. The British Government repeated its stand of August 1887: it rejected any claims which were not founded on occupation and the exercise of authority.[93] Barros Gomes recalled that his Government had protested against the whole of Mashonaland being regarded as within Lobengula's territory. Included within the boundaries of the Zumbo district was only part of Mashonaland which Portugal had always claimed; this was no new annexation. Portugal's position in Africa, and the current of public opinion at home, left his Government no alternative but to keep marching on. But the Portuguese Government remained most anxious to come to an amicable agreement with Britain over frontiers and spheres of influence. Petre remarked curtly that there was no prospect of that if Serpa Pinto kept marching on.[94]

The arrival in London of a bundle of despatches from Buchanan and Churchill increased the indignation of officials at the Foreign Office. Four hundred of Serpa Pinto's seven hundred Landeens were armed with breech-loaders: "This is an army, not an escort," exclaimed Sir P. Anderson. There were reports of reinforcements, to bring the expedition to 6,000 men, and of a steamer (and a British steamer at that) being chartered to carry troops from Portuguese India to south-east Africa. And according to the consul at Zanzibar, who arrived in London at this time, it was no secret that the purpose of this expedition was to checkmate Johnston. Buchanan had perhaps gone too far in declaring a British protectorate, Anderson felt, but since the Portuguese were distributing flags it was only natural for Britons to do the same. The Portuguese were preparing to attack and subjugate tribes sheltering under the British flag, deliberately.[95] The British press reacted strongly to the Nyasa news, and violent articles attacked Portugal.[96]

In Portugal public meetings whipped up enthusiasm. The Society of Geography of Lisbon, for instance, unanimously passed a resolution condemning the British protest, and "trusts that the Government, inspired by the unanimous will of the nation and the unquestioned justice of its cause, will firmly maintain the right and integrity of the sovereignty of Portugal."[97] Portuguese newspapers published articles excited by Barros Gomes and other cabinet and ex-cabinet ministers.[98] Barros Gomes had sent a secret agent to Berlin and Paris to provoke those governments against Britain; he had failed in his mission.[99] Barros Gomes now sent a lengthy circular letter (it ran to 12 pages of white book) to all Portuguese legations surveying Portugal's relations with other powers and particularly with Britain, so that the various ministers might

93 Salisbury to Petre, 21/11/89, 201 Af., CP 5979, pp. 260–1, Nec., SPZ 2, *Neg.*, pp. 100–1.
94 Petre to Salisbury, 25/11/89, 164 Af., CP 5970, p. 276.
95 Anderson, c. [26/11/89] and 26/11/89, memos on Buchanan despatches 30–38, ibid., p. 274; Soveral to Barros Gomes, 27/11/89, 138 A, Nec., SPZ 2.
96 The Minister in London maintained a flow of cuttings to the Minister of Foreign Affairs in Lisbon; most are heavily side-lined (Nec., SPZ 2).
97 CP 5970, pp. 285–6.
98 See the volumes of cuttings in AHU; and e.g. *Novidades*, 27/11/89, CP 5970, p. 277. 99/102.
99 José de Almada, *A Aliança Inglesa*, III (Lisbon, 1949), pp. 405–11. The agent was J. Batalha Reis.

be able to enlist the support of the governments to which they were accredited.[100] This had some effect: the German consul at Moçambique, for instance, instructed by Bismarck, enquired whether the Portuguese had offered assistance to the British settlers on Nyasa, and what were the objects of the Johnston expedition.[101] Salisbury was constrained to instruct his ambassador in Berlin to declare, if interrogated about the treaties Johnston was concluding west of the German sphere of influence, that Johnston was acting without instructions.[102]

Barros Gomes, having circularized his legations, sent an almost equally lengthy despatch to his chargé d'affaires in London for communication to Salisbury, summarizing the Portuguese claims to territory, and expressing confidence that Britain would not wish to infringe the rights of any people, least of all of her old allies, the Portuguese. He cited military expeditions and missionary and commercial penetration and mining enterprises and colonizing ventures from the sixteenth to the nineteenth centuries. He quoted Selous, who had declared that there were numerous tribes of Shona who were not subject to Lobengula but who, whenever his raiding impis arrived, fled into caves and mountain fastnesses. Recent Portuguese expeditions, Barros Gomes insisted, were only re-asserting ancient rights. That of Andrada, supported by António de Sousa, had reached the headwaters of the Umfuli and the Hunyani; that of Cordon had proceeded from Zumbo by way of the Hunyani valley to the valley of the Umfuli and Sanyati. Many chiefs in those regions had acknowledged vassalage to the Portuguese Crown; and so, too, had chiefs subject to Gungunhana lying between the Limpopo and the Bubye Rivers, and along the banks of the Sabi. As for British attempts to restrict Portuguese action north of the Zambezi, Portugal had discovered Nyasa early in the seventeenth century; even Livingstone had acknowledged his indebtedness to the Portuguese for his first knowledge of the Shire and Nyasa; and there was no denying the success of A. M. Cardoso's expedition. The restrictions imposed by the Conference of Berlin on effective occupation applied only to the coasts of Africa, not the interior; if they did, the sovereignty of the Free State could not be enforced over most of the Congo, or of Germany over most of south-west Africa, or of Britain herself in areas of the equatorial lakes and Bechuanaland and Matabeleland. Barros Gomes concluded by reiterating that much could be gained in the cause of civilization and African progress if the questions dividing Portugal and Britain could be amicably settled.[103]

This despatch of Barros Gomes, though dated 29 November 1889, did not leave Lisbon until 2 December; it arrived in London on the night of 5 December and a copy was delivered to the Foreign Office on the 6th; further delay followed while it was being translated.[104] When it was published it added greatly to Barros Gomes's political stature in Portugal, where there was general conviction

100 Barros Gomes, circular letter, 22/11/89, draft in Nec., SPZ 2, *Neg.*, pp. 88–100.
101 Churchill to Salisbury, 6/12/89, 12 Af., CP 6061, pp. 57–8.
102 Salisbury to Malet, 17/12/89, 94 Af., CP 5970, p. 294.
103 Barros Gomes, to Soveral, 29/11/89, CP 5970, pp. 279–85, *London Gazette*, 17/1/90, pp. 275–8, *Neg.*, pp. 102–9, with supporting documents to p. 117.
104 Dantas to Barros Gomes, 9/12/89, Nec., pp. 119–20.

that the substantiation of Portuguese claims must now be acknowledged by Britain.[105] Knowledge began to spread of another expedition, organized by Augusto Cardoso, with assistance from the German trader Wiese, to Mpesene's,[106] and there were renewed attempts to launch a Portuguese chartered company to exploit south-east Africa, though capital was hard to come by, largely because of intrigues by London Jews, according to Barros Gomes's secret agent.[107]

In London feeling was hardening against Portugal. A telegram from Buchanan, received on 1 December, announced Cardoso's arrival at Chikala, on his way to Cuirassia's.[108] The Intelligence Division of the War Office warned the Foreign Office of the expedition to Mpesene, which was to the west of Nyasa.[109] And the BSA Company was making firm plans for an expedition to the interior. In the plans as first conceived entrance was to be forced by way of the Zambezi, with the aid of two Government Nile steamers. Rankin volunteered to lead the expedition which, he recommended, should consist of some 300 Baluchis supported by several 74-foot stern-wheelers in addition to the smaller of the Nile steamers. He anticipated no opposition to the Ruo; a post would be established at Katunga; and he anticipated no opposition to the foot of the Quebrabasa rapids, where a fort would be built to cover the portage of a steam-launch to the middle Zambezi. His objects were two-fold, Rankin declared: to restore British prestige; and to establish firm jurisdiction over Mashonaland.[110] But Rhodes bought Selous, and Selous favoured an overland route. The prospect of having a firm base in dependable Khama's country rather than a swinging hulk in the Zambezi delta appealed to the directors of the BSA Company.[111] While some thoroughly appreciated that money-grabbers were "working the patriotic racket for all it is worth,"[112] the general feeling in London was that national prestige and potential profits together demanded that Britain assert her claims over Mashonaland.[113] One paper, after summarizing Barros Gomes's reply, declared that the amicable delimitation of the territories was by no means a matter of course. Since the original suggestion had been made Portugal's pretensions had immensely increased. The aim of the Portuguese Government was still a belt of territory across Africa which would prevent British expansion northwards. It was to "crumbling walls and bastions, overgrown with tropical jungle" that Portugal appealed for witnesses; but most of that area was known only from the energy of intrepid British explorers. Nyasa, Tanganyika, Victoria, Albert, Edward, were all links in a chain of water communication which could connect British settlements in the Cape to those of east

105 Petre to Salisbury, 12/12/89, 175 Af., CP 5970, pp. 291–2.
106 *Bol. SGL*, 1891, pp. 235–73, 331–430, 465–97.
107 Batalha Reis, Brussels, to Min., 12/12/89, tel., Nec., SPZ 2.
108 Buchanan to Salisbury, 30/11/88, 49, CP 6061, pp. 11–2.
109 Intelligence Div. to FO, received 12/12/89, CP 5970, p. 287.
110 Rankin to BSAC, wrongly dated 6/1/90, CP 6061, pp. 16–22.
111 BSAC to FO, 5/12/89, CP 5970, p. 278; Cawston to FO, 8/12/89, ibid., p. 286.
112 *Stock Exchange*, 7/1/89, declaring that directors of the Ophir Company had received £480,000 for 350 claims which Dr. Balen had hawked about London for £1,000.
113 See e.g. *Morning Post*, 3/12/89, *Pall Mall* 6/12/89, *Times*, 5, 6, 9/12/89.

Africa and possibly even to the Nile.[114] Another did have some qualms as to the possible consequences of the British stand: "It is a horrible nuisance thus to have to contemplate another African war." The paper hoped that Salisbury knew what he was after "in this awkward little broil with Portugal. If he does not mind what he is about he will soon be compelled to order the Channel Fleet to anchor off Lisbon pending the reply of the Portuguese to his ultimatum."[115] Which was very close to what Salisbury had in mind.

On 14 December three cables reached London from South Africa, including one from Rhodes, to the effect that two Portuguese officers and 300 men armed with rifles were building forts in Matabeleland, notably one at the junction of the Umniati and the Nyaboza Rivers, and planting Portuguese flags: "undoubted territory of Lobengula has been invaded."[116] Here was belated reference to the activities of Cordon and the erection of the stockade Luciano Cordeiro.[117] The same day the Universities' Mission received a cable from Zanzibar that Serpa Pinto had picked a quarrel with the Makololo and slaughtered hundreds with Gatling guns and seized two British flags; and that Serpa Pinto had announced his intention of seizing all the Shire country to Nyasa. This was only a garbled version of the account received in November. But the information was rushed out to Salisbury at his Hatfield seat. It was red rag to the bull.[118] Salisbury cabled to the consul at Zanzibar for information. Euan Smith confirmed the information which had emanated from Smythies and Trivier: Serpa Pinto had assured Johnston of his pacific intentions; but he had gone to the coast for reinforcements, picked a quarrel with Mlauri and slaughtered many hundreds, though Buchanan, under provisional authority given him by Johnston, had proclaimed British protection. The Portuguese force at the junction of the Ruo now numbered 4,000 men, with 7 machine-guns, and 3 steamers. They had publicly declared war on the Makololo and had officially announced their intention to retake the whole country to the lake, warning the British settlers to put themselves under Portuguese protection or take the consequences. It was probable that Mponda would accept the Portuguese mission, which Euan Smith regarded as serious, because he could close the Shire. A column of 500 men under Cardoso was supporting Serpa Pinto. Euan Smith added that 350 Portuguese troops were leaving Goa for Moçambique on 31 December.[119] The press campaign against Portugal mounted in anger, prompted, Dantas was certain, by cupidity for gold.[120]

114 *Standard*, 9/12/89, *Neg.*, pp. 120–2; 'Portuguese pretensions in Zambesia' by a Correspondent, *Times*, 11/12/89, etc.
115 *Pall Mall Gazette*, 14/12/89, headed, 'Stop this moment, or —', *Neg.*, pp. 128–9. With reason did *O Dia* 18/12/89, describe Johnston as "a slippery individual, mellifluous and insinuating, who while passing through Portugal acted to perfection the part of a friend of Portugal", CP 5970, p. 300.
116 Shippard, Vryburg, to Loch, 16/11/89, Smyth to Knutsford, 19/11/89, Rhodes, Kimberley, to Colonial Secretary, Cape Town, –/11/89, CP 5970, p. 290.
117 *Novidades*, 13/12/89, CP 5970, pp. 294–5.
118 *Observer*, 15/12/89, *Neg.*, pp. 129–31; Petre to Salisbury, 17/12/89, 179 Af., CP 5970, p. 297.
119 Euan Smith, Zanzibar, to Salisbury, 16, 17/12/89, tels, CP 5970, p. 292; and 18/12/89, 404, extenders of tels. 288, 290, 295, 299, CP 6061, pp. 77–8, received 20/12/89.
120 Dantas to Barros Gomes, 16/12/89, 153 A, Nec., SPZ 2, enclosing, further inflammatory cuttings; 17/12/89, 155 A, ibid., 18/12/89 A ibid.

On 17 December Salisbury telegraphed to Petre a summary of Euan Smith's cable. The attack upon the Makololo, Salisbury declared, was a serious infraction of the rights of a friendly state; the British Government could not acquiesce in such conduct. He requested Petre to request a declaration from the Portuguese Government that the Portuguese forces would not attack the British settlements on the Shire or Nyasa, or the Makololo country or territory under the government of Lobengula, or any other country which had been declared to be under British protection, and that any Portuguese officer who had done so must be recalled. Petre was to report not later than 21 December the answer of the Portuguese Government.[121] This near-ultimatum Petre passed on to Barros Gomes on 18 December, without stipulating a time-limit, but demanding reply with the least possible delay.[122]

On 19 December Petre saw Barros Gomes, and impressed on him the necessity to comply with Salisbury's demands to avoid a rupture with Britain. The Minister of Foreign Affairs was conciliatory, but not acquiescent; he insisted again on the pacific nature of the Pinto expedition; he did not believe the reports of battles with the Makololo, and was certain that there had been no slaughter north of the Ruo.[123] That day Salisbury, in anticipation of a Portuguese rejection of his note planned the withdrawal of the British minister from Lisbon. He advised the First Lord of the Admiralty to prepare operation orders for the ships of the Cape squadron to join the squadron stationed in Zanzibar waters, and for the combined force to occupy the island of Moçambique: ". . . The period between the withdrawal of our Legation from Lisbon and our occupation of Moçambique will be one of great anxiety and all kinds of things may happen. It is a matter of serious importance that the threat should not be separated from the blow by too long an interval."[124]

On 20 December Barros Gomes formally replied to Petre. He gave a calm, dispassionate factual survey of events on the Shire during the year. His conclusion was that the Portuguese had organized an expedition which was of a purely technical character, unprovided with troops for the waging of war; there had been disturbances on the Shire, the result of intrigues against the Portuguese; the expedition, so far from attacking, had been attacked, while Serpa Pinto was absent from it; and this attack had not been in Makololo country but in acknowledged Portuguese territory, south of the Ruo. The Government would not permit any attack on any British station on the Shire or Nyasa. As for allegations about its intentions in Lobengula's country, the Government was only defending the rights of the Portuguese Crown. His Government, Barros Gomes added, still desired to be conciliated with Britain.[125] Barros Gomes invited Petre to read all the correspondence that had passed between Serpa Pinto and the Governor-general of Moçambique, which made it clear

121 Salisbury to Petre 17/12/89, tel. 25, CP 5970, p. 293 and extender, pp. 293–4.
122 Petre to Gomes, 18/12/89, Nec., SPZ 2, *Neg.*, pp. 133–4, CP 5970, p. 299.
123 Petre to Salisbury, 19/12/89, 185 Af., CP 5970, pp. 302–4.
124 Salisbury to Hamilton, 19/12/89, Cecil, *Salisbury*, IV, p. 262.
125 Barros Gomes to Petre, 20/12/89, Nec., SPZ 2, CP 5970, pp. 310–2, *Neg.*, pp. 136–9.

that the agent of the ALC had requested Portuguese intervention.[126] To the Governor-general of Moçambique the Government urged that Serpa Pinto, in accordance with his instructions, use pacific means for his civilizing work and resort to arms only for his defence and to maintain national dignity. A gunboat was to be sent to Chinde, to demand that new vessels entering the Zambezi comply with the regulations; any foreign warship was to be admitted under protest, without the exercise of violence.[127]

Hearing rumours of British naval movements, and fully appreciating the necessity for enlisting the support of as many nations as possible that were represented at the Brussels anti-slavery conference,[128] Barros Gomes, in his extremity, turned to a suggestion made by one of his advisers[129] to have recourse to the Act of Berlin. Article 12 declared:

> In case a serious disagreement originates on the subject of, or in the limits of, the territories mentioned in Article 1 and placed under the free trade system, shall arise between any Signatory Powers of the present Act, or the Powers which may become parties to it, these Powers bind themselves, before appealing to arms, to have recourse to the mediation of one or more of the friendly Powers.
>
> In a similar case the same Powers reserve to themselves the option of having recourse to arbitration.[130]

The Government of the United States of America was agreeable to the idea of arbitration, but made it conditional on resolution of the Delagoa Bay railway case[131]—a case which also helped to explain Britain's resentment against Portugal.[132] The French Government assured Portugal of its moral help and that it would make clear to Salisbury that it desired a satisfactory solution of the dispute. French financiers were negotiating with the Portuguese Government for a concession to a chartered company which, nominally Portuguese, but with mainly French capital, would develop that part of Mashonaland which lay in the newly decreed district of Zumbo. Such a chartered company, it was felt in Paris, was essential to counter-balance the BSA Company.[133]

On 22 December Barros Gomes sent off a circular telegram to all Portuguese legations. He was optimistic of the outcome of his note. But the press of the two countries had aggravated the question, and there were reports of movements of warships. If the conflict worsened, each minister was to make it known to the government to which he was accredited that Portugal would

---

126 Petre to Salisbury, 23/12/89, 194 Af., CP 5970, pp. 318–9; supplemented by an account which appeared in *Diario de Noticias*, 22/12/89, forwarded by Petre to Salisbury, 24/12/89, 197 Af., ibid., p. 326 A; Petre to Salisbury, 28/12/89, 40 Af., ibid., pp. 321–2.
127 Min. to GG, 20/12/89, tel., *Neg.*, p. 144.
128 Min. to Matthias de Carvalho Vasconcellos, 24/12/89, not sent, Nec., SPZ 2.
129 Martens to Barros Gomes, 10/12/89, Nec., SPZ 2, *Neg.*, pp. 122–8.
130 Hertslet, I, p. 30.
131 Roga to Min., 20/12/[89], tel., Nec., SPZ 3.
132 See p. 116
133 Valbom, Paris, to Min., 21/12/89, 31 A, Nec., SPZ 2, Petre to Salisbury, 16/12/89, 178 Af., CP 5970, p. 296 and 21/12/89 187 Af., ibid., p. 310*. By 26/12/89 the Portuguese Government had induced a few wealthy Portuguese to subscribe half a million pounds (Petre to Salisbury, 26/12/89, 198, CP 5970, p. 326 B.)

gladly submit the dispute to examination by a conference of European powers, or to arbitration.[134] At heart Barros Gomes still hoped for belated acceptance of his agreement with Johnston.[135] But the British press was adopting an ever more belligerent attitude. Even the *Pall Mall Gazette*, for instance, which had favoured the Johnston arrangement, called for action: ". . . Pinto, reeking of the blood of our slaughtered allies, flaunts as trophies of his campaigns against the Makololo two British flags which our allies had fondly hoped would secure them immunity from attack. It is another affair to go back on our word after the conflict has broken out, repudiate our allies, and allow the Portuguese to hobnail our honour into the bloody slush of the east African marsh."[136] The International Arbitration and Peace Association urged the British Government to resort to arbitration;[137] but its was a lone voice.

Barros Gomes's note had reached Petre on 22 December; a telegraphed summary of it reached the Foreign Office on 23 December. That same day Salisbury notified Queen Victoria of the cabinet's intentions:

> Lord Salisbury, with his humble duty to your Majesty, respectfully submits that, from the telegraph he has received this morning, it appears probable that the Portuguese Government will refuse to give the undertaking not to interfere with the settlements of British subjects, and the protected chiefs, which has been required of them. In that case, it has been agreed by the Cabinet to recommend that the island of Moçambique shall be temporarily occupied. It is probable that the Portuguese Government dare not give way on account of the strong feeling there is in Lisbon; and that they themselves would not be sorry that Great Britain should take some decided step showing her to be in earnest in the matter. The negotiations are not yet concluded; but in case they should end badly, the requisite naval force is being assembled at Zanzibar.[138]

There was another consideration, and that was the rise of republicanism in Portugal. The Portuguese Republican Party chose this moment to issue a manifesto declaring that the time had come to do away with the monarchy.[139] Crispi, the Prime Minister of Italy, advised Portugal to come to terms with Britain, the home of constitutional monarchy, as quickly as she could, if the monarchy in Portugal were not to suffer.[140] The Spanish and Austrian Governments were also interested in the maintenance of the monarchy; but they would not go beyond expressions of sympathy.[141]

The Netherlands press was favourable to Portugal.[142] The Minister of

---

134 22/12/89, *Neg.*, p. 145.
135 Interview with special representative, *Daily News* 24/12/89, *Neg.*, p. 163.
136 24/12/89, *Neg.*, pp. 159–60.
137 J. F. Green to Dantas and Salisbury, 21/12/89, *Nec.*, SPZ 2, *Neg.*, pp. 145–6.
138 23/12/89, G. E. Buckle (ed.), *Letters of Queen Victoria*, 3rd series, I, 1886–1890 (London), p. 538.
139 *Times*, 21/12/89, *Nec.*, SPZ 2.
140 Carvalho Vasconcellos, Rome, to Min., 23/12/89, *Nec.*, SPZ 3, and 24/12/89, 6 A, *Nec.*, SPZ 2.
141 Casal Ribeiro to Min., 28/12/89, A 9, *Nec.*, SPZ 2; Paget to Salisbury, 28/12/89, 363, CP 5970, p. 323.
142 Pindella, Hague, to Barros Gomes, 23/12/89, 57 A, *Nec.*, SPZ 2.

Foreign Affairs expressed the sympathy of his cabinet for the predicament in which Portugal found herself, but made it clear that his Government would not act against Britain. The South African Republic's minister at the Hague also declared that the Transvaal would not intervene, even if there were a Portuguese disaster at Lourenço Marques; but he felt that Germany would never allow Britain to occupy that port.[143] In Germany there were mixed feelings. There was bitter resentment at the plans of the BSA Company; but Germany was in trouble with the coastal Arabs of east Africa; and it was necessary to define her boundaries with Britain. The Germans, at the end of 1889, were pressing for an African settlement with Britain,[144] and it was realization of this fact that persuaded Salisbury he could take firm measures against Portugal.[145]

On Boxing Day Salisbury put his signature to a despatch which attacked Barros Gomes's communication of 6 December. "Archaeological arguments in the judgement of Her Majesty's Government are not relevant. The fact of essential importance is that the territory is not under the effective Government and occupation of Portugal." Portuguese occupation of the interior ceased more than two centuries before, during the whole of which interval, Salisbury declared, Portugal had made no attempt to govern or civilize or colonize the vast areas she now claimed. Only the advancing stream of British immigration had stimulated Portugal to action. The historical arguments of Barros Gomes did not invalidate the rights acquired by British missionaries and traders, or the lawfulness of the protection which had been extended to Lobengula and the Makololo. Attempts to exercise Portuguese dominion over British settlements, and over tribes under British protection, were an invasion of British rights.[146]

The same day secret orders reached the Commander-in-chief, Mediterranean Station, for the monitors *Benbow* and *Colossus* to proceed to Gibraltar, where they would be within easy sailing of Lisbon.[147] To Gibraltar also arrived, on 2 January 1890, the Channel Squadron, consisting of *Northumberland, Anson, Iron Duke, Monarch* and *Curlew*, ready, according to an Admiralty statement, for any contingency that might arise.[148]

On 2 January Petre communicated Salisbury's despatch to Barros Gomes.[149]

The same day the King opened a new session of the Cortes. He referred to the recent expeditions in Africa which had added to Portuguese prestige and carried administration to regions of the interior. Petre, without justification, told Salisbury that the speech from the throne reflected an unyielding tone

143 Pindella to Min., 25/12/89, 6, Nec., SPZ 2.
144 Cecil, IV, p. 248.
145 Robinson and Gallagher, p. 245.
146 Salisbury to Petre, 26/12/89, CP 5970, pp. 315–7, Nec., SPZ 2, *Neg.*, pp. 153–5; summarized by Ponsonby to Queen, 27/12/89, *Letters of Queen Victoria*, 3rd series, I, p. 543.
147 Journal of Vice-Admiral Sir Anthony H. Hoskins, KCB, C-in-C, Med. Station, for the Quarter ended 31/12/89, PRO, FO 50/385, for 23/12/89.
148 *Daily News*, 31/12/89, *Neg.*, pp. 169–70. *Northumberland*, Flagship of Vice-Adm. Baird, 29 guns, 10,780 tons; *Anson*, flagship of Rear-Adm. Tracey, battleship, 10 guns, 10,600 tons; *Iron Duke*, 14 guns, 6,010 tons; *Monarch*, 7 guns, 8,320 tons; *Curlew*, 4 guns, 950 tons; Journal of Rear-Adm. R. E. Tracey, C-in-C. Channel Sqn. PRO, FO Adm. 50/399.
149 Salisbury to Petre, 2/1/90, 1, PRO, FO 179/276, CP 6061, pp. 2–3; it incorporated a few minor alterations sent by tel.

which did not augur well for any understanding between the two countries.[150]
Petre was probably influenced by receipt of a letter from his informant João
reporting that a strong military expedition, with European troops, was being
organized to the district of Manica and the adjoining territories of Mashonaland; artillery and cavalry officers, especially, were being recruited; Andrada
was at that moment making a treaty with a Shona chief; and he would avail
himself of António de Sousa's sepoys to secure Portugal's position in the
dominions of Gungunhana. A captain in whom the Government had the
greatest confidence had just been appointed to the command of the Zumbo
district. Here was proof, Petre telegraphed to Salisbury, that Portugal was
seizing by force territory which Britain had repeatedly and formally told her
was under British protection. In these circumstances there seemed to Petre
only one course open, and that was to inform the Portuguese Government that
any occupation of any portion of such territories by Portuguese forces, or
refusal to withdraw from them if already occupied, would be regarded as an
act of hostility against Britain.[151]

Meanwhile Salisbury, who had been laid low with influenza on Boxing
Day, and had been seriously ill at the end of December, and was conducting
the campaign against Portugal from his sick-bed at Hatfield,[152] on 2 January
put his signature to a rejoinder to Barros Gomes's note of 20 December. He
regretted that Barros Gomes had not given the explicit assurances that had been
required. A carefully organized and well-equipped military force to the Makololo country had produced the impression that there was deliberate intention to
provoke hostilities and establish Portuguese dominion by force of arms.
Subsequent proceedings had confirmed this impression and compromised
Britain's standing with the native tribes. Makololo action had been prompted
solely by their desire to protect their country against invasion. Serpa Pinto's
campaign must have been extended into territory of the Makololo, who were
under British protection, for the acting consul was the representative of the
British Government. Pinto's defiance of the consul's declaration was contrary
to international practice. The British Government did not ask for an apology.
But it did insist on prompt and distinct assurances that there would be no
attempt to settle the territorial question by acts of force, or extend Portuguese
dominion over districts in which British interests predominated. If the British
Government could not obtain such an assurance, she would take the measures
she considered necessary. Salisbury therefore categorically required an immediate direction that Portuguese forces would not be permitted to interfere with
British settlements on the Shire and Nyasa or any other country declared under
British protection, and that there would be no attempt at exercising Portuguese
jurisdiction in any part of those countries without previous arrangement between

150 Petre to Salisbury, 3/1/90, CP 6061, p. 9, and extract from speech, p. 10.
151 Petre to Salisbury, 4/1/90, 2 Af., PRO, FO 84/2042, part in CP 6061, p. 8. In a minute
   Salisbury ordered it to be printed as a secret despatch and sent to the cabinet. The FO
   authorized Petre to give the informant a further £100; he was to take care that this amount
   did not appear in the accounts (FO to Petre, 8/1/90, Private and Secret, PRO, FO 179/
   276).
152 Cecil, IV, pp. 207, 264.

the two governments. Salisbury demanded answer by the evening of 8 January.[153] Petre incorporated these instructions into a note which he passed on to Barros Gomes on 6 January; that day being a public holiday and Barros Gomes also convalescing from an attack of influenza, Petre addressed it to his home.[154]

A cable from Churchill raised Salisbury's temperature. Serpa Pinto confirmed that the expedition was remaining in occupation of the Shire; several stations, notably Katunga, were being fortified and garrisoned and a governor of the Shire district had been appointed. In the December engagement 180 Makololo had been killed. A governor had been newly established at Zumbo and Andrada had returned to the coast where, Churchill gathered, he was enrolling another large expedition which was about to plant the flag between Sofala and the Matabele and check the projected British expedition to Matabeleland.[155] And the ALC passed on to Salisbury a telegram which confirmed that the Portuguese were remaining at Katunga, and added that the Makololo, trusting to British protection, were refusing to surrender their British flags. ALC steamers had again been searched and ordered to lower their ensigns. "War is imminent."[156] Salisbury, on 6 January, telegraphed Petre that if he had not received a satisfactory answer by 4 p.m. on 9 January, he was to leave Lisbon immediately; H.M.S. yacht Enchantress would be sent to bring him and his cyphers away, and his archives would be left in the charge of an acting consul.[157] Barros Gomes on that day telegraphed to the Portuguese legations in Vienna, Rome, Paris, Madrid, Berlin and St Petersburg, asking his ministers, as an act of urgency, to invoke the good offices of the governments to which they were accredited, individually or collectively, if his reply did not satisfy the British Government.[158] Austria and Italy responded favourably.[159]

Barros Gomes communicated his reply to Petre on 8 January. He repeated that the limited size of Serpa Pinto's expedition proved that it did not have aggressive intent. He again declared that he could not recognize a British protectorate over a territory to which the Portuguese Crown had constantly affirmed its rights. But the Portuguese Government was so anxious to reach an accord that it did not hesitate to repeat instructions that no act of force was to take place against British institutions on the Shire and Nyasa or against the Makololo or any body under the rule of Lobengula or any body over whom there was an alleged British protectorate. Barros Gomes pledged that no attempt would be made to establish or exercise Portuguese jurisdiction in those areas without first

---

153 Salisbury to Petre, 2/1/90, PRO, FO 84/204, with minute on it, "Queen tonight and cabinet. Tel. to Petre tomorrow. Lord Salisbury says it is an admirable despatch." (i.e. it was not written by Salisbury; but he made certain alterations and inserted "categorical"); and CP 6061, pp. 2–3.
154 Petre to Barros Gomes, 5/1/90, Nec., SPZ 3, Neg., pp. 172–3; Petre to Salisbury, 6/1/90, 3, CP 6061, p. 11.
155 Churchill to Salisbury, 4/1/90, tel., CP 6061, p. 9. For Andrada's detailed plans, a description of the projected area of operation, and reference to the BSA Company expedition, see Andrada, Quelimane, to Dir.-gen., 6/1/90, Commissario Regolo nos Muzeruros, 2, AHU Moç., 2 Rep. Caixa 5.
156 ALC to Salisbury, 4/1/90, CP 6061, p. 7; Times, 6/1/90.
157 Salisbury to Petre, 6/1/90, tels., CP 6061, pp. 11 and 12.
158 Barros Gomes, circular tel, 6/1/90, Neg., pp. 191–2.
159 Vasconcellos, Rome, to Min., 8/1/90, 1A Res., Nec., SPZ 3; Martens Ferrão, Vienna, to Min., 8/1/90, ibid.

reaching an accord with the British Government. And Barros Gomes trusted that its ancient ally would give similar instructions to its representatives to abstain also from any new act which would alter the situation, pending the reaching of an accord. With such reciprocity, the two governments could come to an agreement definitively to define their territories. If this reply did not satisfy the British Government, Barros Gomes added, his Government would promptly submit the dispute to examination by a conference of powers signatory to the Act of Berlin. If Britain rejected this proposal, Portugal would appeal to Article 12 of that Act, which made mediation obligatory and arbitration optional.[160] Petre, telegraphing a summary of this note to London, advised Salisbury to obtain explicit assurances for the immediate recall of the expedition to below the Ruo River.[161] The next day Barros Gomes gave Petre an assurance that the most stringent orders had been sent to Moçambique in the sense required by the British Government: Serpa Pinto had long been in Moçambique, and all the force he had organized had returned to Inhambane.[162] He still lacked precise information from Serpa Pinto.[163]

On 8 January the Board of the BSA Company met in London.[164] The directors doubtless discussed the expedition to Mashonaland: Rhodes, a few days previously, had talked Johnson into leading this, on a contract basis, overland from Bechuanaland.[165] The Chartered Company was committed to this adventure; and its directors could not tolerate a guaranteed maintenance of the *status quo*. And that day, 8 January, Petre received from his secret informant further details of the plans of Andrada and the Moçambique Company into Manicaland, the company indirectly subsidized by having its agents carried on the Treasury pay-roll. The Pinto expedition's railway plans were in part at least to develop coal-mines; Ressano Garcia, Minister of Ultramar, had been presented with shares gratis and was chairman of the company; he sought profits. João contended that Andrada and Pinto represented not the interests of Moçambique, or of Portugal, but the private interests of a few influential individuals who had *carte blanche* to do as they liked. João insisted that he was not a traitor; on the contrary, he was repulsed to see his country embarrassed by the personal interests of the governing clique.[166]

Salisbury received advice that the Act of Berlin presented no threat to British ambitions. Article 12 did not apply to Mashonaland, while as for

160 Barros Gomes to Petre, 8/1/90, PRO, FO 179/284, and CP 6061, pp. 13–5; Min. to GG, 8/1/90, tel., Nec., SPZ 3, *Neg.*, p. 194.
161 Petre to Salisbury, 8/1/90, 4 Af., CP 6061, pp. 24–5, 8.50 p.m., received 7 a.m. 9/1/90.
162 Barros Gomes to Petre, 9/1/90, CP 6061, p. 29 and Petre to Salisbury 10/1/90, 6 tel., ibid., p. 29.
163 Min. to GG, 7/1/90, tel., *Neg.*, p. 192.
164 A. L. Bruce to Goschen, 7/1/90, CP 6061, p. 31.
165 Lockhart and Woodhouse, pp. 177–8; Frank Johnson in Pioneer number of *Rhodesian Herald*, 12/9/1930. The CO became worried about publicity given by Selous to Portuguese claims in this area which might clash with "those claims to Northern Mashonaland which Her Majesty's Government wish to establish on behalf of Lobengula and the BSAC" (CO to FO, 8/1/90, CP 6061, p. 15). There were reports that Johnson had offered his abilities to the Portuguese for £4m.
166 Petre to Salisbury, 8/1/90, 4 Af., CP 6061, pp. 60–2. In his next communication João reported difficulty in organizing the expeditionary force for Manica: only one artillery and four calvary officers had volunteered (Petre to Salisbury, 9/1/80, 8 Af., ibid., p. 62).

Nyasaland, Portugal was in a dilemma: she had not placed Moçambique within the territories mentioned in Article 1 within the free-trade system. Consequently, if Nyasaland indeed formed part of her dominions, Article 12 did not apply. If Article 12 applied, it was because Nyasaland was outside her dominion. Britain could in fact then complain that Portugal had violated Article 12 by taking up arms against a territory which was under British protection.[167]

Salisbury, relieved on this ground, without waiting for the arrival of Barros Gomes's note, telegraphed Petre on the evening of 9 January that the British Government was glad to learn that the Portuguese answer met their demands in principle, "but before accepting it as satisfactory they must know that explicit instructions have been sent by the Portuguese authorities at Moçambique applying to the acts of force and exercise of jurisdiction now taking place, already complained of by Her Majesty's Government, as well as to further proceedings of the same nature. This would mean the withdrawal below the Ruo of the authorities and forces now in the Makololo country and removal of all military stations in Matabeleland and Mashonaland." Petre was to demand copies of the instructions sent to Moçambique.[168]

Petre received these instructions on the morning of 10 January. He immediately sought an interview with Barros Gomes, who was not able to see him until the later afternoon. He communicated Salisbury's note, and insisted that instructions be sent to Moçambique at once—"I was peremptory on this point." Barros Gomes was "painfully surprised". He declared that Portugal had already fully complied with considerable demands; and now fresh demands were being sprung on his Government. Barros Gomes told Petre that the matter would be discussed at a cabinet meeting that evening.[169]

Petre now received a further telegram from Salisbury, declaring that the British Government refused to accept Barros Gomes's statement that Pinto's expedition had returned to Inhambane in view of Churchill's telegram of 4 January. "The guarantee that Her Majesty's Government require is an order to the Governor of Moçambique to withdraw all Portuguese troops that are on the Shire, or in Makololo country, or in Mashonaland. Urge the Minister of Foreign Affairs that such a telegraphic order should be immediately sent and that a copy of it should be shown you. Unless this is done Her Majesty's Government must consider the Portuguese assurances as illusory." And, the telegram added, "Should you not receive a satisfactory reply by 10 o'clock on Saturday evening [the 11th] you will telegraph the Captain of the *Enchantress* [at Vigo] to come at once to Lisbon; and if on her arrival a satisfactory answer has still not been sent, you will at once withdraw your Legation and leave the archive in charge of the Acting Consul."[170]

Petre promptly returned to the Foreign Office and saw Barros Gomes in company with the Minister of Marine and Ultramarine Affairs. He communicated the instructions he had received. "It was evident that this announcement

167 Anderson, memo, 9/1/80, CP 6061, pp. 27-8.
168 Salisbury to Petre, 9/1/90, 2 Af., tel., CP 6061, p. 27; 5.15 p.m.
169 Petre to Salisbury, 11/1/90, 7 Af., CP 6061, p. 33, and 12/1/90, 12, ibid., pp. 34-6.
170 Salisbury to Petre, 10/1/90, 3 Af., tel., 9 p.m., CP 6061, p. 30.

produced on them a deep and painful impression, and it seemed to me that until then the Government had not fully realized that it was face to face with a rupture with Great Britain."[171]

Barros Gomes telegraphed all Portuguese legations that Britain was now demanding the *status quo ante*, with withdrawal of all Portuguese forces from the Makololo country and the Sanyati. Portugal could not accept such demands, which had not been formulated in the earlier British note; Portugal demanded the *status quo*. He instructed his ministers to represent this to the various governments to which they were accredited, with the request that they telegraph their recommendations to their ambassadors in London.[172] But Salisbury's continued absence from town made it impossible for the diplomats to bring pressure to bear on him,[173] and the Portuguese Government was well aware of British troop movements.

The Atlantic Squadron, consisting of *Active*, *Volage*, *Ruby* and *Calypso*, had left Portsmouth suddenly in mid December, and had arrived off Las Palmas on 29 December. The squadron practised firing; one ship remained always in view of the consular flagpole lest a telegram arrive.[174] A London newspaper hinted that Britain had in mind the seizure of Madeira.[175] The Portuguese consul at Gibraltar reported the arrival there of a British naval squadron on 2 January, which consisted of the cruisers *Northumberland*, *Anson*, *Monarch*, *Iron Duke*, and a smaller vessel, the *Curlew;* the squadron was reinforced by the two monitors, *Benbow* and *Colossus*. Rumour had it, the consul reported, that the objective of the squadron was Lisbon, to resolve British claims in central Africa.[176] The Governor of Cape Verde reported that the cruiser *Australia* had anchored there without any announced destination; he feared a *coup de main*.[177] The Portuguese consul in Cape Town had reported the departure of three cruisers for Lourenço Marques, rumour had it.[178] The consul in Zanzibar was to report the next day the departure of a squadron of ten warships, accompanied by a transport loaded with coal and supplies, its destination either Quelimane or Lourenço Marques.[179] Dantas from London warned of a likely occupation of Quelimane,[180] while the London press reported general and doubtless inspired rumours that unless Portugal offered prompt reparation a large naval force would occupy Delagoa Bay and other ports on the Moçambique coast; and if the questions in dispute were not settled within three months Delagoa Bay would be added to the British dominions.[181] Private sources of information seemed to confirm that in the event of Portugal offering

171 Petre to Salisbury, 12/1/90, 82, CP 6061, p. 35.
172 Barros Gomes, 10/1/90, circular tel., *Neg.*, p. 196.
173 Dantas to Barros Gomes, 10/1/90, tels, *Neg.*, pp. 195–6.
174 Powlett to Sec. of the Adm., 2, 11/1/90, PRO, FO Adm. 1/7022.
175 *Daily News*, 30/12/89; this section of the cutting in Nec., SPZ 2, is heavily side-lined.
176 J. Maria Tedeschi to Barros Gomes, 2, 10/1/90, A1, A2, Nec., SPZ 3; for details, see Tracey, 'Journal', PRO, FO Adm. 50/399; and Baird to Sec. of Adm., 2/1/90, FO Adm. 1/7022.
177 Gov. to Min., 10/1/90, Nec., SPZ 2.
178 GG to Min., 24/12/89, tel., *Neg.*, 1890, p. 153.
179 Consul, Zanzibar, to Barros Gomes, 11/1/90, tel., *Neg.*, p. 198.
180 Dantas to Barros Gomes, 10/1/90, tel., *Neg.*, p. 195.
181 e.g. *Pall Mall Gazette*, 8/1/90.

resistance there would be simultaneous occupation of Lourenço Marques, Quelimane and S. Vicente, and a demonstration against Lisbon.[182]

In the face of this threat the Portuguese cabinet decided that it must yield. It referred the matter to the Council of State, a small body which considered constitutional matters, and was responsible for decisions on war and peace.[183] Barros Gomes called on Petre on his way to the Council meeting and asked, for his own defence, to be supplied with additional proof of the extreme gravity of the situation. The Councillors, who met under the presidency of the King, appreciated how unprepared Portugal was for defence, and that owing to the time-limit imposed it was impossible to rally diplomatic assistance; they agreed that resistance would be futile. Suggestions were rejected that the surrender should be made conditional on arbitration, and that if Britain broke off the negotiations to settle the question of rights the territory being evacuated should be re-occupied.[184] The Council's decision Barros Gomes conveyed to Petre in a private note on the morning of 12 January. He followed this up with a dignified official communication which concluded,

> In the presence of an imminent rupture of relations with Great Britain, and in view of all the consequences which may perhaps result therefrom, His Majesty's Government have decided to yield to the demand . . . reserving in every way the rights of the Crown of Portugal to the African regions in question, and protesting also on behalf of the right conferred upon them by Article 12 of the General Act of Berlin to have the matter definitely settled either by mediation or by arbitration, will send the orders required by Great Britain to the Governor-general of Moçambique.[185]

The Portuguese Government duly gave orders for its forces on the Shire to withdraw south of the Ruo, and from Mashonaland.[186] It thanked the various powers that had promised their good offices. France had promised her assistance. Crispi had taken the lead in asking his ambassador in London to intervene, and to urge on Bismarck that the monarchical principles to which Italy and Germany subscribed would be prejudiced if the differences were not resolved, and if Article 12 of the Act of Berlin were not applied. Crispi made a similar approach to the Prime Minister of Austria-Hungary, whose ambassador called at the Foreign Office. But these moves were too late.[187]

182 O 'Ultimatum' visto por António Enes (Lisbon, 1946), ed. by F. A. Oliveira Martins (Lisbon, 1946), pp. 197–8.
183 The Council of State also could convene, prorogue or dissolve the Chamber of Deputies, nominate peers, suspend judges and pardon criminals.
184 Petre to Barros Gomes, 11/1/90, memo, Nec., SPZ 3, Neg., p. 198; Petre to Salisbury, 12/1/90, 12, CP 6061, p. 35; Summary of Debate in the Cortes, 16/1/90, statement of Barjona de Freitas, ibid., p. 83. The Army had 16 generals, the youngest 71, and 14 brigadier-generals, the youngest 70 (Petre to Salisbury, 31/1/90, 13, PRO, FO, 179/274).
185 Barros Gomes to Petre, 11/1/90, Neg., p. 199, and CP 6061, pp. 35–6; Petre to Salisbury, 12/1/90, 8, 9 Af., CP 6061, p. 64.
186 Min. to GG, 12/1/90, tel., Nec., SPZ 3, Neg., p. 202, ibid., 16/1/90, Negocios Externos: Documentos apresentados ás Cortes . . . Negociações de Tratado com a Inglaterra, 1890, p. 5; Ferreira to Min., 16/1/90, denying receipt of tel. of 12/1/90, ibid., p. 6; repeated Min. to GG, 17, 18/1/90, tel., ibid., p. 6.
187 Miguel, St Petersburg, 10, 12/1/90, A1 and 2, Nec., SPZ 3; Barros Gomes, 12/1/90, circular tel., Neg., pp. 200–1; Vasconcellos, Rome, to Barros Gomes, 13/1/90, 2A, Nec., SPZ 3; Azevedo Silva, Paris, to Min., 16/1/90, 2A ibid.; Salisbury to Paget, 13/1/90, 1 Af., CP 6061, p. 65; Pandella, Hague, to Ribeiro, 14/1/90, 1, Nec., SPZ 3; Dantas to Ribeiro, 14/1/90, Res. 1A, ibid., stressing the difficulty that ambassadors had in seeing Salisbury, who was convalescing, and Currie was hardly ever at the FO.

When news of the ultimatum and Portugal's humiliation was published there was a great explosion of public wrath. A police guard on the British Legation protected it from possible attack, but a mob shattered every window in the consulate and tore down the British coat of arms and dragged it through the streets. Barros Gomes had the great courtesy, despite the lateness of the hour, to call on Petre (who had in fact retired for the night) to express the regret of himself and his colleagues at this outrage and to assure him that the ringleader had been caught and would be tried. The Portuguese Government made good the damage.[188] In Oporto the police dispersed rioters before they could break more than one window at the consulate, but several British subjects were assaulted, and the consul had fears for British wine cellars.[189]

On 13 January the Chamber of Peers met—the Chamber of Deputies was not yet constituted following a general election—and there Barros Gomes read the correspondence that had been exchanged with the British Government since the middle of December. Speaking in a moderated and dignified tone, he defended the action of the Government. An announcement was then made that the Government had resigned—"in order to facilitate negotiations with Britain."[190]

Petre's conclusion on the crisis was "National vanity alone and a sudden strong desire, far beyond the means of realization, to resuscitate the past colonial glory of Portugal, and not anxiety to convert African races, underlie this African movement which has now placed her in collision with England."[191] But it takes two to make a collision, and the directors of the British South Africa Company were leaning over Salisbury's shoulders and tugging determinedly at the reins, exaggerating the dust that obscured Nyasaland, and emphatic that the Portuguese be forced off the vast, goldiferous plateau of Mashonaland.

188 O'Donnell to Petre, 13/1/90, 1, PRO, FO 179/272; Petre to Salisbury, 13/1/90, 1 and 4 tels., CP 6061, pp. 64, 71.
189 D. Crawfurd, Porto, to Petre, 14/1/90, 1, PRO, FO 179/272.
190 Barros Gomes, 13/1/90, circular tel., Neg., p. 202; Petre to Salisbury, 13/1/90, 2 and 5 tels., CP 6061, p. 64, 72.
191 Petre to Salisbury, 8/1/90, 5 Af., CP 6061, p. 62.

12

THE TREATY OF 20 AUGUST 1890

The ultimatum rocked Portugal and her very institutions.[1] Rage against Britain found expression not simply in denunciation of the perfidious ally (fomented when there were rumours that the Channel Squadron was about to put in at the Tagus)[2] but in a movement against the titular head of State, who had little popular following. The Republicans, previously small in numbers, won wide support as a result of Portugal's humiliation, aided by more than sympathy from Spain, and by the example of the Brazilian revolt.[3] The British press considered that no attention need be paid to "ebullitions of popular prejudice or the frothy vehemence of irresponsible agitators"[4] and Salisbury followed this line.[5] Members of the Portuguese Government, however, were dismayed at the growth of republicanism; anti-monarchical feeling was growing even in the army and navy;[6] the Government regarded the situation as extremely critical if not positively dangerous.[7] Military units were brought to a state of readiness and moved to forts on the outskirts of Lisbon, ostensibly to help appease public opinion as a measure of defence against aggression, but actually to overawe the city in the event of a republican revolt.[8]

Portugal still hoped that her problems would be resolved by mediation or arbitration under Article 12 of the Act of Berlin[9] but Salisbury formally rejected the appeal, declaring that if either state had reason to complain of neglect of

1 Petre to Salisbury, 13/1/90, 3 Af., CP 6061, p. 69; and 16/1/90, 16 Af., ibid., pp. 79–80.
2 Petre to Salisbury, 16/1/90, 4 tels., CP 6061, p. 69, extended in 16/1/90, 17 Af., ibid., p. 80; and 20/1/90, 23 Af., ibid., p. 84; and 22/1/90, 25, 26 and 27 Af., ibid., pp. 94–6; and 27/1/90, 33 Af., CP 6061, pp. 101–2 and Crawfurd, Oporto, to Petre, 23/1/90, ibid., p. 97; and 31/1/90, 39 Af., ibid., pp. 109–13. Placards in Oporto proclaimed:
To the Portuguese people.
Dynamite and more dynamite!!!
Petroleum and more petroleum!!!
The whole world is indignant about the vile, despotic and robber-like proceedings of England, and it appears that the drama is about to commence, as soon as the English fleet shall reach Lisbon!
. . .
War to the death against the English pirates!!!
. . .
Dynamite and more dynamite!!!
Petroleum and more petroleum!!!
(Petre to Salisbury, 27/1/90, 33 Af., CP 6061, pp. 101–2).
3 Petre to Salisbury, 18/1/90, 22 Af., CP 6061, pp. 75–6 and 6/2/90, 49 Af., ibid., p. 122.
4 *Standard*, 25/1/90, encl. in Dantas to Minister, 26/1/90, 10 A, Nec., SPZ 3.
5 Salisbury to Paget, 21/1/90, 3 Af., CP 6061, p. 81.
6 See Luis de Mont, *História do Regimen Republicano em Portugal* (Lisbon, 1932). (I am grateful to Professor R. J. Hammond for drawing my attention to this work.)
7 Petre to Salisbury, 6/2/90, 56 Af., CP 6061, p. 124.
8 [João] enclosed in Petre to Salisbury, 12/2/90, 63 Af., CP 6061, p. 150.
9 Barros Gomes to Petre, 12/1/90.

the provisions of the Act it was Britain; provided, that was, that the territory in dispute lay in the zone designated by Article 1, for Portugal, by sending Serpa Pinto into the area with many thousands of armed men and with Gatling guns had appealed to arms and so infringed the Act. But Mashonaland and Lobengula's country were not in the free-trade zone covered by Article 12.[10]

The Portuguese Government continued to rely on pressure being brought to bear on Britain by the representations of other powers. The Italian ambassador at the Court of St James called on Salisbury and expressed the wish of his Government for an amicable solution of the problem; this was especially necessary to avoid shaking the monarchy, which was allied to the royal house of Italy.[11] The Italian minister in Lisbon, however, declared to Petre that this approach had been made purely on Crispi's own initiative, and did not represent a decision of the Italian Government. The Italian minister doubted whether Portugal would invoke Article 12, and thought that she would prefer the matter to be debated before an international tribunal, not in any anticipation of obtaining her claims, but because curtailment of them by such an international body would satisfy national pride.[12] The Austro-Hungarian Government also warned Salisbury of the danger of a revolutionary movement which might sweep the dynasty away; this republicanism could well spread to Spain, and even to Italy.[13] The Spaniards were certainly expressing an unprecedented sympathy for their fellow Iberians; but the British minister in Madrid commented that a better press could not be expected as long as Britain held Gibraltar.[14] The French press unanimously denounced Britain and supported Portugal,[15] but the French Government refused to commit itself, which was not extraordinary considering the financial links between the Moçambique Company and Paris, and the fact that the Portuguese Republican Party was in communication with the French Government, seeking the latter's support in the overthrow of the Portuguese monarchy.[16] Nor would the German Government support Portugal, in view of her desire to come to an understanding with Britain.[17] The Russian Government condemned British action and it understood that Article 12 was applicable, but made it clear that this was from the expediency of resolving an issue that might lead to war, not from knowledge of the facts of the case.[18] The King of Sweden expressed to the British minister his opinion that the possession of a few square miles of Africa was of small

10 Salisbury, 28/1/90, 25, CP 6061, p. 100. For a Portuguese viewpoint on whether or not Article 12 applied see Martens to Hintze Ribeiro, 31/1/90, Nec., SPZ 3.
11 Salisbury to Dufferin, 13/1/90, 2 Af., CP 6061, pp. 65–6; Carvalho Vasconcellos, Rome, to Min., 17/2/90, 3A, Nec., SPZ 3.
12 Petre to Salisbury, 6/2/90, 50 Af., CP 6061, p. 123.
13 A. Paget, Vienna, to Salisbury, 14, CP 6061, p. 70.
14 C. Ford to Salisbury, 15/1/90, 8, CP 6061, pp. 72–3; and 24/1/90, 1 Af., pp. 98–9; Casal Ribeiro, Madrid, to Min., 28/1/90, A3, Nec., SPZ 3.
15 Azevedo da Silva, Paris to Min., 20/1/90, 2A Nec., SPZ 3.
16 do., 5/2/90. The Minister of the Interior at his interview with the emissary expressed his sympathy but declared that French help could not be kept secret. At a second meeting he advised that the monarchy be overthrown first in Spain, and only subsequently in Portugal.
17 Penafiel, Berlin, to Min., 19/2/90, 1, Nec., SPZ 3.
18 S. Miguel, St Petersburg, to Min., 24/1/90, 1–5, and 26/1/90, and 3/2/90, and 26/2/90, Nec., SPZ 3.

consequence compared with the undermining of the monarchical principle.[19] When the Portuguese minister in Washington was eventually able to see the Secretary of State, Blaine told him that British proceedings in this matter were undoubtedly unjust; but, he added frankly, it was a natural consequence of the unjust proceedings of the Portuguese Government over the Lourenço Marques railway: he who commits an injustice should not complain when somebody else commits a greater one on him.[20]

At the beginning of March 1890, Hintze Ribeiro addressed another circular telegram to Portuguese legations, instructing his ministers to seek the good offices of the governments to which they were accredited. These governments were to be reminded of the violence of Britain's proceedings against her ancient and faithful ally, and the dangerous precedent set of despoiling by threat of force a nation of territory anciently hers; only impartial appreciation could lead to an honest opinion; and as a last resort recourse would be had to Article 12 of the Act of Berlin.[21]

Various foreign governments now expressed their desire that Britain should come to an amicable understanding with Portugal.[22] The French Government, however, would not go beyond the very vaguest expressions of interest.[23] The Austro-Hungarian Government protested that it was quite foreign to African affairs, and so incompetent to venture an opinion; it did not think that intervention by a third nation could serve any useful purpose; but if any third nation did intervene, it should be either Italy or Germany.[24] But neither Italy nor Germany had the slightest desire to stick her neck out.[25] The Belgian Minister of Foreign Affairs confined himself to remarking that this was only an aspect of the battle for influence between Protestants and Catholics.[26] The Russian Government, though remaining sympathetic, would not take isolated action,[27] and only the Spanish Government expressed itself actively in Portugal's favour.[28] Everything must depend on direct negotiation.

The Portuguese negotiator was Barjona de Freitas, a respected member of the Council of State and, according to Petre, a very able man. His public antecedents were impeccable, but his private life was not quite so open to inspection. Petre suggested that if the British Government preferred not to negotiate with him, it might declare that it preferred Dantas to stay. But Dantas begged to be transferred away from London, and the Portuguese Government

19 Plunkett to Salisbury, 4/3/90, 2 Af., CP 6061, p. 221.
20 Souza Roza, Washington, to Min., 25/2/90, 1, Nec., SPZ 3.
21 2/3/90, Neg., p. 46.
22 Salisbury to Lytton, Paris, 4/3/90, 35 A Af., CP 6061, p. 218; Azevedo da Silva to Min., 6/3/90, 5 Nec., SPZ 3.
23 Vasconcellos, Rome to Min., 4/3/90, 6A, and 6/3/90, 8 A, ibid.
24 Martens Ferrão, Vienna, to Min., 6/3/90, 4, Nec., SPZ 3.
25 Penafiel, Berlin, to Min., 10/3/90, A 2, ibid.
26 Macedo, Brussels, to Min., 6/3/90, A 6, ibid.
27 Miguel, St Petersburg, to Min., 7/3/90, A 6, ibid.
28 Casal Ribeiro, Madrid, to Min., 5/3/90, A 11, ibid.

12 Sketch-map of British Central Africa, showing limits of districts intended to be secured by treaties already made and in process of making [1890] (from British Foreign Office Confidential Print, PRO, FO, 403/127)

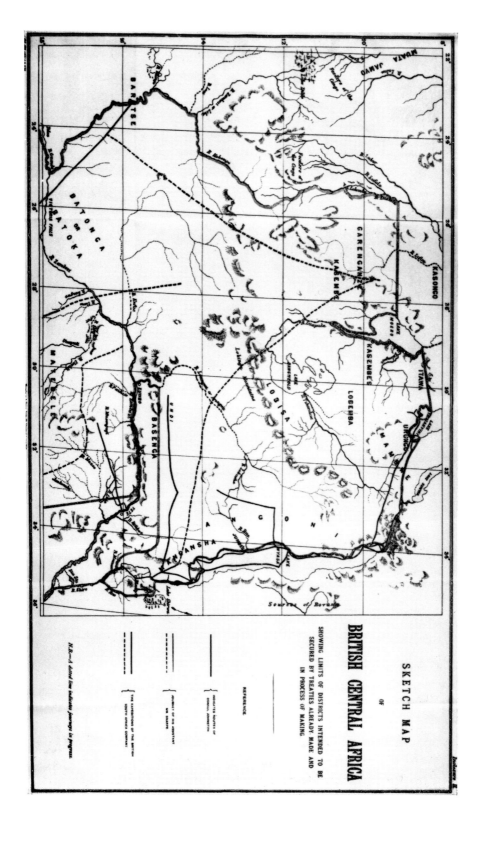

SKETCH MAP

OF

BRITISH CENTRAL AFRICA

SHOWING LIMITS OF DISTRICTS INTENDED TO BE
SECURED BY TREATIES ALREADY MADE AND
IN PROCESS OF MAKING

REFERENCE.

INTENDED ROUTES OF
CONSUL JOHNSTON

JOURNEY OF HIS ASSISTANT
MR SHARPE

THE EXPEDITIONS OF THE BRITISH
SOUTH AFRICA COMPANY

N.B.—A dotted line indicates journeys in progress.

intimated that if exequatur were to be refused Barjona de Freitas there would be such public indignation that the Government would be unable to survive. Petre agreed that for the Government to fall would be nothing short of a calamity.[29]

Barjona de Freitas carried with him instructions to persuade the British Government to agree to an impartial assessment of the differences by arbitration, conference or mediation; if the British Government remained obdurate, the Government would appeal to Article 12 of the Treaty of Berlin.[30] The essence of his instructions was that he was to obtain from Britain some concession which would soothe Portuguese pride.[31] At their first meeting Salisbury told Barjona de Freitas, "*Le passé est passé: le temps est un grand modérateur.*" Freitas stressed the urgent need for a territorial solution. But Salisbury, still convalescing fom his influenza, was leaving London and for the next ten days Freitas's negotiations were limited to discussion with Sir Philip Currie.[32] At his second meeting with Salisbury Freitas presented the Portuguese case and urged that Portugal be relieved from having to propose any cession of territory which was hers by right, which might affect the form of government of Portugal; hence the importance of arbitration, or a conference, or mediation. Salisbury expressed his desire for "an amicable adjustment"; but he rejected reference of the question to a third party, though he undertook to have the proposal discussed in cabinet.[33]

On 21 March Salisbury intimated to Freitas that the British Government could not accept the suggestion of solution by conferences or arbitration. A conference was normally employed where questions were of common interest, whereas in this case only two powers were directly concerned and two others, Germany and the Congo Free State, to a less extent. Recourse was had to arbitration to decide a disputed issue of fact; but Portugal rested her case almost entirely on history, whilst Britain's depended on recent actions by British subjects: the facts were in the main not in question and there was no body of international jurisprudence which could guide the arbitrator. The British Government had hoped that the Portuguese Government would make territorial proposals which would have formed the basis of negotiations, which would lead to the development of unoccupied regions, by immigration, to the common advantage of the world.[34] And, moreover, Salisbury continued, it was not only the territorial question that separated the two countries. The Portuguese authorities were refusing to allow the importation of essential arms and ammunition to the ALC, which was gravely hindered in its fight against Arab slave dealers; perhaps legally Portugal had this right, but her action did not improve relations with Britain. The Lourenço Marques railway was another issue. The

29 Petre to Salisbury, 29 and 31/1/90, tel., PRO, FO 179/274.
30 Ribeiro to Penafiel, 17/2/90, tel., *Neg.*, p. 45; and Ribeiro to Freitas, 6/3/90, tel., p. 46.
31 Petre to Salisbury, 5/3/90, 79 Af., CP 6061, pp. 221–2, reporting a conversation between Ribeiro and the Italian Minister.
32 Freitas to Min., 17/2/90, 1, Nec., SPZ 3 and *Neg.*, p. 44.
33 Freitas to Min., 11/3/90, *Neg.*, pp. 47–8; Salisbury to Petre, 11/3/90, 54 Af., PRO, FO 179/277 and CP 6061, p. 223.
34 Salisbury to Freitas, 21/3/90, CP 6061, pp. 250–1, *Neg.*, pp. 50–2.

Portuguese Government had arbitrarily confiscated the rights of those interested, and was evading the British request for arbitration over the amount of compensation to be paid. And a British naval survey ship had been turned away from the mouth of the Zambezi because she was flying the British flag. In this matter Britain was asserting the rights of the civilized world: the Zambezi was an international highway and not to be treated as the exclusive property of one nation. Salisbury concluded with an ominous warning that the responsibility for any unfortunate collision that might occur would not be Britain's.[35]

These communications of Salisbury's so disturbed the Portuguese Government that it was not until the middle of April that Hintze Ribeiro commented on them to Freitas. Ribeiro still tried to argue that Article 12 was applicable and that the matter should be referred to arbitration or a conference. But since the British Government was adamant on this issue, Portugal would nominate to a mixed commission; he hoped that Britain would abstain from any action in the territories in dispute during the negotiations.[36] This point of view was put before Salisbury on 21 April by Freitas, who added that Portugal was anxious to resolve the question of the Lourenço Marques railway as soon as possible.[37] In Lisbon Hintze Ribeiro called on Petre and again urged recourse to arbitration or mediation, declaring that direct cession of territory by Portugal would affect the institution of the monarchy; he went so far as to declare that Portugal would prefer to cede a larger territory by arbitration or mediation than make a better territorial bargain by direct negotiation. Ribeiro hoped that at least some incidental points might be settled by arbitration or mediation.[38] As far as territorial arrangements were concerned, Ribeiro favoured the agreement between his predecessor and Johnston: "It seems to me to have many advantages if we could only achieve it."[39] Salisbury received this suggestion extremely coldly and Freitas, convinced that the British Government would not consider this plan, asked urgently for alternative proposals.[40] To anxious enquiries in the Cortes about the progress of the negotiations Ribeiro refused to reply, declaring that the negotiations might be prejudiced were information to be divulged[41]—but there was no information to divulge.

Whilst territorial proposals were being considered in Lisbon, Freitas re-examined the Johnston agreement. Britain would not budge from her pretensions to a way up Africa, from south to north, which cut across Portugal's concept of an east-west belt from coast to coast. Where the two met, Freitas proposed to his minister, there should be a common zone, administered by agreement between the two countries. He thought that Portugal should receive

35 do., 21/3/90, CP 6061, pp. 13–4, *Neg.*, pp. 13–4. The *Globe* (17/4/90, *Neg.*, p. 61) commented of the Lourenço Marques question that the property of British subjects had been forcibly seized and confiscated without a farthing of compensation on the most frivolous pretext which constituted scarcely veiled robbery.
36 Ribeiro to Freitas, 16/4/90, Nec., SPZ 3, *Neg.*, pp. 64–6.
37 Freitas to Salisbury, 21/4/90, ibid.; pp. 67–70, and CP 6061, pp. 293–6.
38 Salisbury to Petre, 29/4/90, 80 A Af., CP 6061, p. 311.
39 Ribeiro to Freitas, 1/5/90, tel., Nec., SPZ 4, extract in *Neg.*, p. 90.
40 Freitas to Ribeiro, 2/5/90, tel., Nec. and p. 81; and 7/5/90, ibid., and p. 84.
41 Ribeiro to Freitas, 6/5/90, Nec. and pp. 83–4; Petre to Salisbury, 119 Af., CP 6061, pp. 325–6.

Barotseland and land westwards from there to Angola, and should ask also for Muato Yanvo. Any difference between the two countries should be referred to Article 12 of the Act of Berlin.[42] The Portuguese cabinet endorsed these proposals.[43]

On 10 May Hintze Ribeiro had sent territorial propositions to London.[44] They were not printed in the subsequent white book and there is no record of them in the archives of the Portuguese Foreign Office, but the trusty João promptly reported to Petre that the negotiations would probably result in the appointment of an arbiter to settle the future of the Shire, who would give his award in favour of Britain and the two countries would appoint commissioners to fix the frontiers of Mashonaland. Petre commented to Salisbury that the letter would convey nothing that was new to him; it showed what official circles considered to be the eventual result of the negotiations; the Portuguese Government was under no illusions, but it wished to save appearances; but Petre found it hard to believe that the British Government would be party to a sham arbitration.[45] Petre's Italian colleague obligingly divulged a conversation with the Under-secretary of Foreign Affairs which confirmed that the Portuguese Government was resigned to the surrender of the Nyasa districts and Mashonaland, and that it would ask for Barotseland and the territory stretching to Angola, and for British recognition of Tongaland and Tungue.[46]

On 23 May Freitas called on Salisbury and presented his Government's proposals. Portugal attached the greatest importance to the maintenance of her historic domination in the interior; British emigrants, it understood, attached importance to the development of the industrial resources of the country. The Portuguese Government, therefore, proposed that Portuguese domination be recognized from the east coast of Africa to the west coast; Portugal would guarantee by treaty the commercial, industrial and religious rights of British settlers. Portuguese dominion should be recognized in Nyasaland, and in return Portugal would grant free navigation of the Zambezi and Shire and guarantee all commercial and religious liberty. A mixed commission would delimit the borders of Mashonaland. Freitas then added his idea of a common zone, but failed to explain its significance to Salisbury. Salisbury listened to these proposals with growing amazement. He confined his reply to remarking dryly that at first sight the proposals did not seem to contain the elements of a satisfactory solution; and he added that however enlightened and liberal might be the policy of the Central Government there was no guarantee that local administrators would be imbued with the same lofty ideals. He promised to consider the matter maturely, and to produce counter-proposals.[47]

42 Freitas to Ribeiro, 13/5/90, Nec., SPZ 4, *Neg.*, pp. 91–2.
43 Ribeiro to Freitas, 19/5/90, tel., extract in *Neg.*, pp. 93–4.
44 Ribeiro to Freitas, 10/5/90, tel., ibid., p. 95, with comment by Freitas to Ribeiro, 18/5/90, tel., *Neg.*, p. 93.
45 Petre to Salisbury, 12/5/90, 128 Af., and João's letter No. 22, 10/5/90, CP 6061, p. 353.
46 Petre to Salisbury, 12/5/90, 127 Af., CP 6061, pp. 334–5.
47 Freitas to Ribeiro, 24/5/90, Nec., SPZ 4, extract in *Neg.*, p. 95; Salisbury to Petre, 23/5/90, PRO, FO 179/277 and 99 A Af., CP 6061, p. 349; Ribeiro to Freitas, 9/6/90, tel.; Nec., SPZ 4 and *Neg.*, pp. 98–9; Petre to Salisbury, 10/6/90, 149 Af., CP 6061, pp. 391–2.

The Portuguese Government waited with growing apprehension for these counter-proposals, especially after receiving from Freitas a report that Britain was ceding a great area in southern Africa to Germany.[48] The report was based on rumour of the cession of Heligoland, a proposal made by Salisbury on 13 May, as basis for agreement with Germany.[49] Clearly an understanding with Germany would strengthen Britain's hand in Africa and stiffen her dealings with Portugal. She was planning the forcible opening of the Zambezi by the despatch of two river gun-boats; and the BSAC was about to launch its expedition into Mashonaland which would reach, as the Portuguese Government correctly forecast, areas in Portuguese Zambezia.[50] It protested that the despatch of the gun-boats would alter the *status quo;* it would exacerbate public feelings in Portugal, and embarrass the negotiations.[51] The Foreign Office leaked to *The Times* the Portuguese proposals. Public clamour once again began, especially in Scotland, against Portuguese pretensions to Nyasaland,[52] and at the Brussels Conference Britain insisted on the principle of free and obligatory introduction of arms and munitions to counter the slave-trade in all African territories between latitudes 20° north and 22° south. Portugal agreed that there should be obligatory transit to possessions of another power but not to contested territory.[53] Public feeling in Portugal flared up again and there were angry questions in the Cortes with the publication of reports that Buchanan had burnt a Portuguese flag at Chilomo and supervised the execution of two Portuguese sepoys. It was obviously in the interests of both countries to come to a solution.[54] But Salisbury delayed his presentation of his counter-proposals until the conclusion of the negotiations with Germany. Ribeiro saw a ray of hope in a British-German provision which guaranteed British subjects and commerce unrestricted transit across the German sphere of influence; he thought that this might be applied with equal justice in the case of a nominally Portuguese zone; and he again urged recourse to mediation.[55]

When the British river gun-boats were due on the south-east African coast, and there was still no word from Salisbury, the Portuguese Government was faced with the problem of protesting against this imminent infraction of Portuguese territorial rights and so prejudicing the negotiations forthwith. Freitas considered that Salisbury, for all his dilatoriness, was still prepared to negotiate, so nothing would be lost by protesting. In a note to the Secretary of State he accordingly recapitulated the stages in the negotiation; some weeks had elapsed since Salisbury had said he would formulate his counter-proposals; the despatch

48 Freitas to Ribeiro, 23/5/90, tel., *Neg.*, p. 95.
49 Oliver, *Johnston*, p. 177.
50 Ribeiro to Freitas, 23/5/90, tel., Nec., SPZ 4, *Neg.*, pp. 94–5; and 24/5/90, ibid., p. 95.
51 Freitas to Ribeiro, 25/5/90, ibid., p. 96.
52 do., 30/5/90, ibid., p. 97.
53 Ribeiro to Freitas, 6/6/90, tel., ibid., p. 98.
54 do., 12/6/90, tel., ibid., Petre to Salisbury, 14/6/90, 157 Af., CP 6061, p. 398; Ribeiro to Freitas, 15/6/90, tel., Nec., SPZ 4, declaring that he was 'anxiously' awaiting the counter-proposals; Keene, Madeira, to Petre, 27/6/90, PRO, FO 179/272 reporting unrest among the military.
55 Ribeiro to Freitas 20/6/90, tel., Nec., SPZ 4; Penafiel, Berlin, to Min., 21/6/90, A6, ibid., Ribeiro to Freitas, 26/6/90, tel., *Neg.*, p. 117; Petre to Salisbury, 26/6/90, 165 Af., CP 6061, p. 420.

of the gun-boats was exciting Portuguese public opinion; and the question of the free navigation of the Zambezi was one of the questions pending.[56] Salisbury agreed to postpone entry of the gun-boats, but publication of news of the Pioneer Column's departure for Mashonaland caused Freitas, correctly, to appreciate that the British Government, under pressure from the BSAC, would drive a harder bargain; commercial and financial circles, in fact, did not wish Britain to treat at all with Portugal.[57]

The negotiations proper began only on 6 July, when Freitas outlined to Currie what in his view would be a suitable territorial delimitation. Four days later the two of them discussed arrangements north of the Zambezi. It was agreed that the Rovuma be recognized as the northern boundary of the province of Moçambique. The line would then run to Nyasa and down Nyasa "outside" Lake Shirwa, to the confluence of the Ruo and Shire, and thence to Tete. From Tete a common zone, five miles wide, would run to the Portuguese possessions in the west, except for Zumbo and its immediate surroundings, which would be Portuguese. The Portuguese sphere of influence in the west would include everything south of the Congo Free State and west of the Zambezi. Freitas was jubilant at this arrangement, especially at the recognition of the Rovuma boundary (which would acknowledge Tungue as Portuguese), at the retention of a link between the east coast and the west, and at the enormous gains in the west. In return Portugal would have to accept three articles to be lifted from the Anglo-German Treaty.[58] Article VIII applied the first five articles of the Act of Berlin: there was to be complete freedom of trade; navigation of lakes and rivers and ports was free to both flags; no differential treatment was permitted as regards transport or coasting trade; there were to be no customs dues in the free-trade area defined in the Act of Berlin except those levied in the interest of trade; there were to be no transit dues; there were to be no trade monopolies; and the subjects of either power were at liberty to settle freely in the zone of the other. Article IX provided for the mutual recognition of trading and mineral concessions, and rights to real property held by companies or individuals; the concessions were, however, to be worked in accordance with local laws and regulations. Article X declared that missionaries of both countries would have full protection, and religious toleration and freedom for all forms of worship and religious teaching were guaranteed.[59]

Hintze Ribeiro hoped that it would be possible to widen the common zone, and quoted the 20-mile wide Caprivi strip as a precedent. He requested clarification of the western boundary, e.g. whether it included the state of Muato Yanvo. But he agreed that the territorial arrangement north of the Zambezi was acceptable. He could not agree to the application *in toto* of

---

56 Ribeiro to Freitas, 28/6/90, tel., Nec., SPZ 4; Freitas to Ribeiro, 30/6/90, tels, ibid., and extract in *Neg.*, p. 119; Ribeiro to Freitas, 30/6/90, tel., ibid.; Freitas to Salisbury, 30/6/90, ibid., pp. 120–2 and CP 6069, pp. 1–3.
57 Freitas to Ribeiro, 6/7/90, Nec., SPZ 4, *Neg.*, p. 126; and do., 7/7/90, ibid.
58 Freitas to Ribeiro, 6/7/90, tel., ibid., p. 125; and 10/7/90, ibid., p. 127.
59 Hertslet, II, pp. 649–50.

Articles VIII, IX and X. Portugal conceded free navigation of the Zambezi and Shire; but it could not agree to the abolition of custom-houses at Ibo, Moçambique, Angoche and Quelimane. Nor did Portugal agree to the absolute suppression of transit duties, which were an affirmation of dominion. Article IX could well apply to existing concessions but might prejudice future grants. And Article X Portugal preferred to apply only to new acquisitions, not to areas previously acknowledged as Portuguese.[60]

On 13 July Currie communicated to Freitas the Foreign Office plans for the the region south of the Zambezi. It proposed a frontier which ran from the north-east corner of the South African Republic in a straight line to the Sabi River at 21° south; up the Sabi to $18\frac{1}{2}$° south; to the Mazoe River and along this to $16\frac{1}{2}$° south; and thence a straight line to Tete. Britain also insisted on free navigation of the Limpopo and the Sabi, use of the port of Pungue as a *sine qua non*, with free passage of goods to the British zone and facilities for the construction of a railway line. Freitas immediately declared that such a de-limitation was out of the question: he was reluctant even to report the proposal to Lisbon lest it lead to a rupture of the negotiations. Freitas's instructions required him to insist on the line of the Sanyati to the Zambezi; but, on his own initiative, he recommended as a compromise the Hunyani. Currie declared that if Salisbury accepted this he certainly would not agree to modifications north of the Zambezi, where he had assented to the Kabompo as the western boundary and the Zambezi to Katima, and to a 20-mile wide common zone. Freitas recommended to his minister that despite the loss of territory in the south the proposals be accepted, in view of the favourable allocation in the north-west, the wider common zone, and the necessity to re-establish relations with Britain as soon as possible; Portugal could profit greatly from projected developments.[61] Hintze Ribeiro preferred the line from the South African Republic to meet the Sabi at $20\frac{1}{2}$° south, where it had been shown on the map which had accompanied the 1886 treaty with Germany. He was prepared to accept the Hunyani, but not any river to the east. He thought it possible too to accept free navigation on the Limpopo and Sabi. And Portugal was prepared to be transigent regarding the application of Articles VIII, IX and X of the Anglo-German convention as far as transit dues were concerned and, if necessary, on freedom of religion; but Portugal could not agree to abolishing customs and export duties. Over what had for long been regarded as Portuguese territory she must assert her rights; in the area now granted her she was prepared to make concessions. As for the railway from Pungue, Portugal was quite prepared to construct this line to the frontier, within a given time-limit, and build one also from Quelimane towards the Shire. Ribeiro thoroughly appreciated British desire for easy communications between the coast and her inland possessions; but this must be reconciled to Portuguese rights and interests. The construction of the railway line would be to the mutual advantage of the two states.[62]

60 Ribeiro to Freitas, 10/7/90, tel., *Neg.*, pp. 128–9; and 11/7/90, ibid., p. 129; and 12/7/90, ibid., pp. 129–30.
61 Freitas to Ribeiro, 13/7/90, tel., ibid., pp. 130–1; and 15/7/90, p. 133.
62 Ribeiro to Freitas, 13/7/90, tel., ibid., p. 131; and 14/7/90, ibid., pp. 132–3.

Salisbury, under pressure from the BSAC, refused to accept the Hunyani, and threatened to break off the negotiation if Portugal insisted on it. Ribeiro was most reluctant to see land excised from the proclaimed district of Manica, and considered breaking the negotiations. He decided to let them continue, but demanded compensation in the south, so that Tongaland might be re-united, and placed entirely under Portuguese protection, as had been requested by a recent embassy from the tribe. But Currie intimated that this southern area had been promised to the South African Republic.[63]

At conferences on 17 and 18 July Currie proved more untractable; he talked about having to consult Rhodes, who was now Prime Minister of the Cape Colony; and the BSAC was in fact bringing pressure to bear on the Foreign Office to break the negotiations with Portugal. It was agreed, however, that the line from the South African Republic should meet the Sabi at $21°$ south; that it leave the Sabi at $18\frac{1}{2}°$ south and run east to longitude $33°$ east and up that parallel to $16\frac{1}{2}°$ south, whence it would run in a direct line to Tete.[64] Ribeiro thoroughly appreciated the growing influence of the BSAC, and that it was urgent to conclude the negotiations lest Portugal be compelled to concede even more; but he still had reservations over the articles of the Anglo-German convention.[65]

Currie on 21 July consulted H. H. Johnston, who had newly arrived in London, over the negotiations. Johnston felt that the common strip to Zumbo should be north of the Zambezi only, where it could be 30 miles broad, apart from an area 20 miles in radius around Tete. He was sure that Rhodes would dislike intensely the idea of giving the Portuguese anything south of the Zambezi, for he had the greatest anticipations for the country around the Mazoe River. Of the other directors, Cawston was more conciliatory, but his views did not carry much weight. It was essential, Johnston urged, that Portugal give, sell or lease land at the mouth of the Chinde for the use of the BSAC. As soon as the Shire highlands had been taken under British protection it had become necessary to link that area with other British territories south of the Zambezi. The agreement then being negotiated gained Britain breathing time. It was essential to ensure, perhaps by secret articles, that no other power obtain a footing in Portuguese territory; it was especially essential to bind Portugal not to alienate any coastline south of Quelimane to any other European power without Britain's consent. To Johnston the wealthiest mineraliferous area in central Africa was Garenganze: Rhodes thought that its copper and gold alone would pay all the expenses of BSAC administration. The King of the Belgians was suddenly awakening to its value and was despatching an expedition there. Johnston remarked to Currie that Britain had been far from tender in her treatment of Portuguese rights, traditions and sentiments; he saw no reason why the King of the Belgians should receive special consideration in an area where he had not a particle of interest. Johnston added that he was confident

63 Freitas to Ribeiro, 15/7/90, tels, ibid., p. 134.
64 Freitas to Ribeiro, 18/7/90, tel., ibid., p. 135; and 19/7/90, ibid., pp. 136–7.
65 Ribeiro to Freitas, 19/7/90, tel., ibid., p. 137; and 21/7/90, ibid., pp. 137–8.

that if Britain were to promise to protect Rhodes's rights in Garenganze, Rhodes would be very accommodating as to Manicaland and Gazaland.[66]

The Foreign Office now proposed that the negotiations be restricted to the area north of the Zambezi, but to this Freitas would not agree; and he pressed for communication between Tete and Zumbo south of the Zambezi. Aware that British concession-hunters were active in Gazaland he urged on Currie the necessity for rapid signature to a convention to obtain ratification by the Cortes before it rose in August. Ribeiro also urged on the British minister in Lisbon the necessity for hastening the conclusion of the negotiations, for he was facing angry questions in the Cortes which reached a crescendo with the arrival in Lisbon of *The Times* which contained a leaked report of the latest proposals.

Ribeiro tried to save various *prazos* which might be on the wrong side of the line,[67] but without success. Word reached London that Portuguese officials had arrested the *James Stevenson*. Britain promptly demanded compensation. It was clear that to prevent such incidents it was essential to conclude the negotiations. At the end of July Rhodes, in his capacity as Prime Minister of the Cape Colony, demanded that his Government be consulted in the negotiations. But the draft had already gone to the printers, and on 1 August Salisbury delivered to Freitas a copy of the agreement which the British Government was prepared to conclude.[68] It was Freitas's considered opinion that it embodied the maximum concession which the British Government was prepared to make. Ribeiro attempted to obtain a number of modifications but Freitas could not make contact with Salisbury, who was with the Emperor of Germany, while Currie repeated that British commercial circles did not want any treaty with Portugal at all: the BSAC, he frankly declared, had come to an understanding with Gungunhana, and wished to exploit the situation. Johnston was emphatic that Portugal must not be allowed to take possession of the lands of Mpesene. Salisbury, on his return to the Foreign Office, accepted only minimal alterations and on 20 August 1890 he and Freitas signed the treaty.[69]

By the treaty Britain agreed to recognize as within the dominion of Portugal, territories bounded to the north by the Rovuma River, from its mouth to the confluence of the Msinje and thence along that latitude to Nyasa;

66 Johnston to FO, 21/7/90, CP 6069, pp. 31–3.
67 Ribeiro to Freitas, 22/7/90, tel., *Neg.*, pp. 138–9; and 24/7/90 tel., ibid., pp. 139–40; and 25/7/90, ibid., p. 14, and 26/7/90, ibid., pp. 140–1; and 27/7/90, ibid., pp. 141–2; Petre to Salisbury, 22/7/90, 186 and 188 Af., CP 6069, pp. 37–9, and 23/7/90, 189 Af., ibid., p. 40.
68 ALC to Salisbury, 28/7/90, ibid., p. 41; Freitas to Ribeiro, 27/7/90, tel., *Neg.*, p. 146 complains that the British were now trying to claim Macangira as well; Ribeiro to Freitas, 30/7/90, ibid., pp. 146–7; Petre to Ribeiro, 30/7/90, pp. 147; Freitas to Ribeiro, 30/7/90, pp. 147–8; Salisbury to Freitas, 1/8/90, CP 6069, p. 43. The draft appears in *Neg.*, pp. 167–72, summarized in Freitas to Ribeiro, 2/8/90, tel., *Neg.*, p. 155.
69 Freitas to Ribeiro, 3/8/90, tel., *Neg.*, pp. 156–7; Ribeiro to Freitas, 3/8/90, tel., pp. 158–9; Freitas to Ribeiro, 4/8/90, tel., p. 159; Ribeiro to Freitas, pp. 160–1; Freitas to Ribeiro, 6/8/90, p. 165; Freitas to Ribeiro, 7/8/90, pp. 166–7; Freitas to Ribeiro, 8/8/90, p. 177, with the counter-proposals, pp. 177–9; Freitas to Ribeiro, 9/8/90, p. 181; Johnston memo., received 9/8/90, CP 6069, pp. 57–8; Ribeiro to Freitas, 10/8/90, *Neg.*, p. 181; FO memo., 11/8/90, CP 6069, p. 184; Freitas to Ribeiro, 12/8/90, *Neg.*, pp. 182–3; Ribeiro to Freitas, 13/8/90, p. 186; and ibid., p. 187; and do., 13/8/90, p. 187; Freitas to Ribeiro, 16/8/90, p. 192; and do., 18/8/90, p. 193; and do., 20/8/90, p. 194.

along the eastern shore of Nyasa to 13° 30' south latitude; to the eastern shore of Lake Chiuta; to the eastern shore of Lake Chilwa and to its most southerly point; to the easternmost affluent of the Ruo and down the centre channel of the Ruo to its confluence with the Shire; and then in a direct line to half-way between Tete and the Quebrabasa rapids. Zumbo was also recognized as being under Portuguese dominion, within a radius of 10 miles on the north bank of the Zambezi; it was not to be transferred to any power without the previous consent of Britain.

South of the Zambezi the territories within the Portuguese sphere of influence were bounded by a line which started from a point opposite the 10-mile radius of Zumbo; it ran southwards to 16° south, and along that parallel to its intersection with 31° east longitude; then east to the intersection of the Mazoe River and 33° east; southwards to the intersection of 18° 30' south parallel; westwards to the Masheke affluent of the Sabi; along it and the centre of the main channel of the Sabi to the confluence of the Lundi; and then directly to the north-easternmost point of the frontier of the SAR and along that and the frontier of Swaziland to the Maputo. Portugal engaged not to cede her territory south of the Zambezi to any power without the consent of Britain. Britain engaged not to object to the extension of the Portuguese sphere from the line of the confluence of the Maputo and the Pongola to the coast. Portugal engaged that this territory too should not be transferred to any other power without the consent of Britain.

In the west, the line separating the British and the Portuguese spheres of influence followed the centre of the channel of the Zambezi from Katima rapids to the junction of the Kabompo and up the centre of the channel of that river. The country recognized as Portuguese was not to be transferred to any other power without the consent of Britain. This article did not affect the existing rights of other states. With this reservation Britain undertook not to oppose the extension of the Portuguese sphere beyond these limits. Portugal agreed to recognize as within the British sphere territories north of the Zambezi between this line and Nyasa, with the exception of Zumbo and its 10-mile surroundings and, south of the Zambezi, the territories beyond the line described.

The two governments undertook not to interfere in the sphere of influence assigned to the other; neither it, nor companies nor individuals subject to it, would make treaties or accept sovereign rights or protectorates in the sphere of the other. Mineral and trading concessions and rights to property would be recognized in the sphere of the other power, and worked in accordance with local laws and regulations; any differences would be settled by arbitration. Missionaries were to have full protection, and religious toleration and freedom of worship were guaranteed.

Trade was to be completely free, except that Portugal reserved the right to exclude her ports on the east and the west coasts. Navigation of ports, rivers and lakes was to be free. There was to be no differential treatment in transport or the coasting trade. There were to be no transit dues; but a subsequent paragraph declared that Portugal would not levy more than 3 per cent in transit dues on goods between the coast and the British sphere. No monopolies were to be granted. The subjects of either power were at liberty to settle freely in the territories of the other.

There was to be freedom for the passage of goods and subjects across and along the Zambezi. Within a 20-mile zone on the north bank of the Zambezi Portugal had the right to construct roads, railways, bridges and telegraph lines across territories reserved to the British sphere, and both states would have the same power in a zone 10 miles wide on the south side of the Zambezi from Tete to the confluence of the Chobe, and a similar zone "from the north-east of the British zone south of the Zambezi to the above-mentioned zone." Differences were to be referred to arbitration.

One article specifically declared that the Zambezi and Shire, including their branches and outlets, were entirely free for the ships of all nations; a further article elaborated how this was to be applied. In addition, Portugal was to lease to Britain for 100 years ten acres at the mouth of the Chinde.

Portugal granted absolute freedom of passage between the British sphere and Pungue Bay, and undertook the construction of a railway within a period to be fixed by surveys which would be started within four months of the date of the convention and completed with the least possible delay; in these surveys would participate an engineer to be named by the British Government. If these conditions were not exactly carried out, Portugal would grant an outside company a concession for the construction of the railway. No more than 3 per cent in transit dues was to be levied on goods passing from Pungue to the British sphere, and via the Limpopo, Sabi or other navigable rivers.

The two countries undertook to facilitate telegraphic communication.

All differences concerning the convention were to be submitted to arbitration.[70]

As soon as the terms of the treaty were signed there were vociferous criticisms of it in Portugal, in the Cape Colony, and in the City of London. To account for this tide of protest, it is necessary to glance at events in south-east Africa.

While the BSAC was busily organizing its expedition to Mashonaland, threats that it might be forestalled, and threats to Portuguese claims, came from three directions.

The first threat came from the South African Republic, where on 1 January 1890 a prospectus had been issued inviting farmers to join a northward trek. "The objects of the scheme are: to colonize, form settlements and towns, enter into Treaties with chiefs and Powers, establish law and order in and occupy, hold and work that portion of the north-east Mashonaland contained in the Bowler Concession, granted by the independent native paramount chief of that country." Settlers were invited to take up 930 farms of 3,000 morgen each. L. P. Bowler claimed to have obtained a vast concession through an agent, Pero Rodrigues, at the beginning of 1887, from Chief Mcheza, which had been confirmed in May 1888. Bowler declared that the district granted, in the upper

70 Hertslet, II, pp. 715–26; and *Neg.*, pp. 206–15.

Hunyani, Umsengedsi and Mazoe valleys, lay beyond the Matabele raiding line, and the independent Shona chiefs did not pay tribute to Lobengula, or acknowledge his authority; it was accordingly outside the area granted the BSAC. The British agent in Pretoria considered that Bowler was an adventurer, and that his plans covered a filibustering raid by Boers into Mashonaland. The High Commissioner, prodded by Rhodes, proclaimed that this area lay within the British sphere of influence.[71] And Britain brought pressure to bear on the South African Republic by refusing to complete arrangements for the SAR to assume control of Swaziland and Kosi Bay until it should receive assurances that there would be no northward trek. Selous published a statement that Mcheza was no more than the headman of a small village, and had been credited with unwarranted influence on the strength of an over-large name on Montagu Kerr's map—but Selous was now the paid servant of the BSAC. The Portuguese were equally worried about infringement of their rights, and Cohen, the consul in Pretoria, on 22 January 1890, proclaimed simply that there were no independent chiefs in north-eastern Mashonaland; the land had been conquered and reconquered by the Portuguese, who had a resident at Mcheza's; the Portuguese Government could not recognize agreements with native chiefs unless submitted to the Portuguese Government for approval; but the Portuguese Government would encourage and assist settlers who acknowledged Portuguese sovereignty.[72] Salisbury, as soon as he heard of this notice, requested explanations of the Portuguese Government. But the Government was equally in the dark, and while requesting Cohen for information assured Britain that it asserted no claims to jurisdiction in opposition to the ultimatum of 11 January. The High Commissioner issued a proclamation that the consular notice must have been issued in ignorance of the fact that Mashonaland was within the British sphere of influence.[73]

But Portugal was indeed hoping herself to re-assert her rights in Mcheza's area, which had been included within the proclaimed boundaries of Zumbo district. A resident to Mcheza was appointed, but he was most reluctant to set out to assume his post. He made impossible demands on the Governor of Tete, requiring to be provided with vast supplies, numerous artisans, a considerable military escort and 1,500 sepoys and porters. Hearing that Chief Mtoko was an enemy of Manuel António de Sousa, he saw dangers in travelling by the direct route, up the Mazoe valley. He received 160 porters, but still he lingered in Tete, demanding a minimum of 300, and threatening to withdraw to Quelimane. The Governor ordered him to advance, via Chicoa and Zumbo, where he would find sepoys to strengthen the expedition, and a guide and interpreter. He left Tete, under protest, and arrived at Chicoa on the 11th. By the end of

71 CP 6061, pp. 114, 155, 181–90, 197–212.
72 E. Cohen, consular notice, 22/1/90, CP 6061, pp. 180–1, 226–7.
73 Salisbury to Petre, 6/2/90, 15 Af., CP 6061, p. 119; Ribeiro to Cohen, 7/2/90, *Neg.*, pp. 8–9; Cohen to Ribeiro, 9/2/90, ibid., p. 9; Petre to Salisbury, 11/2/90, 60 Af., CP 6061, p. 132; Cohen to Ribeiro, 17/2/90, *Neg.*, p. 10; FO to CO, 18/2/90, CP 6061, p. 180; CO to FO, 27/3/90, ibid., p. 263.

April he was on the Hunyani, still on his way to Mcheza's. When he was two days' journey from his destination he turned for home.[74]

The Mazoe area was also being claimed by a concern of concessionaries, in competition with the BSAC. W. A. Lippert reported to the High Commissioner in January and to the Secretary of State for the Colonies in February 1890 that he had acquired a concession granted on 25 September 1889—before the grant of the Charter to the BSAC—to Selous by independent paramount Makori-kori chiefs Mapondera and Temaringa.[75] Selous had declared, "This concession is perfectly square, fair and genuine, and nothing can upset it. The Matabele claim to the country is utterly preposterous and cannot hold water for a moment." Matabele impis did not even raid the area; the Umfuli was their limit. And nobody had a sounder knowledge of Mashonaland than Selous. Frank Johnson, who according to Lippert was a traveller in the area second only to Selous, confirmed Selous's view. Both Selous and Johnson subsequently joined the BSAC, and it was significant that the BSAC offered the Selous Exploration Syndicate 100 square miles in the area in dispute in return for the concession. But the Secretary of State for the Colonies would not admit the claims of Lippert, who threatened to look "elsewhere" for support.[76]

Concession-hunters in Gazaland also came into conflict with the rights and the claims of the Portuguese Crown as represented by the Moçambique Company. Members of the post-ultimatum government had, when in opposition, opposed the grant of the original concession. But it had to honour the contract already concluded, though it added that certain new conditions would be imposed on any new concessions. These conditions would require the company to reduce the influence of foreigners, especially in prospecting and mining, and promote national colonization.[77]

A decree of November 1889 had created the post of Superintendent-in-chief for Native Affairs in Gazaland, and provided for superintendents, or residents, in Quiteve, Bilene, Mossurize, Manica, Inhaoche, and Bandire and upper Sabi. The informant João reported that José Almeida, appointed Superintendent-in-chief, was a man of limited intelligence whose main qualification had been his friendship with Ressano Garcia, the late Minister of Ultramar. He had promptly drawn 6,000 milreis (£1,333) against his salary lest the new minister dismiss him, had a gorgeous uniform designed for himself, and departed from Lisbon for

---

74 G. Martins Madeira, Tete, to GG, 10/2/90, AHU, Moç., 1 Rep., Pasta 6; Madeira to Capitão-mor, Chicoa, 12/2/90, 5, ibid., Madeira to Gov., Tete, 27/2/90, 13, ibid.; A.J. d'A Leite Peixoto, Gov., Tete, to Madeira, 28/2/90, 111, and 4/3/90, 119, ibid.; Madeira, Dengoe to Gov., 3/3/90, ibid.; Madeira, Boruma, to Gov., 4/3/90, ibid., Madeira, Chicoa, to Gov., 22, 12/3/90, ibid.; do., 14/3/90, 23, 24, 25, ibid., from Chicoa; do., 23/3/90 to Gov., from Zumbo, ibid.; 24/3/90, 26, to Sec. Geral, summarizing events, and throwing responsibility on Gov., Tete.
75 The area of the concession was described as lying between the Mazoe and the Lind (or Rina): down the latter to its junction with the Shamba Imyama River; to the source of the Muntzi; due south to the junction of the Mapinga with the Mazoe; along the Mazoe to the source of the Umrodzi, thence to the source of the Gurumapudzi and to the source of the Lind (or Rina). (A. Mair, Selous Exploration Syndicate, Cape Town, to Bower, 27/1/90, CP 6061, p. 257.)
76 CP 6061, pp. 255–60, 271.
77 Petre to Salisbury, 29/5/90, 144 Af., CP 6061, p. 360.

Moçambique in March; but he did not enjoy the confidence of the new Government.[78] Almeida warned it that concession-hunters were making their way in increasing numbers to Gazaland, loaded with presents, from Sofala, Chiloane and Inhambane, seeking to persuade Gungunhana to accept British protection. Portugal had lost greatly in prestige from Gungunhana's campaign against chiefs at the doors of Inhambane who had owed allegiance to Portugal, and Almeida feared that Gazaland would go the way of Mashonaland and Nyasaland unless the Government took strenuous steps. He advocated a great increase in Portuguese administration in the district, by creating six sub-superintendents to support the Portuguese residents. But it was impossible for the minister to determine to what extent these proposals stemmed from Almeida's desire to build a personal empire.[79]

On his arrival at Lourenço Marques Almeida heard that Gungunhana had gone so far as to send two ambassadors to England to offer his allegiance to Victoria; it was urgent for him to depart for the interior lest Portugal lose the race. But presents and other goods he wished to take with him had not arrived, and he used this as a pretext for continuing to Moçambique, where he was given the most unsuitable regalia of a sheikh to present to the paramount chief.[80]

More emerged about British pretensions when the South African press published an affidavit by Francis Colquhoun which declared that he had entered Gazaland in May 1889, on behalf of an English syndicate, with the object of obtaining concessions and had stayed there until January 1890. The king and his headmen had denied that they were subjects of Portugal, and Colquhoun declared that in fact the Portuguese had to pay tribute to Gungunhana for their occupation of the coastline; and he had obtained a concession over 3,000 square miles of territory. Cohen, the Portuguese consul in the South African Republic, promptly published a statement recalling Gungunhana's act of vassalage.[81] The British vice-consul in Lourenço Marques alleged (in language reminiscent of Colquhoun's statement) that messengers had reached him from Gungunhana denying the Portuguese claim to his country and declaring that Portugal paid him tribute; but Gungunhana appreciated that the white man was fast spreading over the whole of Africa; when the time came for Gazaland to be taken over by a European power he would prefer that power to be Britain—not Portugal or the South African Republic.[82] But the week after this alleged interview two envoys from Gungunhana paid their respects to the Governor of Lourenço

---

78 Petre to Salisbury, 28/3/90, 93 Af., CP 6061, p. 266, encl., anon., received 27/3/90, pp. 266–7. The Moçambique Company had also proposed that a white school teacher, who had been withdrawn from Gazaland as a result of her intimate association with the chief, be returned to that area to act as an agent of the Company (letter received 12/5/90, CP 6061, pp. 351–2).

79 Almeida to Dir. geral, 5/2/90, AHU, Moç., 1 Rep. Pasta 6. In this file are many documents about Gazaland, 1889–90.

80 Almeida to Dir. geral, 28/4/90, ibid., Pasta 3, and Min. to Gov. Lourenço Marques, 28/4/90, ibid.

81 F. J. Colquhoun, affidavit, 21/2/90, CP 6061, p. 334, Cohen to Ed. *The Press*, 31/3/90, ibid., p. 334–4.

82 Smith de la Cour, Lourenço Marques, to Salisbury, 16/5/90, 13, CP 6061, pp. 292–4.

Marques and reiterated the vassalage of the Gaza people to Portugal and formally agreed to the establishment of a Portuguese administrative post at the mouth of the Limpopo River.[83] Both Machado, the new Governor-general of Moçambique, and Rhodes foresaw the importance of the Pungue as a port. Machado proposed transferring the capital of the district of Sofala from Chiloane,[84] while Rhodes was concerned about an access to Mashonaland, which was close on 1,500 miles from Cape Town. Boats of 6 feet draft could go 60 miles up the Pungue River. The fly belt was perhaps 100 miles across, and beyond it lay the healthy highlands. By this route it was only 200 miles from the sea to Mount Wedza, which Rhodes considered would make an excellent communications centre for Mashonaland. It was essential for the BSAC to secure Pungue Bay; or at least ensure that it became a free port. It was equally essential, for political reasons, that the advantages of this route be concealed from the public of the Cape; pressures and reconnaisances had to be kept secret. He deputed Colquhoun to secure treaties with the chiefs of Manicaland (which was subject to Gungunhana) and investigate the prospects of a railway across this territory.[85]

The wagons of the Pioneer Column were already rumbling before Almeida reached Gazaland. The gun-boat *MacMahon* conveyed him and his party of six whites and one hundred blacks to the mouth of the Limpopo and 30 miles up that river to Chai-chai, where they were met by two hundred Gaza porters, thanks to arrangements made with Gungunhana by Marques Geraldes, who had preceded him from Lourenço Marques overland to Gazaland. Geraldes had been disturbed to find no Portuguese flag flying or even in existence at Zefunha, the head kraal, but Gungunhana had received him warmly. Almeida scored a quick success in persuading the chief to call off a projected campaign against Bilene.[86] But he was disconcerted to find three English concession-hunters waiting on the king. He urged Gungunhana—without success—to declare his kingdom to be Portuguese; but he did at least have the consolation of seeing the Portuguese flag raised again at the king's kraal. He threatened that if the Englishmen conspired against Portugal he would have them arrested. The Governor of Lourenço Marques saw the complications that would result from such action, but the Minister of Ultramar endorsed Almeida's attitude.[87]

And Almeida scored a triumph when he was able to persuade Gungunhana to make a categorical declaration to the English concession-hunters that the Vatua lands had been Portuguese since the days of Umzila; he himself was a

83 They returned to Gazaland with Almeida; they were, in fact the same two headmen who had accompanied him to Lisbon. Gov. Lourenço Marques to Min., 27/5/90, tel., AHU, Moç., 1 Rep. Pasta 3, *Neg.*, p. 96; M. J. da Costa e Couto, Lourenço Marques, 13/4/90, instruções, AHU, Moc., 2, Caixa 9, Almeida to Min., 28/5/90, AHU, Moc., 1 Rep. Pasta 3.
84 GG to Min., 11/7/90, C., AHU, Moç., 1 Rep. Pasta 6.
85 Harris to BSAC, 21/4/90, CP 6061, p. 341.
86 F. A. Marques Geraldes, Zefunha, to Intendente geral, 19/5/90, 1, AHU, Moç., 1 Rep. Pasta 6; and 19/5/90, 2, ibid.; Almeida to Min., 15/6/90, ibid., Pasta 3; and 26/6/90; and 1/7/90, ibid.
87 Almeida to Min., 2/7/90, ibid., and *Neg.*, p. 126; do., 4/7/90, Pasta 3. Gov. Lourenço Marques to Minister, 9/7/90, ibid., Min. to Gov., 11/7/90, do.

vassal of the King of Portugal; and only the King of Portugal could grant concessions. No sooner had the dejected Englishmen departed than a party of four Boers arrived from the South African Republic, sent by the Limpopo Concessions Syndicate to obtain a concession over an area between the Olifants River and the Zoutpansberg, the Limpopo and the borders of the South African Republic. Gungunhana would not even meet the party, and Almeida made the same reply to it as he had been authorized to make to the Englishmen.[88]

Farther south, Portugal was failing in her attempts to extend her influence over Maputo, owing to the agreement between Britain and the South African Republic.[89] Kruger and his executive council were emphatic that they must have access to the sea by some river or other which issued from Swaziland; for long they considered the Tembe or Umbulusi,[90] but then they demanded navigation by way of the Maputo, while a railway would follow the valley of the Umbulusi. When Portugal expressed her reluctance to open the Maputo, and to grant a railway concession unconditionally, Kruger threatened to refuse exequatur to a new Portuguese consul, declaring that by the Act of Berlin an interior state had a right to utilize rivers that ran down to the sea. The British Government approved, on condition that the Republic entered a customs union with the British colonies, that the Republic receive a port. The Portuguese Government conceded this right—and included the right to navigate the Limpopo.[91]

General Joubert proceeded to Europe to further the Republic's claims to Swaziland, and access to the sea. A delegation visited Zambili, queen of Maputo, in an effort to persuade her to grant a concession to enable a railway line to be built across her territory from Kosi Bay; they offered her several hundred pounds, but she rejected the present.[92]

Towards the end of July 1890, a convention between Britain and the South African Republic was signed which recognized the independence of Swaziland. By Article X the Republic withdrew all claim to extension of territory or to enter into treaties with any natives or tribes to the north or north-west of the Republic, and undertook to support the introduction of government by the BSAC within the limits set by the Charter. By Article XI the British Government approved the acquisition of rights by treaty with Chief Umbigesa and Queen Zambili of Tongaland over a strip of land not exceeding 3 miles in width, north of 27° south latitude, for the construction of a railway from or near Kosi Bay; and it promised to use its influence to obtain a concession in the Republic's favour of an area 10 miles in radius on the coast, which would

---

88 Almeida to Min., 4/8/90, tel., ibid.; Gov. Lourenço Marques, to Min., 13/8/90, tel., *Neg.*, p. 188; Almeida and others, *acta*, 20/8/90, AHU, Moç., 1 Rep. Pasta 7. The Boers were W. A. Grobler, H. C. Bodenstein, J. A. Adendorff, P. E. Maré; the syndicate was under the chairmanship of Baron G. Oppenheim.
89 Garson, p. 405.
90 Cohen to Min., 21/3/90, 28/2784, Nec., CPT 1.
91 do., 16/5/90, 31/3105, ibid.
92 Cohen to Min., 6/6/90, 31/3048, do.; J. G. Campos, Pretoria, to Min., 25/7/90, 7A, and 28/6/90, 7A, do.; H. O. d'A. Ferreira, Maputa, to Gov. Lourenço Marques, 23/7/90, 16, AHU, Moç., 2 Rep., Caixa 7; Pindella, Hague, to Min., 29/7/90, tel., *Neg.*, p. 145.

be deemed to be part of the territory of the Republic. By Article XII Britain agreed to recognize the sovereignty of the Republic over land so acquired; and over land acquired by the Republic for navigating the Pongola River, which would not exceed 4 miles in radius from some point on the Pongola River; and over a strip of land, not exceeding 3 miles in width, from the above, for the construction of a railway line north of 27° south latitude. Article XIII proclaimed the right of navigation of the Pongola River.[93] The Portuguese consul in Pretoria promptly protested against Articles XI, XII and XIII.[94] The convention seemed to end Portuguese hopes for reuniting the Tonga people under the Portuguese flag, and there was the danger that the British would force the opening of the Maputo. The consul in Pretoria saw only one hope: the effective occupation, by Portuguese forces, of the Maputo at least as far as the junction of the Pongola.[95]

British and Portuguese territorial claims also clashed north of the Zambezi. There had for long been plans to make effective communication between Angola and Moçambique, and at the end of 1889 two expeditions had been despatched, one from the west coast, the other from the east, to make for Barotseland. The leader of the mission from the Angolan coast, Teixeira da Silva, had the task of persuading Lewanika, the Paramount Chief, to accept Portuguese protection. The commander of the military escort, Captain Paiva Couceiro, would remain at Libonta, build a fort, and begin what would virtually amount to the military occupation of Barotseland. The British ultimatum caused the Portuguese authorities to divert the expedition to the Cubango and Cunene. Couceiro protested strongly against this. He conceded that there would not be much prospect of coming to a satisfactory arrangement with Lewanika owing to the machinations of that "English agent", Coillard; but there were other independent chiefs on the Zambezi, such as Chicofele, ten days above Libonta, who had been often visited by a Portuguese trader: a settlement there would be an important link in trans-African communication. But Brito Capelo, the Governor-general, would have none of it; the Portuguese Government must honour the obligation it gave after the ultimatum to do nothing in the interior of a military or occupational character. The British South Africa Company was organizing an expedition at Walvis Bay which would, it was reported, be making for the Cunene and Cubango; it was essential to forestall the Englishmen, and make treaties with native chiefs in the basins of those two rivers.[96]

The Portuguese expedition was in Bié while this correspondence was going on, close to Silva Porto's house at Belmonte. The local chief, Dunduma, who knew and valued the services of the local traders, was already wondering at the establishment in his territory of a different type of foreigner. Arnot, a Plymouth Brother, had spent nearly four years in Barotseland and Katanga. Publication of his book, *Garenganze*, and his lectures and preachings had caused fourteen

93 Convention, signed Cape Town, 24/7/90, and Pretoria 2/8/90, Hertslet, pp. 868–77.
94 Campos to Min., 11/8/90, 23A, Nec., SPZ 4.
95 do., 15/8/90, "absolutamente confidencial e urgente", do.
96 Fran. Corte, memo., 20/1/90, AHU, Moç., 1 Rep., Pasta 6; Couceiro to GG, 19/2/90, *Artur de Paiva*, I, pp. 159–62; GG to Gov. Benguela, 18/3/90, pp. 162–4.

missionaries to volunteer for service in central Africa. To facilitate communication it was decided to establish a line of mission stations from the coast at Benguela to Garenganze, and one of these was started at Kwanjulu, in Bié, near Belmonte. After the missionaries had been two months in his country, Dunduma, at the instigation of a trader, sent a letter to Arnot demanding that the missionaries leave Bié. To enforce his will he sent a company of warriors. But Arnot knew two of the leaders, and he had in fact bought and liberated one of them from a slaver some years before. The sub-chiefs in the neighbourhood held a palaver and sent messengers to Dunduma asking that the missionaries be allowed to remain. Arnot, accompanied by the doctor of his party and Silva Porto, visited Dunduma, who received them cordially, gave them the road to Garenganze, and permission to engage members of his tribe as porters.[97]

But Teixeira da Silva and Paiva Couceiro made no attempt to meet Dunduma and allay his fears lest their force of 150 soldiers and porters stay in his country and occupy it. He sent them also a letter ordering them to withdraw. They still made no attempt to meet him, but sent Silva Porto to intimate to him that they refused to withdraw. Silva Porto failed to persuade the chief to accept this decision; and he also failed to persuade the officers to take his advice and withdraw to Bailundu. Foreseeing nothing but disaster ahead, the old trader, who had done so much towards opening up the interior, retired to his home, wrapped himself in the Portuguese flag, laid himself on fourteen kegs of gunpowder, and ignited them. A few days later, early in April 1890, word reached Belmonte of the approach of a strong force of tribesmen. Seventeen of the thirty-seven soldiers promptly deserted. The two captains decided that in the circumstances Belmonte was untenable, and withdrew to Cambange, on the frontiers of Bié, where Couceiro temporarily remained, while Teixeira da Silva continued to Bailundu.[98] The Governor-general blamed the two officers for not having withdrawn earlier; but he thought that foreign intrigue might also have been partly responsible for the disaster; he could not understand why Arnot's party had remained unmolested. The Portuguese Government, as soon as it heard of this reverse, ordered the despatch of a punitive expedition. Couceiro demanded to be put in command of it, and he swore not to shave until he had avenged this insult to the national honour. But the Governor-general insisted on his carrying out the Cubango mission, which he did with great efficiency and success.[99] He was still in time to shave in Dunduma's kraal, for it took time to mount the punitive expedition. Portugal could supply no men, and only forty-seven could be spared from Moçambique. But on 15 August 1890 there set out from Humbata a column which included 260 troops, a dozen cavalrymen, four field-guns, two machine-guns, and 80 Boers, who

97 E. Baker, *The life and explorations of F. S. Arnot* (London, 1921), pp. 243–4; Baker, *Arnot a Knight of Africa*, pp. 130–8; R. I. Rotberg, 'Plymouth Brethren and the occupation of Katanga, 1886–1907', *JAH*, 1964, pp. 285–97.
98 Teixeira da Silva to Gov., 1/4/90, *Artur de Paiva*, I, pp. 167–9; Couceiro to Gov., 7/4/90, pp. 169–71; GG to Min., 16/5/90, pp. 164–6; Petre to Salisbury, 18/6/90, CP 6061, pp. 404–6.
99 Paiva Couceiro, *Relatório die viagem entre Bailundo e as terras do Mucusso* (Lisbon, 1892); F. C. Egerton, *Angola in perspective* (London, 1957) p. 92.

were accompanied by 300 Damaras and 40 Basters. The force was not simply to punish Dunduma, but to make effective Portuguese occupation of Bié.[100]

Farther north, Portugal was faced by the growing ambition of the King of the Belgians. The boundaries of the Congo Free State had been defined in the treaties with Germany (8 November 1884), France (5 February 1885) and Portugal (14 February 1885), which had been annexed to the Act of Berlin.[101] A royal decree of 1888 set up eleven districts[102] but in June 1890 a further decree established a twelfth district, of Eastern Kwango, which lay between the Kwango and the districts of Kassai and Lualaba. It was not clear how far south this district extended; but it included Muata Yanvo, which Portugal had regarded as reserved for Portuguese expansion.[103]

Portuguese intentions on Barotseland and Belgian plans for Katanga alarmed Johnston who, with his associate Sharpe, had been treaty-making widely north and west of Nyasa.[104] In April 1890 the High Commissioner cabled London that Barotseland should be included in the British sphere. The Colonial Office agreed that in view of Portuguese ambitions, and to provide an alternative line of communication to Tanganyika, it was essential to secure this territory. The Foreign Office did not think that the time had yet arrived. But the informant João reported renewed plans for Portuguese expansion across the continent, with the construction of a series of forts to provide indisputable evidence of occupation, and in June the Colonial Office again drew the attention of Salisbury to the importance of reserving Barotseland, where the BSAC claimed to have secured concessions, for Britain. The day after the Colonial Office's approach an emissary of the BSAC signed a treaty with Lewanika.[105] Great, accordingly, was the annoyance of the BSAC, and especially of Rhodes, to discover that in the agreement with Portugal it was proposed to recognize Portugal's western-most possessions as stretching to the Zambezi: a boundary which would cut Barotseland in half.

To the north-east, however, the BSAC was meeting with more success. Carl Wiese, who had been a settler at Blantyre, and had left there under dubious circumstances to join Portuguese service, had travelled to the head kraal of Mpesene, an important Ngoni chief between Jumbe's territory and the Luangwa River, in company with Lieutenant Mesquita e Solla. A Portuguese flag was presented to the chief and two of his sons, and he was urged to desist from raiding towards the Zambezi. But he refused to sign any treaty with the Portuguese. Wiese departed for the Zambezi, leaving Solla at the head kraal. Sharpe, on his arrival there in March 1890, was disconcerted to see the Portuguese flag

100 *Artur de Paiva*, I, pp. 172–81.
101 Hertslet, Memo. on the recognized boundaries of the Congo Free State, 7/11/89, CP 5970, p. 236.
102 1/8/88, Hertslet, pp. 201–3.
103 Decree, 10/6/90, Hertslet, p. 204; H. A. Dias de Carvalho, *Expedição portugueza ao Muatiânvua* . . . (Lisbon, 1890), 4 vols.
104 Johnston to Salisbury, 1/2/90, 6 Af., CP 6061, pp. 236–8, with map facing p. 238; Oliver, *Johnston*, pp. 194–5. See Pl. 12, facing p. 234.
105 CO to FO, 13/4/90, CP 6061, p. 282; FO to CO, 5/5/90, p. 316G; Petre to Salisbury, 8/5/90, 121 Af., p. 332, encl. letter dd 6/5/90; CO to FO, 28/6/90, p. 414, and encl. to p. 419; Gann, *Northern Rhodesia*, p. 60.

flying above the house of the Portuguese lieutenant. Mpesene kept Sharpe waiting for nearly a week before receiving him, and then he protested that he was a friend of Wiese and Solla and the Portuguese, and he refused to consider accepting a British flag or signing a treaty. Sharpe left Wiese a letter, in which he offered Wiese £300 a year if he would switch his allegiance to the BSAC. Sharpe then continued down the Luangwa, and a short distance west of that river, on the banks of the Zambezi, he hoisted and saluted the British flag, and airily declared the country to be under British protection. Johnston sent Sharpe back to Mpesene's, with instructions to buy Wiese and make a treaty with the chief. He returned at the end of May 1890, but failed in both his objects. Johnston insisted to the Foreign Office, "The Portuguese *must not be allowed* to establish themselves at Mpesene's." He welcomed the projected settlement with Portugal because it excluded the Portuguese from this area.[106]

The Governor-general and the authorities in Moçambique had been most reluctant to abide by the instructions given from Portugal to withdraw south-wards of the Ruo and from Mashonaland. Posters and inscriptions on the walls of the British consulate in Moçambique and the residences of British subjects had proclaimed after the ultimatum, "War to the death against the English," while the Governor-general announced to his officials that he would do nothing to implement the instructions until absolutely impelled to do so, when he would resign, and allow his successor to supervise what he described as a treacherous surrender of Portuguese soil. It was not until the end of February that Portuguese forces evacuated Katunga and Mebeu.[107] The Portuguese remained in occupation of Chilomo, on the north bank of the Ruo, until 11 March, when Buchanan sailed into the Ruo and landed a mile above the Portuguese fort. He had only ten armed men with him, but the garrison hurriedly dismantled their guns and fled to the south side of the river. He raised the Union Jack, an action which produced protests from the Portuguese authorities; he deposed Mlauri, who was as anti-Buchanan as he was anti-Portuguese, and appointed an officer to police the Ruo post.[108]

Excitement in Portugal was raised to fever pitch when reports reached Lisbon that four sepoys, sent by Ferrão (who had been granted the lower Shire as a *prazo* on the most favourable of terms)[109] on a mission to the Makololo, had been seized and delivered to Buchanan, who had had two of them tied to a tree and shot. Fury was redoubled when it was reported that Buchanan had seized and burnt a Portuguese flag. The feelings so engendered gravely embarrassed the negotiations in London. Salisbury ordered Churchill, the acting

106 Wiese and others, autos of 20/8/89, 11/12/89, 8/2/90, *Bol. Off.*, 24/5/90, pp. 238–40 and CP 6069, pp. 65–6; Johnston, memo received in FO 9/8/90, CP 6069, pp. 53–4; Wiese, 'Mpesene', *Bol. SGL*, 1891, pp. 231–430, 465–97, 1892, pp. 373–599.
107 Churchill to Salisbury, 22/1/90, 4 Af., CP 6061, p. 193; GG to Min., 16/3/90, Nec., SPZ 3.
108 Ribeiro to Freitas, 17/3/90, *Neg.*, pp. 49–50; Buchanan to Salisbury, 18/3/90, 11 and 12 CA, CP 6061, pp. 327, 328–9; João Coutinho, military gov. of Shire, to GG, 26/3/90, 20, *Neg.*, pp. 101–2; Buchanan to Salisbury, 15/4/90, 16 CA, CP 6061, pp. 370–1, with protest by A. A. F. Machado, 12/3/90, pp. 371–2.
109 He had been appointed *capitão-mor*, with the rank of lt.-col., at a salary of 500 milreis p.a. and with a percentage of the *mussoco*; but with obligation to provide 500 sepoys (GG to Min., 1/2/90), 2/12, AHU, Rep., Caixa 2. Mço 7.

consul in Moçambique, to report. J. J. Machado, the new Governor-general, ordered Coutinho to withdraw and collaborated in the enquiry. Ross, the vice-consul in Quelimane, went to the Ruo and investigated. It emerged that the men had not been sepoys, but were simply from Ferrão's *prazo;* they had entered Makololo territory, and enslaved two youths and raped several young girls; tribesmen had seized three of them, the fourth jumping into the river; Buchanan had tried them, and sentenced them to fifteen, ten and eight lashes, after which they had been deported from Makololo territory.[110]

Britain was more concerned about a reported build-up of armed forces on the lower Shire. Some of the troops were British Indians, recruited in Bombay and Goa for railway work, but trained in Moçambique, far from gently, as soldiers; those who sought the protection of the British consul were promptly shipped off to the Zambezi.[111] Johnston reported that Coutinho, "a notorious firebrand", was starting up the Zambezi with 1,000 men and artillery, and there were rumours that he was about to march to Mponda's and punish that chief for the unfriendly reception he had given the Cardoso Catholic mission; he warned Salisbury that unless Coutinho were recalled there would be real trouble; events were drifting to a state of war. Buchanan sent Coutinho a protest, and, exaggerating the size of the force to 10,000, cabled Salisbury, "Portugal threatens destruction British community Blantyre; concentrating overwhelming force Ruo. Fatal results anticipated." Salisbury had already warned the Portuguese Government that Britain could not be indifferent to the despatch of military expeditions into regions which were the subject of negotiations. The Portuguese Government assured Petre that it would not sanction any action that might prejudice the negotiations, and ordered all Portuguese forces to keep below the Ruo. The explanation for the concentration of the force, such as it was, was simple: Massingire had revolted (the revolt instigated by the English, according to the Governor-general) and Coutinho had proclaimed martial law. Ross, on his way up to the Ruo, had seen Coutinho, who had detailed his plans, which Ross had considered perfectly reasonable.[112] The authorities desired too to

110 Jose Cardoso, Massingire, to GG, 12/4/90, *Neg.*, pp. 103–4; Johnston to Ross, 24/4/90, ibid., pp. 110–1; Ross, Vicente, to Churchill, 6/5/90, CP 6069, p. 51; Machado, A/Gov. Quelimane, to V/Consul, 6/5/90, Civil 303, AHU, Moç., 2 Rep., Caixa 7, and to GG, 10/5/90, ibid.; Buchanan to Salisbury, 7/6/90, CP 6069, p. 48; H. C. Marshall, Chilomo, to Ross, 9/6/90, pp. 60–1; Petre to Salisbury, 13/6/90, 156 Af., CP 6061, p. 397; Ribeiro to Freitas, 15/6/90, tel., *Neg.*, p. 100; Ross, Quelimane, to Salisbury, 16/6/90, PRO, FO 179/278, with sketch-map of the confluence of the Shire and Ruo; Ribeiro to Freitas, 17/6/90, tel., *Neg.*, pp. 100–1; Petre to Salisbury, 17/6/90, 38 Af., CP 6061, p. 395; Ross to Churchill, 16/6/90, CP 6069, pp. 68–70; Petre to Salisbury, 18/6/90, 159 Af., ibid., pp. 403–4; Ribeiro to Petre, 20/6/90, *Neg.*, pp. 114–5; Salisbury to Churchill, 23/6/90, tel., CP 6061, p. 407; Petre to Salisbury, 26/6/90, 164 Af., ibid., pp. 419–20; F. de P. Carvalho, Sec. geral, to Gov. Moç., 27/6/90, 2/41, AHU, Moç., 2 Rep., Pasta 7, *Neg.*, pp. 190–1; Machado GG to Min., 11/7/90, AHU, Moç., 1 Rep., Pasta 6 re Coutinho.
111 Churchill to Salisbury, 25/1/90, 5 Af., CP 6061, p. 197; Johnston to Salisbury, 18/3/90, 16, ibid., p. 282A–B.
112 Johnston to Salisbury, tels, 9 and 11/4/90, CP 6061, pp. 273–4; Salisbury to Petre, 11/4/90, tel., ibid., p. 274; Petre, note verbale, 12/4/90, Nec., SPZ 3; Petre to Salisbury, 13/4/90, 28 Af., CP 6061, p. 275; Buchanan to Salisbury, 16/4/90, tel., 17 CA, ibid., pp. 372–3; Min. to GG, 17/4/90, Nec., SPZ 3; Sec. geral to Gov. Quelimane, 18/4/90, *Neg.*, p. 63; Buchanan to Salisbury, 20/4/90, tel., CP 6061, p. 329; Coutinho to Gov., 21/4/90, *Neg.*, p. 105; Ross, Vicente, to Churchill, 7/5/90, CP 6069, p. 52; Petre to Ribeiro, 15/5/90, *Neg.*, p. 90; GG to Min., 16/5/90, ibid.; Min. to GG, 18/6/90, Nec., SPZ 4, *Neg.*, p. 113.

protect a Catholic mission which it was desired to establish at Mlanje to counteract the Protestant influence from Blantyre.[113] And the authorities wished to ensure that there was no repetition of the Valadim massacre.

Lieutenant Valadim had been sent, with a European companion and a Swahili interpreter, supported by 325 sepoys and porters, to extend Portuguese influence to the east of Nyasa. Early in March 1890, reports reached the coast that the party had been wiped out, by Chief Mutaca, who occupied the middle Lugenda (in about latitude 13° south). One report, which came via Cuirassia, declared that Valadim had told Mutaca that he had come to make him a vassal of Portugal, and had offered him thirty loads of presents. The chief and headmen were hesitant, so Valadim threw in a few extra personal gifts. Mutaca then demanded the Europeans' personal luggage and arms. When Valadim refused this attempted extortion Mutaca declared that the Sultan of Zanzibar had warned him against the Portuguese, and ordered the Portuguese to be killed and their sepoys and porters seized. According to another report, which reached Cape Delgado, Valadim was warned at Mutaca's first town not to advance without permission from the chief. Rejecting this advice, he continued to a second town, where he was given the same warning, and where he left his companion, who was ill. He persisted in seeking out the chief, who refused to become a vassal of Portugal. Valadim, however, raised a pole and hoisted the Portuguese flag. A brother of the king tried to take it down, whereupon Valadim struck him. Valadim was beheaded, his sepoys and porters seized, his companion shot. Another report which reached Quelimane suggested that one or both of the Portuguese had been interfering with native women.[114] Whatever the motive, Portuguese prestige suffered a severe blow.

The ALC, all this while, was continuing to demand the right to import munitions in support of its operations on Nyasa. The British Government, while admitting that it could not demand this importation as a right, as long as goods were imported through Quelimane and had to cross Portuguese soil, lent its weight to the ALC requests[115] and brought the strongest pressure to bear on the Portuguese Government; it also did all in its power to accelerate the opening of the Chinde route to the interior. The Lords of the Admiralty instructed *Stork*, of the squadron stationed at Zanzibar, to survey the Chinde bar on her way to Simonstown for a refit. Lieutenant Balfour, her commander, exceeded his orders by trying to penetrate to the junction of the Chinde and the Zambezi. Inside the harbour was a Portuguese river-steamer, the *Cuama*, armed with two Nordenfeldt guns, and manned by three Europeans and a black crew. Her commander requested Balfour to lower the white ensign, since the

113 Thermopylae to Min., 23/4/90, AHU, Moç., 1 Rep., Pasta 6; GG to Min., 7/5/90, ibid.; Esloy [?] to Gov. Quelimane, 7/5/90, ibid.
114 J. Marques Lourenço to Chefe da Missão Civilizadora Henrique de Macedo, Quelimane, 2/3/90, 18, AHU, Moç., 1 Rep., Pasta 7; Johnston to Salisbury, 16/3/90, 13 Af., CP 6061, pp. 279–80; J. A. de Mesquita Guimarães, Gov. C. Delgado, to Sec. geral, 10/5/90, AHU, Moç., 1 Rep., Pasta 6; A. B. de Sousa, Consul, Zanzibar, to Min., 3/6/90, 9A, Nec., SPZ 4, reporting interrogation of a porter who appeared on the slave-market; C. Maples, Kuingini, to Euan Smith, 11/7/90, CP 6069, p. 63. Cf. A. de Matos, 'O tenente Valadin, soldado do imperio', in *Os Portugueses em Africa*, III (Lisbon, 1938), pp. 249–55.
115 CP 6061, pp. 275–7, 316, 318, 336, 339, 343–4.

harbour regulations of the province of Moçambique did not permit of foreign flags being flown on Portuguese waters. Balfour enquired whether this was an invitation or an order. The Portuguese lieutenant admitted that only delicacy caused him to frame his request so politely.[116] Balfour refused to comply, and returned down the river.[117]

This incident caused Salisbury to accede to repeated requests by Johnston, "Want gun-boat badly."[118] It, and the ALC's difficulties, caused the British Government to order two sixty-foot stern-wheeled river gun-boats, for service on the Zambezi and Shire. As they neared completion the Admiralty asked the Foreign Office what instructions should be given their commanders: What was their object? Were they to act against the slave-trade? What were the limits of Portuguese dominion? What were the limits of British protection? The principal object, the Foreign Office replied, was to survey both rivers to the limit of navigation—and carry ammunition for the ALC. Suppression of the slave-trade was not a major object. Fugitive slaves might, however, come aboard from the Makololo, "a slave-trading race"; if in British territory, they were to be freed; if in Portuguese, they were to be handed over to a Portuguese authority. The river-boats were to be taken out to east Africa aboard the *Humber* and *Buccaneer*, which were to be escorted to Chinde by one or more warships from Zanzibar, and remain while they were being assembled and launched. The waterway of the Zambezi and Shire, as far as it was navigable, was common ground [sic], the Admiralty informed the commanders of the two boats; any attempt to stop the expedition by force must be forcibly repelled. If necessary, boats manned and armed from the squadron might accompany the river gun-boats. In support of these instructions Hertslet produced precedents where rivers of great magnitude had been thrown open to the commerce of all nations.[119] Confirmation of the presence of coal-fields near Tete gave promise of suitable fuel—and of a sizeable export.[120]

Britain felt the need to police the waterway when, on 9 April 1890, a Portuguese river-boat fired a shot across the bows of the *James Stevenson* as she was approaching the junction of the Ruo; officers searched her for arms and ammunition, but finding none let her continue on her way to Katunga. Salisbury denounced this "outrage" on a British vessel, and warned the Portuguese Government that if such action were repeated when the British gun-boats

---

116 "Admiralty 13/2/1890 Shire River. Memoranda and information as to the Zambezi Delta and forces in neighbourhood", PRO, Adm. 1/7024; J. C. de Lima, commander *Cuama*, Chinde, to GG, 15/2/90, 38, Nec., SPZ 4; Adm. to FO, 17 and 25/3/90, CP 6061, pp. 240, 260.

117 The GG was sure that he was trying to reconnoitre the defences of the harbour, to see, e.g. whether there were torpedoes, and the strength of the garrison. (GG to Min., 3/4/90, Nec., SPZ 3)

118 Johnston to Salisbury, 3/2/90, tel., CP 6061, p. 113; do., 6 and 7/2/90, p. 118; FO to Adm., 1/4/90, 26/4/90, pp. 270, 303.

119 Adm. to FO, 1/5/90, CP 6061, p. 315; FO to Adm., 7/5/90, ibid., p. 316 I–K; and 16/5/90, p. 336; Adm. to FO, 20/5/90, pp. 354–5; Adm. to FO, 20/5/90, pp. 354–5, and 3/6/90, p. 363; Hertslet, memo, 5/6/90, pp. 366–8.

120 Petre to Salisbury, 11/5/90, 125 Af., CP 6061, p. 350, enclosing a letter from [João], received 9/5/90; he hinted at dirty work in further letters, received 23/5/90, p. 359.

were ascending the river they would defend themselves.[121]   The Portuguese Government requested its consuls at Cape Town and Zanzibar and Aden to report on the movements of the ships carrying the river-boats. As soon as word of the approach of the transports reached Lisbon it ordered the Governor-general to ensure that the ships were challenged by Portuguese naval units on entering Portuguese waters; and Machado himself was to proceed to the area. At the urgent request of the Portuguese Government, Salisbury held the transports at Zanzibar.[122]

In the meanwhile *Stork* returned to Chinde to carry out a survey. Despite all the diligencies of the new Governor-general she entered the river unchallenged. Machado arrived off Quelimane aboard the corvette *Afonso de Albuquerque*, which could not enter because there was no pilot and the commander did not know the entrance. He crossed the bar by launch, meaning to continue to Chinde in the *Auxiliar;* but the *Auxiliar* needed repairs to her engines, and it was only on the 9th that he reached the Chinde bar. He saw at anchor off Chinde the *Tamega*, which had been delayed by a breakdown in her engines; and inside the harbour, proudly flying the white ensign, was the *Stork*. Lieutenant Balfour replied to a demand to lower her flag by the commander of the *Tamega* by clearing for action, and the matter was not pressed. When eventually Machado entered Chinde harbour, on the 14th, he was courteous, and allowed the survey to continue, on condition that Balfour did not ascend the Chinde River. Machado could not but comment to his minister on the disgraceful state of the ships of the naval squadron; most were completely incapable of putting to sea; and those that could had a maximum speed of $5\frac{1}{2}$ knots. The only way to halt the British, he declared, was to anchor the Portuguese ships across the Chinde, and then the British vessels would not be able to proceed without sinking at least one of the Portuguese units. It was with great relief that Machado heard that the British Government had suspended orders for the gun-boats to proceed up the river.[123]

The *Humber* and *Buccaneer* remained at Zanzibar pending the outcome of the negotiations, but the issue was re-opened when, at the end of July, the ALC reported urgently to the Foreign Office that the *James Stevenson* had been arrested at Chilomo and her crew imprisoned. The British Government protested and demanded compensation. The Portuguese Government immediately expressed its regret, and ordered the Governor-general to proceed to Quelimane, and if necessary to the Ruo, to cause its orders to be executed, and summarily to punish those who had disobeyed them; Coutinho had been removed from

121 Buchanan to Salisbury, 17/4/90, 18 CA, CP 6061, p. 374; Coutinho, Mopea, to Gov. Quelimane, 20/4/90, *Neg.*, p. 105; ALC to Salisbury, 18/6/90, CP 6061, p. 400; Salisbury to Petre, 19/6/90, 107 Af., ibid., pp. 400–1; Petre to Ribeiro, 24/6/90, *Neg.*, p. 116.
122 Ribeiro to Consul, Cape Town, 27/6/90 and Aden and Zanzibar, tels, Nec., SPZ 4; Ribeiro to Freitas, 29/6/90, tel., *Neg.*, p. 118; Min. to GG, 1/7/90, tel., Nec., SPZ 4; Consul, Aden, to Min., 2/7/90, tel., ibid.; Consul, Zanzibar to Min., 4, 6, 8/7/90, tels, ibid.
123 GG, Quelimane, to Min., 11/7/90, Nec., SPZ 4; Fremantle, Zanzibar, to Adm., 25/7/90, CP 6069, p. 41; GG to Min., 18/7/90, 2/41, AHU, Moç., 2 Rep., Caixa 7, and tel., 18/7/90, *Neg.*, pp. 135–6; Min. to GG, 19/7/90, tel., *Neg.*, p. 136; V-consul, Zanzibar, to Min., 19/7/90, 13A, Nec., SPZ 4; GG to Min., 21/7/90, 2/45, ibid., *Neg.*, p. 191.

office; if he had refused to leave, and had been responsible, he was to be court-martialled, Ribeiro assured Petre.[124] It was not until the end of August that details of the incident reached London. The *James Stevenson* was carrying Joseph Thomson, the explorer, and J. A. Grant, explorer's son, who, with fifty-five porters, were on their way, as servants of the BSAC, to extend Sharpe's treaty-making west of Nyasa, as well as two white and seven black members of the Universities' Mission, three members of the Free Church, and two employees of the ALC. As she approached the confluence of the Ruo she whistled, to warn the Portuguese officials to prepare for their now customary search. But there was no challenge from the Portuguese side of the river, so she continued to the Chilomo landing stage, and passengers began to disembark. It was only then that three guns were discharged from the Portuguese bank. A boat crossed to Chilomo with a Portuguese officer, who demanded to examine passports and search the vessel. The captain refused to permit the search, declaring that the vessel was in British waters. On 10 July the *Stevenson* returned down the river. As soon as she entered Portuguese waters two shots were fired, the first a blank, the second, of ball, across her bows. She anchored. The commander of the *Cuama* then arrested the vessel and her crew, though without laying a formal charge, sending the latter by the gun-boat to Vicente, whence they were transferred to Quelimane.[125]

The commander of the *Cuama* had presumably taken this action at the instigation of Coutinho, who had indeed refused to accept his recall; he appealed to the War Council in Lisbon, and announced his intention of marching eastwards. He occupied Mount Milolo, which he described as a strategic centre where land and river communications met.[126] This may have brought Portugal local gain; but his action was trivial compared with the prejudice he occasioned the settlement in Europe.

124 ALC to Salisbury, 25/7/90, CP 6069, p. 42; Petre to Salisbury, 29/7/90, 46 Af., p. 42; and 30/7/90, p. 44; Petre, note verbale, 30/7/90, ibid.
125 Ross, Quelimane, to Salisbury, 18/7/90, rec. 26/8/90, CP 6069, pp. 77–8, encl., pp. 78–80, statement by J. Thomson, 7/7/90, and protest by Ross to Gov., Quelimane, 18/7/90.
126 GG to Min., 18/7/90, 3/70, Nec., SPZ 4; and 27/7/90, *Neg.*, p. 143; Min. to GG, 28/7/90, ibid., p. 144.

13

THE TREATY OF 11 JUNE 1891

As soon as the terms of the Treaty of 20 August 1890 were published there was an intensified outcry against them in Portugal. The pro-Government journals and the more responsible of the independent papers considered the agreement to be an honourable solution to the conflict which was not disadvantageous to Portugal. But the Progressista and Republican press loudly proclaimed that Portugal had been degraded and humiliated even more than by the ultimatum of 11 January. The *Novidades* condemned what it called the supreme act of spoliation, and declared that it would be better for Portugal to dispose of Moçambique altogether than retain it under such shameful conditions. The Cortes was convened for 15 September. Petre foresaw weeks of acrimonious debate, but the Government was confident that the convention would be ratified in the second week of October. Hostility concentrated particularly on the repeated provisions that Portugal could not cede territory without the consent of Great Britain; the opposition regarded these as depriving the King of Portugal of sovereignty, if not reducing the country to British vassalage. There was also harsh criticism of the obligation to construct a railway from the mouth of the Pungue to the British sphere which, it was held, would be for the exclusive benefit of the English.[1] The arrival of the British river gun-boats in the Zambezi further complicated the situation. The Portuguese Government had agreed that these might be assembled at Chinde, but insisted that they be not allowed to ascend the river until the convention had been ratified.[2] But the British Navy was opposed to postponement because of the decreasing level of water in the Zambezi and Shire, and the unhealthiness of the valleys once the rains began. When reports persisted of disorders on the Shire, Salisbury gave orders that the transports carrying the river-boats should reach Chinde on 7 September, and that they should start their ascent of the river on 21 September. The Lords of the Admiralty ordered the fleet under the flag of Vice-Admiral Fremantle to concentrate at Zanzibar; a gun-boat was to escort the transports to Chinde; and the balance of the fleet was to enter Moçambique harbour on 24 September.[3] Hintze Ribeiro reiterated his

---

1 Petre to Salisbury, 21/8/90, 198 Af., CP 6069, pp. 72–3; and 23/8/90, 201 Af., ibid., pp. 80–1; and 28/8/90, 20 Af., ibid., p. 84; and 2/9/90, 210 Af., ibid., p. 90; and 9/9/90, 212 Af., ibid., pp. 95–6.
2 Freitas to Hintze Ribeiro, 21/8/90, *Neg.*, pp. 198–9; Petre to Salisbury, 21/8/90, 199 Af., CP 6069, p. 74 (enclosing Ribeiro to Petre, 21/8/90); and 28/8/90, tel., 49 Af., ibid., p. 81; Salisbury to Churchill, 31/8/90, tel., ibid., p. 82.
3 Salisbury to Freitas, 20/8/90, CP 6069, p. 71 and *Neg.*, p. 216; Fremantle to Admiralty, 23/8/90, CP 6069, p. 72; Salisbury to Petre, 1/9/90, tel. 64, ibid., p. 85; FO to Adm., 1/9/90, ibid., p. 86; Fremantle to Adm., 2/9/90, tel., ibid., p. 88.

objections to the gun-boats ascending the river; he feared further excitement, and even violence.[4] Salisbury, led to appreciate that another incident would so arouse public feeling that it would result in the defeat of the Government and the further postponement of ratification, agreed to delay the date of departure from Chinde, on condition that the Portuguese Government pressed resolutely for ratification; but he refused to give any pledge, lest the free navigation of the Zambezi be regarded as resting on the convention.[5] On the eve of the assembly of the Cortes, Pinheiro Chagas, selected by the Government to be the reporter on the bill requesting the treaty to be passed, wrote an article in which he declared that if the British vessels entered the Zambezi before ratification no patriotic Portuguese could vote for the treaty.

The Government pressed for certain modifications in the convention in the hope of placating its enemies and its own wavering supporters. In place of the clauses demanding the previous consent of Britain before she could transfer territory, it suggested that Britain be given the preferential right to acquire them if Portugal should ever decide to dispose of them; it asked for a declaration that the province of Angola was excluded from the free-trade provisions; and it requested that a neutral engineer take part in the survey of the railway inland from the Pungue mouth instead of the postulated British engineer. The Portuguese minister in London sought out Salisbury at Dieppe, where he was holidaying, and obtained his consent to these modifications.[6]

The Cortes reassembled on 15 September amidst great popular excitement. The presence in the streets of numerous troops and police prevented serious disorders, but even so there were scuffles near the parliamentary building which resulted in one man being killed and eleven seriously injured. Hintze Ribeiro spoke firmly in the House of Deputies, but he was repeatedly interrupted, and at times the sitting had to be suspended; the last minute concessions had not reduced the violence of the opposition. The treaty was referred to a joint committee of deputies interested in foreign affairs, the colonies and finance. But before it could report, on 16 September, Hintze Ribeiro resigned, because he had received such poor support from the members of the governing Regenerador party, and some of his own colleagues rejected the convention, holding that it was unsafe to press for ratification in the face of such violent opposition. Illness of the King made it impossible for him to throw his influence behind the convention, the hard core of resistance to which was organized by the Republican party. On 17 September Serpa Pimentel, the Prime Minister, resigned.

Martens Ferrão tried to form a conciliatory ministry, consisting of members of the Regenerador party, which had a very large majority in the Cortes, and also including some Progressistas who were not hostile to Britain. Reports that

4 Petre to Salisbury, 3/9/90, tel., 50 Af., CP 6069, p. 88; Petre to Salisbury, 4/4/90, ibid., tel., p. 89; and 2/9/90, 209 Af., ibid., p. 89, (enclosing Ribeiro to Petre, 1/9/90, pp. 89–90).
5 Petre to Salisbury, 4/9/90, 211 Af., CP 6069, p. 93; FO to Soveral, 7/9/90, ibid., p. 91; Salisbury to Petre, 8/9/90, tel. 65, ibid., p. 92; and 12/9/90, tel. 66 Af., ibid., p. 100.
6 Ribeiro to Freitas, 22/8/90, tel., Neg., p. 197; and 4/9/90, ibid., p. 219; Petre to Salisbury, 11/9/90, 215 Af., CP 6069, pp. 103–4; and 13/9/90, 218 Af., ibid., pp. 110–1; Petre to Ribeiro, 13/9/90, ibid., p. 111; Salisbury to Petre, 18/9/90, 157 Af., ibid., p. 111.

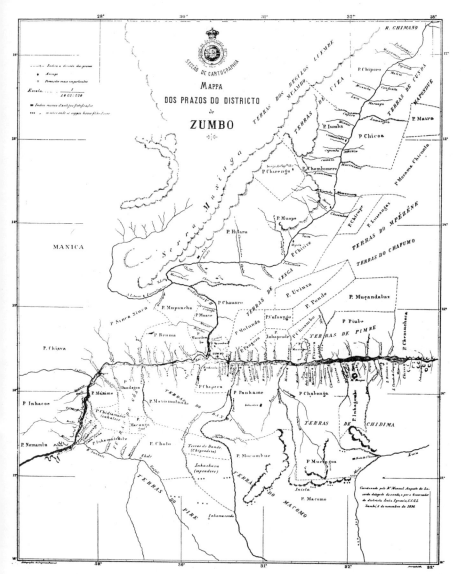

13 Map of the prazos of the District of Zumbo (by M. A. de Lacerda and L. Ignacio, 5/11/1890, published by the Sociedade de Geografia de Lisboa)

the British river-boats were about to leave Chinde complicated matters, and the Progressistas, who had proved so clamorous in opposition, were reluctant to take office. When an official Gazette appeared with lengthy lists of appointments to newly established administrative and judicial districts throughout Portugal there was wild indignation against this attempt at excessive patronage by a tottering government, and the Progressistas refused to associate with the Regeneradores. The crisis continued. Martens Ferrão decided to close the session of the Cortes (which had not met again) and try to obtain further modifications to the treaty which would make it acceptable to the deputies.[7] Salisbury warned Portugal that since an article in the treaty bound the parties to proceed to ratification as soon as possible, the British Government already had cause for grave complaint: if the Government allowed the session to close without ratification the British Government would regard this as equivalent to its rejection, and Britain would not consider herself bound by her signature.[8] He also decided that he would no longer detain the river-boats at Chinde, in view of further information he had received about the shooting at Joseph Thomson, the continued detention of the *James Stevenson*, and the expression of ministerial approbation of the behaviour of Coutinho: he feared further outrages on British subjects and on British property.[9]

Actually in south-east Africa the Governor-general, Machado, had been pursuing a conciliatory attitude; on instructions from Lisbon he had released the *James Stevenson* and he had withdrawn Coutinho from the Ruo, and sent him to an area where, he thought, it would be impossible for the fire-brand to come into conflict with Englishmen: he was to avenge the death of Valadim. Appointed to the command of what was called the Julio de Vilhena expedition, Coutinho was instructed to make for Cuirassia, keeping to the east of the boundary line laid down in the treaty of 20 August, and relieve the Portuguese resident there, if he were still alive, and forward him to the coast, or punish the village responsible if he had been killed. Coutinho was then to reconnoitre a suitable site for a Portuguese centre on the shore of Nyasa north of 13° 30' south, preferably alongside a port, and persuade the local inhabitants to accept the Portuguese. He then had to proceed to the land of Mutaca and castigate some of the main towns, and seize Mutaca and his principal chiefs, killing them if they resisted. He was then to divide his expedition into three columns, which would reach the sea at Mocimboa, at the Bay of Pemba or facing Ibo, and at Fernão Veloso or Moçambique.[10]

The Henrique de Macedo Civilizing mission was encountering adverse weather at Mponda's. The resident, in fact, exasperated by the unfriendly

7 Petre to Salisbury, 16/9/90, 221 Af., CP 6069, p. 164; and 17/9/90, 223 Af., ibid., p. 135; and 18/9/90, 226, Af., ibid., p. 139; and 1/10/90, 236 Af., ibid., p. 166; and 3/10/90, tel. 63 Af., ibid., p. 164; and 4/10/90, 238 Af., ibid., p. 168 (reporting that there were proposals to sell Moçambique rather than make a treaty with Britain); and 5/10/90, tel. 64 Af., ibid., p. 165; and 5/10/90, 239 Af., ibid., p. 174.
8 Salisbury to Petre, 21/9/90, tel. 69 Af., CP 6069, p. 117; and 5/10/90, tel. 74 Af., ibid., p. 166.
9 do., 5/10/90, tel. 73 Af., CP 6069, p. 165.
10 GG to Lieut. J. A. de Azevedo Fragoso de Coutinho, 31/8/90, AHU, Moç., 1 Rep., Pasta 6; GG to Min., 6/9/90, 2/185, ibid.

attitude of the local inhabitants (aggravated by Johnston's treaty with the chief), and the lack of provisions and trade goods, had withdrawn at the end of July.[11] But great things were anticipated from the expedition under Henrique Carlos Lima, which was now reinforced to number fifty sepoys and two hundred porters and had orders to proceed, by forced marches, up the Zambezi, to Muata Yanvo. Muata Yanvo was also being approached by another expedition, under Sarmento, from Angola. These two expeditions, it was hoped, would forestall Congo Free State designs on the land, and make so fair an impression on the people of Muata Yanvo that they would promptly submit to Portuguese dominion.[12]

Machado, beyond proceeding with the reform of administration in the province of Moçambique, had plans for the development of lower Zambezia, especially in and around the area of Tete.[13] But his immediate problem was the relationship between his officials and the officers of the British naval vessels.

The transports carrying the British river gun-boats, escorted by a gun-boat, had entered the Chinde mouth on 10 September 1890. The military commandant refused a request for land to be allocated on which the stern-wheelers could be assembled and coal, etc. stored, so they were assembled and armed on the river, alongside the transports. The steam-cutter, flying the white ensign, set off to examine the Chinde River. The military post fired a rifle-shot in the air, and the commandant warned the boat's commander not to proceed unless he flew the Portuguese flag. When the latter insisted on proceeding the commandant formally protested against "this insolent and unheard-of act of a foreign ship belonging to a European nation for many years an ally of Portugal, disregarding the decisions of His Most Faithful Majesty." The Governor of Quelimane arrived and also protested against this infraction of the Province's port regulations. The British vice-consul from Quelimane also visited Chinde; he too failed to obtain a lease of land; and he counter-protested. As the day approached which had been scheduled for the start of the stern-wheelers up the river, Vice-Admiral Fremantle arrived in Moçambique with a squadron which soon numbered six ships. Machado received the Admiral most courteously. But postponement of the date of the ascent of the Zambezi by the river-boats caused the squadron's stay to become over-extended, embarrassing and somewhat ludicrous. It was not until 8 October that a flotilla set off up the Chinde River, consisting of the two river-boats, the *James Stevenson* carrying the guns and ammunition of the ALC and towing several lighters, accompanied by various boats and canoes, and escorted as far as the Zambezi proper by a British gun-boat.[14]

11 J. A. Teixeira de Souza, Moçambique, to Sec. geral, 27/8/90, 17, ibid.
12 GG to Min., 24/8/90, 2/173, ibid.; and 6/9/90, ibid. (enclosing GG to Governors, 30/8/90; GG to Lima, 30/8/90; GG, 30/8/90, note on boundaries; GG to Lima, 6/9/90, instruçoes; and Lima, Zumbo, to GG, 20/9/90).
13 GG to Min., 23/8/90, 2/171, ibid.; M. C. de Carvalho, Moçambique, to Min., 31/8/90, AHU, Moç., 2 Rep. Caixa 8.
14 Fremantle to Adm., 25/9/90, CP 6069, p. 219, and 29/9/90, tel., ibid., p. 163; H. A. Caldas to M. de Carvalho, 29/9/90, Nec., SPZ 5; N. M. de F. Cabral de Camara to GG, 2/10/90, ibid.; GG to Min., 6/10/90, 2/61, AHU, Moç., 2 Rep., Caixa 7; Fremantle to Adm., 6/10/90, with enclosures, CP 6069, pp. 237-8; GG to Ennes, 15/10/90, tel., *Neg.*, IV, pp. 6-7; Lt.-Cmdr. Floyd to Adm., 12/10/90, tel., CP 6069, p. 135; Lt. Cmdr. Brown to Fremantle, 10/90, with various reports, pp. 325-35.

But opposition remained vociferous in Portugal, where the ministerial crisis continued. Only on 14 October did a new Prime Minister, General Chrysostomo de Abreu, succeed in forming a ministry. Barboza du Bocage was talked into becoming the new Minister for External Affairs. He told Petre that it was impossible for the new cabinet to persuade the Cortes to approve of the treaty in its existing form: this was a case of *force majeure;* and the session of the Cortes, convened on 15 September for a month, would end on 15 October. He hoped that the British Government would agree to modifications to the treaty, when the Cortes would be re-convened. Petre warned Bocage that if the session ended without the treaty being ratified the British Government would regard itself as being released from the obligations of the treaty.[15] This caused dismay, because, to add to the excitement caused by news of the departure of the stern-wheelers, had come an urgent telegram from Moçambique reporting an invasion of the district of Manica by a BSAC force; several Lisbon newspapers in fact urged the Government to obtain ratification of the treaty without delay, else Portugal might lose the whole of the province of Moçambique.[16]

Rhodes would happily have grabbed most of Moçambique. On 27 June the BSAC's Pioneer Column had crossed the Bechuanaland border and headed northwards for Mashonaland. On 11 September the Column camped under Harari hill, and Fort Salisbury came into being.[17] A few days later the BSAC's Kimberley office cabled London a message from Rhodes protesting against the treaty with Portugal: "We are in peaceable occupation of Mashonaland and lose by Treaty large portion of our territories, while gaining absolutely no advantage." He added jubilantly that the BSAC had occupied "probably the richest goldfield in the world."[18]

The only proved gold-fields at this time were in Manica. Extracts from Jeffrey's letters of 1888 and 1889 had appeared in *South Africa*, and samples of gold-bearing quartz had been exhibited at the Crystal Palace in 1890.[19] Rhodes gave A. R. Colquhoun, designated Administrator of Mashonaland, instructions to leave the Column as soon as it had passed beyond the danger of attack by Lobengula, and strike off at a tangent for Manica, there to make a treaty with Umtasa. Colquhoun was accompanied by Selous, and Jameson who was virtually Rhodes's unofficial representative, his secretary, and an escort of troopers. Jameson, heavily thrown from his horse, had to be left at a kraal until well enough to be taken to Fort Salisbury. He sent a letter after Colquhoun, urging him to obtain the most extensive territorial limits that Umtasa would

15 Petre to Salisbury, 14/10/90, tel. 67 Af., CP 6069, p. 182; and 14/10/90, 242 Af., ibid., pp. 188–9; and 20/10/90, tel. 70 Af., ibid., p. 191; and 21/10/90, 245 Af., ibid., pp. 214–5.
16 Petre to Salisbury, 15/10/90, 243 Af., CP 6069, p. 190.
17 Hole, p. 146.
18 BSAC, Kimberley, to BSAC, London, 17/9/90, tel., CP 6069, p. 116; and 22/9/90, ibid., p. 186.
19 J. Jeffreys to Salisbury, 4/12/90, CP 6069, p. 295; R. Clement to Salisbury, 1/1/91, ibid., p. 8 A–C.

acknowledge—"to the sea if possible."[20] The remainder of the party crossed the Sabi and the Odzi, and climbed up to Umtasa's. Colquhoun described the kraal, which was at an altitude of 4,300 feet, as being "situated at the head of what is really a pass, completely concealed from below in mountain fastnesses and lying under a sheer massive granite ridge of rock another five or six hundred feet high—a position, at all events in Kafir warfare, absolutely impregnable." On 14 September Colquhoun and Selous entered Umtasa's kraal and proposed a treaty which Umtasa agreed to sign out of fear of Gouveia, António de Sousa. Umtasa duly set his mark to a paper which described him as "Paramount Chief or King of the Manica nation." He granted the BSAC "absolute and entire perpetual right and power" to prospect for and exploit metals and minerals; to carry out any public works including harbour installations; to engage in commerce and financial transactions; to manufacture and import arms and ammunition; and "to do all such things as are incidental or conducive to the exercise, attainment or protection of all or any of the rights, powers and concessions hereby granted." Umtasa further agreed to bind himself and his successors

> not to enter into any treaty or alliance with any other person, company, or State, or to grant any concessions of land without the consent of the company in writing, it being understood that this covenant shall be considered in the light of a treaty, or alliance made between the said nation and the Government of Her Britannic Majesty Queen Victoria.

In return the company undertook to protect the king and nation from outside interference or attacks, and to maintain the king and his lawful successors in power and authority; it would maintain a resident with a suitable retinue and escort of police for the maintenance of law and order; and it undertook to pay the chief and his successors in perpetuity £100 a year, or the equivalent "in trading goods as on over leaf at the option of the King", the equivalent being presumably in guns and ammunition.[21]

Colquhoun and his party moved to a valley near the Umtali River where there was better grazing. Immediately Umtasa began to have qualms about his action. Had he perhaps backed the wrong horse? Could the British really prevent the Portuguese from taking retaliatory measures?[22] The trimmer sent messengers to Macequece to complain that he had been forced to sign the treaty by threats.

Colquhoun sent Selous, his secretary, and the police officer to Macequece, ostensibly to buy provisions and trade-goods, but also to reconnoitre Portuguese strength. They followed the Umtali valley, and visited the De Kergarion and

---

20 A. R. Colquhoun, *Dan to Beersheba* (London, 1908), pp. 279–80; Lockhart, *Rhodes*, p. 225.
21 A. R. Colquhoun, Manica country, to BSAC, 21/9/90, CP 6086, pp. 22–8, and C 6495, pp. 24–8; Treaty, CP 6086, pp. 31–2 and C 6495, pp. 28–9; Colquhoun, *Dan to Beersheba*, pp. 276–9; L. Cripps, 'The Umtasa Treaty', *NADA*, 1933, pp. 91–5; Warhurst, pp. 14–7.
22 Hole, p. 164; Warhurst, p. 18.

Jeffreys mines worked by Englishmen who frankly admitted that they owed their rights to the Portuguese Government, through concessions from the Moçambique Company. Selous reported that this valley, which was pitted with ancient workings, was one of the richest gold-bearing districts in Manica. They crossed the escarpment, and reached Dambarare, a mining camp of the Moçambique Company, where they were hospitably entertained by De Llamby, a French engineer. The next day they were approaching Macequece, by way of the Revue, when they met a party bearing a message to Colquhoun from Rezende, Superintendent of Native Affairs and Manica manager of the Moçambique Company. Rezende received them with frigid courtesy; he protested against the invasion of Manica by armed force; he pointed out that Umtasa was not a paramount chief, but a subject of Gungunhana; and not even Gungunhana was at liberty to make a treaty without the sanction of the Portuguese authorities. Two English prospectors, working also for the Moçambique Company, entertained the party, and on their advice it followed an alternative and quicker route which brought it to Colquhoun's camp before Rezende's mission.[23]

This mission consisted of Captain A. de Bettencourt and G. A. de Orey, who presented a document, signed by themselves and Rezende, and bearing the marks of Umtasa's father and another induna of the tribe, formally protesting against the entry of the BSAC's armed force in territory long recognized as Portuguese, and against the exaction of a treaty, by force, from Umtasa. Colquhoun denied that force or menace had been used to obtain the treaty which, he insisted, was perfectly valid; and he warned against any steps the Portuguese might take to upset the treaty.[24]

Colquhoun had been instructed also to make treaties with other chiefs on the eastern and southern borders of Mashonaland, and in Quiteve, to the east of Umtasa. But he had run out of rifles and other goods for presents, and so thought it pointless to continue. He sent a message for a further supply of these to reach him at a certain rendezvous, and went to take his leave of Umtasa, who was terrified lest Rezende visit him; Colquhoun left a trooper and an interpreter at his kraal. The arms did not reach the rendezvous, so he left Selous to make treaties with chiefs on the Mashonaland marches, most of whom were relieved to have protection against Gouveia, and only Mtoko remained independent for a while. Colquhoun proceeded to Fort Charter where, on 4 October, he received word of the treaty of 20 August. A telegram from the BSAC instructed its officials to obtain mineral concessions between the Sabi and 33° east; that is in the Portuguese zone. Colquhoun was able to claim that this had been largely done; and one of the results of his treaty with Umtasa, he pointed out to his directors, was that it was a powerful lever towards gaining

23 Colquhoun, 21/9/90, op. cit.; F. C. Selous to Colquhoun, Note regarding visit to Massi-Kesse, 19/9/90, CP 6086, pp. 28–30; F. C. Selous, *Travel and adventure in South-East Africa* (London, 1893), pp. 384–5.
24 Protesto, 16/9/90, by João de Rezende etc., *Neg.*, iv, p. 31–2; CP 6086 p. 32. Colquhoun to Rezende, 18/9/90, C 6495, p. 29, CP 6086, p. 33.

access to the sea, though he had been disappointed to find that Umtasa's authority did not extend east of Macequece.[25]

Jameson and Frank Johnson reconnoitred the route to the sea. Umtasa refused to help them, but Englishmen working for the Moçambique Company found carriers for them. Thirty miles short of the Pungue they sent back their horses because of tsetse fly. They launched their collapsible boat 12 miles above Sarmento, but had to do more dragging than rowing until they reached that Portuguese station. At Beira they connected—just—with a small steamer which the BSAC had sent to pick them up. They reported, rather over-optimistically, that this was a perfectly practicable route to the interior, and Johnson began at once to make plans for a coach-service from Beira to Manica, ignoring alike, as has been remarked, both tsetse fly and Portuguese.[26]

Rhodes was delighted when the Cortes rose without ratifying the treaty of 20 August. He promptly gave instructions for Manica to be effectually occupied.[27] His agents were already doing their dishonest best to anticipate his desires. Trevor, the trooper left at Umtasa's kraal, describing himself as Acting Resident, on 9 October sent out a circular letter, on Colquhoun's directions, to all prospectors on the Umtali and Revue gold-fields, informing them "an Anglo-Portuguese arrangement has been signed, which brings all this portion of south-east Africa including all the Manica country for a considerable distance east of Macequece, under British influence."[28] Colquhoun ordered Captain P. W. Forbes, supported by a detachment of police, to assume command and direct affairs in Manica. "You will occupy as much of Manica as possible under the treaty executed by me on 14 September and you will occupy as much of the Buzi River as possible, after treaties have been executed with chiefs." As for the Portuguese, if Andrada with an armed force were to enter Manica territory and "use force or menace directly or indirectly" against Umtasa, Forbes was to refer him to Colquhoun's letter to Rezende and request him to evacuate Manica territory. "If force is directly used against Umtasa you are empowered to occupy Macequece and any other place in Manica territory which may seem to you important to occupy." Colquhoun directed prospectors to the area, while to assist Forbes on the political front Colquhoun attached Victor Morier, son of the one-time minister, to his force.[29]

In the meanwhile, Andrada, Administrator of the Moçambique Company, had returned to south-east Africa. He was at Moçambique when particulars of the treaty of 20 August 1890 were cabled him, and he was forbidden to cross the line laid down. At Neves Ferreira, on 6 October, he learnt from Kergarion of the BSAC penetration. On 15 October he rendezvoused at Chimoio with António de Sousa, where he received a letter from Rezende confirming the

25 Colquhoun, 21/9/90, op. cit.; and Colquhoun, Fort Salisbury, to BSAC, 11/10/90, CP 6086, pp. 33–5.
26 Jameson, Kimberley, to Harris, 17/11/90, CP 6069, p. 341; Lockhart, pp. 225–7.
27 Cawston to FO, 7/12/90, CP 6069, p. 305.
28 T. Trevor, 9/10/90, CP 6086, pp. 124–5.
29 Colquhoun to Capt. Forbes, 31/10/90, CP 6086, p. 42.

state of affairs. He encountered Jameson and Johnson, and facilitated their journey to the coast. On 19 October he reached Macequece. He sent a message to Umtasa, who delivered three head of cattle to him by way of welcome and peace-offering. But he was in no hurry to call on Umtasa, and for some days he visited the company's stations. Returning from one such excursion he found a police officer awaiting him, with a letter from Forbes, addressed to "General Paiva d'Andrada, Commander-in-Chief of the Portuguese Forces in Oriental Africa." This letter charged him with invading Manica, which was in BSAC territory, threatening Chief Umtasa, and being about to surround the country with his army. The police officer himself was ashamed of the letter, and admitted that his superiors must have been completely ignorant of the actual situation in Manica. Andrada refused to reply to so ridiculous a communication. He pointed out that he could easily have come with an army; but he was accompanied only by carriers and *machila*-bearers, each of whom naturally carried his own fire-arm; and each sepoy had been issued with only five charges of powder.

Andrada sent António de Sousa to make contact with Umtasa. Sousa set off, accompanied by a female companion and her maids, proof that this was no punitive expedition. Umtasa received him cordially and presented him with a large tusk. The chief admitted that the emissaries of the BSAC had presented him with a revolver and thirteen rifles and ammunition, but he denied that he had signed his mark to any paper. Andrada and Rezende meanwhile completed their business, after which Andrada reconnoitred a route for a railway over the escarpment. On the escarpment he received a letter from Forbes warning him not to see Umtasa, and a letter from Sousa, reporting that he had been instructed to leave Umtasa's kraal; Sousa had replied that he was on Portuguese territory, within the kraal of a chief with whom he was on the best of terms, and he would take no notice of whatever might be said to him by a foreigner. Andrada inspected the mining operations in the Umtali valley, and asked representatives of the sub-concessionaires to meet him at Umtasa's kraal. These foregathered on 14 November. The next day Andrada rehoisted the Portuguese flag, where he had raised it two years before; Umtasa declared that the land belonged to him, Umtasa, and the King of Portugal. Immediately after the ceremony Andrada entered the chief's hut. Hearing sounds of commotion, he emerged, to be promptly arrested by troopers of the BSAC. He and António de Sousa were taken to Fort Salisbury, and then sent to the Cape. They remained prisoners until, leaving Tuli, they met Jameson, who ordered their release, since their illegal arrest was causing embarrassment to the High Commissioner. On 17 November Forbes left Trevor and five troopers at Umtasa's kraal, and with the rest of the force at his disposal he galloped for Macequece. He released Rezende and Llamby there, and continued towards the sea, his argument being, "From what I can hear the Gorongosa province extends right down to the sea, and as Gouveia has chosen to carry arms into our territory I think we ought to retaliate." When the party had covered 50 miles a messenger reached it with orders from Colquhoun to withdraw. But the company continued to occupy

Macequece,[30] and to make treaties with petty chiefs in the Pungue and Buzi valleys.

Andrada, as soon as he reached Cape Town, detailed to the Portuguese consul the injustices done to him and to Portugal. The consul confirmed and amplified an earlier protest to the High Commissioner that the BSAC had invaded country which, in the convention of 20 August, had been recognized as under the absolute dominion of Portugal; the agents of the BSAC, to give a tint of legality to this invasion, had extorted a treaty from Umtasa, who was not an independent chief but a subject of Gungunhana, who was a vassal of Portugal, and was therefore incapable of assenting to a treaty, and on 14 September the convention of 20 August was still in force; agents of the BSAC then in conspiracy with Umtasa treasonably arrested, in Portuguese territory, Portuguese subjects engaged in peaceful pursuits, and continued their invasion by occupying Macequece and taking possession of buildings belonging to the Moçambique Company.[31]

The incident at Umtasa's kraal occurred the day after the signature of a temporary agreement between Portugal and Britain. On 15 October the Cortes had met to hear a ministerial declaration to the effect that the Government, aware of the national sentiment, would not recommend ratification of the treaty of 20 August, but would seek modifications which would safeguard national dignity and interests. Bocage telegraphed to Portuguese legations instructing the ministers to ask the governments to which they were accredited to bring pressure to bear on the British Government to accept those modifications when the Cortes would be reconvened. Soveral, chargé in London, was to see that the British Government took no step before it had received the proposed modifications, which would alter clauses which were obscure or injurious to Portuguese commerce, and others which were irritating to national sentiment. For the sake of conciliation Portugal wanted an explanation of the entrance of the river gun-boats to the Zambezi, and the invasion of the district of Manica by agents of the BSAC. Bocage added for Soveral's very confidential guidance two answers which would satisfy the Portuguese Government, and which he could suggest to the British Government: that there was no offensive intent in sending the gun-boats up the river, simply the impossibility of further postponing what had been often announced; and that the British Government was not responsible for the invasion of Manica, but would undertake to maintain the *status quo* until it received Portugal's proposed modifications.[32]

Replies from the legations brought Bocage little comfort. The German Secretary for Foreign Affairs would not go further than expressing sympathy. The Italian minister declared that the sooner a new negotiation was set on foot the sooner would British opposition be stilled. The Austro-Hungarian Minister

---

30 Andrada, Cape Town, to Carvalho, 30/12/90, C 6495, pp. 74–88; BSAC Kimberley, to Cape Government, 9/1/91, CP 6086, p. 137.

31 Carvalho to Loch, 10/1/91, C 6495, pp. 70–4; Carvalho to Min., 14/1/91, 2A, Nec., SPZ 5.

32 Bocage, 16/10/90, circular tel., *Neg.*, iv, p. 7; Bocage to Soveral, 17/10/90, tel., Nec., SPZ 4, extr. only in *Neg.*, iv, pp. 7–8.

of Foreign Affairs advised the maximum prudence in the presentation of the modifications: the British Government, having come to an agreement, could not withdraw; and he considered that most of the clamour against the treaty in Portugal was fictitious. The Russian foreign minister recalled that a previous attempt to bring pressure to bear on Britain had had no response. The Netherlands foreign minister declared frankly that until 20 August European opinion had been in Portugal's favour; but the situation had since deteriorated. The American Secretary of State was not prepared to ask Britain for anything; the Behring Sea and Venezuela were already questions enough. Only a brush-off could have been anticipated from the Belgian Government. The Vatican refused to put the Holy Father to the indignity of a rebuff from a Protestant Government. Only the French Government undertook to make the approach requested.[33] Reports moreover followed of further penetration into Portuguese territory by the BSAC, towards Beira, and to Gungunhana's head kraal. And when the Portuguese Chargé d'Affaires in London intimated to Salisbury the Portuguese Government's desire for modifications, Salisbury declared bluntly that since the Portuguese Government had failed to honour its obligation to proceed to ratification he regarded the treaty as abandoned, and neither government was bound by it. Soveral asked whether the British Government would be willing to embark on fresh negotiations, in Lisbon, for a new treaty. Salisbury agreed to negotiations in either Lisbon or London, but he warned Soveral that alternative proposals would not be confined to one side; the situation had changed since 20 August.[34]

The Portuguese Government continued to maintain that it had not abandoned the treaty.[35] But new negotiations were essential, and these were likely to be protracted—and every day more Portuguese territory was being invaded. Something had to be done, and done urgently. The Portuguese Government, whilst in no way admitting that the treaty of 20 August had been abandoned, proposed a *modus vivendi* covering the most pressing matters. The Portuguese Government was prepared to decree at once the freedom of navigation of the Zambezi and Shire. It was prepared to permit and facilitate transit over the waterways of the Zambezi, Shire and Pungue, and over landways where those rivers were not navigable. It was prepared to permit and facilitate communications between the Portuguese ports on the coast and the British sphere of action in the interior especially regarding postal, telegraphic and transport services. In return it asked for maintenance of the territorial *status quo* laid down in the treaty of 20 August during the new negotiation and until the new treaty had been ratified. Soveral received this proposal on 23 October, but Salisbury was

33 Penafiel, Berlin, to Min., 16/10/90, tel., Nec., SPZ 4; Pindella, Hague, to Min., 17/10/90, tel., ibid., and 20/10/90, A10, ibid.; Carvalho, Rome, to Min., 17/10/90, ibid.; Ferrão, Vienna, to Min., tel., 18/10/90, and 7, ibid.; Prego, St Petersburg, to Min., 18/10/90, 11, ibid.; Rosa, Washington, to Min., 19/10/90, tel., and 24/10/90, 4A ibid.; Macedo, Brussels, to Min., 24/10/90, tel., ibid., Silva, Rome, to Min., 18/10/90, and 24/10/90, ibid.; Dantas, Paris to Min., 19/10/90, tel., and 20/10/90, ibid.
34 Bocage to Soveral, 19/10/90, tel., *Neg.*, iv, p. 8; Salisbury to Petre, 20/10/90, tel. 77 and 79 Af., CP 6069, p. 191; Soveral to Min., 22/10/90, tel., Nec., SPZ 4, extr. in *Neg.*, iv, p. 9, and 21/10/90, ibid., and *Neg.*, iv, pp. 8–9.
35 Petre to Salisbury, 22/10/90, tel. 71 Af., CP 6069, p. 193.

out of town.[36] Bocage used the interval once again to telegraph Portuguese legations informing the ministers of the projected *modus vivendi* and instructing them to ask the governments to bring pressure to bear on the British Government to accept the Portuguese proposal. The Netherlands Government declined, but all the other powers of Europe agreed, laying emphasis on the danger of anarchy and republicanism in Portugal. Particularly massive was the pressure of the German Government. Even the Belgian Government, greatly astonished at such a request coming from her competitor for Muato Yanvo, complied; and Leopold generously offered to cede to Britain some of this territory in dispute between Portugal and the Congo so that Britain might cede it to Portugal as compensation for territorial sacrifices elsewhere, an offer that Salisbury diplomatically rejected.[37]

Soveral saw Salisbury on 27 October. Salisbury approved the idea of a *modus vivendi*, but thought that it should be confined to the area of the Ruo where Coutinho was creating difficulties. He objected to maintaining the *status quo* as in the treaty of 20 August for that had been abandoned and should not be referred to. Soveral reminded him that the BSAC had not waited for the session of the Cortes to end before invading territory awarded to Portugal by the treaty; what would they not do if they had no treaty at all in the background?[38] Soveral remarked to his minister that the delay did not surprise him in view of the hostility of the BSAC and the press; he gathered that the Company's objective was the sea and that if it could obtain a port it would be reasonable on other points; he warned Bocage that Salisbury would not be able to evict the Company from districts it had already occupied; and he advised Bocage that it was essential to obtain an answer before the Commons met in two weeks' time. Bocage agitatedly telegraphed to all the Portuguese legations in Europe yet again.[39] But that day a note reached Soveral from Salisbury: the British Government agreed to the first three bases; but for the territorial clause it suggested an alternative wording:

> The territorial limits indicated in the convention of the 20th of August will be recognised so far, that from this date to the termination of the present agreement, neither power will make treaties, accept protectorates or exercise any act of sovereignty, within the spheres of influence so assigned

36 [Bocage] Projects de *modus-vivendi*, 22/10/90, Nec., SPZ 4 Bocage to Soveral, 23/10/90, tel., *Neg.* iv, p. 10; and 24/10/90, ibid., pp. 11–14; Soveral to Min., 24/10/90, tel, SPZ 4.
37 Bocage, circular tel., 23/10/90, *Neg.* iv, pp. 10–11; Vasconcellos, Rome, to Min., 25/10/90, 16A, Nec., SPZ 4; Penafiel to Min., 25/10/90, A 54, ibid., and 29/10/90, tel., ibid.; Dantas to Min., 26/10/90, ibid.; Ferrão to Min., 28/10/90, tel., ibid.; Pindella to Min., 28/10/90, A 11 ibid.; Prego to Min., 29/10/90, A 10, and 5/11/90, tel., ibid.; Soveral to Min., 29/10/90, tel, do., 4/11/90, ibid.; Vivian, Brussels, to Salisbury, 25/10/90, 25 Af., PRO, FO 179/280, and CP 6069, p. 222; Salisbury to Vivian, 21/10/90, 255 Af., ibid., p. 192; Malet, Berlin, to Salisbury, 25/10/90, 13 Af., ibid., p. 221 reporting that Penafiel had assured him that if Britain would make apparent concessions her attitude would tide Portugal over the crisis and Britain would eventually obtain what she wanted; Malet commented that Penafiel was overwelmingly confident in his own powers and distrustful of Soveral. Salisbury to Petre, 5/11/90, 200 Af., CP 6069, p. 230.
38 Soveral to Min., 27 and 28/10/90, tels, Nec., SPZ 4 and extr. *Neg.* iv, pp. 14–5; Soveral to Salisbury, 28/10/90, ibid., and pp. 17–8, PRO, FO 179/280, CP 6069, p. 218.
39 Soveral to Min., 5/11/90, tel., *Neg.* iv, p. 15; Min., 6/11/90, circ. tel., ibid., p. 15.

to the other. But neither power will thereby be held to prejudge any question whatever which may arise as to the said territorial limits in the course of the ulterior negotiations.

Salisbury suggested a six months' term.[40] Soveral immediately called at the Foreign Office; Salisbury was away, but Currie assured Soveral that the *status quo* of 20 August was conceded Portugal, and informed him that Salisbury had already instructed the BSAC that he would not recognize any treaty made with any chief on the Portuguese side of this line that involved sovereignty; the Company might acquire only mineral concessions.[41] The Portuguese Government promptly accepted Salisbury's proposal[42] and then in an excess of satisfaction leaked the information to the press. The London newspapers, quoting these reports, declared that it would be monstrous if the line of 20 August were imposed and Salisbury was roundly assailed.[43] The BSAC declared that the Portuguese had no rights in Manica, and that it appeared to the Company, "the only safe course in dealing with the partition of Africa is to follow the policy indicated by you, sovereignty or protection to fall to the Power proving bona fide present occupation." Salisbury dryly remarked that he did not regard a treaty made with a chief as constituting bona fide occupation: such a policy could be interpreted in a manner which would be much more favourable to the pretensions of Portugal than of Britain.[44] But those pressures told on Salisbury, whose secretary intimated to Soveral that in his revised wording "this date" (which occurred immediately after reference to 20 August) referred not to August 20 but to the date of the *modus vivendi*. Soveral, as soon as he received this note, called at the Foreign Office. Salisbury was out of town, but Currie made light of the alteration, and declared that the British Government would not acknowledge any act of sovereignty committed on the Portuguese side of the line of 20 August. The Portuguese Government accepted the amendment, and arrangements were made for the agreement to be signed on 12 November. The Foreign Office asked for a postponement, and it was only on 14 November that the *modus vivendi* was duly signed; the final paragraph declared firmly that the agreement came into operation from the date of its signature.[45]

Negotiations for the new treaty, it was arranged, would take place in Lisbon. The Portuguese Government would have to indicate what points in

---

40 Salisbury to Soveral, 4/11/90, *Neg.* iv, p. 18 and p. 19, Alternative fourth article. It is significant that CP 6069, p. 230, and C 6212, p. 28, give the letter but not the enclosure with the wording.
41 Soveral to Min., 6/11/90, tel., Nec., SPZ 4, and extr. *Neg.* iv, p. 15; Soveral added that this was a solution that he had never dared hope for. FO to CO, 28/10/90, CP 6069, p. 216: ". . . HMG wish it to be understood that they cannot undertake to recognize any action by the South African Company within the region which would be Portuguese if the Convention held".
42 Min. to Soveral, 9/11/90, tel., Nec., SPZ 4, *Neg.* iv, p. 17.
43 Soveral to Min., 8/11/90, tel., *Neg.* iv, pp. 16–7.
44 Fife, V-president, BSAC, to Salisbury, 7/11/90, CP 6069, p. 231; FO to BSAC, 7/11/90, ibid., p. 233.
45 Soveral to Min., 11/11/90, tels, Nec., SPZ 4; Min. to Soveral, 11/11/90, tel., ibid. and *Neg.* iv, p. 20; Soveral to Min., 12/11/90, tel., ibid., p. 21; Agreement, ibid., p. 22 and C 6212, p. 29.

the earlier treaty it found unacceptable, and Britain would then present counter-proposals. It seemed to Salisbury that these counter-proposals would be less distasteful to Portugal if they were presented by a third party, and so he asked for the good offices of the Austro-Hungarian Foreign Minister.[46] Soveral conferred with Salisbury the day after the signing of the *modus vivendi*, and found him anxious to begin—and conclude—the negotiation as soon as possible. Britain could not accept a second refusal of ratification, so the treaty would be signed only after it had been approved by the Cortes. Salisbury declared that he could not force British miners to leave Manica; Rhodes might want sovereignty, but the miners wanted only gold; and he suggested to Soveral the advantage of the Moçambique Company and BSAC coming to an accord.[47]

Negotiations between the companies, and between the governments, were complicated initially by receipt in Europe of word of the invasion of Manica by the BSAC. As soon as word of this invasion reached Moçambique and Lisbon the Governor-general protested to the local consul, the Portuguese consul in Cape Town protested to the High Commissioner, and the minister in London protested to Salisbury; renewed protests were made against the arrests at Umtasa's kraal, the lowering of the Portuguese flag, and the hoisting of the British, undoubted acts of sovereignty which infringed the BSAC's royal charter, and broke the *modus vivendi*.[48] Unless the BSAC withdrew from Portuguese territory, Bocage told Soveral, Portugal could not re-open negotiations. But Soveral refused to pass on this threat, declaring that the BSAC had provoked the incident deliberately to excite the Portuguese and lead them to break off the negotiations. He persuaded Bocage that this would be a triumph for Rhodes.[49]

Rhodes was insisting, falsely, that Umtasa's kraal was north of latitude 18° 30′ and in the area falling under British influence—even British maps such as Bartholomew's showed it as south of that line, while Stanford's compiled for Cawston, a director of BSAC, and that of Selous, a servant of that company, showed it as both south of that line and east of the Masheke. The BSAC drew up a memorandum about Portuguese claims to Manica, which contained many

46 Paget, Vienna, to Salisbury, 4/11/90, CP 6069, p. 234; Salisbury to Paget, 14/11/90, 20 Af., ibid., p. 243.
47 Soveral to Bocage, 15/11/90, Nec., SPZ 4, which concludes with an attack on Lisbon newspapers which criticized the *Modus vivendi*, extr. in *Neg.* iv, p. 21.
48 GG to Min., 15/10/90, tel., AHU, Moç, 2 Rep. Caixa 7; Machado to pro-consul, 18/10/90, CP 6069, p. 391; Carvalho to Min., 1/11/90, 21 D, Nec., SPZ 4; and 12/11/90, ibid.; and 29/11/90, *Neg.* iv, pp. 23–4; Carvalho to Loch, 1/12/90, ibid., p. 48; Bocage to Soveral, 30/11/90, ibid., p. 34; Petre to Salisbury, 30/11/90, 165 Af., CP 6069, p. 293; Salisbury to Petre, 1/12/90, ibid., p. 289; Carvalho to Min., 5/12/90, tel., *Neg.* iv, p. 25; Min. to Soveral, 5/12/90, ibid., p. 25; Bocage to Soveral, 6/12/90, ibid., pp. 26–31 and PRO, FO 179/284; and 7/12/90, Nec., SPZ 5, and *Neg.* iv, p. 34; Petre to Salisbury, 7/12/90, tel. 78 Af., CP 6069, p. 304; Salisbury to Petre, 9/12/90, 214 Af., ibid., p. 305; Soveral to Bocage, 10/12/90, *Neg.* iv, p. 36; Carvalho to Min., 10/12/90, 27A, Nec., SPZ 5; and 12/12/90, tel., *Neg.* iv, p. 39; Soveral to Min., 16/12/90, ibid., p. 40; Bocage to Soveral, 16/12/90, ibid., p. 41; Soveral to Min., 17/12/90, ibid., p. 41; GG to Min., 17/12/90, ibid., pp. 43–4; Carvalho to Loch, 10/1/91, CP 6086, pp. 43–50; Petre to Bocage, 27/1/91, *Neg.* iv, pp. 62–3; Soveral to Salisbury, 29/1/90, CP 6086, p. 101, *Neg.* iv, p. 66 and memo., pp. 66–7; Soveral to Salisbury, 4/2/91, ibid., p. 69.
49 Bocage to Soveral 11/12/90, *Neg.* iv, p. 38; Soveral to Min., 12/12/90, tels, Nec., SPZ 5; Bocage to Soveral, 13/12/90, ibid.; Soveral to Bocage, 13 and 16/12/90, ibid.

misstatements, for example it declared that the Portuguese had never climbed the Manica escarpment, and Loch, the High Commissioner, instigated by Rhodes, reported to Whitehall that it was the Portuguese who were the aggressors and recommended the despatch of warships to Lourenço Marques and the Pungue.[50] In these circumstances and since directors of the BSAC had ready access to him, it was natural for Salisbury's views to reflect those of the Company. He refused to admit that Umtasa was a vassal of Gungunhana. He accepted that Umtasa's kraal was on the British side of the line, and declared that Andrada had crossed British territory and torn down the British flag; he refused to give any undertaking that even if Umtasa's kraal were proved to be in Portuguese territory the BSAC would be forced to vacate it because the treaty with Umtasa had been signed before the *modus vivendi*. He did however have the honesty to admit that Macequece was undoubtedly Portuguese and that he would compel the Company to evacuate that place if it were still held.[51] The Company's Board in London ordered the evacuation of Macequece and while undertaking to observe the *modus vivendi* instructed its servants to withdraw only to the watershed. But the Company's agents in South Africa, who were busy making treaties with chiefs between Manica and the sea in the area between the Buzi and the Pungue Rivers, buying their allegiance in return for presents of rifles, had no intention of evacuating Macequece. When Captain Bettencourt returned to Macequece at the end of December as commissioner for Manica and personal representative of the Governor-general, he found the place occupied by the Company and the British flag flying; he was compelled to return to Beira. When the Secretary to the Governor in Manica, Lieutenant Freire, carrying a letter from the consul in Moçambique instructing British subjects to observe the *modus vivendi*, arrived in Macequece he found the place still occupied by the Company, and the British flag still flying; thirty mounted men made him prisoner. When Portugal complained of the arrest of Freire the BSAC declared the allegation "absurdly false" and affirmed that Macequece had not been occupied by the Company. But still the occupation continued.[52]

The British sub-concessionaires of the Moçambique Company protested against this continued occupation. The Ophir Concessions Company (Ltd), and its two sub-companies, the Sabi Ophir and the Manica Ophir Mining Companies, with a combined capital of £480,000, were the first to protest to

50 Loch to Knutsford, 4/12/90, CP 6069, p. 300; Bower to Carvalho, 6/12/90, CP 6086, pp. 62–3; Cawston to FO, 7/12/90, CP 6069, p. 305; BSAC to FO, 10/12/90, ibid., p. 308A, Memo. of information collected by the Company's representatives in South Africa, rec. by FO 13/12/90, ibid., pp. 316–7; Petre to Salisbury, 16/12/90, 283 Af., ibid., p. 340; Min. to Soveral, 22/12/90, *Neg.* iv, p. 45; and ibid., Nec. SPZ 5; Loch to Knutsford, 5/1/90, CP 6086, p. 115.
51 Salisbury to Petre, 10/12/90, 215 Af., CP 6069, p. 308; and 17/12/90, 218, Af., ibid., p. 327; Salisbury to Soveral, 5/2/91. CP 6086, p. 132; Salisbury to Petre, 6/2/91, ibid., p. 132.
52 BSAC London tels to Kimberley, 19/12/90, CP 6069, p. 353. BSAC Kimberley to Cape Government, 9/1/91, CP 6086, p. 137; Petre to Salisbury, 14/2/91, 13 Af. tel, ibid., p. 177; BSAC Kimberley to London, 18/2/91, ibid., p. 186; Petre to Salisbury, 25/2/91, ibid., p. 206; Bocage to Petre, 27/2/91, ibid., pp. 226–8; *O Dia* 30/3/91, CP 6227, p. 29; Bocage to Petre, 11/4/91, ibid., pp. 108–9. The subject is exhaustively treated by Warhurst, pp. 53–5.

Salisbury that the BSAC usurpation was prejudicing the rights of 2,000 British shareholders, whose companies had valid contracts with the Moçambique Company, which was operating in the district of Manica, the capital of which had been Portuguese for generations, in the lands of Umtasa, who was a vassal of Gungunhana, friend, ally and tributary of Portugal.[53] The Zambezi Concessions and the Zambezi Gaza companies protested,[54] and so too did the East African Exploration and Trading Syndicate.[55] Even Lord Castletown, the chairman of the Delagoa Bay and East African Railway, who had always been in the forefront of those who protested to the Foreign Office against Portuguese illegalities, now protested most strongly against Britain taking advantage of her strength to impose her will on a small country which on this occasion was undoubtedly in the right.[56] R. Clement, the representative of a Barberton syndicate, of a Madeira syndicate (mainly British owned) and of the Umsilalana concession, protested; he added that he personally had told two of the directors of the BSAC of the gold values being obtained in Manica, and he had published extracts of Jeffrey's letters in *South Africa*, which had largely directed the attention of the BSAC to those parts.[57] Representatives of the various companies holding sub-concessions from the Moçambique Company met in London; together, they represented a capital of some one million pounds. They protested to the Foreign Office against the "unlawful, high-handed and detrimental actions" of the agents of the BSAC in raiding into Manica country, which was the territory of Portugal, a friendly power, in peaceful occupation of the district.[58] The representatives were concerned not only on principle, but because of the fact that whilst the Ophir concessions had to pay the Moçambique Company only 10 per cent net royalty, and the other companies 20 per cent, the BSAC demanded 50 per cent of its concessionaires.[59] When newspapers reported that the British Government was going to allow the BSAC to remain in possession of Manica, Clement reiterated the justice of Portugal's case: "I cannot think that so manifest a right should be sacrificed to unscrupulous and brutal might."[60]

Negotiations for a new treaty between Portugal and Britain were overshadowed by the Manica question. Several felt that any agreement must acknowledge Portuguese sovereignty over Manica and the rights of the British sub-concessionaires of the Moçambique Company; and it should provide for construction by the Moçambique Company of the railway line from the sea to the Portuguese border. Several, on Lord Rothschild's initiative, suggested to Cawston that Cawston proceed to Paris and confer with a director of the Moçambique Company to bring about an agreement between the companies: his Government would give up many mining rights in return for acknowledgment

53 Major-General N. T. Parsons to Salisbury, 2/12/90, CP 6069, p. 293.
54 Zambezi Concession Company, to Salisbury, 4/12/90, CP 6069, p. 295.
55 10/12/90, CP 6069, p. 309.
56 Castletown to Salisbury, 10/12/90, CP 6069, p. 307; Salisbury in his reply (12/12/90) quoted Rhodes's arguments against Portugal (ibid., p. 315).
57 R. Clement to Salisbury, 1/1/91, CP 6086, p. 8 A–C and Nec., SPZ 5.
58 Memorial of meeting 28/1/91, CP 6086, pp. 126–7.
59 Ophir Concessions to Salisbury, 21/1/91, CP 6086, pp. 75–6.
60 R. Clement to Salisbury, 2/91, ibid., p. 195.

of the boundary of 20 August, and the removal of three objectionable clauses from that treaty. He suggested that the two companies divide the mining concessions in Manica between them; the Moçambique Company would undertake to construct the railway from the Pungue to the British sphere; and the Governor-general of Moçambique would immediately lease land at the mouth of the Chinde to the British Company. Since no territorial adjustments were involved it would be possible, once the companies had come to agreement, to sign a treaty almost immediately.[61]

In Paris Cawston met Bartissol, a member of the French Chamber of Deputies, who had for long been connected with Portugal and had acquired a considerable fortune there. Cawston spoke in "contemptuous and overbearing terms" of the Moçambique Company and its resources, declaring that there was nothing, not even the British Government, which could prevent the BSAC from taking possession of Manica and in fact all the country to the coast. Bartissol assured Cawston he had promise of more substantial funds for the Moçambique Company; and if the Portuguese Government proved incompetent to protect the company he would turn to the French Government. He then put forward a specific scheme for a Franco-Portuguese company which would acquire all the rights possessed by the Moçambique Company, including its concessions and its *prazos*. The Moçambique Company would undertake to negotiate with the Portuguese Government for an extension of its field of operations to cover all territory between the Sabi and the Zambezi. The share capital would be held on account of BSAC friends in Paris, who would nominate the directors. The head office of the new company would be initially in Paris, but when public opinion in Portugal had quietened down it would be transferred to London. The arrangement, whilst respecting Portuguese national pride, would have resulted in the takeover of the Moçambique Company by the BSAC.[62]

Bartissol and his associates persuaded the Portuguese Government to rewrite the Moçambique Company's charter to further this arrangement, and the Government agreed to the BSAC being an indirect shareholder. He arranged to meet Cawston in Paris on 15 December 1890 to discuss final arrangements. But Cawston did not keep the rendezvous: Rhodes had decided to come to England, and the board of the BSAC would take no decision pending his arrival.[63] Rhodes also requested the British Government not to come to any settlement with Portugal until he had reached London; he made no secret of his intention to debar the Portuguese from all the high lands.[64]

The Portuguese Government had not put forward its proposals for a new

61 Soveral to Min., 27/11/90 tel, Nec., SPZ 6; Salisbury to Petre, 1/12/90, Very Confid., CP 6069, p. 289; G. Cawston to Salisbury, 13/3/91, CP 6086, pp. 264–7.
62 Petre to Salisbury, 6/12/90, PRO, FO 179/283, CP 6069, p. 310; Bartissol, memo., [11/89] CP 6086, p. 268; Cawston, 13/3/91, CP 6086, pp. 264–7.
63 Charter, CP 6086, pp. 51–5; Petre to Salisbury, 13/12/90, 83 Af. tel, CP 6069, pp. 336–7; Cawston, 13/3/91, CP 6086, pp. 264–7; Soveral to Bocage, 24/12/90, tel., Nec., SPZ 5; Bocage to Soveral, 25/12/90, tel., ibid.
64 Loch to Knutsford, tel., [17/12/90], rec. FO 18/12/90, CP 6069, p. 338. Carvalho to Min., 13/12/90, 29A, Nec., SP 25. For a survey of the Portuguese attitude at this time see Bocage to Ant. Ennes, 2/12/90, ibid.

treaty pending settlement between the two companies. Salisbury, under pressure, declared that he would not accept the new charter for the Moçambique Company unless Portugal agreed to considerable alterations in the previous treaty to Britain's advantage:

> The Portuguese are living in a fool's paradise if they imagine we are going to take anything less than the Convention of 20 August. We may not require the various stipulations to be in the same proportion. We may take more territory and less communication, or more communication and less territory. But whatever is withdrawn from us in one respect must be supplied in another. If they grant any Charter such as that which they meditate to the Moçambique Company which practically cuts us off from the coast at Pungue, they will have to pay for it by a heavy sacrifice of territory.[65]

Of the seventeen directors of the Moçambique Company, nine were in Lisbon and eight in Paris. Of the Lisbon directors three represented British interests, and the others were light weights. The board in Lisbon delegated financial and administrative control to the board in Paris, where four of the eight directors represented British interests.[66] But despite this Salisbury vigorously assailed the charter and demanded that its signature be postponed until the territorial negotiations had been settled.[67] When Rhodes arrived in England he was emphatic that the only frontier that would suit the company was the line of the escarpment; he was prepared to pay the Moçambique Company a percentage of the profits derived from mines in the Portuguese Company's concession area. Bartissol and one Tiano, representing the BSAC, came to an agreement by which the British Company would have to withdraw to the west of the line of 20 August; and if granted a frontier to the east of that line by negotiations between the two governments, it would pay one-third of the net profits of mines in that area to the Moçambique Company. Further clauses guaranteed the prompt construction of the railway, and the appointment of a British director to the railway board.[68] The board of the BSAC rejected this agreement because many clauses were "of a political nature." A new agreement negotiated between Bartissol and Tiano did not require British withdrawal; the Moçambique Company would receive one-third of the net profits from mines to the east of the line of 20 August, and it and its sub-concessionaires, whose rights in the Revue and Umtali valleys were safeguarded, were granted 1,500 claims in the BSAC area. A Portuguese-French company would be responsible for the construction of the railway, whose directors would be nationals of those two countries in proportion to the amount of capital subscribed.[69] This too the board of the BSAC would not ratify. Two further

65 Salisbury to Petre, 23/12/90, tel., CP 6069, p. 350; and 24/12/90, Cecil, *Salisbury*, IV, pp. 270–1, and Warhurst, p. 68; Petre to Salisbury, 24/12/90, tel. 88 Af., CP 6069, p. 355.
66 C. A. Moreing and F. R. Despard to Salisbury, 28/1/91, CP 6086, pp. 98–9.
67 Petre to Salisbury, 27/12/90, CP 6086, p. 1; Salisbury to Petre, 7/1/91, tel. 2 Af., ibid., 86. pp. 16–17; and 23/1/91, tel. 6 Af., ibid., p. 79.
68 Memo by Bartissol, [2/91]., CP 6086, pp. 269–70, appendix G of Cawston 13/3/91.
69 Memo by Bartissol [2/91]., CP 6086, p. 270, app. H. of Cawston 13/3/91.

directors of the Moçambique Company now arrived in Paris, in the person of Fontes and Pinto Basto, who took over from Bartissol. They demanded that the BSAC withdraw west of the line of 20 August; the Moçambique Company would then make a sub-concession to the BSAC of mineral rights west of the Umtali valley to the line of 20 August on payment of one-third of the net profits. The BSAC broke off the negotiations.[70] In March 1891 both sides approached Sir Donald Currie, and at their request he suggested an accord which respected the mineral rights of the Moçambique Company; if the boundary were to be different from the line of 20 August, the favoured company was to grant one-third of the net revenues to the other; the Moçambique Company would build the Manica railway, its rates not to exceed those obtaining on the Cape railways, nor were transit duties to exceed 3 per cent; definition of the eastern boundary was to be left to the two governments, except that Umtasa was to be acknowledged as within the British sphere, Portugal to be given compensation elsewhere; each company was to subscribe to the other's capital; and if those arrangements were to be agreed to, the BSAC would evacuate Macequece forthwith.[71] After further representations, Currie omitted reference to Umtasa; Macequece was declared to be definitely within the Portuguese sphere, and if representatives of the BSAC were still there they were to evacuate the place.[72] The BSAC required definition of the mining rights, and omission of reference to the right of each company to subscribe to the other's capital, and directors of the two companies signed the agreement.[73] But the BSAC had second thoughts; its lawyer cut Abercorn's signature from the agreement, and terminated the negotiations, to Currie's indignation.[74] The board of the BSAC had been influenced by a cable from Rhodes deploring the negotiations. If they were concluded the company should acquire three-quarters of the capital of the Moçambique Company—provided its charter gave it the coast from the Zambezi to the Limpopo. But "decidedly prefer no settlement." He questioned Portuguese rights; and he had been confidently informed that "Mashonaland and Manica infinitely richer than Witwatersrand. If there is no settlement we shall acquire everything."[75]

In Gazaland an agent of the BSAC, Schulz, had persuaded Gungunhana to come to an agreement in October 1890. In return the BSAC undertook to pay the chief, and his successors, £500 a year "or the equivalent in trading goods,"[76] and to give him a present of 1,000 rifles, and 20,000 cartridges. The BSAC's primary motive was to reach the sea.[77]

The Portuguese resident at Gungunhana's kraal revealed his incapacity to withstand the BSAC pretensions,[78] so Machado, the Governor-general, on receiving reports of Schulz's operations, sent Almeida, the Superintendent-in-

70 Tiano to BSAC, 27/2/91, CP 8086, p. 220; Cawston, 13/3/91.
71 Currie, Memo 1, London, 18/3/91, CP 6086, p. 288.
72 Currie, Memo 2, 19/3/91, CP 6086, pp. 295–6.
73 Currie, Memo, 3, 20/3/91, CP 6086, pp. 302–3.
74 Currie to FO, 9/4/91, CP 6227, p. 49, with enclosures to p. 51.
75 Rhodes to BSAC, 3/4/91, CP 6227, p. 52.
76 Agreement, 4/10/90, CP 6495, pp. 218–9.
77 Warhurst, pp. 83–4, who treats of Gazaland in detail in ch. 3.
78 F. A. M. Geraldez to Int. geral. of Gaza, 25/11/90, AHU, Moç., 1 Rep., Pasta 7.

chief of Native Affairs in Gazaland, on a specific mission to Gungunhana. He was to discover whether the chief had indeed made any concessions of minerals or of land. He was to obtain the chief's approval for the construction of a railway up the valley of the Limpopo to the border of the Transvaal, to navigation of that river, and to the construction of a town on its banks. He was to suggest the establishment of a religious mission close to Zefunha. He was to persuade the chief to permit direct administration by the Portuguese of coastal lands in the district of Sofala, and a transfer of the capital of that district to the mouth of the Sabi. He was to clarify the attitude of Gungunhana to Umtasa, inform him that officials were returning to Manica to prevent further penetration by the British, and seek if possible his assistance. Almeida was also to warn Gungunhana that the British intended to occupy the lands of his brother-in-law, Lobengula, and they would try to drive the Matabele north of the Zambezi. The British would act in an equally hostile manner to Gungunhana and his people if he did not remain loyal to Portugal. If the chief were to become completely submissive the Portuguese Government would pay him a monthly subvention of £30.[79]

On 29 December 1890 Gungunhana held a great indaba, attended by Almeida, four of his residents, three army lieutenants, a Russian and a British subject, and a German and his wife. The chief required Schulz and his party to present themselves. Gungunhana announced that it was his desire to publish to all the foreigners that he, like his father Umzila before him, and his people, were vassals of the King of Portugal, and he had no intention of substituting any other for the Portuguese flag which flew alongside his residence. Englishmen, professing to be his friends, had given him presents; they had tried to obtain concessions from him but he had replied that this was a matter reserved to the King of Portugal. He admitted that he had sent to Natal on several occasions, when he considered himself abandoned by the Portuguese Government and liable to attack from Inhambane and Lourenço Marques, and Schulz had made out that he was the representative of the Governor of Natal; he inisted that he had not betrayed his loyalty to Portugal. Almeida then asked Gungunhana to define the position of Chifambobsico, son of the late Umtasa, chief of Manica. Gungunhana replied that Umtasa had been subdued by Manikusa; the tribe had received a Vatua governor, and paid regular tribute; the governor was visiting Zefunha, and he presented himself to the foreigners. Though the BSAC later disputed the record of this indaba, which bore twelve signatures, including those of the Russian and an Englishman,[80] the company was not able to produce a single affidavit to disprove it.[81]

The position in Gazaland, as Mr Warhurst stresses, was now critical for

79 GG Lourenço Marques, to Int. Geral, 22/11/90, AHU Moç., 1 Rep., Pasta 7. Almeida sought clarification on what action he should take in thirteen eventualities, Almeida to GG, 22/11/90, and GG to Almeida, 22/11/90, ibid.
80 Acta da reunião, Violante (Zefunha), 29/12/90, *Neg.* iv, pp. 97–9; it was signed by the leading Portuguese present, M. T. Bretterman, a Russian, and Alexander Deans, a British subject.
81 Bocage to Petre, 10/3/91, *Neg.* iv, pp. 111–2

the BSAC, which had to deliver the rifles it had promised.[82] The company chartered a 100-ton steamer, the *Countess of Carnarvon*, which sailed from Port Elizabeth with the rifles and a £1,000 bonus in gold, its destination, according to the ship's papers, Pungue.[83] The vessel crossed the bar of the Limpopo River on the afternoon of 17 February 1891, flying no flag. She approached the Portuguese custom-post, turned and anchored for the night near the bar. The junior official in charge of the post boarded her and was so well entertained that he stayed until 10 p.m. When he reached the shore he was completely ignorant—or said that he was completely ignorant—of the name of the ship and her captain, where she was from and the nature of her cargo. On the next morning the *Countess of Carnarvon* ran up the red ensign, and steamed past the custom-post and military detachment, up the Limpopo, to Chai-chai, thirty miles from the bar. There her crew began promptly to off-load her cargo. The next day, the 19th, the official from the custom-post arrived; he did not pause to protest, or even to enquire or observe her name, but made for Zefunha to report to the nearest senior official. The forty-five miles, which would have taken a runner twelve hours, occupied him the better part of three days.[84]

Almeida had already learnt, on 20 February, of the arrival of the steamer from Gungunhana and from Schulz, who told him that the rifles were a present from the British Government. Knowing the weakness of the military detachment, Almeida had sent one of his junior residents, Paiva Raposo, with an interpreter and a lieutenant, an NCO, six troops, a marine, twenty-two sepoys and forty-one Landeens from Inhambane from his own party, backed by a Nordenfeldt machine-gun. Almeida instructed Paiva Raposo to tell the captain that he and his crew were under arrest for smuggling and for having ascended the river with the British flag flying. If the captain submitted, the Portuguese were to immobilize the vessel; if the captain was defiant, and prepared to run down the river, the force was to position itself close to the river where it narrowed, and open fire with the rifles and the machine-gun. But these instructions reached Raposo only on 24 February.[85]

Raposo arrived at Chai-chai at 5 p.m. on 21 February. One thousand Martini-Henry rifles and 90,000 rounds of ammunition had been disembarked and were in three huts for the local chief had refused to transport them to Zefunha until he knew what the Portuguese attitude would be. By the time he had placed a guard on them and pitched camp it was too late in the day, he decided, to board the ship. At dawn sailors cut the *Carnarvon's* cables and she slipped quietly down-stream, leaving eight men ashore. Raposo told Pawley, the senior company servant present, that he had the right to arrest him for smuggling, since he had been caught in *flagrante delicto;* but he did not wish to embarrass

82 Warhurst, p. 85.
83 Warhurst, p. 87.
84 Almeida, Zefunha, to Gov., Lourenço Marques, 20/2/91, 105, AHU, Moç., 2 Rep., Caixa 9; J. Pires, Lieut., Inhampura, to Raposo, 21/2/90, ibid.; Almeida, Zefunha, to Comandante Militar, Inhampura, 22/2/91, 106, ibid.; Almeida to Gov., Lourenço Marques, 22/2/91, 107, ibid.
85 Almeida to I. de Paiva Raposo, Int. of Bilene, 20/2/91, 103 and 104, ibid. and 22/2/91, 108, ibid.

Portuguese relations with Gungunhana, so he would content himself with demanding customs duties. When Pawley offered Raposo a bond for £2,000 to the Portuguese Government, "as security for the payment of any sum of customs dues that may be legally payable to your Government under existing laws of this land," Raposo delightedly accepted it, and withdrew his guards, for here was written acknowledgment by a representative of the BSAC of Portugal's sovereign rights in Gazaland.[86]

On 2 March 1891 Jameson arrived at Zefunha after a strenuous journey from Mashonaland. Gungunhana declared in front of Jameson and Almeida that he was a Portuguese, and a Portuguese he wished to remain. But Jameson gave him an assurance in writing that the rifles were a personal present to him from Queen Victoria.[87] He now persuaded Gungunhana to put his mark on a treaty recording the agreement allegedly made in October. The treaty followed the common BSAC lines, except that it falsely declared "This covenant shall be considered in the light of a Treaty of Alliance made between the said nation and the Government of Her Britannic Majesty Queen Victoria."[88] His frontiers Gungunhana defined as being the Zambezi in the north and the Komati in the south, and to the west a line running through Mangwedzi's kraal, which Jameson defined as being roughly the line of the Sabi.[89]

The *Countess of Carnarvon* refuelled and reprovisioned in Durban; cleared for 'Guam', she returned to the Limpopo to pick up the agents of the BSAC abandoned there, and Jameson and his companions. Reports that a British ship was off the bar reached Zefunha. Almeida rode to Chai-chai, but finding no vessel returned; the next day the *Carnarvon* entered the river. Almeida took no action against her. Six days later the *Marechal MacMahon* anchored a few yards from her. The captain set off for Zefunha to confer with Almeida, but hearing that Jameson and party had passed him on their way to the river he returned. He ordered the *Carnarvon* to lower the red ensign, took Jameson and his companions and most of the crew aboard his ship and, placing a skeleton crew aboard the *Carnarvon*, escorted that ship to Lourenço Marques.[90]

The actions of the *Carnarvon* led to prompt diplomatic action by the Portuguese Government, which protested to Britain against the entry of a merchant steamer into the Limpopo, which was not open to navigation; it protested against the introduction of contraband; and it protested against the BSAC's efforts to incite a Portuguese vassal, within territory reserved to Portugal by the *modus vivendi*, to revolt. Salisbury assured Soveral that Portugal had incontestable right to defend her territories; but the mere entry of the ship

86 I. de Paiva Raposo, Chai-chai, to Int. geral, 22/2/91, 4, AHU, Moç., 2 Rep., Caixa 9; Almeida to GG, 22/2/91, 109, ibid.; A. Pawley to Raposo, 22/2/91, CP 6495, pp. 256–7; Almeida to Raposo, 23/2/91, 112, 114, 115, AHU, Moç., 2 Rep., Caixa 9; Almeida to commander, *Countess Carnarvon*, 23/2/91, 116 A, ibid.; Pawley to Raposo, 23/2/91, C 6495, p. 258; Raposo to Int. geral, 23/2/91, 1, AHU, Moç, 2 Rep., Caixa 9; and 6, 24/2/91, ibid.; and Almeida to GG, 23/2/91, 111 ibid.
87 Almeida to Dir.-geral, 10/4/91, 210, AHU, 1 Rep., Pasta 7.
88 [3/91], C 6495, pp. 218–9.
89 Jameson, Cape Town, to Imperial Secretary, 24/3/91, CP 6227, pp. 86–9; Rhodes to BSAC, 25/3/91, tel, CP 6086, p. 52.
90 Almeida to [Dir.-geral], 4/3/91, 120, AHU, Moç., 2 Rep., Caixa 9; Albuquerque to Dir-geral, 22/3/91, 19, ibid., Almeida to Dir.-geral 10/4/91, 213, AHU, Moç., 1 Rep., Pasta 7.

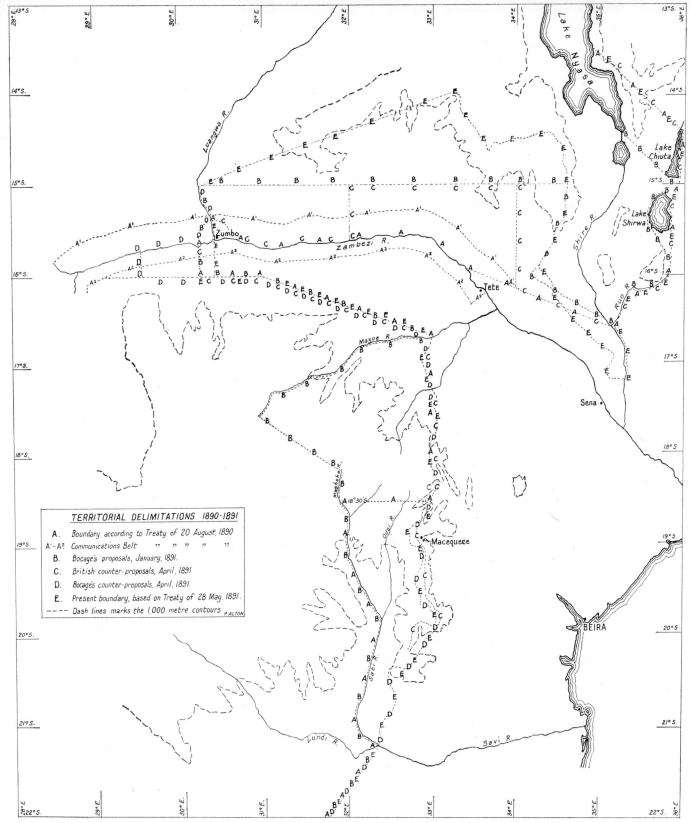

indicated that Portugal did not have the force to police the areas she claimed. The company asserted that Gungunhana was an independent potentate, with whom it was competent to sign a treaty especially since 4 October 1890 was before the date of the *modus vivendi*. The company falsely declared that Almeida was a general (he had never been in the army) and that he was a negro (he was a pure Portuguese, born in Coimbra). It declared that Loch, the High Commissioner, knew in advance of the plan to run in the guns; and it rejected the charge of contraband, declaring that duty had been paid; the company also alleged, falsely, that the *MacMahon* had opened fire on the *Carnarvon*. But Salisbury refused to accede to requests from Cape Town that warships be sent to Lourenço Marques and Beira, and that the Queen receive envoys from Gungunhana.[91] The British Government did not regard the non-ratification of the treaty of 20 August 1890 to be settled fact until 15 October, when the Cortes adjourned: "On 4 October, therefore, it was as far as the Company's agents knew, a Treaty on the point of ratification. An agreement such as was concluded with Gungunhana on that day was clearly inconsistent with the terms of the Convention and the fact of the subsequent refusal of the Portuguese Cortes to ratify the latter does not give force or validity to an Agreement which British subjects were, under the circumstances, not justified in concluding."[92] The Portuguese released the *Countess of Carnarvon*.[93] They had come out the victors in the tussle for Gazaland. The BSAC had suffered a severe blow to its prestige among the tribesmen. It had been deprived of a back-door to the sea. And it had been deprived for weeks of use of the *Carnarvon* on the Pungue route, which was now more vital than ever for supplies to Manica and Mashonaland. It was essential to reinforce the company's forces in the interior because of a double threat from the south and from the east.

The BSAC had received repeated reports that a trek was being planned in the South African Republic to the area wrongly described as Banyailand. Banyai were sepoys, particularly of *prazos* in the Chidima and Dande area south of the Zambezi, but the term had been misapplied by British travellers from Livingstone onwards with respect both to the people and to the area which they inhabited; the area had slipped southwards on successive maps until it was shown (e.g. on a Portuguese map of 1873) as immediately north of the middle Limpopo.[94] Farmers of the Zoutpansberg petitioned their Government to build a road to the Limpopo and a bridge across the river to facilitate communication with the north. Rhodes visited Pretoria and warned the Transvalers to keep out of BSAC reserves. The Transvaal Government enquired of the Portuguese consul whether Banyailand was Portuguese territory. The eventual

91 Bocage to Soveral, 27/2/91, tel. Nec., SPZ 6, *Neg.* iv p. 92; Soveral to Min., 28/2/91, tel., ibid., and p. 95.; and 2/3/91, tel., ibid. and p. 95; Petre to Salisbury, 9/3/91, 47 Af., CP 6086, p. 250; Bocage, circ. tel., 15/3/91, *Neg.* iv, pp. 116–7; Petre to Bocage, 22/3/91, ibid., p. 121; Bocage to Petre, 24/3/91, ibid., pp. 132–3; Petre to Bocage, 3/4/91, ibid., p. 141; Petre to Salisbuty 3/4/91, 73 Af. ibid., CP 6227, p. 36; BSAC, Kimberley to Imp. Sec., 25/2/91, CP 8086, p. 313.
92 FO to BSAC, 14/5/91, CP 6227, p. 247.
93 Dir. geral of Ultramar to Dir. geral politica of Neg. Ext., 3/12/90, Nec., SPZ 5.
94 see map in Livingstone, *Zambezi*.

answer was that the eastern part fell under Portuguese authority, but the western was in the area over which Britain asserted her influence.[95] One S. J. Grobler wrote to the Portuguese consul that he was the leader of a party of Boers from the Waterberg, the Zoutpansberg and Lydenburg, who were planning privately and secretly to emigrate to Mashonaland. They wished if possible to go to an area where they would be completely independent; but if that were impossible, since they did not wish to establish themselves under the British flag, they were anxious to know whether the area they had in mind was legally Portuguese; if it was, they requested permission to settle and enjoy Portuguese protection; they would willingly submit to Portuguese laws, and they would help the Portuguese administration if necessary. The consul commented to his minister that it would be difficult to assimilate the Boers, owing to the differences in religion; and owing to their territorial ambitions, especially their ambition to reach the sea, it would be positively dangerous to admit them.[96] The minister, however, instructed him to assist those Boers who commanded confidence, but he must warn them that frontiers might be reset when the *modus vivendi* ended.[97]

One Vorster, a member of the Volksraad, sought out the Portuguese consul and asked for a concession to build a railway up the Selati valley. He added that 15,000 families were ready to trek with their wagons and cattle, and they waited only for the permission of the Portuguese Government. If, however, the area in which they settled was turned over, by diplomatic negotiations, to the British, they would refuse to acknowledge the British flag.[98] The newspapers began to talk about the proposed emigration, and the Secretary of State confirmed its imminence to the Portuguese consul. He was invited to meet L. D. Adendorff, who was reported to be the organizer of the trek, and General Joubert, whom the consul considered to be the real head of the movement. These two declared that 2,000 Boers were going to assemble on the banks of the Limpopo, and cross that river on 1 June; they would then proclaim a Republic of the North, and defend it by arms against all who sought to oppose it. The consul assured Joubert on his private responsibility that Portugal would not object to the Boers taking possession of territory coveted by the BSAC and lost to Portugal on condition that they respected the Portuguese frontier and helped Portugal against hostile natives and the English. But Bocage felt that this proposal only complicated still further an extremely difficult situation. The proposed trek did not threaten Portuguese sovereignty, so there was no need to discountenance it completely, but there was still uncertainty as to the territorial settlement which must be reached by the time the *modus vivendi* expired. If the Boers went to an area which by agreement was declared to be British, Portugal could not countenance Boer hostility against a friendly power. Whilst Portuguese sympathies were with the Transvaal, Portugal could not do other-

95 Leyds to Campos, 14/10/90 and Campos to Min., 24/10/90, 66A, Nec., SPZ 4; Consul, Pretoria, to Min., 17/11/90, tel., and 20/11/90, 76A, ibid.; Campos to Sec. of State, SAR 7/1/91, Nec., SPZ 5.
96 S. J. Grobler, Smitsdorp, to Port. Consul, 15/1/91 and 26/1/91, Campos to Min., 16/1/91, 2A and Rebello to Min., 2/2/91, A6, Nec., SPZ 5.
97 Bocage E. Teixeira Rebello, 1/3/91, Nec., SPZ 6.
98 Rebello to Min., 6/3/91, 28A, Nec., SPZ 6; and 28/3/91, tel., and 28/3/91, 38A, ibid.

wise than maintain the strictest neutrality. If, however, the *modus vivendi* came to an end without an agreement having been arrived at between Portugal and Britain, Bocage was convinced that the British Government would give the BSAC "full liberty to continue on a course of violence and treachery"; in that event Portugal would be glad to avail herself of the services of 2,000 Transvalers, who would be natural allies; and she would much prefer to see the disputed areas dominated by Boers than by Rhodes's henchmen. Officially, then, the consul was to be careful to abstain from supporting the trek; but privately he was to encourage it.[99] Loch cabled to London that there was no doubt in his mind that the Boers and the Portuguese were about to act in concert, the Boers to occupy Matabeleland, and the Portuguese, with Boer support, to recover the whole of Manica and secure the support of Gungunhana.[100]

The Portuguese certainly were assembling an expeditionary force to go to the relief of Manica. The arrest of Andrada and Sousa had caused the most intense indignation in Portugal. Numbers of volunteers had offered to avenge the national honour, and to assert Portuguese sovereignty in Manica. The Government organized an expeditionary corps to Moçambique, consisting of a battalion (17 officers and 458 other ranks), a brigade of mountain artillery (116 strong), a company of artillery (94 men) and a company of engineers, with ancillary units, a total of 908 men. Lieutenant-colonel Manuel de Azevedo Coutinho received command of the corps, the main body of which sailed from Lisbon on 15 January 1891; it reached Moçambique in February and March.[101] In Lourenço Marques there had been similar protests against the incidents in Manica, and the mayor had convened a public meeting at which 495 citizens enthusiastically volunteered for service against the BSAC. Only one of the four companies was called up, which embarked, 150 strong, on 10 January 1891 with 50 officials and policemen, and 40 native troops, half of them from Angola. This force, under Major Caldas Xavier, reached Beira on 13 January, where it awaited porters.[102] It had been hoped that Sousa would be able to supply these and porters for the corps awaited from Lisbon. Lisbon newspapers talked glibly about Sousa supplying 17,000 carriers. But Sousa had returned to find his subjects in revolt. Eventually 300 Landeens arrived from Inhambane, who joined the Lourenço Marques contingent. The volunteers expressed their resentment at being detained in Beira, and on 14 February they began to ascend the Pungue in a variety of boats, while the porters followed as best they could along the flooded banks of the river. By 20 March the force from Lourenço Marques had assembled at Sarmento, where the Governor of Manica, Major J. J. Ferreira, was waiting. The corps from Portugal remained temporarily on the coast; it

99 Bocage to Carvalho, 29/3/91, Nec., SPZ 6.
100 Loch to Knutsford, 11/4/91, CP 6227, p. 64.
101 J. J. Teixeira Botelho, *Historia Militar e politica dos Portugueses em Moçambique* (Lisbon, 1936), II, pp. 381–2; Bocage, circular tel., 16/1/91, Nec., SPZ 5, *Neg.* iv., p. 51; Crespo, Consul-geral, Zanzibar, to Min., 9/3/91, 6B, Nec., SPZ 3; Gonçalves in *Bol. SGL*, 1950, p. 517.
102 Teixeira Botelho, II, p. 382; GG, portaria, 12/12/90, *Bol. Off.* 13/12/90, CP 6227, p. 26; Bocage to Soveral, 12/12/90, tel., *Neg.* iv, pp. 38–9.

had only eighty Makuas to serve as carriers, and the volunteers, most of them new to Africa, succumbed rapidly to fever. Bocage admitted to Petre that he was not sorry that the rainy season confined them to the coast: the risks were lessened of a collision with the forces of the BSAC.[103]

The BSAC was finding its communications with Mashonaland prejudiced by the rains, and, threatened by the Boers and by the expeditionary force, it was the more intent on opening the Pungue route. Frank Johnson organized a Pioneer Line of steamers which would connect with the mail steamers at Beira, and convey passengers and goods 100 miles up the river to Mpanda's; there first-class passengers would transfer to an American coach and be whisked to Salisbury via Manica in eighty-four hours for a fare of £20, while second- and third-class passengers would do the journey in twelve days by ox-waggon.[104] And before long reports were circulating that 240 Englishmen were on their way to open this route, by force if need be. The Portuguese Government announced that no armed bodies of men would be allowed to land at Beira, and deplored the plan to start a transport service over Portuguese soil without the sanction of Portugal, without even informing her. The consul at Cape Town added that his Government could not sanction such a transport service unless the BSAC first evacuated Macequece.[105] Johnson's company acquired a tug, the *Agnes*, and three lighters; he arranged for these to rendezvous at Beira with the Union steamship *Norseman*, which would bring from South Africa native labourers, carpenters and European overseers. Also aboard her would be Sir John Willoughby, major in the BSAC police, and a Mr Cohen who was going to open an hotel at Mpanda's. Johnson instructed the captain of the *Agnes* to call on the Governor. If the Governor refused to allow the vessel up the Pungue he was to quote the *modus vivendi*. If the Governor persisted in his refusal, the captain was to sail up the river, taking with him, if necessary, any guard that might have been placed aboard his vessel. If fired at, he was to take evasive action, escape if possible, and report by telegraph from Lourenço Marques or Durban.[106]

The High Commissioner was kept informed of these plans. Loch instructed the company to tender 3 per cent customs duties; if passage was still refused, the company's agent was to request a statement in writing from the Portuguese authorities. If the refusal was put in writing, he was to return to Lourenço Marques and cable. If no answer in writing was forthcoming, he was to assert his intention of passing up the river; if the *Agnes* were fired on and forcibly prevented from ascending the Pungue, he was to return to Lourenço Marques.[107] It was only after the party had sailed from South Africa that Loch informed the Colonial Office, and the British Government learnt of this intention to cut a

103 J. de Azevedo Coutinho, *O Combate de Macequece* (Lisbon, 1935), II, pp. 52–8; Teixeira Botelho, II, pp. 381–4; Petre to Salisbury, 13/2/91, 26 Af., CP 6086, p. 178; and 23/3/91, 58 Af., ibid., p. 311; *O Dia*, 30/3/91; CP 6227, p. 29.
104 *Cape Argus*, 7/3/91, CP 6227, pp. 56–7.
105 Petre to Salisbury, 3/4/91, CP 6227, p. 33; Carvalho to HC, 3/4/91 and 9/4/91, Nec., SPZ 7; and to F. Johnson 9/4/91, ibid.; Petre to Salisbury, 13/4/91, 80 Af., CP 6227, p. 79.
106 Johnson to Capt. Andrews 19/3/91, CP 6227, pp. 80–3.
107 Harris to BSAC, 1/4/91, CP 6227, pp. 104–5.

road through Portuguese territory without Portugal's consent; the Foreign Office appreciated that this was a deliberate attempt by Rhodes to force the British Government's hand.[108]

The *Norseman* and *Agnes* arrived at Beira on 13 April 1891, the former with Willoughby, twelve other whites and ninety-one labourers aboard, and 236 tons of stores and provisions. Willoughby was informed that nobody might proceed up the Pungue without permit from the military commandant. Willoughby went ashore in his military uniform and introduced himself to the Governor-general, who had come to Beira, as an officer of the British army serving as second in command of the BSAC's forces in Mashonaland and as the representative of the Chartered Company and of Johnson's company; he intended to carry out his instructions to make a road to Salisbury with as little delay as possible. Machado, who had been expecting a body of armed men, and had proclaimed a state of siege in the province, declared that the company had not evacuated Macequece as she was required to do under the *modus vivendi*, and the company was in a virtual state of war with Portugal; he could not allow officers to pass unless they gave their word of honour to respect Portuguese laws and not instigate the natives to rebellion. This Willoughby would not do, nor would he accept an offer by the Governor-general to forward the mails. The custom-house rejected his offer to pay 3 per cent transit duties on the cargo, which was off-loaded into two lighters. Willoughby does not appear to have attempted to obtain any statement in writing from the Governor-general. Instead, he simply notified Machado that he intended to proceed up the river. A naval officer warned him that he would be fired on first with blank and then with ball if he tried to force his way. Despite this, on 15 April he set sail in the *Agnes*, flying the British flag, with the two lighters in tow, and accompanied by the launch *Shark*. Three Portuguese gun-boats closed in on the flotilla; one fired a blank shot, and the flotilla stopped. Willoughby boarded a gun-boat and protested against this outrage on the British flag. The Governor-general reminded him that the river was not open to ships flying foreign flags; nor was it safe, he remarked, for BSAC personnel to pass through areas occupied by Portuguese army volunteers, in view of the intense feeling against the company.[109]

The British vice-consul in Lourenço Marques cabled Cape Town on 19 April that imperial mails to Mashonaland had been intercepted, British lives at Beira were in danger, and 600 Portuguese troops were marching against Macequece. Rhodes in a telegram to London broadened this into a statement that 600 Portuguese troops were marching against Manica; the British flag had been pulled down; and Transvaal Boers were arranging a trek with Portuguese connivance: "I request gun-boats sent Beira." Salisbury's immediate reaction was to protest against this "deliberate violation" of the *modus vivendi* by

108 CO to FO, 4/4/91, CP 6227, p. 100; Currie to Herbert, 6/4/91, quoted in Warhurst, p. 59; and see Warhurst on these incidents, pp. 58–68.
109 Statement, by J. Willoughby, 20/4/91, CP 6227, p. 262 A–D; Machado to Gov., Manica etc., 17/4/91, AHU, Moç., 2 Rep., Caixa 9, which distinguishes between acceptable foreigners, including Englishmen, and agents of the BSAC.

Portugal; the British minister in Lisbon was to ask whether Portugal regarded the *modus vivendi* as at an end, in which case the British Government would take appropriate measures; unless the Pungue were at once opened and official protection given to British subjects, Britain would be forced to protect their rights by sending gun-boats; and the immediate release was demanded of the *Agnes* and other craft.[110] In the face of this threat the Portuguese Government gave way; it ordered the Pungue to be opened to the company, and the vessels to be released. But though this was done, the British Government ordered warships to Beira: the *Magicienne*, already at Lourenço Marques, and two gun-boats. The Portuguese suggested that a British consul be appointed to help co-operation on the Pungue and the British Government appointed Captain Pipon of *Magicienne* to this temporary post.[111] But the transport scheme was still-born since mules and oxen could not traverse the tsetse-fly belt, and the forces of the company and Portugal came to battle.

The force from Lourenço Marques had, all this while, been struggling into the interior, suffering from lack of porters, floods and fever. On 30 April, however, it was all assembled at Chimoio, with adequate porters, provisions and munitions, including ammunition for four 7-cm. quick-firing Hotchkiss guns which had been buried at Macequece on the arrival of the BSAC. It was essential to occupy Manica before the expiration of the *modus vivendi*, and the column struggled on. On 5 May the company withdrew its caretaker, and the force re-occupied the old Vila de Manica; it numbered 112 Europeans, 47 second-line troops, mainly from Angola, and 93 sepoys from Inhambane who had been employed largely as porters.[112]

Capt. Heyman, commander of the BSAC police at Umtali, warned that Portuguese were advancing on Macequece, had received orders from Rhodes to drive them out.[113] He immediately sent a messenger to Umtasa, ordering him to send an impi, while he himself, with thirty-five policemen and ten civilians, supported by a 7-cm. gun, advanced from Umtali. On 7 May he rode to Macequece under a flag of truce, accompanied by Corporal Morier. The two were led blindfolded into the presence of Ferreira and Caldas Xavier. Heyman asked whether the Portuguese had news of any settlement in Europe. Ferreira said he had not; but he was occupying Macequece on the strength of the *modus vivendi* and he demanded that the company immediately evacuate Manica, else he would force it to do so. Heyman asked that the situation be left as it was until the expiration of the *modus vivendi*.[114]

110 De la Cour to Salisbury, 19/4/91, tel., CP 6227, p. 90; Rhodes to BSAC, 19/4/91, ibid., p. 94; Salisbury to Petre, 20/4/91, tel. 33 Af., ibid., p. 98; and 4/91, tel., 34 Af., ibid., p. 106.
111 Petre to Salisbury, 22/4/91, tel. 31 Af., CP 6227, p. 114; FO to Adm., 22/4/91, ibid., p. 113 and 114; Petre to Salisbury, 24/4/91, tel. 32 Af., ibid., p. 140; Salisbury to Petre, 25/4/91, tel., ibid., p. 143; Salisbury to Pipon, [c. 25/4/91], ibid., p. 145.
112 A. Caldas Xavier, Relatório, Official, L. J. de Azevedo Coutinho, *Combate de Macequece*, 2, pp. 51–62; Teixeira Botelho, II, pp. 381–5.
113 Pipon to Salisbury, 11/7/91, quoted by Warhurst, p. 74.
114 Dr Rolão Preto, Memorias, quoted by J. Gonçalves, *Bol. SGL*, 1950, pp. 519–20; Morier, Memo of interview . . ., [c. 8/5/91], CP 6253, pp. 92–3; Sapte, Outline of Events . . ., ibid., pp. 88–9.

Heyman's force on 8 May reached Chua hill, and began to fortify itself in a position which overlooked Macequece fort, from a distance of only 3,000 yards. One hundred and sixty of Umtasa's warriors moved into a village on the slopes of the hill on Heyman's left. Xavier appreciated that the BSAC would attack as soon as the *modus vivendi* expired; and his position would be untenable. On 9 May he ordered a stockade to be constructed on an elevation 500 yards forward of the fort, to house especially the 7-cm. guns, so that they might come into action as soon as ammunition should arrive. That afternoon he ordered an officer to approach the BSAC position under a flag of truce ostensibly to order the troopers to withdraw, but in reality to reconnoitre the enemy strength. The officer, who was received two hundred yards short of the position, reported that there was no evidence of any artillery (the gun had been concealed). Xavier called for volunteers for a night attack on the BSAC position, but the poor response caused the operation to be abandoned. The next day one hundred carriers arrived with the much awaited ammunition— and *garrafões* of wine; of food the garrison remained desperately short. The carriers confirmed that Umtasa's impi had taken the field; and that night they and other porters decamped. Caldas Xavier, well aware that he would be attacked on 14 May, expecting the approach of BSAC reinforcements from bogus signals used by the troopers, and already thinking of possible retreat, feared his force would be cut to pieces by the battle-axes of Umtasa's warriors, and he determined to try and dislodge them. A display of force, he thought, might be sufficient to persuade at least the tribesmen to withdraw.

At midday on 11 May Caldas Xavier called his men from the cooking of their sparse dinners, paraded them, and announced that all save the gunners and some sentries would attack the British position; he added that if anybody retired before the bugles blew the retreat he would be shot. At 2 p.m. there sallied out of the fort two columns, consisting of a section of police and a section of volunteers, under Captain Bettencourt, followed by forty-three men of the Caçadores under two white officers, and with eighty-two sepoys from Inhambane, under one officer, bringing up the rear. Xavier chose to leave his Hotchkiss and Nordenfeldt guns in the fort. The force had advanced no more than 600 yards when the BSAC gun began to open fire. The Angolans opened fire without waiting for orders and the engagement became general. The Portuguese drove in Heyman's pickets, and advanced to within 500 yards. But their aim was indescribably poor, and though pluckily led by their officers they could not approach the prepared positions in the face of the troopers' superior marksmanship and shrapnel shells. After fifty-five minutes of fire the Portuguese withdrew, to the accompaniment of frenzied fire from Umtasa's warriors, who had been interested spectators of the engagement.

According to BSAC accounts the Portuguese left twenty dead on the field of battle, though Caldas Xavier admitted to the death of only six men, the loss of two prisoners (one white and one black) and the wounding of six men. BSAC casualties were nil. That night there was an anxious conference in the fort, at which the officers decided to evacuate Macequece. Though some porters had arrived that day with ammunition for the Hotchkiss and with biscuits, there was still a shortage of provisions and of munitions and of medical aid; and the fort was powerless against artillery bombardment. Thus the Portuguese abandoned seven Hotchkiss guns after removing the breech blocks and two Nordenfeldts after taking the hoppers, 110,000 rounds of ammunition, and a medley of personal belongings—including a pair of ladies' underwear—and stole out of the fort during the night. They feared pursuit, but the BSAC troopers were standing to that night, expecting themselves to be attacked. Great was the surprise of the troopers at dawn on 12 May to observe that the fort had been deserted.[115] Heyman sent a patrol to the fort, accompanied by a veterinary surgeon to attend any wounded that might be found. By holding revolvers to their heads it persuaded some of Umtasa's men to carry the most valuable loot to the BSAC position. Pennefather, the commander at Umtali, sent ox-wagons and scotchcarts to load up the balance of whatever was worth salvaging. Only three of the machine-guns were brought back; the others, to Pennefather's indignation, were destroyed and Morier, on Heyman's instructions, blew up the bastions of the fort, and burnt down the houses of Macequece. The company was unable to follow up its success by pursuit in strength because its porters also decamped on the day of the battle. Heyman sent out a patrol which was within a few miles of the Portuguese rear-party when it met Ferreira's secretary returning under a flag of truce and demanding to be put in possession of Macequece; the patrol returned with him, and lost a day. On 15 May Pennefather set out with Selous and two troopers to follow the Portuguese; the Portuguese entered Chimoio half a day ahead of them. In view of the lack of porters and the difficulties of the route—the narrow path led through grass up to 12 feet in height, there were many concealed mine workings and game pits, there were expanses of marsh, and the fords were deep—Pennefather decided that he could not keep an attacking force supplied, and he returned to Umtali.[116]

The British High Commissioner in South Africa had at the end of April sent his secretary, Major Sapte, to Manica to ensure delivery of an official letter instructing the BSAC to withdraw from Macequece. Sapte was also to instruct the company's police to avoid, as far as possible, all cause of quarrel with the Portuguese; it was probable that the company would be able to advance to the parallel of 33° east, but Macequece and its surroundings would be reserved to the Portuguese. Sapte was to report on the detention of Portuguese officers who had been sent to communicate with the company. He was to obtain intelligence of Portuguese strengths and movements. And he was to warn the company's officers of the threatened Boer trek into Banyailand.[117]

115 Azevedo Coutinho, pp. 62–9; Teixeira Botelho, II, pp. 385–6; Warhurst, p. 75; Nicholson, Delagoa Bay, to Adm. 27/5/91; CP 6253 pp. 20–1; Pipon to Salisbury, 24/6/91, ibid., p. 58; Pennefather to Loch, [c. 13/5/91], p. 63; Pennefather to BSAC, 13/5/91, ibid., pp. 69–71; Sapte, Cape Town, to Loch, 21/7/91, ibid., pp. 83–6; Sapte, conversation with Cmdt., Portuguese forces, Chimoio, 29/5/91, ibid., p. 87; Sapte, Outline of Events, ibid., pp. 88–9.
116 Pennefather to Loch, [c. 13/5/91], CP 6253, p. 63; Pennefather to BSAC, 13/5/91, ibid., pp.69–71; and 20/5/91, ibid., p. 71.
117 Loch to Sapte, 29/4/91, CP 6227, p. 293; and 29/4/91, Confid., ibid., pp. 294–5.

Travelling by way of Beira and the Pungue, Sapte reached Neves Ferreira only on 19 May, where he heard of the action of 11 May. He reached Sarmento on 25 May, where he was well received by Ferreira. On 29 May he reached Chimoio, where he heard more reports about recent events. The next day he continued his journey. Three miles out he met Lieutenant Fiennes and three troopers. It appeared that on 24 May news reached Umtali that the Portuguese at Chimoio were in a bad way. On 26 May Fiennes and seventeen mounted men set out for Chimoio with orders to turn the Portuguese out, and return with stores and the missing parts for the salvaged machine-guns. They had reconnoitred Chimoio on the 29th, and were planning to open fire on the place from a hill which commanded it from a distance of a few hundred yards at dawn the next morning, when, a mile from Chimoio, they met Knight-Bruce, Bishop of Bloemfontein, who told them of Sapte's mission. Sapte had been too late to obviate the engagement at Macequece but he prevented a second collision at Chimoio.[118] On his arrival at Umtali he conveyed his instructions, and informed the police that Portugal and Britain were on the verge of agreement.

The negotiations for a new treaty had been slow in starting. In November 1890, Barbosa du Bocage had intimated to Salisbury that Portugal was ready to begin negotiations in Lisbon. His hope was, by guaranteeing to construct the railway and telegraph line from the Pungue estuary to the British sphere within four years, by granting other facilities for transport pending the completion of the railway, and limiting transit dues to the rate obtaining from Lourenço Marques, to obtain alterations in the territorial delimitation and in clauses which offended Portuguese susceptibilities.[119] The BSAC's invasion of Manica disturbed the preparation of the Portuguese case, but in the middle of January 1891, Bocage put forward the proposals of his Government. The line of 20 August 1890, Bocage maintained, had deprived Portugal of territories which were Portuguese by historic right and title no less authentic than those alleged for a British protectorate. He insisted on the inclusion of the lands of Makanjila and Cuirassia and part of the lands of two other chiefs who had declared themselves to be vassals of Portugal, but he agreed to abandon Mponda's, site of the White Fathers' mission. He abandoned claim to Mpesene's, prazos on the Luangwa and Kafue, and part of the prazo of Macanga, but asked for the line of 15° south latitude. It was only with reluctance that the Government abandoned claim to the Sanyati area, but it accepted the 1890 line to the Mazoe. It insisted, however, on the course of the Mazoe (a natural boundary and the existing boundary of the district of Manica) to its source, and a line from there to the Masheke, and thence to the Sabi, to include lands explored by Andrada or subject to António de Sousa. The frontier claimed is indicated as line B on map (Plate 14). And in the south a rectification was needed, to leave the Queen of Maputo entirely under Portuguese

118 Sapte to Loch, 21/7/91, CP 6253, pp. 83–6; and Sapte, Outline of Events, ibid., pp. 88–90; G. W. H. Knight-Bruce, Memories of Mashonaland (London, 1895), pp. 88–90.
119 Bocage to Chargé d'Affaires, London, Nec., SPZ 4, Neg., iv, p. 23; Petre to Salisbury, 6/1/91, CP 6086, pp. 55–6.

sovereignty; the boundary must run inland from Sordwana Point; Portugal would honour, however, the undertaking given by Britain to the South African Republic. Bocage also asked for modification to various clauses by which Portugal granted advantages without compensation, notably those referring to the treatment of British subjects, liberty of navigation and of transit, with dues limited to 3 per cent, and the onerous obligation to build a railway line and telegraph from the Pungue to the British sphere.[120]

The impression that these demands made on Salisbury, who had announced that Portugal must yield from her position of 20 August, can be imagined. He decided the negotiations should take place in England. He announced to Luis de Soveral, when he presented his letter of credence, that he wanted peace and conciliation with Portugal; but, he added ominously, he could take no decision until the High Commissioner and Prime Minister had arrived in London from the Cape. The Portuguese consul in Cape Town warned that Loch would be most hostile to Portuguese interests, and would oppose any concession of territory actually in the possession of the BSAC. He advised Bocage to give up any hope of concession by Britain, and to accept the line of 20 August. If Portugal did not come to a speedy accord the BSAC, reinforced by thousands of miners, would invade further Portuguese territory.[121] Two days after Rhodes's arrival Soveral had a most unsatisfactory interview with Salisbury, who rejected Bocage's proposals out of hand, since they were more favourable to Portugal than the line of 20 August. The Manica boundary, Salisbury intimated to Soveral, must follow the parallel of 33° east, or the line of the escarpment; it was possible that compensation might be granted in the neighbourhood of Tete. Soveral immediately declared that this would deprive Portugal of the minerali-ferous area, and the suggestion was quite unacceptable to Portugal even with compensation elsewhere. Bocage confirmed that the Portuguese Government could not accept the line of the escarpment. Portugal had an unassailable right to Manica; and the Colquhoun treaty with Umtasa was both morally wrong, because it was made before the treaty of 20 August had been abandoned, and materially illegal because it had not been confirmed by the British Government according to the BSAC's charter.[122] The Emperor of Germany remarked to the Portuguese minister that the Portuguese Government was adopting too weak an attitude to Britain and he assured Portugal of his greatest interest in events.[123] But Salisbury, no matter what might be his personal opinion of the Freire incident, adopted the BSAC point of view, insisting that Umtasa was an independent chief, the treaty (which he called a concession) of 14 September 1890 valid, and that in any case there was no proof that Gungunhana was a vassal of Portugal; no matter how ably Bocage might present the Portuguese claim

120 Bocage to Petre, 17/1/91, *Neg.*, iv, pp. 51–2; Bocage, memo., 17/1/91, ibid., pp. 52–8, and CP 6086, pp. 86–91; Projecto de tratado, ibid., pp. 58–62.
121 Carvalho to Min., 21/1/91, 1 Res., Nec., SPZ 5. Loch and Rhodes sailed on 14 Jan. Soveral to Min., 28/1/91, tel., ibid.
122 Soveral to Min., 3/2/91, tel., *Neg.*, iv, p. 64; and 4/2/91, ibid., p. 65; Salisbury to Petre, 4/2/91, tel. 9 Af., CP 6086, p. 131; Bocage to Soveral, 6/2/91, Neg., iv, pp. 68–9; and 10/2/91, ibid., p. 76.
123 Penafiel to Min., 11/2/91, Nec., SPZ 6.

to Umtasa Salisbury was inflexible on the subject, and the only concession that he would make was to deflect the boundary to leave Macequece in Portuguese territory. He advised Portugal to come to a rapid agreement: "today", Soveral reported, "we could save Macequece, later would be impossible."[124]

In the middle of February 1891 Bocage requested Salisbury's exact counter-proposals, as a matter of urgency. Soveral gathered that an outline of them had already been sent to Lisbon and the details would soon follow. But Salisbury refused to detail them until he had an intimation from the Portuguese Government as to whether it would accept the line of 33°, excepting Macequece, with compensation in the north. And, since the BSAC refused to surrender its designs on Gazaland, he now proposed a joint guarantee by Britain and Portugal of Gungunhana's independence with freedom to the chartered companies to carry on their operations. To meet the susceptibilities of the Portuguese he was prepared to agree that the provisions forbidding the alienation of territory without British consent might be made reciprocal. The clause about the compulsory leasing of land at Chinde could be omitted from the convention, and arranged by the exchange of notes. But Britain adhered to the clauses about trade, navigation and religion.[125] Bocage could not agree to Portugal being deprived of the auriferous area of Manica, apart from Macequece, which had been the scene of operations of the Moçambique Company, nor could he accept the independence of Gungunhana.[126] The consul in Cape Town warned Bocage that the BSAC was recruiting good riders and marksmen in South Africa, and that the Company would act the moment the *modus vivendi* expired. Bocage, under protest, now conceded to Britain territory around Umtasa's kraal, in return for compensation north of the Zambezi, and assuming that the two companies could come to an agreement over the construction of the railway. He again asked for the British counter-proposals in detail, which he had been awaiting for two months. He circularized Portuguese legations in Europe with copies of documents about Manica and Gazaland which the ministers might use at their discretion. And he issued instructions for the encouragement of Boer and German settlement in Moçambique provided the colonists formally declared themselves subject to Portuguese laws.[127]

On 16 March Petre presented Bocage with a note by which the British Government formally denied that Portugal had any valid claim to territory between 33° east longitude and the Sabi. Failure of the Cortes to ratify the

---

124 Bocage to Petre, 9/2/91, *Neg.*, iv, pp. 72–6; Soveral to Bocage, 11/2/91, Nec., SPZ 6; Bocage to Soveral, 11/2/91, *Neg.*, iv, p. 77; Salisbury to Petre, 12/2/61, tel. 11 Af., CP 6086, p. 167; Bocage to Soveral, 12/2/61, Nec., SPZ 6 and 13/2/91, *Neg.*, iv, pp. 77–8; Soveral to Bocage, 13/2/91, *Neg.*, iv, p. 78; Soveral to Salisbury, 14/2/91, *Neg.*, iv, p. 86; Bocage to Consul, Cape Town, 16/2/91, Nec., SPZ 6; Soveral to Bocage, 18/2/91, *Neg.*, iv, p. 85; Bocage to Soveral, 18/2/91, Nec., SPZ 6; Petre to Bocage 18/2/91, *Neg.*, iv, pp. 86–8.
125 Bocage to Soveral, 14/2/91, Nec., *Neg.*, iv, p. 78; Soveral to Bocage, 18/2/91, ibid., p. 85; Salisbury to Petre, 18/2/91, CP 6086, pp. 184–5.
126 Petre to Salisbury, 24/2/91, 37 Af., CP 6086, p. 205; Bocage to Petre, 10/3/91, ibid., *Neg.*, iv, p. 111.
127 Carvalho to Bocage, 7/3/91, tel., Nec., SPZ 6; Bocage to Soveral, 8/3/91, *Neg.*, iv, p. 110; Soveral to Min., 11/3/91, ibid., p. 113; Bocage to legations, 14/3/91, *Neg.*, iv, p. 114. Bocage to Rebelo, 16/3/91, Nec., SPZ 6.

convention of 20 August 1890 had left that district open to British enterprise and it had been duly and legally occupied by British subjects under the concession from Umtasa. He again urged the approximate line of the thirty-third parallel, with additional land north of the Zambezi.[128] Soveral then tried his hand at an agreement. He suggested the line of $32\frac{1}{2}°$ east to the Odzi and down the Odzi to the Sabi with arbitration over Umtasa, such as had recently been employed over the Newfoundland fisheries. Salisbury would not consider this and quoted the long delay over the Lourenço Marques railway arbitration, but Soveral pointed out that both parties in this case wanted an accord. Salisbury admitted that the BSAC wanted an accord primarily on the building of the railway; if a rapid agreement on that could be arrived at Britain would be more conciliatory on the territorial delimitation. Bocage was prepared to yield to $32\frac{1}{2}°$ east, and 33° if essential, on condition that local modifications were allowed, but he continued to insist that a complete draft of the British proposal be submitted to him; the negotiation could not be conducted piecemeal. He continued to assert Portuguese rights to Umtasa, and would have welcomed the opportunity of arbitration. He appreciated that the position in south-east Africa was becoming critical: the BSAC had refused to obey its Government's orders to evacuate Macequece and was organizing a transport service from the Pungue without consulting the Portuguese authorities; the Portuguese expeditionary force was approaching Manica, and a clash was almost inevitable. He could still obtain no counter-proposals from the British Government; and Salisbury was about to set off on a holiday at Cannes.[129]

In these circumstances Bocage again appealed to the powers of Europe. The Austrian Government responded; its ambassador in London called at the Foreign Office, and requested that the complete counter-proposals be given Portugal. He was told that they had been drawn up, but still awaited Salisbury's approval. This was eventually given. They then had to be submitted to the cabinet, and it was not until 14 April that Petre forwarded them to Bocage.[130]

The British counter-proposals, as far as they concerned south-east Africa, are expressed as line C on map (Plate 14). No territory west of 32° 30′ should be in the Portuguese sphere, and no territory east of 33° in the British sphere. The line was to be deflected, if necessary, to ensure that Umtasa was in the British sphere, and Macequece in the Portuguese. Britain would not object if, south of Delagoa Bay, the Portuguese sphere of influence were to be extended to the parallel of the junction of the Pongola and the Maputo. In the west, the line "shall follow the centre of the channel of the upper Zambezi, starting from the Katima rapids up to the point where it reaches the territory of the Barotse kingdom," which was to remain within the British sphere, its westward limit to

128 Petre to Bocage, 16/3/91, *Neg*. iv, pp. 117–8, CP 6086, pp. 308–9.
129 Bocage to Soveral, 17/3/91, *Neg*. iv, p. 119; Salisbury to Petre, 18/3/91, 52 Af., CP 6086, p. 288; Soveral to Bocage, 19/3/91, *Neg*. iv, p. 120; Petre to Salisbury, 19/3/91, 53 Af., CP 6086, p. 301; Bocage to Soveral, 20/3/91, *Neg*. iv, p. 121; and 24/3/91, ibid., pp. 130–2; Bocage to Petre, 25/3/91, ibid., pp. 133–6; Soveral to Bocage, 28/3/91, ibid., p. 133; Bocage to Soveral, 28/3/91, ibid., p. 137; Soveral to Salisbury, 28/3/91, ibid., p. 139.
130 Bocage, circular to legations, 14/3/91, *Neg*. iv. p. 114; and 30/3/91, ibid., p. 138; FO to Petre, 3/4/91, Soveral to Min., 4/4/91, SPZ 7 (including record of a conversation with Rhodes); Soveral to Bocage, 6/4/91, *Neg*. iv, p. 144.

be established by a joint Anglo-Portuguese commission. Subject to the existing rights of any other state Britain would not oppose the extension of Portuguese administration outside the limits of the Barotse country. All lines were subject to local rectification. If one power proposed to part with territory it gave the other the preferential right to acquire it. Neither power would acquire land or sign treaties or accept sovereign rights or protectorates in the sphere of the other. "It is understood that no companies nor individuals subject to one Power can exercise sovereign rights in a sphere assigned to the other, except with the assent of the latter."

Other clauses repeated that missionaries of both countries were to have full protection; freedom was guaranteed for all forms of religious teaching. Portugal undertook not to impose transit duties on goods being exported, while those on incoming goods were not to exceed 3 per cent. Provision was made for these to be reduced to 1½ per cent when they reached £30,000 a year, while the British Government had the option after five years to claim complete exemption from duties on payment of one million pounds. There was to be freedom of passage for the subjects of both powers across the Zambezi and adjoining territories without hindrance or the imposition of dues. Within a 20-mile zone along the north bank of the Zambezi each power had the right to construct roads, railways and bridges in territory reserved to the other. Both powers had the same right within a 10-mile zone south of the Zambezi between Tete and the Chobe and opposite the British sphere north of the Zambezi. Navigation of the Zambezi and Shire was again declared to be free for the ships of all nations. The clause of the *modus vivendi* regarding the Pungue was made perpetual, and applied also to the Buzi, Sabi and Limpopo, and their tributaries. Portugal agreed to grant absolute freedom of passage between the Pungue and the British sphere of influence for goods, and to construct a railway line with the least possible delay. Should fifty miles of railway not be completed within twelve months, or the entire line within three years, the British Government was to have the right to name a British company to make the line; when the line had been paid for from traffic receipts it would be transferred to the control of the Portuguese Government.[131]

The first protest against these counter-proposals came from the BSAC— before, in fact, they had been delivered to the Portuguese Government. The Board of Directors regretted that the proposals differed from those suggested by Rhodes; they felt strongly that unless the independence of Gungunhana was recognized, and the British sphere carried unequivocally to 33°, the interests of the Company and of Britain would best be served by allowing the *modus vivendi* to lapse and no convention to be signed.[132]

Bocage's immediate reaction was that many of the counter-proposals were

131 Petre to Bocage, *Neg.* iv, p. 156, and counter proposal, pp. 156–61; and ibid., 14/4/91, p. 166, re lease of ground, Chinde.
132 BSAC to FO, 14/4/91, CP 6227, pp. 91–4. BSAC to FO, 18/3/91, CP 6086, p. 293, had requested to be consulted over the draft terms. Cawston was given information on 3 April and Maguire on the 4th; the directors protested against the non-acceptance of Rhodes views on Gungunhana, BSAC to FO, 8/4/91, CP 6227, p. 42.

harsh and obscure. Protracted negotiation would still be necessary before an accord could be reached. And the life of the *modus vivendi* was running out. The British Government had taken three months to formulate the counter-proposals, which had then taken eleven days to travel from London to Lisbon. Soveral was convinced that they had been deliberately delayed so that the shortage of time before the *modus vivendi* lapsed would influence the Portuguese Government into accepting the proposals. And evidence was mounting that Rhodes intended to seize more Portuguese territory after 14 May. Since it was impossible to conclude the negotiations and obtain ratification by the Cortes before that date it was imperative to extend the life of the *modus vivendi*. Bocage instructed Soveral to make application accordingly and asked his diplomats to request the governments to which they were accredited to exert pressure firmly and persuade the British Government to accept the modifications he proposed.[133] He required that the line north of the Zambezi be modified to allow Portuguese *prazos* in the lower Luangwa valley and south of the Zambezi in the Zumbo area to remain Portuguese, and that in Manica and southwards the line follow not the escarpment but the watershed. His proposals are indicated as line D on map (Plate 14). South of Delagoa Bay Bocage asked for the parallel of Sordwana Point to the Maputo River, to enable Tongaland to be united. In the west the line should run simply along the Kabompo River to the Zambezi and down the Zambezi to the Katima rapids. Transit dues could be remitted in return for a lump sum, the amount to be settled by agreement. Construction of the railway would begin within six months and be completed within four years. Differences should be settled by arbitration of a neutral power. Soveral added that in his opinion the delimitation south of the Zambezi could be done only by a mixed commission, like that of Barotseland.[134]

A lengthy interchange of views took place between London and Lisbon, with Soveral, instructed and encouraged by Bocage, yielding only under the strongest pressure to the demands of Salisbury. The British press strongly and unanimously supported the BSAC. The continued detention of the *Countess of Carnarvon* (partly because of the refusal of the Cape authorities to supply copies of the papers under which she had sailed from Port Elizabeth), and the detention of the *Agnes* and the closure of the Pungue, and alleged collusion between the trekking Boers and Portugal, inflamed public opinion in England.[135] Foreign governments now exerted pressure to prevent any precipitate action by Britain, and to persuade Salisbury to be sympathetic in his consideration of Bocage's proposals. The German and Austrian ambassadors in London acceded to the Portuguese request, but urged Bocage that not a minute be lost in re-opening the Pungue to traffic, lest the technical infraction of the *modus vivendi* lead to a rupture in the negotiations. The Spanish and the Italian ambassadors

133 Bocage to Soveral, 17/4/91, *Neg.* iv, p. 173; Soveral to Bocage, 18/4/91, Nec., SPZ 7; Bocage, circular tels., 19/4/91, ibid.
134 Petre to Salisbury, 19/4/89, 88 Af., CP 6227, pp. 132–3; Portuguese modifications, ibid., pp. 133–6 and *Neg.* iv, pp. 175–8; Soveral to Bocage, 19/4/91, ibid., p. 174.
135 see e.g. *Neg.* iv, pp. 180–225, and various despatches from Soveral for this period enclosing newspaper cuttings, Nec., SPZ 7.

called at the Foreign Office. The French Government, after considerable prompting, added its pressure in London, and decided to send a warship to Beira and possibly another to Lourenço Marques to protect French interests.[136] But the strongest support came from the German Government. Hatzfeldt, ill in bed, prevailed on Salisbury to call upon him, and impressed on the Secretary of State the German Government's wish that the Portuguese question be speedily and fairly settled—not, he made haste to add, from any German sympathy with Portugal, but because of the repercussions throughout Europe should the Portuguese monarchy be overthrown; and this was the great anxiety also in the capitals of Spain, Italy and Austria. If the Portuguese Government signed a treaty of which the Lisbon populace disapproved a revolution would probably break out. But if the Portuguese Government could declare that it had sought the advice of the German Government, the people would be less hostile. Hatzfeldt assured Salisbury that he could induce the Portuguese Government to surrender its claim to the Manica plateau in return for modification to the clauses relating to transit duties, the railway and the boundary north of the Zambezi.[137]

Reports of 10,000 armed natives collecting at Sena, under Sousa's command, prompted protests from Britain. Bocage explained that the levies were to act partly as porters to the expeditionary force, partly to suppress a revolt in Barue against Sousa, which had been fomented during his absence by agents of the BSAC. Salisbury warned that if these forces behaved like those under Serpa Pinto on the Shire, the British Government would take measures for self-defence. The consul in Cape Town, reporting that four British warships had left for Moçambique, feared that they might be used against Portugal.[138] Great was the relief of the Portuguese Government when, on 13 May, Soveral and Salisbury signed an agreement extending the *modus vivendi* for a month.[139] The next day the two signed the bases for a convention.[140] The bases were surprisingly well received in the Lisbon press, but Bocage required a number of alterations and clarifications. The German Government warned Lisbon that Salisbury might take advantage of these demands to break off the negotiations at the last moment, for Rhodes was furious at some of the provisions of the convention, notably the recognition of Gungunhana as being in the Portuguese sphere. Recourse was to be had in certain circumstances to arbitration by a third power; at Bocage's insistence this was to be Germany, for he was convinced that Rhodes's intrigues would not stop with the signing of the treaty. and he saw the advantages of appeal to the most powerful of continental states,

---

136 Penafiel to Min., 18/4/91, tel., Nec., SPZ 7; and 21/4/91, tel., ibid.; Bocage to Mins. Rome and St Petersburg, 24/4/91, ibid., Valmor, Vienna, to Min., 24/4/41, tel., ibid.; Bocage to Min., Paris, 24/4/91, tel., ibid.; Dantas to Min., 25/4/91; tel., ibid.; S. Miguel, St Petersburg, to Min., ibid.; Bocage to Min., Paris, 22/4/91, tel., ibid.; Soveral to Min., 22/4/91, tel., ibid.; Dantas to Min., 1/5/91, 9A ibid.
137 Salisbury to Malet, 1/5/91, 107 Af., CP 6227, p. 165.
138 Petre to Bocage, 2/5/91, *Neg.* iv, p. 205; Bocage to Soveral, 3/5/91, p. 206; Bocage, circular, tel., 3/5/91, ibid., pp. 207–8. Petre to Bocage, 9/11/91, ibid., p. 217; Carvalho to Min., 9/5/91, 20A, Nec., SPZ 7.
139 *Neg.* iv, p. 225.
140 Ibid., pp. 228–33.

Reference to Germany was to be suppressed in the convention, however, and a secret note was to specify Germany as the neutral power. On 22 May, Salisbury and Soveral agreed to sign the treaty on the 26th.[141] On the 26th word reached London of the engagement of Macequece, and Germany feared precipitate action by Britain. And in Portugal a ministerial crisis threatened to halt the treaty, but Valbom, Bocage's successor, was just as alive to the urgent necessity for immediate signature. Valbom telegraphed Soveral that it was absolutely essential not to allow the Macequece incident to thwart the negotiation: Soveral must sign as arranged, and the treaty must be presented to the Cortes at a sitting convened for 30 May. Great was Valbom's dismay to receive a telegram that Soveral had refused to sign, because Salisbury had proposed an alteration to the wording of one clause. Valbom authorized him to accept the alteration, and on 28 May Soveral and Salisbury duly signed the draft convention.[142]

The agreement of 28 May gave Portugal more territory north of the Zambezi than she had asked for, as can be seen from line E on map (Plate 14); but south of the Zambezi Britain had her way, and the line ran along "the upper part of the eastern slope of the Manica plateau" southwards to the Sabi. The provision was repeated that no territory west of longitude 32° 30′ should be in the Portuguese sphere, and no territory east of 33° should be in the British sphere; and the line was to be deflected, if necessary, to leave Umtasa in the British sphere and Macequece in the Portuguese. Britain repeated she would not object to a Portuguese extension to the parallel of the confluence of the Maputo and the Pongola. In the west the line was as previously agreed, viz. up the Zambezi from the Katima rapids, except that Barotseland would be in the British sphere; a joint commission would decide the boundaries of Barotseland, with power to appoint an umpire. All lines were subject to rectification, by agreement, for local requirements. The other articles of the treaty were essentially those which had appeared in the British counter-proposal.[143]

It was further agreed on 28 May that notes would be exchanged providing for the Portuguese authorities to lease land at Chinde for 99 years to persons named by the British Government; covering the construction of a road from the coast to the British sphere, and rates on the railway; and forbidding the introduction of spirits by way of the Zambezi and the Shire. A secret note would specify that Germany would be the neutral power referred to in several articles of the convention. And another secret note permitted the passage of British troops across the Portuguese sphere and vice versa.[144]

After dignified speeches by Valbom, Hintze Ribeiro and Barjona de Freitas, the House of Deputies approved of ratification by a hundred and five votes to six, and the Chamber of Peers by eighty-three to six. The Council of State

141 Bocage, circular tel. to legations, 16/5/91, Nec., SPZ 7; Soveral to Bocage, 20/5/91, tel., ibid.; Bocage to Soveral, 21/5/91, tel., ibid.; Soveral to Bocage, 21/5/91, tels. ibid.; and 22/5/91, tel. ibid.;
142 Valbom to Soveral, 23/5/91, tel., Nec., SPZ 7; Soveral to Valbom, 24/5/91, tel., ibid.; Valbom to Soveral, 24/5/91, tel., ibid.; Soveral to Valbom, 25/5/91, tel., ibid.; and 26/5/91, ibid.
143 *Neg.* iv, pp. 252–6.
144 Soveral to Valbom, 26/5/91, 15 A, Nec., SPZ 7.

sanctioned the law, which was signed by the King on 11 June 1891. That afternoon Petre and Valbom signed the treaty, and exchanged complementary notes.[145]

The Portuguese Government decided to send to Moçambique a royal commissioner who would wield wider powers than those exercised by a normal governor-general, the more effectively to settle outstanding questions and to supervise the delimitation of the frontier.[146] There is no need here to follow the activities of António Enes, who arrived to find Barue in revolt — a revolt that cost Manoel António de Sousa his skin.[147] Nor is it necessary to trace the work of the delimitation commissions, which failed to agree on the line of the frontier in Manica so that the dispute had to go to arbitration.[148] Nor is it necessary to detail the steps by which Portugal made effective her authority up to the demarcated boundary, a process which deprived Gungunhana of his throne.[149]

The Treaty of 11 June 1891 marked the end of an epoch for Portugal. The pioneer European power in Africa, she had regarded the hinterland of her settlements on the coasts of Angola and Moçambique as reserved for penetration by her subjects. Lack of financial resources, of manpower, and of will, had militated against extension of Portuguese dominion. She was incapable of withstanding the inroads and onslaughts of the often unscrupulous agents of wealthier, more highly industrialized, more vigorous powers. The Treaty of 11 June denied her the high ground and nearly all the gold-producing areas of Mashonaland. Extra tracts about the upper Zambezi appeared poor compensation. But the powers confirmed Portugal in her possession of what later was found to total 481,351 square miles in Angola, and 302,328 in Moçambique; to develop this vast area proved to be an excessively heavy burden, in view of continued financial crises, and the marked reluctance of Portuguese to export either capital or themselves to Africa. The humiliation of Portuguese feeling by Britain contributed to the rise of republicanism and a resultant period of political instability, while the diplomatic drawing of artificial boundaries during the partition of Africa, without regard to the wishes of the people concerned and often cutting tribes asunder, was to have far-reaching consequences on the Africa of the 1960s — and on Portugal.

145 Petre to Salisbury, 11/6/91, 145 Af., CP 6227, pp. 341–4; 11/6/91, 146 Af., ibid., p. 344; 12/6/91, 148 Af., pp. 345–7. Almada, *Tratado*, V, pp. 400–22; A. C. Barjona de Freitas, *A Questão Ingleza; Discurso proferido na Camara dos Pares do Reino* (Lisbon, 1891).
146 Petre to Salisbury, 12/6/91, 147 Af., CP 6227, p. 244.
147 Teixeira de Botelho, II, pp. 399–405.
148 Conventions and exchanges of notes, 25/5/91 over Lunda, Almada, *Tratado*, IV, p. 165; with Congo Free State, 25/5/91, ibid., p. 157; over Tongaland, 26/6/95, ibid., V, p. 221; arbitration over Manica by Vigliani, 30/1/97, ibid., p. 69; 2/10/97 over Tongaland, Hertslet, II, p. 1070; over Barue, ibid., p. 1069; over Tongaland, 29/12/98, and 25/1/99, ibid., p. 1070; over Nyasaland, 7, and 11/11/99, and accord 8/12/1900, ibid., p. 1070.
149 Teixeira Botelho, II, pp. 433–505.

SOURCES

PRIMARY

MANUSCRIPT

Arquivo Histórico Ultramarino (Lisbon)
Papeis Avulsos
Moçambique Pasta 29 (1875), 30 (1876-77), 31 (1878), 32 (1879-81)
Moçambique, 1 Repartição Pasta 1 (1879–82), 2 (1881–87), 3 (1883–86), 4 (1888), 5 (1889), 6 (1890), 7 (1891)
Moçambique, 2 Repartição Caixa 1 (1883–84), 2 (1885), 3 (1886), 4 (1887), 5 (1888), 6 (1889), 7 (1890), 8 (1890), 9 (1891)

Necessidades (Ministry of Foreign Affairs, Lisbon)
Soberania de Portugal na Zambezia Caixa 1 (1883–88), 2 (1889), 3 (1890), 4 (1890), 5 (1891), 6 (1891), 7 (1891), 8 (1891)
Consulados de Portugal no Transvaal Caixa 1 (1874–90)
Legação de Portugal em Londres Caixa 42 (1875–77), 43 (1878)
Legação de Portugal em Berlin Caixa 9 (1887–90)

Arquivo Histórico de Moçambique (Lourenço Marques)
Selections only from Governo Geral, Correspondencia confidencial expedida ii.1.3 Codice 2–366 FE 4 (1872–79), 2–400 FE 8 (1879–85), 2–317 FD 11 (1881–82), 2–364 FE 4 (1891)
Correspondencia ordinario, para o Ministro ii.2.1B Codice 2–53 FA 8 (1870–73), 2–52 FA 9 (1876–78), 2–492 GE 11 (1878–81), 2–41 FA 7 (1881–82), 2–27 FA 4 (1882–84), 2–28 FA 4 (1884–85), 2–29 FA 4 (1886–87) missing, 2–30 FA 6 (1889–90), 2–33 FA 6 (1891–92)
Correspondencia ordinario para diversos Codice 2–178 FC 2 (Manica, 1884–85), 2–179 FC 2 (Manica, 1891–92), 2–138 FB 7 (Zumbo, 1890), 2–427 FB 7 (Zumbo, 1890)

Public Record Office (London)
Selections only from FO 63/1084 to 1175; FO 84/1643–46, 1657, 1662, 1669–71, 1676–80, 1694–96, 1702, 1708–09, 1722–23, 1724–29, 1730, 1801–26, 1899–1902; FO 179/214 to 285. Adm. 144/10, 6 and 11; Adm. Class 1/7000, 7009–10, 7022, 7024, 7037; Adm. Class 50/385, 399

Natal Archives
SNA 1/1/21–3, 1/1/52; 1/2/2, 9, 13, 14; 1/4/1, 2, 3; 1/5/1; 1/6/1, 2

National Archives of Rhodesia and Nyasaland (searched by Miss Anne Stupart)
HC 1/5/1 and 2 Confidential, HC 3/5/33/1, 2, 10–13

PRINTED

(a) Portuguese Parliamentary Papers
Negocios Externos: Documentos Apresentados às Cortes na Sessão Legislativo de 1888 pelo Ministro e Secretario d'Estado dos Negocios Estrangeiros: Negociações com o Zanzibar. Lisbon, 1888.

Negocios Externos . . . 1889 . . . Limites entre o districto de Lourenço Marques e o territorio de Mussuate. Lisbon, 1889.

Negocios Externos . . . 1889 . . . Bloqueio na costa oriental da Africa. Lisbon, 1889.

Negocios Externos . . . Correspondencia com a Inglaterra e documentos correlativos até 13 de Janeiro de 1890. Lisbon, 1890. Followed by 'Relatorio e documentos acerca do conflicto do Chire', and 'Fundação da missão religiosa de M'Ponda 1888–89'.

Negocios Externos . . . Negociações do Tratado com a Inglaterra. Lisbon, 1890.

Negocios Externos . . . Negociações do Tratado com a Inglaterra iv. Lisbon, 1891.

(b) British Foreign Office Confidential Prints 2790; 2866; 2915; 2921; 3083; 3181; 3686; 3854; 3928; 3915; 4302; 4303; 4395; 4437; 4498; 4506; 4626; 4777; 4785; 4786; 4807; 4865; 4914; 4944; 4960; 4971*; 5000; 5019; 5023; 5033; 5051; 5080; 5103; 5133; 5156; 5157; 5181; 5236; 5271; 5308; 5366; 5370; 5400; 5466; 5459; 5497; 5536; 5565; 5616; 5673; 5727; 5732; 5762; 5770; 5867; 5872; 5875; 5896; 5950; 5966; 5966*; 5970; 5988; 6058; 6061; 6069; 6086; 6088; 7168; 6227; 6253; 6609

British Colonial Office Confidential Points (African) 161; 173; 178; 190; 200; 222; 238; 240; 267; 268; 287; 294a; 302; 358; 359

(c) British Parliamentary Papers C 1361; 4190; 5903; 5904; 5918; 6200; 6212; 6370; 6495

(d) Collection of documents
ALMADA, J. de (ed.) *Tratados aplicaveis ao ultramar.* Lisbon, 1942, 5 vols. and maps.
HERTSLET, Sir E. *Map of Africa by Treaty.* London, 1894, 2 vols.
THEAL, G. M. *Records of South-Eastern Africa . . .* [Cape Town], 1898–1903, 9 vols.

(e) Periodicals
Boletim Official do Governo Geral da Provincia de Moçambique; Boletim da Sociedade de Geografia de Lisboa; *Proceedings* and *Journal* of the Royal Geographical Society, London.

WORKS BY CONTEMPORARIES

1. *Books*

ARNOT, F. S. *Bihé and Garenganze.* London [1893].
────── *Garenganze;* 2 ed. London [1889].
AYLWARD, A. *The Transvaal of to-day.* Edinburgh, 1878.
BAINES, T. *The gold regions of south eastern Africa.* London, 1877.
BATES, L. H. and THOMPSON, M. E. *Sketch of the East Central African Mission Gazaland.* Boston, 1903.
BENTLEY, W. H. *Pioneering on the Congo.* London, 1900, 2 vols.
BUCKLE, G. E. (ed.) *Letters of Queen Victoria,* 2nd and 3rd series. London, 1926–32, 6 vols.
BURTON, R. F. *Two trips to Gorilla land and the cataracts of the Congo.* London, 1876, 2 vols.

CAMERON, V. L. *Across Africa*. London, 1877, 2 vols.

CAPELLO, H. and IVENS, R. *De Angola á Contra-Costa*. Lisbon, 1886, 2 vols.

— — *From Benguella to the territory of Yacca*. London, 1882, 2 vols.

CASTILHO, A. de *Relatório acerca de alguns portos da provincia de Moçambique*. Lisbon, 1884.

———— *Relatório da guerra da Zambezia em 1888*. Lisbon, 1891.

———— *Relatório da viagem da canonheira Rio Lima de Lisboa a Moçambique . . . 1884–1885*. Lisbon, 1889.

COLQUHOUN, A. R. *Dan to Beersheba*. London, 1908.

CORVO, J. de Andrade *Estudos sobre as provincias ultramarinas*. Lisbon, 1883–1887, 4 vols.

DRUMMOND, H. *Tropical Africa*. London, 1889.

FORSSMAN, O. W. A. *Guide for agriculturists and capitalists, speculators . . .* Pretoria, 1874.

FOTHERINGHAM, L. M. *Adventures in Nyassaland*. London, 1891.

FRIPP, C. E. and HILLER, V. W. (eds.) *Gold and the Gospel in Mashonaland 1888*. London, 1949. (Oppenheimer series no. 4.)

HETHERWICK, A. *The romance of Blantyre*. London, [1931].

HOLUB, E. *Seven years in South Africa*. London, 1881.

HYATT, S. P. *The northward trek*. London, 1909.

JESSETT, M. G. *The key to South Africa: Delagoa Bay*. London, 1899.

JOHNSON, F. W. F. *Great days: the autobiography of an empire pioneer*. London, 1940.

JOHNSTON, H. H. *British Central Africa*. London, 1897.

———— *George Grenfell and the Congo*. London, 1908, 2 vols.

———— *History of the colonization of Africa by alien races*. Cambridge, 1899.

JOHNSTON, K. *Africa*. London, 1880.

KELTIE, J. S. *The partition of Africa;* 2 ed. London, 1895.

KERR, W. M. *The far interior*. London, 1886, 2 vols.

LAWS, R. *Reminiscences of Livingstonia*. Edinburgh, 1934.

LEONARD, A. G. *How we made Rhodesia*. London, 1896.

LEWSEN, P. (ed.) *Selections from the correspondence of J. X. Merriman*. Cape Town, 1960, 1963, 2 vols. 1, 1878–1890; 2, 1890–1898. (Van Riebeeck Society, 41, 44.)

LIVINGSTONE, D. *Missionary travels and researches in South Africa*. London, 1857.

———— and C, *Narrative of an expedition to the Zambesi and its tributaries*. London, 1865.

MACDONALD, D. *Africana; or, the heart of heathen Africa*. London, 1882, 2 vols.

MACKENZIE, J. *Austral Africa*. London, 1887, 2 vols.

MANSO, Paiva, visconde de, *Memoria sobre Lourenço Marques (Delagoa Bay)*. Lisbon, 1870.

MARTINS, F. A. Oliveira (ed.), *O 'Ultimatum' visto por António Enes*. Lisbon, 1946.

MATHERS, E. P. *Zambesia, England's El Dorado in Africa.* London, 1891.

MAUCH, C. Carl Mauch's Reisen im inneren von Süd-Afrika 1865–1872. Gotha, 1874. (In Petermann's *geographischen Mittheilungen,* VIII, 37.)

MAYO, D. R. W. B. *De Rebus Africanis, the claims of Portugal to the Congo.* London, 1883.

MOIR, F. L. M. *After Livingstone.* London, [1923].

MONTEIRO, J. *Angola and the River Congo.* London, 1875, 2 vols.

PALGRAVE, W. C. *Report . . . of his mission to Damaraland and Great Namaqualand in 1876.* Cape Town, 1877. In Cape of Good Hope, Votes and proceedings of Parliament, 1877, Appendix 2.

PINTO, Serpa, A. A. da R de *How I crossed Africa.* London, 1881, 2 vols.

RANKIN, D. J. *The Zambesi basin and Nyassaland.* Edinburgh, 1893.

RIBEIRO, Sousa (ed.) *Regimen dos prazos da coroa.* Lourenço Marques, 1907.

SELOUS, F. C. *A hunter's wanderings in Africa.* London, 1881.

————— *Travel and adventure in south-east Africa.* London, 1893.

STANLEY, H. M. *The Congo and the founding of its Free State.* London, 1885, 2 vols.

————— *Through the dark continent.* London, 1878, 2 vols.

STEWART, J. *Dawn in the dark continent.* Edinburgh, 1903.

————— *Livingstonia, its origin.* Edinburgh, 1894.

THOMSON, J. *To the Central African lakes and back.* London, 1881, 2 vols.

VARINAY, P. de Bonnefont de *La Compagnie de Mozambique . . .* Lisbon, 1899.

WALLIS, J. P. R. (ed.) *The Zambezi expedition of David Livingstone, 1858–1863.* London, 1956, 2 vols. (Oppenheimer series no. 9.)

————— *The Zambesi journal of James Stewart, 1862–63.* London, 1952. (Oppenheimer series no. 6.)

WEALE, J. P. M. *The truth about the Portuguese in Africa.* London, 1891.

WELD, A. *Mission of the Zambesi.* London, [1880].

YOUNG, E. D. *Nyassa;* 2 ed. London, 1877.

2. *Pamphlets and Articles*

AMARAL, F and ALMEIDA, J. B. F. de, Apontamentos para a historia do estabelecimento da colonia agricola S. Januario nos terrenos de Humpata. *Boletim Sociedade de Geografia de Lisboa,* 1881, p. 304–17, 456–67.

ANDRADA, J. P. Paiva d' *Manica.* Cape Town, 1891.

————— *Relatório de uma viagem ás terras de Changamira.* Lisbon, 1886.

ANDRADE, A. Freire d' *Região aurifera de Manica, Relatorio.* Beira, 1899.

ANON, *Manuel António de Sousa, Herói de Massangano.* Lourenço Marques, 1936.

ARRIAGA, Visconde da, *Lourenço Marques: exame sobre o tratado . . . 1879*. Lisbon, 1881.

CHIRNSIDE, A. *The Blantyre missionaries: discreditable disclosures.* London, 1880.

COHEN, E. Erläutende Bemerkungen zu der Routenkarta Reise van Lydenburg. *Zweiter Jahresbericht der geographische Gesellschaft in Hamburg, 1874–75*, 1875, p. 173–286.

COMBER, T. J. Brief account of recent journeys in the interior of Africa. *Proceedings Royal Geographical Society*, 1881, p. 20–26.

CORDEIRO, L. Expediçao geographica Portugueza á African Central. *Boletim Sociedade de Geografia de Lisboa*, 1877, p. 126–38.

CUNHA, J. G. de Barros e, *Lourenço Marques*. Lisbon, 1881.

ERSKINE, St V. Journey to Umzila's, south-east Africa, in 1871–1872. *Journal of the Royal Geographical Society*, 1875, p. 45–125.

FREITAS, A. C. Barjona de *A questão Ingleza: discurso proferido na Camera dos Pares*. Lisbon, 1891.

GOMES, H. de Barros *A navegação do Zambeze: discursos proferidos na Camara dos Deputados*. Lisbon, 1888.

———— *Relações externas*. Lisbon, 1890.

HORTA, J. M. da Ponte *Tratado de Lourenço Marques*. Lisbon, 1882.

MACHADO, J. J. Caminho de Ferro de Lourenço Marques á fronteira do Transvaal. *Boletim Sociedade de Geografia de Lisboa*, 1880, p. 71–73.

———— *Moçambique*. Lisbon, 1881.

———— *Questões Africanas: fornecimentos d'armas aos Matabelles, Zambezia Británica e o territorio dos Swasis*. Lisbon, 1889.

———— *Relatório acerca dos trabalhos para a fixação da directriz do caminho de ferro*. Lisbon, 1884.

O'NEILL, H. E. *The Moçambique and Nyassa slave trade*. London, 1885.

REIS, J. Batalha *Os Portugueses na Região do Nyassa*. Lisbon, 1889.

RIDDEL, A. *A reply to "The Blantyre missionaries: discreditable disclosures by Andrew Chirnside"*; 2 ed. Edinburgh, 1880.

SARMENTO, A. C. Rodriques *O governador geral da Provincia de Moçambique, e as conferencias do Engenheiro Machado*. Moçambique, 1881.

TESTA, C. *A politica intercolonial e internacional e o tratado de Lourenço Marques*. Lisbon, 1881.

WALLER, H. *Nyassaland: Great Britain's case against Portugal*. London, 1890.

SECONDARY (Select List)

AGAR-HAMILTON, J. A. I. *Road to the North.* London, 1937.

ALMADA, J. de *A politica colonial de João de Andrade Corvo.* Lisbon, 1944.

────── *A Aliança Inglesa.* Lisbon, III, 1949.

────── *Tratado de 1891.* Lisbon,1947.

ANDERSON-MORSHEAD, A. E. M. *History of the Universities Mission to Central Africa, 1859–1909.* London, 1909.

ANSTEY, R. T. *Britain and the Congo in the nineteenth century.* Oxford, 1962.

BAKER, E. *The life and exploration of Frederick Stanley Arnot.* London, 1921.

BANNING, E. *Mémoires politiques et diplomatiques: comment fut fonde le Congo belge.* Paris, 1927.

BIXLER, W. *Anglo-German imperialism in South Africa, 1880–1900.* Baltimore, 1932.

BOTELHO, J. J. Teixeira *Historia militar e politica dos Portugueses em Moçambique.* Lisbon, vol. 2, 1936.

BRYANT, A. T. *Olden times in Zululand and Natal.* London, 1929.

CECIL, G. *Life of Robert Marquis of Salisbury.* London, vol. 4, 1932.

CONCHAR, M. J. The Concession and Royal Charter (Unpublished B. A. Hons essay, University of Cape Town.)

COUPLAND, R. *The Exploitation of East Africa, 1856–90.* London, 1939.

────── *Kirk on the Zambesi.* London, 1928.

────── *Zulu battle piece: Isandhlwana.* Oxford, 1948.

COUTINHO, J. de Azevedo *Manuel Antonio de Sousa.* Lisbon, 1936.

CROWE, S. E. *The Berlin West African Conference, 1884–85.* London, 1942.

CUNHA, Amadeu *Serpa Pinto e o Apelo de Africa.* Lisbon, 1946.

DARTER, A. *Pioneers of Mashonaland.* London, 1914.

DE KOCK, W. J. Estraterritoriale vraagstukke van die Kaapse regering (1872–1885) *Archives Year Book for South African History,* Cape Town, 11th year, I, 1948, p. 1–306.

DE KIEWIET, C. W. *The imperial factor in South Africa.* C.U.P., 1937.

DIAS, Gastão Sousa, *Os Portugueses em Angola.* Lisbon, 1959.

EÇA, F. G. de Almeida de *História das guerras no Zambeze: Chicoa e Massangano (1807–1888).* Lisbon, 1953–54, 2 vols.

EGERTON, F. C. *Angola in perspective.* London, 1957.

FITZMAURICE, E. G. *The life of G. G. Leveson-Gower, second Earl Granville.* London, vol. 2, 1905.

GARSON, N. G. The Swaziland question and a road to the sea, 1887–1895. In *Archives year book for South African history.* Cape Town, 20th year, II, 1957, p. 263–434.

GOYAU, G. *Un grande missionaire, le Cardinal Lavigeriè.* Paris, 1925.

GRAY, J. *History of Zanzibar from Middle Ages to 1856.* London, 1962.

GREEN, J. *Rhodes goes North.* London, 1936.

HANNA, A. J. *The beginnings of Nyasaland and north-eastern Rhodesia 1859–95.* Oxford, 1956.

────── *The story of the Rhodesias and Nyasaland.* London, 1960.

HARGREAVES, J. D. *Prelude to the partition of Africa.* London, 1963.

HEYSE, T. *Les origines diplomatique du Congo belge.* Brussels, 1934.

HOLE, H. M. *The making of Rhodesia*. London, 1926.

———— *The passing of the black kings*. London, 1932.

KEITH, A. B. *The Belgian Congo and the Berlin Act*. Oxford, 1919.

KRUGER, D. W. (ed.) of VAN DER WALT, A. J. H. *et al*, *Geschiedenis van Suid-Afrika*. Cape Town, [1965].

LANGER, W. L. *European alliances and alignments*. New York, 1950.

LEWIN, E. *The Germans and Africa*. London, 1939.

LIVINGSTONE, W. P. *Laws of Livingstonia*. London, [1921].

LOCKHART, J. G. and WOODHOUSE, C. M. *Rhodes*. London, 1963.

MARTINS, F. A. Oliveria *Hermenegildo Capelo e Roberto Ivens*. Lisbon, 1951–52, 2 vols.

OLIVER, R. *The missionary factor in East Africa*. London, 1952.

———— *Sir Harry Johnston and the Scramble for Africa*. London, 1959.

PINTO, C. de Serpa *A vida breve e ardente de Serpa Pinto*. Lisbon, 1937.

ROBINSON, R. and GALLAGHER, J. *Africa and the Victorians*. London, 1961.

RODRIQUES, D. *A occupação de Moçambique*. Lisbon, 1910.

SLADE, R. M. *English-speaking missions in the Congo Independent State (1878–1908)*. Brussels, 1959

———— *King Leopold's Congo*. Oxford, 1962.

TABLER, E. C. *The far interior*. Cape Town, 1955.

TAYLOR, A. J. P. *Germany's first bid for colonies*. London, 1938.

THOMSON, R. S. *La fondation de l'Etat Indépendent du Congo*. Brussels, 1933.

TOWNSEND, M. E. *Rise and fall of Germany's colonial empire 1884–1918*. New York, 1930.

TRÜMPELMANN, G. P. J. Die Boer in Suidwes-Afrika. In *Archives year book for South African history*. Cape Town, 11th year, II, 1948, p. 1–166.

UYS, C. J. *In the era of Shepstone*. Lovedale, 1933.

VAN DER POEL, J. *Railways and customs policies in South Africa, 1885–1910*. London, 1933.

VAN WINTER P. J. *Onder Krugers Hollanders . . .* Amsterdam, 1937, 2 vols

WALKER, E. A. *History of South Africa*. London, 1947.

WARHURST, P. *Anglo-Portuguese relations in south-central Africa 1890–1900*. London, 1962.

WELLS, J. Stewart of Lovedale. London, 1908.

WILLIAMS, B. *Cecil Rhodes*. London, 1938.

WILLIAMS, W. W. *Life of General Sir Charles Warren*. Oxford, 1941.

WILSON, G. H. *History of the Universities' Mission to Central Africa*. London, 1936.

INDEX

Abercorn, Duke of, 277
Abreu, Gen. Chrysostomo, Prime Minister, 263
Açores, 146
Active, 229
Aden, 257
Adendorff, L. D., 282
Admiralty, British, 58, 202, 221, 255–6, 259
Afonso de Albuquerque, 88–90, 257
African Association, African International Association, *see* International African Association
'African Explorer', *see* Johnston, H. H.
African Lakes Company, 142, 153, 158, 163, 165–8, 171–83, 192, 198–200, 203–8, 211–6, 222, 235, 255–8, 262
Agnes, 284–6, 294
alcohol, 61, 65, 70, 97, 157, 287, 296
Algeria, 185
Alima River, 46
Almeida, J. J., Secretary-gen. of Moçambique, 125–9, 134; Superintendent-in-Chief, Gazaland, 246–9, 277–81
Alsace, 62
Amandebele, *see* Matabele
Amaral, F. J., Gov.-gen. of Angola, 61
Amaramba, Lake, 163
Amatongas, *see* Tongas
Amboim, 38
Ambriz, 1, 39–42, 51, 58, 76, 79
Ambrizete, 39, 42–3, 51
America, American, 38, 110, 118, 135, 269, 284
Amsterdam, 15, 17
Ana Cativa, 139
Andara, 183
Anderson, Sir P., Head of the African Section, British Foreign Office, 74–5, 78, 175–6, 189, 217
Andrada, Capt. J. C. Paiva de, 120–36, 140, 143, 155, 167, 189–90, 196, 203, 206, 215, 218, 225–7, 266–8, 273, 289
Angoche, 3, 125, 240
Angola, Angolan, 1, 20, 38, 41–2, 44, 48–50, 59–60, 62, 66, 75, 80, 87, 166, 186, 189, 195, 197, 237, 250, 260, 262, 283, 286–7, 297
Angra Pequena, 70–1, 73–4
Anson, 224, 229
Antas, d', *see* Dantas
Arab, 2–3, 84–5, 90–2, 94, 118, 164, 170–2, 176–7, 180–1, 183, 202, 208, 224, 235
arbitration, 103–4, 111, 113–6, 198, 222–3, 230, 232, 235–7, 243–4, 292, 294–5
arms, ammunition, 12–15, 24–8, 89–90, 97, 100, 129, 142, 146, 150, 159, 168, 171–83, 192, 194, 197, 200, 202, 204, 210, 214, 216, 235, 238, 255–6, 262, 264
Arnot, Rev. F. S., 250–1
artillery, 16, 58, 61, 143–5, 177–83, 251, 253, 262, 283, 287–8
Aruangua River, 123, 131, 134

Atlantic Ocean, 45, 76
Atlantic Squadron, British Navy, 229
Australia, 229
Australians, 13
Austria, Austrians, 13
Austria-Hungary, Austro-Hungarian, 45, 75, 230, 233–4, 268, 272, 294
Auxiliar, 257
Avila e Bolama, Duke of, 33–4, 36; Min. of For. Affairs, 44
Avila, J. de Almeida de, Gov. of Quelimane, 163–4
Avon, 43

Baden-Powell, George, 99
Bagamoyo, 44
Baião, Major Fran. A. Pinheiro, Gov. of Zambezia, 139–40, 161
Bailundu, 251
Baines, Thomas, 147
Bakedi River, 197
Balalika, 210–1
Balfour, Lieut., 255–7
Baluchi, 219
Banana, 40–1, 43, 57, 60, 82–3
Bandawe, 161, 171, 177, 197
Bandire, 123, 246
Banyai, Banyailand, 281, 288
Bapedi tribe, 16
Baptist Missionary Society, 50, 58, 64
Baptist Union, 64
Barberton, 134, 274
Bargash, Sultan of Zanzibar, 2
Baring, Walter, Sec., Legation, Lisbon, 62
Barjona de Freitas, *see* Freitas
Barnato, B., 147–8
Barotseland, 48, 153, 156, 190, 236–7, 250, 252, 292–6
Barros Gomes, *see* Gomes
Bartholomew's map, 272
Bartissol, E., 275–6
Bartolomeu Dias, 93
Barue, 131–2, 139, 141, 144, 295, 297
Basters, 252
Basto, Pinto, 277
Bazaruto Island, 8
Bechuanaland, 48, 125, 127, 147, 149–53, 190–1, 218, 227, 263
Bechuanaland Border Police, 149
Bechuanaland Exploration Company, 150, 152
Behring Sea, 269
Beira, 134, 136, 266, 269, 273, 281, 283–5, 289, 295
Beit, A., 152
Belgians, King of, 57; *and see* Leopold
Belgium, Belgian, 45, 54, 57, 64, 234, 241, 252, 269–70
Belmonte, 250–1

307

Chagas, M. Pinheiro, Min. of Marine and Colonies, 110, 112, 126, 160
Chai-chai, 248, 279–80
Chaka, Zulu chief, 25
Channel Squadron, British Navy, 220, 224, 232
Chapupat rifle, 183
Chari River, 76
Charmes, 67
Charter, Fort, 265
Chartered Company, *see* British South Africa Company
Chassêpot rifle, 171
Chatara, *see* Cruz, Ant. Vicente
Chegualaguala, 131
Cherim, 213
Chicoa, 132, 143, 245
Chicofele, chief, 250
Chidima, 281
Chifambobsico, Manica chief, 278
Chikala, 219
Chikuse, Makololo chief, 165, 168–9
Chiloane Island, 8, 119, 122, 124, 129, 131, 134, 247–8
Chiloango, 40, 61
Chilomo, 213, 238, 253, 257–8
Chilwa Lake, 243
Chimanimani mountains, 10
Chimoara, 142, 166–7
Chimoio, 266, 286, 288–9
China, Chinese, 57, 101
Chinde River, 183, 202–3, 206, 222, 241, 244, 255–7, 259–62, 275
Chipatula, Makololo chieftain, 162–5
Chironge, 166
Chiuta, Lake, 163, 243
Chobe River, 197, 244, 293
Chopi tribe, 135
Chua hill, 287
Chuma, 118
Church of Scotland, 6–8, 157, 160, 166, 195, 199
Churchill, W. A., acting consul, Moçambique, 215–7, 226, 253
civilization, civilizing, 7, 9, 14, 20, 23, 38, 42, 44–5, 48, 51, 59, 64, 81, 114, 120, 122, 126–7, 146, 153, 164, 169, 186, 218, 222, 224, 228, 238, 261
Clement River, 274
coal, coal-mining, 85, 101, 120, 227, 256
Coelho, Agostinho, Gov.-gen. of Moçambique, 84, 126, 141–2, 165
coffee, 168
Cohen, British consul, Luanda, 59–60
Cohen, E., Portuguese consul, Pretoria, 245, 247
Cohen, hotelier, 284
Coillard, Rev. F., 48, 250
Coimbra, 281
Colonial Office, 16–7, 25–30, 34–5, 152–3, 189–91, 196, 215–6, 252, 284
colonists, colonization, 3, 73, 112, 133, 152, 156
colonos, 137
Colossus, 224, 229
Colquhoun, A. R., Administrator, 263–7, 290
Colquhoun, F., 247–8
Comber, Rev. T., 50

Comité d'Études du Haut Congo, 45
commerce, 3, 7–8, 12–3, 20, 23–4, 26, 28, 45, 51–2, 54–5, 57, 59–60, 62, 64, 66–9, 72–3, 75, 80–2, 84, 94, 110, 113–4, 120, 125–6, 133, 137, 140, 145, 155, 163–5, 178, 182, 188–9, 213, 218, 237–8, 256; *and see* trade
Commons, House of, 54, 56, 58, 65, 152, 174, 178, 188, 195, 200, 202, 242, 264, 268, 270; *and see* Parliament
Comoro islands, 74
Companhia Africana, 123
Conceiçao, 142
concessions, 126, 133–4, 136, 139, 147–54, 175, 190, 222, 239–40, 242–9, 252, 264–5, 271, 277–8, 282, 296
confederation, 14–5, 34
Conference, Berlin West African, *see* Berlin West African Conf.
Congo Free State, 1, 192, 218, 235, 239, 252, 262
Congo River, 1, 32, 37, 39–40, 42, 44–6, 48, 50–79, 83, 195–6
Congo tribe, kingdom, 58
Congo Treaty, *see* Treaties, Portugal-Britain
Congone River, 7, 181, 201–2; *see also* Inhamissengo
Conselho Ultramarino, 4–5
consuls, vice-consuls
  British (Las Palmas), 229
    (Lourenço Marques), 14, 97, 108, 114, 134, 247, 285
    (Luanda), 42–4, 51, 56, 59
    (Moçambique), 2, 92, 97, 123, 134, 159, 162–3, 195, 201, 216, 253–4, 272
    (Nyasa), 161, 164, 175–7, 183, 214, 225
    (Oporto), 231
    (Pungue), 286
    (Quelimane), 134, 159–60, 164, 200, 262
    (South-central Africa), 6
    (Zanzibar), 89, 92–3, 137, 217, 220
  German (Moçambique), 92
    (Zanzibar), 88–9, 93
  Portuguese (Cape Town), 229, 268, 272, 284, 290–1, 295
    (Gibraltar), 229
    (Pretoria), 245, 247, 249–50, 281–3
    (Zanzibar), 88–9, 93, 229
  South African Republic (Lobengula's), 148, 150
Convention, *see* Treaties
convicts, *see degredados*
copper, 39, 120, 241
Cordier, 59
Cordon, F. M. Vitor, engineer, 136, 146, 154–5, 189, 215, 218, 220
Cortes, 29–37, 41, 51, 53, 62, 66–7, 79, 82–3, 103, 113, 120–1, 133, 182, 193, 197, 224, 236, 238, 242, 259–61, 263, 266, 268, 270, 272, 281, 291, 294, 296
Corvo, J. Andrade, Min. of For. Affairs and Ultr., 1, 7, 18, 20–1, 24–6, 29–31, 34, 36, 41–4, 49, 97, 121
Cotterill, H. B., 20, 21, 24
cotton, 4, 6, 65
Cotton Supply Association, 6
Couceiro, Capt. Paiva, 250–1
Council of State, 230, 234, 296
Countess of Carnarvon, 279–81, 294

310

Indian Ocean, 20, 76, 99, 104
Ingoma, *prazo*, 168
Inhaca Island, 12, 96–7, 100, 104
Inhambane, 8–11, 26, 111, 117–8, 122–3, 126, 128–30, 134–5, 227–8, 247, 278–9, 283, 286–7
Inhamissenga, *see* Cruz, Victorino
Inhamissengo River, 7, 142
Inhaoche, 119, 123, 128, 246
Inhaombe River, *see* Chinde River
Inhampura River, *see* Limpopo River
International African Association, 45–6, 52, 57, 59–61, 67–83
International Arbitration and Peace Association, 223
Inyati, 146
Irish, Irishmen, 134
Iron Duke, 224, 229
Isandhlawana, battle of, 29
Isangila, 46–7
Italy, Italian, 45–6, 75, 118, 230, 233–4, 237, 268, 294–5
Ivens, Lieut. R., 48
ivory, 9–10, 23, 39, 119, 130, 135, 146, 163, 165, 206, 213, 267

James Stevenson, 173, 175, 206, 208, 212, 242, 256–8, 261–2
Jameson, Dr S. L., 263, 266–7, 280
Januário, Min. of Marine and Ultr., 34
Jeffreys, J., 263, 274
Jeffrey's mine, 265
Jesuit mission, 117
Jews, 219
João, informer, 132, 189, 225, 227, 237, 246, 252
Johnson, Frank, 149, 227, 246, 266–7, 284–5
Johnston, H. H., 67; negotiator, 195–200, 223, 236; consul, Moçambique, 195, 201–2, 204, 206–8, 215, 217–8, 220, 241, 252, 254, 256, 261
Joseph Nickerson, 43
Joubert, Gen. P. J., 249, 282
Jumbe, sultan, 208, 252

Kabompo River, 197, 240, 243, 294
Kafue River, 215, 289
Kalaka tribe, 188
Kariba gorge, 155
Karonga, 161, 171–3, 177–8, 182–3, 208
Kasisi, Makololo chief, 165, 167–9, 206
Kasoko Island, 154
Kasote, chief, 171
Kassai, 252
Kasson, J. A., U.S.A. Plenipotentiary, 76
Katanga, 250, 252
Katima rapids, 186, 191, 240, 243, 292, 294, 296
Katunga, 205, 207–8, 213, 219, 226, 253, 256
Kebrabasa rapids, *see* Quebrabasa
Keppel, Lieut., 43
Kergarion, E. de, 264–6
Kerr, M., 245
Khama, chief of Bechuanaland, 150, 219
Kilimanjaro, Mount, 195
Kilwa, 90–2, 94
Kimberley, 150, 152, 263

Kimberley, Earl of, S of S for Colonies, 34–5, 37, 52, 55
King George River, *see* Komati River
King of Portugal, 27, 31, 34, 36, 44, 47, 52, 61, 73, 75, 93, 120, 129, 141, 155–6, 167, 183–4, 186–7, 191, 193, 209, 224, 230, 232, 246, 259–60, 262, 267, 278
Kinsembo, 39, 60
Kipini, 87
Kirk, Sir John, consul, Zanzibar, 57, 85–6, 118, 137
Knee, O., acting vice-consul, Lourenço Marques, 114–5
Knight-Bruce, Bishop G. W. H., 151, 154, 289
Knutsford, Lord, S of S for Colonies, 107, 149, 153, 188, 190, 199
Komati River, 9, 98, 110, 280
Konde tribe, 171–2
Kopa-kopa, chief, 176
Kosi Bay, 109, 245
Kota-kota, 208
Kouilou River, 46–7, 79
Kropatchek rifle, 212
Kruger, P., vice-president, 110; and President, S.A. Republic, 101, 111, 249
Kumalombe, 158
Kuruman, 146
Kusserow, 78–9
Kwango, 252
Kwanjulu, 251

La Diligente, 41
Lady Nyasa, 24, 165, 212–3
Laforte, 8
Laing's Nek, 35
Lambermont, Baron Auguste, Belgian ambassador, 77, 79
Lamu Island, 87
Landana, 60–1
Landeens, Gaza warriors, 8, 11, 14, 22, 122, 127, 129, 131–2, 137, 142, 166, 183–4, 210, 212, 217, 279, 283
Las Palmas, 229
Last, 167
latitude, line of, 13, 39–41, 44, 52, 55, 59, 61, 73, 75–6, 83, 86–7, 96, 104, 106, 109–10, 117, 147, 184, 186–7, 191, 197, 214, 238, 240–3, 249–50, 261, 272, 289
Lavigerie, Cardinal, 185, 193, 214
Laws, Rev. Dr R., 7, 157
Leal, Lieut. L. A. Machado, 203
Lebombo hills, 8, 13, 17, 96, 98, 106–7, 109–10
Lefini River, 46
Leopold II, King of Belgium, 45, 47, 57, 67–8, 75, 77, 80, 82, 270
Leopoldville, 46
Le Temps, 54
Lewanika, chief, 250, 252
Lialui, 48
libertos, 18
Libongo, 39
Libonta, 250
Licona River, 46
Lima, H. C., Gov. of Manica, 124, 262
Limpopo Concessions Syndicate, 249

312

313

314

316

318